D1562664

POETIC
INTERACTION

POETIC INTERACTION

Language, Freedom, Reason

John McCumber

The University of Chicago Press
Chicago and London

John McCumber is associate professor of philosophy at Northwestern University.

The University of Chicago Press, Chicago 60637
The University of Chicago Press, Ltd., London
© 1989 by The University of Chicago
All rights reserved. Published 1989
Printed in the United States of America

98 97 96 95 94 93 92 91 90 89   54321

Library of Congress Cataloging-in-Publication Data

McCumber, John.
   Poetic interaction : language, freedom, reason / John McCumber.
      p.   cm.
   Bibliography: p.
   Includes index.
      1. Liberty.   2. Languages—Philosophy.   3. Language and logic.
   I. Title.
   B824.4.M38   1989
   190—dc19   88-19831
   ISBN 0-226-55703-0 (cloth)   CIP
   ISBN 0-226-55704-9 (paper)

For Françoise
dins lou cèu o dins l'afous
inseparablo siéu de vous!

Contents

CONTENTS

Contents

Abbreviations

Citations to these works, unless obtrusively long, will be given parenthetically in the text: the figure after the slash is for the English translation (see bibliography for full references). If there is no such figure, the English version has the pagination of the original edition in the margins.

Aesth.	Hegel, *Vorlesungen über die Ästhetik*
An. Post.	Aristotle, *Analytica Posteriora*
An. Pr.	Aristotle, *Analytica Priora*
de An.	Aristotle, *De Anima*
EF	Kant, *Zum ewigen Frieden*
Enz	Hegel, *Enzyklopädie*
FDL	Heidegger, "From a Dialogue on Language"
GMS	Kant, *Grundlegung der Metaphysik der Sitten*
HW	Heidegger, *Holzwege*
KPV	Kant, *Kritik der praktischen Vernunft*
KRV	Kant, *Kritik der reinen Vernunft*
KU	Kant, *Kritik der Urteilskraft*
Metaph.	Aristotle, *Metaphysics*
NE	Aristotle, *Nicomachean Ethics*
Phdr.	Plato, *Phaedrus*
PhG	Hegel, *Phänomenologie des Geistes*
Phys.	Aristotle, *Physics*
PLT	Heidegger, *Poetry, Language, Thought*
Pol	Aristotle, *Politics*
PRL	Kant, *Prolegomena to Any Future Metaphysics*
Rep.	Plato, *Republic*
RPh.	Hegel, *Philosophie des Rechts*
SF	Kant, *Der Streit der Fakultäten*

SZ	Heidegger, *Sein und Zeit*
TKH	Habermas, *Theorie des kommunikativen Handelns*
UKW	Heidegger, "Der Ursprung des Kunstwerkes"
UzS	Heidegger, *Unterwegs zur Sprache*
WSV	Wellmer, "Wahrheit, Schein, Versöhnung"

Acknowledgments

This book derives from a seminar at the Graduate Faculty of the New School for Social Research, and I am indebted to my students there. Samuel Todes's orientation on the philosophy of small groups provided a starting point for much of the book, and David Hull made some valuable points about how to do intellectual history. Joseph Flay, Rodolphe Gasché and Jürgen Habermas offered advice and encouragement. Three Hegelians taught me what philosophy can be: H. S. Harris, Kenneth Schmitz, and especially Emil Fackenheim.

Many people, in addition to providing that kind of general orientation, have been personally helpful with regard to specific portions of the book. They have steered me past innumerable errors and are hardly responsible for the innumerable ones that remain. R. E. Allen gave me the benefit of his criticism of my views on the *Phaedrus*. Ludwig Nagl first showed me that Kant was not the "monologist" he was generally supposed to be. Allen W. Wood has made valuable criticisms of my views on Hegel and of the final part of this book. David Michael Levin, Graeme Nicholson, and Reiner Schürmann were extremely generous with time and criticism with regard to my interpretation of Heidegger. Thomas McCarthy has done the same with regard to some of my interpretations of Habermas; I am also indebted to the acute criticisms of Nancy Fraser and Françoise Lionnet. Richard J. Bernstein provided crucial criticism of an early version; his concern with Aristotelian phronesis first pointed me back to the Greeks.

Kenneth Seeskin, as my chairman at Northwestern, was extremely helpful in meeting my requests for a complex juggling of teaching loads as I wrote the book. As a Plato scholar, he showed me key features of the Platonic dialogues. Sydney Lenit and Marina Rosiene helped me get part of the book off the typescript and onto the disk. The College of Arts and

Sciences at Northwestern University provided a quarter's leave at a crucial moment.

After adopting and rejeting various strategies for dealing with the intractable sexism of the English language, I decided to make everything masculine (in keeping with the tradition I treat). Future works will simply reverse this emphasis.

Finally, I am overwhelmingly indebted for my views on poetic interaction, and on everything else, to my experience of two small poems named Jonathan and Danielle. They write themselves. But they still belong to me.

General Introduction

This book treats six thinkers from two traditions in three ways, all to make one simple point: that language is oriented to freedom as inherently as it is to truth. More so, indeed, because some language games are intrinsically emancipatory while—in spite of what we think philosophers have told us—none are intrinsically true. I will argue, in fact, that freedom and truth are not only separate values served by speech, but that they are complementary; that language becomes, in certain senses, intrinsically emancipatory when truth claims are not made, and vice versa. To understand language itself, we must seek to understand both its truth telling and its emancipatory functioning; omitting either is somewhat like trying to understand magnets by looking only to their north poles without regard to the south. And, as the effects of such incompleteness would extend beyond physics, so those of ignoring the emancipatory powers of ordinary language may extend beyond philosophy into political science, sociology, psychology, and linguistics.

Between the simplicity of the book's thesis and the complexity of its structure lies a series of problems. It begins once we ask what the terms in my simple thesis may mean. What, to say nothing of "language," is "freedom?" In spite of its importance (especially for Americans), the concept has no agreed extension, and indeed it seems to be without a single universally admitted example. For every person who maintains that the will is free, there are likely to be two others—one to claim that the will is not free, and one to claim that there is no "will" at all. For every American who claims that the United States is a 'free' country, there are 1.16 Soviet citizens to claim that it is not. It is not possible, then, to proceed as if we were dealing with a term for a natural kind. We cannot begin by taking instances of "freedom," as we can of "gold," and then trying to see what they have in common. We have no such instances, a characteristic "freedom" shares with other predicates. "Bloopness," for example, is the property of being 2/3 as just as one is tall, and there are no clear examples of it either. But unlike bloopness, which I just invented, freedom has been talked about for millennia, and a fair amount of that talk has propounded definitions of it: over two hundred of them according to Isaiah Berlin.[1]

Two contrasting approaches suggest themselves, which I will call "positivistic" and "Quinean." The positivistic approach would be to claim that since we cannot empirically discriminate free segments of the universe from unfree ones, the term simply has no meaning and, as B. F. Skinner once suggested on different grounds, would best be abolished.[2] The problem with attempts to adjust political discourse to semantic theory in this way is that they do not work. In spite of Skinner, people have gone right on talking about "freedom" with no consensus on its meaning, just as intervening years have seen no action on Brian Barry's analogous suggestion that talk of "equality" be done away with.[3]

A promising adjustment to semantic theory would be to take the Quinean (or, as we shall see, Hegelian or Heideggerean) approach: to view "freedom" as occupying a position somewhere toward the center of the "web of beliefs" that makes up our cognitive apparatus.[4] The function of concepts such as freedom, we may assume, resides less in telling us about the world than in organizing and coordinating the more concrete forms of cognition which do convey such information. Insofar as "freedom" is a normative concept, we may expect that what it organizes and coordinates will be not merely beliefs but actions. If actions organized and coordinated constitute practices, then we can express the meaning of "freedom" by specifying some of the beliefs and practices it organizes. This may not tell us which segments of the universe are free, for freedom could play this sort of organizing role even if it were a mere ideal and there were no such segments, but it will inform us about what sort of ideal it is.

This approach brings its own idiosyncrasies. The only "web of beliefs" or of practices to which I can claim immediate access is my own. But my own web might be uniquely organized, and whatever functions "freedom" performs in it could for all I know be wholly atypical. If so, my use of the term will be incomprehensible to others, and the only way to find out whether this is so is to ask them. Investigating the meaning of "freedom" thus becomes a dialogical affair in which I measure my intuitions against those of others. But which others?

Those with whom I can speak to begin with—the members of my linguistic community, Americans and other English speakers. But here is another problem: what if they, too, are idiosyncratic, and all in the same way? What if current Anglo-Saxon usage diverges systematically from language usage in other times and places? What if, for example, it disperses practices which could be viewed as members of a single class, designating them by a plurality of terms? What if it fails to recognize practices which, in times past, have given root to important dimensions of "freedom?" Unless we want to maintain, with Aristotle, that the language we happen to speak gives us transparent access to reality, we must at least suspect that such may be the case: that our language and culture themselves occlude practices that other languages and cultures have called "free." Such a fact would be worth knowing in itself. But it may have further implications. For unless we want to elevate ourselves and our kind over all other human beings, present and past, we have to suspect that they, not we, may (in some senses at least) be right. In the face of these suspicions the investigation becomes one of the "post-Foucaultian" sort suggested by Hubert Dreyfus and Paul Rabinow, one which examines "not only systems of thought and the human reality they constitute, but also those practices which persevere even though they seem to be trivial and even subversive."[5] The undertaking must go beyond our own linguistic community, measuring the shared intuitions of its members against those of people belonging to other times and places.

But how can such an investigation be conducted? We could, of course, travel the world as anthropologists do, conversing with all and sundry. But our sample of the human race would be small and probably not random, and would extend only to our own time. Such investigations are hardly to be despised, but I have chosen another way. Examples of the language of previous generations and other cultures remain with us, in the form of texts. Some texts—a relative few—have "canonical" status, in that they are believed to sum up and crystallize the thought of a particular group of people—perhaps a whole culture—on a given topic. So texts give us access to the (written) language of other communities, and canonical texts to their thought. It seems that we can understand how · other cultures view "freedom" by looking to canonical texts on the subject.

The phrase "are believed" in my definition of the canonical status of texts marks off another problem: *who* believes that a given text is "canonical?" The answer is, ultimately, we and our kind. The canonical status of the *Critique of Practical Reason* for contemporary thought about freedom and morality is not a quality resident in the text itself, but derives from the fact that some significant portion of the present generation of educated people holds that text to be central to those topics. Even if an unbroken line of thinkers, right back to its contemporaries, regards a book as important, it can still be dropped from the philosophical canon at any time—as the Neoplatonists, for example, have largely been dropped. We might assume that such decisions, over the centuries, have been rationally motivated. But is that assumption justified? It is certainly possible that some texts are assigned canonical status, not because they really sum up a previous stage of language and culture, but because they highlight what we want them to highlight and occlude what we, on some level, want them to occlude. This suspicion points to a different sort of procedure: to investigating, not canonical texts which have come down to us, but noncanonical ones. Our hope would be to find views in them that subsequent generations have, for one reason or another, suppressed, but which were important in their own times and which may contain valuable correctives for us—as Foucault himself, in his discussion of Greek views on freedom and truth, makes major use of Xenophon in comparison with Aristotle and Plato.[6]

But if canonical texts fall under the suspicion of reflecting the idiosyncrasies of the readers who canonize them, noncanonical texts can be suspected of expressing the idiosyncrasies of those who wrote them. These may be merely individual, as is perhaps the view of epic virtue conveyed by pseudo-Homer in *The Battle of the Frogs and Mice*. But such individualistic texts, by definition, rarely survive; more common are texts which express the shared, but unwarranted, preferences of an entire culture or group. There are reasons why Plato and Aristotle, rather than Xenophon and Isocrates, are regarded as the supreme political thinkers of Greece, and they have to do with the fact that Plato and Aristotle, unlike more pedestrian thinkers, did not simply pass on the common sense of the time. They subjected it to clarification and criticism, refining the rational core of their culture from its dross.[7]

My solution to all these problems of idiosyncrasy will be to take a middle road, looking mainly at texts which are not minor but also not quite canonical, in the sense that they are regarded as lesser or transitional works by major thinkers: Plato's *Phaedrus*, Kant's *Critique of Judgment* and *Conflict of the Faculties*, the political passages of Hegel's *Aesthetics*, and Heidegger's "Origin of the Work of Art," together with the major work of a thinker who, being very much alive, is not yet canonized: Jürgen Habermas's *The Theory of Communicative Action*. Because the writers are major, there is a good chance that the texts do not express the merely individual or cultural idiosyncrasies of their writers. Because the writings are not canonical, there is a chance that they do not reflect the preferences of contemporary readers. There is, therefore, a chance of finding in them something occluded in more widely discussed texts. I will seek to uncover this by playing these texts off against more canonical works of those thinkers—Plato's *Phaedo* and *Republic*, Kant's first two *Critiques*, Hegel's *Philosophy of Right*, and Heidegger's *Being and Time*.

4

This list shows on its face that another principle of selection has been at work: the texts on it come from traditions which themselves are, at least in the English-speaking world, regarded as major but not "canonical." It is a high school platitude that our basic political values and ideas come from the Greeks, but today their political thought is not often deemed worthy of a great deal of attention. Even Habermas, for all his voracious readings of diverse thinkers, has not dealt with it in any length or detail, and a study of Plato published in 1986 could announce itself as the first comprehensive treatment in English of his political theory since Barker's of 1918.[8] Moreover it is, in the strongest sense of the word, "common" knowledge that the German tradition is devoted mainly to deifications of the state (when not, as with Heidegger, of the Führer), backed by reams of turgid metaphysics. Such generalizations, abetted by the difficulty of the texts themselves, have persistence; but, as has often been shown in the past, they have no truth. I will show this again.

My choice of traditions may thus, like my choice of texts, serve as a corrective for distortion and neglect. But there is a further reason for treating the Greek and German traditions and treating them together. We are to investigate the relation of language and freedom, and this limits us to conceptualizations of freedom that view it as arising in and through our speech, i.e., our interactions with others.

One might find good oranges in a hardware store, but that would not be the right place to look first. A glance at two other traditions—the Christian and the British empiricist—suggests that, whatever individual thinkers in those traditions may have achieved, in general they are not promising places to begin looking for the kinds of freedom I want to investigate. John Stuart Mill has, if with almost Calvinist severity, captured the spirit of the former:

> It holds out the hope of heaven and the threat of hell, as the appointed and appropriate motives to a virtuous life: in this . . . doing what lies in it to give to human morality an essentially selfish character, by disconnecting each man's feelings of duty from the interests of his fellow-creatures . . . it inculcates submission to all authorities found established . . . and while, in the morality of the best pagan nations, duty to the state holds even a disproportionate place, infringing upon the just liberty of the individual, in purely Christian ethics, that grand department of duty is scarcely noticed or acknowledged.[9]

Mill's own empiricist tradition, however, tends to see freedom as essentially "negative," i.e., as having to do less with an individual's relations to others than with his own power, resident within himself, to realize his intentions. Thus, for Hobbes, freedom is the absence of external opposition to an individual's actions, and for Hume it is primarily the power of acting or not acting according to the determinations of the will. Hume, indeed, thinks this definition to be so obvious that whether everyone has the power in question is "no subject of dispute;" disputes arise only over whether the will itself is determined.[10] But the capacity to realize purposes is, as Habermas argues, not intrinsically interactive. Its asociality is summed up by Locke's basic example: a man standing at the edge of a cliff is free to jump down (but not up).[11]

Who, here, is the prisoner of cultural idiosyncrasy? If Hume could have told an ancient Greek that no one denies the power of an individual to act according to the determinations of his or her will, the reaction would have been bewilderment: Greek thought, and indeed the Greek language itself, do not even have a word for "will." But Greek thinkers do write about freedom; they just conceptualize it differently. They tend to view it, in fact, as the kind of freedom with which I will be concerned here: the freedom one has, not standing on the edge of a cliff, but only in and through interacting with one's fellow men and women. The same will hold for the German thinkers I have selected.

We will, then, look first at texts: some German, some Greek, and most not quite canonical. And we will look at them as philosophical texts; as bodies of warranted writing, where "warranted" is understood in the wide sense advanced by Stephen Toulmin.[12] There are several things a "text," as a body of warranted writing, is not, and three of those things will determine my general approach.

First, a text is not the product of a concrete human being; the authorial personality provides no philosophical warrant. I will restrict my discussions in the first instance to what is present in the texts themselves and will not try to see in detail how Plato or Kant, the men, were affected by the sociopolitical situations in which they wrote, or how their texts fulfill the intentions they had when writing them. One reason for this is that we usually cannot know how the concrete situation of an author influences his or her writing. Plato was a Greek, a member of an old and supremely wealthy Athenian family, and homosexual. I am an American, notably less wealthy, and heterosexual. There is no question that Plato and I both write differently than we would if these things were not true. But if asked how in detail these facts about me condition my writing, I wouldn't have a clue. How then can I answer the question for him? With a few exceptions—such as Aristotle's account of slavery in a slave society and Kant's ambiguous position vis-à-vis Frederick the Great—the psychological and social circumstances that influence the author of a text, the manner in which they do so, and the intentions he or she has in writing are essentially unknowable. When appealed to by interpreters, such matters are often not even Kantian "noumena," but merely Kantian figments of the brain: unverifiable ideas, arbitrarily constructed by the reader and then dogmatically imposed on the texts.[13]

This dogmatism can have pernicious effects. For it is an imposition, in the first instance, of our own views on what a "personality" is. In particular, because we view a "personality" as something relatively stable and consistent, we tend to overlook surprises which may be presented by the actual texts themselves. Why is it—to anticipate some results of the investigations to come—that Plato is usually regarded, if not as a downright totalitarian, as someone who (in Mill's words) gives duty to the state a "disproportionate place?" In fact his ideal republic is manifestly a sort of minimal state viewed from the top down—where Robert Nozick's conception of a minimal state is one which does not interfere with its citizens, Plato's is structured so as not to interfere with its rulers.[14] The reasons and results, to be sure, are different, but the desire to limit the "political" sphere is of similar intensity.

Why is Kant thought to view morality as an affair of the will of the isolated individual, when in fact that will requires discussion with others for its very power to act? Why has the vehement critique of the state advanced in Hegel's *Aesthetics*, a critique grounded in his *Logic* and alluded to in the *Philosophy of Right* itself, wholly eluded commentators for 160 years? Why is the later Heidegger persistently viewed as a mystic and Habermas as a foundationalist defender of the Enlightenment, when both thinkers are explicitly dialogical in method and believe that all human reason is conditioned by structures of the world which can never be fully known? Given the amount and the quality of the writings on these thinkers, insufficient homework is hardly the answer. I suspect the problem arises in part because of the effects of viewing texts as the productions of a single authorial personality: the *Phaedrus*, then, must cohere with the *Republic*, the *Aesthetics* with the *Philosophy of Right*, the third *Critique* with the first two, and the second volume of *The Theory of Communicative Action* with the first. When the coherence isn't there, we banish the recalcitrant works from the canon and call them "youthful," "transitional," or simply confused. What the texts actually exhibit, I suggest, are violent changes in perspective—changes which themselves may or may not be intended by the author, but which in either case can shed light on his more "canonical" writings.

These claims can only be supported by a detailed and critical, if selective, statement of what is actually to be found in a given text without much regard for what the author says elsewhere. Such a statement, though basic, is harder than it looks—particularly so in the case of the texts I have chosen, all of which have both surface and depth. The Platonic surface is beguilement and ease, with what is really a tightly structured set of arguments presented as a free play of conversation. The Aristotelian texts, on their surface, are collections of fragmentary notes and insights which seem to do full justice to the tradition that they spent a hundred years in a cellar in Asia Minor being eaten by worms. The works of Kant, as Hans Saner has noted, not only refuse to formulate clear meanings for terms in their first use: the meanings change as one goes through the texts, and this continual redefinition is essential to the way the texts operate.[15] Finally, Hegel and Heidegger are simply difficult, and Habermas's main text is so new it is as yet unassimilated by others.

Because of all this, the basic warrants for what a given text overtly asserts are not often explicitly stated, and we must go beneath the embellishments, fragmentations, redefinitions, and difficulties playing upon the surface of texts to engage more basic concepts and arguments. I will refer to this as "analysis," and it is best defined at this point by its goal: to give an accurate, i.e., true, account of the conceptual deep structures of a text on a given topic. Such an account must, for present purposes, be given in ordinary English rather than technical jargon—partly as a matter of discipline, partly because as long as the analysis remains bound to the technical vocabularies of the various writers it will be impossible to tie them together, and partly because, given such a diverse collection of texts, no one reader should be expected to be conversant with all of them.

The analyses are selective: they investigate the respective texts from a particular point of view and are not intended as exhaustive rehearsals of all topics treated in those texts. Here, they will attempt to show that the texts considered contain, not merely isolated insights into emancipatory interaction, but sustained investigations of it. This is particularly important for Hegel and Heidegger. It is possible, for example, simply to look up "language" in the index to Hegel's *Phenomenology* and come away with a set of fascinating (if cryptic) observations. Sustained analysis, however, reveals the book to be largely structured around three basic concepts—those of "recognition," "externalization," and "reconciliation," all of which can be read as referring to various types of interaction. Until we have seen this, we cannot understand the interplay of the three in Hegel's thought or grasp the role of the third, emancipatory type in his conception of freedom. Similarly, Heidegger's view of human discourse as an interplay between an individual's understanding of a particular state of affairs and the larger, encompassing structures of his or her "world" is an important theme in *Being and Time*, and the critique of it is central to Heidegger's later works. Only if that centrality is grasped by a sustained analysis can the real problem be raised, which is that of *why* this particular critique of *Being and Time* should be so central to the later Heidegger; part of the answer is that it yields a new and radical concept of emancipation.

Finally, analysis in my sense is not uncritical. When a body of thought fails to engage its own problematic; when it leaves certain questions unanswered, certain points unclear, or certain formulations strained; and when this can be shown to result, not from authorial laziness or anything of that kind, but from other commitments and presuppositions also exhibited in the text; it is the business of analysis to state that fact. The *analytical* claim, however, is that the text's failures, like its successes, are present in the text itself: they are not "failures" only when viewed from the perspective of some other writer. Criticism dealing with the latter sort of failure will be the prerogative of the book's other two strategies: narrative and demarcation.

Philosophical analysis of texts, beginning with such a diverse collection of surfaces, uses no single set of procedures. In the investigation to come, each such analysis will require slightly different tactics in order to arrive at its goal. But there will be a major distinction among three strategies of textual analysis.

Hegel and Heidegger will prove to be the most important of the thinkers I will be discussing for the topic at hand. And they are also, by far, the most difficult. This is not simply due to the opacity of their texts, though at times that approaches what can only be called perfection. Partly because of their difficulty, both writers have, as I have mentioned, been overlaid with interpretations indicating that they have nothing to do with interaction and little to do with "freedom" in any recognizable or desirable sense. Thus, there is a common view that Hegel's thought is the quasi-theological analysis of something called the Absolute, which is either history, God, or a sort of God-in-history.[16] Heidegger is often viewed as an eremite and mystic.[17] I do not want to argue that both these views are wholly wrong (though in fact I think they are largely so). But I do want to claim that, even if they are right, not every text of each author needs to be read in such terms. In particular, long stretches of Hegel's *Phenomenology* and *Aesthetics* can be understood, not as some sort of historicized theology or metaphysics, but in what I will call "interactionist" terms; their basic concepts can be read as referring to nothing other than modes and aspects of human interaction. The same holds for important parts of *Being and Time* and other works by Heidegger. Showing this demands an extended treatment, which I have placed in part one of this book, "Analysis."

The other thinkers, on whom there is a greater degree of scholarly consensus, will be analyzed in less detail and with more appeal to secondary sources. The purpose for the Plato analysis will be to cut through the playful (and even confused) appearance of the *Phaedrus* to its very serious (and very lucid) core. For Aristotle, Kant, and Habermas, the analysis will critically bring together points dispersed through hundreds of pages of argument in different books.

Finally, the last two chapters of part three of this book will be concerned with analysis, not of texts, but of examples of language in use. Here, as in the earlier analyses in part one, I will be attempting to bring out fundamental structures of utterances; since the utterances will belong to ordinary language, they will be simpler than the enormously complex variety that constitutes philosophical texts. My basic analytical methods will not change greatly, then, when I turn from texts to ordinary language, and my fundamental claim—to truth—will not change at all. But the procedures will become simplified.

Second, a text is not an isolated historical event. It stands in social and psychological contexts which can occasionally be determined with enough precision to be informative. Moreover, the texts we shall be considering relate to each other in ways that can be verified and checked: the Aristotelian texts, once analyzed, can be seen as criticizing the Platonic ones on a variety of grounds; the Kantian texts those of both Aristotle and Plato, the Hegelian texts those of all three; and so on. This fact is of importance here in two broad ways. For one thing, if a later thinker gives an important place to the criticism of an earlier one, then we ought to wonder which came first: was Aristotle an independent thinker who happened to have some thoughts about Plato, or a critic of Plato who eventually pulled his criticisms together into his own unique view? Probably both; but unless we want to deny the latter alternative a priori, we must view Aristotle's texts in connection with those of Plato. In general, the philosophical tradition is such that earlier texts constrain the writing of later texts, which cannot be understood without them.

If the criticisms in question are warranted, they also have the effect of foreclosing certain readings or certain parts of texts where criticized doctrines are presented. If by virtue of the criticisms of Aristotle and Kant, for example, I can no longer accept the Platonic theory of Forms, then a particular dimension of the *Phaedrus* is closed to me—and this, as we shall see, opens up another dimension of the text. If, after Hegel, I cannot accept the abstract character of Kantian morality, the second *Critique* closes off, and the third opens up. In addition, later texts can articulate possibilities not envisaged by earlier ones. Kant's introduction of the sublime (in his particular meaning) into aesthetics opens up concepts and possibilities unavailable to Plato and Aristotle, and this shows us limitations of the two Greek thinkers which would otherwise escape us. Heidegger's appropriation of the sublime both clarifies matters Kant leaves obscure and opens up possibilities not allowed for in Hegel. In this respect, later texts serve to situate those parts of earlier texts which they do not criticize: to show those parts as residing in broader contexts.

In sum, earlier texts constrain the writing of later ones, while later texts constrain the reading of earlier ones. This means that analysis is not enough. Some sort of story stringing the texts together is also required. Positions once criticized do not reappear in this exercise, so it exhibits rational development over time. One can call this "progress." But it is, first, a fragmented and contingent progress, relative only to certain strands or threads within the whole history of philosophy. And even then it is to some degree an artifact of my selection; it is an empirical fact that positions once criticized do, in fact, turn up again later in philosophy. This is why, for example, Quine and Sellars had to do to the logical positivists what Hegel had already done to Kant 150 years earlier.[18]

The reconstruction of this "progress" I will call "narrative," and it has a different goal from analysis.[19] The analysis of a philosophical text claims truth: though one is always imperfect and incomplete, one at least hopes to be accurate. Narrative, by contrast, aims at coherence (and ultimately, I will argue, at freedom). The "re-" in "reconstruct," to be sure, is to indicate that I am not engaged in fiction—the arbitrary construction of a narrative—but I am relying on my analysis. Had I selected different texts, to say nothing of different thinkers and topics, I would surely come up with a different story. But this does not mean that narrative aims at historical truth; the developments narrated may in fact have happened quite otherwise. Indeed, as I carry it out here, the narrative exercise presupposes that events *could not* actually have happened as narrated. In addition to leaving out "backsliders" who take up again positions already criticized previously, I will also, for lack of space, omit many other writers important to the actual events from which my narrative is derived: Plotinus, Rousseau, Schiller, Marx, Nietzsche, and Husserl come to mind. I will also be viewing the confrontation of Hegel and Kant, for example, in only a couple of domains: practical philosophy and philosophy of language. In reality, we know, Hegel's criticism of Kantian ethics was part of a much more generalized confrontation with Kant including issues of epistemology and especially philosophy of religion.[20] Hegel simply did not confront Kant as my narrative will present him doing, and the same may well be true of all the other thinkers. To sum the matter up: the narrative is bound more tightly to the texts actually analyzed than to the historical developments that produced those texts. The narrative claim is that, if what is narrated did not in fact happen, the accuracy of my analysis means that something broadly similar to it must have: the "re" in "reconstruction" refers to a loose similarity, a necessarily distorted one, between narrative and actual history.

Any narrative is then only one of many possible stories, and as more of these possibilities are actualized the better off, narratively speaking, we are. There is reason to believe that our store of philosophical narrative is presently rather low. Why, for example, has no one advanced the idea that our concept of the state, the centerpiece of European political theory (if not of European politics itself), grows from Aristotle's abstruse critique of the Platonic theory of self-motion? Why has it not been suggested that Kant's philosophy not merely takes up Platonic themes, but is largely a rewriting of Plato in which the modern rational mind (one from which eros has been eliminated) replaces the ancient cosmos? Why have modernists and postmodernists, in the lulls between their recurrent skirmishes, failed to see that their respective viewpoints coexist as sweetly as twin embryos in the womb, in Kant's doctrine of reflective judgment? Again, I suspect, the reason for this is not want of intelligence and industry, but rather the conviction that narrative is a form of truth telling, that there can be only one true story, and that the proliferation of narratives would (as indeed it does) undermine the truth claim of any of them. But narrative connecting is like a rope rather than a chain; there is no more need for different narratives to harmonize fully with one another than there is for all the strands of a rope to twist in the same direction at the same point.

My narrative procedure then will be something like the reconstruction of a fossil record: taking structures analyzed previously, I will try to put them into a coherent story. But it will be a minimalist reconstruction; instead of tracing the development of entire species—entire bodies of thought—what I will be doing will be analogous to tracing, for example, just the development of the inner ear. And, because a seminal philosophical text is considerably more unique than the average fossil, I will not take many samples from each stage of the narrative; a couple from each thinker will have to suffice.

Some of the texts I have selected were chosen for their function in the narrative. Aristotle's *De Anima* 1.3, for example, criticizes the account of the soul presented in Plato's *Phaedrus*, and Kant's Third Antinomy criticizes both Aristotelian and Platonic approaches to metaphysics. But in general, a thinker does not really know how he relates to previous thinkers. An example of this is provided by Habermas, who locates the "paradigm change" toward communication theory in the American pragmatists and specifically not in the "German" tradition (*TKH* 1.534/ 397, 2.7–169). In fact, the pragmatists, my narrative will suggest, were in this "interactive turn" merely being good Hegelians—or even good Kantians of the third *Critique*. The same is true of the others I will be dealing with: Heidegger, Hegel, Kant, and Aristotle are all known to be highly suspect when they tell us what their predecessors were really up to and what their own relation to those predecessors is. Because of this, I have made only "episodic" use of texts in which thinkers deal explicitly with their predecessors, and discuss those texts in my analyses—not because they tell us about the predecessors, but because they tell us about their own writers. Most of the texts were chosen, in fact, for their analytical significance; they deal with topics with which I wish also to deal. Their differences with earlier texts are then taken as criticisms, and the warrants for them are analyzed.

The "Narrative" will principally occupy the central section, part two, of this book. Though only loosely related to actual historical developments, it depends directly upon the analytical aspect of the book, and I have—with the exceptions of Hegel and Heidegger—elected to keep narrative and analysis together. But there is nothing to prevent someone who is familiar with a given text, or who is willing to take my analyses on faith, from skipping them and reading the narrative as a continuous whole.

Finally, a text is not the final answer. Any text, of course, has imperfections, like all things human. More to our point, the story of its relation to texts before and after is full of fits and starts, of backslides and new beginnings, of criticisms that don't quite hit their targets. It will be the task of my third method, "demarcation," to mark off some of these which have not been recuperated—those which suggest that, within them, new approaches can still come to be. Thus, Aristotle's critique of the Platonic separation of Forms and sensibles fails to dispose of certain points made in the *Phaedrus*; these stand today as an early portrayal of poetic interaction itself.

While analysis, claiming truth, presents texts as existing in a sort of timeless present, and narrative reconstructs the past, demarcation is oriented to the future. As opposed to narrative, it does not claim coherence; as opposed to analysis, it cannot claim truth either. For what it uncovers are not structures, to which its account could be faithful, but lack of structure, anomaly, emptiness: what Jacques Derrida has called "differance."[21] What demarcation claims is that there is work left to be done, that everything is not settled, that there is a future.

Since demarcation has to do with possibilities for the future, the thinker from whom I must most importantly demarcate myself is the one closest to me: Habermas. "Demarcation" will thus begin, as a separate procedure, when we reach his position in my narrative. Its main task will be to point out discrepancies between Habermas's views (and those of Albrecht Wellmer, which develop Habermas's account in ways important for my topic) and my account of previous thinkers. I will argue that what, from Habermas's own perspective, are relatively unimportant lacunae and uncritical residues of earlier thought actually, when viewed in connection with the concepts of freedom and language emerging from my narrative, connect with each other and reveal a set of phenomena—a practice of freedom. This practice, intrinsically emancipatory interaction, exists today and was discussed by earlier thinkers—though, again, not unproblematically. Solving those problems is a task for the future; revealing them, an aim of the present demarcative effort. Because demarcation depends directly upon narrative, and that upon analysis, I have elected to keep the three methods together in the book's third and final part, "Demarcation."

Analysis, narrative, and demarcation are hardly new with this book. Plato presumably understood his theory of Forms, for example, to "analyze" features of the cosmos not readily apparent on the surface of experience. His dialogues, as rational conversations, have narrative structure and, as we shall see, the *Phaedrus* contains a nonconversational narrative. His early, aporetic dialogues can be considered as a series of fits and starts and new beginnings, which gave rise to something genuinely new—the theory of Forms itself. But since Aristotle, analysis has generally dominated philosophy. Philosophers have seen themselves as providing (or attempting to provide) a set of true propositions about the structure, first, of the cosmos; more recently, of consciousness; and most recently, of language. Such truth has not been the exclusive concern of philosophers, of course; scientists have in fact largely taken it over, and with the rise of science the other forms of investigation began to return to philosophy. In Spinoza's Ethics, the "intellectual love of God," which turns out, in the final book, to animate the whole, is not a set of true propositions but a possible practice of freedom, which Spinoza thinks was occluded by Descartes, among others. And the mode of presentation followed in the latter's *Meditations* is a narrative, aimed at presenting the results of his thought in a particularly compelling form.[22]

More recently, narrative and demarcation have come into philosophy itself as more than a moment of presentation or an ulterior aim. Hegel's *Phenomenology of Spirit* does this for narrative. Demarcation has arrived even more recently in the later writings of Heidegger and their more radical development by Derrida. These developments are not yet well understood; English-language philosophy, for example, has been largely unable to assimilate them. We shall see that such acute interpreters of the *Phenomenology* as Kierkegaard and Marx understand it as the analysis of something, though they do not agree as to what, and that, as soon as it is so understood, it breaks down. Similarly, those who understand Heidegger as advancing a set of doctrines about something called "Being" generally find themselves lost in a welter of arbitrariness, contradiction, and obscurity, unaware that a true "demarcation"—the exposure of gaps in reasoned articulation—must exhibit all these characteristics (just as do Plato's aporetic dialogues).

The methodological innovation of this book, if any, is thus not in making use of these three modes of investigation. It is in using all three of them, for the reasons I have given, and in keeping them separate. Not wholly separate, as some of the texts I will analyze, I have noted, were chosen for their contribution to my narrative. And my narrative of the *De Anima*, for example, will reveal a gap between those criticisms of the *Phaedrus* which proceed on the basis of Aristotle's own substance-metaphysics and those which do not, with a consequent gap or "demarcation" between what Aristotle actually refutes and what Plato actually maintains. But there are reasons for keeping the three methods as separate as possible.

If, for example, we conflate analysis and narrative, then we take ourselves to be analyzing some sort of historical development as it actually happened. This can lead, first, to undue reification, as ideas and approaches come loose from the words and texts in which they are presented and take life as evolving individuals—much as Hegel's "Spirit" is often alleged to do. It can also lead to undue length, as elements which suggest themselves for the sake of coherence and continuity must be sought out in the texts themselves, which then—since they don't quite contain those elements—make what are viewed as further suggestions. There is a place for this. Hegel's thought, for example, develops in a narrative way, and my analyses will attempt to be true to that fact. But in general, separating analysis from narrative can, I suspect, shorten the book.

If, on the other hand, we conflate analysis with demarcation, we take ourselves to be describing gaps and incoherences within texts. This genre lends itself to very short pieces, which point out inconsistencies or omissions and then simply end. But without a sustaining narrative, demarcation uncovers no paths to the future, for the position of a particular text within a larger cultural whole is what enables any demarcation of it to be more than simply a set of plays upon the text itself. And since cultures are never static, to situate a text within a larger cultural whole is to do so narratively: we do not simply relate it to other cultural forms produced simultaneously with it, but relate it to what went before and what comes after (if only, in the latter case, our own writing on it). It is noteworthy that the two philosophers who have most clearly made use of demarcative strategies—Heidegger and Derrida—both rely on what I have called a sustaining narrative, that of the history of metaphysics.[23] Detached from that narrative and applied arbitrarily to various texts that offer themselves, demarcation easily becomes trivial.

Finally, if we conflate narrative with demarcation, we have a narrative in which all gaps and backslides are part of the story, ultimately contributing something positive to it. It would then follow, for us in the present, that all historical gaps have been filled in and all backslides stopped: the past confronts us as entirely recuperated. There is left for us (as for Hegel, who adopted this strategy) nothing to do except await a future which cannot even be spoken of.[24]

It is then, I think, important to keep the three methods separate. Doing so unavoidably gives the book something of a mix-and-match character. A reader could, for example, start with the analyses in part two and then turn successively to those in parts one and three; this would yield a series of intellectual snapshots of what some important philosophers have said about language and freedom. Or one could simply read the narrative sections straight through, obtaining a connected (but incomplete and unsupported) history of philosophy from an interactionist point of view. Someone who simply wants a basic account of Hegel and Heidegger on the topics at hand can read the analyses of them in part one together with the appropriate narratives from part two. Anyone who wants to know what poetic interaction is apart from all historical contexts can turn directly to the last two chapters of the book, and so on.

Using all three methods is also useful. In addition to the considerations I offered earlier, doing so enables me to broach some issues regarding what I call the "situating of reason." This is not a topic that can be directly treated here. Though the historical parts of the book will hazard some discussion of the situating of reason generally (as well as of intrinsically emancipatory interaction), its systematic theme will remain an elementary form of such reason: poetic interaction. The motive for this restriction is simplicity: a discussion of the nature of situating reason would greatly extend what is already a long investigation into difficult areas. Indeed, definitive treatment of situating reason will always escape us; for it is the nature of "situations" to change, and part of the job of human reason is to cope with the changes. Poetic interaction is concerned with this fact, and a brief and preliminary discussion of the topic as it affects my undertaking may be useful here in spite of the unavoidable compression and difficulty.

The genitive in "situating of reason" can be taken either objectively, so that reason gets situated, or subjectively, so that reason is doing the situating. I understand "situation" itself in its derivation from the Latin *sino*, which has to do with permission. Situated reason is reason which has certain things permitted to it, and this implies prior prohibitions or limits; situated reason is in the first instance reason which *cannot* do certain things. For Aristotle (*Phys.* 4.4), to be in a place—*topos*—meant to be encompassed by something which could be left behind. If a situation can be left behind by those who are in it, it is defined by a set of prohibitions which do not hold always and everywhere—limits which are in effect only at certain times and certain places in the universe. When a prohibition is recognized as being of this type, we receive a sort of permission: if not permission to transcend it (which may be beyond our power), permission to think about what other situations we might find ourselves in if it were no longer in force. This sort of changeable or surpassable limit I will call a "parameter." The individual and cultural idiosyncrasies alluded to earlier would then be parameters: limits to a particular thinker or culture that not only could, but for various reasons should, be overcome. Situated reason is then reason that deals with parameters.

Not all limits are parametric in this sense: reason has unsituated forms in which it is the object of situating activity. In those forms, the limits on it are not parameters but what I call "necessities" and "conditions." I am never, if I want to be rational, free to deny logical or mathematical truths, for example, simply because those truths—for whatever reason—cannot be other than they are. Wherever I find myself—or wherever I find rational discourse, as well as in sections of the universe where I will find neither—I will find those truths functioning as limits on what can happen or be said. I shall call such limits "necessities." There are also limits which could in principle be other than they are but cannot be reasonably believed to be so. The temperature of my brain may, for example, exceed 700°F, at least for a time; but I cannot reasonably believe this to be the case here and now. Science and experience teach me that by the time my brain reached that temperature my thought processes would have stopped, and if I want to be rational I must respect that teaching. Similarly, though more profoundly for Descartes: it is quite possible that he did not exist—in fact, he has not existed since 1650—but he himself could not reasonably believe that he did not. Such limits, expressed in propositions whose falsehood is not of itself impossible but in some way (empirically or logically) entails my own nonexistence, I will call "conditions."

Human existence is an obviously complex affair, and conditions are of numerous types depending on how the existence they condition is being understood. That my brain temperature be less than 700° is a condition of my existence qua material object of a certain type. If I must exist as such a material object in order to exist at all, then it is a condition of my existence *tout court*. My existence as a thinking being is a condition of my existence as a doubting being, but as many post-Cartesian thinkers have pointed out, I can (and perhaps even must) exist without engaging in Cartesian doubt. Certain aspects of my culture, in addition, may condition my existence in various respects: capitalism, for example, conditions the existence of the capitalist *qua* capitalist, and if he thinks he cannot exist at all without being a capitalist, then he can no more question capitalism than I can suppose my brain temperature to be above 700°. In such a case, the individual's culture is taken to be a condition of his own existence, and the individual is culture bound. Situated reason, it follows, is not culture bound. It is located within a particular culture and does not occupy any absolutist, Archimedean standpoint. But insofar as it can be shown that its culture is composed of parameters rather than conditions, it is not "bound" to that culture.

Necessities have been explored by philosophers since they first noticed, at least as long ago as Pythagoras, that mathematical truth was special. And they have tried, from the start, to extend the domain of such necessities as far as it could go: Parmenides, for example, can be viewed as taking the Greek mathematical conception of "one," or unity, and making it into his basic metaphysical principle; while Socrates, the *Crito* hints, did the same in ethics.[25] The modern era, with its emphasis on subjectivity, focused on the conditions that make human beings human: the entire critical enterprise of Kant, for example, is a search for the "transcendental conditions" of such things as the experience of objects and moral action (in the first two *Critiques*) and human aesthetic debate (in the third).

Unsituated reason, then, operates with limits that hold always and everywhere, either in themselves or for all or some human beings, and argues for their status as such limits. From its perspective, any limits not of this type are contingent truths and can in general be disregarded: there is no pressing reason to discuss truths that hold only for various periods of time or in various sectors of the universe, unless we ourselves happen to be located in some of those times and places.

Rational activity is often thought of as beginning from local conditions—many of them parameters—and painfully rising via, for example, induction and experiment to universal necessities and conditions, moving from a situated to an unsituated state. It is remarkable that, in the six philosophers presented here, reason is first unsituated. It begins by treating ancient necessities (such as the realm of Forms or the concept of substance) or modern conditions (such as Kant's categories, Hegel's externalized content, or Heidegger's "world"); all else is assigned to the "merely" sensory or empirical realm. Contingent truths become pressing, as we will see, when philosophers come up against the fact that individuals must act in that sensory, contingent realm. For action presupposes, not merely a set of limits which cannot be other than they are, but a specific set of things in the universe that can be changed, and that those changes will affect (but not necessarily destroy) the actor. Those states of affairs, as givens which I cannot deny and which make some actions impossible, are limits; but they are limits which can be other than they are, and which therefore give me permission for action or, at least, for thought about action.

Necessities and conditions, by contrast, yield of themselves no permissions; a permission is always specific, and they are general. The fact that the sum of the squares of the two short sides of a right triangle is equal to the square of the long side provides no *specific* guidance to me here and now, because it is true always and everywhere. To apply that fact in my life, I must recognize myself as in a situation where such knowledge is useful to action, and this requires the adduction of what I am calling parameters. The fact that the temperature outdoors is less than 700° gives me no permission to do anything, provides no important guidance or orientation, again because it is true no matter what situation I may find myself in. But the fact that it is more than 80° outdoors gives me permission to leave my overcoat in the closet and cook dinner on the backyard grill. And it does this because it is also quite possible for the temperature to be considerably colder than that.

If "rational" activity is (in the broad Habermasian sense we will see later) activity that can be criticized by others, then parameters require rational activity. They must be adduced as needed, and the adduction of parameters can be performed well or badly: it too is a rational action. If the temperature is above 80°, I am permitted to dispense with my overcoat when I go outside, and perhaps (if I am male) with my shirt, but not with my pants. The parameters of conduct in my society forbid that, and failure to adduce those parameters, or to adduce them correctly, will lead to misfortune. The words of my language, which change historically, are also parameters, and using such words for thinking (as opposed to making inferences in an artificial language) is another way of adducing parameters. Reason that takes into account parameters, as well as necessities and conditions, is then "situated" reason.

But I can adduce parameters without knowing that I am doing so: I may mistake them for necessities or conditions. Philosophers, with their Parmenidean heritage, are notably prone to this. Aristotle, as we will see, does it systematically, and today the very phrase "natural language" is an invitation to it. Such mistakes are possible because the three types of limits do not always present themselves neatly classified into these types. In the first place, limits do not always "present" themselves at all. The protogeometricians who painted the caves of Lascaux could no more draw on a flat surface a right triangle whose angles added up to more than 180° than could Euclid, but this fact did not present itself until (perhaps) Pythagoras. The articulation of limits is then a human activity, not to be confused with the various ways we adduce limits that have already been articulated (though sometimes, of course, they occur together). And it seems to be an activity which can be performed well or badly: the Babylonians, in some sense, articulated the Pythagorean theorem better than the cave painters, and Pythagoras better than the Babylonians. Such articulation is then an activity that is—somehow—open to criticism if it is performed badly, and it is an exercise in reason.

The second aspect of this kind of exercise is then the decision, for a given limit, of which sort of limit it is. By proving the Pythagorean theorem, Euclid presumably believed he had shown it to be a necessity: always and everywhere true. But Kant argued that, as an a priori geometrical truth, it was not a "necessity" at all but a condition of the operation of the rational mind; and Bolyai, Lobachevsky, and Riemann established that it was not even that. The broadest pattern of Western thought has been viewed, since Hegel brought it into view at all, as a steady increase in the domain of parameters at the expense of necessities and conditions. In this development, all sorts of phenomena once viewed as instantiating universal truths have been shown, at most, to exhibit what is "true around here." My narrative will remain true to this general picture: the metaphysical reasonings of Plato and Aristotle will give way to the Kantian search for conditions, and then to the Hegelian and Heideggerean concern with parameters. Articulating parameters *as* parameters makes clear that reason, as governed by parameters rather than necessities or conditions, is situated; it also makes clear, in general, what sorts of situations it may find itself in. Insofar as the clarification of parameters as parameters is a criticizable, i.e., rational activity, it is distinct from the activity of situated reason which makes use of those parameters in specific circumstances. I will call this activity "situating reason."

The decision of whether a particular limit is a necessity, a condition, or a parameter is not necessarily subsequent to the original articulation of it as a limit: parameters are parameters, at least in part, because they can be articulated in ways that necessities and conditions cannot. But how do parameters get articulated? What sorts of criticizable thought processes does this require? Such questions point us to the introduction into philosophy of two of the strategies I am using in this book, narrative and demarcation. As long as we are dealing with necessities and conditions, we need not make use of these modes of interpretation. The limits we are dealing with are not supposed to be other than they are, and our concern is simply to analyze them accurately and establish that fact—either by deduction from first principles or, more recently, by experimental verification which can be replicated anywhere. When reason, with Hegel, comes to see itself as articulating parameters as parameters, such strategies no longer suffice. For one thing, not all necessities and conditions can be deduced or verified to be such. One way to show that a limit is a parameter, something which could be other than it is without killing us, is to see whether, in human history, it was once other than it is now, to construct a narrative of it or to demarcate ourselves from it.

But narrative, I have suggested, does not aim at truth. It narrates a set of transformations in what is considered to be a single parameter, but it produces only one of a set of possible narratives. Sometimes other phenomena could have been chosen as instances of "that" parameter, and the samples selected can often be put together in different, mutually exclusive ways. Any set of *narratable* phenomena makes possible a variety of stories stringing its members together. Such phenomena are to some degree ambiguous and shadowy, and must be so if we are going to present them in a narrative rather than in something claiming to be the analysis of a development.

When, for example, the elasticity of rubber is observed to decrease as the temperature is lowered, we know which variable we are measuring and which we are varying (at least we do if we are good experimenters). We can express our results in a mathematical formula, which can claim to be true, to be the analysis of a development. When we confront an issue as complex as the development of thought from the *Phaedo* to Aristotle's *Metaphysics* (to say nothing of more remote products of intellectual history), the situation is otherwise. We do not know for sure what is varying or what other changes are produced by that basic variation. We have to stitch together what we do know and construct a narrative of that development. This requires us to make decisions about which sets of phenomena to group together and into what sorts of larger structure to incorporate them. These decisions are based, not only on what we can learn about the phenomena themselves, but also on such factors as the theoretical or practical contexts in which they are encountered, what patterns of rational coherence are available to structure our narrative, and what our purpose is in constructing it. Different decisions will produce other narratives.

Narrative cannot be perfect and complete; it cannot account for all the transformations of phenomena in such a way as to render prediction possible. This is in part, of course, a result of our human cognitive limits and of the way things happen in the quantum universe. But these facts have practical uses. For if narrative could be perfect, our limits would all be produced from the past and hence be products of historical necessity: they would be themselves necessities, changing with time but in ways predictable on the basis of larger, unchanging properties of causal sequences. As Kant argued in his "Critique of Teleological Judgment" (KU 359–474), gaps in the narrative—areas which we do not understand rationally and which mean that new phenomena are possible—are not only inevitable: they are necessary if we are going to act. Such gaps in the narrative do not always present themselves as lacunae left when the limits governing a situation have been listed. Often they appear as persistent vaguenesses or ambiguities in elements of the list—a fact regularly exploited by Heidegger in his discussions of Hölderlin.[26] Demarcation is then a matter not of removing such ambiguity or vagueness, but of showing what is responsible for it.

Thus, in its demarcative as well as its narrative aspects, situating reason begins from experiential ambiguities or obscurities. When such a beginning occurs, not in the mind of an individual but in patterns of human interaction, it becomes what I will call "poetic." For poetic interaction is nothing more than interaction in which the *hearer* of an utterance, rather than its *speaker,* determines its meaning—and does so because the utterance is (in ways also to be explained) either irredeemably ambiguous or otherwise anomalous. Poetic interaction is thus an elementary form of situating reason, in that it is the initial form out of which such reason develops. As I will discuss it in this book, poetic interaction is also elementary in that it takes no account of a major set of issues that affect its developed form, situating reason: issues concerning the standards of criticism to be applied to narratives constructed and demarcations made. Poetic interaction thus stands to situating reason generally somewhat as goodwill stands to friendship in the *Nicomachean Ethics*: it is the simplified initial form out of which situating reason develops.[27]

The questions of how to specify norms for situating reason and what sorts of standing those norms have are many and difficult; my main motive for leaving them aside, as I have mentioned, is simplicity. I will here argue, first, that the poetic determination of meaning cannot claim truth, because the truth of an utterance cannot come into question until after its meaning in the current situation has been determined. But such determination can be, as I will also argue, emancipatory (in several traditional senses also to be explained later). Narration and demarcation, as the two main strategies involved in poetic interaction, thus aim not at truth but at freedom. They do so primarily, I will suggest, by specifying—narrating and demarcating—members of one set of parameters which are supremely important to human beings: the words in the languages they speak.

I have noted that unsituated reason, or what in the philosophical tradition is called "theory," becomes situated when confronted with practical necessities of action. For Plato, Kant, Hegel, and Heidegger, the bridge between theory and action is the analysis, narration, and demarcation of parameters: the situating of reason. And for all of them, though they do not all use the term, this has been most closely associated with what we would call the "aesthetic" realm. This means that my investigation of poetic interaction, though it hopes to lay the basis for a normative and general account of situated reason, will in the first instance deal with aesthetic experience. But it will suggest that the kinds of freedom and emancipation traditionally associated with aesthetic experience may be of significance for situating reason generally.

Philosophy has traditionally been viewed as either universal and absolutist or culture bound. If, instead, it is to play a role in the situating of reason, then it must, as the thought of Hegel and Heidegger indicates, make use of narrative and demarcation: it must not only analyze parameters and constitute them as parameters rather than conditions or necessities, but it must construct narratives of how those parameters came to be in order to show how those narratives break down. This all holds for my investigation here. For freedom itself is not a condition of human life: it is a parameter, something whose nature we know can change in the future because textual analysis shows that it has changed in the past. We cannot, therefore, remain with a mere analysis of it—whether that analysis takes the form of an inventory of ordinary uses of the term or of its uses in past philosophers, as I will undertake here. I will, in addition, try to construct a narrative of those uses. And I will try to show how that narrative itself breaks down: that the set of past transformations in the meaning of "freedom" do not wholly dictate the way we must use the term here and now. This brings us back to the idea of an occluded practice: for only if the set of past transformations have left something out, failed to grasp something, can we hope to free ourselves of them. But what they leave out cannot be something wholly foreign to them, either; for if it has no contact with the tradition at all, it is something too new and different to be called "freedom." Hence, I will look for a meaning—or practice—of freedom present in the texts chosen but occluded from the full awareness of those who have written and read the texts.

Here we encounter the villain of our piece: the malign entity that has systematically repressed the very concept of poetic interaction, in spite of the efforts of earlier thinkers to inform us, and themselves, about it. As in many contemporary tales of intellectual evil, that villain is called "metaphysics;" but metaphysics is many things. In respect to Plato, I will use the term in its Kantian sense: as the purported theory of a supersensible realm. For Aristotle, it will refer mainly to the account of a nonsensible component of the sensible realm, "substance." In regard to Kant and subsequent thinkers, I will use it in its Heideggerean or Derridean sense: as a form of discourse founded on the presupposition of complete presence. Common to all is the view that metaphysics is that area of discourse claiming to provide true propositions about (in my terms, to "analyze") a reality which in some sense is fundamental. If we view all rational discourse as being some one fundamental type, as philosophers have generally done, then the fundamental status of metaphysics gives it prescriptive powers for all other rational discourse. And since metaphysics aims at truth, it will count as rational only those other forms of discourse that aim at truth and that, therefore, are viewed as providing true propositions about nonfundamental realities.

Thus metaphysics in Aristotle, as we shall see, is not *merely* a set of propositions about the supersensible realm of the Prime Mover, or about something nonsensible in empirical objects, i.e., "substance." It undertakes as well to prescribe to other forms of discourse what form they must take, what other forms of interaction they can recognize in their objects, and how those forms are to be interpreted. When it does this for political theory, it demands that political interaction itself exhibit something like the structures of an Aristotelian substance—which means, as we shall see, that it have the structure of a "state." This approach is clearly not without validity; but it has limits. It automatically occludes forms of interaction which, like poetic interaction, are structured differently and aim at different goals, and it views them as marginal or subversive. This view is shared, in varying ways and to varying degrees, by all the thinkers I shall discuss.

Once poetic interaction has been freed from this occlusion, it is possible to go on and ask what sorts of procedures it can contain and what criteria for success it may have. In the final part of the book, I will discuss the procedures, but not the criteria for success. In particular, my accounts of narrative and demarcation will remain concrete, restricted to the examples offered respectively by Hegel and Heidegger. I will not attempt to state in general terms what "narrative" and "demarcation" are. In part this is because narrative is a contextualized matter for which general rules are hard to give; they are even harder to give for demarcation, which, being oriented to the future, includes a good deal of playfulness and guesswork. And in part it is because such an account would be inescapably a priori in character. Narration and demarcation, along with analysis, have never been viewed as three basic strategies of human inter-action, still less as three basic strategies of philosophy; along with poetic interaction itself, they have been accorded marginal status. They thus remain to some extent as possibilities, and to say what they are is to say not what poetic interaction (and philosophy itself, in at least one of its many possible forms) actually is, but what it could be if rescued from its marginal status. This kind of general and normative question would be-long to an investigation of situated reason itself and, as I noted above, is beyond the scope of this book: partly because the book is already long enough, and partly because it would require an extended and critical ac-count of the philosophical techniques of the two most redoubtable of thinkers, Hegel and Heidegger. I will turn to it in later works.

Part One

Analysis

Introduction

As I noted in the general introduction, Hegel and Heidegger present special problems of analysis. The difficulty of their works is such that the reception of them has itself been, in my sense, "poetic:" subsequent readers have had to determine for themselves what those works mean. Not surprisingly, there is little consensus on even basic aspects of their thought. My claim in what follows is that both thinkers can be read as offering accounts of human interaction in general, and of intrinsically emancipatory interaction in particular. At its maximum, this claim entails that their own vocabularies—full of technical terms such as "Spirit," "reason," "Being," and "difference"—can be translated into talk of human freedom and interaction with a gain in clarity and no loss of profundity.

My claim is actually less grand than that. I will argue only that my interactionist reading exposes a single deep structure of their thought—one which occasionally rises to the surface, but which operates elsewhere beneath it. I will consider that claim to be established if my analysis can show that some of the important places where language and interaction are overtly discussed present views which are not merely isolated insights, but coherent accounts of central issues; and that these accounts themselves tie together into larger developmental wholes which show that formulating and improving them was an ongoing, if unvoiced, concern of each thinker over much of his life.

The only way to do this is by selectively analyzing individual passages as parts of a larger development, and this means allowing the works of Hegel and Heidegger to dictate the order of my analysis. My account of Hegel will begin by tracing the theme of interaction through the *Phenomenology of Spirit*, showing the book to be largely structured on the sequential development of three basic concepts—recognition, externalization, and reconciliation—each designating a form or aspect of interaction. I will then argue that the nature of the *Phenomenology* itself prevents a full treatment of the interactive nature of reconciliation and that the lack is made up in the *Aesthetics*, where Hegel's account of intrinsically emancipatory interaction is to be found.

For Heidegger, I will show that *Being and Time* takes up problems of interaction in its treatment of Dasein's two principle modes of Being, authenticity and inauthenticity. I will argue that the account there is unable to present authenticity as an interactive phenomenon because all interaction in *Being and Time* is viewed as unrolling within the overarching context of significance that Heidegger calls "world," while authenticity is, in important respects, a withdrawal from world. "The Origin of the Work of Art," I shall then show, remedies that defect by treating interaction that operates beyond the contexts of world. But that treatment has problems of its own, which are overcome in "From a Dialogue on Language." The account of intrinsically emancipatory interaction presented there is, I will argue in part two, complementary to Hegel's.

Hegel and Heidegger will each furnish, then, several accounts of interaction. The latest of these, in the development of each thinker, turns out to be interaction which is intrinsically free; comparing these final accounts with earlier ones will enable us to see what they are free *from*, and in particular to assess their standing with respect to the kinds of interaction to be found in the political realm. In the part two of the book, I will tie these results into my larger narrative of the occlusion and recuperation of poetic interaction.

Because of the enormous number of competing interpretations of Hegel and Heidegger, not merely in general but with regard to specific passages I will be discussing, I will keep references to secondary literature minimal. The text, as Quentin Lauer has noted, is always there to be checked. If it warrants my conclusions, those familiar with other interpretations can draw their own with respect both to the compatibility of my views with others and to their relative strength.[1]

One

Communication as Recognition
Phenomenology of Spirit B

Reason for Hegel, both in his own sense and in my broader one of criticizable linguistic activity, begins in unsituated form. It is concerned only with universal necessities and, more importantly, with the conditions of its own existence. Those conditions, we will see, are in the first instance various identities which rational individuals are allowed to have. At first particular and empty, those identities are gradually exchanged for more concrete and universal ones. The need for this exchange is posited through what Hegel considers the first and most basic level of interaction: "recognition," to which I will devote this chapter. The exchange itself, "externalization," will occupy chapter 2. Only when externalization is complete can reason, in "reconciliation," understand itself as situated—and as able to situate itself.

Though we will have to turn to the *Aesthetics* for some of them, Hegel's views on human interaction are presented most concretely in the *Phenomenology of Spirit*. But the book has been viewed in many ways: as history, as drama, as education; as conceptual archeology and dialectical ontology; as charlatanry, confusion, and a new religion. The variety of these interpretations, and the fact that 180 years after the book's publication the number of them is growing faster than ever, suggests that the *Phenomenology* engages each reader uniquely, as do Plato's dialogues. Like them, it not only purports to tell us of the nature of reality but also, in some indirect and mysterious way, teaches us about ourselves. It is not my intention here to try and dispel all these mysteries by providing another global interpretation of the *Phenomenology*. But reading it as an account of human interaction will, I believe, clear up some of them.

Most obviously, the book is a narrative. Its protagonist is something called *Geist*, or Spirit, which takes on different forms in different parts of the book. These forms constitute the series of its appearances: the "phenomena" of the title. Within every appearance of Spirit problems arise, often but not always contradictions.[1] The problems it encounters at each stage push Spirit to a new appearance, in which those problems—and no others—are resolved. Because each new stage resolves only the problems with the previous stage, no stage can be located elsewhere than where it is. The series, like any narrative, thus has a structure—a "why and wherefore" or, to use the Greek term for this, a "logos."

The book thus *narrates* the why and wherefore of the appearances of Spirit, and in that sense is a "phenomenology" of it. The narrative exhibits progress: things get better as it goes along. They get better, it will turn out, from a particular perspective which I will call that of a "consolidated ego." This is a self which is at once unified and multiple: a single ego which, fully articulated in all its capacities, is able to deal with the manifold problems and situations of individual and collective life without being threatened by them. The need for such a consolidated self will be decisively questioned by Heidegger, and my own criticism of it will be found in my "narrative" of Hegel, in chapter 17.[2]

Because the *Phenomenology* is a narrative, it develops its accounts of interaction sequentially. The book's basic movement is from "Consciousness" (part A) to "Self-Consciousness" (part B) and finally to Reason, Spirit, and Absolute Spirit (part C). This movement is dialectical, which for Hegel has to do with defining things in terms of their opposites. This provides a clue for understanding the three basic parts of the book:

(A). The opposite of consciousness is the nonconscious. This section, then, deals with awareness and the nonaware object of awareness as they reciprocally define one another. Hence, the chapter titles here refer to "Sense-Certainty" and its object, the "This;" to "Perception" and the "Thing," and to "Understanding" and "Force."

(B). The opposite of self-consciousness is not for Hegel the "non–self-conscious," but what we may call other-consciousness, or the object of awareness which is itself taken to be aware. Here, consciousness defines itself in terms of other consciousnesses as other (i.e., insofar as they are not similar to the first consciousness). The chapter headings thus refer to social relations which are more or less antagonistic: "Master" and "Bondsman," the Stoic withdrawal from society, the Skeptical denial of others' reality, and finally the unrequited yearning for God of the "Unhappy Consciousness." Hegel's concept of recognition can be clarified, for present purposes, without going beyond the first of these.

Now let us consider the relation of (A) and (B), because they, too, if dialectical, are opposed. In (A), we just have consciousness and unconsciousness, present in an interplay of abstract categories; there is no differentiation within consciousness, so to speak. In (B), consciousness is considered to be split up into a plurality of different, antagonistic individuals. What (A) and (B) would seem to have in common is the equation of distinction with antagonism. In (A), both are absent, while in (B) both appear. We can thus expect that in (C) the book explores the possibilities of distinction without antagonism. Spirit here is able to accept the other as other, without attempting to deny the otherness by either submerging it in a general category of "consciousness" or adopting an antagonistic attitude toward it. So we find (C) to be concerned with truly cooperative endeavors, such as science, the family, society, religion, and philosophy. These are structured by two further concepts, "externalization" and "reconciliation." The second of these, "reconciliation," is the most emancipatory form of interaction for Hegel. As we shall see, it exhibits some of the structures of what I will call poetic interaction, in that the hearer of an utterance (or, as Hegel presents it, the appreciator of a work of art) determines its meaning. But we cannot understand reconciliation itself, or its emancipatory character, without first understanding the two lower structures of interaction, recognition and externalization.

This overview, brief as it is, shows two things. First, if Spirit is to be understood as cooperative endeavor, interaction must be central to it, and hence to the *Phenomenology* itself. "Human nature really exists only in an achieved community of minds" (*PhG* 56/43), and an account of concrete humanity will be an account of that achievement by ever more articulate forms of interaction. Second, my analysis must begin with section (B) of the *Phenomenology*. In particular, the important discussion of language in the opening pages of "Sense-Certainty" cannot ultimately concern language as communicative. It is restricted to dealing with it as the way a person makes sense of the world to himself.[3]

Self-Consciousness, Life, and Desire (*PhG* 133–140/104–111)

The first instance of interaction in (B), and therefore in the *Phenomenology* itself, is the "battle of the opposed self-consciousnesses." This results in the community (if we may so call it) of Master and Bondsman. But in order to understand that we must begin with the analysis, a few pages previous, of life and desire. For Hegel as for Plato, it is first of all desire that brings us into genuinely human relationships. True, the desire in question is for Plato (as we will see in chapter 9) erotic, while in the present Hegelian account it is much more destructive. But for both thinkers the desire is ultimately for a certain kind of self, rather than for the other person as such.

Consciousness of self is "essentially the return from otherness," a development of the awareness of the nonself set forth in "Consciousness" (*PhG* 143/105). Any self-conscious being must also be conscious, then, and self-consciousness necessarily has two sorts of object. One is the natural world, with all its sensory richness and diversity. The other is the ego itself, here without content as the "motionless tautology of: 'I am I.' " The general goal of the *Phenomenology*—what I have called self-consolidation—is present as the need to bring these two objects together, somehow to convert the natural world into the self and thus to give content to the latter. This is "desire" (*PhG* 135/105). So defined, desire is boundless. For it is only by virtue of some determinate property of ourselves that we can discriminate objects that can satisfy our desire from objects that cannot and say that we desire this rather than that. Such discrimination is impossible for the abstract "I am I." The very emptiness of its ego means that anything and everything can be viewed as something that can "fill it up."

There is, however, a restriction on this. "We the philosophers," who are following the movement of self-consciousness, know that the object of its desire is really "life" (*PhG* 135/106). The key to understanding this is to recognize that "we" know that the unity of ego and the natural world has *already been achieved*. Both are objects of the same consciousness, in that sense belong to it, and are unified. But consciousness does not know this and is aware only of some sort of felt unity joining all its objects. Since they are supposedly, as natural beings, antithetical to it, that felt unity cannot be viewed as what "we" know it to be, as the unity of consciousness itself. So it must be viewed as some sort of force pervading all those contents: the life-force. Life is thus the dynamism which shapes, and manifests itself in, the unconscious world. And as such it is the object of desire.

The life-force is then the felt unity of the abstract ego, viewed as existing in natural objects. Individual living things are, in consciousness's view, manifestations of it, and it has no content apart from them. The life-force is thus seen as shaping itself into various bodies—into different living things (*PhG* 136f/107). These, as parts of the whole, are not identical to the life-force (indeed, they "disown" their continuity with it). And they, not it, are the reality with which consciousness must deal. In particular, they are what it can consume and thus unite with. Desire thus attempts to convert the natural world into the self in the most direct way possible: by devouring it. But this means that desire cannot be fully satisfied. For desire, we saw, wants to unite with, or consume, the entire natural world. All it can achieve, however, is the consumption of a number of individual living things. This satisfies it—but only partially, and only for a time. There is always more to be desired, and satisfying the desire in this way only produces it, and its object, anew (*PhG* 139/109).

Two things are required to resolve this problem: some sort of universality to the object, so that to consume it will not be simply to consume one living thing among others; and some sort of permanence to the object's destruction, so that the consumption of it will not have to be repeated. The former aspect of the problem is resolved by the "battle of the opposed self-consciousnesses." The outcome of the battle deals with the latter aspect.

Natural objects do not, in and of themselves, make any claim to be more than simply individuals. An apple, for example, is an instance of the species "apple." But we can hardly say that this fact matters to it, or that it behaves as if it were somehow more than just itself. It is otherwise, however, with beings that are themselves self-conscious, as that term has here been defined. For such an entity, in addition to being a natural object, is as well the "I am I," an ego which is over and above its natural being. Such a "tautologous" ego cannot be anything other than a thought-construct. Moreover, it is empty, and as such covers, or is manifested in, all the various activities of the body in which it inheres. As an empty thought-construct which subsumes particulars under it, the ego is in Hegelian parlance a "universal."

When a self-conscious being acts from boundless desire, its behavior shows that its quasi-universal ego is more important to it than its individual natural being: it "effects the negation [of its natural being] within itself" (*PhG* 139/109). Further, this ego is given as indistinguishable from the universal life-force, for both are wholly without content. The behavior of such a being is then an implicit insistence that it is not merely a living thing, but identical with the life-force itself: it claims to be a paradigm of the class of living things. The self-conscious entity thus takes up an attitude toward its genus which, just by being an "attitude" at all, is very different from what is conveyed by natural objects. It is not just another living thing but gives itself a kind of universality, which was the first of the two requirements noted above.

The Battle of the Opposed Self-Consciousnesses
(*PhG* 141-146/111-115)

All these implicit attitudes and claims can be understood by another self-consciousness, which makes them itself in its own behavior. It follows that, for self-consciousness, attacking and destroying another self-consciousness is very different from consuming one natural object among others. For in that special case it seeks to destroy the other, not for what it is (as with a natural object), but for what it means: because of the universal that it claims to be. Consciousness, still seeking to unite with the universal life-force, cannot come closer to it than uniting, not just with any sort of individual entity, but with another universal self-consciousness: it "achieves its satisfaction only in another self-consciousness" (*PhG* 139/110). As with Platonic love, though in much more brutal fashion, the body of the other—his natural being—is significant only through its relation to something non-corporeal and universal.

Consciousness has here made a first move into the symbolic. We can see the nature of this move by comparing the satisfaction consciousness finds here with what it originally desired. That, we saw, was unity with the universal life-force. In vanquishing and destroying another self-consciousness, consciousness achieves unity with a universal—but not with "life" itself. What it destroys is another self-consciousness: a being which implicitly claimed to be a paradigm of the class of living things. The other's body is thus taken as representing the entire class of which it is a paradigm: the "symbol" here is an *example* of what it symbolizes, and constitutes itself as such an example. Its connection with the symbolized is, then, not arbitrary. The body of the other is a genuine member of the class it symbolizes, that of living things, and its symbolic status is not created by consciousness but is given to it—indeed, as we have seen, forced upon it. Language, for Hegel, is a set of arbitrary or conventional symbols, or what he calls "signs."[4] We may therefore say that consciousness has not yet reached language; the "symbolism" in terms of which it operates is prelinguistic.

The satisfaction consciousness obtains is insufficient, because the repetition-compulsion remains. Once consciousness has vanquished and killed another self-conscious entity, its satisfaction is over and, like a gunfighter of the Old West, it finds that it must go out and fight again. What it needs now is some way to render the destruction of the other permanent and ongoing, and this requires a second move into symbolism. The move is made when, during the battle, one of the antagonists submits and the other accepts its submission, making of it a "bondsman." Compelled now to do the bidding of the master in all things, the submissive consciousness renounces its own self: its essential nature is simply to live or be for another. Its claim to be more than a natural object is given up, and it becomes a being for which "thinghood is the essential characteristic" (*PhG* 145f/114f).

The bargain struck between the battling consciousnesses is that the victor will accept the loser's surrender of selfhood as a surrogate for, a symbol of, its actual death. This second move into symbolism is an advance on the first in that the symbol is established as such interactively, by convention. It has no significance outside the agreement that institutes it. Moreover, the agreement is free in that the symbol is not actually a member of a wider class it is taken to symbolize, but merely resembles that which is symbolized: the surrender of self on the part of the bondsman is similar to, though weaker than, the loss of self in death—just as the strength of the eagle, in classical mythology, resembled the much greater strength of Jupiter, which it symbolized.[5] We are thus closer to language than we have been, but because the relation between symbol and symbolized is not wholly arbitrary, we are not yet there.

Let us again compare the satisfaction consciousness has attained with what it originally desired. Desiring consciousness wanted to unite its empty selfhood with the content of the unconscious world. Because this desire was boundless, it could not be satisfied by the consumption of natural objects, and consciousness displaced its desire. It sought satisfaction by seeking to destroy, not the entire natural world, but a paradigm of that world: the quasi-universal ego of another self-consciousness. In order to achieve permanence in this, consciousness again displaced its desire. It no longer sought the actual destruction of the other, but a weakened image of it: the other's submission.

Consciousness now seeks, then, an ongoing relation to another human being: it is capable of sustained interaction with others. But it still seeks to gain content for its own ego from that relationship and, thus, to make that relationship somehow internal to itself. Since we are now on a symbolic level, we may say that consciousness seeks to be "defined" by its relationship to the other. This definition, or determinate content, is supplied by the social roles into which the battlers enter when they become master and bondsman. The empty "I am I" will be overcome, in the one case, by "I am the master" and, in the other, by "I am the bondsman." The two consciousnesses unite, not directly with each other, but with the social roles that form their relationship.

The bargain struck by the two battlers was entered into freely by them: they could have kept up the fight until one of them died. Though thus grounded in individual choice, the bargain results in the interdependence of the two consciousnesses. The master depends on the slave for his self-definition, and the slave depends on the master for that and for his very existence. Further, their interdependence does not destroy their original independence of one another, but instead confirms it: since each depends on the other, neither can kill the other. To put the matter in my terms, it is a condition for the existence of consciousness itself that it be either bondsman or master. Because of that, master and bondsman are conditions for each other's existence.

This complex relationship of interdependence, which entails both the independence of the individuals and their dependence on each other, gives a basic symmetry to the roles they enter. Though in other respects the master and the bondsman are opposites, on this fundamental level they are equals. This symmetry of individual egos as both dependent and independent constitutes what Hegel calls "recognition," the concept which structures this most basic level of human interaction.

Recognition

Recognition is one of Hegel's most important concepts. Elsewhere he says that it grounds society, legality, and the very concept of a person; one of his earliest discussions of it is in terms of language.[6] The German word for it is *Anerkennung*, and is not to be taken merely in the English sense in which we "recognize" an old friend on the street; it is more similar to the sense in which states "recognize" one another (*die Staatsanerkennung*). In Hegel's discussion of it (*PhG* 141-143/111f), recognition is said to be a "many-sided and polysemic limitation."[7] Two of the senses of this limitation are clear by now. In the first place, by recognizing the other, each consciousness recognizes that it cannot destroy the other, and thus recognizes the other's independence. Indeed, by recognizing that the other is independent of me, I leave him free to be what he is: I leave him his own capacity for self-direction, within the context of the social role he has to fulfill. Further, the act of recognition gives limits to the self in the sense that it defines the self: if the master is the master, he is by definition not the bondsman. It is thus in recognizing and in being recognized that each consciousness is constituted by its special nature as having distinct content. Finally, recognition is also a two-fold "supersession" of the other (*PhG* 141/111). In recognizing that the other consciousness is, like myself, a self-consciousness, I undo his foreignness to some extent and "supersede" his otherness.

Recognition is thus rigorously symmetrical; in it, "each [consciousness] does itself what it demands of the other, and therefore does what it does only insofar as the other does the same." The interactive implications of this are clear: in any social arrangement, there is a basic presupposition of the equality of the different participants, no matter how unequal prevailing social conditions may actually make them.

Because of the symmetry of recognition, interaction here cannot be viewed in terms of the conventional separation between the "sender" and the "receiver" of the message. Both participants are doing the same thing—fighting. Similarly, the common distinction between "message" and "noise" loses meaning: if one is in a battle to the death, everything one's opponent does may be significant. Virtually every movement and characteristic of either battler is relevant, indeed crucial, to the other. Recognitive communicators are thus completely absorbed by their interaction, which is constitutive of their identities. We may contrast this "internality" to the self of recognition with Hobbes's conception of the social compact, in which the individual likewise yields some of his freedom in order to gain the much greater freedoms that accompany the interdependence of individuals in society.[8]

The most obvious difference between Hegel's and Hobbes's views lies in the way each presents the concrete situation out of which society arises. Prior to Hegel's "battle," consciousness is seeking to destroy other consciousnesses. This looks very much like a Hobbesian "war of each against all." After the battle we have an enduring society, as we do after the social compact. But Hobbes presents a picture of people entering freely into an agreement, where Hegel depicts the enslavement of one person by another of superior force.

It is clear, I think, why this has to be so for Hegel. The social compact is a rational undertaking: individuals enter into it as the result of calculating their advantage under it and the alternative to it. Once they have entered into the compact they may live longer and will almost certainly live better; but they are the same kind of creature after as before. The battle of the opposed self-consciousnesses is also, in its way, rational: it is the only way to resolve the problem of rendering permanent consciousness's destruction of its other. But this rationality, like that problem, is explicitly present only for "us, the philosophers" who are following the movement of consciousness. The battlers themselves do not know, when they enter the battle, what its result should be. They cannot, for consciousness at the beginning of the battle is still the consciousness, not of a human, but of a brute. If a human is a rational animal, and yet is defined by his interactions, then rationality itself must be defined through interaction. The battle itself, as the first case of interaction in the *Phenomenology*, is thus one of the conditions for reason. Prior to it, there are no "rational animals," and appeal can only be to force.

In sum, the social compact is not definitive of the selves who enter into it the way the battle of the opposed self-consciousnesses is, and this explains its relative gentility. That coercion is essential in taking the first step toward a rational community does not mean that it must be defended in more advanced stages of Spirit's development.[9] Indeed, the most important kind of "coercion" present here is not that exercised by the "winner" in the battle, who makes a "bondsman" of the other, but is of an entirely different order. To understand this, we must look at what the *Phenomenology* considers to be the defects of the encounter.

If we are entitled to call the battle of the opposed self-consciousnesses "communicative" by virtue of its symbolic and recognitive nature, it is certainly a borderline case of communication: it is the most violent sort of "body language." Hegel, however, explicitly locates the problem with the battle not in its violence but in the inequality of its outcome. The battle results in a situation where one consciousness (the bondsman) does all the recognizing and the other (the master) gets all the recognition (*PhG* 142f/111f). To be sure, the battle also begins with the participants unequal, for otherwise there would be no ultimate winner or loser. One of the battlers must be stronger or more intelligent than the other, and it is the weaker and/or brighter battler which realizes the necessity to submit in order to save its life (*PhG* 145/115). This natural inequality may be very slight indeed, and in any case it is not definitive for desiring consciousness. For such consciousness has not yet recognized others, and so cannot be defined by its relative power vis-à-vis others. In the outcome of the battle, the inequality is not natural but social. It is that between master and bondsman, enormous and definitive for consciousness.

The dynamics of the battle thus convert a relatively unimportant natural inequality into an essential social inequality. Whatever concrete human nature might lie latent within the two battlers, whatever talents or dispositions they may have, the battle allows only two possibilities to each: to be master or to be bondsman. It is this coercion, exercised by the structure of the battle itself, which makes the determinate identities of master and bondsman into conditions for the existence of consciousness itself, rather than parametric self-definitions which could be left behind. Reason, which is here able to assert only that it is master or bondsman, is thus unsituated. It is concomitantly unpoetic as well. For every "message" we have seen so far forced a single meaning upon its recipient. Consciousness was not free, for example, to view the other battler as simply a natural object or to ignore it; it was not free to interpret the moves of the other in the battle in various ways, but had to regard them all as aimed at its own death; and it was not free to decide which of the two available identities—master and bondsman—to adopt for itself. In each case the alternative was either death or the failure to attain self-definition.

Lordship and Bondage (*PhG* 146–150/115–119)

The "battle of the opposed self-consciousnesses" thus forces the participants to take on the identities that they do; it does this through the poverty of the possible outcomes it presents. We can see what grounds this poverty of outcome by turning to the next section of the *Phenomenology*, "Lordship and Bondage." This section, positively tranquil in comparison with the raging desire and violence of what preceded, appears to be based on a halcyon view of slavery in the ancient world, where the master enjoys himself and the bondsman does all the necessary work. As elsewhere in the *Phenomenology*, however, the historical source of what is described is less important than the way Hegel appropriates it in his narrative as a stage in the development of Spirit.

We may begin by asking what master and bondsman have in common, and the immediate answer is that both have been through the battle of the opposed self-consciousnesses. This means, first, that each has gained determinate content for his ego. Moreover, that content is definitive for each. Because it was gained in a process of recognition, it has been socially acknowledged and is "real" in a way that the merely interior, unexpressed thoughts of an individual can never be.[10] Finally, because of the symmetry inherent in recognition itself, the determinate egos of master and bondsman are at least formally equal, however unequal the two may be in other respects.

In all those other respects, in fact, the two egos are opposites. The recognition is, as Hegel puts it, "one-sided and unequal" (*PhG* 147/116f). The concrete relationship of the two egos, in other words, is a denial of their basic equality. The bondsman asks nothing of the master (except that the master not kill him). He merely does what the master requires of him. His consciousness "sets aside its own being for self, and in so doing itself does what the other does to it," i.e., sacrifices itself (*PhG* 147/116). But if the bondsman only does what the master asks, his action is really that of the master, who is thus responsible for whatever the bondsman does. The bondsman's loss of autonomy is thus part of what recognition should be: the shedding of one's own natural independence in favor of belonging to a larger social whole comprised of interdependent individuals. But the "shedding" here is one-sided, so that the master is independent of the slave in all things save the basic relation which makes him a master at all. That basic relation constitutes the slave's only hold upon the master, and then only in the sense that it keeps the master from killing him outright.

One result of this disparity is that master and bondsman do not communicate. The master's "essential nature is to exist only for himself; he is the sheer negative power for whom the thing is nothing" (*PhG* 147/116). The reference to "thing" here includes the bondsman, for whose consciousness "thinghood is the essential characteristic" (*PhG* 146/115). Because of his self-absorption, then, the master cannot communicate with the bondsman; to do so would be to talk to a "nothing." Further, as sheerly negative, the ego of the master is empty and abstract. Should he wish to communicate with his servant, he would have nothing to say to him. The consciousness of the bondsman, which we will examine below, is for its part "forced back into itself [and] will withdraw into itself . . ." (*PhG* 148/117). Ignored by the master, the bondsman anticipates what will be the Stoic withdrawal from the world.

Both master and bondsman now have, in a way, what they originally desired: "content" to their egos in the form of social roles. Those roles, in turn, afford them further content. The master's "content" comes in the form of the objects which he uses and enjoys—the food, clothing, *objets d'art,* and so forth which the bondsman produces (*PhG* 146f/115). As in a caricature of contemporary consumer society, he consumes those objects and they "fill up" his inner emptiness for a while. He has come as close as one can to fulfilling the original demands of desiring consciousness.

But the task, it turns out, was to transcend them. This is accomplished by the bondsman. He, too, gets content—not through enjoyment, but in the more permanent form of labor, "desire held in check" (*PhG* 149/118). Hegel presents labor here as the objective rendering of the worker's subjectivity, or (we may say) as the physical realizing of a plan or conception. The master may enjoy a silver goblet, but it is the bondsman who first conceives of that goblet, then draws it, and finally casts it. The cup is thus an expression of his mind, not of the master's. When he yields it to the master he is left not with the thing but with what, for Hegel, is infinitely more: with the knowledge that he is the one who made it. Thus, the bondsman gains self-definition from his relation to the goblet which he has formed (whereas the master's use of it from time to time hardly does this for him):

> The shape does not become something other than [the producing bondsman] through being made external to him; for it is precisely this shape that is his pure being-for-self, which in this externality is seen by him to be the truth (*PhG* 149/118).

Desire checked—labor—is thus desire transcended. This marks the appearance of the second of the three major structuring concepts of human interaction in the *Phenomenology*, externalization. In this first instance, it is labor which externalizes the concrete content of Spirit in the form of a physical object. The bondsman, by his labor, comes to know himself in ways that the master can never reach. He knows his mind, first, as essentially a formative, externalizing agent, and, second, he is aware of the concrete shapes his mind produces. Produced by his creative activity, those shapes are not examples of that activity nor do they resemble it. But, to the bondsman, they signify it. Aware of the creative power of his own mind, he is presumably now able to apply his formative activity to the sounds that can be made by his vocal apparatus and attach them to the very different contents of that mind.

Labor is thus for Hegel the ground of language, as desire is that of symbolism. It is labor which makes signs possible at all and in that it renders them differentiated and articulate. In his earlier *System of Ethical Life*, Hegel had characterized language as "the tool of reason" and had developed its concept from that of the tool—the first product of the laborer, who then uses it to make other things.[11] In the later *Philosophy of Right*, he views the process more concretely. The "building up of language" is there viewed as part of theoretical education, which develops "on the stage" of the multiplicity of objects and situations brought about through labor.[12] We may thus say that it is necessary for Hegel that Spirit be engaged in expressing itself in concrete physical objects before it can constitute the signs used to refer to them. Labor is for him the necessary condition of the ability to attach mere sounds to conceptual meanings as well as the source of the content expressed in the vocabulary of an articulate language.

This enables us to see why the master and bondsman cannot communicate. At the beginning, neither consciousness has labored, and there is no developed vocabulary at all. At the end, the bondsman has labored and presumably possesses a determinate language in which to address the master. But the master has not. He remains trapped in the sterility of sheer enjoyment, knowing neither his own capacity for creative activity nor the specific contents that such activity can bring forth. The bondsman must turn in on himself, becoming the Stoic.

The whole of Hegel's "Lordship and Bondage" bears an obvious, but controversial, relationship to Marx, explored in detail by Alexandre Kojève.[13] For Marx, the problem with Hegel's account here is that he does not conceive of man as a natural being but as a creature of "pure thought." Only on that basis can Hegel take the purely intellectual advance on the part of the bondsman to be essential to human development, and "the appropriation of man's objectified and alienated faculties is thus, in the first place, only an appropriation which occurs in pure thought, i.e., in abstraction."[14] But development so construed cannot, in Marx's view, be really liberating. The bondsman should revolt, not turn inward.

As a critique of "Lordship and Bondage," this view does not take into account consciousness's need, in that section, for self-definition. This comes from earlier stages of the *Phenomenology* and is thus part of its narrative structure. Because of it, the section cannot even claim to treat the real servitude of historically existent bondsmen. What is at issue is a particular way of being a bondsman, viz., defining oneself as such. To the extent that the bondsman so defines himself, his servitude is of his own making. It can be overcome as Hegel portrays: by the bondsman's withdrawal into himself so that no relation to another can define him. This does not, admittedly, address the real problems of his enslavement; a Stoic can, as Epictetus was, still be a slave. But it is not Hegel's intention, I suggest, to address that sort of problem within the confines of his narrative here.[15] Hegel is narrating the self-consolidation of Spirit, not analyzing the structures of ancient society, still less those of modernity (though, as Marx's example shows, reading him in that way can be extremely fruitful).

The same lack of attention to the narrative nature of the *Phenomenology* is responsible, we may note, for Kierkegaard's reaction to the "Unhappy Consciousness" (*PhG* 158-171/126-138). This section narrates consciousness's attempt to relate to the "unchangeable" divine order. As Jean Hyppolite has discussed in detail,[16] themes from Judaism and Catholicism run through it the way Homeric allusions run through James Joyce's *Ulysses*. But to read it as merely a commentary on those religions would be misleading, if only because the implications of the concept of recognition continue to play a crucial role here. We have seen that it is essential to recognition that it be viewed as defining the parties to it. This means here that the Unchangeable, from which consciousness seeks recognition, must be viewed as defined by its relationship to consciousness.[17] The view that God is defined by, and dependent on, his relationship to man is hardly part of the Judeo-Christian tradition, especially not its Jewish and Catholic components. It is thus not surprising to find works with even semitraditional theological standpoints, such as Kierkegaard's *Fear and Trembling*,[18] denying the religious significance of the human community at the same time they deny the possibility of mediation between man and God.

The moral here is twofold. First, a number of people—Marx and Kierkegaard, Kojève and Hyppolite, and others—have taken sections of the *Phenomenology* as analytical in nature, as treating, for example, social reality or religion. Second, in so doing, they underplay the narrative nature of the text: the fact that each stage is defined more by what went before (and, as we shall see, what comes after) than by realities beyond the book. This does not mean that the *Phenomenology* cannot illuminate such realities. But such illumination is not its central purpose, and, as in the above cases, is rarely more than fleeting.

Taking the *Phenomenology* seriously as a narrative, then, means seeing each stage in it as constrained by previous stages, rather than simply by whatever external realities it may allude to. When we do this, we see that both the "Battle of the Opposed Self-Consciousnesses" and "Lordship and Bondage" answer a problem of "Life and Desire:" the need to find content that will define an ego which is at first empty and abstract. That need can only be satisfied, Hegel argues, by entering into interaction with another human being. The most basic level of such interaction, and the presupposition of higher forms of it, is as we have seen recognition. Through recognition, consciousness obtains determinate conditions for its existence. In the next phase, that of "externalization," these conditions will be enriched. But they will remain conditions for consciousness rather than what I call parameters: reason will achieve explicit situated-ness only in reconciliation.

Two

Communication as Externalization
Phenomenology of Spirit C.BB

We have seen interactive reason begin for Hegel as something which in my terms is wholly conditioned. Its truths, the self-definitions achieved by consciousness, are conditions of its existence because consciousness could not exist without them. "Master" and "bondsman" are not the only such defining conditions presented in the *Phenomenology*, and, as we might expect, Hegel arranges them all narratively along a scale from particular to universal. A "particular" self-definition defines consciousness in terms that render it opposed to other consciousness. It is a condition of the master's existence, for example, that he not be a slave, and vice versa. A "universal" self-definition will then be one that applies to all consciousness indifferently. In attaining such a self-definition, consciousness will reach the highest pitch of unsituatedness (which for Hegel is expressed in the Kantian categorical imperative, taken as defining the self which heeds it). The ascent to this pitch is treated by the *Phenomenology* under the rubric of "externalization."

Manifold forms of this are pursued through the central part of the *Phenomenology*. It receives its clearest treatment, and most radical form, in "Culture and Its Realm of Actuality," and I will simply sketch the intervening story briefly. The *Phenomenology*'s section on "Consciousness" began, we noted, without differentiated individuals. Its section on reason begins with cognition as a communal enterprise (in the scientific community's "Observation of Nature"), but one without differentiated content. Since, as we saw, labor provides content, we have a lack of labor as well. The section then moves from theoretical reason (in section C.AA) toward the practical, or from considerations of truth toward considerations of freedom. When the dialectic arrives at a concrete, developmentally acting community, we have not simply reason but "Spirit." This section (C.BB) first looks at the family, which is presented here as founded on love and feeling, and hence as a relatively inarticulate community (*PhG* 318–330/267–278). The dialectical move from the concrete, loving family is to an abstract, indifferent society based on legal status.[1] Eventually the laws come to have more determinate content and evolve into a system of rules governing *all* of an individual's behavior; this is "culture." Thus, though all the sections mentioned have to do with externalization, it is only in "Culture" (C.BB.B) that it is viewed as a freedom-oriented, articulate, global phenomenon. Within that section, it is the first subsection—"Culture and Its Realm of Actuality"—that will be of most importance to my analysis. The next section, on the Enlightenment, begins to overcome externalization in favor of the deeper concept of reconciliation.

Before turning to "Culture and Its Realm of Actuality," I will make some points regarding the social nature of the Hegelian conceptions of both "Reason" and "Spirit" in this section of the *Phenomenology*. In general, where there is a consciousness of community on the part of its members, in Hegelian parlance, the community itself is "conscious." Thus, in the *Phenomenology*'s section on the "Unhappy Consciousness," the Mediator between God and man, the Church itself, "is the unity directly aware of both [God and man] and connecting them, and is the consciousness of their unity . . ." (*PhG* 175/139). This sounds as if Hegel were positing the Mediator as a *Volksgeist* or *Zeitgeist* in the community over and above the individuals which make it up. But the passage also says that "the superseded individual *is* the universal" (ibid.; emphasis added). It is reasonable to think that if the universal is somehow identical with individuals (even superseded ones), it cannot be a *Volksgeist* over and above them. We can clarify this by remembering a basic point of the previous analysis: each individual for Hegel, insofar as he is conscious of commonality with other individuals, takes on and is defined by a certain social content. With an ongoing community present, we can view such content as a set of social "roles." The class of all such roles in a community is a distinct stratum of it, discriminable from the set of individuals in whom those roles inhere and who define themselves in terms of them (*PhG* 257f/213). At this stage of the *Phenomenology*, two important points follow.

First, any given individual will be significant only to the extent that he plays the roles presented to his *communal* consciousness. His merely *conscious* activities and experiences (e.g., eating and perceiving, sensory pains and satisfactions) are of no importance in themselves. Neither are his purely *self*-conscious activities (e.g., his private loves and antagonisms, his search for personal salvation). The categories important for understanding human community at this level turn out to cut across, and even to deny, the manifold nature of the individuals who make up society. If, on a simplistically democratic model, we view society as just an aggregate of individuals, rather than as a structure of roles, we will never understand this feature of Hegel's thought.

Second, the set of social roles in a given society is not merely discriminable from the rest of the phenomena occurring within it the way the set of all red objects is discriminable from the set of all blue ones. It has an organized dynamic of its own and evinces a certain structure. But what has structure is, in virtue of that structure, comprehensible and thus in a broad sense "rational." The overall patterned content of the roles played in a given society is founded on basic rational principles, a sort of "social wisdom" (or what Hegel calls *Sittlichkeit*, ethical life: *PhG* 256/212).

We thus have, from now on, three important levels in society. First is the set of basic principles on which society is structured—the "social wisdom" it incarnates. Second is the set of roles that individuals can play in society and that are structured by those basic principles. Finally, we have the individuals themselves. The interplay of all three levels, which constrains the individuals to act in accordance with roles that express basic principles, is Reason itself, the "unification of individual and universal." Thus it is Reason, in all its Hegelian "cunning," which sees to it that the individual

> with its concrete life, just where it fancies it is pursuing its own self-preservation and particular interest, is in fact doing the very opposite . . . and makes itself a moment of the whole (*PhG* 46/33).

Individuals in complex societies, with all their concrete life, are constrained by patterns of the whole, just as were the master and bondsman—though the constraining relationships are now much richer. Able to exercise such constraints, and to do so in an organized way, Reason seems to be something over and above the individuals who make up society. On the other hand, as a rational system of social constraint, Reason is simply the totality of patterns of interaction occuring within a society: the roles available for its members. Finally, as the individual constrained in action by relationships to others, Reason is the "superseded individual."

Reason thus need not be construed as a property or activity of an individual mind (human or divine) but as a force inhering in society. This usage agrees with ancient writers, most particularly, as we shall see, with Aristotle. If man for Aristotle is the "rational animal," human society is

in his view prior to the human individual. In order to be rational, such
an individual must be born and raised in a good state, in a rational community.[2] Expressed in terms of the dynamism of Hegelian thought, the
view would state that the coming-to-be of Reason is the coming-to-be
of conscious rational community.

The same social character also applies to the Hegelian concept of
Spirit. Spirit, writes Hegel here, is

> the universal *work* produced by the action of all and each as
> their unity and equality [*Gleichheit*] . . . as substance, it is un-
> changing self-equalness; but as being-for-self it is a frag-
> mented being, self-sacrificing and benevolent, in which each
> accomplishes its own work, rends asunder the universal be-
> ing, and takes from it his own share (*PhG* 314/264).

We see, in the first place, a contrast between the simply self-identical
one "substance" and the many individuals. We have seen this before—
first in the unity of the tautologous ego vs. the multiplicity of objects of
desire, and then in the unity of the master vs. the internal multiplicity of
the bondsman.[3] We will see it again, for what the *Phenomenology* narrates,
in the last instance, is the overcoming of precisely this contrast.

Here the unit, Spirit as substance, is actually produced by the multiple. It is the "work" of individuals who achieve a concrete, communal
content or heritage. That simply self-identical cultural content is what
endures. But though it is the result of the labor of all, the common heritage is as well the starting point of the activities of each, which will consist in appropriating it for themselves. And thereby it becomes the
property of the various individuals, "benevolently" sacrificing its own
distinct identity in the process.

The concept of Spirit with which Hegel starts section C.BB of the
Phenomenology is then, like that of Reason, threefold. Spirit is at once an
inherited domain of content; the process by which individuals seek to
appropriate this for themselves; and its own final enrichment through
their labor. "Spirit" thus turns out to be the rational structure of historical development, so that if Reason is politicized wisdom, Spirit is historicized Reason. As such, Spirit provides the basic contexts in which the
individual can do or be, and is the basic determining factor in the individual's own development. Ontogeny does not for Hegel recapitulate
phylogeny, but it develops and enriches the *phylum*. True to Hegel's narrative orientation, however, the parameters in which it does so are set
forth by the *phylum*—the developing community—itself.

In Hegelian terms (as for Aristotle) what *acts* is what in the truest sense *exists.* It is perhaps not surprising, then, that the introductory characterization of Spirit as an active category, quoted from above, should stress its "substantial" nature. The view that a supra–individual Spirit is a "substance" sounds strangely ontological, as if the *Phenomenology* had somehow moved from treating concepts concerning interaction ("recognition") to concepts purporting to inform us about reality in general. But the meaning of the term here is not all that far from some of Aristotle's views.

Metaphysics 7 makes a sustained attempt to define substance. The attempt is problematic because Aristotle wants to say that substance is one and the same in, say, all human beings, and yet is nothing over and above individuals. He considers a number of definitions to convey this, and it is very hard to tell what his final view is.[4] But three of those definitions can be helpful in understanding what Hegel may mean by asserting that Spirit, as he views it, is a substance.

(1) Substance is the essence of an individual thing: it is its "form in matter" (*Metaphysics* 7.6). "Spirit" in this sense would be substantial for Hegel in that it is the "form" of man, of reason, *in* individual human beings.

(2) But essence is also *physis* or nature. Form does not, except in artificial things, simply lie quietly in matter. It is for Aristotle active on its matter, coming to dominate and control it (cf. *Metaphysics* 5.4). The result of this domination is "actuality" (*energeia*, a term we will later consider in some detail). The Hegelian analogue to this process would be what I referred to as reason constraining the individual to act in certain ways, and basic to this process of rational constraint is that the individual himself becomes more and more rational. This is what will here be called "culture" or "education" (*Bildung*). Its result is a group of people who are completely constrained by their acquired culture, and who constitute the "realm of actuality" of culture itself.

(3) Finally, we have form in itself, considered apart from matter. For Aristotle, this is form as universal (*Metaphysics* 7.13). For the *Phenomenology*'s next section it is present as the "realm of belief," which contrasts with the realm of *Bildung* (PhG 315f/265). For Hegel, as for Aristotle, the domain of form separate from real individuals is ultimately a mere conceptual fiction.

Thus, when Hegel refers to Spirit as "substantial," we need not read him as using the term in the sense of Aristotle's primary substances, i.e., as referring to an actually existent individual entity. But Spirit is "substantial" in the sense that it is that which human beings come to have in common. It is actively present in them, yet capable of being viewed separately from them.

Culture and Its Realm of Actuality (*PhG* 350–376/294–321)

The general heading under which this section occurs is "Self-Alienated Spirit," and as we have noted the alienation achieves its high point here.[5] We have, first of all, the distinction between the "realm of belief," which is "universal" and ultimately unreal, and the realm of culture itself. The latter sphere will be the more important, and within it we have the further distinction of state power and wealth (*PhG* 354/300f). The former is the side of identity within the historical situation because individuals, insofar as they are working for the state, work together. The latter (as we shall see) is the side of individuality and dispersal, where each pursues his private gain. The individual himself, first and foremost, is distinct from both these aspects of society. They "confront [him] as objects, i.e., as things from which he knows himself to be free, and between which he believes he can choose, or even choose neither" (*PhG* 355f/302).

But in spite of this capacity to choose, the concrete individual only counts, only "acquires standing and actuality," through culture: through his internalization of all the rules and values of society (*PhG* 351/298). The individual, then, is significant for society only insofar as he plays certain roles, takes on an identity already prescribed. On the one hand, this is good: for it de-emphasizes the random particularities of nature and birth. By requiring the individual to conform to a detailed social code, culture makes him more like other individuals. It raises him out of those particularities and gives him a new and more "universal" self (ibid.). On the other hand, the "natural self" remains part of us all, and its random particularities cannot in fact be wholly set aside. The de-emphasis of nature here thus amounts to a denial of it, and this means that the individual as such is not yet fully recognized.

The side of unity within the historical situation—the state power—is at first viewed as good, while the manifold, wealth, is bad. Both sides are by now composed of entities recognized to be human beings: consciousness is not confronting an unconscious object or a brute, and neither state power nor wealth has abjured its own humanity as did the bondsman. Neither side, moreover, is exclusively identified with consciousness itself, which takes them as its "objects." In viewing both the unity and the manifold as human, and in identifying itself with neither of them, consciousness has taken two steps toward assimilating them to each other. The realm of culture is thus an important advance toward understanding the human individual as the union of One and Many, of individual and universal, as "consolidated."

But while state power, for its part, has been humanized, it has not yet found a really human form. At this stage, which is a sort of early feudalism, it is a nebulous abstraction. It is not located in any constituted governmental institutions or even in any particular human individuals. Because it is free-floating in this way, it does not itself have the capacity to recognize individuals in society, and this means that consciousness "does find in the state its simple essence and subsistence in general, but not its individuality as such" (PhG 357/303). Because of this deficiency, consciousness comes to reject state power as being, not good, but evil. The moral judgment "the state is good" gives way to the dialectically opposed "the state is evil."

All the various modalities of these dialectical reversals are then explored: state power and wealth are both good, both evil, and so on. What is important for us is that the simple nature of state power requires simple adherence. This means that individual consciousness has just two choices. It can identify with state power, accept its detailed codes (the content of the dominant "culture"), and be "noble," in which case it makes a noble use of wealth also. Or it can reject it and be "ignoble," in which case its wealth is also ignoble.

If consciousness opts for state power, it enters the "heroism of service," serving the community and abjuring its own ends. Its talk is the advice it gives the state, or would be if there was as yet a real state to listen. The problem is that consciousness remains an individual, with its own particular interests. The state, requiring simple adherence, cannot recognize this fact, so consciousness's self-interest cannot be openly expressed within the context of its relation to state power. The advice thus becomes bad-faith advice, i.e., counsel whose main purpose is advancing the advisor, rather than the advisee (PhG 360f/306f). And, because the state power cannot recognize particular interests at all, it cannot even know that an individual is distorting its advice; it cannot be critical of that advice.

We saw earlier that the master and bondsman were trapped in the poverty of the outcome of their battle to the death. Here, we have a poverty in the recognition-relation itself which distorts communication. There, the immediate problem was the poverty of content, which the bondsman set about (unwillingly, of course) to rectify. Here, the poverty is structural: the relation of recognition, which ought to hold between the state (itself being composed of human beings) and the individual, is replaced by one of identity. As far as the state power is concerned, individual counselors are totally identified with it, and it is unable to appreciate their differing individual circumstances. The suppression of those circumstances leads not only to bad faith advice but to an inability to be critical of such advice.

Hegel pursues this structural problem into a consideration of the nature of language, one of the most important discussions of the subject in the *Phenomenology* (*PhG*362f/308f). For the problem at hand enables us to see what the nature of language for Hegel really is. To put the matter briefly: the individual can tell the state all sorts of things, but he cannot express his own real nature as individual. And it is precisely the expression of one's inner nature that is the true function of language as "the real existence of the pure self as self."

This characterization of language, we may note, is couched in ontological terms (of "selves" and "existence") rather than in social or grammatical terms. We can understand it by contrasting what is happening here with the discussion of "Sense-Certainty" at the beginning of the *Phenomenology* (79-89/58-66). There language could not fulfill its assigned function, could not express what it was supposed to express—the passing play of sensation. It could express "only the universal," and this discrepancy got the *Phenomenology* going.

When Hegel here asserts that language is the real existence of the self, he seems to claim that it can express at least one thing perfectly—the nature of the self whose existence it is. There are a number of reasons why this view can now be formulated. First, the self is now understood to be not merely a passing content (sensory or other), nor a mere abstract ego, but consciousness acquiring culture, i.e., *in transition toward universality*. This makes consciousness "rational;" for Reason is universal, and to be "universalized" in education (*Bildung*) is to become rational.

Second, not only is the goal of consciousness expressible, its starting point is as well. For this is not, as it was in "Sense-Certainty," raw sensation. Rather, it is the outcome of previous historical labor, i.e., consciousness's definite historical heritage. This cultural heritage is for Hegel "stored" primarily in language (cf. Hegel's remark on the "abbreviation" of thought content at *PhG* 27f/17).[6] Language thus has the resources to express fully the concrete individual's starting point, insofar as the individual can understand it himself.

Third, language itself, as utterance, presents the movement from starting point to goal, the dynamic of universalization. It is characteristic of the spoken word, in contrast to other types of entity, to annihilate itself as uttered. This sort of annihilation is the peculiar, negative sort of being that it has: " . . . it is *not* a real existence, and through this vanishing it *is* a real existence" (*PhG* 362f/308f). The result of this manner of being is that everything about the act of utterance vanishes except the understanding that it elicits: "that it is perceived or heard means that its *real existence dies away* . . . and through this vanishing it *is* a real existence" (ibid.). Its unique form of being is thus to be perceived, heard and understood, by others, and this gives language an intrinsically "universalizing" character. For when someone gives utterance to an idea, those who hear it change and appropriate it—just as the master appropriated the products of the bondsman to his own purposes, which may not have accorded with the bondsman's intentions in making them. Once expressed to others, my message is no longer my own. It exists in their interpretation, and what is effective in that interpretation is the elements of it understood in common by those others. Such interpretation is thus a "universalizing" activity.

Language, then, is not only adequate to express the dynamic of universalization which the individual undergoes in acculturation: it is that dynamic itself.

> The "I" is this particular "I"—but equally the universal "I;" its manifesting is also at once the externalization and vanishing of this particular "I," and as a result the "I" remains in its universality (*PhG* 362f/308f).

Hence, though unable to express things like the passing play of sense, language can capture and express the concrete individual in transition to universality—with respect to the goal of that process, its starting point, and the transition itself. By setting that process into play in the spatio-temporal context of an utterance, language gives to the individual self an existence which is a perfect expression of the dynamism of his higher rational nature. But there is a catch here, as is made plain in one of the *Phenomenology*'s earlier notes on language:

> Speech and work are outer expressions [*Äußerungen*] in which the individual no longer keeps and possesses himself within himself, but lets the inner get completely outside of him, leaving it to the mercy of something other than himself . . . In speech and action, the inner turns itself into something else, thus putting itself at the mercy of the element of change, which twists the spoken word and the accomplished act into meaning something else than they are in themselves, as actions of this particular individual (*PhG* 229/187).

The general discussion we have just looked at would distinguish between speech and work (or action) in this regard: labor may be something which the individual lets get wholly outside him (in its products), but speech cannot be. What remains through the *Phenomenology* is that the act of utterance transforms the self of the speaker. I cannot in fact dissociate myself from my words the way the bondsman could withdraw from the product of his labor: I am *where* they are. They express directly my concrete thoughts at a determinate time and place, and hence give existence to my self: I am *what* they are.[7] Because my words die away as they are uttered, *I* die away as they are uttered. To have them transformed and universalized is to lose my own concrete ego.

A Christian dies with the hope of bodily resurrection. When a word "dies away," another kind of resurrection is possible—not just for the word, but for the human who utters it. Taken up and understood by the community, my words acquire a new and more universal significance. This makes them the expression of a new and more universal ego. At this stage, the original idea that was "in my head" and which, in its uniqueness, made that head "mine" in a unique way, is indeed lost. But the self that is lost is not as important as the self which is now attributed to me, "a self that has passed over into another self that has been perceived and is universal" (*PhG* 363/309). It is only as such a "universal" self that the cultured individual counts or is recognized at all; and what he can utter in this way is only his devotion to the universal state power: his higher rational nature is merely his total adherence to the detailed codes of the state. This circumstance is crucial to the nature of externalization and will be discussed below. What is important for the moment is that the individual's language therefore assumes the form of (honest) flattery. This requires a person as its recipient, so someone gets set up as monarch—is *named* king and becomes the mouthpiece (and earpiece) of the universal (*PhG* 364f/310f).

At long last we have a situation in which two individuals, each conceived as fully human, have different but determinate things to tell one another. The monarch, as a human being himself, is something to which consciousness *in principle* can become equal—but not in fact. In fact, there can be only one king, and he cannot share his kingship (*PhG* 365/311). So equality is still only partial, and there is no real reciprocity (*PhG* 370/315f). Truly reciprocal communication would require fuller reinstatement of the equality implicit in the structure of recognition. The lack of this turns consciousness away from its service to the king, service which still does not recognize consciousness's own full nature, to pursue wealth (*PhG* 367ff/313ff). We need not follow it, however, because the basic structures of externalization are already clear.

Externalization

Recognition, as I analyzed it previously, is essentially a two-term relation. There, the individuals who participate in it are united only by the abstract bond of their common claim to humanity and have very little "unity" at all. Here, individuals, such as the king and the noble, relate to each other through the complex social code they acquire in acculturation. That acquisition alone entitles them to recognition and is the determining factor in how they define themselves. We are now dealing, then, with a three-term relation: one holding among the participating individuals and the concrete social code itself. The structure of recognition is no longer adequate to capture the nature of human relationships, and Hegel introduces the concept of *Entäußerung* or "externalization" to do so (*PhG* 351-353/298f).

The German *Entäußern* basically means to dispose of or even to discard. It contains the word *Äußerung*, or utterance, and we can grasp the connection by noting that "utterance" in English has to do etymologically with "outerance." Its core meaning thus concerns rendering something, such as a thought or feeling, external to oneself by expressing it or, as we saw in the case of the bondsman, by giving it material reality in labor. Labor results in a product that is itself spatiotemporal and fixed. It can be taken away from the bondsman without impeaching his inner self-certainty. When, in "Culture," one's words are "taken away" from him and disseminated through his community, and in the process are transformed, he is transformed as well. Externalization thus takes the form of a double transition:

> it is at once the . . . transition, both of the thought-form of substance into actuality and conversely of the specific individuality into essentiality (*PhG* 351/298; cf. 352f/298f).

As the social code is progressively appropriated by individuals, leaving behind its previous status as a mere "thought form," those individuals are acculturated into it and discard their natural individuality. As applied to the present case, Hegel tells us that it is by means of culture and education that

> what is *implicit* in the substance acquires a recognized real existence. The process by which the individual moulds itself by culture is, therefore, at the same time the development of it as the universal, objective essence, i.e., the development of the actual world (*PhG* 352/299).

One side of externalization is thus the explication, in human interaction, of the "implicit substance" or the unexpressed side of the social wisdom. As such, externalization amounts to labor. Linguistically construed, it is the labor that builds up the common vocabulary missing in "Lordship and Bondage." The product of that labor, however, is not merely a set of words but a new and transformed set of selves existing in an increasingly articulate society.

There is thus a basic continuity between recognition and externalization. Recognizing another person has, since the "Battle," meant recognizing him for what he is and does. By now this includes recognizing one's own commonality with him. What two people have in common here is not merely an abstract and empty ego, but reason in the specific form of the basic principles of their own society or culture. In recognizing another member of my culture, I take cognizance of the "social substance" we both share. Indeed, the more of it we share, the more recognition there will be. Thus, recognition now requires the "externalization" of that substance: its articulation and acquisition by individuals. Transforming the abstract bond of the individuals in recognition into concrete connection by a social whole, externalization is in one sense an Hegelian *Aufhebung* of the concept of recognition: it views the same phenomenon from a richer and deeper perspective. These new contexts are articulated in ontological language: externalization is "the development of the actual world." But the ontology is, so to speak, a social one: the "actual world" in question is the world of culture itself. The individual finds this world existing, apparently independent of himself, realizes it to be in fact his own true "substance," and sets out to acquire it.

But the *Aufhebung* is incomplete. Recognition and externalization remain in disharmony. The problem is that the acquisition of status in the "actual world" denies its own starting point, the untutored particularity of the individual. The social code to which the individual must conform is rigid and universal. As he grows up he must conform to it in every detail, discarding his own individuality. Because of this denial of individuality, externalization also denies equality. The individual counts only through the rung he occupies on the social ladder, and those on higher rungs are more "noble" than those on lower ones. But equality, as we saw, is an essential component of recognition, and this means that externalization is internally incoherent. It came into being to solve a problem with recognition, that of inarticulateness. But it denies recognition's basically symmetrical structure. Recognition and externalization do not yet coexist in the dynamic harmony of complete Hegelian *Aufhebung*.

This is especially true of externalizing speech. To utter something is, from the point of view of externalization, to surrender myself to the "universalizing" interpretations of my audience. It is to place myself in a situation akin to, though much more concrete and civilized than, the situation of the bondsman: my product, my words, are taken up and used by others. With them, in contrast to the case for the bondsman, go my concrete "existence," which is achieved in speech, and indeed my individual "self" altogether. My utterance itself dissociates me from the thoughts and beliefs that I utter and from the concrete self they constitute. Externalizing interaction thus denies its own starting point in the unique perceptions and thoughts of an individual; hence the connection of *Entäußerung* with *Entfremdung*, alienation.[8]

There is another disparity between recognition and externalization. The individuals who recognized one another in the "Battle" were enhanced by that recognition: each gained stable content for his empty ego. Externalization, by contrast, begins from an ego that is already individuated and has determinate content, which it then requires that individual to discard. The self-enhancement that individuals get through recognition is subordinate, in the larger perspective of externalization, to the loss of self brought about by the very act of uttering. If externalization can be said to "emancipate" the individual from the inarticulate poverty of social roles presented in "Lordship and Bondage," it forces him to leave behind his natural being as well. What is required, then, is a form of interaction that will harmonize recognition and externalization; that will accommodate the labor of articulation without forcing an individual onto just one rung of a social ladder; and that will thus allow individuals to recognize their own basic equality. This further emancipatory structure is that of "reconciliation."

For present purposes, the general lesson of all this is that in order to become situated (and situating), reason must for Hegel first be radically desituated. True, interactive reason has been unsituated from the start. We have seen that its genesis in recognition was, for Hegel, a gaining of limits. But the limits gained were, as coerced self-definitions, what I call conditions. In externalization, the individual mind, existing in a network of natural and other particularities, becomes cognizant of a code of behavior claiming universality; adheres to that code; and finally identifies with it. Through this, the individual's original defining particularities, together with all the further ones he appropriates as he climbs the ladder of culture, are revealed in turn to be limits that can be discarded or left behind. Each, then, is what I call a "parameter." But the sequence itself of such self-definitions is a series of states through which individual consciousness *must* pass, and in order of increasing universality. The entire sequence thus constitutes a single giant condition for consciousness, which cannot exist without being somewhere on it. In order for the series of externalizations itself to be seen as parametric in nature, consciousness must be freed from having to occupy, at any given time, some single rung on the ladder of externalization. All positions must be made freely available to it at once. And in order for that to happen, those positions must first be acquired, through the labor of externalization. This is why consciousness must be radically desituated before it can come to situate itself.

The Overcoming of Externalization

The need for radical desituation means, in turn, that in order to become situated, consciousness must first have externalized and transcended all determinate content. This can only result in a state in which consciousness is defined by its utter *lack* of content—or, more precisely, by its own capacity to transcend all determination. This is the level of "absolute freedom," which is precisely defined as the ability to disregard all parameters and to act solely from an abstractly universal self (cf. *PhG* 422/363). As in Kantian moral philosophy, which I will discuss in chapter 14, consciousness here requires itself to act solely from duty, its inner awareness of its freedom—freedom which itself is nothing other than the capacity to deny particularities. The problem with this is that particularity disappears only from the "inner self" of consciousness. It remains in reality, in the form of the manifold unique and unstable situations in which consciousness finds itself and in which it must act. As Marx might put it, consciousness has here, falsely, taken itself to be a creature of "pure thought." This move has moral implications, for in taking itself to be a creature of pure *thought*, consciousness commits itself to viewing all *action* as foreign to it, and hence, as morally wrong. Pursuing this, consciousness becomes first "moral," then duplicitous.

The duplicity results from a tension in the nature of the moral act as here conceived. Because the act is supposed to come solely from consciousness's inner awareness of its freedom, it is supposed on the one hand to be a direct expression of that freedom, of the universal morality which holds for all without regard to concrete circumstances. On the other hand, any act is also a response to a specific set of circumstances, and as such is not necessarily what everybody might do. This means that there is an intrinsic discrepancy between the moral act, performed in particular circumstances, and the moral universal it is supposed to express directly. The result of this is a failure to communicate. For it follows that others may not recognize a given deed as performed out of duty. A wealthy man, for example, may take it as his duty to make a million dollars; but I am free not to acknowledge that as a truly dutiful act, if my inclinations and circumstances are different. There then arises a problem of "other minds:" I know when I am acting from duty, but I can never be sure when anyone else is. Indeed, insofar as the millionaire's actions do not correspond to what my own would be in his circumstances, I am—in conscience—*obliged* to view him, and not myself, as evil (*PhG* 457/394). So the individual deed, precisely because it is supposed to be a direct expression of the inner nature of consciousness, in fact displaces it.

This section can, as I have suggested, be read as an exposition and critique of Kant's moral philosophy.[9] Important to the *Phenomenology*'s narrative, however, is that consciousness now has both unity and multiplicity *within* itself. It has the former in the freedom constituting its inmost self, and the latter in the various actions which are supposed to express that unitary duty. Both have been internalized. But they are wholly at odds.

This problem is resolved by the other kind of externalization Spirit has: language. For language, as we have seen, does not always displace consciousness but can express it perfectly. An action, a unique event in space and time, is irreducibly particular. It cannot "discard" that particularity and rise to the universal. The standpoint of morality, by insisting that actions be direct expressions of the actor's inner freedom, in effect denies this and attributes to the action what is the proper characteristic of language. For speech, we have seen, *is* precisely such an immediate expression: that is why the utterance universalizes the self of the utterer. In the present circumstances, this means that the individual can distance himself from his own actions by talking about them—literally explaining them away. Thus, if the millionaire can talk morally about his actions, his hearer will admit his sincerity and allow that his actions were moral. The millionaire can do this by articulating his acts in a universal way, i.e., by relating them to what is most "universal" in the human self, inner freedom.

This type of speech thus implies, by its very form, that discourse here is among equals (*PhG* 460/397). As such, this form of communication becomes mutual and sets up a community in which speech takes the place of action:

> The spirit and substance of their association are thus the mutual assurance of their conscientiousness, good intentions, the rejoicing over this mutual purity, and the refreshing of themselves in the glory of knowing and uttering, of cherishing and fostering, such an excellent state of affairs (*PhG* 461/398).

Such is the community of the "beautiful souls," a community set up by, in, and for speech itself. What is inadequate in it is the relation of the communicative community to the outside world. However much they may devote themselves to talk, the beautiful souls live, and must act, in the real world. But their individual acts are, as all actions must be, in disharmony with the proclaimed universal nature of those who perform them. The deeds of such consciousness thereby diverge from its words, and this is "hypocrisy" (*PhG* 464/401).

Consciousness now divides. One side pursues its private or individual advantage, but denies that it does so; it is a hypocritical, but active, consciousness. The other side preserves its purity and devotion to duty, and is an honest consciousness which does not act but merely judges (*PhG* 464/401). The two consciousnesses, good and bad, enter into a complicated dialectic of condemnation, recrimination, and confession. The hypocritical consciousness claims that it is, after all, acting in accordance with its *own* law, its own duty. But this amounts, says Hegel, to admitting that it is evil: " . . . when anyone says that he is acting according to his own law and conscience against others, he is saying, in effect, that he is wronging them," i.e., that he is placing his own particular interest above the universal interest. The other consciousness—the one which judges and denounces the hypocrisy—in so doing reveals itself to be as bad as the first: for its denunciation of the "inner duty" of the hypocritical consciousness is based on *its* own inner law. The two laws are equal, and equally bad (*PhG* 465f/402).

Further, the hypocritical consciousness is at least acting; the judging consciousness, on the other hand, does not act but retains its purity by *not* doing anything. Thus, it is "the hypocrisy which wants its judgments to be taken for an actual deed, and instead of proving its rectitude by actions, does so by uttering fine sentiments" (*PhG* 466/403). The two consciousnesses thus prove to have the same hypocritical nature. When the acting consciousness recognizes this, it confesses itself to the other, expecting to be forgiven and make peace. Already aware of the disparity between its words and its deeds in a way that the judging consciousness is not, acting consciousness now realizes that the disparity is not essential. As did the weaker and brighter participant in the "Battle," it gives up the struggle with its other and attempts to found a community with it:

> This utterance is not a one-sided affair, which would establish his disparity with the other: on the contrary, he gives himself utterance solely on account of his having seen his identity with the other; he expresses their identity from his point of view for the reason that language is the existence of Spirit as an immediate self. He therefore expects the other to contribute his part to this existence (*PhG* 468f/405; translation slightly altered).

The battler, we saw, was motivated in its surrender by the desire to retain its corporeal existence. Acting consciousness here has a similar motivation. Rather than seek to escape from or rationalize away its specific actions, it owns up to them and their particularity and evil by seeking forgiveness for them. When the acting consciousness finally achieves forgiveness, the "wounds of Spirit" heal: "the word of reconciliation is the determinately existing Spirit which beholds the pure knowledge of itself, *quâ universal* essence, in its opposite" (*PhG* 471/408).

The moral individual now belongs to a community which he has himself instituted, through his acceptance of his other as basically identical with himself. It is therefore a community which can accommodate both his own universality—his pure knowledge of his own freedom—and his particular circumstances—the "evil" of his actions and the contingencies of the external world upon which they are directed. It is a community of equals, distinct from one another and able to articulate their distinctness as part of their common progress toward becoming rational themselves—and making others rational as well. In this articulation, the natural starting point of the individual is not denied, as it was in "Culture," but is recognized for just what it is—a starting point. The community is thus a "reconciled" one. It is not for Hegel merely one community among others but "God manifested in the midst of those who know themselves in the form of pure knowledge" (*PhG* 472/409).

With this, we may say that spirit has at last become situated. The various particularities it has passed through, as well as the new ones it encounters in specific situations, are no longer shrugged off or dismissed as evil. Consciousness recognizes that though no particular situation or parameter, or sequence of them, is necessary to it, to be in some situation or other is as basic to it as the universality with which it sought to identify itself. The purpose of the universal can no longer be to provide a self-sufficient level on which consciousness can shrug off all particularity, but to provide a general standpoint from which particular features of situations—parameters—can be articulated as parameters. Reconciliation, which I will analyze in the next chapter, is then the exercise of situating reason.

Three

Communication as Reconciliation in Hegel's *Aesthetics*

Through forgiveness, we have seen, the parametric nature of rational content is affirmed as such. Reason can become situated, i.e., rational action can now take parameters into account rather than simply ignore them, dismiss them, or explain them away. The way is now open as well for reason to function as situating: to take over the task of clarifying parameters as parameters. Such clarification, I wish to argue, is intrinsically emancipatory. But in order to see this, we must first view situating (or reconciling) reason in terms of what went before it. My analysis of the *Phenomenology* developed two antithetical structures of interaction. One was "recognition," in which a plurality of egos assume stances of mutual equality and seek the affirmation of their individual selves. The other was externalization, which does not affirm the individuality of those who enter into it but transforms it. This transformation requires a renunciation. In order to assimilate the content available to him in his culture, the individual must give up the "natural self" with which he starts. Because the assimilation of culture is a matter of degree, the self-hood of the cultured person is also a matter of degree. Those who have achieved a higher level of acculturation are given more recognition, and the basic equality of people is denied.

But the original, symmetrical structure of recognition persists as an underlying moment in externalization. We may express this in interactionist terms as follows. If, as Hume wrote, "the skin, pores, muscles, and sinews of a day-labourer are different from those of a person of quality,"[1] nonetheless even these two must understand a common language in order to address one another at all; and they must understand it in the same way. This basic presupposition of the equality of communicating selves is thus at odds with the nature of externalization, in which one side has something to articulate which the other does not. To resolve this problem, we saw a new and higher level of interaction introduced. The word for this is "reconciliation" (*Versöhnung, PhG* 471–408).[2] This concept is treated in the *Phenomenology's* section on "Absolute Spirit" (*PhG* 473-564/410–493). Before discussing it in detail, however, some systematic points need to be made.

The first concerns the possibility of an "interactive" reading of the concept of reconciliation at all. We have seen that when the two-term relation of recognition is replaced by the three-term one of externalization, the *Phenomenology* uses "ontological" language. It seems to be discussing the nature of reality in general, not that of interaction. When externalization passes over into reconciliation, we find language which is not only "ontological" but theological or religious in character. In the final quotation of the previous chapter, for example, we saw that the substance of Spirit had become no longer a social code but "God manifested." I will begin my account of reconciliation, then, by seeing how the *Phenomenology* construes this "deification" of the social substance.

Religion is the "perfection" of Spirit in that the previous moments of consciousness—self-consciousness, Reason, and Spirit itself—have "returned into it as their ground" (*PhG* 477/413). Religion is then constituted, not through relation to a transcendent godhead, but through the unification of human capacities in a "return to Spirit." The change from social substance to religious ground, then, is not a change in the ontological status of the substance, or even in its content. It is a change in the way Spirit now relates to those lower and earlier levels. The above quotation continues as follows:

> they [the previous levels] together constitute the *existent* actuality of Spirit, which *is* only as the differentiating and self-returning movement of these its aspects (*PhG* 477–413)

Those lower levels, as previous moments of the *Phenomenology's* narrative, include the levels on which the concrete individuality of the self was lodged—the levels, then, that were denied in externalization. The deification of the social substance thus amounts to viewing that substance as existing only in and through such concrete individuals. The particular forms it assumes in them are then simply the plurality of ways it exists. As the matter is put in a passage of the *Logic*, which stands almost as a commentary on the present development,

> [The] higher and highest level to which [abstraction] raises itself is only the surface, which becomes ever more destitute of content; the individuality it despises is the profundity in which the Notion seizes itself and is posited as Notion.[3]

We may thus say that if individuals need reconciliation (in its religious forms) in order to consolidate their selves, the deified social substance is itself dependent on them for its very content and existence. All, it appears, are levels of the self, and higher levels can no longer require the suppression—the discarding or ignoring—of lower levels.

If this is all Hegel means here by the "deification" of the social substance, it is clear that "religion" is not being used in anything like the Judeo-Christian sense of the term (and indeed, the next section begins, not with religion in any modern sense, but with the simple deification of natural phenomena, such as the sunrise: *PhG* 483-486/418–421). Religion in its broadest sense is thus what binds together, "heals the wounds," of human life. So understood, the religious language in which Hegel talks about "reconciliation" does not debar an interactionist reading of the concept.

There are other problems. The concluding sections of the *Phenomenology*, even more than earlier portions, bear the traces of what Walter Kaufmann has called the "immense strain" Hegel was under when he wrote it.[4] They are not merely sloppy and infelicitous in places but generally sketchy, and the movement from text to meaning is often a leap in the dark. This is due in part to the speed with which Hegel apparently wrote them, and in part to the compressed form in which they treat such enormous topics as art, religion, philosophy, and their respective histories.

But the problems go deeper. Though the religious framework in which the *Phenomenology* treats reconciliation does not debar an "interactionist" reading of the concept, it turns out to truncate it. The problem is not in the relation of religion, so understood, to reconciliation, but in its relation to the "middle term" between religion and reconciliation, which is art. Like Hegel's later, "systematic" writings, the *Phenomenology* presents reconciliation as, in the first instance, an aesthetic phenomenon. Unlike those writings, in which art, religion, and philosophy are the three moments of absolute Spirit, the *Phenomenology* presents art as a part of religion. It treats, not art as such, but the "religion of art," *die Kunstreligion*. And, because the religion of art flourished in ancient Greece, the *Phenomenology*'s account of art is keyed to classical forms of it.[5]

I have argued that to take the *Phenomenology* seriously as narrative means reading each section as constrained by previous sections of the book. The *Phenomenology*'s treatment of art, however, is constrained in a different way—by the level that will come *after* it in the systematic writings. This means that art is treated in only one of its capacities—that of connecting together, or "reconciling," the members of an entire culture.

As such, art is treated only as a set of public phenomena, such as Athenian drama. At the end of the previous chapter, by contrast, we saw reconciliation presented as occurring in a private conversation between two individuals. We can now see that the conversation was not necessarily private. The kind of dialogue presented there could occur anywhere from the secrecy of the confessional to an individual's public recantation of sins. The *Phenomenology*'s next section, however, treats art as *exclusively* a public phenomenon: as global interaction among the members of an entire community.

It thus seems advisable to turn to the *Aesthetics*, where (as we shall see) art is not treated as exclusively public and where the type of reconciliation afforded in Greek art—and, hence, in the *Phenomenology*—is criticized from a modern standpoint. This means a leap both in chronology and authoritativeness. While the *Phenomenology* was published by Hegel himself in 1808, the *Aesthetics* was put together after his death by pupils and disciples from lectures given after 1820.[6] But the works are not, in our topic at least, inconsistent. The *Aesthetics*, I will argue, in fact develops its concept of reconciliation on the basis of the kinds of recognition and externalization presented in the *Phenomenology*. It is not only consistent with the earlier text but, by virtue of its greater scope, complements it. We thus turn to the *Lectures on Aesthetics*—more precisely, to the systematic treatment of art given in the Introduction and in the first part of that work.

But this text is not without problems of its own. If the religious context of the *Phenomenology* truncated an interactive understanding of reconciliation, the aesthetic context of the *Lectures* at least hinders one. For, much as political philosophy is for Hegel the "science of the state" (*RPh.* 15/11), so aesthetics is for him the science of the work of art. The dominant model with which the *Aesthetics* deals will turn out to be the "monological" one of an individual confronting a work of art. This is not a definitive departure from the problematic of interaction, because Hegel, we shall see, continually wrestles against this model, attempting to construe aesthetic experience as dialogical. "Every work of art," he writes, "is a dialogue with everyone who confronts it" (*Aesth.* 356/264).[7] But his efforts, we shall also see, are strained. In some places, the text recurrently either anthropomorphizes the work of art, attributing to it almost human powers of reconciliation, or radically dehumanizes the spectator, viewing reconciliation as an unconscious, indeed almost natural process. Hegel, in short, is trying to articulate a concept that will not fit in with traditional aesthetics and its emphasis on the work of art. This is the concept I call "poetic," in which the hearer of an utterance determines its meaning. It appears in the *Aesthetics* as the ways in which a spectator determines the meaning of a work of art.

In the face of these problems, I will first analyze reconciliation as Hegel presents it, before moving on to his attempts to construe this as a dialogue and as emancipatory. In the resulting reading, the work of art first *presents* the spectator with an instance of reconciliation. The manner of presentation varies with the kind of art (symbolic, classical, romantic, etc.) as well as with its medium and genre. Second, art *effects* a liberation in the spectator so that his interaction with it is intrinsically emancipatory. The forms of such interaction vary with the historical situation of the spectator.

The dialogue of the spectator with a work of art is thus a complex affair. Any attempt to give separate accounts of its presentative and effectual components is to some extent artificial. I will begin abstractly, with a discussion of the general ways in which works of art can present the dynamics of Hegelian reconciliation. I will then examine the ways in which modern spectators, in Hegel's view, interact with works of art, showing that such interaction itself has a situating, "reconciliatory" character. And finally, in chapter 4, I will return to the work of art itself to see what sort of *political* reconciliation it can present to the modern world. This will enable me, finally, to bring out the basic features of Hegel's concept of aesthetic emancipation.

The Presentation of Reconciliation

Art for Hegel presents

> the *liberation* of Spirit from the content and forms of finitude,
> the presence and *reconciliation* of the Absolute with what is
> apparent and visible (*Aesth.* 14. 580/1236; emphasis added).

Reconciliation, as we have seen the *Phenomenology* develop it, contains the subsumed moments of recognition and externalization. These are what we are to look for first as they are presented by works of art. Only if both can be found in Hegel's account of aesthetic experience can his use of "reconciliation" in the above passage be anything more than a homonym of the term as used in the *Phenomenology*, and only then can aesthetic experience be intrinsically emancipatory.

Insofar as recognition is a mental process, we can hardly assign it to a work of art, which after all is not a mind but a product of mind. But apart from that basic discrepancy, some key features of recognition are present in such a work, in the interrelations of the various concrete details out of which it is composed. For like any beautiful object, a work of art consists of a variety of sensory givens, occurring in harmony with one another (*Aesth.* 156f/108f). These givens are the work's individual details and motifs, and no work of art can exist without them: it cannot be a harmony if there is nothing to harmonize. We may say—paradoxical as it sounds—that the work of art is an advance upon the *Phenomenology*'s community of beautiful souls, who, as we saw, could not accommodate their own individuality any more than could consciousness at the level of "Culture and Its Realm of Actuality."

Art thus has an intrinsic pull toward concreteness (and since for Hegel this pull is present to a high degree in painting, my examples here will be drawn from that area: cf. *Aesth.* 343/255). A painting—at least one of the kinds with which Hegel was familiar—presents us with a number of individual beings: people, their clothes and furnishings, details of landscape, etc. If it is great art, it does so with great concreteness and specificity. The early paintings of Van Gogh, for instance, do not achieve their significance for all humanity by dispensing with the manifold details of peasant life in Holland, but by depicting them. This, for Hegel, is only as it should be:

> on the whole, it is precisely characteristic of the great masters
> to be truly, genuinely, and completely tied down with regard
> to the external natural environment (*Aesth.* 343/255).

Hence, one of the pleasures afforded by art is a "specific contemplation of the external world in all its aspects" (*Aesth.* 331/246). Unlike, for example, a mathematical proof, in which each line is significant only for its relation to the whole, the work of art presents a variety of concrete figures, each of which can be experienced independently (*Aesth.* 226; 14. 29/163, 812). In such experience, we look to each detail alone, singling it out from the other figures in the work and enjoying it for its own sake, as an "end in itself." Because of its independence and finality, such a detail is on an equal footing with all the rest; the various figures in a Bosch would be examples of this. But the independence and finality are only apparent. In reality, each detail in a painting is there only because it serves the larger purpose of the painting, and all form parts of a disciplined composition (*Aesth.* 14. 29, 92f/813, 861f). This account of the concrete "independence and equality" of the details in a painting can be generalized to other forms of art. An individual theme in a symphony or a character in a novel or play can also become an "end in itself" for the hearer or reader (*Aesth.* 14. 136f, 220–226, 251f/896f, 959–962, 982f).

We have here four aspects in which the details in a work of art resemble the "battlers to the death" in the *Phenomenology*'s original account of recognition. First, desiring consciousness, as a living thing, "stepped forth" from the universality of the life force, disowning its continuity with that universal. Similarly, the detail in the painting (or other work of art), ready to be enjoyed in its own right, "steps forth" from the larger whole and cuts off connections to it. Second, it does so as one of a plurality of such individuals, all of which are to that extent of equal worth—as are the "battlers" themselves. Third, it turns out that the individual is what it is, not in virtue of its apparent independence, but only through its relationship to the larger whole—as the battling consciousnesses attained their true self-affirmation only when related as master and bondsman. And finally, this relationship is at first merely latent. As long as we are looking only at individual details in a work of art, we do not have a clear awareness of the work's overall, guiding conception, any more than the battlers to the death had a clear awareness of their relationship as identically human beings.

The individual details in a work of art thus relate to each other in ways analogous to some of the main structures of Hegelian recognition. A major discrepancy between interpersonal recognition as Hegel presented it in the early parts of the *Phenomenology* and what he is presenting now in regard to the work of art centers on the absence of compulsion in the latter. The "living thing" in the *Phenomenology* received its being from nature. Nature itself compelled it to disown its relationship to the whole and to resist reabsorption into it. A detail in a work of art receives its being from the artist and can hardly be said to "disown" or "resist" the whole. This lack of antagonism, as we shall see below, is essential both to the value and to the limitations of aesthetic reconciliation.

Another major discrepancy in structure between recognition in the *Phenomenology* and what we are dealing with now is the absence of symmetry here. In the recognition of the battle, each battler, as we saw, did to the other what the other did to it. The individual detail in a work of art, by contrast, has more concrete relations to the other details with which it cooperates to form the work as a whole. The "universal" connecting them is latent, but not abstract. These relations, and the universal they constitute, are explicated in the course of our encounter with a painting as we step back and see how each individual figure relates to others and contributes to the whole. With art forms such as music and literature, which unfold in time, this process of explication is to some extent performed by the work itself, which, as it progresses, gradually reveals the interrelations of its component motifs and characters.[8] The unfolding of a work of art is thus a temporal process of building up concrete relations among its various details. It leads finally to a presentation of the work's overall guiding conception, which the *Aesthetics* refers to as the work's "content" or "meaning" (*Aesth.* 140; cf. 77f/95, 46f). This subordination of the individual detail to a universal guiding conception exhibits certain features of the building up of concrete content treated in the *Phenomenology* as externalization.

A work of art in fact presents us with two sorts of externalization, only one of which will be party to the final reconciliation. One of them has to do with the relation between the work of art, which is motivated by a single guiding conception, and external reality, which in general is not. I will call it "extraneous externalization." The other type concerns the relation of the details as portrayed in the work to its overall guiding conception. I call this "immanent externalization."

Extraneous externalization affects both the media the artist uses and, more importantly, the external objects the work portrays. Beautiful things in general are for Hegel beautiful because nonsensuous ideas "shine through them." Even natural objects become "beautiful" only through a relation to the human intellect—ultimately, we are told, through a relation to the purity and harmony of thought itself (*Aesth.* 198-202/141–144). Some naturally beautiful things are taken over by the artist to form his media. In this, he makes use of only the purest and most harmonious natural givens. The painter, for example, simply throws away a muddy or impure pigment; the violinist has his instrument made from only the most resonant wood and the clearest glue.[9] And the poet, the "artist of speech," has as his medium language, which is not natural at all but a conventional system of signs.[10] The artist's media are thus free, in large part, from the contingent contamination generally found in nature. They are selected from the most beautiful phenomena nature has to offer and are then further refined.

The same holds for the external objects the artist may depict. It is not the business of art for Hegel simply to *imitate* external reality, but to portray it as a manifestation of deeper content. Art thus "casts aside everything in appearance which does not conform to the Concept, and only by this purification does it produce the Ideal" (*Aesth.* 216/155). The supreme example of this is the portrayal of the human face and figure. In this connection Hegel notes that portraits always flatter, and indeed must do so. The aim of a portrait is to convey its subject's character, and any of his physical characteristics which do not contribute to that guiding conception (such as warts and small scars) must be left out of the painting (*Aesth.* ibid.). On the other hand, a defect which does manifest the character of its possessor, such as the physical deformity of Richard III, must be retained by the artist (or by the producer of Shakespeare's play).

Thus, in order to enter a work of art, an external object must lose those characteristics which do not reflect the guiding conception of that work, or which are recalcitrant to the Ideal it presents. It must "give up its purely objective independence and flexibility in order to evince itself as identical with that of which it is the external existence" (*Aesth.* 341; cf. 160/253, 111). And, just as in the cases of externalization previously considered, the object receives as a result a higher and better presentation of itself. It is

> not just represented in the forms in which it is presented to us in its immediate existence; grasped now by the Spirit, it is enlarged within those forms and otherwise changed (*Aesth.* 226f/164).[11]

In contrast to the apparently global forgiveness presented in the account of reconciliation in chapter 2, some natural characteristics of an individual are simply left behind in this account, as they were in the *Phenomenology*'s account of "culture." There will be no further reconciliation with them, and this means that aesthetic reconciliation has limits. We shall discuss this in more detail later, merely noting for now that there are some aspects of reality—precisely the most troublesome and painful ones—with respect to which aesthetic reconciliation is impotent. Thus, writes Hegel, the oppression of Jews in many countries is simply too evil and repulsive to be a fit subject for art. It is to be fought and, if fighting is useless, to be endured. It is not to be depicted (*Aesth.* 282-287/ 208–211).

An individual entity is not included in a work of art just by being stripped of those features which will not fit the guiding conception. The object in question must also, of course, be rendered by the artist in such a way as to contribute to the expression of that guiding conception (*Aesth.* 240/174). That conception thus serves as a single principle under which a number of individuals fall and according to which those individuals are organized. It is in Hegelian parlance a "universal," and the individual details in a work are therefore "permeated by the universal;" their place within the work as well as their individual characteristics are in harmony with the work's guiding conception. This determinate organizing principle must be present if the work of art is to be a successful one, and it must be capable of being rendered explicit and definite if the work is not to be "stunted" (*Aesth.* 215/155).

Hegel treats this explication of the universal side of the work as a process of externalization occurring within the work itself. In it, the individual ceases to be an end in itself and comes to be defined in terms of its determinate relations to other individuals. Thus, the explication of the work's guiding conception, or "content," means a sort of renunciation, anthropomorphically carried out by the work itself, of the independence of the individual details depicted in the work. But this immanent process of externalization differs both from the type of externalization we saw developed in the *Phenomenology* and from the extraneous externalization we found in the relation of art to external reality. Moreover, it differs in ways which enable the artwork to present a dynamic, not merely of recognition and externalization, but of reconciliation as well. In the first place, as Hegel's characterization of the individual as "permeated" by the universal suggests, this type of externalization is not an arduous process of acculturation, but is immediate. The universal, he writes, must "gleam through" the concrete details of the work of art: "the most fundamental thing is and remains immediate intelligibility" (*Aesth.* 369, 375/ 274, 279). The speed and ease with which the guiding conception of the work of art is presented by its individual details is due, of course, to the process of extraneous externalization the details have already undergone. The hard work, we may say, has already been done.

The immediacy with which it is presented means that the aesthetic universal—the guiding conception of the work of art—cannot be anything abstract or formalistic, like the content of culture. Formulating such a "general doctrine" from a work of art would not be an immediate response, but a matter of "prosaic reflection" which would reduce the work itself to a "useless appendage" (*Aesth.* 83f/51). The properly "aesthetic" universal must rather be fully defined by, and indeed identical with, its function of organizing just the particular set of individual details it does organize, and no others. It must be a universal which is active and therefore concrete (*Aesth.* 108/70f). The guiding conception of the work of art thus turns out to be unique to that work and "universal" only with respect to it. Since there are, of course, a plurality of great works of art, there are a multitude of such universals, none of which is a necessary condition for art itself and each of which would have been different if the details it organizes had been different. As presented by the work of art to the spectator, the guiding conception of the work is not something the spectator can freely invent: it is a limit to his experience. But relative to the work which it guides, it can be other than it is: exchanged for lessons learned from other works, or reinterpreted in light of later experiences. In my terms, such an aesthetic universal is a "parameter," and it is for Hegel part of the business of the work of art to present parameters as parameters.

Finally, the work of art's presentation of its own guiding conception turns out to affirm all the concrete features of the various individuals in the work. This affirmation takes two basic forms, which Hegel refers to under the rubrics of "necessity" and "freedom" (*Aesth.* 165f/115). I will clarify them with examples.

The physical deformity of Richard III must, as we have noted, be included in artistic portrayals of him because it directly manifests the deformity of his character. Such a characteristic is then "necessary" to the work of art's expression of its own guiding conception.[12] If the real Richard also had, say, a wart on his chin, this would have to be excluded from a truly artistic portrayal because it contributes nothing to revealing his character and, by distracting the audience, might detract from that revelation. Richard's real humpback, unlike his putative wart, is then affirmed within the work of art as a starting point for the revelation of his inner character.

In contrast to both sorts of characteristics would stand, for example, the color of Richard's hair. Assuming that Richard is not portrayed as bald, he must have hair of some determinate color. But it is a matter of indifference just what that color is. A given Richard, whether existing as an actor on a stage or in the imagination of the reader of the play, may be blond, brunet, or redheaded; but he must be, and in some very definite way, one of these. This particular detail is "affirmed" by the work of art, not because it manifests something about Richard's character, but because it is essential to showing Richard as an actual, living human being, as an "end in himself." Without hair of some color, he would be only an abstraction.

Because the specific form of such a characteristic is not prescribed by the guiding conception of a work of art, it is for Hegel "free." It is up to the artist or spectator to specify it as he likes. Moreover, it is only by virtue of its possession of such concrete, but not necessitated, characteristics that an individual detail is able to "free itself" from the work's overall structures and step forth as an object of enjoyment in its own right. Any such detail, we may say, has some characteristics which are dictated by the guiding conception of the work and are affirmed as necessary to the expression of that universal conception. It possesses others, however, which go beyond that conception and enable it to be enjoyed as an end in itself as well.

The individual portrayed in a work of art is thus, in a sense, ambiguous. On the one hand, it is presented as an end in itself, affording the spectator an independent enjoyment. On the other, it is subordinated to the work as a whole and can be viewed in terms of the contribution it makes to that work. It is essential to the work of art's presentation of reconciliation that it allow for both: that it present an individual as existing for itself alone, as "free," and for the sake of the whole, as "necessary" (*Aesth.* 165f/115). Hence, aesthetic experience begins with the experience of a detail whose significance is up to the spectator to decide. The rubrics of freedom and necessity here constitute two sides of what we may call the interpretative repertoire of the spectator, who is free to move between them. Aesthetic experience for Hegel thus begins, in my sense, poetically. Construed dialogically, it begins as what I call poetic interaction.

But this is only the beginning. Also required, for full aesthetic appreciation, is the explication of a work of art's guiding conception. This, too, falls to some extent within the spectator, who is "present from the start" in the aesthetic functioning of a painting (*Aesth.* 14. 21/806) as well as in that of the "higher" art forms of music and poetry. But, Hegel points out, a linguistic work of art can contain characters who themselves are able to speak and reflect on their experiences. This enables it to present explicitly its own dynamic of externalization and reconciliation. Thus Oedipus, reduced from kingship to blind beggary, undergoes a fearsome process of externalization. He gives up the commanding self he has at the beginning of his ordeals and receives a sadder but wiser self. And he refers to this process himself when, at the beginning of *Oedipus at Colonus*, he pronounces himself content because through his trials he has learned to acquiesce (cf. *Aesth.* 14. 557f/1219). As the *Aesthetics* puts it for the tragic hero generally, "the ends he pursues are not just taken from him; he renounces them and thereby does not lose *himself*" (*Aesth.* 219/ 157f). But the reconciliation of such a hero with his own experiences is pronounced as an inarticulate "it is so," and thus remains a serene submission to the "cosmic order" (*Aesth.* ibid; 14. 554-558/1216–1220).[13] The reasons for this are, apparently, twofold. First, if Oedipus were to reflect in detail on what he has undergone, to show precisely how and why his experiences have turned out to be reconciliatory in nature, he would no longer be operating merely as a character in a drama. He would be philosophizing, and this would violate the Hellenic view that art, not philosophy, is the highest way of relating to the Absolute. Similarly, if Oedipus were to start differentiating between those of his personal characteristics which manifest his character (such as his clubfoot and blindness) and those which do not, he would step out of the work of art altogether and reflect on his portrayal in it. Thus, any concrete discussion of the reconciliation presented by a work of art does not properly belong, for Hegel, within the work itself. It requires the active participation of the spectator.

Before moving to that topic, however, I will briefly discuss one particular art which will be of special importance to our future investigation of poetic interaction: that of poetry itself. Since Hegel does not recognize the novel or short story as important art forms, "poetry" for him is the "art of speech" in general (*Aesth.* 14. 222/960). We have seen that poetry, particularly its dramatic form, treads the line between immediacy and reflection. It can approach the verge of reflection, and with it the boundary of art itself, because it is the most direct aesthetic expression of Spirit for Spirit (*Aesth.* ibid.). Paint and stone are static and require, at least, the support of a canvas, a floor, etc. There is no danger that a painting or a statue could ever stand out and reflect on itself. A poem is a set of mere words and requires the presence of an active speaker. Hence its nearness to Spirit and the possibility of representing reflection itself.

Because poetry has language for its medium, it has a broader range of content than do other arts (*Aesth.* 14. 230f/966f). A painting of Hamlet's soliloquy, for example, would be unable to capture the concrete content of what he is thinking about. Unless we knew the play independently, there would be no way to guess the subject matter of his reflections. Nor can Shakespeare as dramatist give an exact representation of them: a real Hamlet would hardly have spoken his thoughts aloud. But "externalizing" those thoughts into the mouth of an actor remains more articulate than putting them on canvas.

The plasticity of poetry's medium, language, is in direct contrast to the "alien" element of the material arts apprehended in vision. This means that poetry is able to present reconciliation more fully and effectively than can other arts. Poetic expression organizes and concentrates contents of the "finite" world, and in this is similar to, for example, the abstractive and deductive powers of thought. But it also provides images for those organized thoughts—images and illustrations which are not mere adornments but which are presented as essential to the subject matter itself. In this way, the poem is a "reconciled" whole of thought and intuition. Reconciliation is pursued into the purely sensory realm as well. Sound does not in poetry, as it does in music, convey essential meaning; but it is not in poetry, as in prose, wholly irrelevant. Each word in a poem is, like a detail in a painting, present for itself alone; in stress and accent, it contributes to, carries along, the flow of discourse (*Aesth.* 14. 233, 276f/968, 1002f).

We saw that art's presentation of reconciliation rests upon its extraneous externalization of much of life. Poetry's achievement in presenting, more than other arts can do, the dynamics of reconciliation also rests upon an extraneous externalization. Indeed, as we might expect, the externalization operated by converting a reality or event into speech is more radical than, say, that involved in converting stone into a temple or into the statue of the god placed inside it (*Aesth.* 14. 220/959). The adequacy of poetry's presentation of reconciliation is then the reason why it is the *telos* of art as a whole. The radicality of its extraneous externalization is what threatens to take us beyond art altogether, to thought.[14]

Because of its universality, and because as aesthetic it remains immediately intelligible, poetry is "the most universal and widespread teacher of the human race" (*Aesth.* 14. 238/972). It teaches by taking up dispersed and obscure materials of ordinary life and giving them clear and concentrated presentation under a single guiding conception. In this, as in all art, each detail of the poem remains "free" to be perceived in its own right; more so in fact than in a painting, because a poem is in time. Each detail—each image and locution—is sensorily united with those that precede and succeed it merely by meter and rhythm. Further unity must be supplied by the spectator in recapitulating the details in his mind in order to formulate their common guiding conception. Unlike other artworks, a poem has the possibility to put its guiding conception explicitly into words: a temptation to be avoided, if the poem is to retain the immediate sensuality essential to the work of art (*Aesth.* 14. 253f, 266f/984f, 994).

Thus reorganized, the content of a poem is "truer" than the dispersed and obscure contents of everyday reality. But the two types of content are intimately connected:

> For whatever poetry presents by way of external locality, characters, passions, situations, conflicts, actions, and fates, all this is already to be found, more then some people may commonly believe, in actual life. So here too poetry treads as it were on an historical ground . . . (*Aesth.* 14. 267/994).

But poetry treads its historical ground in two quite different ways, depending upon historical period. Before the development of reflective thought and the prose that expresses it, poetry is "the creation of language." The poets in such cultures find words for as-yet-unexpressed contents of the human spirit and "open the lips" of their nations. Their works are astonishing new creations and are attributed to magic and divine powers. Later, when vocabulary has been articulated and "language is, to so say, common life," things are different. Poetry is no longer a first articulation of ordinary life but finds its concerns already formulated in prose (*Aesth.* 14. 285ff/1009f). In such a (modern) culture, poetry is of course not debarred from coming up with new ideas and expressions; but its main task is to "concentrate . . . into a more fixed center" materials already articulated in ordinary life and language (*Aesth.* 266f/994). Indeed, if poetry seeks after novelty it stands in danger of becoming florid and precious (*Aesth.* 14. 282/1006). In the modern world, we may say, poetry does not create language and culture; it reconciles the individual to them, as they are already present in ordinary life.

We might wish for further discussion of poetry as the origin of language—a point which Heidegger, for example, has made central to his later thought. Hegel does not give us any, in part because he thinks this function of poetry belongs to the past and also, perhaps, because to do so would risk detaching this general function of poetry from the poetic work of art and viewing it as a broader feature of human interaction. But enough has been said to show that poetry is connected to ordinary life, in both modern and ancient cultures, in ways that leave it culturally relative. There is, to be sure, something common to all the situations in which humans may find themselves, and to the extent that it can present those elements, poetry can have something of a universal significance. But its very concreteness mitigates against this, for different languages have different stocks of images and comparisons for the poet to use as well as different values and conceptions for him to "fix" and "center" (*Aesth.* 244f, 287f/977, 1919f). In my terms, different languages provide different parameters for the poet to clarify.

In these treatments of the work of art's presentation of recognition, externalization, and reconciliation, Hegel has labored to view the artwork, not as an inert physical object, but as one which is inherently dynamic. The dynamisms he locates in the work of art are, I think, relatively unpersuasive as long as he is talking about paintings and the like. Is it sensible at all to say, as Hegel's language suggests, that a painting or statue itself engages in recognition among its details, in the explication of its single guiding concept, and in the reconciliation of the two? Can it do so when no one is there to see it?

The anthropomorphisms are less strained when the *Aesthetics* turns to art forms such as drama. The actors on a stage could be said to "recognize" one another, and the drama to explicate its guiding conception, in the performance. This might hold even if the performance is a rehearsal and no one is actually watching. But in such a case, the actors recognize one another, not as the concrete human beings they are, but as the characters they portray. The stage absolution of an actor playing a priest is no real forgiveness.

Hegel's efforts here spring, I suggest, from his basic attempt to construe the work of art as a partner in dialogue with the spectator. This constraint operating on the *Aesthetics* is imposed on it by the interactive account of reconciliation in the *Phenomenology*—an account which, we saw, was itself constrained by earlier sections of that work. Unable to attribute true personhood to the work of art, Hegel attempts to outfit it with an analogue: the triple dynamic of recognition, externalization, and reconciliation which he has articulated in the *Phenomenology*. Concomitantly, he downplays the role of the artist, whom he dismisses as a mere "corridor" for the reconciliatory functioning of art (*Aesth.* 400/298).

The Dialogue with the Audience

Given the importance to poetry of its cultural situation, it is no surprise to find that the interaction of a work of art with its audience is for the *Aesthetics* essentially conditioned by the historical situation of the latter. The main contrast drawn is a dichotomy between the ancient way of approaching art (as well as, to some extent, the medieval way) and the modern. The Greeks in their day would worship art. They could respond to it with the most sublime, and least critical, of feelings. But subsequent centuries have for Hegel established precisely the right of the individual to a more critical response. This critique achieves its proper form in reflection. The appropriate response of the modern individual to a work of art is not merely laughter or the venting of his own subjective reactions, but study and analysis. Art in the modern world does not call us to worship but "invites us to intellectual consideration." We desire to relate art, not to our feelings, but to our capacity for abstract thought. And so the modern community, unlike the ancient, requires art criticism and, ultimately, aesthetics. Thought and reflection have "spread their wings above fine art" (*Aesth.* 30–33, 150f/10–12, 103).

This reference to the spreading of wings recalls Hegel's famous figure of the owl of Minerva, which begins to fly only at the close of the day (*RPh.* 17/13). When moderns reflect upon art, they no longer approach it in a properly artistic way. That art has become an object of reflection means that it is no longer valued as *art*. The passages just cited are very clear that the properly artistic way to approach art is the ancient way: to avoid reflection and to remain content with the immediate apprehension of a given work's guiding conception as "gleaming through" its multifarious details. Nonetheless, Hegel does have a number of observations to make about the modern way of encountering works of art, and these yield the key to understanding his concept of aesthetic emancipation. They can, once again, be organized around the three fold structure of recognition, externalization, and reconciliation.

The modern *recognizes* a work of art in that he sees it as consisting, like himself, in an interplay of intellectual and sensory aspects. Like its observer, and like natural phenomena, a work of art is first of all a sensible object, even if its material component is only the evanescent sound of the spoken word.[15] But natural objects do not evidence, in their perceived structures, single, overriding purposes. Even animals move capriciously, seeking now this and now that; any single, more general purpose (such as self-preservation or survival of the species) is only something that we, as a result of our observations, attribute to them.[16] An individual human being is recognized as such because it presents *itself* as having a single aim. Even the *Phenomenology*'s battler to the death, for example,

78

desired to show itself as an empty self-identity opposed to its natural being. A work of art, as a product of mind, is likewise consciously organized to serve a single purpose, the expression of its guiding conception. Because that guiding conception is a universal which actively organizes the totality of the work, the work itself "belongs to the sphere of conceptual thinking." It appears to its beholders as, like themselves, an interplay of the universal, or intellectual, and the sensible. Displaying in this interplay "subjectivity and life," it can confront its audience "like a blessed god." [17]

As its language shows, this account is strained. The work of art cannot, for one thing, be said to think: it does not, for example, first propose its guiding conception to itself and then carry it out in practice. But neither (to defend Hegel for a moment) do human beings much of the time. Part of the purpose of the *Phenomenology* is to make explicit some of the guiding conceptions which permeate and structure human life, but which are no more known to those whose lives are structured by them than the idea of girlish charm is known to the Mona Lisa. Just as humans are capable of acting "animalistically" or simply of "vegetating," so for Hegel they are capable of acting as works of art. This way of acting is central, in Hegel's view, to the ancient Greek way of life. A Greek confronting a work of art does not, in Hegel's view, reflect on it. He responds in an immediate way, seeing what the work makes him see and feeling what it makes him feel. The most "intellectual" facet of his response to the work is his apprehension of its guiding conception "gleaming" at him through the details. Thus, there is nothing in such a spectator which is not also presented by the work. The Greeks, whom Hegel in his early writings called the "beautiful people," can in a sense be viewed as works of art themselves, responding to other works in an unconscious way. [18] "Subjectivity," in the sense of the ability to formulate and carry out one's own purposes, is not for Hegel to be equated with humanity itself.

Like the ancients, we cannot encounter a work of art as art unless we are aware both of its various sensory details and of the guiding conception they immediately convey. If we begin by confronting a work of art as a sensible object of a certain type, then we encounter it as the Greeks did: by seeing as it makes us see, and feeling as it makes us feel (*Aesth.* 59f, 64f/32f, 36f). As with the ancients, then, our awareness of the work matches, point for point, with what the work presents. We and the work meet in the first instance as equals. Furthermore, the work's guiding conception, which as rational must be something shared by the work and its spectators, remains at this stage latent and inarticulate, just because it is apprehended as a mere "gleam." We thus have a level of modern aesthetic dialogue in which the participants—the work of art and its spectator—confront each other as equals, and in which both are governed by a higher conception which remains latent. The recognitive structures of the *Phenomenology*'s "Battle" return again, but again without the antagonisms present there.

The absence of antagonism is not an absence of otherness. Insofar as the shared rationality of the work of art and its spectator remains latent, the reconciliation presented in the former remains "external" to the latter—here, in the sense that it is not related to his inner self, his capacity for conceptual thought. The next step for the modern is then to formulate explicitly the inner rationality of the work of art via an "externalizing" process. To do so is to relate the work of art to his own inner, subjective self. Such a self, of course, is something the work of art does not have. The equality characteristic of the aesthetic encounter breaks down—just as equality does in externalization.

The first interiority to which the art object is related is religious in character. This means that the guiding conception of the work of art becomes a truth of the human heart and has its proper location in the heart alone.[19] It follows that the work's true guiding conception cannot be presented in the work itself, and if known at all, it must be revealed independently of aesthetic experience (*Aesth.* 13. 104, 132/505, 526). Being independent of the work of art, religious truth can only be alluded to by it: when it portrays, for example, events from the life of Christ (a life whose details and significance must already be understood by the spectator) or when it makes use of allegories and other such devices.[20] The emphasis in such art lies on the spectator's decipherment of its meaning through his background knowledge of that meaning and the cultural conventions by which it can be conveyed. Because of this, the individual details of the work become *in toto* accidental: none of them can directly manifest any of the work's inner content. Even if religious reality is reducible to human experience, that experience is for Hegel in its proper form wholly interior, and no sensible object could hope to capture it (*Aesth.* 13. 144f/536).

The details of a work of art thus yield up their individuality as far as religious or, indeed, modern man is concerned. Amplifying Goethe, Hegel writes:

> In a work of art we begin with what is immediately presented to us and only then ask what its content or meaning is. The former, the external appearance, has no immediate value for us; we assume behind it something inward, a meaning whereby the external appearance is endowed with the spirit . . . .

The meaning is always something wider than what it shows itself in the immediate experience (*Aesth.* 43/19f).

But this negation of external appearance and immediately perceived detail does not give us the whole of the externalization taking place in the aesthetic experience of modern man. Externalization, as we saw it in the *Phenomenology,* was indeed a rejection of man's natural being and, hence, of his sensory experience as well. But that rejection was in favor of something. It was the means by which the individual ascended to the universal or, in the first instance, to abstract thought. Religion, being an affair of the heart, does not yield such thought. Approached religiously, art is "still not compelled to explain itself to the length of complete clarity" (*Aesth.* 13. 150/540). There is thus a further interiority behind the religious one. The "inmost essential nature of Spirit" is in fact thought, not religious feeling. So Spirit comes to require that art be subjected to conceptual treatment. Art thus has, for the modern spectator, a developed theoretical side (*Aesth.* 34f, 163f/13, 114). In view of this, it proves helpful to compare the modern approach to art, not with religious experience, but with a phenomenon of the modern world discussed at some length in the opening sections of the *Aesthetics*: natural science.

A scientist describes (and if he is an experimental scientist, manipulates) nature. But his primary interest is not in the individual phenomenon he studies. The taxonomist of Hegel's day did not, as a scientist, have any personal concern for the individual life-forms he described and classified, any more than a contemporary psychologist is expected to care about the rats he runs through his mazes. The interest of both scientists would lie primarily in the general laws they can extract from or test against individual cases. Like religious truths, such laws apply beyond the specific individuals and circumstances in which they are first revealed; the theoretical or scientific interest, like religion, "lets individual things alone and retreats from them as sensuous individualities" (*Aesth.* 65–67/37f). From the "point of view" of an entity investigated scientifically, to be investigated is to be externalized: the individual rat "gives up" its individuality in order to enter a research report as an idealized abstraction.[21]

The demand for thought and theory requires that the spectator, like the religious audience, see the sensible object before him as the vehicle of a higher meaning. It also demands that he, like the natural scientist, see that meaning as susceptible of rational vindication. Such vindication is in the first instance empirical. Rather than view the details in a work of art as "ends in themselves," the modern audience must use them to formulate a general theory of art. Art critics fulfill this demand by describing and classifying works of art and their various details, hoping to arrive (as

Hegel's contemporary Meyer did) at a theoretical statement of how the details in any work of art contribute to that work as a whole (*Aesth.* 36-43/14–20). Only by virtue of such a general, prosaic theory can a spectator claim to be intelligently critical of a work of art. When a modern critic, for example, discusses various problems in a painting, he measures that painting against a general conception of what a painting ought to convey and of how it should convey it; and that conception itself must have been arrived at rationally.

We can now summarize the kind of externalization occurring within aesthetic experience. Unlike the phenomena studied by natural science, the concrete details of a work of art are not themselves things but portrayals, or appearances, of things (cf. *Aesth.* 67f/38). This means that they have an essential relation to the perceiving subject, whose "appearances" they are. They are to be viewed as consisting, not in a set of actual existents, but in a set of experiences. The modern spectator reduces these sensory and affective experiences to mere starting points for the movement beyond them, inward to religious feeling and then upward to theoretical criticism. He thus rejects those experiences and ascends to the universal. Unlike the scientist, who "leaves behind" concrete individuals that are not appearances and that are not in any sense "part" of him, the reflective spectator externalizes his own experience, in a concrete sense *himself*, as he seeks to formulate universal truths behind works of art.

The difference between this and the sort of externalization we saw in the *Phenomenology* is again the absence of resistance on the part of the sensory individual (here, an individual experience). The work of art, in its original presentation of its various details, allowed them to retreat in favor of the presentation of its guiding conception. The spectator of the work is thus allowed to do the same: he does not violate the individuality of the art object by moving beyond his experiences of its concrete sensory being to whatever universal formulae it may instantiate. He simply refuses to approach it in an artistic way.

The attainment of the theoretical formula for a work's guiding conception corresponds, on the side of the spectator, to what I earlier called the "immanent externalization" presented by the work of art itself. As such, it is itself a situated reflection on the work of art. Limits to its situation are prescribed, first of all, by the work of art itself. For the formula that aesthetic reflection seeks is given, as we have seen, by the work itself: it is just that formula which articulates the guiding conception of that individual, unique work of art.

Second, the spectator is generally conditioned by his culture. A Greek spectator, we saw, reacts differently to a work of art than does a modern. This is not willful; it results from the general characteristics of the culture to which each belongs. This cultural conditioning, we may say, can also be more specific. If, as we saw, different languages contain different images and conceptions for the poet to use in writing a poem, the same is presumably true for the spectator, who has a particular set of linguistic resources to use in articulating it. A modern German and a modern Frenchman might well produce formulations of the guiding conception of a single work of art which cannot easily be translated into the other's language. (Indeed, Hegel writes, the French, because of their "cultural delicacy, have been wholly unable to come to terms with Shakespeare, and when they put him on the stage cut out every time those passages that are our [German] favorites" [*Aesth.* 360/267]).

Cultural conditioning is, however, to some extent undone by aesthetic experience itself. For because the work of art is unique, the parameters formulated by reflection upon it are unique as well. And this means that such reflection is the acquisition of new parameters. These new parameters can, we may say, provide the resources for further reflection on other works of art (and on the present one). They can thus break through the conditioning effects of a given culture—as the French efforts to come to terms with Shakespeare can change French culture, reducing what previously operated as a set of conditions to the status of a set of parameters. In this sense, aesthetic experience as Hegel conceives it is an activity of situating reason.

The other type of externalization—extraneous externalization—is also present. This is because art is no longer for moderns, as Hegel thinks it was for the Greeks, a dimension woven into the fabric of everyday life in the community and a "substantial interest" of that life (*Aesth.* 22f/3). In the modern, prosaic world, art is not part of everyday life, except for a small minority of artists and critics. The individual approaching it must, in order to approach it at all, simply put aside all the cares and burdens of daily life and move into a very different realm of experience: he must approach the work of art, not as a "substantial interest," but with *disinterest*. Far from reconciling the individual to his "station and duties," the work of art opens a much-needed doorway out of them. It "lifts the soul high above all painful entanglement in the real world," and in that sense externalizes those entanglements without coming back to reconcile them (*Aesth.* 13. 240/611).[22]

The final reconciliation afforded the individual through his encounter with a work of art is then only with those sensory and affective experiences the work actually engages. It occurs when the spectator, having penetrated to a clear understanding of the work's guiding conception, returns to the work itself to see how its specific details express that message—both, presumably, in their "freedom" and their "necessity."

This return to the sensory is not paralleled in science, which remains with its general laws or, perhaps, seeks new applications for them, or in religion, which remains focused on the depths of the heart.

This return is for Hegel required by the nature of the aesthetic universal itself. Unlike an animal species or a natural characteristic such as the speed of light, the aesthetic universal is not one and the same for a number of different phenomena. It is itself defined by just those individual phenomena it structures in the work and cannot be understood independently of them. It follows that an aesthetic universal, though possessed of a kind of rationality, does not belong wholly to thought in the way that general laws of science do. It rather stands "midway" between the sensory and the intellectual (*Aesth.* 65-67/37f). The scientist, therefore, can remain content with the universal abstractions of his laws and equations. The reflective spectator, by contrast, must make recurrent reference to the sensory material of the work of art. In so doing, he reaffirms the work itself as a concrete, sensory individual phenomenon, and he affirms as well his own original sensory and affective experiences with regard to it. The encounter with an art object thus "liberates" the spectator, in a sense beyond both theoretical and practical exercises of mind, in that the work of art reconciles him with himself:

> But the self in relation to the [art] object . . . ceases to be the abstraction of both noticing—sensuously perceiving—and observing, and also of dissolving individual perceptions and observations into abstract thoughts. In this [beautiful] object the self becomes concrete in itself, since it makes explicit . . . the unification, in their concreteness, of the aspects hitherto separated, and therefore abstract, in the self and its object (*Aesth.* 164/114).

This liberation is achieved in and through aesthetic experience, which is, as chapter 4 will argue in more detail, intrinsically emancipatory for Hegel. In it, the "universal" which the artwork presents is one whose function is not to be valid at all times and places, but to organize just those details—particularities—which are actually experienced in the work. It is the kind of universal we saw emerge in the *Phenomenology* at the end of chapter 2: a universal whose function is to organize a specific set of particulars. In my terms, as I have noted, it is a "parameter." The work of art's guiding conception has parametric status in that it provides a coherent, reconciling relationship among the details of the work. The spectator's appreciation of this is the institution of a similar relationship between his mind (which formulates the universal) and his senses, and hence is emancipatory.

The dialogue between the spectator and the work of art unfolds in time and, as a reflective process, has a rational structure: it is thus itself, like the *Phenomenology* as a whole, a narrative. We may say, generally, that the situating of reason is for Hegel a process of narration. It begins from something which is itself ambiguous: the portrayal of individual details as both free ends in themselves and as necessary to the whole work. Hegel's stress on the need for both these aspects suggests that even the modern spectator is able to remain on the level of immediate apprehension, viewing the detail merely in and for itself. It is then up to him to decide whether to make the modern rise to the explicit formulation of the work's guiding conception. To that extent, the "meaning" of the individual detail—whether it is an end in itself or a part of the whole—is up to the spectator, and the dialogue with the artwork begins with what I call "poetic" interaction.

But for the modern, the narrative of reflection eventually imposes itself. The course of the narrative is further constrained by its goal, which as we have seen is to view that work as a reconciled whole. If forgiveness in the *Phenomenology*'s depiction of reconciliation was of all particularity, then viewing a work of art as a reconciled whole means seeing *all* of its details as conveying a single guiding conception. Once that has been achieved, the work of interpretation terminates. The standard for judging competing interpretations of the work is thus the completeness of the coherence they attribute to it.

As we have seen, Hegel suggests—though he never actually says— that different cultures might come up with different, but equally coherent, formulations of the guiding conception of a given work of art. This can result if, for example, the French leave some passages out of Shakespeare, as Hegel says they do, and the Germans leave out an equally large, but different, set. But Hegel never deals with this possibility, nor does he mention that two individuals in the same culture—or even the same individual—might come up with two different, but equally acceptable, interpretations of a work of art. We might read this as a case of the cultural determinism for which Hegel is famous. Equally plausible, however, is the possibility that the whole issue is of no great interest to him. The point in appreciating the work of art appears to be articulating it as a reconciled whole. And part of its being such a whole is, of course, that the universal it presents be a concrete and situated one—one, perhaps, among a plurality of others, some of which might also apply to this particular work. If there is anything conveyed by all great artworks, always and everywhere, it can only be this narrative dynamic of reconciliation itself.

This brings us to the general status of reconciliation in Hegel's philosophy. As our most recent quotation tells us, aesthetic experience reconciles the self of the spectator: it makes it into a concrete unity of otherwise separate capacities, sensory and intellectual. The achievement of reconciliation is thus the achievement of what I have called a "consolidated self." True, there are more moves to make before the consolidation is complete: Spirit must still pass through the remaining stages of religion and philosophy. We will not accompany it, because the structures of emancipatory interaction for Hegel are now, for our purposes, completely analyzed. All that remains is to see, in the next chapter, precisely how they are "emancipatory" and to clarify their relationship to the political sphere.

Because it thus coincides with the nature of self-consolidation, reconciliation stands at the end of the *Phenomenology*'s narrative. As far as Hegel is concerned, it is the *telos*, not merely of aesthetic experience, but of the entire account of Spirit. It is thus for him a sort of universal goal, in terms of which not only all great art but all human undertakings are to be evaluated. In virtue of its concreteness, it is not a very constraining goal: all sorts of content—indeed, Hegel has said *all* particular content—can be presented in reconciled form. But even its status as an overall goal is open to challenge, though not from Hegel's own perspective. The challenge, we shall see, comes from Heidegger.

Four

Aesthetic Emancipation and the Politics of Hegel's *Aesthetics*

I have argued that Hegelian reconciliation is, in my sense, situating, and that its first form is poetic. The task now is to understand in more detail how it is "emancipatory." This accomplished, I will apply the results specifically to the political realm as Hegel conceives it. Hegel's concept of aesthetic emancipation, I will argue, leads both to a critique of the existing political order and to a utopian vision of what a better society, from an aesthetic standpoint, would be. The final task of this chapter will be to inquire as to the validity, for Hegel, of this critique and vision.

In general, reconciliation frees us from the problems of recognition and externalization. The *Phenomenology* developed these sequentially. Recognition, treated first, was found to be defective because there was no vocabulary without the labor of externalization: the *merely* recognized self, that of the master, was empty. Externalization was defective because, aspiring to the universality of radical desituatedness, it denied in the concrete what it affirmed in the abstract: the equality of the communicating parties established in recognition. By thus separating individuals on higher levels of acculturation from those lower down, it rendered developed content a condition of the existence of the self. And since all content for Hegel really belongs to a single narrative, this move meant turning the individual against himself, distancing him from the content developed in previous phases of his own development. An emancipated self, then, will be neither empty nor inwardly torn in such ways. It will be both concrete and harmonious, or what I call "consolidated." Such a self is presented in the *Aesthetics*, where the structures of recognition and externalization recur. They recur with a difference, however: both are from the start presented as coordinated by the third structure, "reconciliation."

In a temporal sense, recognition in the *Aesthetics* retains priority over the other two structures. The modern spectator begins from the sensory experience of a work of art and only then inquires after its meaning. But to view something as a work of art is to view it as an interplay of sensory and intellectual aspects, to "recognize" it as being, in that respect, similar to oneself. Aesthetic experience is itself intrinsically recognitive.

Also part of our first experience of a sensible object as a work of art is the immediate apprehension of a single guiding conception "gleaming forth" from the work. Our sensory experience of a work of art is thus, we saw, an experience of an object which presents a dynamic of reconciliation between that "universal" guiding conception and the manifold particular details which make it up. What the spectator recognizes in his immediate apprehension of the work is ultimately this reconciliatory dynamic. The moment of recognition in the aesthetic dialogue of artwork and spectator is from the start conceived and thought through in terms of reconciliation.

Similarly, the universal to which the spectator's reflection on the work of art ascends is also intrinsically reconciliatory in that it directs the spectator back into the concrete details of the work. The process of externalization to which the spectator submits both the work of art and himself does not aim at a universal wholly abstract and hence other in kind from the sensory entity from which it begins. Rather, it seeks nothing more than the organizing principle of that very entity. Hence, in aesthetic externalization—at least of the immanent kind—there is no rejection of the concrete sensory details of the work of art, or of the concrete experiences of the spectator. They are not cast aside or affirmed merely as starting points for the ascent to the universal but are, throughout the process, recognized as ends in themselves and intrinsic to the work. As with aesthetic interaction's recognitive moment, the kind of externalization it contains is also defined and thought through in terms of the reconciliation to which it leads.

But if reconciliation is the key to understanding the other two moments of aesthetic dialogue, it for its part cannot be understood without them. There would be no reconciliation if there were nothing to reconcile. Unlike the defective sublation of recognition by externalization we saw earlier, the relation of reconciliation to both recognition and externalization is a classic case of *Aufhebung* in its double sense of preserving and canceling. Recognition and externalization, having shown themselves to be defective when taken alone, are reformulated as parts of a larger whole. They cease to be viewed as existing independently and are thus conceptually "canceled"; but as parts of the larger whole, they are "preserved."

The success of this *Aufhebung* shows the *Aesthetics* to be a consistent development of the themes traced in the *Phenomenology*. Attention to this solves what may appear to be a problem with the *Aesthetics* itself. In the Introduction and first part of the latter, Hegel's basic concern is to develop the nature of art on the basis of the philosophical concept of the "Idea."[1] That concept itself, developed at the end of Hegel's *Logic*, is simply presupposed in the *Aesthetics*. It may thus appear, especially to the reader unacquainted with the torturous paths of the *Logic*, to be nothing more than a global warrant for allowing Hegel to say whatever he wants to say. Dispelling this suspicion in detail would be an immense task, requiring a detailed and critical commentary on the whole of Hegel's *Logic*.

One result of my investigation of Hegel shows that such an endeavor is, in any case, unnecessary. In place of the logical warrant which Hegel explicitly claims in the *Aesthetics* for the Idea, the *Phenomenology* offers another—a warrant based on an analysis of concrete modes of interaction and their defects. Neither book, moreover, can be fully understood without the other. If we limit ourselves to the *Phenomenology*, we will be unable to grasp the full nature of aesthetic reconciliation, since that reconciliation can only develop out of reflective thought—a moment not yet present in the *Phenomenology*'s "Hellenic" account of art. If, on the other hand, we focus exclusively on the *Aesthetics*, it seems that we will not be able to grasp the necessity for aesthetic reconciliation: aesthetic interaction may appear immediately as a given of human life or of Hegel's *Logic*, rather than as specifically required by other spheres of interaction.

Aesthetic Freedom

The emancipatory character of aesthetic experience is discussed as part of the *Aesthetics*'s general account of the "Idea of the Beautiful" (*Aesth.* 161-166/112–114). It is contrasted with the two basic modes of "finite" human existence: the theoretical and the practical. Each mode has defects from which aesthetic experience is free and frees us; because of this dual contrast, aesthetic emancipation will itself have a twofold character.

The theoretical approach assumes objects to exist independently of the mind. The mind's task can then only be their passive apprehension. On the level of sensation, this means perceiving the objects as accurately as possible. On higher levels, it means viewing their perceived properties as instances of concepts, themselves viewed as abstracted from perceptions of similar objects in the past. In adopting such an approach, the spectator must exclude from his experience of the object such "merely subjective" aspects of his cognitive apparatus as imagination, preconception, and prejudice, as well as personal wishes, desires, and interests. The subjective dimension as a whole is then "subjugated." As objective perceivers, we "make our minds prisoners to our belief in things" (*Aesth.* 161f/112).

The object, by this approach, is left "free" to be what it is. But this freedom is merely apparent. An object perceived in such a passive way presents itself not as an "object" at all but as no more than an aggregate of sensory data. Any internal dynamics it may have remain undiscovered, and in their absence the object is perceived as purely natural. But a natural object is precisely not "free" to be what it is: it stands at the intersection of a network of causal chains and is therefore dependent on other things for its origin and continued existence (*Aesth.* 163/113). A work of art, of course, has such natural being: a painting, for example, is prey to vicissitudes of climate and can be destroyed in hundreds of ways—fires, floods, being dropped or defaced, and so on. But it has, in addition, a sort of coherence that natural objects lack, a coherence not determined simply by the sum of causal chains in which it may stand but rather by the painting's "guiding conception," i.e., immanently to the work itself. It is this self-determining side of the work of art that constitutes the "objective" side of its freedom. It is not accessible to the purely theoretical attitude because appreciation of it requires not the mere perception of the work but recognition of it as a reconciled interplay of sensory and intellectual components.

In the other mode of the "finite" mind—the practical—we seek to make objects conform to our purposes or desires by altering or even annihilating them. In such activity the subject now appears "free," able to conceive and carry out its own ends; the object, viewed merely as a means or obstacle to those ends, is "unfree." But this freedom of the subject is, again, only apparent. It is a fact of life that external reality can never be made to conform completely to the purposes of an individual agent, so they must continually be modified to take into account changing circumstances. Further, those purposes themselves are often aroused from outside, as drives and passions. Thus, the subject, in the practical sphere, is no more able to determine himself than was the object in the theoretical sphere (*Aesth.* 162f, cf. 64f/112f, 36).

Two conceptions of freedom are thus advanced and rejected here. One is the "objective" freedom to be what one already is—a view of freedom which, as we shall see, was of importance in ancient Greece (see Chap. 8). The other conception of "freedom" is as the ability to pursue one's own purposes and to gratify one's own desires—also important in the ancient world, but more familiar to moderns. Both of these concepts have obvious political implications, for Hegel's "finite" world contains the political realm; and both have been found wanting with respect to a further concept of freedom, "self-determination," which is afforded by aesthetic interaction.

As with the theoretical attitude, aesthetic contemplation alters nothing in the object—but neither does it reduce it to a mere place holder in a set of causal chains. Rather, the beautiful object appears as something "whose own concept is realized." The "concept" or guiding conception of a work of art finds adequate embodiment insofar as it organizes the work as a whole. It was in virtue of this organizing activity, we saw, that the work presented a dynamic of reconciliation. Thus, what is here called the "self-determination" of the work of art turns out to be its reconciliation with itself as a unity of sensory and intellectual components. Insofar as a work of art is a reconciled whole, its various sensory details are presented as organized from within rather than as determined by a causal chain from without.

This sort of freedom is not the exclusive property of the art object. The self as well, as we saw at the end of the last chapter, is reconciled with itself in its dialogue with the work of art. Only as thus unified can the self be a whole whose various aspects determine each other and whose rationality, more particularly, is able to organize and express itself through sensory perception (*Aesth.* 163f/114). The self which is, in aesthetic interaction, reconciled with itself is thus one which is both unified and concrete—or, in terms of the *Phenomenology*, is one whose single, unitary side is at one with its own multiplicity.

On the practical side, because we do not seek to alter art objects to make them conform to our purposes, we approach them in a disinterested way. Our finite purposes are "canceled" (*aufgehoben: Aesth.* 164/114). Our encounter with the object as an end in itself enables us to reconcile ourselves with ourselves. Through it we achieve, not one of the many particular desires and purposes we may have, but what Hegel perceives as the basic, overriding purpose of any rational being: to be self-determining in a concrete sense, to be "reconciled," to be free. This emancipation, which makes reconciliation possible, is performed by the element of extraneous externalization we uncovered in aesthetic experience. By reconciling an individual with only a portion of his concrete sensory and affective experiences, the aesthetic encounter dissociates him from the rest. It "lifts him above" the struggle with externality that, in the finite world, is constant and unending.

We thus arrive at two sides of Hegelian aesthetic emancipation. On the one hand, our experiences with art raise us out of our manifold entanglements with the necessities of life and society and give us an escape into another realm. On the other hand, this refuge is not a realm of abstract thought completely detached from the sensory realm (as it will be for the

Plato of the *Phaedo*: see chap. 8). It is rather a complex whole containing an interplay of both intellectual and sensory components. Art, in other words, is a part of this sensory world but it is nonetheless "other."

In aesthetic self-determination, freedom and reconciliation run together and prove to be synonymous. But they coincide only within aesthetic experience. In the finite world, freedom means, on the object's side, the ability to persist as what one is; on the subject's side, it means the ability to set and carry out one's own purposes. In both, self-determination is an unachievable goal, and reconciliation with the sensory givens out of which abstract concepts are formed is neither sought nor possible. It is thus open to doubt whether this view of aesthetic emancipation can have any political consequences at all.

An argument that it does have political consequences would have to have two sides, like the concept itself. From the "theoretical" side, a politically relevant type of reconciliation would have to be presented in aesthetic form: an artistic depiction of an ideally reconciled society, not merely an abstract idea of "reconciliation." On the "practical" side, an account would have to be given of which aspects of finite political reality have been cast aside in art's presentation of that ideal picture—and which would have to be done away with in actuality were that picture to be realized. The *Aesthetics*, we will see, provides materials for both accounts but does not really develop either. Hence, Hegel never achieves a full account of poetic interaction, or (it follows) of situating reason. The reasons for this failure will be important for our understanding of the occlusion, over millenia, of both phenomena.

The Aesthetic Critique of the State

We will begin with the second, "practical" requirement. The affirmation, in the *Aesthetics*, of the emancipatory character of extraneous externalization suggests that certain types of reality stand in opposition to aesthetic reconciliation and must be cast away if it is to take place. Our task is to see if any of these realities are social in nature. In the *Philosophy of Right*, social reality is presented under three forms: the family, civil society, and the state. The latter two will be more important for us, and we will treat them in turn.

Civil society is the market-oriented realm of practical individualism which the state is to regulate, not annihilate.[2] If I, as an individual, am to survive in the modern economy, I must have something to sell— something which other people want to buy. In selling to them, especially if what I have to sell is my own labor and skill, I subordinate myself to their purposes: I make myself a means to the achievement of their ends, and they (of course) do the same for me (*Aesth.* 207f/149). In this, the individual in civil society exhibits the same sort of unfreedom that the object had in the practical sphere of finite existence. He becomes merely "useful" for the ends of others.

By entering into the economy, the individual gives himself a role and position in a chain of production and consumption. Though not perhaps a strictly "causal" chain, this is still a series of dependencies: as long as the individual holds a place in such a chain, he is at the mercy of those who produce what he needs and who need what he produces. The key features of the modern economy are the ever-increasing complexity of these chains as wholes and the concomitant simplification of their individual links—the roles allotted to individual workers and consumers. The *Aesthetics* gives two extreme examples of this simplification.

In institutions such as the assembly line, modern society has carried the division of labor to such extremes that any single worker has only an "abstract," mechanical job to do. Instead of the complex involvement with concrete materials characteristic of the craftsman, the modern laborer merely repeats a very few actions. These are simple enough to be susceptible to relatively exact description and codification in norms and regulations: "every one of his activities proceeds, not in an individual living way, but more and more mechanically, according to universal norms." This leads to an irruption of the "harshest cruelty of poverty" into the midst of the productive cycle of civil society (*Aesth.* 350/260).

The argument here in the *Aesthetics* is highly elliptical, and is hardly less so in the *Philosophy of Right* (cf. *RPh* 200f/149f). But in student notes of Hegel's earlier lectures, we find it spelled out a bit more: the simplified nature of labor in modern society means that the individual who performs such work can be more easily replaced than could a skilled craftsman. Hence, his wages can be reduced toward mere subsistence—and ended altogether, when he is thrown out of work by a machine.[3] The bondsman of the *Phenomenology* was, by comparison, in much better state: his labor began with a conception and ended with a finished product, an external expression of his own productive activity.

The other main example of the oppression of civil society is, of all things, the rich man (*Aesth.* 350/260). Standing at the opposite end of the economic chain from the worker and "no longer stuck in the sordidness of gain," he is able to satisfy his needs without making himself a means to others. But his dependence on others is hardly removed by this. The objects with which he surrounds himself

> have been taken from the supply of what was already available, produced by others, and indeed in a most mechanical and therefore formal way, and acquired by him only through

a long chain of efforts and needs foreign to himself" (*Aesth.* 350/260)

Together with the diminution of the place of the individual worker in the chain of production goes a similar reduction in the scope of action of the ultimate consumer, the rich man. He does not order or plan the creation of his possessions, but simply takes them over ready-made. Just as the objects made by the modern worker do not manifest his productive activity, so when they are bought by the rich man they express nothing about his character other than its acquisitiveness.

Like natural objects perceived in the theoretical attitude, the worker and the consumer in the modern economy are both reduced to mere placeholders in long chains of dependency. As such, like those objects, they can be said to be "externalized" in modern production. Their individual characteristics, abilities, and skills are not permitted to determine their contributions to the economy and are thus "left behind." It is not surprising to find civil society referred to in the *Philosophy of Right* as the "external state" (*den äußeren Staat*, RPh 165/123) or in the *Aesthetics* as a domain of "universal culture" (*Aesth.* 350/260).

With respect to the next higher level, the state itself, the *Aesthetics* presents in places what seem to be reverberations of the *Philosophy of Right*'s famous paean to the state. The state is., e.g., "a perfect totality in itself, rounded off and completely perfected . . ." (*Aesth.* 145f/99). More precisely, the "genuine state," as opposed to a mere "combination of individuals," is rationally structured. Laws, customs, and public affairs in general are not matters of individual feeling or a sovereign's whim, but are clearly and explicitly stated and valid for all; their form is "universality and abstraction" (*Aesth.* 250/182). As to their content, "all the laws and institutions are nothing but realizations of freedom in all its essential characteristics" (*Aesth.* 144/98). As rational, they are in agreement with the structures of the mind of the individual citizen: "if he obeys those laws he coincides, not with something alien to himself, but simply with what is his own" (*Aesth.* 144/98) The state would thus seem to offer a type of reconciliation superior to the aesthetic variety. By living in accordance with its laws, the individual brings rational structure to his own actions and achieves "self-coincidence," or reconciliation, not simply in occasional encounters with works of art, but throughout his daily life in society.

This is without doubt the standard picture of how Hegel views life in the modern state.[4] But the *Aesthetics* denies it. In spite of what we have just cited, it claims as well that the state remains something external, "even to those who stand at the head of affairs and feel the whole thing as their own" (*Aesth.* 208/149). A magistrate, a general, a field marshal, or even the monarch himself, confronts the state as the worker confronts the economy: as an enormously complex affair in which his own sphere of activity is vanishingly small. His official functions, prescribed by others, address only a few of his manifold human capacities. He operates, within his set limits and according to regulations, not as the concrete individual he really is but as "stamped with the universal" down to the tiniest detail. Hegel's view of the statesman presents him, not as a self-contented wielder of power or even as a self-aggrandizing manipulator, but as akin to a trapped animal. He is unable to escape the snares of his position "no matter how much he may twist and turn."[5]

The texts cited indicate that the pitiful situation of the statesman is only an extreme example of what all citizens of the state must undergo. While, for example, those who administer justice are described as functioning in this restricted way (*Aesth.* 252/183f), the ordinary citizen who seeks legal redress is also present in court, not as the concrete individual he really is, but only insofar as he has standing in the particular case at hand (*Aesth.* 145f/99).

Thus, Hegel's account of the relation of the state to those who compose it amounts to a global indictment:

> the position of separate individuals in the state is that they must attach themselves to this regime and its real stability, and subordinate themselves to it . . . . As happens in genuine states, the whole details of their mental attitude, their subjective opinions and feelings, have to be ruled by this legislative order and brought into harmony with it (*Aesth.* 250/182).

This global quality comes from the fact that the modern state is founded on the principle of law. The success in art of aesthetic reconciliation was due in part, as we saw, to the concrete nature of the aesthetic universal: it was defined as organizing the particular content of the work whose basic principle it was, and it could not be understood independently of that content.

The published laws and regulations of the modern state are not of this type. They are codifications, and hence organizing principles, of the behavior that is to be allowed in the state. But though they may be rooted in the ancient mores of the people they govern, they are not themselves defined in terms of the individuals who come under them. Rather, they apply equally to anyone who is, or may come to be, an inhabitant of the state. They are thus, in their form of "abstraction and universality," akin to a scientific description of an animal species, which is intended to apply not only to animals who have been observed but to any member of that species which may in the future be observed. The difference, of course, is that the abstract regulations of the state have normative power. They can be enforced, as scientific descriptions cannot, against individuals who fail to conform. The modern state, as a regime of laws,

> exists as an inflexible necessity, independent of particular individuals and their personal mentality and character . . . When regulations and laws have been brought to our minds in their universality, they are also actual externally as this universal which goes its explicitly orderly way and has public power and might over individuals if they undertake to oppose and violate the law by their caprice.[6]

The very universality of the laws and institutions of the state thus turns out to mean that there is an "actual cleavage between the universals of the legislative understanding and immediate life" (*Aesth.* 250/182; translation slightly altered). Though the "political sentiment," patriotism, has an important place in the maintenance of the state (*RPh.* 218f, *Werke* 7. 414/163f, 282), the legal basis of the modern regime means that justification for an individual's acts is to be found in the published laws and regulations, not in his own experience, mind, or heart. It follows that if the individual does "find himself" in the rational structures of the state, he finds only an abstractly rational self, which as far as the state is concerned is all that he will be allowed to be. If his obedience is in this tortured sense to his own *higher* nature, it is nevertheless an oppressive obedience which requires the individual to renounce his own *concrete* nature and "immediate life."

Hegel allows that the "harmonizing" of the individual with the state need not be by force. It is possible for an individual to recognize the rationality of the state's strictures and demands, and to view his harmonization with them as the achievement of his own higher rationality. But this makes no difference: "even in that case separate individuals are and always remain only incidental, and outside the reality of the state they have no substantiality in themselves" (*Aesth.* 250f/182f).

This demand for conformity and obedience results in an oppression which the individual knows and feels in his everyday life. If the demands of the state are a fact of the modern world, another such fact—and one of the major points of the *Phenomenology*—is that "the modern person is in his own eyes, as subject, infinite in his heart and character" (*Aesth.* 266/194). This knowledge is not entirely inward, moreover: in the social domains of family life and personal relations, the individual is loved for himself, and his character and "subjective" side still count (*Aesth.* 264/193).

We are now in a position to appreciate the subtlety with which our earlier quote from the *Aesthetics* is worded. Though the state does "form a perfect totality within itself," it is necessarily oppressive to those who compose it, and even to those who lead it. The freedom it grants to them is restricted and abstract. It is accompanied by an oppressive refusal to acknowledge, much less to incorporate, their individuality. We thus have a split within modern social reality: concrete individuality stands on one side, and "substantiality" within the life of the state on the other. Each side, moreover, rejects its opposite. The state demands conformity from the individual, and the individual responds in the only way open: by feeling oppressed.

A typically Hegelian approach to this sort of situation would be to recognize validity in both sides of the split and try somehow to mediate it. That Hegel does not do this points to the fact that, for him, the split in question is not a mere contingent feature of the state, "nor an unpleasant consequence of a basically sound structure; it is rather necessitated by the very principle or "concept" of the state itself, and is therefore something which cannot be remedied within the political sphere the state structures:

> But the *principle* itself, the actualization of which is the life of the state and wherein man seeks his satisfaction, is still once again *one-sided* and inherently abstract, no matter in how many ways it might be articulated without and within; it is only the rational freedom of the *will* which is present here—it is only in the *state*—and once again only in this *individual* state—and therefore again in a *particular* sphere of existence and the isolated reality of this sphere that freedom is actual (*Aesth.* 145f/99).

The problem with the state is thus a deficiency in its basic principle, which is the "rational freedom of the will" (cf. *RPh.* 45, 48/33, 35f). This points us back to the development of the concept of the will in the *Science of Logic*'s discussion of the "Idea of the Good".[7] That discussion is rather murky, even for Hegel, but two points in it will enable us to see how the critique of the state in the *Aesthetics* fits together with the celebration of it in the *Philosophy of Right*.

First, the will is a development of purposive activity in general. As such—and clearly as in the case of the discussion of the practical sphere of finite existence in the *Aesthetics*—the will confronts a reality which is other than it, in which it seeks to realize its purposes. Second, what in the *Logic* distinguishes the will from mere purposive activity is that the single purpose of the will is the "Good"—in general, the developed structures of rationality. For purposive activity, the goal was merely one or another subjectively formulated aim.

The reference of the will to a reality external to it means that freedom of the will cannot consist in making external reality conform completely to the purposes of the will, because in that case there would be nothing left to "will" at all: rather than the consummation of the will, that would be its dissolution. The fact, noted in the *Aesthetic's* discussion of the "practical" attitude, that the world cannot be made completely to conform to the purposes of an individual turns out to be a fact, not merely about the world, but also about the will itself.

The distinction between purposive activity in general, where goals are fortuitous, and the will, where they are rational, is treated in the *Philosophy of Right* as holding between two sorts of will.[8] One of these, the "subjective will," takes as its purpose the gratification of needs which are purely individual or even whimsical or arbitrary, and which would fall under the *Logic's* classification of "purposive activity." The other type is the "absolute" will, which not only has a rational or "objective" content (one derived, ultimately, from the nature of willing itself) but which explicitly recognizes and consciously pursues that "absolute" purpose (*RPh.* 35f, 40-44/25f, 29-32).

Even absolute will retains a relation to a reality which is other than it is. Within the social sphere, that reality includes the "subjective" wills of the individuals who make up society.[9] From the point of view of the state, particular wills, insofar as they diverge from the legalistic prescriptions of the state's own rational will, are simply "perverse."[10] They must either conform entirely to the rational will, when the individual by virtue of his moral education recognizes that will as rational, or else are to be suppressed by force, as in the punishment of crime (*RPh* 158f, 196/117, 146).

The state, even as presented in the *Philosophy of Right*, is thus to be located in the context of the *Phenomenology's* general treatment of culture. Just as in the self of the individual there are both the natural self, from which he started, and the universal self to which he desires to come, so in the modern state the universal mores of ethical life appear to the citizen, on the one hand, as something existing over and above him in their own right, invested with "absolute power and authority," and, on the other, as his own higher nature or "essence" (*RPh.* 143f/105f). As did state power in the *Phenomenology*, though in the modern world in a more complex way, the state demands complete adherence from its members in the form of their conformity to its laws and decrees. Those concrete aspects of an individual's life which do not come under the state are, as in "Culture," simply ignored; those which run counter to it are destroyed.

The split articulated in the *Aesthetics* follows from two circumstances.

First, the will is for Hegel essentially directed against a reality which is other than it, and which is (as far as the will is concerned) not what it should be. It therefore seeks to make that reality conform to its own purposes, or to the Good. Second, the political life of the state contains an interplay, not merely of different wills, but of different *types* of will, each of which takes the other to be an "external" reality. The state requires that the subjective will conform to its own structures and demands, while the subjective will—too weak to take action against the state—feels its oppression.

The *Philosophy of Right* is the "science of the state," and "expounds the principle of the state in its own proper sphere," which by definition is the sphere of its success (*RPh* 15, 222n/11, 166n). In it, this fundamental split is only alluded to, as when the universal mores of ethical life are said to exist in the state both as the higher nature of the individual and as an "absolute authority over him," or when the state, with respect to the subordinate institutions of family and society, is said to appear both as an "external necessity and higher authority" and as the "end immanent within them" (*RPh.* 215/161).

We may view the *Philosophy of Right* and the *Aesthetics* as each developing one side of this ambivalent relation. The former views social institutions as the "essence" and "immanent purpose" of the humans who compose them; the latter treats them as external "power" and "necessity." Far from being, as Lukács maintained, a domain in which Hegel could escape from political considerations altogether,[11] his *Aesthetics* proves to contain a critique of social reality which is both global, in that it articulates the oppression of everyone in the state, and radical, in that the oppression follows from the very nature of the state itself. That Hegel, here or anywhere, should view the state as inherently oppressive to everyone within it is perhaps surprising. The critique of the state is no mere aberration, however. As we have seen, it is grounded in the *Logic* and is articulated in different terms in the *Phenomenology*'s section on "Culture."

The Critique Disarmed

But Hegel's political thought and his aesthetics are not coordinate moments of his system; the latter, because later, is also a "higher" standpoint than the former. In fact, as the *next* higher standpoint, it ought to be expected to "negate" it (cf. *Logic* 1.35f/54). Furthermore, this negation, or critique, directed against the "principle itself" of right, is carried out from the "principle itself" of art. For to claim that the political sphere contains an unresolvable split between the general structures of the law and the particularity of individuals is to claim that it is "unreconciled" reality.

The aesthetic status of this critique thus assigns it to a certain place in Hegel's system, and this determines both its rights and its limits. Within the *Aesthetics* itself, the critique is construed as a statement of what is unaesthetic, or prosaic, in modern life; from an aesthetic standpoint, to call something "prosaic" is to criticize it. It is to say that, in order for an aesthetic order to come to be, it must all be swept away—"extraneously externalized."

If the aesthetic critique of the modern social order is not to remain merely aesthetic, then it must be shown that something resembling aesthetic reconciliation is possible in the political realm. Otherwise, the critique merely states that the modern social order is not art, and this would be analogous to advancing the fact that cows are not sheep as a "critique" of them. The properly aesthetic way of showing that the concept of reconciliation applies to social experience would be pictorial: to depict a reconciled social order. What Hegel calls "ideal art" does this by depicting a time (archaic Greece) when there was no state, and each individual met his own basic needs:

> in such a mode of life, man has the feeling in everything he uses and . . . surrounds himself with, that he has produced it from his own resources and therefore in external things has to do with what is his own and not with alienated objects lying outside his own sphere . . . Each and everything produced and used by human hands is . . . prepared and enjoyed by the very man who needs it (*Aesth.* 352f/261f).

The archaic social order is, moreover, the opposite of the "legal regime" of modernity. In it, justice does not repose on laws publicly proclaimed and binding on all. If heroes transgress,

> there is no public authority with powers to call them to account and punish them, but only the right of that inner necessity which is vitally individualized in particular characters (*Aesth.* 252f/184).

The authority of the rights and customs which constitute the ethical order rests upon individuals alone, because of the greatness of their hearts and characters. As thus "vitalized," the ethical principles of society function as do aesthetic universals: they "keep an individual shape in that they depend exclusively on individuals and reach life and actuality only in and through them" (*Aesth.*, ibid.) If Achilles's sense of justice differs from Agamemnon's, that is for Homer only as it should be. Similar moral principles organize different characters in different circumstances, and do it differently. There is no one standard to which all must conform.

In such a situation,

> the universal wins concrete reality only through the individual, just as the individual . . . finds only in the universal the impregnable basis and genuine content of his actual being (*Aesth.* 247/180).

A heroic individual is then integrated in a way the citizen of the modern state can never be. He is the "unity and interpenetration of individuality and universality" that constitutes true "self-reliance" (*Selbstständigkeit, Aesth.*, ibid). Moreover, the "reconciled' lifestyle is no mere figment of artistic imagination. It achieved actuality in ancient Greece, where it was lived by people not wholly unlike ourselves because they were our own cultural ancestors (*Aesth.* 366f/272). The ancient world thus provides material for art to portray a society in which individuals are naturally expressive of the social order instead of being alienated from it, as are moderns.

The lessons of art are therefore not restricted to the so-called aesthetic sphere. If art first educates a distinctively aesthetic sensibility, this in turn leads to comparison with other sorts of content and more general points of view (*Aesth.* 82/49). The ultimate content of art is nothing other than humanity itself, and through its portrayal of particular people in particular cultures, art discloses to its audience the most universal of truths: "the higher interests of Spirit and will, what is in itself human and powerful, the true depths of the human heart" (*Aesth.* 375/279).

Finally, art's modern audience is not specialized. Savants may, of course, convert works of art into subjects for specialized discussion, especially of historical minutiae. But "the first thing (*allererste*) is and remains immediate intelligibility": specialized knowledge should not be necessary to understand art, and art's lessons are for the people as a whole to reflect upon and enjoy (*Aesth.* 367-369/273f). Conveying material for reflection and enjoyment, art has an educative function, not merely with regard to the individual's abstract intellect but encompassing his whole range of sensibilities and affects (*Aesth.* 80f, 83/48f, 50).

Aesthetic dialogue thus brings modern spectators—the people as a whole—before their true identity as human beings. But because modern society and the modern state are so opposed to the social order portrayed in ideal art, to identify oneself with that order and with one's "true nature" means to cease to identify oneself with one's political environment. To learn one's true nature as a human being is to learn that that nature is being stunted and deformed by the modern social order. Art thus provides an account of what is defective in modern social structures and presents a picture of what an adequate social structure would be. In sum, it teaches the people as a whole that the modern state is fundamentally inhuman, and that other and better forms of society have actually existed. It would seem that the state, as a rational will seeking to change or annihilate the wills of its individual inhabitants, can hardly tolerate this. Because the aesthetic critique of the state proceeds from the basic principle of art—its presentation, and achievement in the modern audience, of reconciliation—art cannot itself be changed to accommodate it to the state. The state, it appears, must attempt to annihilate art.

Such annihilation would, for what it is worth, be philosophically unjustified. Art stands, as we have noted, on a higher level of Hegel's system than does politics. As a dimension of human life, the *Aesthetics* goes so far as to claim, that art stands to the "finite" spheres, including that of practical politics, as reality to appearance:

> . . . it is precisely this whole sphere of the empirical inner and outer world which is not the world of genuine actuality; on the contrary, we must call it, in a stricter sense than we call art, a pure appearance and a deception . . . . Art liberates the true content of phenomena from the pure appearance and deception of the bad, transitory world and gives them a higher actuality, born of the Spirit. Thus, far from being mere appearance, a higher reality and truer existence is to be ascribed to the phenomenon of art in comparison with [those of] ordinary reality (*Aesth.* 28f/8f).

Art's negation of social reality is thus "truer" than politics's affirmation of it and is to be accepted over that affirmation.[12] But the negation, or critique, is itself made from a standpoint which reconciles the sensory and intellectual components of the individual in a way unique to art. Neither of the other two moments of absolute Spirit, religion or philosophy, can take it up.

That Hegel's own public philosophy did not take it up is obvious enough. In the *Philosophy of Right*, the state is "the actuality of the ethical idea," "rational in and for itself," an "absolute, unmoved end in itself" membership in which is the "supreme duty" of the individual, the "divine will as present on earth," and indeed an "earthly divinity" (*Irdisch-Göttliches*).[13] Our analysis of the *Aesthetics* may render some of this suspect. But even there, Hegel normally writes as if art, as a higher truth, leaves lower levels (including the state) undisturbed (cf. *Aesth.* 139, 146/94, 99f). And he is notably reluctant, after detailed and admiring discussion of the heroes' provision of their own physical needs, to discuss their non-alienated social life (*Aesth.* 355/263). We can attribute this to the fact that

Hegel lived, when he wrote the *Aesthetics* and the *Philosophy of Right*, in a state which was not only (relatively) modern, but an embryonic dictatorship to boot. But more respectable reasons, derived from his views on religion, keep Hegel from these matters.

Religion is essentially characterized by a withdrawal into subjective interiority: this was presented in the *Phenomenology*'s transition from classical to revealed religion and is underwritten in the *Aesthetics* in terms of the relation of religion to art.[14] Protestantism, the highest (because most "interior") form of religion, coexists in an "abstract harmony" with the state, and "religion does not have principles of its own which contradict those in force in the state." Any intrusion of religion into political life takes the form of sectarianism, when religion gains control, or of rigid opposition when it does not.[15]

But religion, as a moment of Hegel's system, actually goes further and, in a sort of intricate reversal, provides material for a philosophical rehabilitation of the state. From a philosophical point of view, the aesthetic ideal cannot, and should not, be realized. This is shown by considering the implications of art's moment of extraneous externalization. The state, as the *Philosophy of Right* puts it, "is no ideal work of art. It stands on earth, and so in the sphere of caprice, chance, and error" (*RPh* at *Werke* 7.404/279). Though the artist must wrestle with his medium, he has a freedom with regard to it that other workers lack. The farmer cannot throw away flooded fields, as the painter can throw away muddy pigments, and a road builder cannot simply ignore boulders the way a portraitist can ignore warts. On the subjective side, too, those who frame and administer social policy cannot simply shove aside the complex contingencies of human character and desires the way the modern spectator, in aesthetic interaction, shoves aside the details and peculiarities of his daily life.

The erection of a social order on the basis of aesthetic reconciliation would incorporate such externalization into politics, where whole groups of people would have to be "shoved aside." A society founded on Homeric heroism would ignore nonheroes as the artist ignores the Protean muddiness of human and natural reality. And the human species does not consist solely of people with the strength of character to become Homeric heroes: nonheroes are the norm.

But how do we know this? The Greeks, in a sense, did not believe it. For them, only heroes were in a sense truly human, and elitism was a basic principle of the Greek world. That world achieved its nadir in the slavery of classical times, which was no mere blemish on the face of the "beautiful people" but the necessary condition and ultimate nemesis of the Greek achievement.[16] In Homeric times the elitism was less malign.

There could be no "slavery" as a fixed juridical status because there was no law, and few underlings would be required by a person who met most of his own needs. But the common people, if not the hero's slaves, were not his equals either. They obeyed him, writes Hegel, out of their own psychological needs, not from external compulsion. But obey him they did, in all his caprice. If not driven into battle like herds of serfs, they functioned only as ancillaries to the hero: as witnesses to his exploits, or as his defenders in time of need. Humanity is thus already divided in the Homeric age, if not yet into free men and slaves, then into heroes and companions.[17]

For Hegel, religion, especially modern Christianity, teaches that in the depths of their souls, if not on the surface explored by art, all men are brothers—that freedom is inherent in their common nature. It is only the modern state, among social structures, which recognizes this fact and attempts to safeguard the freedom of all individuals, precisely by codifying and publishing law.[18]

Thus, religion has for Hegel no specific principles in terms of which to criticize the state because it has, in general, accepted the state's existence: or rather, the state, by existing as a state, has accepted the basic premise of the true religion, Christianity. The legitimacy denied the state by art is thus restored to it by the philosophical comprehension of that religion. And, as a higher stage of the system, the religiously derived legitimation of the state takes precedence over the aesthetic critique of it, just as that critique took precedence over purely political affirmations of the state. It is therefore the mutual acceptance of religion and the state which is to be grasped and justified in the philosophical "reconciliation with reality" (RPh. 27/12). Art is *allowed* to make its critique of the state, for that critique is essential to art. But while art is exhorting the inhabitants of the modern state to sweep away its structures, religion is teaching them that they cannot do this. It maintains that all men are brothers, and that the state is the only social order attempting to accommodate this fact. Its oppression is something that each must put up with for the good of all. And this view, promulgated by religion, is underwritten by philosophy. The aesthetic critique of the state is thus disarmed, and art is made safe for the state.

We saw previously that aesthetic experience for Hegel is a situating exercise in which the audience of the work of art determines its meaning. We saw that the very act of such determination is an act of reconciliation. Now we see that as thus reconciliatory, aesthetic experience is inherently free in a way that active life in the political sphere cannot be—to say nothing of the passive life of those who are oppressed by that sphere. Aesthetic experience is thus intrinsically critical of the political sphere (as well as of the theoretical enterprise of science), and it is important for Hegel to disarm the critique—to show the state that it need not, in fact, try to annihilate art.

We shall see this general problematic, in which intrinsically emancipatory interaction is viewed as something which subverts the state, throughout this book. It will be phrased and avoided, resolved and repressed, in different ways by different thinkers. A full understanding of it must await the treatment (in part three) of Habermas. But we can already suggest that the problem here is misconstrued by Hegel's emphasis, in the *Aethetics*, on the work of art. The state can perhaps try to annihilate art by gaining control over art objects and institutionalized aesthetic discourse. But the dialogical aspect of aesthetic experience for Hegel, which we have seen him straining to articulate, would be effected by this only to the extent that it is dependent on works of art. If these could be replaced in Hegel's account of aesthetic dialogue by utterances in ordinary language, the problematic itself would disappear. For no regime can set out to destroy the language of its people.

In such a replacement, an ambiguous utterance would take the place of the ambiguous detail in the work of art. The hearer of such an utterance would have to decide on its meaning, and such a decision would be reached through a narrative process similar to (immanent) externalization and reconciliation. Like them, this process would articulate parameters as parameters and would be an exercise in situating reason. As interactive, it would share in the intrinsically emancipatory character Hegel attributes, if indecisively, to aesthetic experience. I will undertake such a replacement in the last two chapters of this book. The result will be one form—the normal form—of poetic interaction. The bases for an account of poetic interaction (and, perhaps, for an eventual account of narrative situating reason itself) are thus laid in Hegel's philosophy.

Five

Communication and Community in *Being and Time*

Like Hegel, Heidegger can be read as offering a series of accounts of human interaction. These accounts, I will argue, culminate in the presentation of a form of interaction which is intrinsically emancipatory. Like Hegel's, Heidegger's views of such interaction and its emancipatory power will adumbrate structures which my own account of poetic interaction, in part three of this book, will attempt to reinterpret and capture. But the structures themselves will be very different. Heidegger's thought concerns and exhibits not a sustained narrative but fits and starts and new beginnings. It takes the form of what, to use the title of one of his major books, are called *Holzwege*—paths that lead nowhere, or in my term "demarcations." My interpretation (in part three) of demarcation as interactive and emancipatory will then articulate a type of poetic interaction which is complementary to its Hegelian, "normal" form. I will call it "abnormal poetic interaction."

Because of their demarcative character, Heidegger's writings make no pretense to be ordered in any systematic way. Motifs from one work are retracted and illuminated by others. What lurks obscurely in the background, say, of Heidegger's interpretation of Nietzsche may be focal to his discussion of Heracleitus, and a clear ingredient in his discussion of Hölderlin. The reader, following out these Heideggerian tracks, only gradually becomes aware of a tremendous discipline behind it all, giving it direction and development. The result of one such gradual discovery is what I will be giving here.

My analysis will focus first on Heidegger's largest and most ambitious work, *Being and Time*. But uncritical analysis of *Being and Time* is impossible, if only because the book so openly critiques itself. Its second section, introducing temporality into structures previously exhibited, analyzes the deficiencies of its first, atemporal approach. Though supposed to be a direct exhibition of phenomena, it speaks for the most part

in what it characterizes as a "derivative" mode of interpretation, assertions (*SZ* 27–39, 154–160). And, most important for us, Heidegger
states that *Being and Time* leaves the nature of language undecided: "even
the horizon for the investigative question remains concealed" (*SZ* 166).
His own discussion of the nature of language is, he adds, strictly prepara-
tory to exhibiting Dasein's everydayness, or inauthenticity.

Since critique is inescapable, in what terms should we undertake to
criticize *Being and Time*? Clearly, our own. But as in the case of Wittgenstein, the most telling critique of the "early" Heidegger of *Being and Time*
is perhaps carried out by the "later" Heidegger. It is then necessary to
engage in what Reiner Schürmann has called a "retrospective hermeneutic" of *Being and Time*[1] We must seek, not to expound or refute it on its
own terms alone, but to interpret and locate it with respect to Heidegger's later works. Of these, I will first concentrate on "The Origin of the
Work of Art," which solves a problem about language adumbrated in
Being and Time. The problem is that, for *Being and Time*, emancipatory
interaction of any sort is impossible: all interaction is, in ways to be explained, not emancipation but subjection. My articulation of this problem in the present chapter will proceed by progressively more concrete
analyses of *Being and Time*'s views on authenticity, interpretation, language, and finally interaction itself. In the next chapter, I will argue that
Being and Time tries, and fails, to deal with this problem by articulating
a concept of emancipation—that of "resoluteness"—that can at least co-
occur with interaction. I will then turn to "The Origin of the Work of
Art" to see the successful resolution of the problem, and finally to "From
a Dialogue on Language," which carries still farther the insights acquired
in "The Origin of the Work of Art."

Like Hegel's *Phenomenology*, *Being and Time* was published rather
hastily;[2] and, like the *Phenomenology*, it is tremendously difficult. The two
books resemble each other more substantively in that both are works of
"phenomenology," but the term has very different senses in each. We saw
that for Hegel "phenomenology" was the study and portrayal of the *logos*
of *phenomena*. The individual phenomenon, or "appearance" of Spirit,
was a part of a narrative, and its *logos* was its relation to the whole story.
Heidegger, to begin with, is not in agreement with this idea of *logos*. For
him, in true *logos*, "what is said is drawn from what the talk is about"
(*SZ* 32). Each phenomenon, as individual, is unique, and its uniqueness
is to be expressed in a unique phenomenological description. Phenomenology is then the "direct exhibition" of phenomena; and a "phenomenon" is defined, in section 7 of *Being and Time*, as what can be the theme
of such a presentation in virtue of the fact that it "shows itself in itself."

This definition is nothing more than a translation-cum-paraphrase of the Greek *phenomenon*. It means, at a minimum, that a phenomenon has complexity to it. For if it "shows itself in itself," it must be at once shower and shown; it must possess a structure which reveals—its structure. Such self-revelation is over time. The mere perception of, say, a patch of color—what philosophers have called a sense datum, or a Humean idea—is thus not a "phenomenon" in Heidegger's sense. Such a datum is just there, all at once; we do not get led on to anything within it. It is, in short, too simple to "show itself," and is a case of what Heidegger calls the "vulgar concept" of phenomenon (*SZ* 31), rather than the "phenomenological" conception. For sense data, as simply present to us, require no special descriptive techniques. They need no "phenomenology."[3]

The main topic for phenomenology is then "obviously what, first off and usually, does *not* show itself, which is . . . *concealed* and yet which belongs essentially to that which does, first off and usually, show itself" (*SZ* 35). The very existence of the phenomenological method thus presupposes, not only that phenomena have internal structures, but that some phenomena are relatively hidden and can only be properly shown in terms of phenomena which are not so hidden. The supreme case of this, of course, is Being.

The aim of *Being and Time* is to exhibit Being in terms of one particular kind of being, Dasein. Dasein is characterized as the type of being concerned with Being in a way which can be thematized (viewed) as inquiry. Since it is we as readers who are undertaking the investigation of Being, Dasein is the kind of being we are. Presenting our understanding of our own Being will then clarify our relation to Being itself and will uncover the limits of our possible understanding of it (*SZ* 11–15). Those limits are, from the point of view of *Being and Time,* the concrete structures of temporality (*SZ* 1, 17). The main problem of the part of *Being and Time* that was actually published (about one-third of the whole: *SZ* 39f) is to show how Dasein inheres wholly in a temporally structured field.

We can understand the book's general approach to this problem by referring to what Heidegger says is the key statement in the history of philosophy about the relation of the kind of being we are to the question of Being itself. This is Aristotle's thesis from *De Anima* 3.4 that "the soul is, in a sense, the things" themselves which it knows (*SZ* 14). If we view *Being and Time* as a critical rethinking of this ancient insight, its main results can be set forth briefly as follows:

(1) "The things" must be reinterpreted to include, not merely the entities that we encounter in our everyday dealings with the world or that we regard in a purely theoretical way, but "world" itself, as the ultimate

horizon of significance which makes beings meaningful to Dasein, as well as the smaller horizons called "contexts of significance" (*Bedeutungsganze*) or "contexts of involvement" (*Bewandtnisganze*).

(2) "The soul" must be viewed as Dasein, which comprises the basic structures of the human being as it interacts with the world itself; with entities it encounters as significant within that overarching context; and with other humans. Those structures, which are many and complex, operate in two basic modes, authenticity and inauthenticity, and these will be crucial to our understanding of the view of communication in *Being and Time*.

(3) The "sense" in which Dasein "is" all things is not a simple identity. It is rather the manifold ways in which significance is disclosed to Dasein, and in which Dasein appropriates it: for "Dasein is its disclosedness" (*SZ* 13). The basic structures of this disclosedness Heidegger calls "felt orientation" (*Befindlichkeit*), "understanding," and "discourse"; our concern will be with the latter two.

Contexts of Involvement and Authenticity

If "Dasein is its disclosedness"; and if world is a condition for disclosedness; then Dasein must be in a world in order to exist at all. In my terms, the disclosedness of world is then a "condition" for Dasein. But insofar as disclosure is to be understood in terms of Heidegger's conception of phenomena, then it seems that certain structures of the world, at least, can change without destroying Dasein. For Heideggerean phenomena, as experienced, reveal themselves only gradually over time, and this means that they can be disclosed as other than they were. Such phenomena are then what I call "parameters." To the extent that Dasein is located among a set of parameters, it is situated from the start. But the situatedness is a matter of degree, for we do not know how far this parametric domain extends. Which structures of our experience are to be classed as parametric and phenomenal, and which as falling under the condition of world?

I will return to these issues later. For the moment, I will note that one way in which the mode of disclosure can change for Heidegger is that our encounters with beings in the world can take either of two fundamental forms. We can understand entities merely theoretically— contemplating or studying them as they lie before us; such entities are, in Heideggerean language, encountered as "present-at-hand." Or we can encounter them by using them, in which case they are "ready-to-hand" (*SZ* 67ff). The use to which a being ready-to-hand is put connects it with a number of other things in what Heidegger calls a "context of involvement." While I can, for example, hold a pen before my eyes anywhere in the world and just look at it (as long as there is sufficient illumination and my eyes are good), if I am going to write with it I need to have paper, a writing surface, certain definite kinds of illumination, and so forth. I also need something to write, someone to write it to, and a language in which to write it. The "context of involvement" of an entity thus contains elements to which philosophy has traditionally assigned sharply distinct ontological statuses—for example, physical objects, spatial relations, social structures, and beliefs. A major aim of *Being and Time,* and of Heidegger's thought in general, is to undercut these metaphysical distinctions.

An encounter with something as mundane as a pen, then, ultimately refers us to matters like our command of language itself and our relations with those to whom (or for whom) we are writing. This is an example of a general truth: if we trace out the contexts of involvement within which we encounter beings ready-to-hand, they get very wide indeed. But the process is not endless. Eventually it reaches a reference point that does not itself "fit into" any wider purpose or structure. This ultimate involvement is with Dasein, for the sake of which our various interactions with things and people are carried out (*SZ* 84). "World" is the totality of such contexts of involvement and it follows that there is not a great deal that can be said about it apart from its "reference" to Dasein; human involvements are too rich and diverse for the set of all of them to have any very definite structure. This means that world is not only unthematized in our daily activities; it lacks determinate content and is inherently unthematizable. Though individual entities may stand in various contexts that we can trace out explicitly, we can never become explicitly aware of the totality of all of them.

This raises the question of whether Heidegger is not reifying unduly when he writes of "the world" as if it were a single entity instead of a collection of contexts of involvement: why refer to "them" with a singular term at all? The answer will be that, though we cannot thematize "the world," we have a nonthematic "feel" for it. Our awarenesses of more restricted contexts of involvement *presuppose* our awareness of broader ones. I cannot be aware of a pen as something to write with unless I am already aware of what it means to possess a language, to have people that I want to write to, and so on. Hence, if there is to be any unity to my experience at all, those individual entities and contexts must be encountered in terms of a single, overarching (if structurally indeterminate) context of significance. This is world, a sort of concrete, unthematic a priori for my everyday encounters with entities ready-to-hand (*SZ* 85).

The nature of the reference to Dasein made by entities ready-to-hand provides a key for understanding how Heidegger views our relations with others. Such references, taken in the concrete, disclose entities to me in terms of their uses. As concrete, they point to concrete characteristics of myself, of the individual Dasein who is to use them. But the Dasein so referred to is, very often, not the individual, unique person that I think myself to be, but a sort of average "mock up" of a human being.

Consider, for example, public transportation. In my use of it, if I am to use it correctly, I have to be aware that it is intended to be used by people other than myself. Trains and busses do not run precisely when I arrive to catch them, and they do not go exactly where I want to go. The existence of others is presented to me, in a nonthematic way, every time I hurry to catch the bus or pore over a subway map trying to figure out which train to take. Such would be the case even if, *per impossibile*, I always use public transportation in the dead of night and never actually see another passenger. The existence of other people is part of my use of public transportation. It is not something I need to step back and infer, but it governs my correct use of the technology in question—just as grasping a hammer by the handle is part of using it correctly. Public transportation, along with other such ready-to-hand entities as clothing, books, typewriters, and so on, is not bereft of reference to Dasein. But it refers not uniquely to me but to "the random, the average"; and in my use of such entities, I have a felt awareness of this (*SZ* 71).

Thus, my basic encounter with entities ready-to-hand in the world discloses to me other beings who, like myself, are not pieces of equipment or objects of theoretical contemplation. They are in a word users and not tools, and they are a constant accompaniment to my everyday activities. If the "a priori" context of world allows us to encounter individual entities as concretely significant, it does so "in such a way that together with [them] we encounter the co-Dasein of others" (*SZ* 123). World is thus always shared world, and Dasein is always *Mitsein,* or Being-with others. Indeed, since Dasein generally "finds itself" in its encounters with entities ready-to-hand, my knowledge of others is as basic as my knowledge of myself (*SZ* 119).

The "others" who are given to Dasein in that way are not given as concretely distinct from Dasein itself. They are others "from whom, for the most part, one does *not* distinguish oneself—among whom one is too" (*SZ* 118). My use of public transportation does not tell me about some set of beings, "mass man," that I am not, but about the mass man that I *am.* My Being-with others is thus a stratum of my own Being. It is the level on which I am addressed by the world in ways average, random, and indistinct from how it addresses others. As defined by the world's address to it, that stratum itself shares all those characteristics: it is average, random, indistinct from others.

There are, it seems, only two attitudes an individual can take toward his own aspect of Being-with others. He can recognize it as what it in fact is, as one aspect of his entirety; or he can treat himself as wholly identical with it. The latter is normally the case (*SZ* 131). Indeed, every time I function as indistinguishable from others, I function as identical with just one aspect of myself: my Being-with comes under the "dominance of the other" (*SZ* 126). I act as others do and my actions are, to that extent, characterized by the "random, average" character of Being-with. In such cases, Being-with is referred to as "the 'they,'" or *das Man*. Das Man, as we shall call it, is thus intrinsic to Being-with and hence to Being-in-the-world. It is a basic property, or *existential*, of Dasein. As such, it cannot be overcome and left behind by authentic Dasein. Authenticity itself is in fact a "modification" of it and a sort of "breakthrough" from it (*SZ* 129, 131, 179).

The reason why Dasein ordinarily does not make that "breakthrough" is quite simple. Dasein is intrinsically disquieted by its "distance," or distinction, from other Dasein. To overcome this disquiet, Dasein takes das Man as a standard, forsaking its own concrete individuality and seeking to "blend in" with the crowd (*SZ* 126f). The reason for the disquiet is also simple: concrete individuals die, while das Man does not. To the extent that I can ignore the "depths of my Being" and identify myself with such mundane, but ongoing, structures as mass technology or (on a more intellectual level) the values, insights, and prejudices that permeate my society as a whole, I can achieve a spurious sort of immortality (*SZ* 249–267).

The world itself is always a shared world and "refers" to me as an average person. My inherent tendency is to identify myself with the average. Insofar as I try and understand another person on the basis of such an identification, I will presuppose that he is like myself, assuming that his concerns and purposes are similar to mine. Such "inauthentic solicitude" does not allow the other to be what he truly is. Instead it "leaps in" for him, predetermining his encounters with world and the entities within it. It violates his individuality, then, and can lead to a relation of dominance and dependency (*SZ* 122–124). Occasionally I rise above this and take explicit account of the fact that though the world as such is always shared, certain of its aspects in certain situations are not. To understand another authentically then means to take into account the wider contexts in terms of which his concrete encounters with entities ready-to-hand may be significant to him, but not to me. It means allowing for the totality of contexts which are responsible for his side of our common encounter. That totality is one aspect of our shared world, but it is not necessarily the aspect which is, at a given moment, significant for me. Occasions when I recognize this, though important, are rare. Because of the implication of mortality that comes with them, they are also painful.

In spite of the unequal status of authenticity and inauthenticity as modes of Dasein's Being-in-the-world, the two cannot be reduced to each other. This means that *Being and Time*'s accounts of speech and communication will be double. To the speech and interaction of das Man will be opposed the forms of interaction of authentic individuals—or rather, of individuals insofar as they are authentic.

Understanding and Interpretation

This double structure applies to *Being and Time*'s account of Dasein's "cognitive" activity, of which understanding is a more basic form and interpretation a more developed form. We "understand" entities ready-to-hand in terms of their "for the sake of which," i.e., their ultimate reference to our Dasein, and this means in terms of the possibilities they offer us. "Understanding" in Heidegger's sense is thus what reveals to Dasein its own possibilities—its own future. It is Dasein's primary way of relating to equipment, to things present-at-hand, and to nature. To the extent that my possibilities change, my self-knowledge changes with them; in disclosing entities within the world in terms of their possibilities, understanding also discloses Dasein to itself (*SZ* 144f, 337). Indeed, *Being and Time* goes so far as to say that Dasein does not just *have* possibilities but *is* its possibilities, since they are constitutive of the disclosure that Dasein is (*SZ* 143–145). As so constitutive, Dasein's possibilities are inherently determined by the concrete givens of its present situation.

> In every case, Dasein . . . has already got itself into definite possibilities. As the potentiality-for-Being which it *is*, it has let such possibilities pass by. . . . Dasein is Being-possible which has been delivered over to itself (*SZ* 144).

All this means that understanding operates in terms of Dasein's own purposes and perspective, and in terms of the possibilities given and denied to Dasein by its environment and by its own past decisions. The concrete structure of understanding is called "projection," and in this Dasein becomes aware of certain possibilities as possibilities *for it*; it moves toward them, or "projects itself upon," them (*SZ* 145f). Projection is then double in structure: upon Dasein's own purposes, its "for the sake of which," and upon the concrete contexts of significance present to it at a given moment.

Understanding partakes as well of the generally double nature of the "existential" character of Dasein analyzed in this section of *Being and Time*: it can be either authentic or inauthentic. In the former case, Dasein understands itself and entities primarily in terms of its own unique "for the sake of which," i.e., primarily in terms of its own purposes. In the latter case, Dasein allows its possibilities to be determined mainly by whatever presents itself in the world and according to the world's common structures: it "understands itself out of its world" (*SZ* 146).

If a possibility is to be a "phenomenon" in Heidegger's sense, it cannot reveal itself all at once. Its true nature becomes gradually apparent only with time, and this means that we must commit ourselves to realizing possibilities before we understand fully what they are. *Auslegung,* interpretation or explication, is the "working out" of possibilities. It is, we may say, the reciprocal interaction between a concrete possibility (say, that of marrying this person rather than that one) and the Dasein which is transformed by the possibility it chooses (and becomes a different person with one spouse than he or she would have been with another; *SZ* 148). *Being and Time* sums up the nature of interpretation as follows:

> when something in the world is encountered as such, the thing in question already has an involvement which is disclosed in our understanding of the world, and this involvement is one which gets laid out [*herausgelegt*] by the interpretation [*Auslegung*] (*SZ* 150).

To interpret something is thus to encounter it *as* something. We can clarify this "as structure" by adopting the rather un-Heideggerean schema "x as y" and asking about its various parts.

The "y" here is supposed to tell us what involvements or applications a thing has for us in our current situation: it tells us how to *take* the thing in question. It thus makes explicit what has already been understood by Dasein in virtue of Dasein's Being-in-the-world (*SZ* 148f). The "y" should not then be understood as a conventional predicate, but as locating the entity in question within a particular context of involvement. When I interpret something as a chair, for example, I am not simply applying to it any sort of abstract or "unsaturated" concept. Nor am I simply asserting the applicability to that entity of a set of defining criteria for "chairhood." I am, rather, committing myself to dealing with the entity in question in terms of all my concrete information and habits regarding chairs: to sitting on it, or placing it in the "right" location in a room, or perhaps jumping up on it if I see a mouse.

The "as," Heidegger says, is preassertive: in order to make an assertion about something, we must already have interpreted it—if only *as* something about which we can talk, the possible referent of a true proposition. This means interpreting it as something which has properties: if we are not going to say simply "this is this," or some equally empty tautology, we must already be aware of some complexity in the object. Thus, the "as" is almost a primitive term. It cannot be explained in terms of some yet-more-fundamental phenomenon, because all explicit speech presupposes it. "Epistemic bedrock" for Heidegger, such as it is, is not "simple ideas" that can be connected with one another in judgments and propositions, but structures or phenomena that are, in our first awareness of them, already complex.

They are also already interpreted, because our awareness of their complexity is ordinarily guided by the concrete situation in which we find ourselves. If I say "the cat is on the mat," for example, this is very likely to be because someone else is looking for the cat (or the mat), and I want to be helpful. The utterance is not part of an overall description of the universe (or even of the room), but is produced in the context of my overall interpretation of the sensory data and the interpersonal situation.

If epistemic bedrock is interpreted structure, it follows that the "x" in the "x as y" schema does not have a nature of its own, independent of the "as-structure." To consider it apart from such a concrete structure is to fail to locate it within a context of involvement (actual or possible), and this is simply not the way we ordinarily do things. In *Being and Time,* it is argued that this in fact requires an artificially "theoretical" frame of mind (*SZ* 149). As we shall see in the next chapter, aesthetic experience, without being either "artificial" or theoretical, can also encounter entities without locating them at once in any larger context.

In light of Heidegger's basic concept of "phenomena," his accounts of understanding and interpretation claim, in effect, that reason can be situated. For Heidegger's "phenomena," as we have seen, are what I call parameters. It is the task of understanding and interpretation to adduce them, and when such adduction can be criticized it is an exercise in situated reason.

The Heideggerean articulation of parameters, again, can be either authentic or inauthentic. In the latter case, Dasein relies on structures of its shared world, in terms of which it understands the phenomena it encounters. The uniqueness and inner development of individual phenomena—their phenomenality itself—is then overlooked in favor of the random, average meanings furnished to inauthentic Dasein by its world. Since Dasein's world is, for *Being and Time,* a condition for Dasein's own existence, its structures are viewed as conditions of the phenomena they help to clarify. Inauthentic reason, then, clarifies parameters. But not as parameters, for the clarification ultimately consists in reducing them, via interpretation, to a set of conditions for Dasein's existence. Inauthentic understanding and interpretation, we may say, are situated but not situating. Only their authentic counterparts, it seems, could be situating as well as situated. They could be such only under two conditions: First, they could not commit themselves to any preexistent set of structures of meaning, but the meaning would have to be truly "drawn from what the talk is about." Second, by not overlooking the phenomenality of phenomena, they would have to articulate those phenomena as capable of being other than they are.

Discourse and Language

The nature of articulation is further specified in *Being and Time*'s account of discourse. We saw that understanding projects Dasein both upon its own purposes and upon the contexts of significance that are presented to it by virtue of its Being-in-the-world. These are distinguished in words reminiscent of Gottlob Frege: the context in which an entity ready-to-hand stands is called the *Bedeutungsganze*, the totality of significance, while the meaning worked out by an individual Dasein in its own appropriation of that context for its own current purposes is called the *Sinn*.[4] This distinction between *Sinn* and *Bedeutung*, with the former being arrived at through understanding and interpretation, raises the question of how the latter is presented to Dasein. In what manner do I become aware of the contexts of significance in which entities stand so that I can project my own understanding upon them?

As we saw, epistemic bedrock for Heidegger is always interpreted structures. Granted that significance is something that can be put into words, then it seems that significance itself must be present through some sort of interpretive activity. Such activity must, in order to be distinct from the kind of interpretation that functions together with understanding, proceed without reference to the concrete situation and purposes of individual Dasein. It must itself be an articulating and thematizing, but one given independently of Dasein's own "for the sake of which." Heidegger calls this "given articulation" discourse (*Rede*) and says it is the "existential-ontological foundation of language" (*SZ* 160).[5] We may view discourse as language insofar as language is viewed not as a vehicle of communication but as the medium in which a human being makes sense of the world. If for the early Wittgenstein "the limits of my language are the limits of my world," Heidegger, for whom discourse is always Being-with (*SZ* 161f), would take seriously the private-language arguments of the later Wittgenstein and amend the dictum: the limits of *our* language are the limits of my world.[6]

We can clarify the nature of discourse with an example. Language, according to *Being and Time,* contains an interpretation of the understanding of Dasein (*SZ* 167); and it is generally true that the various languages actually spoken in the world manifest the concerns of the people who speak them. Thus, French possesses a much more refined and subtle vocabulary for discussing food than does English, and according to some writers this is part of the latter language's heritage of Puritanism.[7] The "food world" of an English speaker is then simpler than *le monde culinaire* of a Frenchman. Food, we may say, stands for the latter in a much richer network of significance. These relatively rich contexts are not something which an individual Frenchman creates or projects; they constitute a meaningful totality in which he finds himself, which is "given" to him when he learns his native tongue. But it is not a given of nature any more than *escargots bourguignons* are a natural kind. It is, rather, the outcome of a long history, of the interpretive efforts of previous generations. Only as such an outcome can discourse be both interpretive and "given."

Heidegger will later explicitly assign this interpretive function to language, going so far as to say that *"nur wo Sprache, da ist Welt,"* that world is only found together with language.[8] But in *Being and Time* he attempts to separate discourse, as the "articulation of intelligibility," from language *per se,* which is what is actually spoken (*SZ* 161f). As the "foundation" of spoken language, we may say, discourse discloses to Dasein the basic structures of significance which make up its world. Such disclosure need not be explicit: when I use the word "pen," for example, I evoke the entire context of light, desk, illumination, script, language, and audience within which alone writing instruments can exist as such. This, then, is the *Bedeutungsganze*—the totality of significance or, in a more Fregean vein, the referential totality (*SZ* 160).

But my utterance does more than just that. With it I am able to thematize, or call to explicit attention, one component of that totality: the pen itself. I can do this virtue of my language, which has a word for that component (as English does not, for example, have a word for the leading edge of the mark that my pen traces, though that too is a component of the overall context). The individual components of a totality of significance which are important enough to have names "accrue" to them are then individual significances or referents (*Bedeutungen, SZ* 160). *Bedeutungen* are "articulations of the articulable," historically given to the individual Dasein who speaks a language; as such, they belong to discourse. But they are also *"immer Sinnhaft,"* always related to the understanding of an individual Dasein (*SZ* 160). It is for purposes of my own, for example, that I choose the pen, rather than some other component of the *Bedeutungsganze*, to talk about.

Similarly, I can often refer to an entity by any of a number of names and thereby can locate it within one context or the other. To take a standard Fregean example, "the morning star" and "the evening star" have the same referent, but different meanings or senses: the same *Bedeutung* but different *Sinne*. For Heidegger, the phrases have different *Bedeutungen*. One locates the entity within the overall context of the coming of day, and for the ancients was to be worshipped in one way. The other puts it into the opposite diurnal context, and thus into a different context of activity and worship. For *Being and Time,* then, the referent is not primarily the "objective" entity, as it is for Frege, but is, consonant with Heidegger's account of the "as-structure," the entity *as* standing within a supraindividual context of significance. The Fregean referent is reached only by abstracting from that structure in a "theoretical" undertaking. The *Sinn*, for Heidegger, is whatever meaning that context may have to an individual Dasein: time to milk the cows, for example, or deliver the papers, or nurse the baby.

An actual utterance, we may say, is always the product of an interplay between contexts of significance articulated in discourse and constituting Dasein's shared world, and the sense articulated with respect to an individual's understanding of his current situation within that world. It results, then, from an interplay of *Sinn* and *Bedeutung*. As a component of Being-in-the-world, discourse always functions together with the other components of Dasein's essential disclosure, understanding and felt orientation. It is, we may say, the historically derived vocabulary at Dasein's disposal. The other two components determine the way that vocabulary is used in a given utterance.

Fleshing out the Heideggerean account of situating reason with his account of discourse enables us to see two things. First, the scope of variance in the structures of world is, for *Being and Time,* wide indeed. For *all* Heideggerean *Bedeutungen* now seem to be, if given historically in discourse, capable of being other than they are and hence parametric. Only world itself, which as the horizon for all *Bedeutungen* can have no further *Bedeutung*—and which, we saw, is inherently unthematizable—seems exempt.

Second, as will be seen in more detail below, inauthentic discourse, like inauthentic understanding and interpretation, would take parameters of language as unchangeable conditions for speech and would dissolve all utterances into such conditions (cf. *SZ* 168). If the parametric domain is so wide, this amounts to nothing less than an attempt to escape from situatedness itself. More than merely not situating, inauthentic discourse is, like externalization in Hegel, desituating. The extreme case of such desituating would be someone who managed to achieve a purely "theoretical" view of the universe, regarding it as simply a set of entities without any contexts of significance. This apex of inauthenticity, like Hegel's apex of externalization in the "beautiful souls," destroys concrete significance. It leaves in place of real talk only empty assurances that everyone is really just alike.

Communication and Authenticity

We can now analyze *Being and Time*'s account of articulate interaction, or communication, to see how it fits in with the double structure of authenticity and inauthenticity, or of situating and desituating. Communication is first characterized by *Being and Time* in negative terms:

> communication is never anything like a conveying of experiences, such as opinions or wishes, from the interior of one subject to the interior of another. . . . In discourse Being-with becomes "explicitly" *shared*: that is to say, it *is* already, but is unshared as something that has not been taken hold of and appropriated (*SZ* 162).

What does *not* happen in communication, then, is this. One person has a mental state consisting, for example, of a belief or wish. In accordance with various linguistic rules (syntactic, semantic, pragmatic, etc.) he produces a sound which someone else hears. That other person, who knows the same rules as the first, deciphers that utterance so that, in his mind, he duplicates in some fashion the content the first person wanted to convey to him.

The picture of communication that is rejected here is so common that it is hard to see what it is to be replaced with; doing so will require us to recapitulate our entire analysis of *Being and Time*.

To begin with, both speaker and hearer are in a world. They both interact with other beings in terms of a set of contexts of significance, and insofar as they can communicate at all, this set is a shared one. The "world" in which they are is a public one, and they are together in it. Thus, the "rule competence" that is shared by the interlocutors in the more ordinary view of communication is here supplemented by the broader set of pragmatic "competences" each individual has for interacting with public objects. Such competence is not a purely intellectual matter but includes such "know how" as the ability to use a hammer or a subway, to solve a differential equation or ride a bicycle, or to talk about Cinderella.

In addition, each of the interlocutors has his own understanding and interpretation of the environment and of the entities within it. In order to be communicable at all, this understanding must be grounded in Being-with. It must then be a special aspect or subset of the overall set of contexts of significance which both interlocutors share, one which concerns him explicitly and which he thematizes, in his choice of words, for the other.

In communication (*Mitteilung*) I share with (*teile mit*) my hearer my own understanding of, or openness to, some entity. Communication is thus, for *Being and Time,* ultimately a public and sophisticated way of pointing things out or letting them appear. In it, the speaker calls attention to some entity which is "present," not necessarily sensibly but in a shared context of significance. Aspects of the overall situation which did not previously concern his hearer come to do so, and the hearer understands the situation differently than he did before.

If we keep in mind what has been said about communication so far, it is easy to see what inauthentic communication is. It is communication which never gets beyond the indeterminate stratum of Being-with, and in which the element of understanding remains restricted to the purposes and perspective of das Man, or everyone in general. Two points about it are particularly important for us. First, by restricting understanding and interpretation to that of everyone in general, inauthentic discourse (*Gerede*) loses Dasein's primary relationship to the entities it is speaking about. For that primary relationship, as conditioned by understanding, is an interpretation of the entity in terms of one's own, individual purposes and situation—not in terms of "everyone's." An inauthentic interpretation of an entity, then, does not tell us what that entity really means for the speaking *individual* who encounters it. It informs us only of the prevailing opinions and attitudes toward that entity in the culture at large (*SZ* 168). In such a case, Being-with functions, not as the basic horizon within which understanding and interpretation function, but as their final criterion: "the matter is so, because people say it is" (*SZ,* ibid.).

Second, inauthentic discourse is grounded, no less than its authentic counterpart, in the nature of language and discourse itself. We have seen that discourse is the articulation of contexts of significance which is carried out by an individual's language itself, independently of his own purposes and situation. To it, in inauthentic discourse, are added those purposes and situational givens which, by and large, hold for everyone around him. But it is precisely those general, non-individualistic purposes and givens which constitute his Being-with, the fundamental level on which he can relate to others. Thus, it is in terms of inauthentic speech that we first and foremost interact communicatively (*SZ* 167f). Just as individual authenticity was to be viewed as a modification of inauthenticity, so authentic communication is a modification of the kind that simply remains on the level of Being-with: "in it, and out of it, and against it is performed all genuine understanding, interpretation and communication, rediscovery and new appropriation" (*SZ* 169).[9]

Such inauthentic communication then effects our relations to one another and sets up a particular type of community, in which

> the other is proximally "there" in terms of what "they" have heard about him, what "they" say in their talk about him, and what "they" know about him. Inauthentic discourse [*Gerede*] now slips itself into primordial Being-with one another (*SZ* 174).

In such cases, I relate to the other not as the unique individual that he is but in terms of the way my surroundings prescribe that I ought to relate to him. The philosopher who views the businessman as somebody inescapably crude and greedy, the American who thinks all Russians are evil, and the Englishman who is certain any Frenchwoman is a good cook, are all interacting with their respective others in an inauthentic way.

Furthermore, in identifying an other in terms of what I have "heard about him" from other people, I identify him as a representative of other people in general. I constitute him as himself nothing more than das Man, and this makes him the standard by which I measure myself. Thus,

> everyone keeps his eye on the other first and foremost, watching how he will comport himself and what he will say in reply. Being-with-one-another in das Man is by no means an indifferent side-by-sidedness in which everything has been settled, but rather an intent, ambiguous watching of one another, a secret and reciprocal listening-in (*SZ* 174f).

But, of course, the other is not just that and will never do exactly what I am expecting him to do. His being-with me is only one aspect of his concrete nature, just as is my Being-with him; and "under the mask of the 'for-one-another,' an 'against-one-another' is in play" (*SZ* 175).

Being and Time, then, presents us with two models for communication. In one, the common set of contexts of significance is counterbalanced by the individual ways in which individual interlocutors are open to that overall context, their common world. In the other, such divergencies are suppressed. Instead of honest communication, we get only repetitions of whatever attitudes, values, and concerns are shared by the interlocutors. Those attitudes, values, and concerns are thus conditions for all such speech.

It is relatively easy to see the deficiencies of inauthentic communication. But there is a problem as well not so much with authentic communication itself as with *Being and Time*'s account of it. If *Bedeutung*, as articulated in discourse, is to be the "foundation" of language, it must also be recognized that language itself plays a constitutive role in setting up the contexts of significance in which individual *Bedeutungen* stand. It follows that, simply by learning my mother tongue, I am adopting, and adapting myself to, the understanding and interpretations of an indeterminate mass of other (older) people. I cannot make myself understood to my interlocutors of today except insofar as I have done so, and the history of my mother tongue is a condition for my intelligible speech here and now. The problem with this is not that the discourse in which that history results cannot be other than it is (as inauthentic discourse presumes it cannot), because history reveals that language does change. The problem is rather that discourse, as the work of previous generations, articulates significance without regard to my own unique situation as an individual Dasein. My mother tongue, it seems, addresses me, not as the unique individual I am, but as simply one more of its speakers: as "average," indistinct from others. As das Man.

Heidegger does not actually say this. To do so would be to assign to language a specific sort of Being: that of equipment, and indeed of the kind of technology exemplified in mass transportation. But the very passage which admits indecisiveness about the Being of language also, as we noted, states that *Being and Time* approaches language in terms of the phenomenon of inauthenticity. And this is consonant with other views I analyzed in the work: that inauthentic language forms the basis with which all authentic communication must constantly wrestle (*SZ* 167f), and that inauthentic Dasein "understands itself out of its world," i.e., out of what is primally articulated in discourse (*SZ* 146). Indeed, writes Heidegger, "inauthentic discourse is the mode of Being of Being-with itself" (*SZ* 177).

We will pursue these matters in the next chapter. For the moment, the problem is that linguistic communication seems to be incompatible with authenticity. Authentic experience of some phenomenon would, it appears, remain authentic just until it was articulated in terms comprehensible to others; at that point, its assertions would be "leveled" down into the repertoire of das Man, and it would become "inauthentic" (cf. *SZ* 158, 220). Authenticity appears to be an inarticulate and irreducible solitude. If so, my analysis of *Being and Time* has indeed led nowhere. If the achievement of authenticity is to be construed as an "emancipation" of Dasein from its everyday domination by das Man, emancipation and interaction cannot go together. Emancipatory interaction, to say nothing of intrinsically emancipatory interaction, is impossible.

Six

Heidegger beyond *Being and Time*: "The Origin of the Work of Art"

Being and Time

Being and Time, like all of Heidegger's writings, is not a unified set of arguments for a single thesis but exhibits a set of what I call "demarcations." In it, approaches are tried and fail, and their failures suggest new approaches. The first place to look for a Heideggerean standpoint beyond *Being and Time* is therefore *in* the book itself. One of its demarcations, I will argue, concerns the issue we have raised of solitude and authenticity.

I have analyzed the earlier failure as follows. Though Being-with is fundamental to Dasein, *Being and Time* tends to portray authenticity as an irreducible solitude. It is brought about, not in and through one's relations to others, but in one's stance toward one's own death—and in authentic Being-toward death, "all [Dasein's] relations to other Dasein have been undone" (*SZ* 250; also cf. 238–240, 263). Heidegger takes this motif so far that, as Karsten Harries has commented, the authentic person is presented as a "homeless stranger who, like Kierkegaard's knight of faith, has suspended his ties to the world."[1]

The "knight of faith," Kierkegaard's Abraham, "suspended his ties to the world" to the point that he could no longer speak.[2] Heidegger, in keeping with this, posits authenticity as a mode of Dasein's existence beyond the homogenizing operation of communicative interaction. Quite consistently, he locates it beyond determinate language as well. The "call of conscience" which summons Dasein to its "ownmost possibility," death, is a wordless *Schweigen,* a keeping silent (*SZ* 273f, 296). It presents no specific significance or meaning. Heidegger calls it "indefinite"; we may call it "inarticulate," because it stands outside the articulateness of both discourse and understanding (*SZ* 273, 322f). Standing as it does *outside* those contexts, it calls Dasein *away* from them: "Dasein, as which [the self], understood in worldly terms, is for others and for itself, gets passed over in the call" (*SZ* 273; also cf. 307). Authenticity, then, places Dasein beyond its world.

But we have also seen *Being and Time* maintain, as its central thesis, that Dasein is Being-*in*-the-world. Because world is the ultimate horizon of significance, of *Bedeutsamkeit,* beyond the concrete contexts of significance that make up Dasein's world there is only the famous Heideggerean "nothing," here understood as the meaninglessness (*Unbedeutsamkeit*) to Dasein of those contexts themselves (*SZ* 187, 343). In accordance with what we have seen to be Heidegger's conception of *Bedeutung,* the "nothing" of the world would be the incapacity of specific entities and contexts to be understood, to offer possibilities to Dasein. Since Heidegger understands the most radical absence of possibilities as death, the call of conscience is ultimately a call toward death (*SZ* 307, 262f). Authentic Being-toward death "reveals that all Being-alongside the things with which we concern ourselves, and all Being-with others, fail us." But since Dasein is essentially Being-in-the-world, authentic Being-toward death neither reduces us to an "inner life" nor elevates us to an absolute, "free-floating" ego above and beyond world (*SZ* 263, 273, 189). Heidegger puts the case most clearly in his discussion of "resoluteness":

> resoluteness . . . does not detach Dasein from its world; nor does it isolate it so that it becomes a free-floating "I" . . . Resoluteness brings the self precisely into its current concernful Being-alongside the ready-to-hand and thrusts it into solicitous Being-with others (*SZ* 298).

More concretely,

> The "world" which is present ready-to-hand does not become a different one, the circle of others is not replaced; and yet . . . one's solicitous Being-with others [is] now determined by [its] inmost potentiality for Being [i.e., by one's own authentic Being-toward death] (*SZ* 297f).

Resoluteness thus returns Dasein to its world, to the concrete contexts of significance and the relationships it had before. It must; there is no place else for Dasein to go.

It appears, then, that *Being and Time* gives two accounts of what happens to Dasein when it ceases to be inauthentic. On one account, which has its own textual support, Dasein "suspends" its ties to the world, and "authentic" Dasein is a homeless stranger. On the other account, which is articulated in terms of "resoluteness," Dasein does not leave its world but is returned to it, to understand and interact with others in terms of its awareness of its own death. On the former view, the basic structures of the world are parametric in nature, for they can be left behind; on the later, authenticity simply affirms the specific features of Dasein's world as conditions of its being-in-that-world. The two accounts share the view that meaning resides within the world: that whatever *Bedeutungen* I can be open to are parts of the larger context of meaningfulness that constitutes my world. The former account suggests that there is someplace else to go, some sort of "suspended world." The latter denies this.

The concept of "resoluteness" is then to be demarcated from that of "authenticity." If we take *Being and Time* seriously as demarcative in nature, to ask whether these two accounts are ultimately consistent with one another is beside the point. The point is that they are different, and that resoluteness, in terms of our problematic, takes up where authenticity left off. It takes authentic Being-toward death back into what it had seemed to escape, the context of human interaction. By returning to its world in this way, resolute Dasein at least *commits* itself to that world. Its specific relationships and contexts of significance are now, if not created by Dasein or even invested with significance by Dasein, at least chosen by it. This choice makes Dasein, for Heidegger, "free for its world" (*SZ* 297f.; also cf. *SZ* 188). But the freedom is very restricted: no alternatives to its present world are possible for Dasein, and it can only confront, authentically or inauthentically, the single world that it has.

Heidegger's next step in developing an interactive account of resoluteness is to try and vindicate such freedom as a basis for interpersonal relations. As he puts it, authentic Dasein can "become the conscience" of others (*SZ* 298f), "calling" them in the inarticulate way its own conscience calls it. The "call of conscience" from one Dasein to another is itself, of course, inarticulate. Heidegger does not give any concrete examples of how it is supposed to work, and one suspects they would be hard to come by. The lack of concreteness shows again when sections 74ff. of *Being and Time*, going beyond personal relations, attempt to show how individual Being-toward death is the "hidden ground" of historical community (cf. *SZ* 386). The historically destined community, the authentic *Geschick*, is founded on "being-with-one-another in the same world and in the resolve for determinate possibilities" (*SZ* 384). This resolve, though "for determinate possibilities," is itself "indefinite" and therefore partakes of the inarticulate character of the call of conscience to which it responds (*SZ* 298, 307f). We are told that the power of the authentic community is "set free in communication and struggle" (*SZ* 384). Again, in view of the inarticulateness of the resolve which founds authentic community, it is unsurprising that we are not told more.

Being and Time here attempts to ground authentic community, not on linguistic interaction, but on an inarticulate resolve. This very inarticulateness shows the limits of the account of discourse and language in *Being and Time*. For it amounts to the recognition that language and discourse, both of which are characterized by communicative interaction, have no role in resoluteness itself and cannot contribute in any positive way to the constitution of resolute, or authentic, community. The inadequacy of this account is attested by the later Heidegger's elevation of language and dialogue to the central position in his concept of man, in the "dialogue that we *are*."[3] It was brutally illustrated by Heidegger's own inability to cope with a political movement which not only negated communication within the community (leaving the individual no option except the "inarticulate resolve" to do the Führer's bidding) but denied "exoteric" communication in the most radical possible manner: by exterminating those it defined as "other."[4]

If we ask why communication, as construed in *Being and Time,* seems incompatible with authenticity, the answer is simple—and devastating. It is that Dasein is Being-in-the-world. In our original discussion of Being-with, we saw that it is constituted through Dasein's encounters with entities ready-to-hand in the world which refer not to concrete and unique individuals but to the "random, average" dimension of man's existence. Considered in this perspective, language reveals to us what previous generations understood about their encounters with entities and contexts within the world. The significance of individual terms in a given language is then itself something "average." It is articulated as the lowest common denominator of the concrete individuals who, by their interactions with the world and one another, created various contexts of significance and gave names to their more important components. Insofar as Dasein must, to be understood, use words in their accepted senses, Dasein is given over to the homogenized, and therefore inauthentic, structures of its world.

It is thus no accident that Heidegger should say that inauthentic Dasein "understands itself out of its world" (*SZ* 146,187); or that "inauthenticity . . . constitutes an outstanding mode of Being-in-the-world, which is completely enthralled [*benommen*] by the 'world' and by Being-with others in das Man" (*SZ* 176); or that "inauthentic discourse is the mode of Being of Being-with one another itself" (*SZ* 177). *It is world itself, as the cultural complex constituted in part by others, to which inauthentic Dasein has been subjugated and from which, in some sense, it must be freed.*[5] *Being and Time* tries to articulate such freedom via its account of authenticity. But as long as language and discourse are seen wholly in the perspective of Being-in-the-world, emancipation can only be either solitary or brought about through an inarticulate resolve.

But it is not certain that language and discourse are irretrievably "world bound." As we have seen, nothing is settled in *Being and Time* regarding the basic nature of language: "even the horizon for the investigative question remains unclear" (*SZ* 166). Can a stratum or type of concrete utterance be isolated which somehow really does articulate significance, as does discourse in *Being and Time,* without being subject to the strictures of a pregiven language and world? If so, an account of emancipation from the world which, unlike that of *Being and Time,* is inherently linguistic and articulate would find a purchase.

"The Origin of the Work of Art": Language and World

This essay, written just after Heidegger's Nazi activity and at the beginning of the *Kehre,* or turn, in Heidegger's thought, has been called by Walter Biemel a work of "passage" from the early to the later Heidegger.[6] Like Plato's *Phaedrus* and Kant's *Critique of Judgment,* it opens up a new conceptual constellation via a critical confrontation with the old. As such, and like *Being and Time,* it is not a finished work. In both texts, Heidegger writes, the relation of Being and human being is unsuitably conceived. But the "tacit path" of that problematic leads, in the later work, to a discussion of language and poetry.[7] That discussion, at the end of the essay, is thus not an appendix or an *obiter dictum,* but the place where the entire essay "comes together." We will, for our part, read the essay as, from first to last, a discussion of the nature of language. That discussion begins with three conceptions, taken from the history of philosophy, of what a "thing" is. Two of them are of special importance for us: the views of the "thing" as a substance with attributes (*UKW* 12–14/22–25) and as equipment (*UKW* 16–20/26–30).[8]

The view of the thing as a substance with properties is, in its first articulation at the beginning of Aristotle's *Categories,* derived from the subject/predicate structure of propositions.[9] The other relevant view of the "thing" is also couched in Aristotelian terms: those of matter and form. Both form and matter, Heidegger writes, are ultimately determined by what a thing is to be used for, and the view of a thing as a composite of matter and form is for Heidegger derived from the nature of equipment (*UKW* 18/28). So understood, language is to be viewed in terms of its serviceability for human purposes, notably communication (*UKW* 60f/73).[10]

These ontological interpretations are recognizable as, respectively, *Being and Time*'s categories of present-at-hand and ready-to-hand (*SZ* 66–72, 92–96). They fail to capture, we are now told, a certain aspect of at least some things. In the case of the substance/attribute interpretation, this is the thing's *Eigenwüchsigkeit,* or "self-grownness," and its *In-sich-Ruhen,* or its coming-to-rest in itself (*UKW* 14/24f).[11] In the other case, it is the "self-sufficiency" of the class of things that are art works (*UKW* 18/29).

These terms point to the idea that a "thing" has, as such, an internal, dynamic structure of its own. From the one point of view, a "thing" is something that grows up by itself and comes to rest within itself. From the other, a "thing" is something which makes, and fulfills, demands upon itself. Some parts or phases of it, we may say, place constraints which are met by other parts or phases. The qualities of self-grownness, coming-to-rest in self, and self-sufficiency thus refer to the sort of internal dynamic that, we saw, was part of the concept of "phenomenon" advanced in *Being and Time.* Both the basic categories advanced in that work—that of the present-at-hand and the ready-to-hand—thus fail to grasp fully the character of the "thing" as phenomenon.

The substance/attribute schema fails to capture this because it embodies an "assault" on the nature of the thing (*UKW* 14f/24f). We may regard this "assault" as the attempt to understand the nature of things in terms of a conceptual construct—the idea of substance itself—rather than in terms of our lived experience of them as belonging to contexts of involvement. (The relation of the concept of substance to ordinary lived experience will be discussed in part two, chapters 11, 12, and 13).

The understanding of "equipment" misses the internal dynamic of the "thing" because it comprehends the thing in terms of something other than itself—its usefulness (*UKW* 18f/28f). In the terms of *Being and Time,* we encounter an entity ready-to-hand by looking beyond it to the context of its significance and to the meaning it may have for an individual Dasein. Such an entity is defined in terms of its context, and that context is, therefore, not wholly other than it. But there is still some distinction between entity and context, for encounters with entities ready-to-hand leave those entities unthematized. This is why the proper concern of phenomenological description is not entities as such but the contexts in which they stand: a distinction which could not be drawn, and a procedure which could not be followed, if encounters with entities as present-to-hand really revealed the internal dynamics of those entities.

Both views of entities offered in *Being and Time* thus fail to capture what we might call their "phenomenality."[12] But is such a capture necessary? Is there a phenomenality to things at all, or is Heidegger merely constructing an arbitrary concept and then criticizing other approaches (including his own previous one) for not capitalizing upon it?

At least one class of entities, we are told, can and must be treated as "phenomenal" in the sense indicated: works of art. In discussing Van

Gogh's painting of a pair of peasant shoes, Heidegger contrasts our experience of those shoes in the work of art with the peasant woman's experience of the originals. She simply wears them, puts them on and takes them off, and in that context of daily use is not aware of them (*UKW* 23/ 34). It is *we* who see them, in the painting. They are equipment for her, but they are objects of explicit awareness for us. This awareness is not a "theoretical" one which posits the shoes as spatiotemporal objects with various properties. We are not, in the work of art, made aware of a series of properties of the shoes which, simply because they are of the *shoes*, tell us little or nothing about their wearer. The whole work-world of their wearer shines forth in their presentation by the artist:

> the more simply and authentically the shoes alone are [presented], the more directly and engagingly do all beings attain to a greater degree of being along with them" (*UKW* 44/56).

But Van Gogh does not *portray* the relationship between the shoes and the world of their wearer. He does not, for example, show the peasant woman wearing the shoes as she trudges through the fields. The shoes are not even portrayed as lying in a closet or on the floor; they are in an "undefined space" (*UKW* 22/33). The world of the wearer of the shoes, their context of significance, is evoked entirely through the various facets of the shoes themselves that are portrayed. In a lyrical description of what the picture reveals to us, Heidegger shows that the entire context of the shoes' use is evoked by the way the artist draws them. The rugged heaviness of their construction, the dark opening of their insides, the dampness of the leather as painted call up the climate, landscape, and labor in which and for which they are worn (*UKW* 22f/33f). *This* pair of shoes, worn through in just these ways, we may say, cannot be conceived apart from hard farm work. The shoes themselves, as presented, do not merely "evoke" the work-world of their possessor; they define that world, and are defined by it. The interplay between the shoes and their context of significance is thus internal to the shoes themselves. It is that internal dynamic which makes the shoes what they "truly" are as phenomena (*UKW* 24f/35f).

The work of art thus presents entities to us in a distinctive way. As in our encounters with entities present-at-hand, it presents the entity in question explicitly or "thematically." As in our encounters with beings ready-to-hand, it also presents the context in which that entity is significant. The work of art thus sets up its own context of significance and "belongs, as work, uniquely in the realm which is opened up by itself" (*UKW* 30/41). Because this realm is opened up by the work itself, it is not the realm in which the beholder of the work normally lives: "in the vicinity of [Van Gogh's] work, we were suddenly somewhere else than we usually tend to be" (*UKW* 24/35). "Where we usually tend to be," of course, is in our own world. Our displacement from that world is clearest when the work of art presents a context of significance which itself is strange to us, as in the case of art works which have survived from previous historical periods (*UKW* 29f/40f). The fact that works of art can remain meaningful even when the "world" that produced them has vanished means that the context of significance the work "opens up" is independent of the overall context of significance that is the world of its beholders—or of its makers (*UKW* 29 f./40 f.).

In opening up its own realm of significance, the work of art is "self-sufficient" in a way that entities ready-to-hand within a preestablished world cannot be. Further, the process by which this realm is defined and explicated in the work of art is one of self-contained dynamic development, or *Eigenwüchs* and *In-sich-Ruhen*. Heidegger is thus ready to replace the dichotomous "ontology" of *Being and Time* with a trichotomy of "mere" thing, equipment, and work of art (*UKW* 18/29). There would then be a corresponding trichotomy for language: it could be viewed theoretically as a set of propositions; pragmatically as a set of tools for communication; and aesthetically as opening up new contexts of significance.

The realm of significance opened up by a work of art is as unique as the work itself and, hence, not necessarily a part of the world of those who behold the work. They cannot "use" the work, and it does not "refer" to them as inner-worldly entities do. The work's significance is a totality unto itself, and as such can itself be called a "world." It is then the function of the work of art, as Heidegger puts it, to "set up a world" (*UKW* 33; also cf. 31/42, 44). But what, here, does it mean to "set up" a world? What sort of situation precedes such "setting up?" The answer is twofold.

First, world arises only through and for human beings (*UKW* 33f/44f), and human beings are always already in a world. So any world must arise from a previous world. If "world" is the overarching totality of contexts of significance to which Dasein can be open, then a new world arises when people find themselves open to a new such overarching context.[13] In this, *all* structures of the previous world are revealed as parameters. "World" itself no longer designates a condition of Dasein's existence but a state of affairs in which all determinate content is capable of becoming other than it is, or is parametric in nature.

Moreover, because the context in question is "overarching," the new world cannot emerge from the old via any sort of dialectical negation or otherwise-conceived rational critique. If it did, the very concept of "dialectical negation" (or "rational critique") would be one in terms of which both worlds could be understood: it, and not they, would be (as in Hegel's *Phenomenology*) the "overarching" context of intelligibility. The emergence of a new world from an older one must be the emergence of something new and truly "incommensurable" with the old, out of which it takes us (*UKW* 54, 61, 64/66, 74, 77). Thus, the setting forth of new parameters is demarcative, in that the world preceding the new one opened up by a work of art is incommensurable with that new world. Art is historical, not merely in that it changes with history, but in that it grounds history, here understood as the emergence of new worlds incommensurable with old ones (*UKW* 64/77). As such, art also, we read, grounds true human community (*UKW* 55f/68).[14]

If Heidegger wants to say that worlds as such originate in works of art, we need not read him to say that *all* works of art originate worlds. Originating a world is doubtless the most radical form in which art can articulate new *Bedeutungen*; but presumably there are, though Heidegger does not mention them, works of art which do not set up wholly new worlds, but rather develop new meanings that fit into the world in which they come to be. In any case, we do not yet have a complete account, even in outline, of the way a world arises in a work of art for at least two reasons. For one thing, there are many "new worlds" spun from the heads of artists, but only a few are accepted by society at large and become great art; there must be something beyond imagination and whimsy to account for this (cf. *UKW* 37f, 60/49, 72). Second, phenomenologically speaking, there is more to art than ideas spinning from artists' heads: there is also the concrete, "thingly" character of the work of art, and this remains to be brought out (*UKW* 55/46).

To every work of art there belongs a "material," not in the traditional Aristotelian sense of a quiescent matter into which the artistic form is projected (cf. *UKW* 18/28), but in the sense of something dynamic and configurating, which Heidegger calls "earth" (*UKW* 31, 35, 37f/42, 46, 48f). The aim of the artist, then, is not to impose his intentions upon matter, which offers, at best, a sort of inert resistance (as when, from various different pieces of wood, a furniture factory turns out hundreds of virtually identical tables), but to liberate forms already present in the medium (cf. the remarks on Dürer at *UKW* 58/70). This medium is, of course, not to be construed as a mere physical entity; that would mean giving the attempt to explicate the nature of art over again to the category of the present-at-hand. Heidegger's discussion seeks rather to bring out what we might call the "natural significance" of the various materials artists can use. It portrays the stone of a Greek temple as interacting with the rock on which it stands, with the weather and sunlight, with the nearby sea and local life forms. These natural givens of its site and material define the temple. They are themselves evoked by it and thematized in our encounter with it. Like the world of the peasant woman, they become what they "truly" are through their relation to the work of art which stands in their midst (*UKW* 31/42).

Earth, we may say, functions here as a realm of "pre-significance" with which the work of art interacts in its own unique way. The prefix is important. On the one hand, the "pre-" indicates that the work of art comes from, belongs within, and thematizes the natural contexts of the earth (*UKW* 35f/46). On the other hand, as being a realm of "pre-" significance, the earth is not significant in and of itself: it is and remains undisclosable (*UKW* 36/47). A given piece of marble, in other words, may have the *Pietà* in it. But the marble itself cannot "know" this; it cannot be "open" to the interrelations of veins and stress lines which make that statue uniquely expressible in it. Since that statue, once carved, remains a thing of marble, it never loses its dependence upon a domain inherently undisclosable. There is always a tension between the marble or the site, and the statue or the building; and the essay goes so far as to call this tension a "strife" (*UKW* 37f/49f). It is its strife with the domain of natural pre-significance, then, which gives the work of art a "resolute foundation" (*Entscheidendes*) and keeps it from being a mere play of whimsy (*UKW* 38/49). The world opened up in a work of art is thus in tension with, and dependent upon, an original domain of natural pre-significance. World is not ultimate, as it is in *Being and Time,* but is grounded and defined by its relation to that other domain.[15] It is by virtue of their relation to that domain as well that works of art can transcend the world within which they come to be and open up new worlds.

Earth, as we saw, offers only pre-significance, not significance, because purely natural entities cannot be "open" to one another. It is through language, Heidegger tells us, that man is open to things and contexts (*UKW* 60f/73); language, then, which ultimately allows pre-significance to become significance. It performs this function, not in being a set of propositions or an instrument of communication, but in its aesthetic function of opening up a world. The vehicle of such opening is the name (*UKW* 60f/73).

This point depends, first, on the fact that names (except in certain artificial languages) always convey information about the object named. That such is the case for "common names," like "horse" or "red," is indisputable; it has not always been held to be the case for names of individuals, or "proper names." A proper name, so viewed, designates an object, but conveys no information about it.[16] But while it is true that we can, and logicians in fact often do, give names to objects which are entirely arbitrary and convey no information whatever about them, it is easy to see that such is not the case with names in ordinary language. As *Being and Time*'s account of words accruing to significations has suggested, the name of any entity in natural language conveys to us one crucial piece of information about it: that it is important enough to *have* a name. Pike's Peak has a name; the individual stones lying on its summit do not. The statistical curve of normal distribution has a name, the "bell curve"; the curve of a baby's foot as it sleeps does not. And so on.[17]

Thus, any name in ordinary language tells us, at a minimum, that its bearer is important enough to have been responded to, at some time, by an act of naming. Most names, especially common names, tell us a good deal more than that.[18] In terms of *Being and Time*, names tell us "as what" the named entity is to be understood (*UKW* 61/73). The "as-structure" of a being thus requires, at a minimum, a name in order to be thematized or made explicit. Since to understand an entity *as* something is to put it into a context of significance, such contexts—and the worlds they constitute—are themselves impossible without names. Thus, for example, a stream of water can be "present" to a stone lying on its bottom, if we wish to speak that way. The water touches it, moves it along, gradually grinds it into an ellipsoid, and so forth. But the water is not present to the stone *as water*—as something resembling what runs in other streams and falls from the sky, as clear or muddy, as what can be drunk or bathed in, and so forth. All this "internal" complexity of water, the structure which constitutes it as the phenomenon that it is for human beings, remains, so to speak, unknown to the stone.

It is then in being named that a thing is for the first time brought into, or, in Heidegger's term, "projected" onto, a context of significance—a context which is then unique to itself. Such "projective" speech is always poetic in nature: it thematizes a being in terms of a new and unique context of significance (*UKW* 60f/73f). We can understand the artistic, world-originating nature of poetry for Heidegger in the following way. A poem is an articulated whole of significance—a "world"—compounded out of the words available to the poet in the language in which he writes. In his poem, individual words take up positions in an articulated whole, and in that sense are given significance: each word is defined, to some extent, through its relation to the other words in the poem. Their "pre-significance" would be the meaning that they had before the poet actually put them to work in the poem, i.e., the sum total of the information they convey, of their denotations and connotations, or of their possible uses in the language.

There is, therefore, a double relation between a poem and the language in which it is written. On the one hand, the poem attempts to "wring the most" out of each word it contains, to make the fullest use not only of its denotative capacities but of its associations and even of its sound. That is why notions such as synonymy, paraphrase, and translation have no meaning within poetry. On the other hand, the poem remains in tension with the language in which it is written, because the poet is using the language to say new things. In Heidegger's view, the poet is bringing forth new aspects of pre-significance in the individual words he uses.

But pre-significance does not belong to world. World in fact is only "opened up" when the dimension of pre-significance is addressed in a particular way by the work of art (*UKW* 61/74). It is not *we*, in other words, who make water something that runs in streams, that falls from the sky, that can be drunk or bathed in, and so forth. Water is those things independently of us, and the word "water" can be used to convey them all. They lie, so to speak, "latent" within that word the way the grain of wood lies latent within a tree, until it is brought out by a sculptor. A change in the pre-significance of water—some new way of relating to it—means a change in the grammar of "water," and such innovations get articulated in poetic language.

Because they present us with independent givens which, like the meaning of "water," can condition our lives in important ways, poetic names articulate what I call "limits." Because these limits can fall prey to innovation, they can change and are therefore, in my sense, "parameters." Poetic naming is thus the articulation of parameters. But this articulation does not come about, as for Hegel, via a narrative process in which the new can be grasped as a specific transformation (or, in Hegel's terms, a "determinate negation") of the old. A poem is rather a breakthrough to a stratum of language inherently beyond world. As such, it can introduce radical discontinuities into world. In using words poetically, we are not merely conforming to the understandings and interpretations of other Dasein in our world, or to those handed down to us in our language; we are ultimately conforming as well to that nonhuman domain of pre-significance. By bringing natural pre-significance into the openness of world, poetic language grounds and transforms world (*UKW* 61-63/74-76). If world is historical, poetic naming is also historical in that, like all art, it grounds history (*UKW* 64/77).

"The Origin of the Work of Art," then, takes the step beyond world that was required, as I argued, by the failure of *Being and Time*'s accounts of authenticity, resoluteness, and their respective relations to interaction. Poetic naming, in fact, meets the two conditions I laid down for authentic interpretation of a phenomenon. First, it is true to the phenomenality of the phenomenon, i.e., it articulates it as a complex whole which shows itself (as we shall see in more detail in the next chapter).

And second, it does this without reliance on previously given structures of meaning. Because *Being and Time* saw all significance as world bound, its own accounts of authentic understanding, interpretation, and discourse were unable to achieve this.

Art and Emancipation in "The Origin of the Work of Art"

Heidegger has now taken the step beyond world that was required, I argued, by *Being and Time*'s accounts of authenticity, resoluteness, and their relations to interaction. As we will see in the next chapter, a new concept of emancipation is opened up with this. But any attempt to mine "The Origin of the Work of Art" for political philosophy faces major obstacles. For in detaching poetic language from world, Heidegger has also detached it from ordinary linguistic practice. Everyday speech hardly consists of a series of breakthroughs to radically new contexts of significance. It proceeds, as Habermas will argue, against the unchallenged background of the world of the speakers. But Heidegger restricts the discussion of "The Origin of the Work of Art" to great works of art (*UKW* 29/40). There is no account of what the language of such works has to do with our ordinary efforts to find our way around in the world and to help others to do the same. As Werner Marx has put it for Heidegger's later works in general,

> The "everyday" modes of the Being of man, which played such an important role in *Being and Time,* are no longer studied. Nor is it asked how the creative modes of man might determine the everyday modes or whether and how these everyday modes are "derived" from the creative modes.[19]

Not only is the poem in tension with the language in which it is written; poetic language itself is in a "tension" with ordinary speech which seems to be so slack as to amount to mutual indifference. This brings us to the question of just how the work of art, and in particular the poem, is supposed to found human community with its obvious everyday dimension. We can begin with a passage, which I will quote at length, in which Heidegger discusses the way the work of art affects those who behold it:

> The more solitarily the work . . . stands on its own, the more cleanly it seems to cut all ties to human beings . . . the more essentially is the extraordinary thrust to the surface and what seems to be the long-familiar thrust down or overthrown [and] . . . the more simply does [the work] transport us out of the realm of the ordinary. To submit to this displacement

means: to transform our accustomed ties to world and to earth, and henceforth to restrain all usual doing and valuing, knowing and looking, in order to stay within the truth that is happening in the work. Only the restraint of this staying lets be what is created by the work. . . . This letting of the work be a work we call the preserving of the work. (*UKW* 54/66; translation slightly altered).

In "cutting all ties to human beings," and in the way that it "transports us out" of our world, preserving the work of art functions similarly to Being-toward death in *Being and Time*. Heidegger in fact goes on to relate the preservation of the work of art to the concept of "resoluteness" presented in that book (*UKW* 55/67). But the difference is unmistakeable. The inarticulateness of resolve in *Being and Time* is replaced with the concrete individuality of the work of art, which speaks to us, not from within our world or as an indeterminate "call" out of it, but from another concrete world, one unique to itself (*UKW* 63/76). This way of experiencing a work of art is a condition for its being a work of art at all (*UKW* 54f/67). An art work which does not deserve an audience, we may say, is no art work. This is why, in experiencing a work of art for what it is, we "preserve" it; and it is why, for Heidegger as for Hegel, the work of art is intrinsically a communal and (in a broad sense) a communicative entity.

If world originates in works of art, and if Being-with is an element of Being-in-the-world, then it, too, must originate in works of art. This means that our original Being-toward the work of art, our preservation of it, is also our primal Being-with one another (*UKW* 55f/68). We may then say that the primordial community is now the community of preservers of the work of art. This community, again, will be a "resolute" one, if preserving the work of art is a resolute mode of existence. But it is not grounded in an inarticulate resolve, ready for whatever demands the community (or dictatorial leader) might make on the individual.[20] It is a limited and definite sort of community, one dedicated to experiencing the work of art for what it truly is.

One member of the community, we may note, and no more essential to it than the "preservers" of the work, is the artist himself (*UKW* 58, 64f/71, 78). Like Hegel, Heidegger is able to present art as a social, communicative phenomenon by refusing to view it exclusively as the creation of an individual genius. Both writers, in fact, refer to the creator as a mere "passageway" or "corridor" for the truth his work expresses (*UKW* 29/40; *Aesth.* 400/298).

In a short and, it must be confessed, mystifying list of the "essential ways" in which truth "establishes itself," we find included—along with art—the "act which grounds a political state" (*UKW* 50/61f; translation slightly altered). Clearly, there is supposed to be some relation between the artistic grounding of history and the grounding of political structures. We may understand it as follows.

The "destiny" of an historical people is constituted in "simple and essential decisions" (*UKW* 37, 43f/48, 55). These decisions themselves, however, comply with "paths," which the people presumably follow toward their destiny (*UKW*, ibid.). We shall consider Heidegger's concept of "path" more closely in the next chapter, but we have seen enough not to be surprised by the language here. In order to make decisions, we must be aware of alternative possibilities. But a possibility, as we have seen, reveals itself only gradually over time. It can never be understood until it has been followed: I cannot know what it is like to marry this person rather than that one unless I actually do so, and even then achieving the knowledge may take a few decades. A possibility thus has something of the nature of a "path," which is also something we can follow or not, and which we will not understand even in part until we have gone where it leads.

Thus, social decisions imply the awareness, on the part of the decider, of alternatives and presuppose the givenness of possibilities. As we also noted previously, in *Being and Time* the overarching context in terms of which possibilities are given to Dasein is world. It plays the same role here:

> The world is the self-disclosing openness of the broad paths
> of the simple and essential decisions in the destiny of an his-
> torical people (*UKW* 37/48; also cf. 33f/42).

Such decisions respond to the pre-significance of earth in terms of the open significance of world. They are then responsive to the primordial "strife" between world and earth. Insofar as a social decision partakes of the radicality of the art work, then, it would be an opening-up of radically new social significance. As in the Paris Commune or in the Declaration of American Independence, a new social order would appear within, and opposed to, the old one.

What, we may now ask, is the relationship of what I have called "social significance" to the concept of the state? Is the state to be identified with the realm of social significance opened up by a radical social decision? If so, then Heidegger is identifying the state as an overarching context of intelligibility, in itself a "world." Such an identification could only be totalitarian in character, and Alexander Schwan has argued at length that such is the case.[21] On the other hand, if Heidegger is not making such an identification, the relationship of what he has to say about social significance and social decision to concrete political structures like states remains to be clarified. This view is, I will argue, the more plausible.

In the first place, Heidegger accords to world, as the "all-governing expanse" of human destiny, things which in any possible analysis fall outside the scope of the state as a form of political organization. Birth and death, disaster and blessing, endurance and decline cannot be understood, as they relate to individual human beings, in terms of political structures *alone* (*UKW* 31/42). If I contract cancer at the age of thirty, that is a tragedy and may bring death, no matter what sort of state I live in.

The reason for the generality, I suggest, is that based on Heidegger's account here aesthetic language is the primary articulation of significance itself. The basic type of human community is the community of all those who speak a single language; and language cannot arise in the total absence of cooperative endeavor and community.[22] Heidegger's account of aesthetic language as the origin of significance itself is then coordinated to an account of that primordial cooperative endeavor. But this makes it a theory of human community as such, not a theory of that particular, sophisticated type of community that we call a "state." Language and linguistic communities pre-exist states, and they pre-exist by far the modifications of modernity that constitute totalitarianism. Heidegger, then, is operating on a level which leaves undecided the question of the nature and derivation of specific political structures.[23]

This does not mean, however, that the views Heidegger presents are entirely irrelevant to political thought. We have already seen him referring to the "grounding" of a state, and this can be interpreted to correspond to his views of the "grounding" of the work of art. A work of art is not a mere play of imaginative whimsy, but it must be oriented to the pre-significance latent within language and nature. Similarly, the structures of the state cannot be spun from the heads of thinkers without regard to the world and the earth of the people who are to inhabit the state.

Another general corollary to what Heidegger has said in "The Origin of the Work of Art," and a further point against totalitarian readings of the essay, is that even the "governing expanse" of the world is a response to, and is conditioned by, something else—the realm of pre-significance, or the earth (*UKW* 31f/42f). This means that all "essential" social decisions are based on earth, on something "not mastered . . . concealed, confusing" (UKW 43f/55). It follows that a "Heideggerean state" could never be rationally legitimated by some transparent train of reasoning. Nor could it be pragmatically legitimated by the way it serves the needs of the individuals who make it up, since those needs are themselves the products of interpretation and thus conditioned by the world and the earth in which those individuals dwell. It follows that nothing a state or society does can ever be fully justified. All social decisions are open to challenge.

Further still: earth, as inherently undisclosable, not only *denies* full legitimacy *to* existing institutions; it tends to *withdraw* legitimacy *from* them. Earth "tends always to draw the world into itself and keep it there" (*UKW* 37/49). Because the world, including the political realm, is for Heidegger grounded on earth, it is always open to the possibility of a complete loss of legitimacy, to a radical and total change. And this is in fact entailed by the view that the world, and political structures, originate in works of art. For a work of art confronts man with radically new significance and, hence, is intrinsically revolutionary:

> The truth that discloses itself in the work can never be proved or derived from what went before. *What went before is refuted in its exclusive reality by the work* (*UKW* 62/75; emphasis added).

As grounded in the preservation of the work of art, we may say, human community is constituted through the confrontation of human beings with radically new significance. Any attempt to deny the possibility of basic transformations of world, and hence of political and social structures within a particular world, denies this basic fact.

We may sum up the political insights we have derived from "The Origin of the Work of Art" in the following theses:

(1) Political and social structures do not legitimate themselves and are not wholly determined by the conscious efforts of men. They are under limits imposed by nature and language.

(2) These limits can never be fully known.

(3) They are also susceptible to change, i.e., are what I call "parameters."

(4) They are originally disclosed, not in social interaction that is in any narrow sense "political," but in the kind of interaction which takes place in the preservation of works of art.

(5) This original disclosure can be one of genuine newness.

These are not theses of political philosophy as such. They do not tell us anything about the norms according to which societies ought to be constructed, nor do they tell us how to evaluate societies which actually

exist. They would, in fact, permit us to argue that the authoritarian Soviet system is "grounded" in the nature of the homogenous, nonmobile,
agrarian society of Russia just as Anglo-Saxon democratic structures are
"grounded" in the cosmopolitan world of imperial British commerce.

But if so, then those structures can change: for earth is an unmastered
mystery. We must hence conclude that Heidegger's political thought, as
we have worked it out so far, is radically and intractably subversive. All
political structures belong to world, and world is "the ever non-objective
to which we are subject" (*UKW* 33f/44). In transporting us from our
world, the work of art transports us as well from its political structures.
It can in this way "free" us from those structures. This emancipation does
not come about, as in *Being and Time,* through an inarticulate "call" beyond those structures, one which causes them to fade into "nothingness"
and then returns us to them, but through the articulate presentation of
fundamentally different structures.

Because the work of art frees us from the dominance of the basic structures of our current world, it reveals those structures to be parameters
which can be left behind. Insofar as old parameters are in fact left behind,
the Heideggerean concept of emancipation analyzed here seems similar
to what we called "externalization" in Hegel. But in Hegel's view, the set
of parameters (or particularities) that was left behind was less universal
than the set arrived at. This enabled the two sets to be placed into a rank
order, so that the movement from one to the other, and thence to a third,
became a continuous ascension—a narrative which was a condition for
consciousness itself, and one which could be fully recuperated when its
starting point was recovered in reconciliation.

For Heidegger, the two sets of world parameters do not stand in such
a hierarchical order, any more than did authenticity and inauthenticity.
There is no continuous movement from one to the other, and no reconciliatory recuperation of both. Indeed, when the two sets of parameters
retain their differences down to very basic levels, they become incommensurable worlds. In any case, the better acquainted one becomes with
both sets, the more determinate and decisive the differences between
them become. The emancipatory movement from one set of parameters
to the other (and, since they are not ranked with respect to each other,
back to the first) neither reveals nor constitutes their harmonization into
some larger narrative. It only brings about an increasing differentiation
of each from the other. Such differentiation I call "demarcation." Along
with narrative, it will be shown to be one of the two basic strategies of
poetic interaction.

Given theses (2) and (3) above, we cannot expect Heidegger's thought ever to yield a set of definitive standards by which to judge societies, as Hegel's concept of reconciliation did (at least from the standpoint of art itself). But the nature of the basic parameters of world and society, and the ways these parameters can be (at least partially) disclosed to us, can nonetheless be set forth more clearly than they have been. We will examine such a presentation in the next chapter.

Seven

Heidegger's View of Intrinsically Emancipatory Interaction: "From a Dialogue on Language"

The preceding analysis of Heidegger has resulted in four models of interaction, one of which has already been criticized by Heidegger himself. We may list them as follows:

(1) Interaction in which all parties to the conversation share both significance and meaning, *Bedeutung* and *Sinn*. Their conversation serves, inauthentically, only to reiterate their common understanding.

(2) Communication which does not reiterate common understanding but establishes it. In this model, all parties are in the same world and are open to the same contexts of significance; but they understand and interpret those contexts differently. In the course of their communicative encounter, their differing understandings and interpretations get leveled out or homogenized.

(3*) Also treated in *Being and Time* was the silent and inarticulate "call" to authenticity, which can either be the call of Dasein's own conscience or the call of another Dasein. My analysis of "The Origin of the Work of Art" showed it to be an implicit critique of this model in this list. Accepting Heidegger's self-criticism as the basis for our own critical reading of his thought thus means discarding this model and substituting for it the last one.

(3) We shall call this final type "aesthetic" communication. Through the art work, as we have seen, we are transported out of our everyday world and, together with other "preservers," are placed into a different one. In this experience, we interact with others and, most importantly, with the work of art itself.

We now have a neat hierarchy of modes of communication. In (1), both *Sinn* and *Bedeutung* are shared; in (2), *Bedeutung* is shared but *Sinn* is not. Both these models, since they presuppose shared *Bedeutungen,*

143

view communication as taking place against the horizon of a single world within which the interlocutors dwell. In (3) we interact with an entity which shares neither *Bedeutung* nor *Sinn* with us, and whose *Bedeutung* and *Sinn* we must work out for ourselves, in the preservation of it. Such preservation is then (in my sense) "poetic," and this type of communication is across worlds, or "interworldly."

There is a problem with Heidegger's account of interworldly communication. He introduced it, we saw, in order to articulate our experience of works of art. But it seems to make no sense to *deny* a common understanding to the work of art and its beholders, as (3) does, because it makes no sense to *attribute* any sort of understanding or interpretation to anything but a human being. Does a work of art "interpret" the world differently than we do? Heidegger thus encounters a question we saw to be troublesome for Hegel: that of how the experience of a work of art can be an interpersonal interaction. In one sense, the answer is clear. The preservers of the work interact with one another in preserving the work. But they do so, it seems, only by virtue of common *Bedeutungen*: those opened up by the work itself, and those of the ordinary world out of which they confront it. Such communication, then, would fall under (1) or (2) and would not be a distinctive form of interaction.

Thus, if a truly novel, interworldly form of communication is present in "The Origin of the Work of Art," it must be found in the interaction of the preservers with the work itself rather than with each other. Heidegger's reference to the art work's essential "createdness" provides a clue to understanding the interpersonal character of this interaction. Because the work of art brings earth into world, we may say, it is essentially something that has been produced by human beings. This is what makes it a "work" at all (*UKW* 46/58). But the nature of the work of art is ultimately to be understood in terms of the interplay of earth and world, not as the creation of a single artist (*UKW* 48f/60). The artist, therefore, can signify aesthetically only insofar as he enters into that interplay. He must be defined in terms of his work rather than vice versa. The result of this is that, while it is essential to the work of art that somebody has made it, in a sense it does not matter who:

> Precisely where the artist and the process and the circum-
> stances of the genesis of the work of art remain unknown, this
> thrust, "*that* it is," of createdness, emerges into view most
> purely from the work" (*UKW* 53/65).

This does not mean that the work of art cannot put us in touch, as it were, with the artist as a concrete human individual. But the individuality of the artist is aesthetically defined through the concrete individuality of the art work, not the other way around. The work of art "makes the creators possible in their nature" (*UKW* 58/71). Aesthetic experience is not dialogical, then, in the sense that the artwork is taken as an utterance of the artist, so that in appreciating the work we really communicate with its maker. Rather, the artwork itself, not the artist, is the true partner in aesthetic dialogue. If the artist was for Hegel a mere "corridor" through which absolute Spirit found expression (*Aesth.* 400/298), for Heidegger he is a "self-destructing passageway" for the creation of the work (*UKW* 29/40). In such locutions, Heidegger tries, as did Hegel, to construe aesthetic experience as both the experience of a particular type of object, a work of art, and as essentially dialogical in nature. Unlike Hegel, Heidegger will overcome this tension. "From a Dialogue on Language," as we shall see, will detach the structures of interworldly communication brought forward in "The Origin of the Work of Art" from the work of art itself.

Like other writings of the later, post-*Kehre* Heidegger, this dialogue can be viewed as an exercise that is itself similar in some ways to the preservation of works of art. In such works as *Holzwege*, Heidegger undertakes to restore to their originary meaning the thoughts of ancient Greek philosophers and modern ones like Descartes, Kant, Hegel, and Nietzsche—all thinkers who lived in different historical periods from each other and from Heidegger himself. He also writes, e.g., in *Unterwegs zur Sprache*, on the poetic "worlds" of Hölderlin, George, Trakl, and Rilke. These various interpretations do not result from the application of a single method, in the sense of a procedure aimed to bring about intended results; but they all exhibit a certain structure, which I will call the "way structure."[1] The very titles of some of Heidegger's later books (*Wegmarken, Holzwege, Unterwegs zur Spache*) testify to this, and as early as *Being and Time* Heidegger had said that Dasein is always, in a sense, "underway" (*SZ* 79). His own works thus illustrate the declaration that "the lasting element in thinking is the way" (*FDL* 99/12). Ways, whatever other features they possess, can be considered as having beginnings, middles, and ends. We shall examine these three elements in "From a Dialogue on Language."

This particular work is chosen because in it Heidegger engages in dialogue, not with someone who lived long ago and who is available only through his writings, but with a living person actually present. The specifically communicative structures of the encounter thus lie closer to the surface of the text. But they derive, as I will argue, from the dialogue's basic character as a way and, therefore, are common to all the interpretative writings of the later Heidegger—a fact the reader may verify at his or her leisure.[2]

"From a Dialogue on Language" explores language in terms of what I have called interworldly communication. It develops a basic theme of "The Origin of the Work of Art": that of the preservation of the art work through interaction between its world and a radically different one. But though the whole dialogue is inspired by an attempt to understand the nature of art (*FDL* 86/2), it treats no individual art work at length, making only a few remarks on the film *Rashomon* and on Japanese No plays (*FDL* 104ff/16ff). Nor does it say much about "art" in general, or even "aesthetics," except to note that Western aesthetics rests on the metaphysical distinction of the sensible and supersensible realms (*FDL* 86f, 101ff/2f, 14ff). In sum, aesthetic experience is here taken, not in its own right as a way of responding to a work of art, but as a clue to the broader nature of language itself. This approach, though not that of "The Origin of the Work of Art," is suggested by it. For we saw that it asserted that all language is primordially poetry (cf. *UKW* 61/73f). It would follow that subsequent investigation of the nature of language can proceed only by investigating poetry. Following out that investigation will also, I have suggested, overcome the problems involved in construing the experience of a work of art as essentially dialogical in character. Once again, then, we have a "demarcation" in Heidegger's thought: a new departure from an old approach, which may or may not be consistent with that approach but is clearly suggested by it.

The climax of the dialogue is the Japanese's characterization of language as *Koto-ba*. This phrase is itself, clearly, no work of art; it is introduced as simply the Japanese word for language (*FDL* 142/45). It translates partially as "petals that stem from Koto" (*FDL* 144/47), and thus is hardly a *conceptual* description or definition of language as a substance with attributes (*FDL* 142/45). Nor is it a "serviceable" clarification (*FDL* 153/54), in the sense that it will of itself enable those who understand it to exchange information about language. The term must therefore, as we will see in more detail, be used aesthetically, i.e., to open up a new context of significance for the person who encounters it. This person is the "Inquirer," clearly Heidegger himself. The context that the term opens up for him is the whole "East Asian" experience of the nature of language (*FDL* 94, 113/8, 23). Thus, it is a Japanese word—not a work of art—that brings Heidegger into confrontation with what is for him a radically new context of significance. The same is true reciprocally for the German words Heidegger explains for the Japanese (*FDL* 145f/47). The dialogue then reaches a level on which, for Heidegger, *all* language is aesthetic. Such aesthetic dialogue, I will now argue, exhibits what I have called the "way-structure."

The Beginning

I have suggested that "From a Dialogue on Language" implicitly demarcates itself from the problematic approach of "The Origin of the Work of Art." The dialogue begins by explicitly distancing—demarcating—itself from another past failure. The Japanese, who is not identified here,[3] has come to Germany to try to gain better understanding of the aesthetic concepts his own teacher, Count Kuki, had learned in Germany and had tried to apply to Japanese art (*FDL* 86/2). Kuki's attempt had failed, in that he had been unable to explain clearly to his Japanese students the meanings of the German terms (*FDL* 95/9). Kuki had failed at the other end as well. Even his main teacher in Germany, Heidegger, had been unable to understand the Japanese aesthetic terms, which he thinks have significance only within the Japanese world, or "house of Being" (*FDL* 89/4f).

Kuki's failure was partly the fault of his students. They were too desirous of "handy information," of certain knowledge and clear explanations (*FDL* 100/3). Such explanations could not be given in Japanese, presumably for the same reason the Japanese terms could not be translated into German: the languages are, we may say, fundamentally incommensurable (*FDL* 94f, 101/8, 13). The basic words of each language do not stand in one-to-one correspondence with basic words of the other, and neither do the words which could explicate those basic terms. Each language appears then to be totally closed in on itself, with no entry point for terms from the other. The demarcation thus turns on the mutual incommensurability of ordinary languages, a characteristic which—partly as a result of Kuki's failure—the Japanese has now recognized. We can understand this sort of incommensurability as follows.

It is a matter of debate whether the differing syntaxes of ordinary languages can be reduced to a single overall paradigm, or whether, if not, they somehow cause speakers of those languages to "view the world" differently.[4] But Heidegger here engages a different issue, one about which there is, I think, less room for debate. It is perfectly possible, in principle, for languages to have the same *syntax* but wholly different *vocabularies*. Scholarly or professional articles, though nominally written in English or some other vernacular, often approximate this.[5] A language in which no word had the same meaning as any other word in another language would suffice to produce the kind of misunderstandings Kuki encountered, issues of syntax entirely aside.

The languages people actually speak exhibit such lexical incommensurability. Though terms for some natural kinds appear to be cross-cultural (like "bird" and "horse"), other seemingly similar ones ("poodle," "Percheron") do not. Once we leave the relatively small portion of a language's vocabulary devoted to such terms, the incommensurability increases. Words for actions, for example, tend to vary widely from culture to culture: "walk," for example, has no single equivalent in German. The closest one can come is *zu Fuß gehen,* "to go on foot," or simply *gehen,* "to go." Similarly, English speakers, when they learn French, are taught that *manger* means "to eat," and *boire,* "to drink." Though this works in the vast majority of cases, it remains what Heidegger will call a "foreground" or "superficial" assimilation of the terms (*FDL* 87/3). *Boire* actually means "to ingest a liquid"; *manger,* "to ingest a solid." The English distinction is quite different: "to eat" means to ingest one's main nourishment, whether this be in solid or liquid form. One test case for this is an infant at the breast: in English she can quite well be described as "eating"; in French, she *boît.* Similarly, when the child gets a little older, her mother may tell her to *bois ta soupe,* which can only be translated as "eat your soup."[6] If such mundane activities as eating and walking have words "accrue" to them so differently in languages as closely related as English, French, and German, we can appreciate Kuki's problems in trying to explain German philosophical terms to Japanese students. If language is, in Heidegger's phrase, the "house of Being," then it seems clear a "dialogue from house to house remains nearly impossible" (*FDL* 90/5).

Kuki's project of applying Western categories to Japanese art made certain presuppositions. It assumed, first, that both types of art are fundamentally the same, for otherwise the undertaking would be without point. On the other hand, it also presumed that Western and Eastern ideas *about* art differ: otherwise the undertaking would be needless. What Kuki intended to do, then, was share the Western understanding of art with his fellow Japanese. His intention thus fits model (2) of communication given above. Beginning with a shared context of significance (the phenomenon of art itself) and with unshared understandings of that significance (the differing interpretations of art in Eastern and Western cultures), Kuki sought to achieve a common (or homogenized) understanding. The problem was that the two languages themselves resisted such homogenization—even though their speakers desired it (*FDL* 94f, 100/8f, 13). Kuki had, like his pupil Tezuka, "wandered between the languages" (*FDL* 115/24); he was to some extent at home in both. But his Japanese students and his Western teacher, bound to their respective languages, simply could not understand his explanations of terms from the other.

In spite of this past failure and the problems it raises, Heidegger and

Tezuka undertake a dialogue "from house to house," apparently with some success. But the failed dialogue of the past is essential to their undertaking, since it provides a concrete case from which to investigate the broader question of the natures of German and Japanese, and of language altogether. Thus, the *failure* to reach a common understanding—the absence of common *Bedeutungen,* to say nothing of common *Sinne*—demarcates the situation at the beginning of the dialogue from Kuki's previous attempt. By that demarcation, the nature of art, as well as model (2) of communication itself, is shown to have parametric status: communication can, perhaps, take other forms, and there is, possibly, no such thing as "art." Thus disclosing parameters as parameters, the dialogue is situating from the start.

The Middle

The dialogue moves on from that beginning in an apparently random way. Heidegger and Tezuka reminisce about their mutual friend Kuki and then begin a series of discussions of various Japanese and German words. As in an actual conversation, the discussions tend to run together and to be accompanied by less scholarly meanderings. But a rough list of them, and of the pages they cover, shows two interesting things:

hermeneutics	95-98/9–12
iki, iro, ku	100-102/13–15
gesture	107-109/16–19
Being	109f/19–21
language, hints	113-118/22–28
hermeneutics	121f/28–30
relation	125f/32f
expression	128-131/34–36
appearance	132-135/36–40
ku	137/41
iki	139-142/42–45
koto-ba	142-145/45–47
Saying	145-151/47–54

First, the discussions of individual words cover almost the entire course of the dialogue. They are interspersed with reflections by the interlocutors about what they are doing, usually phrased in terms of the dialogue's "path."[7] The first nine pages are devoted to reminiscences of Count Kuki and to general considerations. Thus, we may say that the actual progression or "way" of the dialogue consists in a series of meditations on individual words.

Second, that progression appears to be entirely random. Words occur and recur without any obvious reason why they should occupy the places that they do. But it does not follow that the dialogue is disunified; its unity is expressed in two stages. On pages 111f/21f, the interlocutors notice, to their own surprise, that their seemingly random conversation has up to that point been focused on the single problem of the Being (or nature) of language. Heidegger then asks Tezuka for the Japanese word for language, which the latter hesitates to give. His hesitation continues to page 142/45, where he finally gives the Japanese word, *Koto-ba*. After that the discussion turns to Heidegger's own word, "Saying," which is seen to have great similarities with that Japanese word. The dialogue thus "comes to rest" in these two names, to which its previous development has—apparently unbeknownst to the speakers—been directed.

The dialogue thus portrays a series of meditations on individual words which, independently of the intentions of the participants in the dialogue, somehow "homes in" on the meaning of a single (or, here, because of the two languages, double) name. Because it results in a name, we may say, the dialogue is an instance of what Heidegger in "The Origin of the Work of Art" calls "projective saying," or poetry (*UKW* 61/73). It is in the final unification of what first appear to be random meditations on words, then, that the dialogue reaches the basic, poetic level of language. We can understand that level better by asking what gives the conversation this peculiar structure.

The dialogue's progression is, first, not the product of the participants' conscious efforts to stick to a single topic; otherwise they would not be surprised to discover the narrow focus of their meditations. It cannot be the product of an unconscious effort, in a broadly Freudian sense, either. On that sort of model, a repressed drive can direct the responses of an individual in free association; and Heidegger and Tezuka certainly seem, throughout the dialogue, to be engaged in some sort of free association. But on the Freudian model, the analyst refrains from all reaction and commentary to the analysand's utterances and would hardly enter into free association himself. Here we have two people whose "free associations" somehow harmonize into a larger whole. The content which is ultimately expressed cannot, therefore, be viewed as "belonging" to a single mind. It must be something intersubjectively accessible.

The unifying force in the dialogue also cannot be interpreted as some sort of common cultural preconception embedded in ordinary language and articulated by the participants, the way the interlocutors in a Platonic dialogue clarify the nature of the Greek language which they speak, because here two unrelated, mutually incommensurable languages are dealt with and ultimately harmonized. Whatever is focusing the dialogue must then be, not only intersubjective, but intercultural as well.

We might, finally, suspect that what is being articulated is some sort of universal structure of human reason itself, and that the dialogue moves toward formulating it in a way somehow similar to the progression of Hegel's *Phenomenology* as it leads inexorably to the decisive formulation of the universal in absolute knowing. But this, too, cannot be. In contrast to the narrative of the *Phenomenology,* where every stage can in principle be precisely located as part of a transparent dialectical development, we cannot see why, in "From a Dialogue on Language," just *these* topics, considered in just *this* order, arrive at the result they arrive at—though we can see *that* they do so. To call such a progression "rational" would be to say that the operation of reason itself cannot be understood: that reason, which supposedly enables us to understand other things, is itself unintelligible. Though not necessarily un-Heideggerean, that would be a very nontraditional use of "reason." It also would not explain why something we cannot understand or control should be called either "structured" or "human."

The only conclusion is that something radically other than the interlocutors—other to them at least insofar as they are rational beings—is responsible for the direction that the dialogue takes. Heidegger characterizes this "otherness" (*FDL* 100/13) as an "indefinable something [which] displays its gathering force ever more luminously in the course of the dialogue." Something—the essence of language—is (so to speak) moving toward speech, as the dialogue homes in on the two key words that express it. The function of the interlocutors in such a development is then not to "pump each other" for their opinions and information, but to "release into the Open whatever might be said" (*FDL* 123/30).

Heidegger's use of the term "Open" here enables us to relate what happens in this dialogue to the earth/world schema of "The Origin of the Work of Art," where the Open was identified as world (*UKW* 34, 37f/45, 48f). When the essence of language (if we may call it that) is given the two names "Saying" and *Koto-ba,* it takes its place within the contexts of significance the names open up. Prior to receiving those names, the essence of language was "pre-significant"—latent within the meanings of words like "hermeneutics," *iki,* and "Being," in somewhat the way that a statue is latent within the piece of marble the sculptor has chosen. In view of their cooperative efforts, Heidegger and Tezuka are able to articulate that pre-significance, each in his own language. To put the matter in the terms of *Being and Time,* the two speakers participate in the self-revelation of a phenomenon. To put it in my own terms, they participate in the clarification of a parameter—the "essence of language" itself. If criticizable (an issue I will not discuss here), their dialogue would amount to an exercise in situating reason.

The End

The dialogue's final names, "Saying" and *Koto-ba* , are thus grounded on, or situated by, the terms previously discussed in it. "Saying," for example, is an allowing-to-*appear*, not a human *expression*, which *hints* at man's *relation* to the Two-fold as adumbrated from a *hermeneutical* perspective, and so on back through the dialogue (*FDL* 145/47f). "Saying" and *Koto-ba* can only have the *Bedeutungen* they do on the basis of the meanings earlier established. Conversely, we can only begin to understand those meanings, and their presence in the dialogue, when we see how they make possible the final naming of the essence of language. As the Greek temple makes the landscape and living things around it "enter into their distinctive shapes" (*UKW* 31/42), so the final words of the dialogue clarify and redefine the linguistic terrain that precedes and situates them. In that sense, the dialogue "comes to rest" in those final names.

This shows one further major difference between "From a Dialogue on Language" and "The Origin of the Work of Art." Though Heidegger makes a few passing references to the "worlds" of the interlocutors (cf. *FDL* 89/4), he never refers to the domain of pre-significance as "earth." It is rather the "hints" and "traces" he finds in language.[8] Nature, and with it the concrete work of art, has thus ceased to be central to his concerns. Language, in the peculiarly "creative" sense which interests him, exhausts the field of investigation. In and of language, "From a Dialogue on Language" does not attempt, as *Being and Time* did, to *describe* the general structures and ultimate conditions of the self-showing of phenomena (cf. *FDL* 149f/50f). Rather, the dialogue *is* the self-showing of the phenomenon, the gradual self-manifestation of the essence of language. It is because that self-manifestation is unique that the words in which it occurs are unique, then, and are relative to—situated in—the dialogue in which they occur. The dialogue has itself provided their meanings.

In addition to situating previous words in the dialogue itself, *Koto-ba* constitutes a new and unique intrusion of pre-significance into German discourse. For to join together the word for "petals" with the highly abstract (and perhaps unfathomable) meaning of *Koto* is unheard of in German. Coming from another language, the phrase opens up possibilities for future thought in German; indeed, together with Heidegger's own term, "Saying," it is "inexhaustible" for such purposes (*FDL* 144/47). With their *Bedeutungen* now articulated, these words can form a new domain within which new significance can take shape. When the dialogue comes to rest, then, its way is only provisionally over. Its conclusion does not close off future topics for thought, in the way a definitive conclusion in the natural sciences can put an end to discussion about a topic. Rather, the dialogue has no firm results. It settles nothing but opens up new possibilities for thinking.

Heidegger expresses as much by referring to "Saying" and *Koto-ba* as "hints" (*winken, FDL* 145/47)." Hinting," the dialogue suggests in its brief discussion of this crucial term (*FDL* 114-117/24–26), is the basic character of the word as such. Understood as hints, words are completely nonmetaphysical and belong to the primordial nature of language as "Saying." They are, then, not to be viewed in terms of the metaphysical dichotomy of sensible and supersensible (for which cf. *FDL* 86f, 101f/2,14). They are not sensible objects (sounds or marks) which convey clear (or unclear) conceptual meanings but are "riddlesome" or enigmatic. They do not try to convey information univocally but to orient us on more basic levels. They "beckon to us; they warn us away. They beckon away, to that from which they unexpectedly bear upon us." In this, hints function as "signs" do in *Being and Time*. If Dasein is, in the words of *Being and Time,* "always underway," (*SZ* 79), it is the function of writings like "From a Dialogue on Language" to help Dasein along its path—insofar as its path is in fact one of "thinking"—by opening up new regions into which thinking might go.

A road sign, pointing in one direction, does not tell the traveler to go in that direction. That is a matter for the traveler himself to decide, depending upon his own projects and circumstances. What the sign does do, however, is open up the terrain in that direction for the traveler. It directs his attention to it. A word encountered on the way of Heideggerean thinking opens up further terrain which is linguistic in nature. It presents further words through which thinking can travel. The shape of the terrain, and the pathways that may be taken into it or avoided by future travelers, is not laid out definitively by the hint, which remains enigmatic. Rather, it is presented as something for other thinkers to develop in their own ways. Because its meaning is left open for the reader of the dialogue in this way, the dialogue itself is an instance of what I will call poetic language. Since the hints of the dialogue—the words it traverses—are its basic level, we may say that situating reason, in Heidegger's account as in Hegel's, begins poetically.

The final words of the dialogue are situated by earlier words, as the universal articulated in Hegel's concept of "reconciliation" is situated by the specific contents it organizes. But those words do not stand, as the universal in Hegel's concept of "reconciliation" stands, as the conclusion to a narrative. Rather, they sum up one approach, from which others may one day take off, demarcating themselves from it as it demarcates itself from earlier approaches. If reconciliation revealed the contents of externalization to be narratable parameters, the kind of thinking Heidegger undertakes in his later essays shows parameters to be demarcatable. Thus, for Heidegger, demarcation takes the place that narrative occupied for Hegel. As a mode of articulation which shows that what it articulates can be other than it is, it is the way parameters get construed *as* parameters. When in part three I show the roots of this in ordinary language, we will have the non-Hegelian type of poetic interaction I call "abnormal."

The Limits of Aesthetic Interaction

"From a Dialogue on Language" not only contains dislocations, it is in a sense dislocated itself. We saw Heidegger maintain in *Being and Time* that words are not to be understood as things merely present-at-hand, and the basic words in this dialogue do not function as such entities either. Entities ready-to-hand, for their part, are encountered "within the world" in terms of their contexts of involvement. They can, therefore, only be understood by people who share those contexts. The Japanese words discussed in the dialogue do have such a "context of involvement." This is, ultimately, the whole Japanese language in which they have their distinctive roles to play, and the Japanese way of life which those roles help to formulate and constitute. But that context is not made very clear to Heidegger. The only specific information he gets about Japanese life and language is the meanings of four words and some remarks about No-plays and the movie *Rashomon*. A good novel, to say nothing of a work of history or a travelogue, would teach him much more about the Japanese as a people. Tezuka, for his part, is in Germany and knows German: he understands Heidegger's world to a broader extent than Heidegger understands his. But the dialogue hardly teaches him very much new about what it really means to be a German in 1953.

The fact that the German and the Japanese stand within two different worlds or, as Heidegger puts it here, two different "houses of Being" (*FDL* 90/5), means for him that they *cannot* understand one another's worlds. In another context, that of understanding the Greek world, Heidegger speaks of

> the futile intention of reckoning up historically, and that means philologically and psychologically, what once was really present in the man named "Anaximander of Miletus" as the situation of his representation of the world.[9]

If that reservation holds for the Greeks, who are among Heidegger's own intellectual ancestors, it may be presumed to hold as well for the

Japanese world.[10] It follows that Heidegger (and perhaps Tezuka) cannot hope to understand the beings ready-to-hand within one another's worlds, including the words in which information about those worlds gets communicated. And the conclusion to be drawn here is, I think, that such understanding is simply not what the dialogue aims at. Its purpose is rather to understand man's linguistic encounter with the self-revelation of phenomena that is Being—and to understand the Other, one's interlocutor, *only insofar as he embodies such an encounter.* Thus Heidegger, like the Western reader with no background information, understands Tezuka out of his dialogue with Tezuka itself—just as, for Heidegger, we are to understand the artist strictly in terms of the work of art he produces. The rest of Tezuka's concrete human existence—and the rest of the concrete Japanese world—do not signify for such understanding.

But to understand the Japanese and his world as embodying a linguistic encounter with Being is for Heidegger not simply to understand one restricted aspect of them; it is to understand their basic nature itself. In his study of Nietzsche, Heidegger writes as follows about the nature of the ego:

> Through dwelling in the region of the Unconcealed, man belongs within a fixed periphery of what is present to him. Through his belonging within this periphery, a limit is taken over against what is not present. Here, therefore, man's self becomes determined as this or that ego, through the limitation of itself to the surrounding Unconcealed. The limited belonging within the periphery of the Unconcealed co-constitutes the selfhood of man.[11]

If we interpret "what is present" in this passage as words, then we see that it is of the nature of man, for Heidegger, to dwell within a limited environment of word meanings. No language has the absolute lexicon or can express everything. Concomitantly, no human being can "transcend" his particular world, or mother tongue, in the sense of entering into another world or language and understanding it as those who live in it do: or rather, no one can do that without having his personal identity transformed. But all languages, through their very limitations, are related to something which is other than they: to the ongoing self-presentation of radically new phenomena. This, then, is presumably what Heidegger refers to as the source of language which "remains concealed from both language worlds" (*FDL* 94/8) and yet is "the Same" in both (*FDL* 112/22).

The limited understanding we can have of the words of our interlocutor in such interworldly dialogue, to which Count Kuki unwillingly testified, is thus for Heidegger a *precondition* (not in my sense a condition) of aesthetic interaction. For it means that we can understand the words of our interlocutor neither as entities present-at-hand nor as ready-to-hand. We *can* understand them, however, immanently to the communicative encounter in which they occur. In the present case, this means understanding the key words of the dialogue, listed above, in terms of their roles in bringing to pass the unique self-manifestation of the essence of language that constitutes Heidegger's encounter with Tezuka. But to understand words in terms of such a self-manifestation is precisely to understand them in terms of their relation to the primordial event of Being, which is not part of any one world but is "the Same" in all determinate worlds. And this is to understand the fundamental reality of our interlocutor, who is himself an encounter with Being from a world other than our own.

As Walter Biemel has noted, communication in *Being and Time* is possible only on the basis of a shared world. It "does not [originatively] create community, but presupposes a lived community which through communication merely experiences its explicit articulation."[12] The type of communication presented in "From a Dialogue on Language" also presupposes shared worlds—but not worlds shared by the interlocutors themselves. It presupposes, rather, the dwelling of each interlocutor in a different language or "house of Being."

Such communication, like authenticity in *Being and Time,* is incompatible with intraworldly dialogue, which presupposes and reproduces the particular structures of the world which "governs" it. In order to confront a different world, then, the thinker must withdraw from his own. As in an encounter with a work of art, he must cease for a while to engage in the kinds of interaction for which his own world is the Open and basis. In this, however, he only enters more deeply into his own nature. For he is opened out into a dialogue which itself brings its participants together in a community. They are persons who dwell in different worlds, but who belong together in the opening-up of Being—who "dwell in the claim of the Two-fold" of Being and beings (*FDL* 135f/ 40). The question of the significance of Heidegger's thought for political theory, then, will ultimately be that of what sort of difference such interworldly communication, rarified and special as it seems to be, can make to more mundane forms of human interaction.

I have suggested that interaction for Heidegger is in general an interplay of meaning and significance, of *Sinn* and *Bedeutung*, in their Heideggerean acceptations. This means that the meaning of an utterance in dialogue is determined by the speaker only in the first of the three Heideggerean models of communication listed at the beginning of this chapter. In the second model, the meaning is determined in part by the hearer, who applies his own *Sinn* to the *Bedeutungen* of which the utterance is compounded. Because the utterance is understood by its hearers in ways the speaker cannot predict, it can be said to "escape" the speaker—just as an utterance in Hegelian externalization was understood by its hearers in ways differing from how the speaker intended it. As with Hegel, this type of interaction is not for Heidegger truly emancipatory: not because it denies the individual *Sinne* which the speaker and the hearer both have (as does type 1), but because it remains bound to the more basic parameters of the world.

As for Hegel, emancipatory interaction is found on a further level, that of "aesthetic" dialogue. This level is not, however, one on which individual *Sinne* are organized and harmonized by a concrete universal, so that the individual becomes "reconciled" with himself and his particular culture. To function on the level of aesthetic dialogue for Heidegger means to leave behind one's concrete situations and commitments, one's own world as a whole, in order to enter into something which cannot be understood in terms of that world. Aesthetic emancipation for Heidegger is just as much a "discarding" of the previous self, together with one's own concrete *Sinne*, as externalization was for Hegel. Only after the new significance, with which the hearer is presented, has been articulated and understood—has "come to rest" in a name—can it have a *Sinn* for an individual. Only then can it present him with concrete possibilities for living a transformed life, or for recommiting himself to his present life. Hence, aesthetic interaction, unlike other types, is not an interplay of *Sinn* and *Bedeutung*. It makes no reference to *Sinn* at all.

Aesthetic Interaction and Emancipation

Aesthetic dialogue for Heidegger is thus situating: first because it begins from previous dialogue, particularly, as we have seen, from dialogue which has in some respect failed. Insofar as it seeks to redeem such failure, it takes the presuppositions of that previous approach (even when they are as basic as the metaphysical distinction between sensible and supersensible) to be susceptible of change, and hence as parameters. Such dialogue is also situating in that it meditates, not timeless truths, but the concrete words of a particular language. Insofar as those words take up new meanings within the dialogue, they themselves are revealed to be changeable parameters. And insofar as they are, on their basic level, not merely parameters but, in Heidegger's term, "hints" capable of orienting a hearer along any of several paths of thought, they function as (in my sense) "poetic." The problem now is to discover how aesthetic dialogue, given its limitations as analyzed above, can in any concrete sense be emancipatory. I will proceed here in two steps. First, I will analyze in more detail the way in which such dialogue frees us from our world, now conceived as the overarching contexts given us by the language we speak. Then I will ask after the ways this view of liberation can be made more concrete.

"The Origin of the Work of Art" presented the basic limits on human life in the "naturalistic" vocabulary of "earth." The present text construes them as the limits of linguistic understanding, and this enables us to see in more detail how the language we speak puts us under the domination of a particular world. For a language is able, as "From a Dialogue on Language" has shown, to articulate some things and not others and tends to "foreground," or direct our attention to, what it can articulate. As we saw previously, for example, any name in natural language tells the speakers of that language that its referent is important. To the extent that two languages tend to foreground the same sorts of thing, they share contexts of significance, or *Bedeutungen,* and can serve as the basis for the first two types of communication in the Heideggerean hierarchy. "From a Dialogue on Language" does not deny that this happens, even for languages as different as German and Japanese; but when it does, communication between the worlds instituted by those languages remains "foreground" (*vordergründig*) in character (*FDL* 87/3).[13] Insofar as we limit ourselves to such forms of interaction, the particular foregrounding action of the language we ourselves speak remains presupposed, not examined; and insofar as the overall context within which this foregrounding takes place is world itself, we can say that we remain dominated by our world. In sum: the limits which ultimately determine human social structures are themselves instituted by world and cannot therefore be uncovered by language insofar as it remains world bound.

But these limits can be elicited, though as we have seen only partially and provisionally, through dialogue with other worlds. By experiencing articulate contexts of significance which do not belong to our own world, we learn what our world is not—and learn it in an articulate way. Thus, in "From a Dialogue on Language," Tezuka comes to learn what, at the beginning, he only suspected: that his world, unlike the Western world, is not organized in terms of a basic dichotomy of sensible and supersensible, with the elements of the latter arranged hierarchically (*FDL* 86f, 100-103/2, 14–16). Similarly, Heidegger is confirmed in his suspicion that those two basic structures of his own world, while historically given and valid within it, are not themselves ultimate (*FDL* 109, 147/20, 48f). He is "emancipated" from metaphysics, we may say, in the sense that he comes to understand it, not as the neutral view of the cosmic order that it claims to be, but as a set of basic parameters of his own world. The emancipation from that world, in turn, undermines its legitimacy. Governed as we are by incompletely known limits, the hidden parameters of Being or the "hidden rules" of Saying,[14] we will never have language or nature entirely under our control. It follows that we are always open, whether we like it or not, to the possible advent of radical newness. We will never be able to set up structures, including social structures, which are anything more than provisional. Heidegger's thought remains as I characterized it in the preceding chapter: implacably subversive.

Let us imagine how such subversion might actually work. We saw in the last chapter that human societies are grounded on certain "earthly" parameters. Two of the basic parameters of Heidegger's own Western world, we have seen, are mentioned in "From a Dialogue on Language" in the form of basic principles of Western metaphysics. These are the distinctions between sensible and supersensible, on the one hand, and that of hierarchical organization, on the other (*FDL* 86f, 101f/2,14). These parameters can be applied to social phenomena. We could read the former one, for example, into Marx's fundamental distinction between mental and physical labor.[15] The latter could be taken in the spirit of contemporary management theorists who advocate the participatory planning and basic flexibility of Japanese corporate structures, as opposed to the quasi-military hierarchies which characterize many Western business firms.[16] Aesthetic dialogue teaches us, then, that the basic metaphysical principles on which such concrete social structures are founded are mere parameters, and that other societies—such as Japan—have different ones. It would enable us, then, to question and challenge certain of our own social structures. In this way, an emancipation from the limits of one's world could bring about as well an emancipation from political and social structures inhering in that world.

But this kind of analysis, showing Western economic structures to be concrete applications of fundamental principles of Western metaphysics and opening them to comparison with analogous components of the Japanese world, would be an inner-worldly analysis proceeding on the basis of what is gained from aesthetic dialogue. It would not itself be an instance of such dialogue. And for a person, or group of people, to take such analysis as the basis for action to change those structures would mean for those people to take the analysis as offering concrete possibilities for them in their current situations. It would be a matter, not of *Bedeutungen* at all, but of their individual *Sinne*. That Heidegger does not discuss such possibilities—does not, in fact, refer to *Sinne* at all here—is, I suggest, no accident. For the radicalization of the self that we saw operating in aesthetic interaction for Heidegger was a leaving-behind of all levels that were not basic, of all the concrete structures of a particular world, in order to experience an alternative that could not be articulated within those structures.

Nothing in Heidegger's writings, however, forbids the kind of concretization envisioned here. "From a Dialogue on Language" shows how a particular type of interaction can elicit the basic parameters of a world—and hence of a political system. Only such elicitation, however, would allow us either to commit ourselves to our world anew, escape it entirely, or introduce into it structures we have learned to understand from our encounter with another world.

Indeed, such possibilities are adumbrated by Heidegger's earlier works. Insofar as an encounter with another world leads us to recommit ourselves to our own world more intelligently, it can be viewed as a development of the "inner-worldly" view of freedom advanced in *Being and Time*.[17] But it does not return us to our everyday world by eliciting from us an abstract or inarticulate resolve for it. It shows us, rather, and in a determinate way, what that world is not, and hence, with equal determinateness, what it is. In "The Origin of the Work of Art," the work of art, understood as the irruption into a preexistent world of a radically new context of significance, takes us out of our world by introducing us to a new one, which we can dwell within and preserve. The same would presumably be true of the kind of interaction evidenced in "From a Dialogue on Language." It is in principle possible for the "Inquirer" to be so motivated by the wisdom of the Japanese world that he commits himself to that world by moving to Japan, learning the language, and so on. And the middle case, presumably, would likewise be possible: introducing structures of the Japanese world, uncovered by aesthetic dialogue, into our own world. In all three cases, we see that aesthetic dialogue can reveal to us a determinate alternative to our present world. This is something that intraworldly communication, bound to the contexts of significance that make up a particular world, cannot do.

But in all these cases, aesthetic interaction does not function as *intrinsically* emancipatory. It furnishes only a basis for concrete emancipation from the structures of our world. Aside from what we have called its function of revealing the "basic parameters" of our worlds *as* parameters, and in that sense "liberating" us from them, aesthetic communication has only very limited applications to the concrete problems of life in the world. Heidegger views aesthetic dialogue as, in my sense, "poetic." Developing those views into a more concrete account of intrinsically emancipatory interaction will mean, not making the kind of analysis I have envisioned here, but detaching aesthetic dialogue from its concern with basic meanings at the expense of others.

Finally, any attempt to take Heideggerean ideas in these (or any other) directions runs into the basic question of the extent to which the contemporary Western world is still "metaphysical" at all, or whether we are already, in Heidegger's terms, in a epoch of fundamental historical transition.[18] My concrete account of poetic interaction, then, will not be exempt from the demand to show whether and how it is "beyond metaphysics." The relation of metaphysics to poetic interaction is an antagonistic one and will be a central theme of the following narrative.

Part Two

Narrative

Introduction

Both Hegel and Heidegger, as I have analyzed them, are interactionist philosophers. They discuss types of human interaction which are directed upon freedom and in which freedom in some sense is actually achieved: intrinsically emancipatory interaction. For Hegel, my dialogue with the work of art not only clarifies parameters as parameters, but also harmonizes my various sensory and intellectual capacities over time. Giving me a "consolidated self," it liberates me both from the inarticulateness of recognition and the alienation of externalization. For Heidegger, aesthetic dialogue clarifies the parametric ways my own language and world articulate reality. It enables me to understand this functioning— constitutive for language and world—concretely and determinately, and, by establishing its parametric nature, undoes its dominion over me.

The articulation of parameters *as* parameters is thus for both thinkers an intrinsically liberating activity. But their views of such articulation, and of the kinds of emancipation it can achieve, remain wholly disparate. For Hegel, as we have seen, we articulate a parameter as a parameter by telling a story about it, and then showing it to have ultimate validity only as a moment in that particular story. The key notion both exhibited in and treated by Hegel's writings is that of narrative: the idea of a rational development unfolding over time. The gradual articulation of the "substance of Spirit" is for him a steady ascent to the universal, and the final liberation in language—reconciliation—comes about when the universal at which the ascent arrives is seen to be, not an independent stratum of thought or of the self which could dictate to lower levels, but simply the basic principle unifying what has gone before. In this, the universal is defined in terms of the narrative which it ends, and it is recuperated for that narrative.

Heidegger's writings treat and exhibit a very different notion: that of demarcation. In his view, the *emancipatory* articulation of a parameter is the experience of something so new and different as to be, like "Saying" and "Koto-ba," incomprehensible. We cannot articulate it in terms of what we already understand, for its newness forbids this. We can only experience it immanently to itself, as a "phenomenon" or a "way," a whole of parts which refer to one another over time. Eventually we can (perhaps) accommodate our speaking and dwelling to this way—or else return to our old ways with a clearer understanding of their limits and of the provisionality of those limits.

A number of questions remain. The first is that of the relation between these two very different forms of intrinsically emancipatory interaction. Both have somehow to do with aesthetics, and I have just referred to both of them as "the articulation of parameters *as* parameters." But neither of these points gives us a very clear notion of the nature of such articulation itself, let alone of how the very different practices dealt with by Hegel and Heidegger are related. Is it possible to find a more articulate set of categories that will accommodate both thinkers? If so, given the degree to which Hegel and Heidegger both consider themselves to respond to and extend the philosophical tradition, whatever common ground they share ought to be buried somewhere in that tradition itself. Before proceeding to my own views, then, I will analyze what I take to be the historical locus of Hegel's and Heidegger's common ground: in Kant's doctrine of the "judgment of taste."

Still other problems will force us back beyond Kant into the history of philosophy. We have seen why Hegel and Heidegger call the kinds of interaction they treat "emancipatory" or "free." But why should we accept their usage? As I noted in the General Introduction, freedom is a concept furnished us, not by the natural world, but by the cultural tradition in which we live. It is itself a parameter, not a necessity or condition. What developments in the philosophical tradition warrant applying it to what Hegel and Heidegger are talking about?

Second: we saw no fewer than three basic domains of modern culture interfering with Hegel's articulation of emancipatory interaction: religion, which truncated it; aesthetics, which hindered it; and politics, which set out to destroy such interaction itself. Similar situations arose for Heidegger (with the exception of religion, on which his views are much more diffuse than those of Hegel). "From a Dialogue on Language" got Heidegger beyond the identification of aesthetic experience with that of a work of art, but the problem of relating emancipatory interaction to the political sphere remained: aesthetic dialogue in Heidegger's presentation was so rarified as to have almost nothing to do with other dimensions of life, and in particular left the political sphere behind. Heidegger, in effect, has taken the opposite tack from Hegel. Where

Hegel reconciles aesthetic experience and politics by disarming the former's radical critique of the state so as to install a superficial harmony between the two points of view, Heidegger demarcates aesthetics and politics from one another so radically as to leave them mutually irrelevant. Before we can solve this persistent problem, we must see how it arose. Why is the political sphere construed as so intolerant of intrinsically emancipatory interaction?

Third: I have not even alluded to Hegel's and Heidegger's complex and iconoclastic views on the nature of truth. That was by design, for I want to ask about intrinsically emancipatory interaction's relation to truth in its ordinary acceptation as the correspondence of a proposition to a state of affairs. Do freedom and truth, viewed interactionally, need each other? Is one of the pair basic to the other? Or are they, as I suggested in the General Introduction, complementary? If so, how is it that truth, not freedom, has come to be viewed as essential to language?

Finally: at the end of chapter 7, I noted that any theory of poetic interaction which presents itself as, even in part, a concretization of Heidegger must clarify its own relation to metaphysics. And it is possible that the three problems I have just mentioned also have something to do with metaphysics. The correspondence theory of truth is often called "metaphysical" in nature, and as we shall see, the state can be construed as, in some respects, a sort of "metaphysical" entity. Is it then metaphysics that has for millenia occluded what I will come to call poetic interaction? What is metaphysics from the point of view of such interaction? How, from that viewpoint, is our current relation to metaphysics to be articulated?

These questions will, in this second part of the book, carry us back to Western philosophy's original presentation of intrinsically emancipatory interaction, in Plato's *Phaedrus*. They will, in the third part, take us forward to Habermas, and eventually to my own views. In ranging so far, I will undertake to narrate what amounts to an entire philosophical tradition—one that has persistently been occluded and marginalized. This tradition sees language (and, indeed, philosophy itself) as connected, not merely to truth, but to freedom; understands the meaning of an utterance to be determined by the hearer, not the speaker; and directs attention to the vocabulary, not the syntax, of language. My narrative of this tradition will hardly be complete. I will selectively analyze just enough of a few of its major stages to enable me to tie them together into a story. The story itself will be presented in the "narratives" which from now on will accompany my analyses. Their overall gist is as follows.

Intrinsically emancipatory interaction was first articulated in Plato's *Phaedrus* to solve problems with the conceptions of freedom treated in earlier dialogues. In the *Phaedrus*, such interaction is understood in terms of Platonic metaphysics, with its dichotomy of Forms and sensibles; but the presentation itself is warranted independently of that metaphysics.

Aristotle's critique of Plato's metaphysics thus does not hit the *Phaedrus*'s account of emancipatory interaction. But Aristotle's formulation of his own metaphysics, based on the category of "substance," occludes it in two ways. First, intrinsically emancipatory interaction cannot be understood in terms of substance. Because metaphysics for Aristotle is "prescriptive" for more concrete investigations, whatever cannot be articulated with reference to the category of substance cannot be rationally articulated at all. On Aristotle's account, then, no interaction is *intrinsically* emancipatory: freedom resides within the individual soul.

Together with this theoretical occlusion of poetic interaction goes a practical proscription of it. For Aristotle conceives of human interaction as dominated by the polis, which has some of the characteristics of a substance and which therefore, as we shall see, cannot tolerate intrinsically emancipatory interaction. As long as human beings seek to organize themselves into such quasi-substances as the ancient polis and the modern state, such interaction is viewed, if at all, as something marginal or even subversive. Hence the problems that Hegel and Heidegger have with the political sphere.

Intrinsically emancipatory interaction begins to be recovered theoretically in Kant's critique of metaphysics, which in his Third Antinomy, as we shall see, directly hits both Plato and Aristotle. The recuperation is carried out, though obscurely, in his *Critique of Judgment*, and has two sides: that of the beautiful and that of the sublime. Hegel's philosophy, I will argue, develops the former side; Heidegger's, the latter.

The elementary form of intrinsically emancipatory interaction is what I call "poetic interaction." Once this has been theoretically retrieved, the problem arises of how to deal with its practical proscription by the modern state. Kant, like Hegel and Heidegger, will face this problem; like them, he will not solve it. The solution will come only in the second volume of Habermas's *Theory of Communicative Action*, which allows, in addition to the state, a second domain of interaction in some respects antithetical to it, which Habermas calls the "life-world."

The outcome of my narrative is that we are, at present, in a situation where the conceptual tools for the final recuperation of at least the elementary form of intrinsically emancipatory interaction are at hand. On the theoretical side, all that we need to do is, first, articulate the insights of Hegel and Heidegger as structures of two species of one genus of ordinary linguistic interchange, without reference to works of art: this will mean articulating intrinsically emancipatory interaction as poetic inter-action. Then we can show such interaction actually to be emancipatory in several traditional senses. On the practical side, we can locate such interaction in the Habermasian life-world and examine its status as pro-viding norms for social and political critique.

Eight

Freedom and Metaphysical Aporia: *Republic* 8 and *Phaedo*

Analysis

Plato's *Phaedrus* portrays a form of interaction that is (as I will argue in chapter 9) intrinsically emancipatory. It is also (as I will argue in chapter 10) an exercise in situating reason whose elementary form is poetic in nature. But the account of intrinsically emancipatory interaction in the *Phaedrus* is advanced to solve problems arising in earlier dialogues, in particular one concerning the nature of freedom.[1] In the *Republic*, as we shall see, Plato argues against the common, "democratic" view of freedom. In the *Phaedo*, he tries to formulate his own alternative, locating freedom in the supersensible realm of the Forms. Like other Forms, freedom ought to have an empirical image in the sensory domain. But problems arise in Plato's attempt to articulate that image, and these call for a fundamental rethinking of the conceptions of "freedom" and "soul" advanced in the earlier dialogues.

In general, Platonic texts speak of freedom (*eleutheria* and derivatives) in the most diverse ways. There is "freedom" from debt and from worry, freedom as opposed to slavery and disgrace, and there are even emancipatory effects to disease. But in their most extended discussion of the term, in *Republic* 8.557b–564a, the texts imply that, in political discourse, "freedom" can have only one meaning: the power to satisfy unnecessary desires.[2] This characterization is drawn from the more general view that freedom is the capacity to do as one likes. Many of the things we want, and want to do, are not required for our life or even our well-being. Desires for them can be diverted or suppressed, and so are unnecessary. But one who is able to do just as he wishes will undertake to satisfy them anyway. Thus, human beings necessarily desire healthful, nourishing food—any human without such desire will not remain human for long. The "free" human being has, in addition to this, the opportunity to eat pastries and such other unhealthy delicacies (cf. *Rep.* 4.404d). The argument thus turns on a commonsense distinction between desires which an individual must satisfy in order to remain alive, and desires which are not so pressing. Its conclusion, however, is not commonsensical at all. If freedom is reducible to the opportunity for eating pastry, it seems to be nothing very estimable.

The condemnation continues with a second argument, on a political level. Freedom is nothing more than the supreme value of a low form of government—democracy. The main problem with democracy is its instability. Because the democratic character is bent on satisfying desires as they arise one after the other, it is unable to make a sustained effort at anything, and its democracy cannot last long. The increasing anarchy of the pursuit of individual objects of desire eventually leads to a desperate instatement of tyranny (*Rep.* 8.562a seqq.). When pursued as a basic social goal, freedom turns into its opposite—which means that it cannot be consistently pursued as such a goal at all.

Each of these arguments against freedom—the one on an individual, the other on a social level—appeals to a distinct type of warrant. In the first argument, it is argued that freedom (a) is nothing other than the opportunity to satisfy unnecessary desires, and as such (b) is not worth having. Discussion of the second of these claims must be deferred for the moment; the first of them is, I noted, derived from the view that freedom is the opportunity to do as one likes. This view is not itself argued within the dialogue and can be sustained only as the formulation of some ulterior agreement on the meaning of the term. This must in turn be either dialectical agreement explicitly achieved elsewhere; or the kind of agreement implicit in common usage; or something in between.

If backed only by such ulterior agreement, part (a) of the argument would not hold for someone who maintained that freedom was something else entirely (such as, for example, the power to make one's actions conform to moral law). Like other dialectical arguments in the Platonic texts, then, this one holds only ad hominem, for those party to certain agreements: here, about the nature of freedom. In this case the parties apparently include, not only Socrates's interlocutors in the *Republic,* but such able advocates of democratic freedom as Callicles (cf. *Gorgias* 491e seqq.) and, Aristotle informs us, the run of people in democratic states (*Pol.* 1310a25–36).

The argument is thus close to ordinary language analysis. By adducing some commonsense premises, Plato transforms the ordinary view that freedom is the power to live as one pleases into his own view of it as the opportunity to satisfy unnecessary desires. In general and with respect to one of their important theorists, the democrats stand refuted by their own words—once part (b) of this first argument goes through.[3]

The second argument asserts a necessary progression from democracy to tyranny via anarchy. If a society gives itself over to attempts to gratify individual desires, it will destroy all social bonds, from which state of affairs it will pull back by instating a tyrant. The "necessity" of this progression is not apparent.[4] A democracy whose members have the power to gratify their unnecessary desires is not, it would seem, inevitably one in which they will actually attempt to do so. And it is possible for a society to disintegrate wholly into anarchy, i.e., simply disappear altogether, rather than instate a tyranny. The first step in the progression is the more important for us: why does the *opportunity* to satisfy unnecessary desires turn into actual *attempts*?

Warrant for this can be supplied if we bear in mind that, in the *Republic*, unnecessary desire is consistently viewed as disorderly motion which comes into the soul from outside—from the object which arouses it.[5] It is a matter of empirical fact (later elevated to a basic truth in Aristotle's impetus physics) that when a moving object impinges on a stationary one, it imparts to it something of its own velocity (cf. for example *Timaeus* 87c–90a). Objects of desire are always around; given the opportunity, they will impinge upon the soul. The "actual attempts" to satisfy them are nothing more than the motions they impart to the soul once they have entered it. The problem with desires, then, is that they are chaotic and disorderly motions in the soul, originating from outside it. The problem with freedom, as the democrats define it, is that it licenses the soul to be ruled by that sort of motion.

The fact that they are disorderly motions suffices, in the Platonic scheme of things, to render desires evil. For all goodness, in Plato's universe, resides in the eternal and unchanging realm of the Forms.[6] Hence, allowing scope for desires beyond what is required for life is also evil. The thesis that desires are disorderly motions in the soul provides warrant as well for part (b) of the first argument, which asserted that, on the individual level, the opportunity to satisfy unnecessary desires was no great boon.

This condemnation of freedom, then, is not a single argument which unfolds within what thinkers of later eras would call social or moral philosophy. One of its warrants—the claim that the ability to satisfy unnecessary desires will lead to actual attempts to satisfy them—is backed by a thesis about motion, or by what Aristotle (and later thinkers) would call "physics." Another—the assertion that unnecessary desires, being disorderly motions, are bad—is metaphysically underwritten by the Theory of Forms. And a third—that democratic "freedom" is nothing other than the opportunity to satisfy unnecessary desires—is the result of linguistic analysis.

According to the argument thus far, not all desires are to be condemned, if only because not all desires are unnecessary. Indeed, the "mob of motley appetites" is contrasted with the "simple and moderate appetites, which are guided by reasoning with intellect and right opinion" (*Rep.* 4.431b seq.). One such appetite would presumably be that for the "pure and stable pleasure" of beholding the Forms (586e seqq.). In that state, pleasure and desire do not come in from outside the soul, but are *oikeiotaton* to it, or most its own. Such desire is not manifold but rather is that single desire proper to the true and unified nature of the soul: the love of wisdom, or philosophy (*Rep.* 10.611e).

There is a further state of the soul with which freedom, as understood in *Republic* 8, must be contrasted: that in which a plurality of desires in the soul are led by its reasoning capacity and harmonized with it. Plato calls this state "justice" and posits it as the prime political value (see *Rep.* 4.443d-e, 444c-e; 9.591b-c; 10.609b-610e). Justice is then immanent to the individual. It is an affair, not of his relations to others, but of the relation of the parts of his soul to one another. In the just soul, this relation comes about under the rule of the best part, reason. The rule of the best part is "natural" to the soul and is also, as are all virtues, "beautiful" (*kalon* 4.444d-e).[7]

These states of soul stand in a moral hierarchy. From lowest, we have "freedom," in which the soul is pushed and dragged by its desires; "justice," in which it rules them in harmony; and "philosophy," in which the soul leaves behind both the disordered state of freedom and the well-ordered one of justice, following the single desire that it most truly has: the love of wisdom.

The restriction of "freedom" to designating merely the worst possible way of relating to one's desires was, I suggested, in part a response to views in common circulation at Athens. But there were other views about. One of them in particular, though not incompatible with the democratic view, was in some respects quite distinct from it. This view arose from the obvious fact that in Athens some people were "free," and others were slaves. "Freedom" in this sense did not designate a psychological property at all, and escaped the instability that characterized freedom in the democratic view. It designated a juridical status, fixed at birth and changed thereafter only with difficulty. This view of freedom as an enduring, even static condition finds expression in Pericles's Funeral Oration, where the freedom of Athens is first asserted to consist in the autochthony of its citizens—in the fact that the land has always been populated by the same group of people, handed down from father to son. To be "free" is simply to belong to that group: to be a landowning (adult, free, male) Athenian.[8]

Such a juridical (or genealogical) definition would have been acceptable to moderate democrats (of whom Pericles, in fact, was one); none
of them was advocating the abolition of slavery. But the radically democratic view of freedom, the sense condemned in *Republic* 8, would require
that the juridical definition be supplemented. What made a free man free
was not simply that he had inherited land in Athens, but that he was
(because of that) able to do whatever he wanted. Belonging to the group
of free Athenians would then be just a means to an end. What for Pericles
himself was the great restraint on the citizen—the fear of disgrace—
would, as *Republic* 8 suggests, have been viewed by a radical democrat as
an unwarranted restriction on his capacity to live as he wished.[9]

The main problems with the democratic view of freedom had to do
with its instability and disorderliness. If freedom is to be given any positive meaning at all within Platonic thought, it will have to be considered
in terms that are, at least, in partial accord with this moderate, Periclean
view. It will have to be considered as a fixed and enduring state, rather
than as a condition of instability which is itself condemned to its nemesis,
tyranny. But Plato, like a full-blown democrat, would have had reservations about Pericles's formulation as we have seen it.

Those reservations would, of course, have been very different. Any
claims Athens may have had to be eternal were highly dubious, even at
the time of Pericles's speech, which is reported by Thucydides to have
taken place during a particularly perilous moment of the Peloponnesian
War—not long before the great man himself fell victim to the plague.[10]
In the *Timaeus*, genealogy is "no better than the tales of children": the
most that can plausibly be claimed is not that Athens has always existed,
but that it is descended from a noble and mighty people. Even that is
claimed only in a myth (*Timaeus* 23b seq.). The realm of the eternal is
not to be found on earth, then. In the long run, there is only one "fixed
status" among men, and that is death. If a Periclean view of freedom as a
fixed and enduring state is to be admitted into Platonic thought at all, it
must be located after death, in the "other world"—the world of Forms,
which in the *Phaedo* had already been asserted to be eternal and unchanging and thus to provide a "fixed status" for the soul.[11]

The freedom of the soul after death is not discussed systematically in
the Platonic writings. Indeed, the realm of Forms, and the soul as it
dwells within it, are repeatedly asserted to be matters which we on earth
cannot really understand.[12] But Plato does portray life after death mythically, most importantly for our purposes in the dialogue which first advances the theory of Forms in explicit form. This is the *Phaedo*, itself
named for an emancipated slave.[13]

At *Phaedo* 114b-115a it is asserted that those who have lived good lives are, after death, "set free" (*eleutheroumenoi*) from a confinement below the earth; those who have been philosophical carry this liberation further and "live completely without bodies for the rest of time." True freedom, as I will call it, is thus an eternity of disembodiment. Those who are not qualified for this must return to earth and, while there, abandon the pleasures of the body, devoting themselves to knowledge and thereby adorning their souls with various good qualities, among which is again "freedom."[14]

The view that liberation is, in the fullest sense, liberation from this world *in toto* is not simply tacked on mythically at dialogue's end. It is implied, for example, at *Phaedo* 80a–84b. The soul is kin to the Forms. It is immortal, indissoluble, self-consistent, and invariable. The body is the reverse of these things and contaminates the soul. Earthly life is inescapably a "bondage to the body," and the soul in it a "servant of the god" (*Phaedo* 62b, 83d). Worse, the soul in such bondage "rolls in ignorance" within the body, like a prisoner roaming his cell and peeking at reality through the bars. The soul which follows philosophy is "released"[15] and after death arrives in an environment congenial to it, where it can exist "in accordance with itself"—as what it really is.[16]

Freedom is then that state of the soul in which it attains its true being. Like all "true being" in the Platonic universe (cf. *Phaedo* 74d seqq., 78d, 83b, etc.), that of the soul is a fixed—indeed, an eternal—status. Only as thus eternally fixed can the soul be truly what it is. Whatever being it has in the sensible world is merely a poor imitation of the true being it has among the Forms (*Phaedo* 66e seq., 81a, 84a seq.). As in the Periclean formulation, to be free here means to exist within a congenial and unchanging environment. But the environment is metaphysical, not social, and adherence to it is determined at death, not at birth.

We saw the freedom of the democrat to be a kind of disorderly motion within the soul. The truly liberated soul, dwelling among the Forms, is not mobile at all. The freedom the soul has on earth when it abjures corporeal pleasure and devotes itself to knowledge is then, even when brought about in philosophical discussion and dialogue, at best a necessary preliminary to true liberation. It is not that liberation itself. And philosophical dialogue—in this life, at least—is at best a condition for true freedom; it is not itself intrinsically emancipatory.

True freedom thus finds an empirical image, not in such dialogue, but in the soul's dominance over the body. For the soul of the philosopher is alone what guides his life, and it guides it solely with a view to its own well-being, disregarding the well-being of the body (cf. *Phaedo* 66b–d, 82a–c, 94b–e). The highest example of this sort of empirical freedom is

Socrates's decision, in the *Crito*, to refuse the escape offered by his friends and to stay in Athens to die (cf. *Phaedo* 98e seq.).

The self-mastery of the philosophical soul is thus sharply distinct from the "release" of the philosophical soul after death.[17] In referring to the rulership of the soul over the body, it seems more akin to the conception of "justice" advanced in the *Republic*. But self-mastery in the *Phaedo* is not the ideal "psychic harmony" presented in the *Republic*, and is far indeed from the lofty simplicity of "philosophy" in that dialogue. Rather, it is portrayed as a constant battle, in which the philosopher's body continually hampers and distracts his efforts at philosophical cognition (*Phaedo* 94a–e). The motion of the philosopher is, to be sure, at least partly determined by his soul, which simplifies and directs it to the single quest for wisdom rather than to the manifold of pleasant earthly objects. And, given the *Phaedo*'s strong assertion that the "self" of a human being is his soul alone (*Phaedo* 115c seqq.), such motion would be that most proper to the soul, if the soul must "move" at all. But it must continually fight against all the other motions impelled by the body.

The nature of freedom is thus articulated, in the *Phaedo* as in the *Republic*, in terms of the relations between the rational soul and the desires it feels. In both dialogues, there is a triplet of such relations. The soul which gives in to its desires, allowing itself to be governed by them, is in the *Republic* (democratically) "free"; in the *Phaedo* it is "imprisoned" in the body. The other two parts of the triplet in the *Republic*—justice and the love of wisdom—are in the *Phaedo* conflated into the empirical image of true freedom in which the soul, progressing toward wisdom, dominates the body. This conception is then supplemented with the view that the soul is truly "free" only when dwelling for all eternity among the Forms. Is it possible to derive from these two classifications, separate but related as they are, a single concept of freedom?

This question is not to be viewed as part of an attempt to extract a single set of Platonic doctrines concerning the soul and its well-being from the *Phaedo* and the *Republic*. Such a procedure is always perilous, and in this particular case seems impossible; the *Phaedo* does not attribute "parts" to the soul, and hence makes no reference to the "psychic harmony" of those parts. What the *Republic* treats as the rulership of one part of the soul over others is expressed in the *Phaedo* as its mastery over the body.[18] I will therefore limit my question to the concept of freedom and put it as follows: Freedom can, from the *Phaedo* and *Republic*, be viewed in three ways: as the license to heed unnecessary desires; as the soul's true being in the world of Forms; and as the empirical image of the latter, the difficult mastery of the soul over the body. Is there a common formula to all this?

The first and second of these views seem in general to concern the soul's relation to its environment. On earth, the soul inhabits a body which, as a physical object, is in constant, unstable interplay with other physical objects. Freedom is nothing more than the capacity for total engagement in that interplay. It is the individual's ability to pursue any desirable object that offers itself (and, presumably, to flee any object it finds undesirable). If, recalling Hegelian developments, we call a relationship in which the two related sides tend to become similar to one another a "reconciling" relation, we can say that the democratic soul has a reconciling relationship to its sensory environment.

In its true sense, "freedom" is the ability to know and be with the Forms; since the Forms themselves are fixed and unchanging, the soul's relation to them will be as well. By assuming its fixed and enduring, or true, nature among the forms, soul reveals its "kinship" with them and has what I have called a "reconciling" relationship to them.

If the third type of freedom is the empirical image of the second, then I suggest that it cannot, on the basic principles of Platonic metaphysics, be defined independently of it. The sensible world in general is neither one species (together with the world of Forms) of some wider genus of "world as such," nor does it share a "common character" with the other type. It is, as R. E. Allen has argued, a copy of the world of Forms, and nothing more.[19] It follows that the nature of self-mastery is fully expressed by saying that it is the empirical image of true freedom. The truly free soul has a "reconciling" relation to the realm of Forms, and so does the soul of the philosopher on earth. But in the empirical world, this reconciling relation to the Forms is also manifested as an antagonistic relation to sensibles.

If, then, we take the notion of "relation to environment" to be basic to the Platonic concept of freedom, we find soul relating to two very different environments. Reconciling relation to the Forms, with no relation at all to sensibles, is true freedom, while reconciling relation to the sensory world is democratic freedom. Self-mastery comports with both a reconciling and an antagonistic relation: the former to the Forms, the latter to sensibles. But the reconciling always goes in one direction only. Both the sensible world and that of the Forms are metaphysical necessities which cannot be other than they are: the world of Forms cannot change in any way, while that of sensibles cannot alter its basic character of instability. Hence, soul in a reconciling relation to either is fundamentally determined by necessities, rather than parameters. It is thus, in my term, unsituated and, in the case of the truly free soul among the wholly unchanging Forms, radically so.

Common to the two "sensory" forms of freedom is the idea of the motion of the embodied soul. This can be classified in two ways: as single or multiple, or as coming from within or without. The two classifications, in the texts considered so far, coincide. Motion from without is inspired by a variety of sensible objects, each of which incites a desire within the soul, whose motion then becomes a disorderly succession of pursuits. Motion from within comes from the soul itself (in the *Phaedo*) or from its leading part, the reason (in the *Republic*). This motion is directed by the soul's single "ownmost" appetite, the love of wisdom, and is itself simple—and free.

There is thus a relatively unified, if complex, conception of freedom to be extracted from the two dialogues under consideration. But whether it can furnish a conception of the truly free life is another matter. The problem is posed most clearly by the *Phaedo*. For there, as we have noted, the soul of the philosopher is not in a harmonious condition. It must constantly fight against the body, which, for its part, constantly obtrudes with its desires. No man, it appears, can completely master his body—at least not in the sense of having his body follow the dictates of his soul without any resistance whatever. He who attempts to be master of himself is thus at variance with himself, and Socrates's admonition to Callicles (at *Gorgias* 482b), that it would be better to have all mankind disagree with him than for him to disagree with himself, would hold out an ideal impossible for any human being. Complete mastery of the body is as impossible in this life as separation from it, and separation from the body is (at *Phaedo* 66b–67b) the only true "liberation."

But there is one crucial exception to this: Socrates himself. We have noted that his decision, in the *Crito*, to reject his friends' offer of escape is presented in the *Phaedo* as the paradigm of self-mastery. His calm demeanor throughout the *Phaedo* is essential to its purpose of moral exhortation. For the dialogue aims, not merely at justifying a set of propositions (e.g., the immortality of the soul), but at getting its readers to become good: to become like Socrates.[20] Part of Socrates's message, as a moral hero, thus appears to be that we living mortals can come much closer to complete self-mastery than we usually think.

There are problems with this use of Socrates as the empirical image of true freedom, however. For there is clearly a difference, a moral gap, between him and the rest of mankind. Socrates's nature is in fact occasionally asserted to be the gift of a "divine fate" (*Phaedo* 58e seq.; *Phdr.* 230a), and the serenity of his death, in view of what we know about the ways hemlock really works, has been much idealized.[21] Nor is this gap between the portrayed Socrates and the rest of mankind something Plato ignored or tried consistently to downplay. Indeed, Kenneth Seeskin has argued that it is intrinsic to the moral strategy of the dialogues.[22]

Even if the empirical image of true freedom can be presented on earth as the individual moral genius of a Socrates, and even if other mortals could live up to it, there is no reason to think that very many of them could ever do so. True freedom, in Platonic terms, might be a *moral* ideal. But since it is defined as an escape from everything human in the sensory world, there seems no way to make it a *political* or interactive ideal. It is perhaps no surprise that the *Republic*, written after the *Phaedo*[23] and concerned with the best form of society, refers in its political discussion of freedom only to its "democratic" variety, painting self-mastery in idealized colors and calling it, not "freedom" or even its empirical image, but justice.

Is freedom, in any sense other than the democratic, possible in the sensory world? And, if so, is it possible in a political order? The answer to both questions, based on the analyses of freedom we have just examined in *Republic* 8 and the *Phaedo*, is No. As long as desires are viewed as simply opposed to reason, and as long as we have desires, we are not truly rational and cannot be masters of ourselves. Nor need *all* desires be viewed as inimical to reason for this problem to arise. *Republic* 10.611e, as we saw, adumbrates the concept of a desire which is itself rational: the love of wisdom. But the problem with self-mastery remains. For the desire for wisdom must still compete with, and try to assert itself against, the other desires. As long as there are *any* such desires—as long as the soul is receiving sensory inputs which attract or repel it—victory will be incomplete. Unless Plato is to be construed as an unequivocal enemy of freedom in all senses,[24] he has a problem here: how can freedom, attainable in its "true" nature only in a supersensible realm, be given a convincing empirical image?

The problem lies in the opposition between the many desires which come from without, to which we are prey as long as we have bodies, and the single desire for wisdom, which comes from within. More deeply, perhaps, it lies in the whole classification of desires by origin and number. On the former classification, desires are viewed as motions which originate either within or without the soul. As long as the soul has both types of desire, self-mastery will be impossible. But this is all dependent on viewing the soul as a "physical" container of motion, i.e., on a rather crude metaphor. Why not simply drop it? It is, of course, possible that Plato does not view it as a metaphor: that he simply has no other way to conceive of soul than as something extended in space and capable of receiving motion from without. But we have noted above that the passages in which the doctrine is implicit are highly metaphorical, even flowery, in character.

It is hard to see, however, what could replace the view in question if we wish to retain the notions (a) that desire is a form of motion, (b) that desire affects the soul, (c) that the soul is somehow localized in space and time, and (d) that desire must originate either inside or outside the soul. And these notions are not easily dropped. Desire comes and goes in time, even animals seem to feel it, so it seems obvious enough that desire is some sort of physical process or "motion"; even Kant will not abandon that doctrine. That desire affects the soul is, though in the Platonic view unfortunate, wholly beyond question. But if desire is a motion, then—unless we are going to allow action at a distance, unacceptable to physicists until Newton—it is hard to see how it can affect the soul without impinging on it. And if the soul is something that can be affected by some movements and not others, it must somehow be localized.

The only thing left to abandon is the idea that desires must come either from within or without the soul. This disclaimer could take either of two forms: we could say that desire comes from neither within nor without the soul, or that it comes from both locations at once. But where, on the first alternative, would such a motion come from? If the soul is localized in space and time (and if, having parts, it is not to be construed as a point), it seems reasonable to think that all space can be divided into that portion which is within it and that which is outside. A desire which came from neither of these areas would not be "spatial" at all, in which case it is hard to see how it could be a movement. If, on the other hand, desire comes, not from a single locale either inside or outside the soul but somehow from both the external realm and the soul at once, then the entire distinction of "within" and "without" seems to be impeached. How can we distinguish the soul from the world if one and the same motion can arise "in" both? And how, then, can there be any desire which is "proper" to soul?

But Plato need not in fact abandon the container model. For there is a way of undercutting the distinction that needs to be undercut, while retaining the idea that the soul contains motions, some of which come from within and others from without. This is to temporalize the distinction: to say that a motion "from without" can over time become a motion "from within" (or, perhaps, vice versa). To say this is to make the soul, not a passive container, but an active one. It is then not merely something that is pushed around by motions from outside, but something that can appropriate such motions and make them its own. In so doing, it reveals the locus of motion to be itself parametric in nature: motion from without can become motion from within.

The *Phaedrus*, I submit, shows us how this is supposed to work. In so doing, it presents, for the first time, a view of freedom as neither metaphysical (*à la* the *Phaedo*) nor physical (*à la* the *Republic*) but interactive: the "environment" into which the free soul fits is itself human.

Nine

Eros and Emancipation: The Three Speeches of the *Phaedrus*

Analysis

That a reconstrual of the views of freedom found in the earlier dialogues takes place in the *Phaedrus* is evidenced in the sequence of its three "set speeches." Each of these portrays a distinct type of interaction. The interaction is in every case erotic, and this might seem to detract from whatever treatment of freedom the dialogue contains. For what connection, we may ask, does freedom have with seduction? There is, I suggest, a close one. If "freedom" is the ability to gratify desire, then interactive freedom would be the ability to gratify one's desires with respect to other people. The most intense form of this would occur where the other person is not simply a means to satisfaction, but is in fact the desired object itself. Hence, in speaking of an erotic relationship, the first speech is able to treat it, as do the other speeches, as an intensification of other types of human interaction, rather than as wholly distinct from them. It treats, in general, interaction that would be engaged in by someone bent on satisfying his desires, or by a member of the lowest, "appetitive" class in the ideal state of the *Republic*.[1] The second speech is, by contrast, purely logical. If it cannot be held to portray the kind of interaction that takes place among souls in the realm of Forms, it comes close to it. In the third and last speech, the *Phaedrus* proposes its own alternative to the views presented in the first two, and in this advances its view of the nature of intrinsically emancipatory interaction. The three set speeches then give way, in the second part of the dialogue, to a more explicitly general treatment of language.

In the first speech (*Phdr.* 230e–234c), love is viewed as simply "a name for unrestrained sexual desire."[2] The speech is centered on two characters, both of whom aim only at gratifying such desire. One, the "lover," is so overpowered by his lust that his capacity to think is impaired. Since his exclusive goal is to gratify his own desires, he seeks neither to understand his beloved nor to tell him the truth. His utterances, as portrayed, simply express his own feelings of the moment. Beyond this, they are no more than stratagems designed either to enhance him in the eyes of his beloved or to keep the youth from consorting with others. The result of this is an absolute minimum of communication. It consists wholly of egoistic professions of emotion, quarrels, and attempts to stop further speech with other people. The entire affair is conditional upon desire for the youth. Once that has cooled, the lover repents of the whole thing.

The other character, the "non-lover," who also purportedly makes the speech, retains some capacity to calculate his own interests. He exhibits the same degree of subjectivity and lack of understanding as the lover. His discourse with the youth is likewise for the sake of "pleasure," and his distinction from the lover can only be in terms of the intensity of their respective desires. If, for example, he does not discourage the youth from associating with others, this is not for the youth's sake: the non-lover simply operates on the relatively sophisticated assumption that those who shun his beloved pass negative judgment on him as well. He, too, has no knowledge of his beloved, as is indicated by locutions such as "if you are anxious because you judge it to be difficult . . . (232b5f), and "if you respect established convention . . ." (231e3)—the latter surely an early thing to learn about anyone!

If the non-lover's stratagems are more complex, their intended result is the same: no benefits accrue to the youth, and all to the "non-lover." True, we are told that the non-lover "administers to the future advantage" of the loved (233b6ff). But the ministry turns out to amount to nothing more than the non-lover's relatively mild expression of his own mental state (233c1–5), and no positive advice is portrayed. Nor, in view of the non-lover's ignorance of his beloved, could any be given. The non-lover, like the lover, is concerned only with himself and knows only himself. Thus, the first speech fully lives up to its own opening words: "concerning my affairs." Both lover and non-lover speak for the sole purpose of advancing those affairs. The result of this egoism, in both cases, is an absolute minimum of communication with the youth.

The second speech (237b-241d) begins with the phrase "concerning everything" and represents the opposite, impersonal extreme of discourse. It is uttered, not by a known democrat, but by Socrates himself (though disguised, 237a), and it begins with an attack on "the many" who do not know that before debating it is necessary to know what the debate is about. Where the first speech had no overall structure, with points succeeding one another at random, the second falls into two parts, both structured by the Platonic method of "division." The first of these is a definition of "love"; the second, a description of its harmful effects.[3]

Both parts of the speech are entirely general and without reference to either speaker or hearer as individuals. The speech, for example, merely enumerates the evils for any youth in having a lover. It takes no account of personal characteristics which might set this youth apart from others. As for the supposed speaker, he is entirely hidden behind his complicated dissimulation as a non-lover—just as the real speaker, Socrates, is hidden behind his cloak. The non-lover (the pretended identity of the speaker) is not discussed at all. The impersonal content of the speech is in marked contrast with the Palinode, or third speech, which is avowedly for Phaedrus's sake (243e6f, 257a5); even the first speaker, as we saw, makes a few blind stabs at what his hearer might be like. The impersonality of the second speech is also evident from its rhetoric. The youth is not addressed once after the process of division gets underway; for the rest of the speech he is referred to only in the third person. This is in contrast to the Palinode, where the youth is addressed at least eight times, and to the first speech (23 times).

It is thus clear that the second speaker, though he has gotten beyond the purely subjective egoism of the lover and non-lover in the first speech, can come to know another human being no more than they. For the divisions of the second speech reach, not an individual, but only a sort of lowest class or *infima species*.[4] Human individuals therefore have no place in the second speech, which avoids the subjectiveness of the first at the price of making its discourse purely universal.

The third speech has, for our purposes, four main parts: a positive definition of love in terms of madness (244a–245c); a discussion of soul as self-mover (245c–e); one narrative of the soul's fall from heaven and resurrection to the Forms (246a–250d); and another of an earthly love affair (250e–256e).

In this third speech, soul is no passive container. Its very nature, in fact, is to move itself. It has, indeed, not one principle of motion but three. These are presented metaphorically as a wing and two horses. The wing gives it what we may call "metaphysical" motion. It enables the soul to rise toward the Forms, and the loss of it causes the soul to fall to earth. When this happens, the wing shrivels to a mere stump, and the other principles of motion take over. The horses, which can be broadly viewed as desires, pull the soul like a chariot across the surface of the earth. But its motion is erratic. While one horse is good and cooperative with the driver of the chariot, the other (a creature of mean but intense passion) seeks to go its own way. The result is that the soul can be pulled in two directions at once or be suspended between alternatives—as Phaedrus himself is suspended between Socrates and Lysias, and as the smitten soul will be said to be later in the Palinode.[5] It is possible for such a soul, when it sees a beautiful person, simply to take after that beauty at the behest of the evil horse: "like a four-footed beast." But if it is of higher quality, the soul restrains itself and experiences a very different sort of motion. It catches and holds a stream of particles emanating from the beauty it beholds. These particles nourish the stump of its wing, causing it to regrow.

At this point, we have a metaphorical presentation of motion from without—the stream of particles emanating from the loved one—being caught and held by the soul, thus becoming motion within—the regeneration of the "most divine" part of the soul, its wing (cf. 246d–e). Where in *Republic* 8 the swarm of desires buzzed into and out of the inert container (or citadel) of the soul, and in so doing pushed it around, the Palinode turns to another physical possibility—called for, as we saw, by the problems with the "passive container" model. The soul itself is likened to a living organism rather than a mere container. It is dynamic enough to capture, retain, and actually derive nourishment from outside motion.

Those particles that the soul is not strong enough to retain within itself do not escape into the environment at large. They are reflected back to the beautiful person, by now the soul's "beloved." His soul, catching and holding them, is affected in a way similar to, but less intense than, that of the lover's soul. Lover and beloved in this way come to constitute a couple, a closed system of mutual mirroring. This systemic closure of the loving couple means that the motion in their souls is no longer a linear wandering after sensory objects of desire, but circular interchange. As the *Timaeus* and *Laws* will tell us, circular motion is less mobile than other kinds, for it involves no change in place.[6] Their relatively settled motion at last brings the lovers to the quiet of the couch, where the final victory is to be won: the lovers do not succumb to their sexual attraction, but transmute it into the "ordered rule of the philosophical life." In this they have been liberated. The "power of evil in the soul has been subjected, and the power of goodness set free" (*eleutherôsantes*, 256b3). After death, they are further rewarded with the first of the three victories they will require for their final liberation, the definitive rise to the Forms.

The account of the love affair in the Palinode is structured, in part, on a pair of oppositions between appearance and reality. In the first of these, what appears to the lover's soul as an emotional or psychological affection—his reaction, inexplicably strong to him, to the sight of the youth—is really a wholly physical phenomenon: the flow of particles from without becomes motion proper to the soul, as the quest for the beloved is transmuted into the rise to the Forms. In this process, both the higher and the lower parts of the soul come to be directed upon one and the same object. The horses and the driver, we may say, no longer quarrel about the direction in which to go, but only about the speed with which to go there (cf. 254a-e). The soul as a whole ceases its wandering and suspension, and comes to have a single, unified motion.

This motion, as proper to the soul, is "self-motion" (245e), and the sense in which self-motion is attributed to the soul in the *Phaedrus* has been a matter of much scholarly controversy.[7] One point at issue is the precise meaning of *psychê pasa* (245c5), which can mean either "all soul," collectively, or "any soul," taken individually. Some commentators have even taken it to refer to the "world soul," the single soul which, in the *Timaeus*, is said to animate the whole physical world.[8]

Without attempting to resolve all issues, we can note for our purposes that since soul moves throughout the different levels of the Platonic cosmos, manifesting itself differently in each, the predicate "self-moving" presumably has different meanings in different contexts. Indeed, if Raphael Demos is correct in the view—which Aristotle, as we shall see, also imputes to Plato—that to say that soul is a self-mover is to say that it in fact has no determinate nature at all, then self-motion cannot be unequivocally assigned to anything.[9] But two implications the passage draws for the nature of soul from its characteristic of being a self-mover—that its motion never ceases, and that it is the source of all motion in the universe—are hardly characteristic of the individual soul as contained in a human body. The sense in which this sort of soul can be "self-moving," if any, is then specific to circumstances and must be derived from the context of the Palinode itself. And there are several senses in which the individual soul in the Palinode is portrayed as *not* self-moving. Its original fall from the heavens is caused, somehow, from without. Its early, confused wanderings across the earth are also motivated externally, as by its "horses" which drag it after desired objects. Even when seized by the vision of the beloved, the soul is not portrayed as a self-mover: it is a sort of mirror which catches and appropriates the motion of visual particles.

Self-motion does, it seems, apply somewhat more clearly to the conjoined souls of the loving couple. That couple constitutes what I have called a closed system, in which each part—each individual—derives its motion from the other.[10] Each part of that system—each individual—is moved from without, by the desire for (or particles from) the other. But the couple as a whole is moved from within, as the linear pursuit of desired objects becomes a circular transfer of particles. Eventually, in the "final victory" on the couch, the souls achieve "self-mastery" (256b) and presumably become self-moving, as individuals, in yet another sense.

But the loving couple also is moved from without. For the lovers are, unbeknownst to themselves, being guided and indeed "possessed" by a god (252e seq). And divine possession is not understood Platonically as an "indwelling of the spirit." Rather, as Léon Robin puts it,

> . . . le mot de doit donc pas être entendu en ce sens que l'être serait habité par le dieu qui l'inspire. L'homme inspiré est au contraire hors de lui-même: le dieu . . . l'élève et le tient suspendu à lui comme des anneaux de fer sont suspendus à la pierre magnétique.[11]

The "self-motion" of the loving couple is thus not to be interpreted in terms of the autonomy that modern humanism will attribute, for example, to the state. It is a characteristic of the couple only as a sensory phenomenon, whose movements can be captured in a "physicalistic" myth. Insofar as their movement is not that of erotic desire entering the soul, but that of the couple itself toward the Forms, it is indeed quite passive; but of that they are ignorant. This is the second of the oppositions between appearance and reality that I mentioned above. What appears (to the reader of the dialogue, if not to the lovers themselves) to be a physical exchange of particles is really a "metaphysical" process, in which a non-sensible entity—a "god"—draws the souls of the lovers upward, toward the Forms. Those two oppositions thus result from an interplay of three levels of discourse—psychological, physical, and metaphysical.

The loving couple is not then a simple empirical object, as are such objects of desire as food, drink, and beautiful bodies. In its unique capacity for self-movement—and in the fact that the individual soul, unmoved by anything outside, lives wholly within it—the loving couple can be said to constitute an environment for the individual soul, detached from the sensory world of inanimate objects of desire as well as from the realm of Forms itself. The phrase "self-motion" captures this double detachment admirably. As detached from the Forms, the human environment of the loving couple is in motion. As detached from sensibles, it constitutes the "selves" of its two members. It is by adhering to this human environment that the members of the loving couple achieve their liberation while on earth.

Seen in this way, the emancipation achieved by the love affair is the instilling of wholeness in the soul. In it, the soul becomes a smoothly functioning whole of heterogenous parts. It does this in and through interaction with another human being, for only as belonging to the human environment of a loving couple does the individual soul achieve unity. In that sense the erotic experience recounted in the Palinode is constitutive for the individual human soul. Without such experience, the soul will be disunified and will indeed be, not "a" soul at all, but a mere collection of diverse motions.

On its ultimate, metaphysical level, this entire process of liberation is grounded in the Platonic metaphysics of beauty (*to kalon*). Beauty, of all the Forms, is the most "apparent" and "lovely" in the sensible world (250d). The beholder of it in the body of another is thus presented with an alternative. He can regard it as a purely sensory phenomenon and operate as a beast. Or he can perceive its true nature as an image of beauty itself and have the kind of love affair the Palinode depicts.

The Palinode is addressed specifically to Phaedrus. It is designed to evoke in him resonances with his own experience as a "loving disciple," showing him possibilities in such experiences that he had not realized were there (257a; also cf. 243e, 265c). But its story is not *about* Phaedrus. It presents, not the adventures of an actual human individual, but the more general narrative of "a soul." We may assume that it is addressed also to eventual readers of the dialogue, and that it is intended to function in the same way for them. Indeed, unless the reader of the dialogue finds the description of the soul's experience in the Palinode to be similar enough to experiences he himself has had to be at least possible for human beings like himself, the entire myth fails to be anything more than a pretty story. It can convey no serious doctrine whatsoever.

The portrayal of the love affair, on its psychological level, has the status of a description of a general type of human experience. This description is to be verified by the reader in the light of his own experiences. We may, in this loose sense, call it "phenomenological" in spite of its narrative structure and the metaphorical language it contains. We may venture further to suggest that the Palinode is a *successful* piece of phenomenology. The fact that it is read and admired millenia after its composition testifies that many, if not all, human beings have indeed found its portrayals to be verified in their own experiences.

As phenomenological, the portrayal of the affair does not appeal directly to metaphysical truths. That such affairs, or ones approximating them, do in fact occur does not presuppose any facts about a supersensible domain. It is rather the *significance* of the affair, we may say, that is metaphysical: the idea that the self-mastery attained in it leads to the escape, after death, from the sensible world altogether.

But the description of the affair contains, on its second and third levels, dimensions which, in addition to its metaphors and rhetorical flourishes, would distinguish it from classical phenomenological description.[12] One of these is the Palinode's emphasis on motion. The Palinode does not simply describe phenomenologically, for example, the experience of a soul which sees an attractive member of the appropriate sex. It goes on to suggest that this experience is to be understood as something entirely separate from the feelings and awarenesses of the soul in question. What *really* happens, on this level, is that a stream of small particles emanates from the youth and strikes the soul of the lover, causing a succession of changes, beginning with the regrowth of his wing. Finally, on the metaphysical level, what is *really* happening is that a "god" is drawing the lovers toward himself.

Narrative

That the *Phaedrus* can be read as narratively following other Platonic texts is open to doubt; at the dawn of modern scholarship on those texts (but following a tradition as old as the third century A.D.), Friedrich Schleiermacher noted that the *Phaedrus* contains "the germs of nearly the whole of [Plato's] system" and argued that their germinal state must mean that the *Phaedrus* was the first of the Platonic dialogues written. More recently, Chung-Hwan Chen has argued that the *Phaedrus,* containing doctrines associated with both the "early" and the "late" Plato, is the key transitional dialogue in the Platonic corpus. Martha Nussbaum has noted that it actually contains critical retractions of themes presented in earlier writings.[13] Among these, based on my analysis of the *Phaedrus*, is a new concept of emancipation, advanced via a critique of those presented in the *Republic* and *Phaedo*.

The type of interaction presented in the first speech, with its portrayal of momentary desire as the only motivation for human interaction, approximates democracy and the lowest class in the *Republic*'s ideal state. It is presumably no accident that the speech is put into the mouth of Lysias, a noted democrat and orator at Athens.[14] Indeed, the very form of the speech, in which each fragment is worked out for itself but is connected with other parts in a haphazard and mechanical way (cf. 235a, 264b-e), mirrors linguistically what the *Republic* portrays as the meaningless succession of desires in the democratic soul. The second speech, by contrast, seems to present a mode of discourse appropriate to the *Republic*'s rulers. Without personal property, family, and private relationships, each individual ruler is completely subsumed into the ruling group, just as the individual youth of the second speech is regarded as a mere instance of his own general class, that of "Athenian young men."[15] The rulers' discourse is not only wholly general, being about the Forms, but presupposes a denial of their own individuality; more specifically, the rulers in the ideal state represent the ideal of self-mastery as achieved in a communal, philosophical (but earthly) life.[16] The very presence of the Palinode after the second speech thus suggests a critique, not only of that speech and of the mode of discourse it portrays, but of the concept of freedom as self-mastery advanced in the *Republic* and *Phaedo*.

Emancipation in the *Phaedrus* begins in fact with a failure of self-mastery: when those who have some memory of a Form first apprehend a sensory entity which shows some likeness to it, they "are amazed, and no longer masters of themselves, and know not what has come over them" (250a). Only in their final victory on the couch are the members of the loving couple said to achieve "self-mastery" (256b); the concept is then not wholly rejected, but reinterpreted. For one thing, it is no longer viewed as the internal dominance of one part of the human being (or soul) over other parts, but it is grounded on the peculiar status of beauty. At once sensory and intellectual, the beauty of another human being affects both the senses and the reason of the soul: it brings them together in the desire of a single object which appeals to both. This is unification, not by the power of one's own reason, but by the "madness" of love itself, i.e., by the soul's participation in a loving couple.

This has two further results. One is that it makes the final victory seem easy: where self-mastery in the *Phaedo* was presented as something immensely difficult, in fact unattainable on earth, in the *Phaedrus* (256a seq.) it is narrated as coming naturally, almost of its own accord. Second, it makes the failure to achieve the final victory completely a matter of some indifference; even if the couple, on occasion, gives into sexual desire, no great harm is done. Self-mastery, in sum, is no longer *the* empirical image of the soul's true freedom, but one stage—and not one which must be wholly achieved—in the soul's emancipation.[17]

In the *Republic*, we found a cross-classification of motions in the soul, by locus of origin and by number: the multitude of motions originating outside the soul was contrasted with the single motion originating within. Neither classification survives the Palinode.

This does not at first seem to be the case. We read that any being which derives its motion from without is soulless, while any which derives it from within has a soul (*Phdr.* 245e). The dichotomy between movement from within and from without is not only, it seems, restated, but is used to define self-motion. But if, as we noted, self-motion only applies to the individual soul in a tenuous way, the dichotomy in terms of which it is defined would also apply only tenuously to the human soul: thus, the "flow of particles," as circular, has no distinct starting point—it both begins from and impinges upon the individual soul. The allocation of self-motion, not to the individual soul but to the couple to which it belongs, thus undermines the rigid classification of motions into those from within and those from without that is presented in the *Republic*.

Even as impinging upon the individual soul from without, motion in the erotic experience of the Palinode is not manifold: only one desire is felt by the soul, that for the beloved. The only direction for this desire is toward the beloved, to the intimacy of the couch. The overpowering erotic attraction of the lovers thus becomes their detachment from the manifold motions of the sensory world.

The concept of emancipation as the interactive attainment of human wholeness differs from the views of the *Phaedo* and the *Republic* not only in content, but also in the mode of discourse advocating it. Self-mastery in the *Phaedo*, defined as an image of the soul's life in the metaphysical realm of Forms, had but one empirical image: Socrates, a person so unique that others have no real hope of imitating him. The Palinode's presentation of liberation is to be verified, not in terms of its fidelity to the life and character of the historical Socrates, but by its ability to capture experiences the reader of the dialogue has had. It is those experiences of the reader, then, which "image" the kind of emancipation depicted in the *Phaedrus*; and, I have suggested, that imagery has been validated in the only way that it can be—by the assent of readers from disparate cultures over long epochs of human history.

In my terms, the true freedom advanced in the *Phaedo* was radically unsituated: the soul which attained it, dwelling among the Forms, related to an environment consisting only of metaphysical necessities rather than parameters which could be left behind. The second speech of the *Phaedrus,* though it takes account of its hearer's status as an Athenian youth, derives its view of that status by division, and hence appears to claim that it exhibits some sort of logical structures. It treats those structures, not as things that can be left behind by the youth, but as what I call conditions of his existence: the speaker claims to teach the youth how to cope with his status in Athens, but not how to stop being a youth.

The Palinode is clearly different. Through his love affair with an older man, the youth abandons whatever social status he may have and becomes a philosopher (the same is true, of course, of his partner). Social status is seen as what I call a parameter, as something that can be left behind. The lovers leave behind the statuses they have in Athens by entering into a new and different environment, that of a loving couple. Their new situation is conditioned, not socially by status, but physically (and ultimately, as we saw, metaphysically) by eros. The next chapter will examine some of the implications of this change in situation.

Ten

Speech and Politics
in the *Phaedrus*

Analysis

The narrative of emancipation in the Palinode, we have seen, can be read on several levels. It is at once a "phenomenological" account of the experiences of a soul, a physical account of the movement of particles from one body to another, and a metaphysical account of the operation of beauty in human lives. It can also, I will now argue, be seen as an account of speech itself, and this dimension shows it to portray what I call intrinsically emancipatory interaction. For though vision is the clearest sense and is the one with which we most readily apprehend sensory beauty (cf. *Phdr.* 250d), speech, like any sensuous phenomenon, can also be beautiful. Those who have the true rhetoric, founded on dialectic, will be able to speak "well and beautifully" (259e seqq., 273b seqq.). That Plato could do so is evidenced on every page of the Platonic writings and is suggested in the *Phaedrus*'s myth of the cicadas. The beauty of their song is tied, on the one hand, to Calliope and Urania, the muses who give the most beautiful expression to discourse human and divine, and on the other, to philosophers, for those who live philosophically "do honor to music" (259b seqq.). A beautiful body is such because of its relation to the supersensible or intelligible world of the Forms and, in particular, to its "most apparent" denizen, beauty itself. Unless "beauty" is to be in some strange way equivocal, beautiful speech must have a similar relation to the Forms.

But the soul in the Palinode, on first seeing a beautiful body, does not know that its beauty manifests its relationship to an intelligible world. Indeed, the soul of the youth does not make that discovery until the final victory of the lovers on the couch. This means, we noted, that the soul on first apprehension of a beautiful body might go in one of two directions: either straight after that body in beastly fashion or, after hesitation, upwards toward the Forms.

A similar, but more complex, choice is present in the case of certain words (*logoi*), those whose meanings are disputable. When confronted with such words, we "wander" intellectually. Different people are "carried" by them in different directions (263a seq.). Some speakers—Lysias, for one—simply operate with the words anyway, using them without clear meanings and hence, presumably, for their sound alone. The result of this, says Socrates, is that their discourse itself wanders. Thoughts follow one another with no overall plan or consistency (263d seq., 264b). Just as the right procedure with physical beauty is not to go straight for it but to allow oneself to see it as the image of an intelligible entity, so the right procedure with such a word is not simply to use it for its seductive and intriguing sound but to look to its meaning.[1]

But Lysias does not represent the only sort of speaker to misuse words by not adequately investigating their meanings beforehand. The speaker of the second speech has a predetermined thesis—that love is harmful—and he clarifies the meaning of "madness" only to the extent necessary for him to state that thesis clearly and to argue for it. He does this, we are told, accurately enough but incompletely. He leaves out the divine half of madness and delivers a speech that is not only false, but sinful (242d seqq., 265a seq.). If a speaker is to use a word correctly, it is necessary to perform both "collection" and "division." He must allow his mind to be carried to the word's single root meaning, and then in a disciplined way to see all the various specific meanings that it has, irrespective of how he actually intends to argue with it (265a-266b). When this happens, the resulting discourse can be called beautiful. As Socrates says of his own final definition of "madness," it may be well or badly put in itself—but it did give his speech clarity and coherence (265d).

Thus, proper procedure with words mirrors proper procedure with loved ones. More than that, they coincide. For the souls of the philosophical lovers eventually concern themselves, not with actions, but with words. The lovers do not use words to pursue earthly purposes but examine them on their own account, allowing themselves to be carried upwards to their true meanings: the Forms (cf. 256a seq.). Their love thus turns into dialectic, the disciplined investigation of language; it is no wonder that Socrates should refer to himself as a "lover" of dialectic (265c-266b). For to encounter another erotically, we saw, was to encounter him as, not merely a body, but as a body with a particular (though still unknown) relation to the Forms. So, too, with dialectic. The interactive examination of word meanings requires us to encounter, not that person's body, but his words as themselves having a particular (though still unknown) relation to that supersensible domain. The erotic roots of dialectic are thus attenuated roots. But dialectic cannot dispense with them.

The attainment of self-mastery by the philosophical lovers can be seen as the victory of *logos*, or speech, over the body: for it is on the couch that the lovers decide not to consummate their relationship physically, but to love one another in words alone. At that point, they can at last become real philosophers (256a7). Aware of their true motion as the metaphysical motion toward the Forms, they enter into that motion as their own. To do this, we saw, is to liberate their own capacity for virtue. This liberation, then, is not something subsequent to the interaction of the philosophers (as was true freedom in the *Phaedo*), but part and parcel of it. The kind of erotic, yet rigorously conceptual, interaction portrayed in the Palinode is both necessary and sufficient for the kind of emancipation it brings about. Such interaction is then intrinsically emancipatory.

Prior to their final victory, when the lovers first become truly philosophers, such dialectic would not be possible for them. They are still bent on seducing each other physically and will use persuasive words for the purpose. The speech depicted in the Palinode is thus not restricted to the dialectical examination of word meanings portrayed at its end. There is nothing to exclude from it the kind of rhetorical seduction that Socrates, through the Palinode itself, uses upon Phaedrus to turn him toward philosophy. Indeed, if such language were to be excluded from the lovers' encounter in the Palinode, their speech would relapse toward the merely logical sort portrayed in the second speech.[2] Because the erotic and seductive uses of language persist, the interaction of the Palinode—like the lover's original vision of his loved one—engages all aspects of human personhood, and so unifies the self.

The emancipatory process depicted in the Palinode is thus not to be understood merely in psychological, physical, or metaphysical terms, but as a type of discourse as well. As such, it comprises, not merely motions of the soul, but the words and arguments of dialectic and the kind of persuasion brought about by rhetoric. Its ultimate goal, as in the earlier Platonic writings we have discussed, is emancipation from the vagaries of the sensible world (to reach, not propositional truth, but the apprehension of the true beings, the Forms: 247c seq.). What it achieves itself is the unification of the soul, the liberation of the capacity for virtue. Because the unification of the self does not leave behind affective and even erotic elements, the lovers can (and Socrates does, in the Palinode and throughout the dialogues) use speech that, while not itself true, appeals to the senses and emotions. The philosophers thus engage their entire selves in their dialogue.

I have suggested that the emancipation depicted in the Palinode comes about through the soul's inherence in an environment which is neither the sensory world nor the world of forms, but is essentially human: the loving couple itself. Let us now broach the question of whether such an environment can be a political order. Can society itself, as an organized whole, consistently pursue, or even tolerate, such emancipation?

The very setting of the *Phaedrus* hints that the kind of emancipation it portrays is somehow incompatible with the polis; for the *Phaedrus*, alone among the Platonic dialogues, takes place outside the walls of Athens.[3] This is no accident. Socrates and Phaedrus must leave the polis in order to be alone together (cf. 227b seqq.). More generally, the loving couple of the Palinode is not simply put together out of two wandering souls who pass each other in the night, but is rather precipitated from society at large. Couple formation is the selection, for an exclusive relationship, of one person from the mass of available partners of various natures (cf. 252e seqq.). Since the "mass of available partners" is, at its widest, the polis itself (or at least its adult male members), the formation of the couple is actually the denial of the city. The human environment constituted by the loving couple is then detached, not only from the realms of Forms and sensibles, but from the political order as well.

The metaphysical reason for this, presumably, is that erotic madness, as a gift of the gods, is not properly part of the human concerns that make up the polis. The contrast is in fact drawn as the lover as madman stands aside from human affairs and looks to the divine (249c seqq., 273e). But the lovers of the *Phaedrus* do not simply stand aside from the political order. They actively reject it. For the lover, possessed by a god in the image of his beloved, comes to disdain all established custom and is "ready to be a slave" (252a). The willingness of a free man to embrace slavery is "mad" indeed—and in the Platonic view, altogether incompatible with political life. For the effacement of the distinction between free and slave was asserted in *Republic* 8 to be the highest pitch of the anarchy brought about by democratic freedom (*Rep* 563b). The erotic emancipation of the Palinode is thus neither political nor apolitical. It is antipolitical, and in Eric Voegelin's words, "The *Phaedrus* is the manifesto which announces the emigration of the spirit from the polis."[4]

But it does not follow that the kind of interaction portrayed in the Palinode is entirely without political significance. This is made clear in the second part of the *Phaedrus*, which is concerned with rhetoric (*Phdr.* 259e–279c). The love affair of the Palinode culminated, as we saw, in the dialectical study of word meanings. Such study is the foundation of rhetoric, the art of persuasion, for we cannot persuade others of the truth if we do not know it, and we cannot use words to that end if we do not know what they mean (cf. 271b-d). Rhetoric, by the account of the *Phaedrus,* is highly political. It applies, among other things, to lawsuits and public speechs, and via the latter, one may address rhetorically anyone in the city or even a god (261b seqq., 273e). Small wonder, then, that Pericles himself, arguably the greatest statesman in Athenian history, was also "most consummate of all with regard to rhetoric" (269c).[5] The rhetorical art, if it cannot guarantee to each practitioner the status of sole power in the city, at least enables him to play an active role in its governance (cf. *Politicus* 303e seqq.). Dialectic thus gains political significance as the necessary foundation for rhetoric. As the interactive context of dialectic, the love affair of the Palinode does the same: it is a form of interactive investigation which provides stable meanings to the words in which political man is to articulate himself. The political sphere, as a rhetorical domain, is thus dependent upon the erotic interaction of the Palinode.

But even as dialectic, the interaction of the Palinode is not *part* of the political sphere, for it is neither directed to nor conditioned by the political order. It is not directed to it because the word meanings it investigates are, in the Platonic view, not political but divine—they are metaphysical necessities, the Forms, which are not to be found in the polis but in the "space beyond the heavens" (*Phdr.* 247c seqq.). Dialectic is conditioned, not by the political order, but by the physical processes of biological "madness," in which the distinction among men most constitutive of political life—that between slave and free—is replaced by metaphysical distinctions among types of soul (252e seqq.).

Detachment from the political sphere is also required in order for dialectic to serve as an appropriate foundation for rhetorical, and hence for political, discourse. The political sphere is one in which people formulate purposes and work toward them. Even the crudest of politicians seeks to achieve something with his speech—if only to make himself look good (258a seq.). He uses words to this end, or to the more noble ends he may have. When it becomes political, the art of language is a way of "contending with words" (261c seqq.).

But, as the second speech shows, it is not enough to examine a word with respect to the particular purposes one hopes to achieve by using it on a particular occasion. *All* the various meanings of the word must be investigated and seen in their conceptual relationships in order to have a truly firm basis for speech of any kind. Operating with a word whose meanings have only been partially clarified is as bad as operating with a term which has not been clarified at all. The the loving couple's detachment from the polis thus has, from this point of view, the effect of providing an interactive context free from such practical constraints. The interaction of the Palinode can be of significance for society—but only by virtue of its detachment from, and indeed its rejection of, the political order with its established certainties.

Though the political sphere is dependent on the kind of interaction portrayed in the Palinode, the two remain foreign to one another. We can now see several reasons why this is so. The political order is not divine, nor is it directed to divinity: it is a part of the sensible world in which people formulate and pursue various purposes. Their interaction is grounded, not on love or beauty, but on a set of fixed social distinctions. The most basic of these distinctions has to do with purposive action; it is between those who are "free" in the juridical sense, who are able to formulate and pursue their own purposes, and those who are not. Both this particular distinction and the purposive activity which grounds it apply to political orders well beyond those of ancient Greece. So, then, might Plato's account of what lies outside them.

Narrative

The concept of emancipation invoked in the *Phaedrus* has clearly changed from those implied in earlier writings. In the *Republic*, the state can at least facilitate true liberation—primarily by affording to the individual the right sort of education, one which culminates in the vision of the Forms (cf. *Rep.* 8.504a seqq.). This model is more clearly stated in the *Symposium* (210a-211b), where the individual begins, as in the *Phaedrus*, with the love of a single beautiful body. But he proceeds from that to admiration for all beautiful bodies, and continues thence through the study of law, institutions, and the sciences to that of philosophy, which culminates in the true vision of Beauty. Properly then, political study can only begin after the pupil relaxes his love for a single other and devotes himself to all beautiful bodies. The *Symposium* suggests that this is the achievement of what we have called self-mastery: for to make it, the pupil must "bring his passion for the one into due proportion by deeming it of little or no importance."[6]

Part of the educational process in the *Symposium* is facilitated by society as a whole, which provides the laws and customs to be studied. But the achievement of self-mastery, like the other educational transitions presented there, is primarily the work of the individual alone: his "preceptor" may tell him what to study, but the pupil himself must by his own effort "grasp," "consider," and "discover" new truths. In contrast with the antipolitical, interactively achieved self-mastery of the Palinode, the youth in the *Symposium* achieves his liberation as his own work, guided by his preceptor and facilitated by society in accordance with his own intentions.

In the *Phaedrus*, the relaxation of interest in the single beautiful other is never reached. The highly charged erotic relationship is retained, I suggest, because of the *Phaedrus*'s concept of emancipation as the unification of the self. On that view, as in Hegelian reconciliation, lower levels of the self cannot simply be left behind or, as in the *Symposium*, denied importance.

More generally, we can tie the *Phaedo*, *Republic*, and *Phaedrus* together as showing a unity, not of doctrine, but of approach: the later writings treat problems presented in the earlier, improving the earlier treatment at the cost of some doctrinal revision. The most basic problem I have analyzed here is that of whether "freedom" can be defined in such a way as to be the subject of consistent pursuit in the sensory realm. A fixed point in the development of this question is that democratic freedom—the ability to live as one pleases—cannot, and the *Phaedo* then advances two further concepts of freedom: those of the soul existing among the Forms and of self-mastery as its empirical image. But freedom of the soul among the Forms is obviously incapable of realization by embodied human beings. The calm dignity of the death of Socrates shows that earthly attainment of self-mastery is possible, but Socrates is unique; for the rest of us, self-mastery is as unattainable as true freedom.

The *Phaedo* and *Republic* together thus set up a dilemma. Freedom as defined by, and in terms of, the sensory order is incapable of consistent realization, and would be an evil if it were realized; the two types of freedom formulated in metaphysical terms are incapable of sensory realization (except, as with Socrates, by "divine fate"). The dilemma is overcome when the *Phaedrus* articulates freedom as the individual soul's reconciling relation neither to Forms nor to sensibles, but to a specifically human environment. The formula for this environment, I suggested, is "self-movement": "movement" signifies its detachment from the realm of Forms, and "self" shows its detachment from the sensible world, where all is flux and there are no "selves."

The achievement of such freedom is an exercise in what I call situating reason. For Platonic dialectic begins with the view that human argumentation proceeds on the basis of ulterior conventions—such as the one we saw in *Republic* 8 concerning the democratic sense of "freedom." Like other conventions, those of interest here are binding upon the parties to them and, hence, function as limits on what those parties can say or do; but unlike other forms of convention, they are not always known by the parties to them. They are, in the first instance, the meanings of the words those parties use in other forms of interaction (such as rhetorical and political). To be "situated" is hence to be bound to unknown limits, and the aim of dialectic as situating reason is to articulate those limits (in the first instance, word meanings).

Such articulation must begin with the sensory realm, for a word bereft of its meaning is only a sound. When discourse remains on this level, it becomes the rhetoric of a Lysias (or a Gorgias): it uses words for their sounds alone, without regard to their meanings. The emancipatory dialectic of the Palinode, then, only begins with the sounds of words. Instead of using those words, it seeks to discriminate their various meanings via collection and division. In discriminating those meanings, it may reveal that a term is used wrongly in ordinary language—as, the *Phaedrus* argues, "eros" is wrongly used in Athens. Such dialectic thus takes the meanings of terms in ordinary language to be changeable—not conditions of discourse, but parameters for it. True, those parameters are ultimately grounded in metaphysical necessities, for the true meanings of terms are the Forms themselves. But even these, in the *Phaedrus*, are always viewed perspectively; the soul "sees," but does not possess, true and unshakeable knowledge of them (*Phdr.* 247d seq.). Moreover, the perspective is constantly changing and incomplete (251a). Hence, the Forms, though themselves metaphysical necessities, are always given parametrically to humans: our knowledge of a Form, if not the Form itself, can always become other than it is.

Situating reason as presented in the *Phaedrus* is, in addition, essentially interactive. For the individual, left to himself alone, has open to him only his own subjective desires and the abstract operations of logical dissection. These can only come together in concrete discourse through an encounter with another human being. Word meanings, we may say, are not accessible as such to the isolated individual; only consensus with others can verify that what I suspect is the meaning of a word holds in my language generally. Situated reason, then, cannot be conducted by an individual alone any more than an individual alone can operate the two-handled saw used by lumberjacks.

Clarifying the meaning of a word, on the model of the *Phaedrus,* brings one part of the sensory world—the sound of that word—into harmony with the rational, supersensible domain of the Forms. We saw the harmonization of sense and reason to be emancipatory in the *Phaedrus,* and the only form of such harmonization left to the lovers after the victory of speech over body is this sort of rationalization of language itself. Dialectical discussion, achieving this, is then intrinsically emancipatory.

Finally, erotic interaction, the specific "situation of reason" in the

Phaedrus, is initiated through what I call a poetic use of language. For the lovers can only become *philosophical* lovers if they are capable of taking one another's words, like one another's bodies, in either of two ways: to achieve sensible purposes (here, seduction), or to raise the soul to the Forms. The truly philosophical, of course, will choose only the latter. But the choice is theirs; and couples who occasionally take their words (and actions) back into the overtly erotic domain are almost as meritorious as the philosophers (*Phdr.* 256a–e).

In sum, poetic interaction is already to be construed in the *Phaedrus* as an elementary phase of the situating of reason via intrinsically emancipatory interaction. But my narrative cannot end here, for it is also the story of how poetic interaction became lost—theoretically occluded and practically proscribed. It is time to introduce into this narrative the complicating factor which will sustain its future plot: metaphysics.

The *Phaedrus* exhibits metaphysics—here, the Platonic theory of Forms—playing a particular sort of role which will contrast with later developments. "Freedom" is clearly a notion of immense complexity for Plato. Even to define it, in its various senses, has required him to draw on the domains that we would today call physics, psychology, metaphysics, ethics, aesthetics, and sociology. They are not yet separate here: throughout the Platonic dialogues, arguments move at will through regions which the contemporary specialization of intellectual life keeps rigidly separate.[7] They roam, however, only as needed. Freedom in the sensory world, the soul's permeability to motions from outside, would require for its complete definition specifications of the nature of soul as an extended locus in space and time, as well as of the nature of motion. Only the latter is actually carried through in the Platonic writings, and only in the very late *Laws* 10. The partial explication given in *Republic* 8 serves, not to state completely the nature of freedom in the sensory world, but to allow for a condemnation of it. Similarly, a full and non-metaphorical account of freedom in the realm of Forms would require a lengthy discourse on that realm itself; it would in fact amount to a systematic metaphysics, which the Platonic texts never offer. But again, what they do offer suffices to make the point that true freedom comes through wisdom alone, rather than from sensory goods.

Together with the enormous diversity of subject matter drawn upon for the definition of freedom goes a diversity of modes of argumentation. *Republic* 8, as I analyzed it, engaged in something akin to ordinary-language analysis; and its second, political argument anticipates modern dialectic: freedom when pursued by a society necessarily turns into its opposite. The use of Socrates as an empirical image of true freedom in the *Phaedo* relies upon empirical description: Socrates must actually have pursued his philosophical life to the end, as the dialogues report, if true freedom is to have any empirical image at all. The second speech of the *Phaedrus* contains what purports to be an *a priori* conceptual dissection of the notion of madness. And the Palinode, drawing on the Platonic physics of sense perception, also uses "phenomenological" narrative and vindicates the philosophical use of rhetoric.

But one mode of discourse has priority over the others: that which consists of assertions about the supersensible realm of Forms (including, most fundamentally, the assertion that it exists). The conclusion of the ordinary-language argument in *Republic* 8, for example, is reached by what seem to have had the status of commonsense premises. But common sense will not tell us why the argument should be offered at all, for its purpose is to show the worthless nature of what Athenian democrats called freedom; yet that view of freedom is fully justified as an empirical report of usage. It is to be condemned only if one wants to argue that there is another, better type of freedom: one which, in the *Phaedo*'s view, is to be found in the supersensible, metaphysical realm of the Forms.

The account of the death of Socrates, even if its historical accuracy is conceded, is also undertaken in part from metaphysical motives. If the wish of the man, Plato, had been merely to memorialize his teacher, he could have erected a stele or written (or commissioned) a poem. The death of Socrates is the subject of a philosophical work because that death has philosophical significance: the *Phaedo* presents Socrates's death as the paradigmatic case of self-mastery, the empirical image of the true freedom which can only be understood metaphysically.

Finally, the depiction of the love affair in the Palinode is sufficiently similar to actual love affairs to be recognized by the reader as, in some large sense, "true" to his own life; it bears comparison with other erotic writings in which a person finds his or her own identity through erotic experience, such as the *Story of O*. One major difference between the Palinode and such writings, however, is that in the Palinode the love affair is asserted to raise the lovers out of the sensible world altogether, to a wholly intellectual domain, which is also a better one. This assertion is, again, grounded in a theory of the supersensible world: in metaphysics.[8]

Each of the various types of discourse we have referred to proceeds on its own terms. The ordinary-language argument is to be evaluated as ordinary-language analysis; the empirical description of Socrates as empirical description; the phenomenological and physical accounts of the Palinode as phenomenology and physics. But all are conducted as means to conveying a metaphysical view: the larger purposes they serve are vindicated by the theory of a supersensible realm. Because it provides the motives and reasons for the use of other forms of discourse, without making them rely on assertions which only it can justify, metaphysics plays what I will call a leading or "hegemonic" role in the texts we have examined.

Because its role is merely hegemonic, metaphysics can tolerate a plurality of other modes of discourse; it is not itself the seat of all validity. Indeed, philosophy as presented in the Palinode not only has no distinct body of doctrine, but no distinct modes of discourse and argumentation either. What distinguishes it from other modes of interaction is the specific sort of love on which it is based—eros without touch—and, of course, its specific goal. And because of all this, the metaphysical dimension is not really necessary at all: for the new concept of freedom is articulated, we saw, in the phenomenological narrative of the Palinode. Whether love affairs really happen that way, and whether we want to call the resulting experiences "emancipatory," are empirical and linguistic questions independent of both Platonic physics and metaphysics.[9]

But there is another, stronger role for metaphysics in the Platonic writings which serves to occlude the full scope of the interaction portrayed in the *Phaedrus*. In the *Republic*, the poet is expelled from the polis (*Rep.* 10.595a seqq.). It seems that, in all consistency, a like fate should meet the lovers of the *Phaedrus,* for most of the accusations made against the poet can also be made of them. Like the poet, the lover is—at least in the early stages of his affair—ignorant of the truth, of what he is doing and of what is happening to him. Like poetry, his attraction to his beloved is an affair of the lower elements of the soul, to which it gives expression; and it leads him, like the poet, to despise the basic distinctions on which society is erected (cf. *Rep.* 10.598e–607a).

But the *Phaedrus* sharply distinguishes the "lovers of beauty" from the poets, mere crafters of imitations (*Phdr.* 245a, 248d seq.), and the erotic interaction of the Palinode differs from poetry in several ways. First, it does not remain as it starts, in ignorance and low desire, but becomes the pathway to knowledge and restraint. Second, it is not a public affair the way poetry is. A poet must have an audience; the lovers of the Palinode want only to be alone together. They constitute a closed system; their mania does not spread through the larger society. But, most important, love is not mimesis, or imitation, of a sensible object. The poet produces images of sensibles, which themselves are images of Forms, and is thus at two removes from reality (*Rep.* 10.595e–598d; *Phdr.* 248e). The lovers, too, fashion and adorn images as do sculptors (*Phdr.* 252d); but the "images" in question are each other, and—far from being twice removed from reality—are themselves the most beautiful human reality possible.

The commonality between the experience of poetry and the interaction portrayed in the Palinode is thus obscured by the texts' insistence that art is mimetic in character. This occlusion is not just another instance of what I have called the hegemony of metaphysics. Here, the metaphysical theory of Forms seems actually to determine how a sensory phenomenon is to be understood. "Imitation" is a standard Platonic way of characterizing the relation of sensibles to Forms.[10] Given that sensible reality is always a matter of imitation, the only question to be asked about the work of art is—what does it imitate? The answer cannot be the realm of Forms, for the sensible realm itself does that; nor can it be any specific Form or set of Forms, since (as *Republic* 10 says repeatedly) all manner of things get represented in art. So it must be sensibles that art imitates. The theory of Forms thus provides a basic premise—that all sensory reality is imitative—from which the view that art, too, is imitative follows deductively. By providing such a premise, rather than a guiding goal, metaphysics here is what I will call "foundational" rather than merely hegemonic.[11]

In the case of Plato, the metaphysical location of poetry at two removes from reality makes aesthetic experience seem to be something quite different from the erotic experience of the lovers in the Palinode, and in particular deprives it of the liberating character of that experience. Appreciation of the emancipatory power of aesthetic experience will then have to await, in the modern era, the collapse of the foundational status of metaphysics.

Eleven

Metaphysical Prescriptions and the Aristotelian Concept of Freedom: *De Anima* 1.3

Analysis

With the philosophy of Aristotle begins, I will argue, the systematic occlusion of intrinsically emancipatory interaction. The agent of this is his metaphysics, which occupies for him a position much more dominant than the hegemonic status it had for Plato. Aristotelian metaphysics maintains, we will see, that language is essentially a medium for truth telling. It follows from this that intrinsically emancipatory interaction contravenes the essence of language itself and is impossible. Since the view that language has some privileged relation to truth, among all values, continues to dominate the efforts of philosophers and linguists today, the occlusion of intrinsically emancipatory interaction persists into the present, though in somewhat different forms. We cannot understand those forms, then, without recourse to Aristotle. To show this will require, first, a brief account of the key concept of Aristotle's metaphysics and its role in his thought generally. In the next chapter, I will show how that concept—substance—structures Aristotle's account of freedom, and in the following section I will show how this, in turn, occludes intrinsically emancipatory interaction. I will then turn to the attack on the primacy of metaphysics in Kant's Third Antinomy, in order to show how that attack leaves metaphysics surviving, so to speak, its own death.

The primary dispute between the Platonic and the Aristotelian texts centers, for my purposes, on the issue of whether the cause of an entity's being is to be found outside it, separately existing like a Platonic Form, or is immanent to the thing itself. Aristotle articulates the latter alternative in terms of the concept of "substance." My analysis of this will begin with the Aristotelian critique of Platonic philosophy, and since my account is to have special relevance to the *Phaedrus*, I will concentrate on the treatment of self-motion in *De Anima* 1.3. But that text is virtually impossible to understand on its own. It calls, first, for the broader investigation of self-motion in *Physics* 8, and eventually for a brief discussion of substance itself.

Neither the *De Anima* text nor the *Physics* makes direct mention of the *Phaedrus*, and in fact the Aristotelian corpus in general avoids doing so.[1] But the doctrine that soul is to be defined as that which moves itself is clearly held by Plato, and Aristotle would hardly have exempted him from his critique. The doctrine is not specifically Phaedran. As Harold Cherniss points out, it is also to be found in the *Laws* (895e). But that the *Laws* is not the only target of *De Anima* 1.3 is suggested when that passage directs its criticism against those who "wish to wander" in their thought (*De An.* 1.3.406a27). As Cherniss notes, this has in view Platonic myth, and the *Laws* passage is not mythological.[2]

De Anima 1.3 thus bears prima facie reference to the *Phaedrus*. Its second part (1.3.407a2ff), however, is directed mainly to an attack, irrelevant here, on the self-motion of the world-soul as portrayed in a third dialogue, the *Timaeus*. The five preceding arguments are directed against the thesis that the soul "essentially" moves itself. A corollary of this is the assertion that soul is not moved by anything else, except "incidentally": for if its essence is self-motion, its essence cannot be to be moved by others (*De An.* 1.3.406b7–11). The corollary is acceptable in Aristotelian terms, but the main thesis is not. The soul moves, not itself, but the body it is in. If it is then carried along with that body, that is merely "incidental."

I shall briefly set out the five arguments, calling as needed on the *Physics* and other texts.

> (1) (406a12–22): There are four kinds of motion: locomotion, alteration, diminution, and growth. Soul must be moved, if essentially moved, by some or all of these. But all these motions are in place.[3] So if the soul essentially has any of these motions, it must essentially be in place. But the soul has no place, and therefore no essential motion.

The denial that the soul is in "place," in the Aristotelian sense, does not entail that it is not in "space," in the modern sense. Two analogies in argument (1) compare the soul's status with respect to the body to those of the body's color and length. This suggests that soul is to be viewed, not as somehow hyperphysical, but as intimately connected to the sensory realm. To understand the true force of the argument, we must distinguish—as does Jean Tricot here—*topos*, or "place" in the sense of a thing's proper place (which will be referred to in the third argument), from place in the more general sense of *Physics* 4.4 (212a5ff, 20f): the innermost boundary of what contains a thing.[4] One feature of such a place is that it can be left behind by that which it contains: to be *in* a place means to be able to *change* places (*Phys.* 4.4 211a5). The body can move around, exchanging one spatial place for another; but the soul cannot change bodies. Hence, soul is not "without place" in the sense that it does not belong anywhere within the sensory realm. Rather, it is too intimately wedded to just one part of that realm to be construable as "in a place." In my terms, it is conditioned by, rather than situated in, its body.

> (2) (406a22–27): If the soul is moved by nature, it can also be moved by force. But it would be hard to say what a "forced" motion of soul would be, unless we wish to "wander" mythologically.

Several Aristotelian texts argue that if an object can be moved by force, it can also be moved by nature.[5] Warrant for the converse proposition can perhaps be stated as follows. All motion, as we shall see, comes from contact with a mover. This mover is either within the moving entity or without. If within, the motion is "natural"; if without, "by force." The only entity that could move itself by nature and yet be unmovable by force would be one which could not come in contact with anything outside it: the world-soul, which is discussed in the later part of *De Anima* 1.3.

> (3) (406a27–30): If the natural movement of the soul is upward, it will be fire; if downward, earth.[6] But soul is neither of these—nor one of their intermediates, water and air.
>
> (4) (406a30–b5): Since the soul appears to move the body, it would be reasonable to assume that the movements it communicates to the body are those by which it is itself moved. But if so, there can be a reversal: movement of the body can be communicated back to the soul. And since the body's basic movement is in place (cf. argument 1), it would follow that the soul could change place, either wholly or in part.[7] But then it would be possible for the soul to leave the body and come back to it: for the dead to live again.
>
> (5) (406b11–15): All change is *from* something *to* something,[8] and all motion is hence "displacement" of the moved in whatever respect in which it is moved. Whatever has as its nature to move itself must then be "displaced" with respect to its nature. But it is absurd to say that something can leave its own nature behind.

These arguments rely on two metaphysical doctrines. One is that there is a cosmic order which contains the proper places to which motions, when natural, lead, and which also contains a proper place for the soul, its individual body. The other is that everything has a determinate nature, which it cannot leave behind. One of Plato's main problems, says *Physics* 3.2 (201b24ff), was precisely that he thought motion itself was somehow indeterminate in nature. But the indeterminate cannot be defined: to *define* soul as self-mover is therefore incoherent—a nondefinition. Moreover, motion does have a determinate nature, and defining it is in Aristotle's view difficult but not impossible: motion is the actualization of a potentiality *qua* potentiality (*Phys.* 3.1.201a10f). This definition makes self-motion impossible. It does so by triggering a series of arguments and doctrines that go to the core of Aristotelian metaphysics, and the most useful thing here is perhaps simply to quote W. D. Ross *ad loc*:

> An aggregate of bricks, stones, &c, may be regarded (1) as so many bricks, stones, &c, (2) as potentially a house, (3) as potentially being in the course of being fashioned into a house. The movement of building is the realisation (1) not of the materials as these materials (they are, previously to the movement of building, already actually these materials), nor (2) of their potentiality of being a house (the *house* is the realisation of this), but (3) of their potentiality of being fashioned into a house. Similarly every movement is a realisation-of-a-potentiality which is a stage on the way to a further realisation of potentiality, and only exists when the further potentiality is not yet realised.[9]

Motion is thus the reception, by something which already exists, of some quality which it is capable of having but does not yet have.

In Aristotelian terms, no potentiality can actualize itself. Actualization must come from an agent which already possesses the quality in question (cf. *Metaph.* 9.1049b18–29). For something to "move" itself, then, it would have to possess some quality both actually and potentially, i.e., both to have it and not yet have it. Some entities can in fact be that way. If one of the sticks in a bundle of wood is on fire, and is igniting the rest, we could say that the bundle as a whole is both imparting and receiving heat. But such an entity is a mere artifact (cf. *Metaph.* 5.6.1015b36ff), not something organically unified or in "actual existence" as a unit. It is then only for such an actually existing unit that it is a contradiction to assert that it both has and does not have the same quality in the same way: "insofar as a thing is an organic unity, it cannot be acted upon by itself; for it is one and not two different things."[10]

Motion thus is inseparable from, in fact is a mode of existence for, the moving entity. It cannot be hypostatized as something in itself. In order for motion to occur, in fact, two actually existing entities are required. One is the entity which moves or changes: this actually exists as something determinate but has the potential of acquiring other characteristics. The other is the mover, which actually has those characteristics which the moving entity (the "moved") acquires in motion. *All* motion is thus induced from outside the moved, by contact with a mover, and therefore is directional: from mover to moved.[11] Ignoring this leads to philosophical trouble, because the communication of motion has the peculiar characteristic of being one actualization of two potentialities: the potentiality of the mover to cause motion, and that of the moved to be moved. Hypostatizing motion thus means looking at that single actualization in abstraction from the actual entities in which it inheres. If we do this, we have one actual existent with an active and a receptive side. To act is then conflated with being acted upon, and teaching, for example, with learning (*Phys.* 3.3 202b6f). Plato and others, we may add, were open to this because they attempted to consider soul without providing a precise account of its relation to the body (*De An.* 1.3.407b13ff).

Because nothing can move itself, if we want to trace a single case of motion back to its source we must (barred infinite regress) eventually come upon a first mover which (a) is not identical to the moved, and (b) does not move itself: an "unmoved mover" (*Phys.* 8.5.256a3–258b9). Though not identical with the moved, the mover need not be outside it: it can be part of it. If so, it must be a single, unitary part, for if there are two parts, each of which moves the other, there would be no first mover. Further, the directionality of motion would be impeached. We can perhaps put this second argument more completely in the following way: suppose entity A imparts quality Φ to entity B, and B imparts it again to A. If A has in the interim lost Φ, then we do not have a single case of motion at all, but rather two successive communications of a quality, in each of which the entity is "moved," i.e., receives the quality from another agent which actually possesses it. If A has not lost Φ, then when it receives it back from B it is both imparting and receiving it, and the directionality of motion is impeached. In neither case can either A or B, or both together, be the first mover. Such a mover, as unmoved, must be a unit: a single, actually existing entity.

I have recounted this argument at some length because it will have application in the Aristotelian *Politics,* where the single "mover" of the polis will be the form of its government. The idea that the human community is or should be structured in such a way is also taken up, we will see, in the modern concept of the state. But for the moment, it is clear that the Aristotelian arguments against self-motion rely on the view that no "actually existing entity," in virtue of the kind of unity that it has, can both receive and impart the same quality at the same time in the same respect.

The concept of an actually existing unit is central to Aristotelian metaphysics and is treated at *Metaphysics* 9.6–8.[12] Actual existence, or actuality (*entelecheia, energeia*) is connected with motion: indeed, it has been thought to be identical with it (*Metaph.* 9.3.1047a30 seqq.). In truth, however, actuality is the complete form of something of which motion is the incomplete correlate.[13] Actuality is not then merely a static state. It is a condition of dynamic self-maintenance and can be viewed as "motion" whose end is present within it. An example of this is vision. Seeing is not something static, but an activity which maintains itself over time because there is no exterior goal it aims at. If there were, seeing would stop once that goal were achieved, just as motion stops when the moving entity acquires the characteristic it previously had only potentially (*Metaph.* 9.6.1048b18–34).

The actuality of an individual thing is thus its dynamic self-maintenance as the thing that it is, a movement whose goal is nothing else than the thing itself (*Metaph.* 9.8.1049b9f). Because a thing which exists actually is not changing with respect to its basic existence, it has its substantial form—that character which makes the entity what it is, and thus makes it exist at all—within it. A thing's actual existence is then the dynamic presence of that substantial form, or "essence," within it. And because, strictly speaking, a thing is to be identified with its substantial form (cf. *Metaph.* 7.6.1031a15–1032a12), we can say that what gives an entity actuality is that entity itself. Where self-motion was a contradiction, self-actualization is a redundancy. The cause of a thing's being, then, resides in that thing.

A self-actualizing thing must be a single unit. It is in full possession of its form, and nothing else can actualize that form in it. That form, moreover, is itself unitary and gives unity to the matter in which it comes to be (*Metaph.* 7.17.1041b5–32). Therefore, something is "actual" by virtue of something unitary within it which maintains it as the entity it is, giving unity to its other components and furnishing the necessary *prius* for any further properties it may come to have (cf. *Categories* 5; *Metaph.* 7.17).

The view that anything which exists, in the fullest sense of the term, is of this sort is for my purposes the core of the Aristotelian doctrine of substance.[14] This doctrine provides a basic warrant for the arguments that soul cannot be defined as a self-mover, or as self-moving motion. Souls, in sum, cannot move themselves because ensouled beings are substances, i.e., have within them principles which give them unity. Whatever changes they undergo may come from other things or from one of their parts, in which cases those changes can be called "motions" but do not originate in the "self" of the moving entity. Or they may come from within, not from a part of the entity but from its substantial form. In this case they are not "motions" at all, but "actualizations" of that primary unitary principle—or, in the terms of *Metaph.* 9.6, they are "actions" (*praxeis*, 1048b22 seq.).[15] Aristotle's arguments against self-motion, as he states them here, thus depend on his alternative to Platonic metaphysics: viewing the source of the being of things as, not separate from them, but immanent to them. I will argue in the ensuing narrative that the arguments do not all *have* to be stated that way.

The concept of substance is in fact *prescriptive* for all Aristotelian science.[16] For scientific knowledge is knowledge of causes (*An. Post.* 1.2.271b8 seqq.). The most general types of causes are those studied by the most general science, "first philosophy," and first philosophy studies them by examining their paradigm, which is substance itself (*Metaph.* 4.1–2.1003a7-b19, 1004a32 seqq.). But the causality most fully illustrated by substance is just the self-causality of the actually existing individual thing, and this leads to two sorts of prescriptions for the rest of Aristotelian science. Formally, substance is known through syllogisms, and all Aristotelian science proceeds syllogistically (cf. *An. Post.* 1.1f; 2.13). It eschews myth and narrative, along with metaphor and equivocation, and aims solely at truth.[17] In terms of content, first philosophy furnishes to Aristotelian science the basic presupposition that there is, in any entity, a single substantial form which gives unity to that entity and from which its actions must all be derived. To understand this substantial form is to understand the entity itself. The political texts, as we shall see, remain true to both prescriptions.[18]

But not wholly true. To know the causes of things is to know why they cannot be other than they are, and the physical world for all we can know is full of things that do not fulfill this condition.[19] In particular, the science of politics (together with its introduction, ethics: *NE* I.2.1094b7ff) studies affairs of such confusion and complexity that it is only a sketch of a science; it concerns regularities and likelihoods, not laws and necessities. It begins, not from metaphysical premises, but from the "facts of life."[20]

But those facts of life are already interpreted in terms of the concept of substance. Political science (as well as ethics and other sciences of the physical world) makes a sort of hermeneutic use of the concept of substance. It uses that concept, prescribed to it by metaphysics, to interpret the givens of political life.[21] Hence, in Aristotelian physics we find appeal to the single source of the actions of each entity: all things which exist "by nature" are said to have in them a single source (*archê*) of motion and rest—their nature itself—and are "substances" (*Phys.* 2.1.192b8–36; *Metaph.* 5.4.1014b19–26). This is carried out yet more concretely: for persons, the unified source of action is their reason.[22] For households, it is the master and husband.[23] For armies, it is the general (*Metaph.* 12.10.1075a14f).

Finally, polises too exist by nature. Their unitary form is the constitution, the arrangement of the ruling principles or "magistracies" (*archai*).[24] A polis, to be sure, is not really a single "organic unity" or an actually existing entity. It is composed of individual people, who themselves are substances. But its unity, though weaker than that of such individuals, or of the families to which they belong, is not different in type. In particular, as a unity of heterogenous elements, the polis exhibits the same sort of unity that *Metaphysics* 7.17 attributes to the syllables in a word, or to the components of a substance.[25] The fact that we can understand a polis by examining its constitution (*Pol.* 3.7.1279a22–30) means that we approach it as, if not a substance, something which exhibits a weak approximation to the kind of unity that a substance exhibits in paradigmatic form. I will express this weak unity by referring to the polis, in its Aristotelian conception, as a "quasi-substance."

Narrative

The Aristotelian texts, like the Platonic, will define freedom by drawing upon an enormously diverse variety of investigations—in the domains of metaphysics, physics, and psychology, as well as ethics and political philosophy. But the mode of organizing these diverse discourses has changed: instead of providing the motivation for modes of argument that have their own, independent validity, Aristotelian metaphysics actually supplies the fundamental form of scientific knowledge and the fundamental concept in terms of which the "facts" basing more concrete investigations are interpreted. The Platonic writings, we have seen, are more pluralistic; the ordinary language argument of *Republic* 8, or the phenomenological insights of the *Phaedrus* may retain their validity even if the Theory of Forms is rejected. But the views of freedom in the Aristotelian corpus, we shall see, are prescribed by Aristotelian metaphysics, particularly by its account of substance. If individuals are not substances, or if polises are not quasi-substances, those views will fail in important respects.

This role for metaphysics, which I will call "prescriptive," differs from both the hegemonic and foundational roles we saw metaphysics play in Plato. It is stronger than "hegemony" because it prescribes a general form for rational inquiry; it is weaker than a "foundation" because it does not, of itself, guarantee the truth of propositions in more concrete investigations: the polis, for example, is not a substance but a quasi-substance, and this means that an individual polis may in fact exhibit features which are not those of a substance (such as several ruling parties struggling for power in it). In its prescriptive role, then, metaphysics tells us not how things are but how they must be if they are to be rationally accounted for. Such prescription can become practical: if human beings adopt rational justification, so construed, as something desirable, they will try and make concrete entities—people or polises—conform to what it prescribes. We have seen an instance of this in the *Phaedo,* where the human being—not very much like a Form, or even like a soul among the Forms—was told to make itself resemble such entities as much as possible. The practical, prescriptive role of metaphysics will be radicalized in Kant, who will deprive metaphysics of its claims to truth and hence to foundational status, but will continue to accord it prescriptive roles in his social and political thought. This prescription will take the political form of the state as an ideal of human community.

In general, the Aristotelian writings deny what they consider to be the main doctrine of Platonic metaphysics, the "separation" of Forms from the sensibles which are their instances.[26] The next stage in my narrative—Kant—will render detailed rehearsal of those arguments unnecessary; but it follows from them that human liberation cannot be viewed on Aristotelian principles as an escape to a supersensible realm. Such freedom is to be found in, and defined in terms of, the sensible world alone. This means that the Aristotelian account of freedom will develop some of the features we found in the *Phaedrus,* as opposed to the *Phaedo.*

On the Platonic model of participation, a sensible being participates in (or imitates) an indefinite number of Forms, each of which explains one of its various properties. On the Aristotelian doctrine of immanent form, a thing has its substantial form in it from the start; only on the basis of that does it come to have other properties. On this model, then, a human self is "formed" when matter (in the mother) receives the form implanted by the father, and cannot be constituted as a self through interaction with other human beings; further developments are merely "actions" (*praxeis*) of this previously existing substance. The kind of interaction presented in the Palinode is thus, on Aristotelian terms, *ontologically* impossible. For Aristotle, what happens would have to be construed as two complete human selves, already unified, alternately imparting information to each other.

The prescriptive status of metaphysics in Aristotelian philosophy should not be taken to entail that, if the concept of substance is rejected, everything Aristotle says falls to the ground. This is important for evaluating the criticisms of self-motion in *De Anima* 1.3. Though my analysis showed them to appeal to the doctrine of substance, such appeal is not always logically required: alternative, non-Aristotelian warrants can, in some cases, be supplied. Separating this purely critical side of Aristotle's treatment of self-motion from the positive account with which he wants to replace it reveals something interesting.

The denial, for example, in arguments (1) and (4) that soul is "in place"—that it can leave the body—has its *Aristotelian* warrant in the doctrine that the soul is the substantial form of the body. But we need not, of course, subscribe to any such view to hold that soul is inseparable from body. Any materialist, should she or he be willing to use the term "soul" at all, would agree with that. If we ourselves do, then we must reject the conception of true freedom advanced in the *Phaedo* as the product of a misguided metaphysical imagination.

In terms more specific to the *Phaedrus*, the doctrine that if the soul moves at all it must move in place, and hence in a broader sense in "space," points to a basic incoherence in the Platonic account of soul as self-motion. For the soul in the *Phaedrus*, as in the *Phaedo*, knows the Forms by virtue of its likeness to them (cf. *Phdr.* 250c); this makes it hard to see how it can move at all—let alone move itself. For motion, as ordinarily understood in both classical and modern times, is primarily motion in space. It is so presented, not only by Aristotle (e.g., in argument (1) above), but (mythically) in the *Phaedrus* itself. Plato's later *Laws* implicitly accepts the idea (10.893c), as do the *Parmenides* (138b seq.) and the *Theaetetus* (181c seqq.). But the Forms are not in space, and do not move or change. In short: if the soul is essentially in motion, and thus in space, how can it ever—outside of a myth—"approach" or come to know the Forms?

Argument (2), we have seen, is directed against the mythological status of the *Phaedrus* account, and is likewise conducted from the principles of Aristotelian philosophy: the formal prescription made by Aristotelian metaphysics to more concrete investigations systematically precludes resort to myth. But the error cannot be repaired by any facile demythologizing. The mythological "wandering" to which argument (2) refers is, we saw, an account of the forced movement of the soul. In the Palinode, such unnatural motion is the soul's fall from heaven, which results from the loss of its wing—a fall explained only as the "decree of Adrastus" (*Phdr.* 248c). This movement, nothing less than the soul's irruption from the realm of Forms into the sensory world, turns out to be inherently contradictory: for it would have to be a motion in space which began from a starting point outside of space itself. Thus, the mythology of the Palinode serves to fudge the same fundamental incoherence in its account of the soul that we saw above: soul is at once able to know the Forms, outside of space, and yet is a type of motion within space. But again, we need not accept Aristotle's views either on metaphysics or on science in order to say either that philosophy should eschew myth or that motion in space cannot begin from outside space; most philosophers since Plato have held such views.

Finally, argument (5) states that something which by nature moves itself must leave its nature behind. This is nonsensical in view of the Aristotelian claim that everything has a substantial form, and thus a determinate nature. But the Platonic writings do not make that claim: we have seen *Physics* 3.2 assert that Plato himself did not believe that motion has a determinate nature.[27] The view that the human soul has no determinate nature is not, moreover, simply absurd: it was to have a remarkable career in philosophy, down to Sartre's elevation of it to a basic ethical principle.[28] Aristotle's argument thus appears to be wholly external to the *Phaedrus*.

But the *Phaedo* itself implies that soul, though in a non-Aristotelian sense, at least ought to have a determinate nature. For Plato, to have a determinate nature is to approximate the Forms, which *are* determinate natures; if the soul is to be like the Forms it must, then, have some sort of determinate nature: one which the *Phaedrus* asserts to exist, but of which it defers discussion (*Phdr.* 246a, 270c–272b). The deferral is probably a shrewd one: for how, among the unchanging Forms, can there be one of self-motion?

The interesting thing shown by all this is that when we disregard those aspects of *De Anima*'s arguments against the account of soul as self-mover, which are based on the principles of Aristotle's own metaphysics, the remainder turn out not to attack the concept of self-motion directly at all: they argue instead that the concept of soul as self-moving is incompatible with the view that it is like the Forms, and hence that it can know them or exist among them. The reason for the incompatibility is that the Forms are viewed as existing outside space, in an unchanging realm of their own, while the soul as self-moving must be wholly spatial and unstable or indeterminate in nature. The arguments are ultimately directed, in other words, against the "separation" of Forms from sensibles.

To them we may add another, similar difficulty, noted in my discussion of the *Phaedrus*: while the Palinode is able to give a "physical" account of the couple as self-moving, when it comes to the metaphysical level even this tenuous sense of "self-motion" fails. For the motion on that level is really brought about, not by an exchange of particles between the partners in the loving couple, but by the "magnetic" attraction of the god they both resemble and who, as an external paradigm of their own souls, is either a Form or something very close to one (cf. *Phdr.* 249c, 252d seqq.). Again, the ascription of self-motion to the soul is incompatible with the Theory of Forms.

In sum: the arguments of *De Anima* 1.3 against self-motion all depend, as I have analyzed them, on the Aristotelian account of substance. But those parts of the arguments which can be separated from that dependence are directed, not against self-motion per se, but against its compatibility with the separation of Forms from sensibles. They show that the *Phaedrus*'s account of self-motion, and hence of emancipation, is not only separable from the Theory of Forms, as we noted in the preceding narrative, but incompatible with it. But that does not "refute" the *Phaedrus*'s views on emancipation—for we are always free to throw out the Theory of Forms.

This is what Aristotle does; but it is only his first step. The Aristotelian view of freedom will take up the Phaedran view of liberation as the unification of the self, while discarding the Platonic metaphysics of separation with which that view turns out to be incompatible. Into the gap, however, will step another metaphysics: the unification of self will be conceived in terms of substance, and hence as brought about, not interactively, but internally: by a formative principle inherent within the human self from the moment of its generation. By not resting content with getting rid of the Forms, but taking the further step of injecting a new metaphysics, Aristotle will put philosophy into a bind. For Aristotle's metaphysics, as I noted, takes the opposite view from Plato's on one key question: it views the cause of an entity's being as inside it rather than outside it. And Kant will show, in the Third Antinomy, that to assert either of these views as a fundamental metaphysical principle requires us to assert the other as well.

The introduction of Aristotle's new metaphysics is going to occlude the poetic interaction of the *Phaedrus*, and two levels of that occlusion are already apparent. First, as we have seen, in terms of Aristotelian metaphysics the *Phaedrus* account is ontologically impossible. The self, as substance, is a given ontological unit; its fundamental unity cannot be achieved through interaction with another human being. Such interaction can only, as we will see, enhance its unity in various ways. More generally, the prescriptive status of substance in the Aristotelian universe means, as we saw, that science is keyed to the nature of substance itself. In the fullest sense, a substance is something completely finished, and the object of true science is then something which cannot be other than it is (*An. Post.* 1.2). But there is nothing for us to do with such a necessity but describe it: we certainly cannot intervene in it or change it.

216

Hence, the highest form of language—the rational language of science—
becomes purely descriptive. It does not change the objects it is about,
but merely represents or mirrors them. The highest and primary function of language then becomes telling the truth, and because for
Aristotle (as we have seen) we are to understand everything in terms of
its highest and best exemplars—i.e., those most closely connected with
substance in one way or another[29]—this gets generalized to all language.
The idea that the core of language is descriptive, with all its other functions ancillary—an idea whose importance for our culture cannot be
overstated—here shows its metaphysical roots.

Twelve

Freedom and the Soul in the Aristotelian Political Writings

Analysis

In the Aristotelian texts, to be "free" ultimately means to be a certain kind of moral agent, one with a certain structure of self. The self in question is one exhibiting something like the kind of unity that the *Phaedrus* portrayed, but which, as we shall see in this chapter, has been reconceptualized in terms of substance metaphysics. In the next chapter, I will argue that this reconceptualization occludes the kind of emancipatory interaction the *Phaedrus* presented, and does so in several different ways.

Emphasis on the individual, rather than larger social units, in formulating a concept of freedom seems foreign to Aristotle. If to be a "substance" means to be something independent and self-actualizing, then the human being, considered politically, is more like a part than like a substance.[1] Man is even more political than other gregarious animals, such as bees and ants, because unlike them he has speech. He can communicate, not only pleasure and pain (as do animals), but also his apprehension of advantage and justice, of harm and injustice, of good and bad. While other animals can presumably bond together for the sake of leading a pleasant or advantageous life, humans can do so for the sake of a good or noble life. Achieving such a life is the purpose of the polis. The goodness of the individual requires, in fact, that he be brought up in a polis. For virtue is formed from habit, and we acquire good habits from being brought up in a good polis.[2] The individual also requires the polis, as we will see, to exercise his virtue once it is formed.[3]

Though argued for in the political writings themselves (the *Politics* and the *Nicomachean Ethics*), the view that there is no human life outside the polis is, as we might expect, metaphysically prescribed. For the polis as a quasi-substance plays the role of form with respect to the individuals which are its parts—just as the parts of the living body are informed by its soul.[4] And the form in a substance is, as the *Metaphysics* has it, the "limit" of the entity in question: it is or determines the point beyond which no part of the thing can be found.[5] Hence, no part of an individual's body can be found beyond the form or shape of the body itself, and no human being can be found—for long—separated from his polis.

Given the comprehensive nature of politics in human life, it is not surprising to find that the two nouns which in the Aristotelian texts are related to the adjective *eleutheros* both refer to characteristics of human beings within a polis. One, *eleutheriotês*, refers to the psychological property (or virtue) of liberality, or the disposition to spend money in the correct ways, and is thus concerned with economic action (cf. *NE* 4.1 passim). The other, *eleutheria,* refers primarily to the kind of juridical status that we saw in Pericles: that of not being a slave.[6] "Freedom" thus appears to be a political predicate, one applied to individuals by virtue of their behavior or status in society. I will argue that this is not exactly the case.

The distinction between slave and free, according to the *Politics*, is of greatest importance in democracies, because in them "freedom" is a precondition for political power. This is opposed, for example, to what happens in oligarchies, where only the wealthy have power, and the distinction between a poor man and a slave is of relatively minor import (*Pol.* 3.8.1280a 1–7).

In extreme democracies, freedom is sometimes taken to be just what *Republic* 8 takes it to be: license for each person to live as he likes. It is also held to be the principle that each citizen have the opportunity to rule, either successively (by rotation of offices) or in virtue of majority rule, a principle which guarantees that the polis as a whole will do as most of its citizens like.[7] But "freedom" in both senses is badly defined: for both these sorts of freedom, if carried into practice, eventually coincide with irresponsibility, and through that with meanness or evil. Aristotle's argument here, simply put, seems to be that (1) there is evil in human beings, and (2) only an undemocratic constitution of the polis can restrain it. This principle of political coercion is denied by the extreme democrats, with the result that their form of government produces evil.[8] Democratic freedom is therefore, as was the case for Plato, incompatible with life in a political order. In addition, it fails to take account of two major distinctions among human beings. One is that between good and bad men. As we shall see, that which restrains evil in the good man is not the society he lives in but his own substantial form—his reason. It is because the polis is not compounded only of good men that the government itself has to play this role with coercion (*Pol.* 3.4.1276b36 seqq.).

In addition to ignoring the distinction between good and bad men, the "democratic" view unquestioningly accepts the standard juridical distinction between slave and freeman. Though not critical (or modern) enough to see that slavery is bad in any and all forms, the *Politics* is able (at 1.5.1254b31f, for example) to see that there are at least some cases in which slavery is unjust, and to ask after the conditions under which someone should justifiably be enslaved. The reverse of this question is, of course, to ask after the conditions under which someone can justifiably be free. But freedom here, if justifiable, is not simply a factually existing juridical status or a fortuitous characteristic of certain people (cf. *Pol.* 1.6.1255a5ff). It is a normative condition which requires and can receive legitimation. This normative condition, the ground for justifiable juridical freedom (and slavery), is not itself political. It is defined in terms of the condition of one's individual soul.

The legitimation of slavery, which occupies *Politics* 1.5–7, consists of showing that slavery, where justifiable, is a natural phenomenon. Among living beings, the *Politics* tells us, there is a threefold distinction. One group of humans—the masters and free men—possesses reason and can think. Another class—slaves, children, and to some extent women—do not have reason themselves, but can apprehend it in others.[9] The third group, which neither has nor apprehends reason, is that of animals.[10] The *Nicomachean Ethics* supplements this with the claim that even a master has in his soul a faculty which can apprehend, but does not itself possess, reason. In addition to this part of the soul, which master and slave both have, the master has a further part which the slave simply lacks: the part which enables him to make an active use of reason. The master's reason thus does not give orders to, and is not obeyed by, the slave alone: it also commands and, if he is morally good, is obeyed by the lower part of his own soul (*NE* 1.13.1102a-3a). The legitimate master then dominates his slave in just the same way as his own rationality—his immanent human form—dominates his body; the slave is merely a "separated" part of the master's body (*Pol.* 1.6.1255b11f). The political distinction between slave and free is thus, where legitimate, grounded in natural characteristics of individual souls. The legitimately free man is the one whose own body obeys his reason. The slave is one whose body obeys the reason of another. Freedom is here considered as, like Platonic "justice," a property immanent to the individual, a relation of his constituent parts to one another.

The immanence of freedom to the individual soul is brought out more fully in the *Nicomachean Ethics*'s discussion of the "voluntary" and of rational choice, or deliberation (*NE* 2.1–4 passim). An act is performed "voluntarily" if its cause is "in" the agent. If the cause is outside, and the agent "contributes nothing," the act is nonvoluntary. What sort of contribution an individual can make to his own acts can be seen from what the discussion excludes from the category of the voluntary. These are acts performed in ignorance (especially ignorance of the particular circumstances of the act), from compulsion, and, less strictly, from fear of a greater evil. The thrust of the latter three exclusions is to restrict the category of voluntary acts to those performed from desire. This move involves a departure from modern, and indeed from some ancient, usage. We often speak of an act which results merely from an irrational desire (as in neurosis) as "compulsive," rather than as voluntary; the Platonic conception of sensual desires as motions into the soul from without would accord with this. But the Aristotelian concept of "compulsion" cannot exclude desires of any kind from the production of "voluntary" acts. It is a term from natural science, and denotes any movement which does not proceed from the nature of the mover. Hence, a stone, which "naturally" moves all the way to the center of the universe, rests on a mountaintop by "compulsion," though hardly against its desires.[11] In general, a natural object moves from compulsion when its movement is directly caused, not by anything in itself, but by some other natural object: examples given for this in human affairs are sailors carried by the wind, or a man being carried off by others. Thus, any desire—even an irrational appetite—is a cause of action located in the agent, and if he knows the circumstances of his action, that action is voluntary. The "irrational passions are thought to be no less human than reason is, and therefore the actions which proceed from anger or appetite are the man's actions" (*NE* 3.1.1111blff).

In sum, there appear to be two sorts of thing which can be "in" the agent and which can contribute to his actions: knowledge of the circumstances and desire. Neither of these, however, requires the active use of reason, which we saw to be the defining characteristic of the politically free man. Children and animals can act voluntarily (*NE* 3.2.1111b8ff), and so presumably can slaves whose actions are motivated by fear of the master's punishment. The actively rational part of the soul which we saw to characterize the free individual is thus missing from the account of the voluntary: its specific contribution to action is the process of "deliberation" and "rational choice" (*NE* 3.2–4).

The Aristotelian accounts of deliberation are confusing, and have given rise to a rather extensive literature.[12] According to the discussion in *Nicomachean Ethics* 3.3, deliberation is in general a ratiocinative process which begins from a presupposed end (ultimately, happiness) and decides what actions are the most efficient means to that end. It concludes when it reaches an action that can be performed by the deliberator at the present moment.[13] *Nicomachean Ethics* 7.4 adds the idea that the beginning points of practical reasoning are universal premises: "dry food is good for a man" and "I am a man" are required in order to formulate "dry food is good for me," a practical principle which, in the actual presence of dry food, can produce the conclusion that I should eat it.[14]

But that conclusion is not itself rational choice. Having decided rationally what to do, the agent must also desire to do it. Choice is thus "deliberate desire" of things in our power, and it is this combination of deliberation and desire which causes the act. The *Nicomachean Ethics* later specifies that the causality here is "efficient": reason plus desire constitute the choice, which then produces the act. These two causes in the agent are the only two morally relevant factors in him and, in effect, constitute the moral agent as such: "choice is either desiderative reason or ratiocinative desire, and such an [efficient] origin of acts is man" (*NE* 6.2.1139b3ff). When a man acts from deliberation, then the cause of his acts is not *in* him; it *is* he. The active use of reason which distinguishes the free man thus brings about the unification of his self. For the moral agent is nothing over and above his desires and reason, which are unified in his choice. This is why actions, in the strict sense of things deliberately done, reveal the actor (*NE* 3.2.1112a2f).

The democratic definition of freedom, we have seen, takes no notice of the distinction between those who are legitimately slaves (or free) and those who are so by law. The other distinction it ignores—that between good and bad men—will provide us with more detail regarding the internal relation of "faculties" which constitutes rational choice. The good man is one whose "opinions are harmonious, and he desires the same things with all his soul" (*NE* 9.4). The soul of the bad man, by contrast,

> is in discord, and one element of it, because of its wickedness, grieves when it abstains from certain acts, while the other part is pleased, and the one draws him hither and the other thither, as if pulling him apart (*NE* 9.4.1166b19–23).

There are for Aristotle four types of less-than-good, i.e., less-than-unified, souls. Worst off is the man who only apparently lives for the well-being of his rational principle. According to *De Anima* 3.10 (433a26–29, b11–13), an object of desire is presented either in imagination or by reason. Reason, operating in accordance with deliberative procedure, is always right. What it identifies as desirable is always either a means to or a component of happiness. Imagination, by contrast, can be either right or wrong. So, it follows, can the appetite or desire which follows it. A person who pursues objects of desire given only in imagination, without regard to reason at all, is thus in fundamental error about how to pursue happiness. He pursues, in fact, a multitude of objects which only appear to lead beyond themselves to his own well-being. His pursuit of that well-being is only apparent. In reality he is dragged around by diverse desires and is "at variance with himself," disunified and unfree (cf. *NE* 9.4.1166b6–8, 21 seq.). A second type of soul is that of the man whose reason gives the correct orders but whose desires will not follow them. He is "incontinent," unable to act from rational choice, and in that sense unfree (*NE* 7.1–10 passim).

Without desire, as we have seen, there can be no action. In order for a man to pursue his own well-being, the objects of his desires must be presented to him by reason, and his desiring faculty itself must accept what reason presents to it. If the man's desires follow his reason but reluctantly, or if he must act against some of his desires in order to follow his reason, he is "continent." If they follow willingly, he is not only free but good: desire and reason both pursue the same things, and he is not at variance with himself.[15] Only in such a man does desire assume its proper place in the soul, as that element which is not in possession of reason but which can apprehend and follow it (*NE* 1.3.1095a10; 3.12.1119b6–18). The Aristotelian moral hierarchy is thus one of self-unity. It begins with the man who pursues a conflicted multiplicity of objects his imagination tells him are desirable. The incontinent and continent men are both afflicted with a single basic opposition between their desires, *in toto,* and reason. The truly good man is also, then, truly unified—and truly "substantial."

In addition to "democratic" and juridical freedom, then, the Aristotelian texts advance the view that he is free who is able to act from the confluence of active reasoning and desire that constitutes rational choice. Though it is empirically not always the case, in the best polis—one composed of "free" men—political agency will follow upon moral agency as thus described.[16] Goodness (of whatever sort) is the same for the polis as for the individual, and political debate and decision is a form of deliberation (*Rhetoric* 1.4.1359a36–b1). It follows that only those who are themselves deliberately good can make their polis good. They alone are able to determine what actions and policies will conduce to the best life for the community.[17] Such determination is made by the rulers in the deliberative council, in which individuals—each capable of practical reasoning on his own—together examine whether a proposed course of action will contribute to the common good. It is this deliberative element which is the "authoritative" part of the polis.[18]

Political agency is then distinct from juridical freedom: it is possible to be juridically free and yet to be one of the ruled, rather than one of the rulers. The difference between these two classes is that the ruled will have only right opinion to guide them, while the rulers will have the capacity for practical reasoning itself (*Pol.* 3.4.1277b11f, b25–29). This is not because the two classes are composed of different types of people, but because the ruled are still young. Once they have learned how to obey, and have acquired moral insight from their obedience, they will in their turn become the rulers (*Pol.* 7.14.1332b32–43).

Moral agency, or the unity of the self, is thus the ground of political freedom for Aristotle. But such moral agency is not without problems when viewed in terms of the general Aristotelian account of movement. I have noted that, in terms of the *Physics*, actions which are undertaken for external ends are "motions," as opposed to actualizations. It would follow that the moral agent, or truly free man, is one whose actions are not externally induced. But the necessary role of desire in action suggests that such "internally induced actions" are impossible.

Let us grant that desire for some good is something somehow present "in" the individual who feels it, and that it can be a cause of actions. It can still be maintained that all desire is aroused by the perception of a good object outside the self, and hence is caused from outside. On this view, the desired object functions as, in Aristotelian parlance, a final cause (cf. *De An.* 3.10.433b10–18). Since no action occurs without desire for its object, it would seem that all action is caused by objects outside the agent. I will call this the "external causation" thesis.

On this thesis, an action can be called "voluntary" if it is (in part) caused by a desire present within the individual. But "voluntary" now refers only to desires as the *proximate* causes of actions. These causes are themselves ultimately caused from outside, by their objects. Hence, an action which is proximally "voluntary" is nonetheless ultimately "compelled": its ultimate cause is not in the agent, but in another sensible object. It is now hard to see how the voluntariness of an action could be the basis for ascribing it to the agent in any but a trivial sense. To claim that an agent is "responsible" for a particular action would mean nothing more than that the broader causal chain which produced the action passed through the agent, so to speak, in the form of a desire. But the agent did not, in any morally meaningful sense, "originate" his act.

Something akin to the external causation thesis is stated and rebutted at *Nicomachean Ethics* 3.1 (1110b8–17). But *De Anima* 3.9 offers, I think, a more perspicuous treatment. There, the question concerns what sorts of "movers" reason and desire are. Reason is not strictly speaking a mover at all, since reasoning can tell us that something is to be pursued or avoided without any action resulting. Desire alone can bring about movement, and is strictly speaking the moving cause of action.[19] But it is not an unmoved mover, for desire or appetite is always directed toward something other than it, and is moved by that object. It is that object which, in causing motion within the "organ of desire," itself undergoes no change and is not moved, but is an "unmoved mover" (*De An.* 3.10.433a27–29, 433b15–17). So the *De Anima*, perhaps surprisingly, *accepts* the external causality thesis. All desires are caused by their objects, which are unmoved movers of the desiring faculty. The problem now is not to refute the external causality thesis, but to disarm it. Aristotle must show that, in spite of the fact that desires are caused by their objects, sense can nonetheless be made of the idea of a causal chain which has its ultimate mover, as well as its proximate one, within the acting agent.

As we have seen from the *Physics*, no causal chain can terminate in a mover which is moved by anything else or by itself. Thus, if we wish to define "voluntary actions" as actions whose ultimate, as well as proximate, cause is within the agent, that ultimate cause must be an "unmoved mover" within the agent. But an unmoved mover, *Metaphysics* 12.7 tells us, moves by being, like the Prime Mover, an object of desire. If there were to be an object of desire within the self, then the causal chain producing desire would indeed terminate within the self. The desire would still be for, and caused by, something external to it—but not by something external to the individual moral agent. Such an object of desire is human reason itself. For desire is not merely, in human beings, a part of the soul which pursues external goods; it is also that part which is capable of apprehending and following reason. To "follow" reason, as an activity of the organ of desire, is not to be intellectually persuaded by it. It is to desire active reason itself, as one's final cause.[20]

This point is put even more strongly at the beginning of the *Nicomachean Ethics*. There is one thing which is desired for its own sake, and for the sake of which everything else is desired: happiness. But happiness is nothing other than the excellence of the active soul, i.e., of that part of the soul which possesses, rather than merely apprehends, reason.[21] Thus, the excellence of the rational soul is the ultimate aim of human action, as well as the ultimate object of human desire. Desire for an external object is only proximate. If I want, say, a drink of water, that is ultimately because drinking the water will conduce to (or perhaps be part of) happiness, the well-being of my reason. My desire for the water is only proximately caused by the water itself, then. Its ultimate cause, or the final object of desire, is my own well-being (*NE* 6.3.1139b3ff). The same is true, presumably, of desire for another person, of *eros*.

The movements of living things, though in part caused externally, are thus ultimately caused from within. Though they may require movement for the attainment of their aim, the ultimate goal is always the well-being of the agent himself. Though an action may involve motions, in the last analysis it is a real or apparent attempt at actualization: at securing or manifesting the dominance within the individual of his unifying substantial form. All actualization, we have seen, is (in the case of an entity that already exists) self-actualization; and a person's reason, as the substantial form immanent within him, is in the strictest sense to be identified with that individual himself. Hence, to desire reason is to desire, or love, one-self.[22] The individual who pursues the excellence of his own rational faculty has himself for a goal. His acts spring from rational choices pro-duced by his reason, which in the strictest sense he *is,* together with desires which have their ultimate source in that same reason. And with this we have the full—and notably nonpolitical—Aristotelian definition of the free man: as the one who "exists for his own sake, and not for that of another" (*Metaph.* 1.2.982b25ff). Such a man's acts are performed by, and for the sake of, his reason, his substantial form. He, and he alone, is in the fullest sense an Aristotelian "substance."

Narrative

The Aristotelian texts thus follow the Platonic ones in condemning the "democratic" view of freedom; and, like them, they turn to a metaphysi-cal theory for warrant in doing so. But the theory is different, and so is the warrant it supplies. This can be seen by asking the same question here as we did there: what reason is there to believe that, in a society in which every man lives as he likes, people will actually undertake to do things which go against the common interest?

The Platonic answer was that people who can live as they like will attempt to satisfy unnecessary desires, and this in turn was predicated on a physicalistic model of the soul as a sort of passive container which could, and would, be impelled from without. On the Aristotelian model, desire is not construed in such physicalistic terms: it is a species, not of efficient, but of final cause. Yet all desire is for something external to the organ of desire: proximally for external objects and ultimately for reason. *All* motion of the human being is impelled from without, because nothing can move itself. It might seem from this that the satisfaction of *any* desire would be a bad thing. But the Aristotelian writings are not ascetic: they distinguish, if not between necessary and unnecessary de-sires as Plato did, between desires whose satisfaction will really contrib-ute to the rational well-being of the agent and desires for which this is only apparently the case. Since satisfaction of the latter sort of desire does not benefit the desiring agent, such desires are in fact ultimately, as well as proximately, desires for external objects and correspond to Plato's un-necessary desires. This distinction is not, for Aristotle, evident from the character of the desires themselves, however. It must be drawn by the individual's reason, operating via practical syllogisms.

Hence, only those who are able to make active use of their reason can, in the absence of external authority, act well. In the case of others (including evil men, children, slaves, and women) reason acquires authority only through external constraints. Radical democracy weakens those constraints, and hence impeaches the authority of reason. And reason itself should govern the polis: those who are not fully rational should obey those who are. This follows, again, from the ontological status of the polis as a quasi-substance; its actions ought to be directed by just one of its single components, which should be reason. Thus, as in the Platonic texts, democratic freedom contradicts the nature of the polis and cannot be consistently pursued by, or made the basis for, a polis. The warrant for the Aristotelian condemnation of democratic freedom is ultimately, like that for the Platonic, metaphysical in nature.

The Platonic condemnation of democratic freedom was made without regard to the specific set of fixed distinctions constituting the state: such freedom would be bad for anyone, because everyone's soul—even the philosopher's—is a sort of "container" of motion. The Aristotelian condemnation, by contrast, applies to specific groups within the state, not to everyone. That some members of the state would not be harmed by the introduction of democratic freedom is true to the Aristotelian denial of the Platonic "separation" between forms and particulars. If the forms are to be found in this world, the rational life must be present there as well, and must in fact be the life of the highest group within the polis, the class of "serious" men.

The *Phaedo*'s view of emancipation as an escape to another world thus has no place within the Aristotelian scheme of things. It is not surprising that the Aristotelian concept of freedom should be a conflation of the two Platonic views of freedom which remain if we reject both democratic freedom and the "supersensible" freedom advanced in the *Phaedo*. These are self-mastery and the unification of the self. The Aristotelian free man is master of himself because he *is* his reason, and his actions are all guided by reason. But this does not mean that he must, like the Platonic "self-master," continually struggle against his desires. For the Aristotelian free man's desires follow his reason of their own accord: he is in something similar to the situation at the end of the Palinode, where the evil horse has become responsive to the good horse and the driver. This unification is, however, performed by the free man himself in his deliberations; it does not come about interactively.

The Platonic texts, we have noted, have a name for this state: it is "justice," as defined in the *Republic*. From a Platonic point of view, we could say that the notion of justice has usurped the name of freedom (with "justice," in *Nicomachean Ethics* 5, being assigned to the lawful and the equitable). The reason for this is that, in the Aristotelian approach, freedom is no longer defined interactively; it is not a reconciling relation to one's environment, but an immanent state of the soul of the free man. This is again metaphysically warranted: if a human being is a substance, then it must contain a single principle which gives unity to the rest, and which is in fact the basis for any other characteristics that it has. It is therefore impossible for a human being to be unified "from outside," in and through interaction with others. This is why the good man is able to control his desires all by himself. For desires to withstand his reason would mean that his reason would not be the source of his entire life, would be for him not to be a substance.

But, as we have seen, not all human beings are "substantial" in this full sense: bad men and slaves, as well as women and children, all lack the authority of reason that is required for "substance;" so do the two lower levels on the Aristotelian moral hierarchy.[23] The category of substance is here playing what I have called a prescriptive role: not all human beings can be empirically observed to act like substances, and not all are even able to do so. But a rational account of human life must interpret it in terms of substance, and a human being who wants to live a rationally justifiable life must undertake to act from and for his substantial form—his reason—alone.

Thirteen

Freedom and Interaction in the Aristotelian Polis

Analysis

If the cause of the being of an individual thing is to be found within that thing, then each political being—each human—must act for his own sake, and is "free" when he can do so. But then, it seems, there is no place for an overarching human order. The social universe will consist of a set of individual substances bouncing off one another in more or less random ways, a conception more Hobbesean than Aristotelian. Aristotle in fact is able to occupy a middle ground between the interactive concept of emancipation articulated in the *Phaedrus* (as well as in Hegel and Heidegger) and modern individualistic views. That middle ground may be understood in terms of his views on equivocity. At *Metaphysics* 11.3, in a discussion of this, we read that both

> a medical discussion and a knife are called medical because the former proceeds from medical science and the latter is useful to it. And a thing is called healthy in a similar way: one thing because it is a sign of health, another because it is productive of it (*Metaph.* 11.3.1061a3–7).

This threefold classification, I suggest, can also be applied to the Aristotelian accounts of freedom.[1] In and of itself freedom, as we have seen, is defined in terms of the mutual relation of the parts of the free man's soul, and hence without reference to the environment in which the free man may find himself. But both the production and manifestation of such a soul require the political environment of the polis. The accounts of interaction in the Aristotelian political writings, my ensuing analysis will argue, consistently interpret it as either a necessary (but not sufficient) condition for freedom or as a manifestation of it. In this, Aristotle is faithfully following the prescriptions of his metaphysics, for as I have argued in chapter 12, the free man is for Aristotle simply the most "substantial" of humans. To interpret human interaction as producing or manifesting freedom is to interpret it with the category of substance as

229

one's guiding conception. But to interpret it that way is to deny, implicitly, that interaction can itself be intrinsically emancipatory. Aristotle's approach thus occludes the kinds of poetic interaction portrayed in the *Phaedrus*. It also constrains his views of language in general and places certain limits on Aristotelian social critique.

Two important ways of producing free souls are training for the young and tragedy for their elders. At *NE* 1.9.1099b9–11, training is said to have two main parts, habituation and learning. Habits are formed by repetition: a person who performs just acts, even without doing so from deliberate choice, will become a just person (*NE* 2.1.1103a33-b2, b14–26). One who cannot make deliberate decisions about what sorts of acts to perform must be forced to perform those which will produce good habits. This coercion must first be exercised by parents and teachers, and later by the polis itself.[2] Habituation, like motion, thus depends upon at least two actually existing individuals, and is a form of interaction. One individual, the child, has a human nature and thus the potential for developing the ability to deliberate. The other is the source of the prescription: the parent, teacher, or the rulers of the polis itself. This second participant must know what the appropriate actions are, if it is to prescribe them to others. And it cannot know this unless it has itself acquired the appropriate habits (or is composed of legislators and magistrates who have: cf. *NE* 10.9.1180b 3–5).

The other side of training is learning. This is not merely like motion; for the *Physics*, it is a standard example of it.[3] Again, the form or characteristic that learning implants in the learner must previously exist in another: all learning requires a teacher as "mover" (*Metaph.* 9.8.1049b23–28). Both habituation and learning, then, are asymmetrical. One participant, the "master" of the encounter, already has a property which in the encounter is passed to another.[4] Once the child has become well-habituated, and has learned enough, it is possible for him to "live for his own sake" and be free. But the interaction which makes this possible is not constitutive of freedom itself.

The same holds for the paradigm of Aristotelian aesthetics, tragedy. This is conceived as interaction between the tragic poet and the members of his audience. The tragedian makes a statement "about what such and such a kind of man will say and do, according to either probability or necessity" (*Poetics* 9 1451b8–10): he aims at conveying a universal. This universal provides the basic structure of the plot, the action the tragedy "imitates."[5] The various deeds and acts on the part of individual characters, which are parts of the plot, are thus revealed, as the play proceeds, to exist in a rational context determined by the kind of actions they are.

This in turn discloses to the audience the rational possibilities implicit in action of that kind. And because action reveals character, it also discloses to them the basic structures of human personality (*Poetics* 4.1448b9–18).

Tragedy is thus, on this level, a form of teaching, and as such aids in the production of free souls. In making its disclosures, the language of tragedy approaches that of politics, which also aims to disclose to the audience rational possibilities implicit in courses of action.[6] But tragedy differs from political speech in two ways. First, it links its disclosures to the emotions of pity and fear. While political speech, we noted, sets forth "advantage and justice, harm and injustice, good and bad," tragedy is restricted to presenting people who suffer terrible fates.[7] Identifying with these characters, the audience sees the terrible things that befall them as the kind of thing that might befall themselves also—and soon.[8] The situation presented in tragedy is never affirmed, then, as offering the possibility of a rational course of action; it is rejected, as something to be fled. The audience does not in fact flee because, however caught up in the horrible tale it may become, it eventually recognizes that what is being presented is not actual, but merely possible. It is not as similar to the life situations of the audience's members as they had thought. At the end of the tragedy the audience finds itself, not fearful, but relieved—purged, in "catharsis," of its fear (*Poetics* 14.1453b12ff) and restored to what Hannah Arendt called the "political virtue *par excellence*," courage.[9] Since, we may say, without courage no one can be free, the cathartic effect of tragedy also plays a part in the production of free citizens. In both its educative and purgative dimensions, then, tragedy is valuable for the polis, and the *Poetics* argues against the (Platonic) view that it necessarily debases the people (*Poetics* 26.1461b27–1462a13).

The second contrast between the languages of politics and tragedy involves "authoritativeness," and because of its future importance in my own account of poetic interaction, I will discuss it in some detail. Political oratory, according to the *Rhetoric*, aims to demonstrate the expediency or harmfulness of a possible course of action, and seeks to win its audience over. It is at once "authoritative," in the sense that the audience is supposed to accept it, and straightforward.[10] Tragic language is neither. It achieves its effect by lengthening and shortening words, as well as using metaphors and a special vocabulary. "Other than the authoritative," it "comes to be as something different from what is accustomed" (*Poetics* 22.1458b1–5). This, presumably, helps the audience keep in mind that the fearsome events being presented do not *really* affect them.

It also means, however, that the audience is repeatedly pulled up short by the language of the tragedy, which contains incongruities or anomalies in the form of unusual words or "enigmas": combinations of words which appear to be impossible (*Poetics* 24.1461a32).[11] It is wrong in such cases for critics to assume that the tragedian is mistaken or obscure in his usage (*Poetics* 22.1458a26ff). They ought to accept his authority (if not that of his utterances) and apply special understanding procedures. These include understanding words in terms of unusual meanings, rather than their normal ones (as when, in English, "mule" is used to refer to a machine for spinning cotton); construing them as metaphors; examining possibilities of syntactic ambiguity; and looking to linguistic custom, or what today would be called background knowledge. Wine mixed with water, for example, is conventionally called "wine" in Greek, though some propositions true of the mixture are not true of wine alone (e.g., alcoholic content, and consequent effects on the drinkers, are lower for conventional "wine" than for real wine: *Poetics* 25.1461a9-b8).

The strangeness of poetic diction, then, requires the audience—especially the critics—to examine in how many senses a word can be used, performing for that word the kind of investigation of "things said in many ways" that Aristotle's first philosophy undertakes for "Being," "One," and of many other terms (in *Metaph.* 5).[12] Such a response presupposes that the tragic poet knows exactly what he is doing with his strange language. Like the more complex universals conveyed by the plot, the meanings of individual terms are present in the mind of the writer (cf. *Poetics* 9.1451b27f). Concomitantly, the writer himself is not, as for Hegel and Heidegger, a self-effacing corridor producing meanings greater than he. For Aristotle, he functions as a sort of "master" of aesthetic interaction.

The mind of the spectator must for its part possess the resources for deciphering poetic language: knowledge of unusual meanings, syntactical knowledge, and background information. Thus, again in contrast to Hegel and Heidegger, poetry is not for Aristotle an origin of language. It is a determinate message from the poet which makes use of unusual linguistic tools but does not create new ones. The only exception to this is metaphor, which I will consider in the more general discussion of language below.

In addition to habituation, learning, and tragedy, which are productive of freedom, there are forms of interaction which manifest it. Preeminent among these, in addition to the communal deliberation we saw to be exercised in political agency, is the highest form of friendship. The good man does not require friends in order to be good in the first place, for he is already that. He needs them because friendship is a normal and natural consequence of goodness.[13] Friendship will, however, make the already good better, first with respect to action and the moral virtues:

> . . . the friendship of good men is good, being augmented by
> their companionship; and they are thought to become better
> too by their activities and by improving each other; for from
> each other they take the mould of the characteristics they
> approve (*NE* 9.12.1172a11–13).

Friendship so construed is a form of reciprocal imitation. Its proper
locus, as with everything human, is the polis. In fact, it "holds the polis
together": when men are friends, they have no need of abstractions such
as legal justice. But if friendship thus *secures* the unity of the polis, that
unity is *first* achieved through the constitution of that same polis. Indeed,
friendship, like all community, is subordinate to the polis, for the polis's
constitution determines what sorts of friendship will flourish among its
citizens. In a tyranny there is almost no friendship, for ruler and ruled
have nothing in common. True friendship flourishes where the citizens
are equal and the government is fair.[14]

In sum, the polis is the field in which the freedom of its citizens can
be manifested in friendship. Its constitution, its single "ruling principle,"
determines whether and how this will come to pass. Making friendship
"political" in this way goes together for Aristotle with its divorce from
erotic attraction. Love, in fact, is an "excess" of friendship and is felt
toward only one person. Furthermore, it begins with the pleasures of the
eye; friendship, by contrast, begins with goodwill and is enhanced by a
period of time spent living together.[15]

It is necessary, as we have seen, to be a good person before one can be
a good friend. A good man must be free: he must be capable, in terms of
the definition from the *Metaphysics,* of living "for his own sake, and not
for that of another." But when brought into connection with friendship,
this formula undergoes qualification. For one thing, the good man,
as we have seen, identifies himself with his own rational principle:
this is what he loves in himself, and whose good he seeks (cf. *NE*
9.4.1166a10–28). But this love of self is not exclusive. It is for the most
"noble" element within him, and this means that the good man loves
himself, not qua himself, but qua noble. Whence it follows that he will
love the nobility of another with the same love he feels for himself and
will be ready to sacrifice anything for the nobility of that other. So
friends will give one another their wealth and honor and office; they will
die for one another, and more: they will even yield to each other the very
opportunity to act. For "it may be nobler to become the cause of the
friend's acting than to act himself." Since it is in action (*praxis*), we saw,
that self-actualization takes place, the friend is ready, for the sake of the
noble, to sacrifice his own self-actualization—his very opportunity to
manifest his own freedom.[16] The final cause of his action—of his own

concrete self-actualization—is then not in himself but in something else. In such a case, though the Aristotelian texts do not say so, one's action is derived from a "separate form": the reason, the substantial form or nobility, of the other. In this sense, as Thomas Gould has remarked, the Aristotelian account of friendship remains wholly Platonic.[17] Friendship, then, presents anomalies to basic claims of Aristotelian metaphysics.

The final manifestation of freedom I will consider—fragmentarily, after the example of the texts—is the "freedom" of philosophical activity itself. At the very beginning of the *Metaphysics*, the paradigm of such activity—first philosophy—is asserted to be, among many other things, "free," and in the very sense that we have seen Aristotelian thought most directed to articulating:

> . . . as the man is free, we say, who exists for his own sake and not for another's, so we pursue [first philosophy] as the only free science, for it alone exists for its own sake. Hence also the possession of it might justly be regarded as beyond human power; for in many ways human nature is in bondage . . . (*Metaph.* I.2.982b24–29).

First philosophy is directed to the main Aristotelian divinity, the Prime Mover itself. As such, it is carried out, not strictly speaking by man, but by the "divine element" within him—his intellect—and the excellence of the intellect is something "separate" from other excellences of man. As directed to and accomplished by something divine rather than strictly human, first philosophizing is not a political activity: the polis exists for the sake of theory, not theory for that of the polis. Since the polis is the field of human interaction, theory is also not interactive. First philosophizing is something the philosopher can perform entirely by himself; friends are helpful but (as with virtue in general) are only aids to performing it *well*.[18]

Two things follow from this. One is that theory has no essential bearing on politics: it is possible to be a first philosopher and as such to leave the polis entirely to itself. On the other hand, a leisured class, and the degree of political order which can produce this, is necessary for first philosophy. When the existence of that class is threatened, the philosopher must involve himself, critically if need be, in political affairs.[19] This brings us to the question of Aristotelian political critique. It is a vexed one,[20] and I will limit myself to sketching some of its basic limits. In general, my view will be the one stated by Ritter:

> [Aristotle's] procedure does not consist in first defining the nature of man through reason, and then deducing the polis from that. The concept of man as a rational being can

rather only be found and developed when the polis is already there. . . . Theory can produce no concept of essence and nature which has not actually come to be. Therefore it must, in every step, proceed hermeneutically as the reflection on what has come to be: it must "speak out of" that. . . . [The rational nature of man] cannot be deduced, it must be given as present; the concept is derived from that given.[21]

This is not to deny that Aristotelian political science can be critical; *Politics* 2.1 (1260b32ff) certainly proclaims critical intent. The criticism, carried out theoretically by Aristotelian political science, has its ideal—the preconception of its "hermeneutical" reflections—metaphysically prescribed: it is the polis as quasi-substance, as an active unity with a specific form.[22] Hence my view, consistent with Ritter, will be that Aristotle is critical of existing polises, but not, as is Plato, of the polis itself as the all-encompassing domain of human interaction.[23]

The exercise of political critique does not for Aristotle question the polis itself because such critique is, for one thing, confined to its leisured class. Far from disregarding social distinctions, then, critique is founded on them and cannot challenge the political order which embodies them. But a more important restriction on social criticism can be seen from examining its relation to language. We saw that language, because it "sets forth" the advantageous and harmful, the just and the unjust, is the differentiating characteristic of the human community (*Pol.* 1.2.1253a13ff). Hence, if language does these things wrongly—is loose enough to set forth what is unjust as "just," for example—the consequences would be serious indeed. But in the general Aristotelian view of language, such a mishap is impossible.

Words, in the Aristotelian conception, serve not to express cultural consensus (which could be mistaken) but to designate things.[24] This follows from the view, noted earlier, that the highest and primary function of language is to describe entities that cannot be other than they are. The status of word meanings as "likenesses" of external things is in fact so crucial to the nature of the word that it is not words which, in the standard Aristotelian formulation, are ambiguous, but the *things themselves* which are said in many ways (*ta pollachôs legomena*).[25]

The sound of a word is associated with its meaning by conventions. These vary for different languages and must be learned.[26] But in order to learn the conventions by which sounds are attached to meanings, one must already have knowledge of those meanings. And our knowledge of those basic significations cannot be learned from others.

Prior to learning, in the formation of a free self, went habituation. An analogous process in the case of language learning would be as follows:

the child sees others grouping various entities together, presumably by uttering the same sounds in their presence. By imitating them, he forms the habit of uttering the same sounds when in the presence of the same sorts of things. The child thus acquires the meanings of words from his elders. The "universals" with which his mind comes to be furnished are habitual ways, predominant in his culture, of grouping things together. "Justice," for example, would be a word which grouped together entities (actions) that the society in question happens to group together, though they may look as different as making a war, allotting custody of an orphan to his uncle, or giving a criminal 20 lashes instead of 25. It would not only designate a class of actions, but it would express a cultural consensus that those actions are similar in some important way.

This, however, is precisely what is *not* portrayed in the Aristotelian texts on the soul's acquisition of universals. It is only the sounds, not the meanings of words, which are acquired by imitation.[27] The meanings are acquired by induction, the "stabilization" of a universal, or form, within the (individual) soul. This begins from sensory experience, when some sensory form persists—"makes a stand"—in the soul. When a number of these have done so, the higher-order forms which they all possess make stands as well. The mind, if powerful enough, thus rises to apprehension of even the most general universals by a process which is at once individual and natural.[28] Further, since the Aristotelian universe has no separate Forms, those universals are exhibited fully in sensory experience itself. Since all people have sense perception, they can in principle come to know the meanings of all terms. There is no class of intrinsically vague words, as there was for Plato.

Even higher-order species and genera exist naturally. Hence, though the sounds of different languages may differ, the meanings of those sounds are the same for all languages and for all people (*De Interpretatione* 1.16a3ff; 4.17a1ff). As natural givens, they cannot be criticized. Word-meanings for Aristotle are not only definite; they are unchangeable.

There are two restrictions on this. First, such a word meaning may not be fully known to all competent speakers of the language as a whole. It may be the case that a given word, in the mouths of some speakers, fails to express adequately the nature of what it designates. We have for example noted that, in Aristotle's view, many speakers of Greek do not know the real meaning of "freedom." But the Greek language itself is not at fault. The critique of the usage of such people will be conducted in light of the usage of most speakers, or of the particularly competent ones.

Second, a language may be incomplete. There may be certain general features of the sensory world which have not yet been brought inductively to the attention of its speakers, and hence not yet formulated in words. Bringing them to light is the function of metaphors (and, we are told, of philosophy). Unlike other aspects of nonauthoritative speech (tragedy), the coining of metaphors thus extends language.[29] But this is a case of one acute individual taking induction farther than others have done. It fills in gaps, but is not a critique of what has previously been accomplished.[30]

Thus, political discourse is, for Aristotle as for Plato, inherently rhetorical in nature. But it is no surprise that it does not presuppose the kind of analysis of word meanings we saw in the *Phaedrus*. In fact, the Aristotelian rhetorician, unlike his Platonic counterpart, gains clarity not from preliminary dialectical investigation of word meanings, but precisely by using words with their *ordinary* meanings.[31]

This status of ordinary language is consonant with the view that, as Ritter notes, the actuality of reason is for Aristotle to be found only in the polis. For language is presupposed by both the polis and the household (*Pol.* 1.2.1253a18).[32] Since the polis is the circumscribing field of all human interaction, it cannot be the locus in which its own presupposition first comes to be. It follows that language must be formed, not interactively, but in the mind of the individual. Considered apart from all interaction, the individual mind, if its ideas are not to be wholly idiosyncratic, can only draw them from external nature itself. Language so construed cannot be other than it is, any more than can the nature from which it is drawn. It serves as a condition for the use of reason, not as an object of rational critique. Hence, in my terms, reason is for Aristotle bound to its language, which itself is necessitated by nature. It is unsituated, and there is no such thing as the clarification of parameters as parameters: no such thing, then, as situating reason.

Narrative

The thrust of all these accounts of interaction has been to show it either to lead to or follow from freedom—not to be, as was the poetic interaction of the *Phaedrus,* intrinsically and of itself emancipatory. Together, they occlude poetic interaction, and intrinsically emancipatory interaction generally, in at least three interrelated ways. First, they apply to all interaction (with the exception of friendship, which we saw to be anomalous to Aristotelian philosophy) a single formal model, on which poetic interaction is not possible. Second, they bring such interaction into the polis, reinterpreting it so that it will not be a threat to the political order. And third, they disperse the complex nature of poetic interaction as presented in the *Phaedrus* into a variety of seemingly disparate practices.

On the Aristotelian view as here analyzed, all interaction shares a common structure, and one model is appropriate for it. On this model, something (in learning, a piece of information; in habituation, a state of character; in poetry, a tragic plot) exists first in the mind of one person and then is transferred, via language, to that of another. Plato, presumably, would not deny that this happens. But he would deny that all inter-action is of this type. In particular, Platonic dialectics, especially as presented in the Palinode, is a form of interaction in which neither member of the loving couple at first has any idea what is happening to him and in which they acquire such knowledge, simultaneously and gradually, by a cooperative labor of argument and analysis.

On the Aristotelian model, all interaction has by contrast a "master"— one who knows, whose message is transferred to the others. To use Aristotle's own terms: the speaker makes active use of reason, while the hearer merely apprehends reason in another. Dialectic, therefore, is replaced by instruction as the knowledge existing in the soul of the teacher passes into the soul of the student; since tragedy has an instructive component, the same holds for it.[33] Warrant for this comes, proximately, from Aristotelian physics, which asserts that anything which has a quality must receive it from some entity which already possesses it: since knowledge, like character, is a "form" in the soul of the knower, it comes only from preexisting knowledge or from solitary induction.[34] This physical warrant is in turn warranted by the metaphysical proposition that forms exist eternally, as for Plato, but are immanent to things. Prior to coming to exist in one entity, a form must have been somewhere; if there is no separate domain within which it can exist, it must have existed within some other sensible entity. If Plato had been right—if forms were separate and substance were not the central category of the most general study of things—there would be no warrant for regarding the phenomena of political and ethical life in terms of substances, still less of quasi-substances—and poetic interaction would not be ontologically impossible.

When we view interaction in terms of its location rather than its formal structures, we again find Aristotle's account making a global and anti-Platonic claim: all interaction belongs to the polis. This claim, like the imposition of a single formal model on all cases of interaction, is, as we saw, prescribed by Aristotle's metaphysics: the most important quasi-substance in Aristotelian political philosophy is obviously the polis itself, beyond which nothing human can be found. In part, the Aristotelian texts view the polis in terms similar to those of the *Phaedrus*: it is a realm of fixed social distinctions (free/slave; leisured/working) in which men pursue purposes. The innovation on the *Phaedrus* is that as parts of a quasi-substance, humans can no more interact outside the polis than a kidney, for example, can live outside its body. Moreover, interaction within the polis can no more be dangerous or damaging to the polis itself than the possession of a kidney could be dangerous or damaging for the body. This means that in Aristotle's texts, certain forms of interaction, which for Plato stood outside the polis and threatened it, must be made safe for it. This leads to a second set of occlusions.

We saw the *Phaedrus* (together with *Republic* 10) present four such forms: eros and friendship, on the one hand; the dialectical examination of word meanings and poetry on the other. Aristotle attempts to render these safe for the polis by first interpreting them, on his single model of interaction, as having "masters." He then maintains that these perform tasks valid and sustaining for the polis itself. Thus, the *teacher* is responsible for producing active citizens—not for educating a class of contemplatives who will reject political life or attempt to overthrow its structures. The *tragedian* produces properly courageous citizens. The *philosopher*, as such, stays out of politics altogether: his interventions into the political sphere are in order that he may be able to perform his activity well, but so are everyone else's. In all this, poetic interaction, in which the hearer decides the meaning of an utterance and the interchange therefore has no single master, is occluded. With it go more developed forms of situating reason and intrinsically emancipatory interaction generally.

From the point of view of poetic interaction, the success of these arguments is less important than the fact that they are undertaken. They show that the presence within interaction of a master is a device by which the communicative infrastructure of a society reproduces the quasi-substantial character of the polis itself. This makes education, poetry, and philosophy safe for the polis.

The texts analyzed undertake to make friendship, too, safe for the polis: their general claim is that the types of friendship present in the polis are coordinated, as everything in it must be, to its constitution. The first step in such coordination—a necessary one, as the example of the *Phaedrus* shows—is to exclude from friendship erotic attraction. This guarantees that true friendship will not cross the basic distinction between citizen and noncitizen that constitutes the Aristotelian polis: though members of the lower classes can be beautiful, no one will have a character suitable for true friendship unless he is a full citizen.[35]

This move reveals the third way in which poetic interaction gets occluded in the Aristotelian texts: it is split up into other, apparently disparate forms. As I analyzed it in the *Phaedrus,* intrinsically emancipatory interaction was a confluence of the first three of the four forms of interaction mentioned above: eros, friendship, and the dialectical examination of word meanings. Friendship and eros have been definitively separated, and word meanings, for Aristotle, are examined in two disparate ways which have nothing particular to do with either of them. In the experience of a tragedy, the audience (and critics) accept the authority, both of the tragedian and of the language he uses: anomalies in tragic speech are recuperated as merely unusual instances of basic structures that need not be challenged. Outside the polis, apparently, is the philosophical examination of "things said in many ways." But this, we noted, takes itself to be examining, not words, but the things themselves in which ambiguities reside.

In the *Phaedrus*, a specific relation to another is not only an essential means to freedom—it *is* freedom, because it is constitutive for the free soul. With this interactive view of freedom goes a rejection of the polis as its appropriate terrain: adherence in a loving couple in fact emancipates the couple from that society, among other things. Aristotle does not, as we saw, *refute* the Palinode's account of interaction: he does not show that such interaction is impossible, unless we accept his own substance metaphysics. But he renders it invisible by separating its ingredients into different spheres; by interpreting these as contributing to the polis, rather than threatening it; and by applying a single formal model of communication to all cases of it. There is simply no room, on the Aristotelian schema, for intrinsically emancipatory interaction.

But even when separated from eros, friendship cannot be brought into line with the "quasi-substantial" model used for dealing with the other forms of interaction. For there is in true friendship no master, and a pair or group of friends is thus not a quasi-substance: none of its members is its single source of action and unity. But the group cannot for Aristotle be constituted through poetic interaction as in the *Phaedrus*, either: that, we saw, is ontologically impossible on Aristotelian terms. The texts here fall back on a sort of pre-Phaedran model of participation: the friends live for the noble in each other as well as in themselves, and when necessary they will act accordingly. In such cases, we may say, the friend lives for something separate from himself: the nobility of his friend.[36] We have seen that the concept of substance is applied to human individuals only equivocally, in any case: women, children, slaves, and less-than-good free men are not as "substantial" as free adult citizens because they are (by nature) not able to live for their own sakes. Now it appears that the concept is of only limited application when applied to good and free men as well: that men form friendships indicates that all interaction, even among them, cannot be interpreted by a substance model.

This anomaly may be a question of the chronological development of Aristotle's thought. I have avoided most such questions in dealing with

Aristotle, not because chronology is unimportant but because it is a scholarly thicket best left untrod here.[37] But Werner Jaeger, to whom this approach can be traced, advanced the thesis that Aristotle began as a Platonist, convinced of the separate Forms and using "idealistic" conceptual constructions to formulate his ethical and political norms. Later, on the basis of his own metaphysics, he became more empirical. Could we not say that Aristotle began with the Platonic conception of friendship just mentioned, but that this became outdated with his denial of the separation of forms and sensibles?

In the first place, this is not how Jaeger himself develops the thesis with respect to the topic of friendship; Jaeger in fact claims that the discussion of friendship in the *Nicomachean Ethics* is relatively late.[38] A further problem is that no account of friendship on the basis of the substance metaphysics is to be found in the Aristotelian texts. Nor could one be easily provided: for an account of friendship which took the individual substance to be the supreme factor in human affairs would deny the importance of the polis.[39] The "Platonic" dimension of the Aristotelian account of friendship thus points, not to Aristotle's growth and development, but to the limits of a substance ontology as a basis for ethical and political thought.

The Platonic theory of Forms makes, in one sense, much heavier commitments than does Aristotelian metaphysics: it postulates, in addition to the world we actually live in, a whole second world of Forms. But because metaphysical reality is located in that completely different realm, Platonic philosophy, when it deals with the sensible world, is much less constrained than its Aristotelian successor. Hence, Plato can retain self-mastery as one stage in human emancipation without having to claim that it is always and necessarily the manifestation of a single person's internal nature. He can recognize fundamentally heterogenous types of communication without having to apply a single formal model to each. Thus again, in the Platonic model as in the Aristotelian, the ultimate meanings of words are entities which exist extralinguistically and cannot be changed: they are the Forms. But because the Forms are located in another realm, one which living humans cannot really come to know, humans may not know the meanings of their own words. There is in fact a category of words with which we necessarily "wander," and it is possible for an entire language community to be mistaken about the meaning of such a term.[40] Hence, for Plato not only the sounds of a language are conventional, the normal meanings of its terms may be so as well. If all speakers of Greek call a particular set of actions "free," that is in part because they, following their forbears, have agreed to do so (whether they know this or not). Only in an ideal society, such as the *Republic* sketches, might the true meanings of terms have a chance to become current in the mouths of ordinary speakers.

Such an ideal language, whose names refer only to universal necessities, would be radically unsituated. Because Aristotelian thought accepts none of this, it seems to be more situated than the Platonic variety: the only way to decide what a word means is to look to the practice of those who use it, here and now, in order to see which aspect of the world they are referring to. One can, as I have noted, look both to the run of people and to the best minds they have produced, and preference is to be accorded to the latter. But in any case, there is for Aristotle no appeal from such empirical facts: where the facts of usage for Plato are what I have called parameters of discourse, i.e., can be changed, for Aristotle they are conditions of it, founded in turn on the physical necessity of nature and the metaphysical necessity of substance. Reason is thus not for Aristotle "situated" in a particular culture or language, but bound to it. There is then no place for situating reason, and intrinsically emancipatory interaction is definitively occluded.

This brief rehearsal of Aristotelian and Platonic views on freedom has, as a first lesson, the extreme complexity of the topic. My analysis has had to move from ethics through psychology and physics to metaphysics, and back again to politics and aesthetics. In part because of this breadth, neither the Platonic nor the Aristotelian approach provides an unambiguous locus for freedom: neither can tell us unequivocally where freedom, in its primary sense, is to be found. Is it in the individual soul, so that freedom would be an ethical and/or psychological concept? Is it in society, so that a person can be "free" only in and through his interaction with others? If the latter, is such free interaction to be situated among the fixed distinctions and purposive activities that characterize the polis, or elsewhere? Is freedom a metaphysical characteristic, which the individual acquires in and through the appropriate relation to an eternal realm? Or is it a physical property of certain types of bodies?

The Platonic texts I have analyzed give conflicting answers. The *Phaedrus* implicitly criticizes the view that true freedom is to be found in the metaphysical realm of Forms and articulates a new one. But it never wholly abandons the earlier view and, as my analysis of *De Anima* 1.3 made clear, resorts to mythological presentation to fudge the discrepancies. The Aristotelian texts also waver: freedom is first said to exist within the soul of the good man, as (like Platonic justice) the arrangement of its parts; but it turns out that the good man also lives for the communal pursuit of the noble among his friends, and for the isolated contemplation of divine things—a freedom which, if not strictly "human," is to some degree available to human beings.

Two points of agreement, and several more of disagreement, illuminate these dark and indecisive bodies of thought. For both the Platonic and Aristotelian texts, freedom is not what democratic theorists consider it to be: the ability to live as one wishes. And both approaches presuppose that the only way to establish a different account is to appeal to metaphysics: to a global account of reality, itself anchored in something non-sensible. Hence, the Platonic texts begin with freedom as located in the non-sensible world of Forms; their attempt to account for freedom in the sensible realm is mythological, and is such (in part) because it is inconsistent with that earlier view, which persists into the *Phaedrus*.

On the Aristotelian approach, a person is also free, not in the empirically observable world, but in another one: within his or her own self. Freedom is thus assigned, not to a different level of the cosmic order, but to the inner world of deliberation and choice. A free man is ultimately free because of the interrelation of the parts of his soul, and Aristotle interprets phenomena of the public realm as leading to, or following from, such non-sensible freedom. The polis, with such forms of interaction as instruction and tragedy, can enhance the authority of the rational nature and the ability to deliberate. But these are, in themselves, activities that the individual carries on within himself and are not properly speaking political.

However complex the Aristotelian and Platonic concepts of freedom may be, their disparities have roots that are basically metaphysical in nature. Platonic metaphysics claims that the ultimate sources of the existence and nature of things are not to be found in those things, but as the eternally existing Forms; the self, from the start, has existence and freedom only as related to something other than it. Moreover, the Forms, as outside the sensible world, can call into question everything within that world, including the polis itself and its language. On the Aristotelian view, the existence and nature of a thing is to be found within that thing itself, as its substantial form; hence the immanence of freedom to the individual soul. And, as exhibiting ultimate ontological grounds, elements of the sensory world cannot be called into question. Individual and polis, in particular, are as substance and quasi-substance justified in their basic natures. There is no getting outside them for deeper questioning.

These metaphysical roots themselves will be challenged by Kant's Third Antinomy. But the view that the polis exhibited any sort of ultimate ontological ground was already empirically questionable in Aristotle's day. After the battle of Chaeronea in 338 B.C., Athens was no longer independent except in name, and hence did not contain any immanent source of action and unity; it was, in short, no longer a polis. Without the polis as a form of social organization, there was no way to become "free" in the Aristotelian sense, and no field within which to manifest one's freedom.

It is thus no surprise that for Epictetus, the Roman slave, for example, freedom has become something entirely interior to the individual; it is found in his inner self, the only realm which an individual can wholly control and which comprises his capacity to give or withhold assent, to desire, and to prefer or choose.[41] The free man is concerned solely with the advantage of these capacities, not with their outward manifestation: if, for example, what is noble is to his own advantage, he will desire it; if not, then not.[42] The order of nature is divine and rational, and hence necessary; the only possible response to it is to harmonize one's desires with it, by willing what actually happens.[43] Such acquiescence is the prime political virtue: those whom the divine order places in a city or polis must fulfill the duties of citizens, even though these have nothing to do with the good of their true selves.[44]

And so freedom becomes entirely immanent to the Stoic sage, whose image Kant would call the "ideal of wisdom" (KRV B. 597). The impotence and melancholy to which the free man has been reduced is aptly expressed in the following:

> He wishes . . . disinterestedly, to establish the good to which that holy law directs all his powers. But his effort is bounded. . . . Deceit, violence, and envy will always surround him, although he himself will be honest, peaceable, and kindly; and the righteous men with whom he meets will, notwithstanding all their worthiness, yet be subjected by nature, which regards not this, to all the evils of want, disease, and untimely death, just like the beasts of the earth.

But this is not some ancient describing the life of the Stoic sage; it is Kant, describing Spinoza.[45]

Fourteen

The First Foundation of Kantian Political Philosophy: The *Critiques* of Pure and of Practical Reason

Analysis

As will become evident in the final chapters of part three, the practices which constitute intrinsically emancipatory interaction did not cease to exist because of Aristotle's metaphysics; they did not vanish from everyday life. But they were generally ignored by philosophers, who remained fixated upon truth as the essential value served by speech. Poetic interaction, together with situating reason and intrinsically emancipatory interaction generally, begins to break forth into theory again with Kant's attack on metaphysics.

In his (unusually succinct) letter to Kästner of August 5, 1790, Kant puts his attitude toward metaphysics thus: "my efforts . . . in no way aim to work against the philosophy of Leibniz and Wolff. . . . I aim to achieve the same end, but by a detour which in my opinion those great men held to be superfluous."[1] The aim is to retain the content of metaphysics—the ideas traditionally exhibited in it. The critical detour is to abolish the claim that those ideas have objective referents.

The need to retain the content of metaphysics can be understood in terms of the moral status of nature in Kantian philosophy. Empiricism had subjected the view that the universe is good, as well as the supporting view that God had created it, to a searching critique. For neither God nor the goodness of nature can ever be a sensory given, and Hume's account of causality had shown that we have no reason to infer them from such givens.[2] The moral status of nature in Kantian thought is evidenced by two passages omitted from the long quote at the end of chapter 13:

245

But his effort is bounded; and from nature, though he can expect here and there a contingent accordance, he can never expect a regular harmony agreeing according to constant rules (such as his maxims are, and must be, internally) with the purpose that he feels himself obliged and impelled to accomplish. [. . . .]

So it will be until one wide grave engulfs them together (honest or not, it makes no difference) and throws them back—who were able to believe themelves the final purpose of creation—into the abyss of the purposeless chaos of matter from which they were drawn.

There is no denial here of the lawfulness of nature, the basic Kantian definition of which is law-governed sensory appearances.[3] What is asserted is that, in order to be good, nature would have to agree, not contingently but lawfully, with at least some human purposes, and that this is not the case. No moral guidance, it follows, is to be drawn from the study of sensible nature. Hence, moral values, if they are to exist at all, must inhabit some nonnatural, supersensible realm: a realm that, in a sense somewhat like the Platonic, would be "ideal." Man could be a moral being only in virtue of a relation to such a realm. Metaphysics, as the account of that realm, would be the basis for morality. Yet the first *Critique*'s "Transcendental Dialectic" argues that we can have no knowledge of any such nonempirical domain. Metaphysics can yield no "account" of anything. In sum: because of the amoral status of nature, some account of a supersensible realm is morally necessary. But it is cognitively impossible.

The Kantian answer to this dilemma will be to replace metaphysics with the "culture of reason." Moral ideals cannot be known, but they can, in culture, be constructed by human minds according to rational formulae. They inhabit, not an objective metaphysical realm, but human reason itself. Thus, the *propositions* of metaphysics cannot be true or provide basic premises for other sorts of discourse. But the *content* of metaphysics—the "ideas" with which it operated—makes us good. We have those ideas, not because they inform us of how the world actually is, but because they serve our moral interest (*KRV* B.384–386, 498ff; *KPV* 50ff). Though deprived of the cognitive status it had for Aristotle, metaphysics here remains entitled to play a prescriptive role in all aspects of life. The result of this will be that Kant is able to conceptualize speech that does not aim primarily at truth. Unlike Aristotle, he can at least begin to talk about poetic interaction as intrinsically emancipatory. But the residual prescriptive power of metaphysics for the practical sphere will mean that as soon as the discussion starts to have practical implications, it is cut off. Instead of being allocated to everyday language itself, which has implications for all human behavior, poetic interaction gets restricted to just one very special activity: that of experiencing objects as beautiful or sublime. We have already seen this situation with Hegel and Heidegger. It originated, I argue here, with Kant.

The prescriptive status metaphysics retains for Kant is perhaps nowhere as clear as with the concept of freedom, which was one of the three basic ideas of traditional metaphysics and is now to be the "keystone of the whole edifice of pure reason" (*KRV* B.7, 394n; *KPV* 3). The old, metaphysical concept of freedom is now to be replaced by a "transcendental" one—one grounded, not in a theory of the universe, but in the critique of the rational mind.[4] That grounding begins, for present purposes, in the third of the first *Critique*'s four "Antinomies of Reason" (*KRV* B.473–480). An "antinomy," in the Kantian sense, is a pair of contradictory propositions, both of which can be proven (*KRV* B.432–435). The third antinomy undertakes to prove that "everything in the world takes place solely in accordance with laws of nature"—and, contradictorily, that "to explain appearances, it is necessary to assume that there is also another causality, that of freedom."

The argument for the latter proposition—the thesis—is a reductio ad absurdum. It assumes that nature is entirely law-governed, i.e., that every event follows from some previous state of affairs according to a rule. This must also apply to that previous state of affairs, which then presupposes a further state prior to itself, and so on ad infinitum. But if such were to be the case, then nothing would ever happen: for in order for something to happen, the causal chain leading to it must be completed, and no infinite series can be completed. Thus, no complete set of rules can be given by which any event follows from previous states of affairs. But this contradicts the proposition that the universe is wholly law-governed, from which it is derived. That proposition is therefore contradictory, and there must be a type of causality which does not depend on a previous state of affairs for its action. Such causality is freedom.

The argument for the antithesis is also a reductio. If there is a cause which is not determined by any previous state of affairs, then there are events which are not caused by anything preceding them in time. Suppose that such an event itself has a cause (e.g., the human or divine will). This cause, which produces the event via some uncaused effort, will then exist successively in states which have nothing to do with one another. The state of not-yet-causing the event will be noncausally, i.e., spontaneously, succeeded by the state of causing it. But this is unthinkable:

it denies the principle of sufficient reason, and in favor of nothing more than "blind causality," which it seeks to locate in the human (or divine) will.

The antinomy thus has a peculiarly subtle structure. The thesis assumes its opposite and proves itself; the antithesis does the same. Thesis and antithesis turn out to prove each other, a state of affairs Kant calls "dialectical." The Kantian solution (*KRV* B. 566–586) is to claim that the antithesis represents, not a fact about appearances, but a cognitive demand made on them by the mind, which insists that all events be caused in lawful fashion. The thesis represents a moral demand. This demand cannot be met within experience. But it may in fact be satisfied in some supersensible realm—the "noumenal realm" which we cannot know, but which may exist. More interesting for us than this solution of the antinomy, however, is Kant's account of its generation. How could such a problematical concept as that of "freedom" be formulated in the first place?

The Kantian construction of the idea of freedom begins in the third antinomy with a negation of natural causality. Any event in time is produced from a previous event in time and is unfree. A free event (or "action") must then be one which is produced by something other than a previous event in time. Here, we arrive at a concept of freedom simply by conceiving of an event which could not be wholly explained by causes—like proton decay in quantum physics. But any human action, which as an empirical given comes under causal laws, can in principle be traced back to previously existing states of affairs in accordance with such laws.[5] It follows already from this first, and conceptually poorest, characterization that freedom cannot be thought of as manifesting itself in the empirical world.

Freedom so defined has no moral bearing. Simply to claim that an act is "free" if it does not arise in accordance with causal laws makes room, not for freedom, but for "blind causality" or chance (*KRV* B. 826f; *KPV* 95). We can specify the concept of freedom in a morally relevant way by considering in more detail what sorts of causality a free act must be exempt from. Natural causality applies to human actions either physically (as the law of gravity forbids us to fly) or, more importantly, psychologically, by way of what Kant calls "inclinations." Inclinations are desires and impulses elicited in the human psyche via some chain of natural causality—such as my desire to eat when my stomach is empty. Thus freedom, as the ability to act independently of natural causation, must include the ability to act against one's inclinations (*KRV* B. 561f; cf. *KPV* 72, 118f, 161). This second characterization of freedom is implicit in the first: an inclination is a natural cause prior in time to any act it causes and, therefore, suffices to render that act unfree.

That human beings can act against *some* of their inclinations is an observable fact. It amounts to nothing more than the capacity to defer rewards. That they can act against *all* of them, however, is by no means empirically given. For all empirical observation is of objects and events conditioned by other objects and events, and no amount of empirical experience ever yields absolute universality. In the Kantian framework, our cognitive faculties are constituted for the purpose of knowing the empirical world. They do not require us even to pursue, much less attain, the sort of universality conveyed by the idea of an act which is independent of *all* inclinations. That which bids us to inquire into unconditioned entities is, in general, not our cognitive faculties, but reason itself (*KRV* B.362–366, 379ff). So the original attempt to conceive of an event which is independent of all empirical givens was itself inspired by reason. This means that it is not an arbitrary undertaking. For reason forms concepts of unconditioned entities, or "ideas," via a syllogistic procedure in which, proceeding from one of the logical forms of the syllogism, it demands totality: demands, in effect, that all possible premises be fed into the syllogism (*KRV* B.379ff, 441–448).

This can be clarified from the procedure in the third antinomy. The construction of the concept of freedom begins there from a hypothetical syllogism, one with an "if-then" structure:

1. If A, then B
2. If B, then C
3. If A, then C.

Such a syllogism is explanatory: "C" in line (2) designates the explanandum, and "B" a condition for it. Line (1) adds a further condition. Starting from such a syllogism, reason presses forward toward completeness, which means adding further lines in front of line (1): if Q then A, if P then Q, and so on. The antinomy's thesis then states that complete explanation must start somewhere. No explanation can, if it is to be complete, actually contain an infinite number of premises, tracing the origin of the event ever back in time. The beginning point of such a complete explanation would then be a cause wholly unconditioned by any antecedent events: a "free" event as defined.

The concept of freedom is thus not reached by imaginative play or intellectual insight. Nor is the move from excluding *some* inclinations from the causal context of a free act to excluding *all* of them an empirical generalization. The concept of freedom is constructed from the form of the hypothetical syllogism according to the principle of unconditionality.

As such, it is wholly a priori and forms part of a coherent system of "ideas of reason" likewise produced from the various forms of the syllogism (*KRV* B.390–396).

An "idea," in the simplest formulation, is "nothing other than the concept of a perfection which is not found in experience."[6] An idea of reason is thus a rationally constructed standard by which empirical actions can be judged. It is no accident, says the first *Critique*, that the term is borrowed from Plato (*KRV* B.370ff). The Kantian concept of an idea claims in fact to be the Platonic one, stripped of the metaphysical excesses which hypostatized the ideas as actually existing outside human reason and then extended them far beyond the moral realm. As such an idea, freedom for Kant can have no empirical examples; but it is not in need of any. For the system of ideas itself, constructed by the systematic application of rational procedures in and by a faculty which is common to all human beings, is "objective" in the sense that human beings can come to agreement about its nature and resolve disputes with respect to it.

A free act is one which is not produced from a preceding event in time. It does not follow, however, that we must regard it as wholly uncaused. Its cause may be understood as reason itself. For reason is not sensed or intuited, and therefore, for Kant, is not in time (cf. *KRV* B.46, 50). It has no "before and after," and an event caused by reason would therefore stand outside natural causality. Thus, by a further rational operation, we arrive at the third and deepest of the first *Critique*'s characterizations of freedom: that it is the capacity of reason itself, apart from all inclination, and thus independently of natural causality, to initiate action (*KRV* B.566ff).[7] Reason does this lawfully, and the *Foundations of the Metaphysics of Morals* and later writings simply accept the moral law as a "fact of reason." The idea that freedom is the causality of reason in accordance with the moral law is, finally, the Kantian conception of "autonomy," the "highest principle of morality." While the concept of freedom discussed in the first *Critique* was to be thought of as the formulation of something merely possible, i.e., as a concept which we *could* construct, the concept of autonomy is a "necessary" one, one which we *must* construct because of our knowledge of the moral law.[8]

Autonomy or freedom, defined as the ability of a rational being to "give the law" to its actions, is generally considered to be the property of an isolated self: an inner mental ability which only subsequently has effects with regard to human relations.[9] Such a view, I will argue, is oversimplified and in fact misses two intersubjective dimensions of Kantian autonomy. These are the ideal "Kingdom of Ends" and its empirical counterpart, the "culture" (*Bildung*) of reason.

The *Foundations of the Metaphysics of Morals* characterizes the Kingdom of Ends as what the world would be like if everyone really followed the moral law: if humans really were the kind of pure moral agents that reason tells us they ought to be. In order to form a conception of this, we must abstract from all the "empirically conditioned" purposes which human agents in fact set for themselves: purposes such as the possession of various sensory goods. There remain only those purposes which are "posited through freedom," i.e., dictated by the legislation of reason. Because these purposes are rationally posited, they stand in systematic interconnection, established through reason.

In setting its own purposes strictly through the moral law, each member of the Kingdom of Ends legislates that law to itself and is autonomous. But, unlike our actual moral legislation, the legislation of a member of the Kingdom of Ends is always actually heeded by that member in all respects. Thus, at the same time that he gives himself the moral law, he obeys it. Because all his activity is determined through such legislation, the member of the Kingdom obeys only laws that he himself has made, and because each member is at once legislator and subject of the laws, all are equal. The kingdom is thus an ideal community, composed of free and equal members. It is in its content very similar, as the first *Critique* recognizes, to Leibniz's "kingdom of grace."[10] But it is not advanced, as is Leibniz's kingdom, as a doctrine about the nature of reality. Even if natural causality is the only kind there is and freedom a mere chimera, the Kingdom of Ends would still be a rationally constructed idea, and one which is practically necessary if there is to be any moral action at all (cf. *KRV* B.372).

As such a political ideal, the Kingdom of Ends should play the role of ideal state in a political philosophy proceeding on a Platonic model. The aim of political philosophy, once in possession of this ideal, would be to go on and judge existing states of affairs in terms of how closely they conform to it. This sort of problematic is advocated in the first *Critique*:

> A constitution of the greatest human freedom in accordance with laws . . . is at least a necessary Idea, which one must place at the foundation, not only in the first project of a state constitution, but also with regard to all laws. . . . Though a [perfectly constituted society] may never come to pass, the Idea itself remains completely correct, which posits this maximum as an archetype, in order to bring the legal constitution of man ever closer to the greatest possible perfection, in accordance with the archetype. What the highest level may be at which man must stop, and how great therefore is the gap which necessarily remains open between the Idea and its re-

alization—that is a matter which no one can or should determine [in advance]—precisely because it is Freedom which can
transgress any assigned limit (*KRV* B 372–374).

With this, I have sketched the outlines of the ideal standard which the
first foundation of Kantian political philosophy will apply to political
reality. The passage just quoted goes on to allow that it has been formulated by an abstraction from certain "hindrances"—hindrances which are
discussed in detail in the later political writings. Two of them are already
clear. In the first place, sensory nature is external to the human person,
and the free determination of the human will by the moral law—the legislation of reason—may not succeed in altering its course.[11] Overcoming
such natural "hindrances" to a good society requires, not merely increasing the physical capacity of the willing subject, but also increasing his
knowledge of the course of nature. It requires empirical knowledge far
more concrete than those relatively few natural laws which can be known
a priori. It requires, in short, natural science.[12]

The second hindrance is nature in us: the inclinations aroused in us by
natural causality which lead on, also by natural causality, to responses.
These are always present in finite beings (*KPV* 20ff, 83f) and compete
with the moral law to be the determining grounds of human action. This
hindrance is overcome by the "culture of reason."[13] For human reason,
unlike the human feet, is not something practice alone will tell us how to
use (*KPV*162f). The human being, as morally free, is capable of acting
against all inclinations; but he must be taught how to do so, how to
oppose the inclinations aroused by external objects with the feeling ("respect") aroused by the moral law (*KPV* 84f, 117, 160f). This educational
process has three main phases, all of which are interactive in nature. The
first of these is the articulation and systematization of moral ideas. This
is accomplished by the Kantian writings themselves (in validating freedom, for example, as a rational idea, rather than a mere imaginative figment of the brain: *KRV* B.845f). The second part comprises making
other individuals aware of the moral law thus formulated. The third part
is accustoming those individuals to using the moral law once they are
aware of it.[14]

As brought about through the culture of reason, human autonomy is
not simply the exercise of legislative reason by an isolated individual. It
requires for its establishment the development, by society, of the individual's reason. This development is historically conditioned: if everyone
had to start anew from the natural state, without leaning on the achievements of those who have gone before, he would be trapped in a maze of
false starts or "faulty attempts" (*KU* 283; cf. *KRV* B.845, *KPV* 64f). We
today, then, are capable of moral action in ways our ancestors were not.

The concept of the culture of reason points us to two further discrepancies between the Kingdom of Ends and the empirical world. These discrepancies call for a more concrete account of politics[15] and thereby relegate the points we have considered in the first two *Critiques* to the status of an abstract "foundation" for political philosophy.

In the first place, the historical development of the culture of reason underlines the fact that human societies are in time. The Kingdom of Ends, which is not an appearance but the rational idea of a nonempirical, perfect community, is not (cf. *KU* 444). Such a community must however be viewed in temporal terms, as a future goal: as the concept of a future life, says the first *Critique* (*KRV* B.836f), or as heaven. In the sensible realm, its analogue is the never-ending human progress toward communal autonomy which, since the perfect community can never be realized, becomes the "real object of our willing."[16] More than a standard by which to judge human communities—and by which to find them all, in various degrees, wanting—the Kingdom of Ends is to be a goal which, though unrealizable, can be approached by human action.

A political philosophy armed with the concept of the Kingdom of Ends can specify in what ways and to what degrees any human society fails to accord with that standard. But it cannot show how to improve the society so as to increase the accordance. For that, we require means-ends thinking, or, in Kantian terms, thinking which proceeds in accordance with "hypothetical maxims." Such maxims, the first foundation assures us, are in need of no special treatment, for they are not moral maxims. They relate empirical givens to desired ends, are themselves empirical, and cannot be prescribed in advance by theory (*GMS* 414–421; *KPV* 20). But this is not to say that they have no standards at all, for clearly some maxims are better than others for realizing particular purposes. Political philosophy will eventually, if it wants to offer concrete guidance, have to explain what those standards are. Thus, the importance for politics of hypothetical imperatives points political philosophy beyond the purely moral realm of the first foundation, toward a more concrete discussion.[17]

This will also require a more concrete account of human interaction than the Kingdom of Ends can provide. Since the members of the Kingdom obey the moral law, they all treat one another as ends rather than as means: each respects the moral legislation of the others. And since each member of the Kingdom is thought of as doing nothing more than engaging in such moral legislation, it would seem that there is nothing for them to interact about. All maxims present in the Kingdom of Ends, for example, are derived from a single formula, the moral law (*GMS* 66f); every member of the kingdom has that moral law within him and is able, as legislator, to prescribe maxims for himself on its basis. It thus seems that the necessary "interaction" of members of the kingdom must be restricted to the purely negative character of mutual noninterference. And a Kantian idea, as a rationally formulated and coherent conceptual whole, contains just what is rationally necessary for it and nothing else. Any further content, such as accounts of interaction over and above what is necessary for moral legislation, would be mere "figments of the brain" (cf *KRV* B 595–599).

These two formal discrepancies between the Kingdom of Ends and empirical reality—the temporality, and hence purposiveness, of the latter and the necessary presence within it of human interaction—are both themes taken up beyond the first foundation, in the *Critique of Judgment*. It is there that reason becomes for Kant truly interactive, and, in my terms, situating and emancipatory.

Narrative

This analysis of Kant shows that two things have happened to metaphysics in his thought. On the one hand, its truth claim has been destroyed, and its career as, in my sense, "foundational" for other forms of discourse has been ended; on the other, its claim to the sort of prescriptive status it had in Aristotle has been maintained. Both these aspects of the fate of metaphysics serve to tie Kant's thought in with what has gone before, and my narrative will examine them in turn.

The Kantian antinomies aim to destroy metaphysics's truth claim by showing that such concepts as causality and necessity, applied beyond the limits of experience, generate contradictions. In this, the two sides of the third antinomy can be viewed as modern formulations of the metaphysical positions of the Platonic and Aristotelian texts.

The theory of Forms holds, first, that no sensible thing has the source of its being and nature within itself. This position, the antithesis of the third antinomy, is already "metaphysical" in the Kantian sense: we can never experience all sensible beings and thus could never verify it empirically. Moreover, motion for Plato is a characteristic of sensibles, and according to the principle of causality from without, sensibles must derive that motion from other sensibles (it certainly cannot come from the unmoving Forms). But any sensible being which is in motion can also cease to be in motion, whence it would cease to impart motion to others; and, over infinite time, "the whole universe. . . . would collapse into immobility" (*Phdr.* 245c seqq.). When thus generalized to infinity, the principle of causation from without cannot hold, and there must be an entity which derives its motion from within: soul as self-mover. The incompatibility of self-motion with the Forms is thus an instance of its broader incompatibility with the principle of causation from without. It prefigures the third antinomy's proof of its thesis from its antithesis.

The antinomy's thesis states that there exist causes which are not determined by anything prior to themselves: in Aristotelian terms, such causes would be actually existing entities such as a human being or, paradigmatically, the Prime Mover. We come up against the third antinomy if we consider the activity of such a cause. If, on the one hand, its causal functioning is entirely independent of anterior circumstances, it must be independent of previous states of the cause itself, and in that case it is hard to say why it should be attributed to that cause. If it is not independent of anterior circumstances, then its relation to those circumstances is to some extent lawful, and then we have merely another case of lawful behavior of a cause.

The Aristotelian texts actually say something rather different. The Prime Mover is a being which cannot be other than it is, and it does not change. Its causal activity is thus not a "state" within it that can be discriminated from what went before and what will come after. The causal activity of the Prime Mover at time t, we may say, is related to it at some previous time $t-x$ not by causal laws, but by identity. This for Aristotle is the point of saying that it is an "unmoved mover," and that it is a final, not an efficient, cause: for it is such causes, like objects of desire, that move without being changed themselves (*Metaph.* 12.7.1072a23–33).

The final cause operates for the "good" of everything it affects (*De Generatione Animalium* 731b20 seqq.). Aristotle is thus able to escape the third antinomy by maintaining that the cosmos, as caused by the Prime Mover, is inherently good. But we have seen what Kant thinks of the moral status of nature. For him, the assertion that the cosmos is "good" is not only unverifiable but is not cognitive at all (cf. *KRV* B.ixff). Hence, the third antinomy does not directly attack Aristotelian metaphysics, but it is embedded in the modern denial of moral goodness to nature. If we accept that denial, it hits Aristotle. Absent final causality, the causal functioning of a finite substance is either unconnected with previous states of that substance, or is connected to those states in lawful ways: if I decide to eat dry food now, I am either acting wholly spontaneously, and hence irrationally; or my act is caused by my character and by the events that formed that character in me.

The basic metaphysical doctrines of Plato and Aristotle cannot, then, claim truth, and that was of course their main purpose. But, as my previous analysis has argued, they had an important practical effect. This was to invalidate the democratic idea of freedom: to provide warrant for asserting that the best life for humans is not adequately formulated as the attempt to "live as one likes," as long as this means gratifying desires. The fall of metaphysical truth affects the warrants for this invalidation. For one thing, freedom can no longer be defined, on the model of the *Phaedo,* as an escape to an actually existing supersensible realm. Nor do we have to define it, as did Aristotle, as the internal state of a certain type of individual soul. The way is open to reinterpret freedom as both this-worldly and interactive, on the emancipatory model of the *Phaedrus*—a model which, we saw, was presented independently of metaphysical warrant.

We will see Kant resurrect the *Phaedrus* model in chapter 15. But for the moment, if moral goodness is banished from the cosmos, it returns in the object of critique. For critique will study the mind as metaphysics studied the cosmos, and indeed the "proper" content of metaphysics— the ideas of God, freedom, and immortality (*KRV* B xxixff, 395n)—will be restored because it is good for the mind to have it. The Kantian ideas of reason destroy metaphysics, then; but in terms of the prescriptive function it had in Aristotle, they replace it point by point.[18]

For Aristotle, metaphysics was "prescriptive" in two basic ways. Theoretically, it prescribed that all philosophical science must operate syllogistically, rather than by taking over heterogenous forms of discourse for its own ends as it did in Plato. Metaphysics also theoretically prescribed that other investigations operate as if their objects were substances, even when—as in the case of the polis—they were not. Practically, metaphysics prescribed that a moral agent (or a polis) should exhibit the structure of a substance: all his (or its) actions ought to originate in reason. These types of prescription will be present also, then, in Kantian moral and political thought.

For Kant, it is not metaphysics but critique which theoretically prescribes structures for all rational discourse. All such discourse, it claims, must be capable either of empirical justification by appeal to the givens of sensibility, or of transcendental justification by appeal to the structures of the human mind laid out in critique itself. Not all discourse validated by this theoretical prescription aims at truth: talk about human freedom, for example, does not tell us that we are in fact free, but aims to make us good. But the idea of freedom to which it appeals must in its way be sanctioned by critique: it must, as critique prescribes, be constructed by the a priori syllogistic procedure I have analyzed.

Critique for Kant not only resembles metaphysics for Aristotle in its generally prescriptive character, it prescribes more specifically as well, and in the name of substance. For critique teaches us that reason, unrelated to external objects, is immanent to the mind of the autonomous moral agent; when in moral legislation it (possibly) causes the body's actions, it does so (somehow) from "within." Reason is thus the single source for the actions of a moral agent, and this holds even more stringently for Kant than for Aristotle. For Aristotle, reason had to persuade desire, tell the desiring faculty what it should want. For Kant, a truly moral act does not "persuade" the inclinations but is performed without regard to them, from respect for the moral law alone. Hence, the Kantian moral agent functions like an Aristotelian substance, only more so. It is thus not surprising to find that, as Hans Heimsoeth has noted, the discussion of the "pure idea" of such a Kantian moral agent in the Kingdom of Ends is concerned with what we saw to be a basic question in Aristotelian social philosophy: that of how substances—for Kant, the individual members of the kingdom—can come into mutual relation.[19] Insofar as the noumenal realm, to which the third antinomy allocated its "Aristotelian" thesis, has moral significance, it remains structured like an Aristotelian substance.

Its inherence in reason means that the concept of substance will continue to play a further theoretically prescriptive role for Kant, one which governs not rational discourse in general but philosophy itself. Insofar as philosophy is the work of the human reason, it will be viewed in terms of the kind of unity that substance had for Aristotle: it will be conceived, not pluralistically, as making use of divergent types of warrant and discourse, but as a single type of discourse, carried into different topics but founded entirely on the basic warrants of critique. The theoretical prescription of Aristotle's metaphysics, though in very different form, will continue in the Kantian "architectonic."

This leaves one rather large area essentially free from metaphysical prescription: the empirical realm. If human reason is noumenally structured and considered in terms of an Aristotelian substance, that strictly tells us nothing about human beings as we empirically know them to be, and such beings are not necessarily "substantial" in nature. Thus, even the capacity to judge autonomously, though *noumenally* part of the a priori capacities of the human mind, is not *empirically* the sort of self-actualization we saw Aristotelian substance to exhibit: such judgment empirically requires the interactive "culture of reason" for its development. Aristotle's concept of substance is thus deposed, at least, from its claim to tell us about the way things are in the empirical realm. As with Plato, Kant is free to construe the human being in the empirical realm in a variety of ways. He does this in the *Critique of Judgment*.

The reason why Kant had to go on and write that work is now apparent. The Platonic and Aristotelian forms were causally efficacious in the sensible world, in that they made sensibles what they were. Kantian ideas, since as far as we can know they inhabit only our reason, can have causal efficacy only through human actions (if at all); the concept of freedom as the causality of reason, discussed above, is nothing more than a general formulation of this. The question then arises of *how* moral ideals—including that of the ideal polity or Kingdom of Ends—can be realized in human action.

In spite of its destruction of metaphysics, the Kantian approach is here in a more difficult position than the Platonic. For the *Phaedo* had one, if only one, empirical example of "true" freedom as the proper relation to the supersensible world—that of Socrates in prison. For Kant, no empirical examples of moral freedom are possible at all, and in our terms his moral philosophy is here, in the first foundation, radically unsituated. True, freedom is not a metaphysical *necessity*: it is not always and everywhere true that human beings are free. It is, however, a moral *condition*: any human being, in order to act morally, must be able to think of himself or herself as free, and that can never change. But moral action (as we have seen Hegel argue) always occurs in a particular set of circumstances, some of which are parametric in nature and can be left behind. Some of them, indeed, will certainly be left behind, because it is the purpose of any action to change some of the circumstances of the actor. Since freedom as the a priori causality of reason itself takes no account of empirical givens, parametric or not, thinking of oneself as free can provide no guidance with regard to concrete moral choices. It will not, by itself, tell us which of our current circumstances can and should be changed by our action.

The existence of such circumstances, which must be articulated empirically and dealt with by means-ends thinking, was recognized by Kant in terms of what I called the "discrepancies" between the Kingdom of Ends and the empirical world we live in. When the *Critique of Judgment* discusses how moral ideals can be realized in the face of these discrepancies, however, it adumbrates a completely different conception of freedom—one with its ancient roots, not in the *Republic* and *Phaedo*, but in the *Phaedrus* and to some degree in Aristotelian thought. The Kantian movement from the first two *Critiques* to the third can thus be seen as reenacting the Platonic movement from the unsituated view of freedom in the *Phaedo* and *Republic* to the situated view of the *Phaedrus*. The reason, as we shall see, is the same: if "freedom" is a radically unsituated concept, it makes no sense for either an individual or a society to pursue it in the empirical or sensible realm.

Fifteen

The Second Foundation of Kantian Political Philosophy: The *Critique of Judgment*

Analysis

Though its interactive and emancipatory characteristics will remain obscure, situating reason as presented in the *Phaedrus* begins to emerge from the occlusion induced by Aristotelian metaphysics in Kant's *Critique of Judgment*. That *Critique* starts with the question of how and why we should use means-ends thinking to realize moral ideals: in particular, how can we formulate moral ideals as moral purposes which apply in concrete situations? Such thinking, we saw, was lacking in the Kingdom of Ends. Kant does not want it to stay lacking, for if it does human life will remain trapped in the impotence and melancholy we saw him attribute to Spinoza, no matter how much freedom we attribute to ourselves in the noumenal sphere. But it does not appear that purposive thinking can be justified according to the prescriptions rational discourse must satisfy for Kant. Theoretical reason, as explored in the first *Critique*, operates in the empirical sphere strictly in terms of the mechanical category of natural causality. Like the Aristotelian efficient cause, this makes no reference to purpose. It cannot provide any warrant for viewing human society and history in purposive terms (*KRV* B.232–256, 289f; *KU* 372). Practical reason, likewise, teaches us nothing concrete about the empirical world and, hence, nothing about moral or historical purpose. We are thus faced with the possibility that the mechanical causality of nature is not amenable to the achievement of such purposes. Yet in the "mechanical" world of empirical experience, there do exist beings which formulate goals and purposes, and seek to achieve them; and such activity is clearly of moral significance. If the empirical world is to have any moral relevance—if, indeed, there is to be any moral action at all—there must be some warrant for viewing the empirical world purposively. Kant must seek, so to speak, a "site" in nature for moral purposes. In my terms, the attempt to achieve a moral purpose is, like all action, situated among limits that can be other than they are (some of which the action aims to transcend). Insofar as the articulation of such purposes and of the circumstances in which they apply is a criticizable activity, it is an exercise in situating reason which, I will argue, begins poetically.

To view the phenomenal world purposively means, in moral terms, to view it as amenable to the realization of moral ideals, and this means somehow uniting it with the noumenal realm in which those ideals reside. The project of unifying the intelligible and empirical worlds is announced in the "Introduction" to the third *Critique*, and it has two sides. On the one hand, purposiveness must be vindicated for the sensory realm in order to keep the two worlds from falling apart. On the other hand, some nonconceptualizable dimension of empirical experience must be found in order to keep them from collapsing together. But the *Critique of Judgment* will do far more even than meet these two demands. For the "bridge" that is thrown from the sensible to the supersensible world will turn out to be, not only different in kind from the realms that it bridges, but—like the "limit" in Hegel's *Logic*—independent of both and more important than either.[1] The *Critique of Judgment* will turn out to adumbrate a concept of freedom wholly different from that of the transcendental causality of a noumenal reason. It is this new concept that will be taken up in the philosophical recuperation of poetic interaction.

In the apprehension of an object as beautiful, as the third *Critique* has it, my faculty of *sensibility* presents me with raw data.[2] These are recapitulated by my *imagination* in such a way as to conform to the basic nature of my faculty of *understanding*, which is a requirement for form.[3] None of the understanding's own stock of "pure concepts" comes into play here. The object is perceived, not as one or many, as cause or effect, as substance or accident, etc., but simply as a harmonious form. Such apprehension is then a cooperative achievement of my cognitive faculties (sensibility, imagination, and understanding) in which they refer to one another without being tied to any determinate concept. Their mutual reference is a "free play" of my cognitive faculties and is experienced as aesthetic pleasure.[4]

Because no determinate concept is involved here, the experience of beauty is nonconceptualizable. And because we can only talk about objects if we have determinate concepts in which to do so, to call something beautiful is not really to say anything about that object at all. It asserts, rather, something about myself: namely, that my faculties are put into free play by the imaginative presentation of that object. This lack of cognitive status means that the free play, though occasioned by the object, is in a sense independent of it. It depends, not on accurate cognition of the object, but on how I receive it, and is thus disinterested (*KU* 191, 204ff, 350). Because I have no concept of the object I experience, I have no guidelines for producing it: unlike moral experience, aesthetic experience does not require us to bring about any state of affairs in the actual world and is disinterested in a second sense.[5] Such disinterested satisfaction is again "free" (*KU* 210, 350).[6]

To be "free" here means, first, to have my cognitive faculties put into the free play of mutual reference; and it also means to be disinterested, in the two above senses. Freedom so construed resides, not in the self conceived as part of a noumenal realm of reason, but in the sum of the cognitive faculties of an individual who is *in* nature but not subject *to* it. We now have two senses of "freedom" which complement one another but are formulated independently of the "transcendental" senses articulated in the first foundation.

The judgment that an object is beautiful is radically distinct from the assertion that it is pleasant. Aesthetic pleasure, unlike for example the pleasure of sitting in a comfortable chair, has a transcendental ground: it is not merely a good feeling, which as purely sensuous is private and, in Kantian terms, subjective. As the result of the free play of cognitive faculties, aesthetic pleasure has reference to the understanding, which, unlike sensibility, is not merely private but has contents identical for all human beings. My experience of something as beautiful is thus one which others can, in principle, share, and this is attested by the fact that an aesthetic judgment (a "judgment of taste") claims to be valid for everyone. It is, the *Critique of Judgment* would inform us, of no concern to me if others do not find my favorite chair as comfortable as I do. But if I find the Mona Lisa beautiful, and they do not, then I am disturbed and undertake to argue them into agreement.[7]

These passages specify that, in a judgment of taste, agreement from others is only "imputed," not "postulated" (*angesinnet*, not *postuliert*: *KU* 216, cf. 284f). The validity of such a judgment cannot be decided by proof alone (as can, for example, that of a mathematical judgment). For it begins from an individual's perception of an individual object, and the assent of others will be forthcoming only if they have perceived the same object in the same way. This means that the validity of aesthetic judgments can only be decided dialogically: by discussing the matter with others, rather than by reasoning it out on one's own. I can in principle discover whether a mathematical judgment is true by proving it or its contradictory. If my proof is valid, I know, without having to ask them, that all rational beings will agree with that judgment. The validity of an aesthetic judgment can be decided only by discussing it with others who have also experienced the object occasioning it—and this means, not with all "rational beings" (for some of them, e.g., God, may be disembodied) but with other *human* beings (*KU* 210, 216, 284f.). Judgments of taste are thus not truly "universal" or "objective" in a Kantian sense. They hold, at most, only for all human beings, i.e., for all embodied rational creatures. Their universality is a human one, and their objectivity at most a form of consensus.

This dialogical character of aesthetic judgment has methodological import. Ernst Cassirer has noted that Kantian critique is always related to a specific fact whose conditions it investigates. In the *Prolegomena*, pure physics and mathematics constitute such facts, arising from experience yet pointing to something independent of it. In the *Foundations of the Metaphysics of Morals*, ordinary moral consciousness and, in the a priori realm, the "fact of reason" are further examples (cf. *PRL* 274f., 294f.; *GMS* 393f.). Here, the fact in question is one about how humans interact with one another. It is that, as Ingrid Stadler has put it, we take certain "risks" in making aesthetic attributions, saying things which can only be verified by agreement from others and which we are committed to defend if agreement is not forthcoming. This sort of dialogue is, we shall see, institutionalized in art criticism, which then plays the same sort of role that physics and natural science do in the *Prolegomena*: it is an empirical fact which requires a transcendental foundation.[8]

If aesthetic consensus is possible, then other people must be able to experience an object in imaginative recapitulation just as I do. This is the presupposition of a "common sense" shared by all human beings (*KU* 237ff). That common sense is presupposed by aesthetic judgment does not prove that it actually exists. Empirically speaking, not all my aesthetic judgments find assent from others, and it is possible that, when they do, the reason is mere chance. If such is the case, then common sense is a mere ideal norm—a "regulative principle" in terms of which to think and speak, but not one which tells us about the world or, as here, about our minds (*KU* 239). But the *Critique of Judgment* makes a more compelling case than this for the existence of common sense. It shows it to be a condition for other phenomena which do exist, and which thus constitute evidence for it. These phenomena reveal the importance of aesthetic judgment for human life in general, and for politics in particular.

One of them is "sociability" (*KU* 296ff, 306). Because human beings are social animals, they enjoy communicating with each other—to such an extent that in advanced societies only those feelings and sensations which can be communicated have any value. So humans like as well to communicate their aesthetic enjoyment. And, as the interest in society

incites aesthetic communication, so such communication increases sociability—increases the range of things human beings can communicate
about. Thus, common sense, as a presupposition of the communicability
of aesthetic enjoyment, plays a role in the "harmonization of the representative powers of different people" (*KU* 217). For it brings, not only
their intellects, but also their feelings into agreement (*KU* 231f.), and
does so in a way which, because preconceptual, is free of all constraining
or arbitrary rules (*KU* 306–308).[9]

In addition to this fundamentally pragmatic argument for presupposing common sense, the *Critique of Judgment* also argues that it is a necessary condition of empirical cognition.[10] Cognitive judgment, in which
the understanding applies its own concepts to experience, is "determining" in nature. Aesthetic judgment is "reflective," in that it begins without any predetermined concept under which the sensory manifold is to
be brought (*KU* 179f.). But in order to be brought under a determinate
concept of the understanding, the sensory manifold must first be rendered accessible to the understanding in general. It must, then, be recapitulated by the imagination in a harmonious form. Unless human beings
shared this capacity for recapitulation—common sense—they would
never be able to formulate determinate empirical concepts or mutually
intelligible cognitive judgments. The fact of human cognition is thus further evidence for common sense (*KU* 189, 238f.).

Since empirical concepts are formed from experience, it follows for
Kant that all empirical judging begins without one. The first human being to see a horse, for example, had no concept of the "equine" under
which to bring it (cf. *KU* 286f.). In order for someone even to begin
looking for such a concept, we may say, two conditions must be met.
First, the object presented must be sufficiently organized that it seems
possible that the understanding could say something about it—could
form a concept of it. Second, if the conceptual realm is not to be a "useless duplication" of the empirical, we want to have fewer concepts than
there are entities. This requires us to assume that the universe is sufficiently well organized that the object in question comes under a relatively
small number of yet-to-be-discovered general concepts and laws. This
latter assumption is about the "form" of the universe itself and is not
entailed by empirical givens. It is, the third *Critique* argues, a basic principle of reflective judgment, and gives such judgment heuristic value
(*KU* 183–185). The former condition, rather than a principle of reflective
judgment, is reflective judgment itself: the presentation of a harmonious
form is a "judgment" which is aesthetic in nature and from which all
empirical concept-formation begins.[11] All empirical judging operates this

way, and aesthetic judgment is simply judgment in its pristine form as an (empirical) activity of the subject (*KU* 286f.). It is then to be found in such fields as social science and even in politics itself. It is through the function of aesthetic judgment in empirical concept-formation that the *Critique of Judgment* can be viewed as a "second foundation" of Kantian political philosophy.

Aesthetic experience falls, in the *Critique of Judgment*, under the two main headings of the beautiful and the sublime. Though both provide aesthetic pleasure, a beautiful object does so in virtue of its form, while a sublime one does so in virtue of its formlessness (*KU* 244f.). This difference gives rise to two distinct types of aesthetic interaction.

Interaction which concerns the beautiful has two main types. In what we may style the "communication of genius," one person, a pupil, feels himself inspired by a work of art produced by an original creator and undertakes, not to replicate it, but to equal it—in originality if in no other respect (*KU* 307f., 318). Such communication, being wholly unreflective, or "natural," is a matter of chance: the intuitive creativity of the genius is as capable of producing nonsense as art (*KU* 319f.). "Nonsense" is not only not art, it cannot even be beautiful, because it violates common sense. Other people do not view a nonsensical work of art in the same way that its creator does, and in fact they do not generally look at it at all. In order to be truly communicative—and in order to have significance beyond the "natural" sphere, e.g., in the areas of action and politics—genius requires the discipline of taste, or of common sense (*KU* 319f). But this discipline, as interactive, informs us not *through* a work of art but *about* one: its paradigm is not the creator communicating to his pupil, but the critic talking about a beautiful object to the public.

Sensory objects can be either natural or artificial, and about the beauty of the former art criticism has relatively little to say. Indeed, the pure judgment of taste says it all, which is that one person finds that the natural object in question affords him aesthetic satisfaction, and that it should do so as well for others. Works of art are different,[12] and it is in commenting on them that communication of the beautiful takes on its richest and most important form. As products of intentional activity, works of art exhibit not merely purposiveness in general, which is a characteristic of all beautiful objects (*KU* 180, 219f.), but more or less definite purposes. There is something that a work of art is supposed to be, a message which it is supposed to convey. In Kantian terms, there is a "concept" for which it is the vehicle. This reference to a concept means that critical judgments on a work of art are not pure judgments of taste. In formulating what the work is supposed to achieve, such judgments assign a sort of "nature" to the work of art and view it as a realization of that nature, thus coming close to teleological judgments of final causality (*KU* 311–313).

Though critical discourse tends to assimilate aesthetic judgments not to judgments of taste but to teleological ones, an art object preserves its properly aesthetic character in the way that it "realizes" its own basic concept. For though a work of art can be fully recapitulated by, and present in, the imagination, this recapitulation itself can never be wholly grasped in concepts. If I recognize an object as, say, a horse, I have a single concept which gives me the nature of that object. I can judge the horse's "perfection," say that it is a good horse or a bad one, depending on how closely it comes to whatever specifications are contained in my concept. But there can be no doubt that the object, in some preeminent way, is captured by or brought under the concept "horse" (cf. *KU* 226–229). Similarly, a teleological judgment simply assigns a purpose to a natural event and stops (as when we say that a bird makes its nest in order to lay its eggs). If other natural purposes may be assigned to that event (perhaps the bird makes its nest to attract a mate), these are matters for wholly different teleological judgments: their multiplicity is not an inherent feature of such a judgment itself (cf. *KU* 36)

An aesthetic object, by contrast, furnishes to the understanding, not the concept of a single nature under which to subsume its various features, or of a single purpose which it is to fulfill, but an unbounded number of such concepts, each of which partially expresses its purpose or nature. Its "true" or complete concept can never be stated and, hence, is not strictly speaking a "concept" at all. It is an idea, a mental content for which no adequate empirical presentation can be found (*KU* 314f, 342f). Thus, the work of art offers to the critical judgment an infinite number of possible conceptualizations, each of which may be acceptable as an articulation of the work's beauty, but none of which can claim to settle the matter permanently.[13] Concomitantly, a critical judgment carries, as such, the implication that it is one among an infinite number of such judgments which could equally well be made. The aesthetic domain thus exhibits, not a complete ineffability, but rather what we might style an infinite "effability:" a work of art always suggests more to the critical eye than can actually be put into words, and is thus inexhaustible. This contrasts with the cognitive employment of the faculties in which the imagination must "conform" to a particular concept that the understanding provides and stop its free play (*KU* 316f.). The free play of the faculties in the apprehension of the beautiful is then primarily the freedom of the imagination from determinate concepts of the understanding. The condition for this freedom of the imagination is the disinterestedness of the aesthetic judgment, which means that it is not "about" a real object at all, and hence that the cognitive faculties are "free" to remain in their play without producing any sort of final statement about the world (*KU* 204–210, 217).

When a critic takes a work of art as an example, then, it is not an "example" of any definable class. Rather, it is ultimately a case of a "rule which I cannot give," or (better) of an unbounded number of such rules. If the critic goes on and formulates, on the basis of such examples, more general rules for evaluating works of art, those rules can never be definitive. The natural gifts of the genius and the inexhaustibility of works of art themselves guarantee that new rules are continually being found for art, and this means that—unlike the case, for example, with products of handicraft or industrial art—works of art are in a sense "free" of all arbitrary rules. Each generates its own rules out of its own intrinsic character, rules which can then be articulated in critical judgment (*KU* 304, 306, 309f, 317). The general rules of the critic function only to educate the taste of the audience. They cannot serve as prescriptions for making beautiful objects, or even for recognizing them. This freedom of art from preestablished rules grounds the interactive freedom of the public to judge each work of art on its own terms, and this interactive freedom is itself grounded in the capacity of the imagination to furnish material over and above that which can be grasped under any single concept

Expressing these senses of "freedom" in terms of the interaction proper to aesthetic experience, we find that such interaction is, first, free from theoretical and practical exigencies. Those who engage in it do not have to commit themselves to any truths about the world or to the realization of any particular state of affairs. They are also "free" in that they are unified within themselves. The unity, moreover, is "playful," not achieved through the dominance of the understanding (or of reason). Finally, they are free in that they are constantly deriving new articulations and rules from their experience rather than being bound to any previously articulated set of such rules.

In spite of its inexhaustibility, this sort of interaction contains what we may call partial stopping points. Each new rule that is articulated in the course of it captures one aspect of the aesthetic object and articulates it in the form of a concept. Such a concept or rule, once spoken or written down, is no longer dependent on the apprehension of beauty from which it arose. Its intrinsic reference to other possible articulations of that particular art work is suspended, and it can stand as an empirical rule to which various objects do or do not conform. At this stage, interaction is no longer purely aesthetic in character. When, for example, a rule derived from the perception of one object as having a harmonious form is generalized to cover a number of other objects perceived as having similar forms, we have the generation of the "aesthetic normal idea," which is the normative idea of the class to which those objects belong. Such a "normal idea" determines correctness in representations of that class and can be articulated into the concept of that class. It is then a rule for judging the class membership of various sensible objects (*KU* 232–235), or what we usually call an "empirical generalization." It is in providing such generalizations that aesthetic interaction is the primary mode of human concept formation.

Since it is by virtue of aesthetic form that the imagination brings sensation into accord with the understanding, such accord is not possible with regard to the sublime, the principle of which is formlessness and a concomitant limitlessness.[14] But the limitlessness presented by the imagination in the perception of something as sublime is consonant, so the "Analytic of the Sublime" tells us, with the unconditionality of reason (*KU* 244f.). The sublime is in fact an imaginative analogue of how reason attempts, for example, to think the sum of all causal chains in infinite time.

Because the sublime as such has no form, something sublime cannot be recapitulated by the imagination in the way that something beautiful can. The imagination of a quantity requires for Kant two steps. First, the mind must successively perceive each unit in that quantum. Then it must combine the units perceived into a single larger unity, which can be present all at once in an immediate awareness (*KU* 251f.; cf. *KRV* B.202–207). In the perception of something sublime, the units are either too many or too great for the imagination to combine in a single intuition, or they are themselves incommensurate with one another; the whole is too large to be made present. Such presence is, however, a demand of reason (*KU* 251, 254, 256f.). In attempting to meet that demand, the imagination fails: it can "present" only its own inadequacy. The feeling of inadequacy with regard to a given demand can, however, have a positive aspect, for it can instill "respect" for the entity which poses that demand. The great example of this in the second *Critique* is respect for the moral law (*KPV* 131ff.). Here in the third *Critique*, the respect is for reason itself, which is revealed to be of sufficient magnitude to pose a demand which the imagination cannot fulfill, and which is in the strictest sense the only "sublime" thing (*KU* 245, 256, 264). The mind as a whole gains consciousness of its independence of nature and, hence, realizes its "inner freedom" (*KU* 268f., 271).

The formlessness of the sublime means that the experience of it can result in no positive rule or concept—not even a partially adequate one.

Transcending both sensibility and the understanding, as well as imagination, the experience of the sublime confronts them with an abyss in which all empirical rules and concepts lose standing and count for nothing (*KU* 257f.). The "abyss" is reason itself, which is its own standard and hence incommensurate with anything else. Indeed, reason itself is not "present" even to itself in any positive sense, except as an "undetermined concept;" the awareness of it in the experience of the sublime is merely the mind's feeling itself set into "unending motion" by the effort to imagine the sublime, rather than "brought to rest" in a play of contemplation, as is the case with the beautiful (*KU* 244, 257–260).

Though not as closely bound to sociability as is the experience of the beautiful, that of the sublime can also be interactive (*KU* 275f.). As a conflict of faculties which are present in every individual, the experience of the sublime makes the same sort of imputation of validity for all humans as does that of the beautiful (*KU* 265f., 275f.). And, just as common sense requires cultivation, so does the ability to experience the sublime as such. The cultivation required is the development of the moral ideas which inhabit reason, or the culture of reason. Without that, the individual experiences the sublime merely as terrifying (*KU* 264f.).

The articulation of the sublime would then be a mode of interaction in which all concepts and generalizations are undermined in favor of an indeterminate abyss-in-unending-motion. Such interaction achieves no harmonization of the faculties: it rather "deconstructs" harmonies achieved elsewhere, in that all empirical concepts are undone and the imagination is revealed as unable to conform to the demand of a higher faculty. The awareness of this is pain. But it is pain which brings forth the "higher pleasure" felt in respect (*KU* 257–260). Such interaction is then free, as is interaction concerning the beautiful, first because it is disinterested: awareness of the sublime does not depend on the object (which, we noted, can be merely terrifying), but on how we take it. And it is free because it teaches us that ultimately we are neither in nor subject to nature. This truth brings with it "freedom," we may say, not merely from previously articulated rules and concepts, but from all rules and concepts as such.

The experience of the sublime is not, strictly speaking, to be found in works of art. Yet in a sense such works, if in their scope they transcend the comprehensive power of the imagination, can excite the feeling of the sublime: the *Critique of Judgment*'s example is of Saint Peter's basilica in Rome, which is simply too large to be "taken in" by the mind (*KU* 254); the same would presumably hold for novels and poems, if of sufficient scale. The way is thus open, though Kant does not develop the idea, for a criticism of the sublime, which would make use of the scale of such works, or of incommensurabilities within them, to undermine any concepts or generalizations that could be derived from them.

Narrative

In general, Kant's doctrine of reflective judgment recuperates the basic features of situating reason, the articulation of parameters as parameters. The first step in seeing this is to note that the *Critique of Judgment*, as I have presented it, gives Kant's solution to the *Phaedo*'s problem: given that true freedom exists only in a supersensible realm, how are we to find an empirical image of it? The solution is not presented, however, in the *Phaedo*'s terms, as the self-mastery of the individual soul, but moves beyond that. It has in some respects obvious affinities to the *Phaedrus* and to the Aristotelian texts; in others, it stands beyond them.

In the first place, the individual's aesthetic experience involves all the cognitive faculties in harmonious cooperation and is a relation of his psychological "parts" to one another and not to anything outside: an affair of the "self-contained" free individual, as is Aristotelian deliberation. In contrast to such deliberation, Kantian aesthetic judgment does not begin with a concept (such as happiness), nor does it issue in action (action, in the Kantian framework, originates with the will—a faculty absent from the Aristotelian account of the mind). The result of this is that where for Aristotle action is basic, and aesthetic experience, in the *Poetics*, is the "imitation of an action" (*Poetics* 1448a), the third *Critique* grasps aesthetic experience in terms independent of action altogether.[15] Beginning without any concept, reflective judgment is the basic vehicle for what, in an Aristotelian view, is a natural and individual process: articulating meanings.

In this, reflective judgment is similar to the erotic interaction of the Palinode. There, as we saw, the soul begins with the perception of something—the body of another—as beautiful, but without any awareness of what this in fact means. This inarticulateness, moreover, makes the soul in a strange way "disinterested:" the mute soul cannot directly approach the beloved but only admires him from afar. The soul acts, we may say, only when it has achieved enough harmony among its parts to be able to express intellectually (or linguistically) what it is feeling. And this, too, has its counterpart in the Kantian account: once an empirical concept has been formulated, for example, various cognitive and practical interests can enter into play.

The two accounts differ over the type of object the perceiving subject encounters. For the Palinode, this object is the body of another, and it is encountered erotically: in terms of desire. That is why "disinterestedness" is in the Palinode so difficult to achieve—and so unpleasant. On the Kantian account, the individual encounters merely any beautiful object, and the generality of this suffices to ban from explicit discussion any erotic element. The body is present only as perceiving, not as desiring. This means that the unification of the self achieved on the Kantian account, though free in the sense of the *Phaedrus*, is from a Platonic perspective incomplete: it is a unity only of transcendental faculties, not of the concrete properties of a living human being.

It also means that the interactive dimension of reflective judgment is subsequent to its primary function of unifying the self. I encounter the other, in aesthetic debate, only *after* my faculties have been unified by the experience of a beautiful object; only then am I able to begin the debate by saying that the object is beautiful. I am thus not unified by my experience with the other—rather, the reverse: the free play of my cognitive faculties in aesthetic enjoyment, with its imputation of universal human assent, brings me out of myself and into relation with others. Interaction, we may say, expresses, or is the field of manifestation of, aesthetic freedom. It is not constitutive of it.[16] In my terms: if situating reason is to some extent recuperated here, its interactive dimension, together with its intrinsically emancipatory quality, remains obscure.

If this relegation of freedom to immanence within the individual sounds Aristotelian, there are differences. The Aristotelian reason for entering into friendship with another was the nobility of that other, and this was conceived as the rule of reason in all the concrete activities of his life; the "imputation" of such a rule was the content of goodwill. In the Kantian account, what is imputed is not the rule of reason (which no one could manifest even in a single deed), but common sense: and it is imputed, not to a few mature citizens, but to all humans. Thus, what the Kantian text takes as the keynote of Athenian life is the very thing the Aristotelian account of friendship is designed to downplay: friendship among persons on different social levels.

Two further points separate the Kantian account of aesthetic interaction from the Aristotelian and Platonic ones, and both involve limits. Both the Platonic and the Aristotelian metaphysics are predicated, as we have seen, on the existence of eternal forms; they disagree only in where they take such forms to reside. This view is behind the Aristotelian assurance that metaphysics is prescriptive of other disciplines: the basic "form" is substance, and whatever other disciplines study, their subject matter cannot, in principle, be viewed as other than a substance or a quasi-substance. In the Platonic account, the fundamentality of form governed the hegemonic role of metaphysics: though other forms of discourse have independent validity, they are always directed to providing awareness of a specific set of entities, the Forms.

Hence, in the Platonic and Aristotelian approaches, a beautiful object can have only a finite set of "meanings:" there is only a finite set of Forms to be meant. In the Palinode, a beautiful body can, to begin with, signify in two ways: it can be taken in its relation to the Form of Beauty, or as a merely sensory object of animalistic desire. Similarly, though for Aristotle individual poetic utterances can have several different interpretations, there is a finite set of these: the possibilities are given in the syntax and vocabulary of the language and in the background knowledge of its speakers. The "meaning" of a tragedy as a whole is the single rational organization of its plot. On the Kantian approach, by contrast, an infinite set of meanings can be generated out of the experience of a single beautiful object. Such experience is empirical, and there is no hegemonic or prescriptive metaphysics of form to prescribe limits to it. Hence, new rules are always possible for art; new empirical concepts can always be generated.

Finally, for both the Platonic and Aristotelian approaches, the ordered domain of forms is an ultimate value for the human mind: no experience of formlessness, no "sublime," can have moral worth, let alone political. The Aristotelian principle of the cosmic order denies even the possibility of the radically formless. The Platonic approach allows the "unlimited" chaos of the unformed sensible world, referred to in the *Timaeus*,[17] to undo all our predications and rules, because it puts sensible entities into radical flux and change. But this does not teach us anything of value about ourselves; such flux is the lowest form of reality, and in fact is a sort of nonreality.

The Kantian account, embedded in Christianity with its positive evaluation of infinity and limitlessness,[18] has a different view. There are, of course, limits to the human mind which cannot be transgressed: reason cannot know objects, and cognition cannot achieve anything "unconditioned." But reason's "non-knowing" of objects that are too great for the imagination confronts reason, not with valueless flux, but with itself, in all its uniqueness and power. For our purposes, it is in its articulation of the concept of the sublime—not in its supposed freedom from metaphysics—that the Kantian approach advances most significantly upon the Greeks.

With the third *Critique*, reason—if we use the term, not in Kant's sense, but to cover the activities of the judgment of taste—has become situated. It is not concerned with metaphysical necessities or even with conditions for the functioning of the mind as such; but it is concerned with concretely given sensory objects, which are significant for it not in virtue of their position in causal chains but because of the opportunity they offer for imaginative recapitulation as beautiful. The concepts reason forms from the experience of these objects, as empirically derived adumbrations of an aesthetic idea, can be changed or left behind by the mind—and, in the experience of the sublime, are in fact left behind. They are thus, in my term, parameters. The judgment of taste, then, is not an "aesthetic" phenomenon in any narrow sense: it is that faculty of the human mind which articulates parameters as parameters, and hence is what I call situating reason.

Such reason is situated, first, among a variety of articulable objects. A second aspect of its situation concerns, not such objects, but other people. As we saw, the judgment of taste's imputation of universality applies, not to all rational beings, but specifically to other human beings—to embodied rational beings. The judgment of taste thus presupposes me to be located, not in an ideal Kingdom of Ends, but in the human community itself. Moreover, for me actually to make such an imputation of universality, I must be situated, not merely within humanity at large, but within a specific, actual human community—among people with whom I can speak and against whose judgments I can measure my own.

The judgment of taste is not merely situated in these two different ways, but is (in my sense) poetic. For it begins with the experience of a beautiful object—one which can be recapitulated by the imagination in a harmonious way and is susceptible to an infinite variety of conceptual articulations. It is (in some sense that Kant does not explain) up to the observer to determine which articulations he or she actually produces. In the experience of the sublime as well, it is up to the observer to relate what he or she sees to reason itself, and to see it as sublime rather than as terrifying.

Finally, aesthetic experience, as the achievement of the disinterested free play of the faculties, is intrinsically emancipatory in senses highly reminiscent of the *Phaedrus*. For it is unconstrained by theoretical or practical exigencies; it is the gaining of a unified self; and one who engages in it is not bound by previously existing rules but can leave them behind, as Socrates and Phaedrus leave the polis, in order to articulate new rules or to confront the infinitude of reason. With Kant's account of aesthetic judgment then, basic structures of situating reason, as we saw it in the *Phaedrus*, begin to be recuperated. With the account of the sublime, a new structure is introduced, which, as we shall see, constitutes a second basic structure of poetic interaction.

But several obstacles remain to a full recuperation. One of them is the Kantian theory of transcendental faculties in the human mind: the unification of understanding, sensibility, and imagination remains, as I noted, highly abstract in comparison with the erotically concrete account presented in the *Phaedrus*, and this is not merely a result of Plato's greater capacities as a writer. The separation of the human mind into empirical and transcendental levels must itself be overcome.

A second obstacle is the separation of the situation of reason into two distinct components: the aesthetic object and other people. The only truly emancipatory experience, we have seen, is that of aesthetic objects; aesthetic interaction, as with Aristotle, either manifests such freedom (when a person explains to others why he finds something beautiful) or, presumably, produces it (when the other is led by the discussion to see it as beautiful also). This second obstacle is not unconnected with the first. If a "critique" of judgment is to be possible for Kant, it is because the faculty of judgment has transcendental principles. But if the unification of the faculties constituting the judgment of taste is to be transcendental, it must be a priori, independent of the experience of any particular or type of object. This transcendentality is bestowed on the judgment of taste by the imagination. For, as we saw, it is the object as given in its imaginative recapitulation that can be beautiful, not directly as given in the senses; we need only imagine a beautiful object, not experience it, to find it beautiful. But in order for me to talk to others and compare my judgments with theirs, it is not enough that those others be imagined; they must actually be present. Dialogue cannot be an a priori experience; hence, Kant must view it as occurring subsequently to the operation of the judgment of taste itself. Both this and the previous problem I mentioned—the abstractness, in Kant's account, of the unification of the faculties—are the result of what we might call intrusions of the transcendental level into what should be an empirical account of the judgment of taste.

Hegel and Heidegger, in my analysis of them, made no mention of transcendental faculties of the mind and, hence, were able to give much more concrete accounts of aesthetic emancipation than does Kant. Hegel discusses, in the *Aesthetics*, a wealth of examples of it; and, though "wealth" is never a good term to apply to Heidegger, he did furnish a concrete example in his "From a Dialogue on Language." We have also seen both thinkers strain to construe aesthetic experience in dialogical terms, thus bringing together the two aspects of the situation of reason that Kant has separated; and we saw Heidegger finally detach the "aesthetic" realm from works of art altogether.

But there is a third intrusion of the transcendental level into the empirical for Kant. This consists of the practical prescriptions of reason, to which I have referred as the first foundation. As for Aristotle, for Kant (as we will see in the next chapter) the state is structured like a substance and is unable to countenance intrinsically emancipatory interaction. Hegel and Heidegger, as we have seen, do not solve this problem. It will have to await Habermas.

Sixteen

Kantian Political Philosophy in Its Double Foundation

Analysis

With the third *Critique*'s account of reflective judgment, situating reason emerges from the occlusion it underwent in Aristotle and can once again be thought of and talked about; we have seen Hegel and Heidegger, behind their very different vocabularies, talk about it. But the fact that it can be recognized to exist, and that the words are being forged to discuss it, does not mean that its recuperation is complete. For both Plato and Aristotle, poetic interaction was not safe for the polis: Plato located it outside the walls; and Aristotle, who allows for nothing human beyond the polis, suppressed it altogether. It, and its developed forms in intrinsically emancipatory interaction, are for Kant still unsafe. Theoretically, recognition of the interactive nature of situating reason would, I have argued, impeach the distinction between the empirical and transcendental realms which is fundamental to Kant's entire philosophy. His political writings, I will now argue, show him trying to cope with the practical implications of reflective judgment as we saw it developed in what I called the second foundation for his political philosophy. The coping has two sides: First, Kant institutionalizes reflective judgment in the "philosophical faculty" of the university. Second, he tries to set this up in such a way that the state, grounded itself in the first foundation, can tolerate and even support it. For present purposes, this attempt to harmonize the first and second foundations is basic to Kantian political philosophy. The main problem Kant encounters is not that the *accounts* he gives of state and philosophical faculty are inconsistent, but that these two types of communities themselves cannot, apparently, coexist.

The standard texts for Kant's political philosophy are a string of essays he wrote late in his career.[1] But Hannah Arendt has challenged this. Largely dismissing the essays, she writes: Kant "expounds two political philosophies which differ sharply from one another—the first being

275

that . . . in his *Critique of Practical Reason,* and the second that contained in his *Critique of Judgment.*"[2] Kant's political philosophy is in fact to be found both in the *Critiques* and the essays; the *Critiques* contain, not a full political philosophy, but the abstract premises or foundations for one—if not, as Arendt suggests, for two. To verify this claim, we must see how political philosophy is built, in the later texts, upon those two foundations. What I have called the "first foundation" is clearly operative in those explicitly political essays, and especially (for our purposes) in *Perpetual Peace (Zum ewigen Frieden).* The second, in a dark and quasi-subliminal way, seems to direct the portrait of the "philosophical faculty" in the *Conflict of the Faculties.*[3]

The application of the first foundation to political theory begins, for my purposes, with the affirmation in *Perpetual Peace* that political philosophy, to be self-consistent, must begin from our a priori awareness of the moral law.[4] The only other possible beginning point would be from principles of (empirical) advantage. Since violations of justice will always be to someone's advantage, a political philosophy which takes this as its supreme principle will ultimately consist of nothing more than the rationalization of unjust acts.[5]

The *Fundamental Principles of the Metaphysics of Morals* contains two formulations of the categorical imperative which are restated in the "First Definitive Article" of *Perpetual Peace* to yield such an a priori political beginning-point. The first or "objective" formulation requires that human beings act lawfully—that they act in accordance with practical laws valid for all rational beings. Politically phrased in the "First Definitive Article," this asserts that all members of society must be equally subject to a single common legislation. The second or "subjective" formulation requires us to treat other moral agents as ends and never as means. It requires us never to transgress their own capacity to legislate for themselves, and to respect their autonomy or freedom. In the "First Definitive Article," this becomes the principle of the freedom of all members of society.[6]

Just as the first two formulations of the categorical imperative lead in the *Foundations of the Metaphysics of Morals* to the idea of the Kingdom of Ends, so in *Perpetual Peace* the principles of equality and freedom, taken together, refer to the idea of the moral agent as "citizen of a supersensible world" (*EF* 350n). The aim here, however, is not to reiterate the doctrine of the Kingdom of Ends, but to consider the moral law as furnishing standards for a constitution possible in the temporal, empirical world. Such a constitution is "republican" in nature, and the society it structures is a "civil society" (*EF* 350n.)[7] The Kingdom of Ends is what the *Conflict of the Faculties* refers to as a "respublica noumenon," and what *Perpetual*

Peace calls the community appropriate to a "race of angels;" civil society is a "respublica phaenomenon." It not only applies as a moral idea to human beings as they actually are, but it would even serve, in Kant's famous phrase, for a "race of devils, if only they have understanding" (*EF* 365f.; *SF* 91).

Although civil society is the only kind of society which moral philosophy can justify, it is not itself a "moral" entity. Its principle is not freedom (which can, we have noted, never appear empirically) but coercion. For the purpose of the laws which constitute the "legality" of civil society is to force people to do, on prudential grounds, what they ought to do on moral grounds.[8] Coercion is also present on the basic, constitutional level of Kantian civil society. Though dictated by the moral law, for example, the republican form is also required by nature itself, which, as Hobbes showed, forces men to enter into a social compact to obtain gratification of their inclinations for a long and comfortable life (*EF* 360–368, 375n.). Other humans can also force the institution of a civil society. On an individual level, they may compel reluctant neighbors either to place themselves under its laws or to leave the area. Collectively, they may, as a state, threaten another society and force it to constitute itself as a republic in order to gain greater unity and cohesion in preparation for a coming battle.[9]

Such coercion is necessary, of course, because people possess inclinations to seek their individual advantage at the expense of the moral law. The operative principle of civil society is to oppose such inclinations with legally instituted ones (such as the inclination to stay out of jail) and thereby, through a quasi-Newtonian balancing of forces, to cancel them out.[10] Freedom as the ability to legislate for oneself thus remains, in Kantian political philosophy, a predicate of man qua noumenon. Its empirical appearance is, as it must be in the Kantian framework, a form of natural causality which, when affecting human beings, is coercion.

The idea that a just society can be founded only on the coercion and canceling of inclinations is a far cry from the third *Critique*'s presentation of a form of freedom consisting in the integration of the various levels of the human psyche. So far, indeed, it seems that the second foundation has no "founding" role at all in Kantian political philosophy. However, we can see that such is not the case by looking more closely at the defining characteristic of civil society, its lawfulness.[11] Legislation, the *Metaphysics of Morals* tells us, has two parts. One is the law itself, which specifies an action (or omission) as necessary; such specification, we are told, is a merely theoretical activity. In *Perpetual Peace*, Kant consistently refers to the contents of laws—their formulation, prior to being enacted—as "maxims." In order to be practical rather than merely theoretical—in order to have an influence on conduct—a law must also have a "motive," which can be either internal or external. In the case of moral legislation, duty itself is the "internal" motive. In political or juridical legislation, the "external" motive is the penalty fixed for transgression. To legislate, or to enact, is then to attach a motive to a law or a subjectively valid maxim.[12]

Without "motive" there can be no "interest" (*KPV* 79, 119f.), and it is only through such legislation that laws come to have an "interest" for society. The task of legislating rightly thus reduces to the task of seeing to it that what is in the interest of society as a whole is also in the interest of individuals in society. This shows why the third *Critique* is apparently so unimportant to Kantian political philosophy. For if the essential characteristic of a just society is legality, and if interest is intrinsic to law, then the "disinterested" discourse explored in that *Critique* has no apparent relation to either. On the other hand, the *Metaphysics of Morals* does claim that, while aesthetic pleasure is not an "indigenous" (*einheimisch*) concept for practical philosophy, there are to be "episodic" mentions of it.[13] My account of the Kantian view of social legislation will aim to uncover and explain those episodes.

Such legislation is determined by two basic principles. One is the right of each citizen to obey only those laws to which he "could have given" his consent: to violate that right is to violate his autonomy.[14] The second principle furnishes the criterion for whether a given piece of legislation meets this requirement: the "principle of publicity." This holds that any law (or policy, such as making a war) which can be made known to the entire populace without harming its own chances of success may be held to be legitimate (*gerecht*). Any which must be hidden from them is illegitimate (*EF* 381–386).

The principle of publicity is held to be a "transcendental" one, meaning that it follows from the rational idea of a civil society. It is, in fact, nothing more than the restatement of a principle structuring the Kingdom of Ends: that each of its inhabitants obeys only laws which he himself has made. Its first use is merely negative, for from the proposition that any proposed legislation that cannot be made public is illegitimate, I cannot conclude that whatever legislation *is* susceptible to publicity is therefore legitimate. This is then supplemented with a "positive" formulation, according to which all legislation requiring publicity to achieve its goals must be just. But there remains a broad middle ground of cases in which publicity is neither necessary nor inimical to success. The details of the regulations of a country's transportation industry, for example, do not need to be laid before the entire citizenry in order to achieve their goals; while the fact that a proposed speed limit for that country must be made known to the citizens in order to achieve its goals does not decide whether it should be 55 or 60 miles per hour. The principle of publicity, in both applications, is merely "formal" in character (*EF* 381–386).

The nature of the "material" content of the laws of a society can be understood by considering the purposiveness of such laws.[15] When laws are enacted in order to achieve certain purposes (such as happiness, e.g., *SF* 21f.), they are empirically conditioned in two senses. First, the purpose itself (here, happiness), because empirical, is not necessarily one and the same at all times for all men; it varies with respect to the desires and inclinations it is formulated to satisfy.[16] Second, any attempt to achieve purposes requires knowledge of natural causal processes in the form of hypothetical imperatives.

Let us sketch, in a preliminary way, some characteristics of the sort of discourse by which such an empirical law would be formulated. Assuming that a civil society already exists, formulation of a new law is made necessary by the empirical discovery of a defect in the present laws, a given case of injustice or unhappiness (cf. *EF* 372). The recognition of a particular event as unjust requires evaluating it against the standards provided by the a priori ideas of civil society and the Kingdom of Ends and would be carried out, in Kantian terms, by a determining judgment. But the formulation of an empirical law goes beyond such recognition: it attempts to diagnose the specific case and formulate a general, legal prescription for avoiding it in the future. It thus moves from the particular to the general and partakes of the nature, not of determining judgment, but of reflective judgment.[17]

The aim of such formulation is, moreover, analogous to the use of reflective judgment in directing empirical research. For it aims, ultimately, to discover that set of empirically derived laws constitutive of a harmonious society, just as in science reflective judgment provides the controlling idea of a harmonious nature.[18] Such formulation is not enactment. It does not decide that the maxims it produces are in the interests of society, since that is up to the legislators themselves. But, in advancing those maxims as subjects for discussion, it must at least impute the legislators' consent. Since it only imputes and cannot force that consent, it makes no decisions about interest. It is, as we shall see in more detail, interest free.

The kind of discourse we have just sketched would have, if actually engaged in, all four moments of the judgment of taste. In quality, it would be disinterested. In quantity, it would impute the consent of all (legislators). In terms of relation, it would be purposive with respect to the harmonious society. And in terms of modality, it would impute the necessary agreement of all (cf *KU* 203–240). Though it could culminate in a general rule for society, and hence might be more like teleological than aesthetic judgment, such rules could never be definitively attained. Man will always remain "crooked wood,"[19] and the social whole will always present new material for the reflective formulation of laws.

As disinterested, this sort of formulation cannot be carried out by the government, which has an interest in the established order and must act to maintain it—a necessity which "inevitably destroys the free judgment of reason."[20] It cannot be carried out by the people as a whole, who aim at material well-being without regard to moral goodness, and who are not free of government influence on their opinions.[21] Though any citizen should be free to communicate to the authorities his views on social injustices,[22] for the true "public use of reason" a further condition is required: that he be learned, possessed of intellectual expertise relevant to his subject. The learned public is however institutionalized, not in the legislature, but in the university (SF 17f.).

Among the university's faculties (jurisprudence, medicine, theology, and philosophy), it is primarily the philosophers who are to be listened to by the authorities. As the "secret article" to Perpetual Peace has it, this is because they alone are able, not merely to expound and apply the law, but to criticize it and investigate its need for improvement (EF 368f.; cf. SF 24f.). Thus, what for those other faculties is "content," doctrines to be taught, is for the philosophical faculty the "object" of its examination and critique.[23] Insofar as this critique is an affair of reflective judgment, it will have to begin from individual cases.[24] All action, we may say, requires the subjective determination of the will—an individual's decision of what to do in his or her unique situation of the moment—and hence has a "maxim."[25] An unjust act proceeds from bad maxims, and in such cases the philosophical faculty's task is to analyze and criticize these, penetrating beyond the silence or rhetorical disguises which seek to conceal them. At this point, the philosophical faculty exercises its function as *the* source of social critique.[26]

The case for or against a maxim is decided when reason makes a "verdict" (SF 33). Such a verdict has, of course, no compelling power. It is envisioned, as early as the first Critique, as the "consensus of free citizens" (KRV B.766). It may be formulated in a determining judgment, to the effect that an action or social arrangement is or is not in accord with basic moral principles. But it can also, presumably, be a reflective one— an articulation of a problem, or of the maxims that produced it, which is imputed to capture the nature of the basic injustice which is being reflected upon. In either case, the philosophers are also able to go on and formulate positive alternatives, for a merely negative critique is socially irresponsible, and rulers need advice on how to achieve their intentions (*EF* 368ff., *SF* 35).

When such a positive formulation is reached, we may say that a new rule has been gained for society—just as, in the critical reflection on an art object, a new rule is gained for art. And, as is the case with aesthetic criticism, the new rule gained is never definitive or final. For all laws of men—especially the empirically derived "positive" laws—are fallible and in recurrent need of updating (*SF* 33). The social critique engaged in by the philosophical faculty thus operates via basic procedures similar to those of art criticism. Beginning from a given case of injustice, as the art critic begins from a beautiful art object, it articulates that injustice as purposive or as determined by a maxim. It then goes on to formulate new rules from that given case, just as art criticism can analyze the failings of even a great work of art and derive rules for understanding further successes. As in the case of art criticism, those rules as formulated have no prescriptive standing. In the case of social critique, they may subsequently acquire such standing through legislation, but that is outside the scope of the faculty which first enunciates the rules in question.[27]

In all this, the philosophical faculty judges in accordance with reason. In determining judgment, it subsumes individual cases under individual concepts; while in reflective judgment, it formulates new concepts out of reflection on specific cases (cf. *SF* 19f., 27f.). The ability to judge in accordance with reason goes together with human autonomy itself, and this means that the philosophical faculty stands under the legislation, not of the state, but of reason. The exercise of its rational powers is then a kind of freedom which the government may not transgress (*SF* 17, 19f., 27f.). This kind of freedom is grounded on another, deeper and more complex: freedom from action itself. For the philosophers are wholly unable to act—even to the extent of advocating their ideas publicly or of forming interest groups to do so. Otherwise, they would inevitably come under the influence of government (*EF* 369, *SF* 18f.). For government is never disinterested. True, it serves the general interest rather than particular ones. But this overarching interest of the government brings with it other ones. The government must, for example, be able to see to it that its orders are carried out, and this means that it has an interest in influencing popular opinion (*SF* 21f.).

The "inner freedom" of the philosophical faculty is then grounded on the fact that it does nothing but investigate truth, thereby developing reason itself.[28] Its inability to act results from this basic disinterestedness, itself a kind of freedom. But it is not freedom in the sense of autonomy, which, precisely, legislates to moral agents. It is freedom as the ability to relate merely to oneself in one's activity without requiring anything outside: freedom, then, as characterized in the third *Critique*.

The "First Definitive Article" of *Perpetual Peace* gives three principles for a just constitution: the freedom of members of society, their equality, and their common dependence on a single legislation.[29] The philosophical faculty is founded on the freedom of its members, as rationally judging scholars, and on their equality as such (cf. *SF* 23). All, we have seen, come under a common legislation, that of reason. The philosophical faculty can thus be said to constitute a sort of subpolity within the larger political whole. But it is not a polity of coercive laws. Reason is engaged here, not in legislating to the will, but in developing itself; the individual inhabitants of this "republic of ends" need no coercion, because antisocial inclinations are already mastered. For, in addition to being knowledgeable and free, the philosophers are also, we read, moderate in pleasure and patient in distress, restraining their desires and handing the governance of their lives over to reason. They are in no position to seek power or to do injustice, and unlike the "people," they do not seek material goals such as health, property, and eternal bliss except insofar as those goals are sanctioned by reason (*SF* 30).

To sum up this sketch of Kantian political philosophy: the normative account of the structure of the social whole is given in the concept of civil society. The first foundation provides the basic norms for a just and free society, while the second provides those for critical discourse within that society. The philosophical faculty, in its use of aesthetic judgment, then stands to civil society as the aesthetic to the moral, or as reflective to determining judgment. Because, as we saw, all political action must begin from the a priori, it is the discourse of the second foundation which must be integrated into, subordinated to, that of the first—not vice versa.[30] But there is a serious question as to whether such integration is possible. Can a disinterested, autonomous institution, such as the Kantian philosophical faculty, ever come to exist within the system of counterbalancing natural coercions that is Kantian civil society?

The account of the status of the philosophical faculty (at *SF* 21) is notably obscure: it even *claims* obscurity. The university in which that faculty exists is an "idea of reason" which, like that of freedom, is supposed to prove itself in empirical reality. But unlike freedom, which shows itself empirically in a system of coercions, i.e., through the self-cancellation of its opposite, the philosophical faculty is supposed to achieve some sort of direct realization. It is "darkly grounded" on a rational principle, without the state—which institutes it—even being aware of the fact. This "dark grounding," I suggest, covers a variety of deep difficulties. For it leaves undecided whether the philosophical faculty is to be understood as (1) something which actually exists in the world; (2) something which could exist in it but does not yet; (3) an idealized presentation of something which actually exists; or (4) a wholly *a priori* idea of reason.

In favor of (1) is, first, Kant's language. Throughout the *Conflict of the Faculties*, he speaks in the indicative mode, as if describing something that actually existed. A second set of considerations is provided by the relationship between the kind of interaction in the philosophical faculty and art criticism. The latter is, we saw, an "empirical fact" of reason: it is not a fact about the rational realm, but one about the empirical realm which reason itself, in critique, encounters and must admit. If true of aesthetic criticism, we could argue, this is also true of the political criticism exercised by the philosophical faculty: for both present, at bottom, the same sort of interaction.

But a university enjoying complete freedom from political interference was sadly counterfactual in Kant's Prussia, though he clearly hoped for better days (cf. *SF* 5–11). If his hopes were serious, we must move to some version of (2): the philosophical faculty does not exist but is something that Kant thinks can come about, and which he (perhaps) wants so badly that he uses the indicative mode to describe it. But this does not work either. There are, first, serious problems with construing the philosophical faculty as something which, even if not yet present, could conceivably exist in the world. In the first *Critique*, we find it asserted that no true philosopher has ever existed: such a person, who can direct reason toward its essential ends, is only an "ideal" (*KRV* B.866–868). That there could have been no intelligent change of mind between the first *Critique* and the *Conflict of the Faculties* is indicated by considering what is entailed by the latter's account of the philosophical faculty's disinterestedness. For if an interest is a concept which founds a desire, and if the philosophical faculty creates concepts of what is good for society, its disinterested character would have to entail that it would not be affected, as a faculty, by whether or not those concepts were actually enacted in law: it could have no desires for the realization of its suggestions. Can we imagine, for example, that philosophers, about to advise the sovereign on whether to make war (*EF* 368), would be capable of such disinterest?

If institutionalized critical discourse does not yet exist, we must ask where Kant gets the idea of it, and this leads us on to (3) and (4): either it is already realized in some defective form, and Kant is "dressing up" reality for adjuratory purposes; or it is some sort of a priori idea. If the former, however, Kant is engaged not merely in pleading but in special pleading. He is taking his start from an empirical reality and, after "dressing it up," is advancing it as an idealized norm—which is just the sort of thing done by the "moralizing politician" against whom he inveighs in *Perpetual Peace* (even when that politician's intentions, like Kant's, are good: EF 370–380).

We are thus left with (4): the philosophical faculty is a wholly a priori idea. In order for it not to be a mere "figment of the brain," there must be a sort of "transcendental recipe" for its construction (as the idea of freedom was constructed by taking a particular type of syllogism and extending it to infinity). If we ask what sort of rational operation might be expanded into the idea of the philosophical faculty, we could say that it is (in part, at least) reflective judgment. We could, perhaps, eventually arrive at the idea of the philosophical faculty as a community of individuals engaged in the unrestricted use of such judgment, just as the Kingdom of Ends was the idea of a community of agents engaged in unrestricted moral legislation. But then the question arises of how such a "pure idea of reason" can ever find empirical instantiation. If it cannot, then we come back to the problem of its relation to aesthetic critique, mentioned above: Why should one be an empirical fact, but not the other?

Whether he could have solved these problems or not, Kant does not mention them, and the "dark ground" of the philosophical faculty remains dark. The comments offered here on the status of the philosophical faculty thus remain speculative. But they do suggest that it cannot be integrated into civil society, and that it can in principle have no clear "ontological" or "critical" status within a Kantian framework. And it follows that the first and second foundations cannot be integrated with one another. The first, by making freedom a noumenal idea, gives empirical reality over, not to institutionalized reflective judgment, but merely to mechanical causality, in which an entity like the "philosophical faculty" can have no place. It thus seems that no coherent Kantian explanation can be given of how the abstract and formal considerations set forth in the first foundation are to be concretized by the considerations presented in the second.[31]

The Kantian account of reflective judgment is, I have argued, an account of reason as situating: reflective judgment articulates parameters as parameters. But this activity turns out to have uncomfortable political consequences. Avoiding these consequences leads Kant to say some peculiar things about the philosophical faculty. This need to keep reflective judgment somehow apolitical goes together with his view of it in the third *Critique* as primarily an aesthetic phenomenon, one which is only secondarily interactive.

Narrative

The reflective judgment of the philosophical faculty is similar in several ways to the poetic interaction portrayed in the *Phaedrus*. It formulates basic empirical concepts for the understanding of social experience (though not, apparently, of other kinds) and to that extent gives stable meanings to some words. This articulation is inherently "sociable" and interactive—more so than in the *Critique of Judgment*, because a pattern of social injustice is not something that can be immediately presented by the imagination but something whose very existence can be a matter for discussion and debate, like the meaning of an inherently vague word in the *Phaedrus*. As thus referred to common sense—and because in that reference it begins without a concept—the final verdict of the philosophical faculty presupposes subjects who are unified within themselves: whose sensibility, imagination, and understanding all cooperate in free play. Rendered by a group of disinterested people who stand apart from the political order, such a verdict is both a manifestation of freedom and, when necessary, a critique of the political order within which its members exist.

The free play of the faculties achieved in the judgment of taste differs from the self-actualization of an Aristotelian substance, for no individual faculty dominates. But, as for Aristotle, self-unification is always achieved by the individual as a condition for his participation in the community, rather than through that participation itself. Thus, as I have suggested, the Kantian texts, in spite of their overtly antimetaphysical character, continue to take a broadly "substantialist" view of the self. In the empirical world, this is because of the concept of disinterest. The judgment of taste is "disinterested" because what allows me to see an object as beautiful (or as unjust) is not any verifiable sensory quality of that object, but the way I recapitulate it in my imagination. Such recapitulation is as private as the imagination itself, and so is immanent to the self.

Disinterest fills the role, in the Kantian empirical world, of substance in the Aristotelian world (and in the Kantian Kingdom of Ends): it makes possible the articulation of the unity of the self as something achieved immanently to that self rather than as arising in and through interaction with others. And, as we saw, it is because the philosophical faculty is "disinterested" that it poses no threat to civil society, but can be integrated with it. It is thus, we may say, through the concept of disinterest that the first foundation—the "otherworldly" doctrine of noumenal free-dom—intrudes into the second. In the *Phaedrus*, as my account of the Aristotelian *Physics* suggested, the theory of Forms constitutes a similar intrusion. The eventual fate of the Kantian view that aesthetic experience is disinterested will be seen in later chapters. For the moment, we will just note that the Platonic texts, though free of a substance metaphysics of the self, do not operate with any conception of disinterest as morally valuable: what stands between the soul and action in the Palinode is merely its inability to speak to the beloved. This permits Plato to view the primal unity of the individual as achieved interactively.

Because the empirical realm in general escapes the Kantian demotion of substance as prescriptive for all philosophical discourse, empirical dis-courses can take a variety of forms.[32] This holds on the political level, where we have what may be styled the "discourse of legislation." When carried out in civil society, this is grounded in the rational idea of moral autonomy which, in the first foundation, provides the conceptual basis of that society and consists of the communal decision that a proposed rule is in the general interest of society. But also present is what we may call the "discourse of criticism," which formulates that rule in the first place. As an exercise of reflective judgment, this does not rely on ideas validated "noumenally" but provides its own concepts by giving what is agreed, in a "consensus of free citizens," to be a true and coherent for-mulation of reality.[33]

Though it has lost prescriptive status for our understanding of the empirical world, however, metaphysics continues to play a prescriptive role with regard to philosophy itself. This reveals a new form of prescrip-tion: metaphysics performs, not a truth telling, but an integrating and systematizing, or "regulative," role in discourse.[34] Different areas of philosophical discourse are not simply taken up and used according to the needs of the moment, as happens in the Platonic writings. Rather, each field is to have its allotted place and function within a larger totality, whose "key concept" is the rational—formerly metaphysical—idea of noumenal freedom. Albert Hofstadter's claim that Kant "initiated the at-tempt to think through the idea of freedom as the central systematizing idea of philosophy itself"[35] thus points to what is, on my terms, Kant's greatest achievement and his greatest limitation. By deposing metaphys-ics and relocating its contents to the human mind, Kant makes freedom central to philosophy: but philosophy still has a center, governed by that very concept.

This means, with regard to political philosophy, that its two founda-tions must be shown not only to cooperate but to cooperate necessarily by virtue of the respective positions, in a larger integrated whole, of the discourses they found. This requires that both types of discourse be institutionalized: that of the "first foundation" in civil society itself, and that of the second in the "philosophical faculty." As a result of its institutionalization, reflective judgment loses the global character it had in the *Critique of Judgment* and which poetic interaction had in the *Phaedrus*. For it does not provide the vocabulary of politics itself, but it only diagnoses patterns of injustice. Though the political sphere, where people use language to pursue purposes, presumably requires the broader exercise of the Kantian judgment of taste, as it required Platonic poetic interaction, it does not require the university as such; like an Aristotelian substance, the state is independent of other forms of interaction. This means that Kant's theoretical demand for the unification of the two foundations runs up against an empirical reality. For Kant, the state, as a substance, would at least like to have the overarching dominance which the polis has in the Aristotelian framework; it would like to influence even the most intimate opinions of its subjects. It follows that the institutionalization of critical discourse cannot be given a convincing discussion: just why the state would allow there to be such a thing as a philosophical faculty is left resting on "dark ground."

The preeminence of the state in the political sphere also accounts, we may suppose, for the absence in the Kantian political writings of any effort to recuperate the sublime for political discourse. For although the reflective judgment of the beautiful can be held to be of use to the state, in that it enables injustices to be remedied before they become dangerous, the sublime would have no such redeeming value; it casts all empirical rules (and laws) into the "abyss" of reason and shows them—and the entire empirical realm of politics—to be as nothing.

Thus, where the Aristotelian approach assumes a basic order to the cosmos, and thereby legitimates the polis as the basic field of human interaction, the Kantian approach assumes a basic order to the human mind and derives the state as the prime political object. In the Aristotelian case, this is legitimated by a set of metaphysical propositions asserted to be true. In the Kantian; it is done through a set of rational ideas asserted, in critique, to be good.

The Aristotelian legitimation, then, relies on what I call necessities; the Kantian, on conditions. This difference, from the perspectives of the thinkers to follow, will not prove to be a great one. The incompatibility between the first and second foundations leaves only two basic options: either we remain with the merely formal and abstract guidelines given in the First Foundation, viewing them as inescapable conditions for human society; or we abandon it, together with its "noumenal" justification, and attempt to found political thought on empirical considerations as developed in the *Critique of Judgment*. This requires viewing society, not in relation to an a priori moral law (or "fact of reason"), but as purposive, as part of the larger development of human culture, and as composed more of parameters than of conditions (or necessities). It is this path that Hegel and (with major modifications) Heidegger will take.

Seventeen

Hegel

It is now time to integrate Hegel and Heidegger, as previously presented in part one, into my narrative. The analysis of Hegel aimed, first, to uncover the interactionist and narrative dimension of the *Phenomenology* and the *Aesthetics*. The overall Hegelian narrative analyzed was structured by five main concepts, two of which, reason and Spirit, presented the main fields of interplay for the other three, recognition, externalization, and reconciliation, which articulated structures of interaction in general. The philosophical tradition I am narrating here has now been uncovered sufficiently to permit us to see how Hegel's articulation of these five concepts fits in with the general occlusion, and subsequent recuperation, of poetic interaction; the crucial links in this narrative will be Hegel's appropriation of Kant's third antinomy and doctrine of reflective judgment. Once we have seen how Hegel develops those doctrines, we can turn critically to his conception of self-consolidation and to the precarious harmony he has tried to introduce between art and the state.

Hegel as a Philosopher of Interaction

Reason, I argued, could be viewed as the structured system of constraints upon an individual's behavior in society—a definition which held as much for the state in the *Aesthetics*, "rounded off and fully-perfected" in its rational freedom of the will, as for the master and bondsman in the *Phenomenology*. Reason is thus an empirical phenomenon, one which takes no single form in the texts I have analyzed but is manifested in different ways; for example, in the variety of different states, founded on various dynamics of externalization, and in different works of art, where reason becomes in manifold ways reconciliatory. Nor, in the texts we analyzed, is Reason ever fully present. Externalization inherently distorts language and meaning, and works of art present their guiding conceptions inexplicitly: it is up to the reflective spectator to formulate their rational structures. Those structures themselves, as concrete, are particular in nature. There is no inherently universal content for art, except its lack of abstract universality. The texts analyzed thus impose no need to posit Reason as any sort of metaphysical entity, whether we conceive "metaphysical" in the sense of a theory of the supersensible realm; as the articulation of something universal and necessary in the empirical realm; or even in the Heideggerean sense as a discourse founded on the idea of complete presence. The same held for Spirit, which I presented as the set of historical transformations of Reason in a quest for cooperation and articulateness among people—for the achieved community of minds which, as early as the *Phenomenology*, is said to constitute Spirit's "real existence."

I have talked of Spirit's "quest," and of Reason's "constraint." But such reification is, though convenient, not necessary: it is individuals who, in the Hegelian narrative, want increasing cooperation and articulateness in their relations to others. They want these as they are themselves embodiments of past cases of cooperation and articulateness—as biological products of man and woman, and as vehicles of a cultural heritage. In the pursuit of cooperation and articulateness, individuals and collectives can transform their cultural heritage, and these transformations, in my analysis, were Spirit.

Neither Reason nor Spirit has any clear ancient ancestry, unless we call in Kant as the narrative link between Hegel and the Greeks. Plato and Aristotle were obviously aware that society constrains its members in numerous ways. But for Plato, to call those constraints "rational" would have been an unholy joke, a blasphemy of the Forms; for Aristotle, the polis is indeed rational, but is so by virtue of its position within the cosmic order: as an organization of people pursuing the noble—ultimately, the Prime Mover—in a distinctively human way. If the Kantian account of reason (in Kant's own view) developed the Platonic concept by making ideas inherent in, and formed by, reason itself, it is Hegel who then makes the Aristotelian move and brings reason down to earth, conceiving it as an actually existing system of social constraints. But in contrast to Aristotle, this system is itself viewed, along Kantian lines, as generating its own contents—its own constraints. Because it generates those constraints, it can also leave them behind: they are not, as for Kant, conditions either of cognition or of moral action, but a set of parameters about which a story can be told. Reason for Hegel, then, makes no appeal either to metaphysical necessities or to transcendental conditions: in my terms, it is wholly situated.

The first of the three main headings under which the *Phenomenology* conceptualized human interaction was that of "recognition," the inter-active character of which has been clear since Kojève (and indeed since Marx). It provided the basic form of communication, indeed, of human relations in general: in order for any two (or more) beings to be related at all, they must resemble each other in some respect. Moreover, they must *signify* for each other: another human being must be perceived as more than simply a natural object. On both the Hegelian and Platonic accounts, the other human comes to signify for me through desire—erotic in Plato, edacious in Hegel. In both cases, my desire is provoked by the relation of the other's body to something non-physical—beauty or an abstract ego. My own body also has this relation, and so I and the other are equal; the "pure concept" of recognition, presented in the "Battle of the Opposed Self-Consciousnesses," saw it as the acting out of such equality, indeed as rigidly symmetrical.

On the other hand, there must also be *some* dissimilarities among in-dividuals if they are to constitute a plurality: one of the lovers is younger, and one of the battlers is stronger. In the *Phaedrus*, this dissimilarity was overcome as the lovers came more and more to resemble both each other and their common god. In the "Battle," which because of the structure of Hegel's narrative had to be much more antagonistic—and for which the guiding "god," in the form of Hegelian reason, had still to be created by the battlers themselves—the differences overwhelmed the similarity, and the basic presumption of equality was denied.

Dissimilarity leads to inarticulateness: for the possession of a language is both a constitutive feature of the self and a concrete bond to others, an enormous mass of similarities with them. The overcoming of inar-ticulateness is achieved by externalization. In this, an individual puts forward—makes external to himself—some thought or idea: he "exter-nalizes" it into a material object (in labor) or into words (in speech). Through speech, then, something new comes to be in language: as ma-terial is reconfigured in labor, so language can be reconfigured in exter-nalizing speech. And through the efforts of others to understand those configurations, further new configurations come to be. These new forms can be higher-and-higher order abstractions, since, as the circle of those to whom the thought has been communicated widens, it is measured against the ideas and experiences—the concrete selves—of more and more people. Externalization is thus a process of articulation, an interac-tionist equivalent to what the *Phaedo*, *Republic*, and *Symposium* depicted as the solitary rise to the Forms, or to what Aristotle had viewed as the solitary natural process of induction. As with Plato, such articulation be-gins from something vague or unclear—in the beginning, one's own de-sirous self, a mere abstract ego; at the end, the ambiguity of the detail in the work of art, which was both "free" and "necessary," and which stood in a variety of relations, themselves unclear, to other details. Unlike Platonic dialectic, externalization ends not with determinate form but with inner freedom, which itself is nothing more than the ability to cast aside all content. It thus culminates in the awareness that all content, not merely of society but of language itself—its entire vocabulary—is a set of parameters, and can be discarded. If externalization was already, in my sense, "poetic" because consciousness was formulating its own universals, reconciliation is where consciousness learns that it was poetic: that the universal contents it has formulated in externalization were not something given to it, but were things it produced.

With the achievement of a common linguistic heritage, the two-term relation of recognition becomes a three-term relation among speaker, hearer, and their common language. Such language and its influence on the individuals who grow up within it lend themselves more to reifying talk than do the obviously interactive structures of recognition; Hegel, we saw, articulates externalization in an ontological vocabulary. But the texts I have analyzed remain oriented, not to some suprahuman entity, but only to the phenomena of human interaction itself, as structured by the dynamism of a common cultural heritage dispersed among various individuals, in the first instance, as the language they speak.

The appropriation of that heritage by different individuals can differ, and so can their subsequent articulation of it: externalization is a realm of difference, and words are brought forth through human dissimilarity. This fact occludes the equality present at the recognitive base of all interaction. Only when the culture is completely articulate—i.e., has traversed the human mind all the way to its subjective depths in the realization that everyone is both sinner and saint, both universal and particular—can externalization and recognition be reconciled.

Reconciliation, viewed interactively, is thus a "free play" in which differences can arise, but they arise as overcome in principle: a common vocabulary exists which, with perhaps some modifications, can cope with them. There is thus, at once, reconciliation of the individual with his language—indeed with his concrete self, which attains recognized existence in a language that he knows will be adequate to express whatever he has to express—and reconciliation of the individual with the other, to whom he will be able to express it and by whom he will be understood. Because reconciliation is at once of the individual with himself and with the other, there is no clash between "within" and "without," or between "us" and "them:" in forgiving my sin, you forgive your own as well. The claim that forgiveness must be self-forgiveness, i.e., brought about by the sinning, human parties themselves, actually imposes here an interactionist reading of reconciliation; for if the reconciled community is "God manifested in the midst of those who know themselves," the manifestation is their work—not His. This forgiveness, though not without obvious Christian antecedents, had its original pagan form in Platonic sexual desire: desire that was for the other's mind without losing or setting aside interest in his body. *Hegelian reconciliation is thus a reinterpretation of the unification of self presented in the* Phaedrus.

The foregoing is not meant to put an end to what David Kolb has called "large-entity" interpretations of Hegel: views of his philosophy which see it as exposing some sort of supraindividual or suprahuman thing such as "Spirit," or "the Absolute."[1] I have treated only a few of Hegel's texts, and my analysis of those has been too partial to authorize judgments about his philosophy as a whole. But we have seen that fairly lengthy stretches of that philosophy have a good deal to say about human interaction and that, for those stretches, Hegel's texts do not require large entities for the interpretation of even some of their most basic concepts. His philosophy is then narratable, not as an unfortunate reinstatement of metaphysics after its salutary destruction by Kant, but as operating within the terrain left by that destruction.

Hegel, Metaphysics, and the Third Antinomy

Hegel's relation to that destruction is evident from his response to Kant's third antinomy, which I argued spelled the end of both Platonic and Aristotelian metaphysics.[2] Kant, we saw, allocated the antinomy's thesis and antithesis to separate realms: everything empirical was governed by causal laws, wholly determined by previous events in time; while the capacity to begin new chains of events was "noumenal" in nature. Hegel retains the critical import of the third antinomy but not its Kantian solution, and therefore must interpret *both* of its sides as having to do with the empirical realm. In this, he is true enough to empiricism to deprive the category of causality of its universality. For Kant, empirical experience offers no certain generalizations: the category of cause imposes itself on all appearances, not empirically, but by virtue of being a "pure concept of the Understanding," a category. The antinomy itself was begun, not by empirical experience, but by Kantian reason, when it asserted that *all* entities and events (not merely appearances) were naturally caused—an assertion which reason itself, with its moral prerogatives, could not accept.

Hegel, more empirical than Kant, refuses to consider seriously the a priori claim that all entities have causes; refuses to consider the equally a priori claim that all appearances exhibit causes; and in fact refuses to make any a priori claims at all about the domains of application of the concepts of freedom and necessity. This indifference to the field of application of the concepts, as Michael Allen Gillespie has noted, transforms the third antinomy from a conflict of propositions to an incompatibility of concepts.[3] The same entity or event cannot be described both as "free" and as "caused," at least not in the same time and in the same respect. But the categories themselves are interdependent: if we are going to make use of the concept of "freedom" to describe some things, we are committed to the use of "caused" for other things. Moreover, everything real is in time and changes with time. This applies to us as well, as observers. If we use "free" to describe an entity at one *time*, we are contrasting that with earlier and later states of the universe in which that entity (or whatever precedes and succeeds it) is "caused." If we describe the entity as "free" in some one *respect*, we are opening ourselves to describing it as "caused" when further, contrasting aspects of it come to view. Which things come under which description in which respect at which time is a matter for contextualized and pragmatic consideration.

We see this sort of contextualized use of the concepts of freedom and causality, though not the words themselves, throughout the *Phenomenology*. Each of its "certainties" is a new beginning for consciousness, which views itself as undetermined by what went before: it is then "free." But once adopted, that certainty is subjected to a chain of events not under the control of consciousness but determined from outside it, and thus—in a sense that goes back at least to the *Republic*—it is "unfree." Having learned the untenability of its certainty, consciousness then makes another new beginning. Though Hegel uses instead the terms "immediate" and "mediated," the entire development of the *Phenomenology* can be viewed as a dialectic between freedom and causality.

But the freedom here is only apparent: in actual fact, though unbeknownst to consciousness, its "certainty" is not truly a new beginning but has been necessitated by what has gone before. Freedom thus arises only through consciousness's forgetting of previous experience, i.e., through the occlusion of necessity. What for Kant was a way of defining "freedom"—the negation of empirical causality—is for Hegel the genesis of freedom itself.

The Hegelian point here is not to dismiss the occlusion of necessity as something wholly subjective, as if it were just a lapse in attention or an act of "forgetting" in any ordinary sense. As Heidegger argues in "The Origin of the Work of Art," it is essential for phenomena to pass out of conscious experience, "occluding" themselves in earth. Sometimes—as in the *Phenomenology*—this is even necessary to allow something new to begin. "Freedom," as the occlusion of necessity, is thus a useful category for articulating aspects of our experience. For such occlusion can happen anywhere in our experience, and anything can be looked at as free in this sense. As the *Science of Logic* puts it,

> there is nothing, nothing in heaven or in nature or in mind or anywhere else that does not equally contain both immediacy and mediation, so that these two determinations reveal themselves to be unseparated and inseparable and the opposition between them to be a nullity.[4]

The dialectic of freedom and necessity can be seen in the living thing's rigid "disowning" of its continuity with the environment and its forcible reabsorption into it, and in the bondsman's withdrawal into himself. In externalization in general, something necessary to consciousness is occluded: its natural being. And, again, the denial of one's natural being raises one to inner freedom: consciousness becomes free by occluding natural necessity. Such occlusion is also present in the Hegelian account of the highest pitch of externalization: that of the assembly-line worker in modern society. The worker, we saw, is dependent on a long causal chain reaching back along the assembly line to the original raw materials; reaching on through the market to those who, he hopes, will eventually buy the products; and reaching up through the company itself which has hired him and which is bent upon reducing his pay and increasing his output. We must describe him, then, as "necessitated" or "caused" in all possible ways. But that causality simply generates another description of him as, in a different respect, "free," for the very modernity generating his economic oppression also generates his religious awareness of his own freedom. That awareness is, again, merely a disregarding, an occlusion, of the fact that in reality the worker *is* completely caused in all his (working) acts: his freedom, politically and economically speaking, does not exist except as a mere feeling of oppression.

Externalization can thus be understood, in terms of the third antinomy, as the empirical occlusion of natural necessity. For cultured consciousness, this occlusion is itself necessary in that it defines consciousness itself: the degree to which the cultured individual, for example, can set aside his own particular nature is the degree to which he has a recognized social standing or is a "really existent" individual at all. The occlusion of natural necessity is thus what I call a condition of externalized consciousness. Viewing externalization in terms of the third antinomy then means seeing it as a process in which consciousness generates conditions for itself by defining itself in terms of certain occlusions. If enough occlusions are made, consciousness rises to a "universal" level—but that level, as with Kant, will be empty. Thus, what Kant did, and what the Plato of the *Phaedo* and *Republic* did, was simply to exclude various factors from the human individual; if both thinkers reached ethical universals, that is merely a result of this more basic activity of occluding necessities.

The situating of reason is for Hegel an overcoming of such conditioning occlusions. In our experience of an artwork, individual details step forth from the whole, are perceived on their own account, and then are reabsorbed into it: the whole, as external to the individual, is in turn occluded and explicated. That movement, we saw, was an unconstrained version of previous developments: nothing coerces the detail to step outside the work as a whole, because (unlike the worker or the living thing) it is at no point defined as merely an increment in the whole. And nothing in the detail impedes its return into that whole: it is not defined as something outside the whole, either. Rather, it defines itself—or is defined by the spectator—as something whose nature consists precisely in, by turns, stepping forth from its surroundings and retreating into them. The same holds for how the spectator defines himself in interaction with the work: by turns, he approaches it, perceiving it and letting himself be guided by it, and then steps away to reflect upon it. Nothing forces him into one or the other mode of apprehension, and neither mode is a condition of his consciousness, which is then in a free play of occlusion.

This structure can be generalized to many sorts of unconstrained interaction, and it is for Hegel ultimately (but not unproblematically) a structure, not of aesthetic experience, but of interaction itself. Suppose, for instance, that I formulate a thought or message; in this, I am operating differently from my interlocutors, who themselves (presumably) have not formulated it. I perceive my thought as something unique to myself, which is why I view it as worth expressing, and in so doing, I "occlude" those others, operating in terms of my difference from them. I also occlude the factors of language, culture, and personal experience which have conditioned the formulation of my message, perhaps rendering it not so new and different after all. My message formulated, I then return to the interpersonal context and express it. Others understand it, if not exactly in the way I intended, in ways conditioned by the common culture and language we share, and it thus becomes something which adds to the cultural complex binding us all together: a new parameter.

Externalization in speech, considered apart from its capacity to define those who engage in it, occurs when one or the other of these moments is dominant: when, because vocabulary has not been developed or because my hearers will not countenance my message, I cannot formulate my thoughts to others but must keep them to myself as inarticulate feelings and interests, as was the case with the noble consciousness's advice to the state; or when I am forced in the name of the universal to disown them completely, explaining them away as does the member of the community of beautiful souls. The first two speeches of the *Phaedrus* can be seen as examples of these two sides of externalized speech. The speaker of the first speech, while he does speak, has no established vocabulary in which to do so. He is thus inarticulate, "wandering" with his words; they draw their meaning exclusively from his own personal situation and are no more than so many blind arrows fired in the general direction of his hearer. The second speaker, identified with the universal, is unable to relate either to the youth or to himself as individuals. Only speech resulting from the unified self of a true lover, in the Palinode, is able to move freely between universal arguments and persuasive speech appropriate to the particular individual being addressed.

The Kantian realm of noumenal freedom, then, is precisely the sort of necessary occlusion that Hegelian reconciliation is designed to overcome. In this, Hegel makes a massive appropriation of the third antinomy, viewing experience—and freedom itself—as a successive occlusion and explication of various moments or details. "Reconciliation" for Hegel can thus be seen in general as the free and fluent, indeed playful, alternation between occlusion and explication of external determination: it is his resolution of the third antinomy. His departure from Kant is into the empirical, not the metaphysical, realm: the "earthly" realm of the *Phaedrus*'s love affair, not the "space beyond the heavens" of its metaphysics. *The Hegelian Absolute, insofar as it inhabits aesthetic experience, is not a fully present entity, but merely a free play of occlusion.*

Reflective Judgment and Hegelian Narrative

Hegelian philosophy therefore treats development in time—there is indeed nothing else to treat. But the narrative dimension of Hegel's philosophy suggests that more is to be said, for there is as yet nothing to keep these successive moments from occluding each other in aimless oscillation. The Hegelian narrative is further structured by the fact that consciousness keeps arriving at new general truths—new "certainties." *What accounts for this, I suggest, is another massive appropriation from Kant: the doctrine of reflective judgment.*

We saw that the separation of freedom and nature became a problem for Kant himself in the *Critique of Judgment*; in the opening sections of his *Encyclopedia*—sections which bear on the nature of his own philosophical method—Hegel has some strongly positive things to say about Kantian reflective judgment, the strongest of which is perhaps that it is the "Idea" itself.[5] In making this claim, Hegel specifically downgrades the first two

Critiques. In contrast to them, the doctrine of reflective judgment is the "genuine relation" of concept and reality, and the "very truth;" Kant's problem—one which I have followed out into the *Conflict of the Faculties*—was in not recognizing this and in attempting to maintain the validity of what I called the first foundation together with the second.[6] Hegel's philosophy, then, remains not only within the Kantian empirical domain, but within the conceptual terrain of reflective judgment. The entire *Phenomenology*, for example, is a process in which consciousness forms new concepts for itself out of its experience. It can be viewed as a series of reflective judgments—or as a giant aesthetic dialogue in which the interlocutors (here consciousness and its object) reciprocally test one another in order to arrive, not at the definition of a metaphysical entity existing outside of them (as in a Platonic dialogue), or at the simple agreement that their faculties have been unified (as for Kant), but at a concrete articulation of the nature and content of their own minds.

There are, however, important departures from Kant in Hegel's account, both in form and content. Without the Kantian noumenal realm to support it, the concept of substance does not apply even practically to the mind. With this, Hegel's philosophy destroys the claim of metaphysics to be a set of "good" propositions about noumenal reality. Hence, those propositions of metaphysics cannot prescribe moral acts, and freedom must be (for Hegel following Kant as for Aristotle following Plato) a wholly empirical phenomenon. Hegel thus has no need to view the unification of the self in aesthetic experience either as something purely immanent to the subject or as merely the interplay of a couple of abstract faculties. The specific features—perceptive, affective, physical, intellectual—which are harmonized in a case of aesthetic interaction vary concretely.

Together with the greater concreteness of Hegel's account, as opposed to Kant's, goes greater detail in describing the form of such interaction. Hegel has construed the reconciliation of the spectator's self as a narrative: as a rational structure which reveals itself over time. This means that, in contrast to the free play of the faculties in the *Critique of Judgment* (and similarly to the situation in the *Conflict of the Faculties*), aesthetic reconciliation is not immediately given but is achieved in ways which themselves can be criticized and hence are, in a broad sense, rational. The ascent to the universal is a step-by-step process which advances hypothetical formulations of that universal and tests them against other details of the work, ideally stopping only when it has accounted for the necessity of all such details.

The ascent ends in a universal: dispensing with the first foundation in Kant does not mean to abandon universality but to reconceptualize it in two ways. First, the universal is not argued for in analytical fashion, as for example the Pythagorean theorem is argued for by Euclid, but is presented as the final stage and organizing conception of a narrative. It is to be evaluated, then, in terms of the whole narrative in which it is embedded. If that narrative captures aspects of the reader's or hearer's own experience, then it, and the universal with which it ends, are acceptable; if not, then not. The Hegelian universal thus makes what Kant would call an "imputation" of universality: it advances a formula as universal but cannot argue for this in a compelling way. It leaves it up to others (as did the Palinode) to see whether the universal formula can apply to their own experience as well. Second, the "validity" of this universal is not that it somehow holds always and everywhere, but that it fulfills its assigned function within the narrative itself—i.e., that it really accounts for *all* the details of the development it culminates. Hence, the concreteness of the Hegelian universal as opposed to the abstract Kantian demand for form.

The concreteness of the Hegelian universal would explain why the question of whether other narratives and other universals are possible does not, as I noted, seem to be much of an issue for Hegel. But Hegel certainly would not, unlike Kant, view an irreducible plurality of interpretations as indicating that some further content—an "aesthetic idea"—was lurking behind the work of art and its interpretations. The work of art is for Hegel neither ineffable nor infinitely effable, because for him to "eff" something is simply to place it into some narrative or other. Hence, Hegel rejects the doctrine of the "aesthetic idea:" if a product of the imagination cannot be brought under a concept, that is no big thing but a mere result of its origin in some external contingency, such as individual genius. The key to the nature of reflective judgment thus does not reside for Hegel in its lack of concepts but in what Kant would call its purposiveness: the attribution to experience of a guiding center (in a work of art, of its guiding conception) which organizes that object over time and does not apply to any other.[7]

Philosophy and Self-Consolidation

But there appears to be for Hegel one sort of narrative for which this is not true—one case where a plurality of narratives would be troubling to him. This is philosophy itself. We saw that metaphysics for Hegel, in contrast to Kant, cannot prescribe practically: the concept of substance has no moral bearing for Hegel. But metaphysics for Kant also prescribed theoretically in two ways: generally to all rational discourse, which had to be either empirical or transcendental; and specifically to philosophy itself, which had to have an overall guiding structure, an "architectonic."

Hegelian philosophy divides things up differently. The *Phenomenology* is, I argued, a narrative in which each stage is primarily defined by those before it. To ignore its narrative dimension, construing it as analytical of something outside, is to misunderstand it. Philosophy then does not for Hegel, as for Aristotle, provide basic concepts for articulating the empirical world: that is left to empirical science, to art, and presumably to religion. But it cannot follow that the Hegelian narrative is wholly self-contained, mere word play. Two sorts of external reality to which it relates in very different ways will be important for us here: human individuals and other forms of discourse.

Hegel's philosophy, like Kant's, recognizes a plurality of discourses as rational: empirical science, valid in its sphere, has fundamentally different aims and procedures from aesthetic dialogue, and this again differs generically from philosophy itself. Philosophy therefore relies upon, indeed presupposes, the validity of other forms of discourse. This seems untrue to Hegel, for we saw him claim that his account of aesthetic interaction had been developed solely from the nature of the idea as developed in the *Logic*. But Hegel's approximation of the idea to reflective judgment shows that there is no problem here: the idea itself is, if an a priori conceptual construction, the a priori construction of the general notion of learning from experience—of articulating certainties in reflective judgment, seeing how far they work, and formulating new ones when they fail. Hence, it is essential to the idea, as the conception of such procedures, that experience be present to it.[8] To say that Hegel's interpretation of the nature of art—or of any of the other stages he treats—is developed from the idea is in fact to *deny* that it is founded on a conceptual construct derived from elsewhere, and to claim that it is the result of a long process of formulating and testing hypotheses. The Hegelian narrative of art, or of anything, then, does not spin itself out of logical space: it takes up experiences actually present before the philosopher, as a child of his time and place.

But philosophical discourse, though recognizing other discourses, is the *telos* or goal of them all, and this hegemony is both more radical and less imposing than the Platonic variety. It is less imposing because philosophy is now sharply distinct from other modes of discourse. For Plato, philosophy had no single essence but really was the soul's love of wisdom, a collection of various forms of discourse with independent validity and a common purpose. Hence Plato, we saw, simply took up arguments from all sorts of domains and used them for metaphysical purposes; his texts recognize the distinctness of different forms of discourse, but accord them no distinction from philosophy itself. Hegelian philosophy, by contrast, has a determinate nature. It cannot simply incorporate at will elements and procedures from empirical science, from art criticism, or indeed from art itself. But it views those other forms of discourse, though external to it, as leading up to it; this means that philosophy takes up such discourses and *arranges* them, supplying them an ordering and ranking—a systematic place—which will in theory still be true to what they empirically are. The Hegelian narrative is then structured on a basic conception in terms of which other modes of discourse, if not reality itself, are interpreted: they are allowed validity only as so organized and interpreted. The concept of philosophy itself for Hegel plays a hermeneutical role with regard to other discourses similar to that which metaphysics played in Aristotelian philosophy for natural and social reality itself.

Philosophy's basic structuring principle, in my analysis, was "self-consolidation." At the beginning of the *Phenomenology,* in the section on sense certainty, consciousness is presented as in crisis between the manifold contents of sensuous experience and the abstract, impoverished identity of what it can say about them (*PhG* 79/58f). This basic dilemma is repeated in the other sections I analyzed. Desiring consciousness, for example, was in crisis between the simplicity of its empty ego and the multiplicity of objects of desire; cultured consciousness, between the unity of the state and the multiplicity of wealth; moral consciousness, between the identity of its single ultimate duty and the manifold circumstances in which it had to act. This series of crises is not resolved until "Absolute Knowing," where we have at last cognition which is at once, in John Findlay's words, "a pure knowledge of self . . . which is also the knowledge of all the moments of content which self distinguishes from self."[9] At that point, we have not only philosophy, the *telos* of all discourse, but a particular kind of self, which is the *telos* of Hegel's phenomenological narrative: a "consolidated self," one which is at once complex and unified and which, like the Hegelian work of art, engages in a free play of occlusion between its unity and its multiplicity.

As a fundamental structuring principle, self-consolidation is always the basic goal of consciousness. It provides, in fact, the motivation for consciousness's entry into communicative relations: for it is, we may say, impossible for an individual consciousness alone to consolidate itself, if only because, as long as consciousness is construed as merely individual, some of the elements to be consolidated seem to lie outside consciousness itself. Thus, for the consciousness of the bondsman, unity resides in the person of the master, not in itself; while the master, as we have seen, has no determinate content at all: multiplicity for him lies in the bondsman.

At the other end of the development, the judging consciousness was unitary; the acting consciousness, conceived as the "other," was manifold.

It is, indeed, because consciousness is in quest of self-consolidation that the human individual not only need not but cannot be conceived for Hegel on the model of an Aristotelian substance: as for the *Phaedrus*, there is for the Hegelian narrative no human self which first exists in its own right and subsequently comes into relations to other such selves. The kind of relation to the other which can consolidate the self of the individual is, as with Plato, a "reconciling" relation, in which the *relata* are not simply made to resemble each other in some static way, as the Platonic soul comes to resemble the static Platonic Forms, but in which they are placed in a free play of mutual occlusion, as I forgive your sin and recognize your freedom, and you do the same for me. Only in and through the forms of this reconciliation, revealed in the first instance in aesthetic dialogue, is the unity of intellect united with the multiplicity of sense. The beginning of the narrative—in "Sense-Certainty's" abstract confrontation with the sensuous—is the least-consolidated possible self.

Let us now inquire about the status of self-consolidation as the goal of all discourse for Hegel, particularly as the goal of the *Phenomenology*. The book is supposed to be a "ladder to the absolute standpoint," handed to the individual (*PhG* 25/14). If someone hands me a ladder, I have at least one choice: whether or not to climb it. Does the individual reader have to "climb" the *Phenomenology*?

There are, to continue Hegel's analogy, two general ways in which I can be forced to climb a ladder: if I am pushed or pulled up it. It seems from my analysis that the individual can be pushed along the *Phenomenology's* narrative in one of two ways. First, if each stage of the *Phenomenology* contains a contradiction which can only be resolved by moving to the next stage, then it seems that the individual is pushed up the ladder: the price for not climbing it is to contradict oneself. Another sort of push, visibly operating in "Lordship and Bondage" and "Culture," would come from the need to be articulate, to have words in which to express whatever one wants and needs to express. But neither sort of push is validated within the *Phenomenology* itself. Why, we may ask, does consciousness have this fear of contradiction? Why should the individual not respond to Hegel by saying, for example, that a foolish consistency is the hobgoblin of small minds, and let it go at that? And we can also ask why someone would want to express one's various "contents": in ordinary life, there are manifold things which are better left unsaid. Why is this feature of everyday experience abrogated in the *Phenomenology*? The answer, I suggest, is that the individual is pulled, not pushed, up the *Phenomenology's* ladder: pulled along by the goal of having a self which is at once completely articulate and completely harmonious, or what I have called a "consolidated self."

But the value of self-consolidation is then *presupposed* by the *Phenomenology* and the *Aesthetics* from first to last, not explicitly argued for (much less established) by them. The entire Hegelian narrative is thus, from the perspective of the individual, hypothetical in nature. Its basic claim is that, given self-consolidation as consciousness's goal (and given certain other constraints not relevant for us here),[10] consciousness will go through processes similar to the stages of that narrative. Like the plot of an Aristotelian tragedy, the Hegelian narrative explores the rational consequences of an action: of adopting self-consolidation as one's goal. But is this adoption itself a free action? Whose action is it? What sort of warrant might it have?

One Hegelian answer to this is historical. As early as the *Phaedo*, we have seen that freedom was presented as a "reconciled" relation of the individual soul to its environment, and in the *Phaedrus* we saw such reconciliation to be given an empirical, "phenomenological" portrayal as the unification of the individual self within an environment which was exclusively human. This conception of freedom was taken up in the Aristotelian account of deliberate action within the polis; and, in the Kantian reenactment of the Platonic aporia of freedom, it surfaced again in the life of the philosopher within the philosophical faculty. The concept of self-consolidation thus turns out historically to capture a long tradition of thought about freedom; and freedom turns out historically, in Hegel's day as in ours, to be a good thing. The adoption of self-consolidation is then the act of history itself, not of any individual.

Further warrant can be supplied. An interactive reading of the Hegelian concept of history would view it not as a "large entity," governing the individuals and events that make it up, but simply as the sum of intelligent critiques of what has gone before. The historical adoption of self-consolidation is then to be warranted rationally—first, in terms of my narrative, by its independence from theories about a supersensible realm. Already in the *Phaedrus*, self-unification, unlike the existence of the soul in the realm of Forms, could be given a convincing empirical image; and, as a free play of occlusion, we saw reconciliation to remain within the terrain left by the Kantian destruction of metaphysics. Second, the account of freedom as reconciliation is able to retain the ancient condemnation of "democratic" freedom as simply the capacity to do as one wishes. Hegel does not merely regard this as contradictory to the organized political life: as we have seen from his accounts of the repressions of modern society, he views it as wholly unattainable in the modern world, where no one can do as he or she likes. It is every bit as unrealistic as was the escape of the soul to the domain of Forms. If the field of definitions of freedom handed over by the tradition is exhausted by democratic, other-worldly, and "reconciling" views, as it appeared to be for Plato, then we can say that "history" itself has made the most rational choice from the available alternatives. The individual, as historically situated, has no choice but to climb the ladder. *Hegel's narrative, alone among narratives, is for him a compulsory one.*[11]

The Hegelian narrative then arranges and interprets the results of this process according to its own principle of self-consolidation. The degree to which it can remain true to as many of those results as possible, while reinterpreting them in terms of its own *telos*, is the degree to which philosophy can "consolidate" not only the individual self but the whole of culture, providing it with the kind of purposive center that the work of art presents in itself and provokes in the spectator, and which is missing from the "non-consolidated" individual lives lived in modern society.

Aesthetics, Politics, and Hegel

It is by virtue of its position on the philosophically established scale of interaction that art stands above politics: it is more harmonious than the political sphere because aesthetic interaction does not entail a conflict of wills; and it is more articulate because, as an "ideal" realm, art can organize its content more thoroughly and thus, as we noted, be "truer" than is the finite domain of politics. Similarly, art is less articulate and cooperative than religion: less articulate because aesthetic consciousness does not penetrate the depths of the human soul and discover the freedom inherent there; less cooperative because, remaining on the surface, it is elitist.

Aesthetic response for Hegel is thus situated, as an empirically given form of discourse, between politics and religion. Hence beauty, for Hegel as for Aristotle, belongs in the human community: he will not banish poets from society. But it does not belong to the state. Not only is the artwork's presentation of aesthetic reconciliation inimical to the state, but it also, as it did for Plato (though without the erotic aspect which led to this for him), disregards the basic distinctions of the state: rich man and poor man, field marshal and king, judge and plaintiff and defendent—all are oppressed by the state, and all alike require the reconciliation afforded by art, whose message is for the people as a whole.

This puts Hegel up against the same problem that Kant faced: since for Kant reflective judgment could not be exercised in solitude, it had to be institutionalized in the philosophical faculty. Since its exercise was potentially critical of, and hence threatening to, the state, Kant had to maintain that the philosophical faculty was wholly disinterested in its criticisms, i.e., it would not push to have them acted upon or even put before the people; but even then, he was unable to show why the state would ever countenance such an institution as the philosophical faculty.

For Hegel, there is no separate "institution" for reflective judgment, unless perhaps an art museum. But art is still communal and, therefore, must stand in some sort of relation to the state as the overriding human community. Furthermore, the problem is even more intense for Hegel than for Kant: art for Hegel is not merely *potentially* critical of state policies, but *inherently* critical of the very nature of a state as such. Moreover, aesthetic experience for Hegel is not disinterested: its "interest" is the reconciliation of the human mind with itself, and hence the highest and most general of interests. Those who are aware of this reconciliation are for Hegel historically compelled, as we have seen, to try and realize it, and they therefore constitute a major danger to political authority. Because, finally, the state for Hegel is essentially will, bent upon working its way in the world, the question for him is not how to get the state to subsidize or institutionalize art; it is how to exempt art from the workings of that will, which in this case—given the inherently critical attitude of art to the state—would mean rooting art out of life altogether. Hegel's answer to this, as we have seen, is to allow art to make its critique of the state, but to disarm that critique through philosophy. *Philosophy, therefore, allows art to make its critique—but assures everyone that the critique is ultimately invalid.*

We can see that philosophy for Hegel, in spite of its recognition of a variety of heterogenous discourses, in the end becomes prescriptive. Philosophy takes political and aesthetic experience in terms of the idea, i.e., empirically and on their own terms, allowing their contradiction to develop to the full. But as the ultimate *telos* of all discourse itself, philosophy then restores each domain to the rank order it has established, thereby disarming the aesthetic critique with its own comprehension of religious teaching. This is the price paid, in Hegelian terms, for the philosophical consolidation of culture.

In sum, my analysis argued that Hegel's account of interaction culminates in an intrinsically emancipatory type of interaction which is both situating and poetic. His view of such interaction as exhibiting features of a narrative enables him, we now see, to spell out the Kantian conception of interaction regarding the beautiful in ways Kant himself could not do, and, in so doing, to resuscitate certain points originally made in the *Phaedrus*. But both the empirical and the systematic sides of Hegel's philosophy keep him from fully recuperating poetic interaction. On the empirical side, Hegel takes up aesthetic discourse as it stands in his world, and this gives him one side of the "situation" of aesthetic reconciliation: it is situated near works of art, and is not possible without them. Systematically, aesthetic experience is situated between politics and religion, and this impeaches its status as furnishing norms for social critique. Both these aspects must be undone, then, in my final account of poetic interaction. Doing so will mean challenging the status of self-consolidation itself as the ultimate goal of all discourse. That challenge is delivered, most effectively, by Heidegger.

Eighteen

Heidegger

Heidegger fits into my narrative in the following way. Like Hegel, he is an interactionist philosopher who develops views of situating reason and intrinsically emancipatory interaction present in the Kantian second foundation. He starts, however, not from that foundation's account of the beautiful but from its treatment of the sublime, thereby developing the other half of Kant's doctrine of reflective judgment. This means, first, that instead of attempting to unify the two sides of the third antinomy, as did Hegel, Heidegger stands altogether beyond it: he uncovers and denies a presupposition of both the antinomy's thesis and its antithesis, which I will call the "postulate of unified source." Heidegger's appropriation of the sublime also enables him to articulate a concept of emancipation which goes beyond Aristotelian and Phaedran conceptions in ways that Hegelian self-consolidation did not. In all this, the prescriptive status of metaphysics, a status it had from Aristotle through Hegel, is definitively undone. But undoing the prescriptions leads back to hegemony: the "Question of Being" motivates Heidegger's writings somewhat as the theory of forms motivated Plato's. Heidegger welcomes this hegemony, and indeed exploits it when he encounters the same problem with the state that Kant and Hegel encountered. For it allows him to leave political issues aside in favor of a supposedly deeper and independent sort of questioning, that of Being itself.

Interaction and Metaphysics

Of the three Heideggerean texts analyzed previously (in part one), the last, "From a Dialogue on Language," is more overtly interactionist than those of Hegel; the earliest, *Being and Time,* is less so. These texts, like the Kantian ones, have thus made an interactive turn. But *Being and Time* does accord fundamental importance of phenomena of human interaction for Dasein, and thus confronts what for us is now a very old problem: how to provide empirical examples of moral categories. In the *Phaedo,* the problematic moral category was freedom as the soul's existence in a supersensible realm; in the Kantian texts, it was freedom as the causal action of a nonempirical realm; in Hegel's *Phenomenology,* it was the freedom of the beautiful soul which could not express itself directly in action. In *Being and Time,* the problematic category is authenticity, which is persistently viewed as residing in the realm of an individual Dasein open in a solitary way to unique contexts of significance. The solitude is so great, indeed, that the authentic individual is inarticulate, which leads to Heidegger's attempt, problematic in theory and ultimately shameful in practice, to ground authentic community on inarticulate resolve. Heidegger, as did Plato, Kant, and Hegel, finally turns for a solution to an interpretation of aesthetic experience. "The Origin of the Work of Art," in its insistence that the preservation of the artwork is a communal experience, begins to open up a view of authenticity as inherently communal: the preservation of the work of art is not its sensory apprehension and enjoyment, but its appropriation and discussion by a community. A step beyond this—and, as well, beyond Kant and Hegel—is taken in "From a Dialogue on Language." There, concern is no longer directly with works of art at all: *it is language itself which is "aesthetic."*

This divorce of aesthetic language from the work of art was prefigured, in my analysis, by Hegel's conception of the breadth of poetry: at least in the ancient world, where prose is not yet present, the poets are creating language. Though Hegel did not develop this idea, he at least adumbrated a view of poetry as not merely first in art, but first in language itself. The move away from the work of art also follows, at greater distance, on the *Phaedrus.* For Plato, basic structures of what would later be called "aesthetic" experience were preeminently to be found, not at all in confronting works of art (which are for him mere imitations of sensibles), but in our erotic attraction to other human beings—an attraction which culminated in a certain type of speech.[1] The emphasis on the work of art as defining the nature of aesthetic experience dates in my narrative only from Aristotle's *Poetics,* and it can be viewed as another of the metaphysical prescriptions characteristic of his thought: the work of art, embodying the rational structure of its plot, is itself one of the metaphysically prescribed quasi-substances which direct concrete Aristotelian investigations, just as the concept of the polis directs the political writings.

This emphasis on the work of art, wherever we find it, tends to occlude the interactive side of aesthetic experience. Aristotle accounted for tragic effect, for example, by appeal to two processes immanent to the individual: learning and catharsis. Kant distinguished the wholly "subjective" unification of the faculties from the subsequent communication of this to others in the discourse of art criticism. Hegel's *Aesthetics* attempted, by contrast, to construe our encounters with art objects in terms of the dialogical structures of recognition, externalization, and reconciliation; but the work of art was not really a person, and the construal was strained. Finally, the continuing obscurity of the interactive side of aesthetic experience for "The Origin of the Work of Art" is shown in the fact that the text's insistence that authentic preservation of the work of art is a communal phenomenon remains just that: an insistence (*UKW* 55f/68). Why it should be that way—why private enjoyment cannot be accorded the status of "preservation"—is warranted there by the role that art plays in history rather than by any account of the nature of aesthetic experience itself. Only the later Heideggerean conception of thinking as a "way" reassigns the aesthetic dimension to language itself, whence it follows at last that it cannot be merely private or subjective. In its divorce of the basic structures of aesthetic language from those of the work of art, the "way" concept is not only an interactive reconstruction of what, in *Being and Time,* was the self-showing of the phenomenon; it is also a restatement, in avowedly nonmetaphysical (and nonerotic) terms, of the communal upward path of the lovers in the *Phaedrus.*

But in what sense are we to call that restatement "nonmetaphysical?" Is there any such sense? Or are Heidegger's texts, in spite of their repeated claims to be nonmetaphysical, really what Carnap assumes them to be: a restoration of metaphysics?[2] A similar question was relatively easy to answer for Hegel: Hegelian thought clearly responded to the Kantian third antinomy and situated itself further in the interactive use of reflective judgment. Heidegger's texts pose more difficulties. Heidegger never, in his major works on Kant, discusses the third antinomy.[3] Those works take, moreover, a strongly "unitarian" line regarding the three *Critiques,* claiming (in *Der Satz vom Grund*) that *all* Kantian philosophy is a "critique of pure reason."[4]

This unitarian line, and the downplaying of the third antinomy, are not mere eccentricities. Together they suggest that Heidegger stands, if beyond the metaphysics that Kant demolished in that antinomy, more importantly beyond further metaphysical dimensions which remain in Kantian thought from first to last. "From a Dialogue on Language" has in fact uncovered one of those dimensions: approaching the world in terms of a distinction between sensible and supersensible realms. *Being and Time*'s conception of the "context of significance" undercuts this: for such a context may indifferently contain components that are traditionally assigned to objective, physical, or sensory realms, such as the layout of equipment in a room, and also components normally assigned to subjective or intellectual realms, such as the background knowledge of the users of that equipment and their purposes of the moment.

It is such contexts, reinterpreted as "earth" on the one hand and "world" on the other, which make possible the Heideggerean interactive turn. For in the "Origin of the Work of Art," it is the artwork's relation to an earthly context which enables Heidegger to view it as founding history and, in that role, as inaccessible to a merely subjective enjoyment. In "From a Dialogue on Language," the way of thinking itself is a play of contexts—Western and Oriental—which is not an empirical object to be described, nor a metaphysical one which Heidegger would have to argue for; it is a structure of dislocation presented in and as the dialogue itself.

But, however "From a Dialogue on Language" may phrase matters, the distinction between a sensible and a supersensible realm was not, in my narrative, necessary for thought to be "metaphysical." The term applied as well to the Aristotelian account of substance, which made no unequivocal appeal to a supersensible realm and, in fact, denied the Platonic separation of Forms from particulars. In "Vom Wesen und Begriff der *Physis*. Aristotles' *Physik* B.1," Heidegger acknowledges the affinity between his views and those of Aristotle on this point, interpreting "*physis*" in terms of the self-showing or arising of phenomena that is his own central concept.[5]

But Aristotle's thought, too, remained "onto-theologically" grounded in an account of the highest entity (for Aristotle, the Prime Mover as the paradigm of substance) and in an account of Being in general (as actual existence). Both accounts rest on a presupposition of pure presence: on the idea of a being which is wholly existent at once, rather than showing itself gradually, as do Heideggerean phenomena and ways. In particular, the Aristotelian concept of actuality, which is nothing other than the full presence within the individual entity of its substantial form, comes under this stricture: though not founded on any radical distinction of sensible and supersensible realms, it is a "metaphysical" doctrine in that it makes what Heidegger calls the onto-theological presupposition of pure presence.[6]

A Heideggerean phenomenon or way, though an interconnected whole, has by contrast no single substantial source to its being and activity. Particularly in its later formulation, it is a set of stages joined by the dislocations which occur along it. Heideggerean thought, in addition to rejecting the sensible-supersensible distinction, thus rejects what we might call the "postulate of unified source," the view that there must be a unitary, and hence fully present, source for the being and activity of any entity.

The Third Antinomy and the Postulate of Unified Source

This enables us to clarify, more than Heidegger's texts themselves do, Heidegger's relation to Kant's demolition of metaphysics. For the third antinomy, no less than the metaphysical doctrines it criticized, was bound to the postulate of unified source. Only with that presupposition can it get underway, for only then does it make sense to ask whether the source of an entity's being and activity is inside or outside the thing. And Kant's solution of the antinomy was to maintain that acts have two types of fully present source: empirically, the set of all inclinations that cause them; noumenally, with even greater unity, the will itself. "Being" or the "Twofold," by virtue of its dislocating feature, is not such a unified source, and the metaphysical problematic Kant demolished in the third antinomy cannot even arise.

But Kant remained metaphysical in this sense well beyond his solution of the third antinomy. The Kantian practical postulate of a free will was not theoretical: it was not an appeal to fact, because we cannot *know* that the free will exists; but it was an appeal to an ideal, because we must *act* as if it does exist. This ideal was given political formulation in what I analyzed as the first foundation of Kantian political philosophy. Indeed, the postulate of unified source governed the basic structure of Kantian philosophy itself. For in that philosophy, the single source of knowledge was to be critique, which prescribed that all knowledge be brought into a coherent whole; that certain forms of discourse (such as classical metaphysics) be excluded; and that such concrete investigations as remain be located within the systematic place which critique assigned to them.

The theoretical and practical prescriptions of metaphysics from Aristotle through Kant and Hegel were thus applications of what Heidegger's thought enables us to formulate as the postulate of unified source. It is Heidegger's denial of it that enables him to state so baldly in "The Origin of the Work of Art" that the work of art can be a "beginning" of history (*UKW* 63f./76f.). For the new beginning presented by the work of art is merely one of the dislocations in a much larger story: the working out of the history of the West as founded on metaphysics. *Works of art, in beginning history anew, show that the history of the West has no unified source, any more than they themselves do.*

Presenting one such dislocation, a work of art is an occlusion, as it was for Hegel. Coming forth from the earth, it allows the earth to retreat; it also, we may say, occludes previous worlds in that it presents an alternative to them. But these occlusions are not the kind of free play which we found in the Hegelian account of aesthetic interaction. The work of art does not encounter us as an increment of a larger whole to which it retreats without resistance (as does the detail in the work of art), but it stands forth in a "battle" with that larger whole, with the earth—a battle which is not merely in the eye of the beholder, and which the mortals who experience the work are not free to direct, as the Hegelian spectator directs his own appreciation of the interplay of detail and the work. On the other hand, the occlusion of earth and previous meaning achieved in the work of art is not, as for Hegel, the occlusion of what later turns out to be an external necessity, for there is no recuperation of the work of art by a larger context which produced it. To put it differently, the immediacy with which the work of art confronts us is not mediated back into a larger whole; in Hegelian language, mediation and immediacy, necessity and freedom, do not themselves rejoin; the two sides of the third antinomy are not dialectically reunited. Hence, the occlusion is simply—immediately—occlusion: we do not come later to know what it occludes; we can never know the depths of the earth.

The experienced unrecuperable immediacy of the work of art for Heidegger is why, for him, the key question to ask of philosophical aesthetics is directed to Hegel's thesis of the death of art (*UKW* 66–68/80f.). Art died for Hegel, as we saw, because the modern era is reflective: in ancient times, art was the highest form of spiritual expression and was immediately experienced as a divinely inspired creation of language. For Heidegger, works of art today continue to have this characteristic: they present us with an immediate creation of new meaning, and hence art—though Heidegger does not explicitly say so—has not, in Hegel's sense, "died."

More important than this single issue for "The Origin of the Work of Art" is that Hegel's verdict on art is warranted by the totality of Western metaphysics (*UKW* 67/80). Metaphysics, we may say, since it ignores the dislocations that constitute phenomena and history itself, is unable to articulate the possibility of radically new meaning. And this in turn is said to lie in the nature of metaphysical thought about one concept: the beautiful. The beautiful, we read, was conceived—in Hegel as well as previous thinkers (including Kant)—in terms of form. The metaphysical nature of this should be evident by now: as long as the work of art is understood in terms of its form, rather than as conditioned by dislocation, it is viewed in terms of the postulate of unified source; the single factor responsible for the being and activity, or effects, of the work of art is the aesthetic form that resides in it. But if the work is to be a source of new meaning, the presence in it of aesthetic form cannot tell the whole story. The work must also be dislocated from all that has gone before, and this dislocation cannot be wholly explained in terms of its form or in terms of the beautiful. Hence, Heidegger's denial of the postulate of unified source leads him, within the interactionist terrain of the third *Critique,* away from its analysis of the beautiful.

Heidegger and the Kantian Sublime

The beautiful was not, in my narrative, the only way to conceive of the nature of aesthetic experience. There was also, in Kant, the failure of presence in the experience of the sublime. Gary Shapiro has suggested that, as Hegel is a philosopher of the beautiful, so Heidegger can be construed as a philosopher of the sublime—though, as Shapiro notes, Heidegger does not actually use that word.[7] If such were the case, Heidegger's thought, like Hegel's, would develop the Kantian second foundation. Do our current texts support this view?

As was the Kantian sublime, so the Heideggerean earth is something undisclosed and unexplained, something which unfolds itself in an "inexhaustible variety of simple forms" and which "shatters" every attempt to open it up to a full presence. As thus unpresentable, it is also something dynamic: like the Kantian raging sea, the work of art contains an "inner concentration of motion," and with this motion it "drives beyond itself" to its unfathomable source, the earth (*UKW* 35-38/46-50). Finally, as did the Kantian sublime, the Heideggerean work of art transports us away from the fixed and regulated certitudes of our current life (*UKW* 54/66).

But the difference between the two conceptions is as striking, perhaps, as these similarities. It can be seen by considering the terminal point of the "transport" referred to. For Kant, our experience of the sublime puts us into a motion which culminates in a feeling for our own true nature, for the infinite abyss of reason itself. For Heidegger, the terminus is in a finite realm of determinate significance—what I have called another world. And this, of course, is because for Heidegger there is no "infinite," noumenal realm—not even in thought—to which the experience of the sublime could bring us. There is only determinate, finite significance, and if we traverse an abyss (or a Nothing, a dislocation) to get there, that is nonetheless where we eventually arrive.

The Heideggerean dynamic is thus a withdrawal, not from all fixed determinacy, but from the concrete set of determinacies that constitutes an individual world; and it is, just as much, the setting up of a new world, the "fixing" of earth into a new form. As such, the Heideggerean art work sounds more like the Kantian aesthetic idea than like the Kantian sublime: just as the aesthetic idea was itself unconceptualizable but provoked an infinite variety of new "rules," formulations, and concepts, so for Heidegger is art. But in fact Heidegger cannot distinguish the aesthetic idea from the sublime, as Kant could, in terms of the role of the imagination. In the aesthetic idea, understanding was unable to come up with a single formula which would capture everything in it; but imagination was able to recapitulate the sensory givens into a coherent, fully present whole, and the aesthetic idea was thus grounded in the full and harmonious presence of a sensory object. Heidegger, without the postulate of unified source (and also without a Kantian faculty psychology), cannot allow such functioning to the imagination or indeed to the spectator at all: his discussions of art objects—e.g., the Greek temple or the peasant shoes—show that such objects are constituted through what they do not themselves show directly, their "battle" with earth. Thus, the Heideggerean work of art operates, as does the Kantian sublime, through the very inability of the art object to be made fully present. Though the *temporal* terminus of the aesthetic transport for Heidegger is another realm of determinate content, the abyss it traverses is not left behind: it continues to yawn open in every apprehension of the work of art as such, and it is the true "origin of the work of art." *Heidegger's concept of the work of art, we may say, absorbs the Kantian aesthetic idea into something like the Kantian sublime, and also absorbs Heidegger's thought as a whole into the second foundation.*

Hegel, too, rejected the Kantian conception of the aesthetic idea—but in the opposite direction. For Hegel that idea, in its ineffability, was something merely "subjective" which could be overcome in the full conceptual articulation of the guiding conception of the work of art. He thus viewed the aesthetic idea from the perspective of the unity of the intellectual and sensory which constitutes the idea of the beautiful, and regarded it as a deficient example of that certain idea. Heidegger, by contrast, rejects that unity—in favor of the sublime.

It is, again, no accident that Hegel's *Aesthetics*, while defining the sublime very much as Heidegger does, gave priority to the beautiful. The sublime was a "multiplicity of shapes which do not yet correspond to the Idea" (*Aesth.* 116, cf. 408/77, 303), and the key word in this characterization is "yet:" the sublime for Hegel was, like the aesthetic idea, merely a subordinate moment in the unfolding of the idea of beauty (cf. *Aesth.* 495/372). The reason for the subordination was different: the sublime is not something merely subjective, as is the aesthetic idea, but is grounded in the abstract (and hence in its own way inarticulate) nature of the guiding conception of the sublime artwork itself (cf. *Aesth.* 482ff/362f). For Heidegger, what the work of art does not articulate may be the mute otherness of earth itself; derived from that dislocated otherness, the sublime is never overcome.

Emancipatory Interaction in Heidegger

The structures of the interaction involved in the Heideggerean preservation of the work of art might thus be understood to follow those of the Kantian account of the sublime. They would as such center on anomalous utterances—utterances which are so new or so different (like the Japanese words in "From a Dialogue on Language") that their very functioning as words is incommensurate with and cannot be understood in terms of one's established world. Confrontation with such utterances is then, in my sense, poetic: it is the hearers who must determine what they mean. In questioning and articulating such utterances, the hearer is transported out of his old world: its unity and harmony is lost, just as the harmony of the subjective faculties is lost in the Kantian account of the sublime. As the painful discrepancy between imagination and reason "deconstructed" the Kantian self, so the wrenching between old and newly presented frameworks of significance is presented as difficult and painful—as a "wandering back and forth between two different language realities" (*DFL* 115/24). And, just as we could not live wholly within the supersensible realm to which the sublime conveyed us, so for Heidegger we cannot live "within" the work of art or the utterance as we have lived within our own world: we are either returned to our world in a new way or else installed wholly in the new world; no synthesis or mediation of the worlds is possible. The experience of such preservation, then, is not narrative in character. It presents, not developments which can be seen as rationally related to what went before, but upsurges of genuinely new meaning. The articulation of such newness is what I call a demarcative articulation of parameters.

This wandering between worlds, like the "wandering" characteristic of Heideggerean ways of thought in general, is not a motion with an inherent end. This is in contrast to the Platonic situation: there, we did indeed "wander" with our words, but the wandering had its "end" in the sense both of goal and of termination: to put into words the nature of a Form. For Heidegger, such an "end" could only be one's return to the established world or one's definitive installation in a new one. But as the close of "From a Dialogue on Language" indicates, no end is *inherent* in aesthetic interaction as such: for aesthetic encounter is a play of worlds generating new meaning, and for it to end the generation of new meaning must come to an end. Since there is no inherent goal to such wandering, it follows that Hegelian self-consolidation is not such a goal. Indeed, the general importance of dislocation for Heidegger means that the self is not consolidated by aesthetic interaction, but rather is radically disjoined from itself. It exists, not as a harmonious play of occlusion within a reconciled whole, but as a painful wandering among incommensurable worlds which leaves behind much of each world and, indeed, much of its own nature as dwelling within that world. Hence, the basic structuring principle of Hegelian narrative is impeached: *self-consolidation is at best only one of two ways of existing. It is neither necessary to seek it nor always possible to achieve it.*

The sublime in art, for Hegel as for Kant, "liberates" the Spirit from "every immediate existent;" Hegel's subordination of the sublime to the beautiful did not deny this emancipatory quality to the work of art, but he interpreted it in terms of his fuller view of freedom as reconciliation. For Heidegger, propositions so general as to refer to "every immediate existent" are impossible. His concept of liberation is a liberation, not from *all* determinate content, but from a specific set. It thus frees us, not for the kind of abstract universal that Hegel would diagnose as the "destination" of the sublime, but for a concrete, wholly new, set of determinacies. Thus, the liberation brought about by the work of art for Heidegger is, as for Hegel, situated—not in a single world which, as reconciled, receives some sort of aesthetic sanction, but in a plurality of worlds among which those being liberated wander, poetically articulating alternatives to their own world. It becomes situating, rather than merely situated, when the wanderers either remain with those alternatives or return to their own world with a more decisive understanding of it.

Heidegger and the Hegemony of Being

Heidegger's thought thus recognizes a plurality of discourses: indeed, we may say that each world will have its own peculiar types, as incomprehensible to other worlds as Western metaphysics is to the Japanese world. Some of those discourses—those of the poets and the philosophers, for example—are taken up by Heideggerean thought, and in this their heterogeneity is recognized if not made entirely clear.[8] But when this happens, it happens for a single purpose: to accomplish a disclosure of Being, an interplay of only the most basic contexts of given worlds. This is why, as we saw, there is no concern in "From a Dialogue on Language" to teach Heidegger anything about Japanese ways of life, social structures, or the like. It is also, I suggest, why Heidegger maintains that all Kantian philosophy is the "critique of pure reason:" for it is as such a critique that

Kantian thought analyzes, for Heidegger, the basic parameter of Kant's world—the nature of Being.[9] And this single purpose is behind the general absence of concrete concerns evident throughout Heidegger's later writings.

I have referred to "phenomenon" and its later articulation as "way" as Heidegger's central concept; it is remarkable that a thought so dedicated to the elimination of all metaphysical components should retain a single purpose with such hegemonic force. But in fact, the hegemony of Being in Heidegger is at least as strong as that of metaphysics in Platonic philosophy: every word in a Heideggerean dialogue is aimed at the disclosure of Being.[10] There is, however, a contrast. I noted above that aesthetic interaction as analyzed in the *Phaedrus* has an essential termination in the complete formulation of the nature of a Form. It was through such formulations that the dialectic furnished the basis for rhetoric and could be politically relevant. Heideggerean thought, not construing aesthetic dialogue as having any terminal points at all, attempts as well to eschew such relevance: it never goes on to discuss concrete matters of how, on the basis of aesthetic interaction, new worlds may be put in place against old ones, or how those in the old world may be educated about its nature. Heideggerean thinking, as we saw, remains a sphere unto itself, indifferent to political, social, and indeed to all concrete reality.

Because Heideggerean aesthetic interaction has no inherent stopping points, such indifference is possible: there is no intrinsic requirement to sum up an acquired result or to face questions of the broader implications of such results. But that hardly means that such indifference is necessary: that terminations *need* not occur does not mean that they *do* not occur, that there is not a moment when the preservers turn away from the work of art to confront their former world or when Heidegger and Tezuka return to their own cultures bringing new insights with them.

We know that Heidegger's single attempt to deal with concrete political realities was a shameful moral catastrophe, and it is far from unlikely that this catastrophe was the reason for Heidegger's subsequent proclamations of indifference to concrete questions. But there is more to the matter than personal indifference, or even personal pain. We have seen that aesthetic interaction, whether articulated as the erotic *paideia* of the Palinode, as the reflective use of judgment, or as the aesthetic expression of the true nature of spirit, was hostile to the state or polis: questioning old concepts and formulating new (or, as in Hegel, even older) ones, such interaction was liable to deny the basic presuppositions on which the established political order, as the pursuit of purposes within fixed social distinctions, depends. Hegel and Kant, we saw, attempted in their different ways to make such interaction safe for the state; Aristotle denied it altogether, and Plato resorted to metaphors of nature and a "space be-yond the heavens." Heidegger takes a new approach: his thought allows heterogeneity to reign to such an extent that the different aspects of hu-man life—politics and aesthetics, for example—may have nothing at all to say to one another. And this, in turn, is possible for him because of what I call the hegemony of Being. *For as long as emancipatory inter-action is directed to the articulation of a single privileged parameter—Being itelf—it can formulate no concrete critique of political or other realities.*

Heidegger's account of aesthetic interaction, then, views it as both situating and poetic. He occupies, not merely the terrain left after Kant's destruction of metaphysics, but a level where that destruction itself (like all "revolutions") is seen to retain a component of metaphysical thinking, in the postulate of unified source. The denial of that postulate means that philosophy can no longer for Heidegger prescribe either theoretically to other discourses or practically to ethics and politics. It cannot even, as it could for Hegel, organize other discourses while seeking to remain true to their empirically given natures. As for Plato, philosophy for Heideg-ger—if we continue to use that term at all—is without a single method and without a unitary organizing principle of its own. But, as for Plato, it has a single, hegemonic goal: the disclosure of Being. The presence of this hegemony within philosophy itself, and the absence of any prescrip-tive relation to other discourses, means that philosophy for Heidegger can be taken as a discipline entirely unto itself, a domain without concrete relevance. This remaining vestige of metaphysics must be undone if we are to complete the recuperation of poetic interaction. How to undo it without reawakening the problems of the relation of poetic interaction to the state, to which we saw Hegel and Kant fall victim, will be shown by Habermas.

Part Three

Demarcation

Introduction

My narrative has now broken down. Up to now, the story has been one of critical progress: not because such progress is universal or necessary, for I do not purport to reconstruct more than a few threads in the tapestry of philosophical tradition, but because those threads could, with some exceptions (notably presented by Aristotle), in fact be tied together in a narrative so as to exhibit progress. Aristotle, for example, showed how the Platonic metaphysics failed to cohere with the *Phaedrus*'s views on soul and interaction: Kant showed how both the Aristotelian and Platonic metaphysics were fundamentally misguided; Hegel liberated Kant from talk about the noumenal realm and transformed philosophy into (in part) the conceptual articulation of the moral dimensions of different forms of interaction. And all this exhibited, first, an occlusion of what I call poetic interaction and, then, its gradual recuperation.

Does not Heidegger's thought stop this progress? Does it not present us, not with an improvement upon Hegel's philosophical disarming of the aesthetic critique of the state, but with a new problem? Is not the question no longer how to make aesthetic interaction safe for the state, but how to find a middle ground between allowing it to be dominated by the political order and allowing it to be completely cut off from that order? Indeed, does Heidegger's account of aesthetic interaction *follow* on Hegel's at all? Might it not, perhaps, complement it?

For Heidegger himself, Hegel was merely the final stage in the modern "philosophy of subjectivity," which interpreted subjectivity in terms of the "parousia" or presence of the Absolute, and which therefore installed the Absolute as the highest form of unified source.[1] My interactive reading of Hegel has at least provisionally exempted him from this: insofar as it is presented in the texts I have analyzed, the Absolute is no "parousia," but a play of occlusion. Hence, Hegel will not fit into Heidegger's own narrative. Heidegger's thought does not criticize or recuperate Hegel but differentiates—demarcates—itself from him, taking a different line of departure from Kant. To note this fact is itself an exercise which opens up possibilities for future thinking—it is to demarcate Hegel from Heidegger, and ourselves from both.

Where Hegel takes his start from the Kantian beautiful, Heidegger takes his from the Kantian sublime: both remain within what I called the second foundation. Hegel's account deals with the reconciliation of the individual with the domain of already articulated content that constitutes his culture (if not its political order). Can Heidegger dispense with this? Does not the entire Heideggerean account of the formation of new worlds and meanings presuppose the articulation of old worlds, as well as the concrete belonging or reconciliation of individuals to those old worlds? How else could Heideggerean thinking seek, not to abandon metaphysics, but merely to understand it better, to situate it within the more radical interplay of worlds evidenced in Heidegger's historical investigations?

Similarly, Hegel can dispense with Heidegger only by making the claim that no fundamental new meaning can now be generated, that the world has achieved a final articulation, and that art is truly "dead." But are these doctrines not decisively refuted by history? Have they not rendered Hegel's systematic project among the most suspect that philosophy has ever undertaken?

Can we, then, mark off an area in which both the interaction of the beautiful and that of the sublime can be situated? Can we show that this dimension, while distinct from the political sphere as defined so far, can yet speak to it? Even, so speaking, to situate it?

Three points that have emerged so far will be of help here. The first, common to Hegel and Heidegger (as well as to Plato), is the recognition that not all rational discourses are of the same nature: in particular, that aesthetic interaction is fundamentally different from other types. The view that they *are* all somehow alike is itself a product of the prescriptive character of metaphysics in Aristotle: all discourse made use of the basic concept of substance and was therefore to be explicated syllogistically.

The second point emerged from my narrative of Hegel. I suggested that the narrative of the *Phenomenology* and the *Aesthetics,* as analyzed here, reposed on the concept of self-consolidation. I suggested further that, for Hegel, the choice of self-consolidation as a fundamental goal was one that had been made, rationally, in the course of history; and that it therefore imposed itself on us as the only rational alternative. But Heidegger has articulated a very different conception of liberation, one which has to do with what I called the "deconstruction" of the self rather than its consolidation. This makes the Hegelian narrative only one of two alternative approaches to emancipation—freeing it from absolutistic claims. The way is open to say, for example, that in some areas of discourse art is indeed "dead," as Hegel thought—that some areas of life have been taken over by prose. But we are not committed to saying that all of them have been taken over, or that art is completely dead, or that self-consolidation is the single *telos* of philosophical discourse.

The third point (and it is in one area where we have seen progress from Hegel to Heidegger) concerns the relation of aesthetic language to works of art. Heidegger's account of aesthetic interaction was, finally, independent of the work of art: "aesthetics" ultimately concerned a level of language itself. This suggests that the area we seek to demarcate need not be confined, as in Hegel, to the vicinity of works of art. We can take Hegel's accounts of aesthetic interaction and apply them beyond the artistic realm. The relation of aesthetic interaction to politics may thus become a little clearer.

Here, too, there is help. Over almost two decades, Jürgen Habermas has developed a general theory of interaction which, though it does not itself articulate the distinctively aesthetic sphere adequately for our present purposes, can (I will argue) be amended to do so. And in his recent (1981) *Theory of Communicative Action,* Habermas articulates his general account of interaction in terms of a sphere which is both different from and crucial to the political sphere: that of the "life-world." It is to that text, then, that we will now turn.

We will not turn to it, however, merely to analyze its strengths and weaknesses and to relate them narratively to what has gone before. If only because he is the last thinker in my narrative, Habermas (together with Wellmer) necessarily poses questions that remain open. Those questions can be formulated by seeing, not where Habermas has built upon the previous thinkers in the narrative, but where he has *not* appropriated from them. Articulating these gaps in the Habermasian account will open up a path beyond that account, terrain as yet unexplored. This opening will be neither analytical nor narrative in character, but demarcative.

Though we have not discussed its nature in general (if it has one), we have seen demarcation before: it was exhibited by and treated in Heidegger's thought as old approaches suggested, but did not dictate, new ones. Heidegger himself, I have just remarked, fails to undo Hegel, and there another demarcative gap opens up. Aristotle's critique of the *Phaedrus,* centered on its metaphysics, failed to refute its account of poetic interaction, which was not warranted by that metaphysics. There was a gap between what Aristotle attacked and what the *Phaedrus* really said, a gap which began to be filled by Kant's doctrine of the judgment of taste, and which has been filled in further by Hegel and Heidegger.

But demarcation will now become a thematic part of my investigation, and I will present it in separate sections of the remainder of this book. The first three chapters of this third and final part will concern Habermas and Wellmer and will seek to mark out the path opened up by their own demarcation from the tradition previously narrated. The last two chapters will actually follow that path to the point where the structures and emancipatory characteristics of the elementary form of situating reason—poetic interaction—have been analyzed. I will narrate the relation of poetic interaction to previous developments, and I will finally suggest that the limits and deficiencies of my own account may themselves open up future pathways.

Nineteen

The First Foundation in *The Theory of Communicative Action*

Analysis

Jürgen Habermas's thought, I will argue, exhibits a general movement we have seen in previous thinkers: beginning with an account of reason that is in some respects unsituated, it moves to situate it by an interpretation of aesthetic experience. This situating is actually carried through by Albrecht Wellmer. My primary Habermasian text will be *The Theory of Communicative Action* of 1981, on which Habermas himself wants discussion of his work to be based.[1] On my analysis, the unsituated first foundation is presented in volume 1 of that work. The second foundation is adumbrated in volume 2 and carried out in Wellmer's "Wahrheit, Schein, Versöhnung."

The Theory of Communicative Action, like all of Habermas's writings, aims to produce a critical theory of society. Such criticism is to be carried out in terms of positive standards articulated and justified in the theory itself.[2] But the standards in question are not to be derived from "transcendental" approaches, such as the Kantian first foundation; together with metaphysics, such approaches belong to the genus "foundationalism," against which Habermas inveighs.[3] Also explicitly dropped is justification in terms of the development of history. The contemporary outcomes of that development—primarily, organized capitalism and bureaucratic socialism—are not fit for canonization, and social theory must be freed from the sort of "ballast" of historical approaches that the classical Frankfurt writers gave it. What these two rejections mean is that Habermas, I will argue, actually rethinks here the relation of the first and second Kantian foundations. His rejection of foundationalism will then mean in some sense depriving them of the status of "foundations" at all. I will analyze the Second Foundation in the following chapter; the remnant of the first—Habermas's theory of "formal pragmatics"—is advanced in *The Theory of Communicative Action*. It is not claimed to be transcendentally valid for all rational beings, as are the statements of the first foundation in Kant, but is put forth in order to explicate a concept of rationality which is itself derived provisionally from discussions of ordinary language and anthropology.[4]

That derivation, in outline, proceeds as follows. Habermas begins with an analysis of ordinary language uses, concluding that an utterance is "rational" if it is open to criticism. This concept of criticizability is then extended to cover three sorts of claim. One is the claim that one's utterance is true. Another is that it is in accord with an accepted social norm (I will refer to this as the "appropriateness claim"). The third is the claim that one's utterance accurately expresses one's own state of mind (which I will call the "sincerity claim"). Habermas again extends this concept of rationality to apply not merely to persons and assertions, but (a) to the conduct of an entire life, and (b) to cultural complexes or world views. Finally, he moves to a "more exact explication" of the concept of rationality by considering four "sociological concepts of action" in which the validity claims discussed are embodied, together with the "ontological presuppositions" of those types of action (*TKH* 1:25—151/8–101).

When we raise or examine claims to truth, normative rightness, or subjective sincerity, we presume that there is in each case a domain, knowable in principle by all, against which those claims can be tested. When I make a truth claim, for example, I presume that there exists an "objective" domain of facts, independently ascertainable, in which the state of affairs my assertion describes is in fact the case. Similar presuppositions are, as we shall see, made for the other validity claims, and each such domain is a "world." These worlds are not to be understood as ontological domains in the normal sense: Habermas is not claiming, for example, that mental states can be proven to belong to a domain irreducible to physical states of affairs. The worlds, for one thing, have arisen historically. In mythical world views, and in the cultures expressed in such world views, they are not separated from one another. But, whether they actually exist independently or not, they must be presupposed if we are to raise and examine validity claims.[5]

Different types of action, already treated by social theorists, turn out to be coordinated to these worlds. Thus, an action is "teleological" when it aims at realizing a preset end.[6] Since the end is given, the action consists basically in the choice of means to achieve it. When the choice can take into account the reactions of others to the actor's plan, it is "strategic"; strategic action may then include the manipulation of other people. When the action does not involve others but manipulates only states of affairs in the objective world, it is "instrumental." Teleological action has been central to philosophical action theory since Aristotle and is today fundamental to utilitarianism, in which an action is to be evaluated in terms of its usefulness at achieving (in the most common formulation) "the greatest good of the greatest number." Through utilitarianism, the teleological form of action has become the presupposition of contemporary decision-theoretical approaches in economics, sociology, and social psychology. There is good reason for this emphasis. Actors are always following more or less determinate goals, even when they engage in non-teleological forms of action. In all types of communication, for example, one could hardly speak without having the goal of saying what one has to say. Teleological action is therefore fundamental to all action.

The ontological presupposition of teleological action is that there exists one "objective" realm to which the actor can fit his subjective experiences (as perceptions of and opinions about that world) or which he seeks to bring into conformity with those experiences (as values or goals). Through its presupposition of an objective world, teleological action becomes criticizable. Subjective perceptions and opinions can be criticized for being untrue, i.e., for not corresponding to that world. Plans and intentions which form parts of realizing larger goals can be criticized for not being efficacious.

Social norms incorporate an agreement among members of a social group to render obligatory, always and upon each individual, behavior prescribed by the norm. Actions which come under such binding social norms are "norm-regulated" actions and have been studied by a number of researchers.[7] A norm-regulated action which successfully carries out an actor's intention while violating a social norm is thus open to criticism, where a merely teleological action would not be. Though social norms can be regarded as complex facts about the objective world (it is a fact about modern Western societies that they have laws against murder), this does not mean that the world in which such norms reside is the objective one. For I have no obligations to states of affairs, and I cannot be criticized for failing to observe the law of gravity. This means that a norm-regulated action can be criticized with regard to two different worlds: the objective one of given states of affairs, which all action presupposes, and the social one of norms in force. Emphasis lies, however, on the social world, and the actor's relation to this one can again take two forms. He can either make his action correspond to the norms in force, or he can attempt to remake the norms to correspond, if not to his actions, to actions that he would like to perform.

Finally, my states of mind—opinions, intentions, wishes, feelings—are private, in that whether or not they are revealed to others is to some extent under my control. Such self-revelation is "dramaturgical action," examined first by Erving Goffman.[8] It, too, has ontological presuppositions: the totality of subjective experiences to which the access of others can be controlled constitutes a third, "subjective world." Here there is only one direction of relation, for the expression either conforms to, or expresses, the subjective world of the actor or it does not. In the latter case he is, intentionally or not, dissimulating. In no case, apparently, do an actor's subjective experiences change to match his words or actions. Dramaturgical action, in its pure form, pays no attention to social norms, and hence is also a two-world relation: the subjective world is given expression in an "outer," objective world of physical and social entities.

These three types of action share two characteristics. First, they are not themselves necessarily linguistic: I can manipulate others, act in accordance with norms, and express my own subjectivity all with gestures. Second, each relates to at most two of the three worlds Habermas has isolated. Both characteristics contrast with the case of communicative actions, in which participants sort out their common situation in a cooperative way, assigning elements of it to each of the three worlds—as when we undertake to find out if the "objective" world really contains a state of affairs someone has asserted to be the case. As thus directed upon the question of which are the relevant constituents of the three worlds, interlocutors in communicative action take up a reflexive attitude toward those worlds. The aim of their reflection is to achieve an agreement on the nature of their common situation, an outcome which Habermas calls "understanding" (Verständigung). The medium in which all of this is done is language, and there are no nonlinguistic communicative acts.[9]

This making and evaluating validity claims by relating utterances to the respective worlds they presuppose, is Habermas's fullest conception of rationality (TKH 1:114/75). It still requires some filling in, because in communicative action the participants relate themselves to all three worlds; in the other forms of action, they relate to at most two of them. Each of the other types of action then has a partial view of language. Teleological action views it as a means of conveying information about the world (or of manipulatively conveying misinformation). Norm-regulated action sees it as a medium in which we take up legitimate interpersonal relations with one another, recreating the basic consensus of our culture. And dramaturgical action makes use only of the "appresentative" function in which we use words to reveal ourselves. In communicative action, by contrast, all four dimensions of language are reflected upon. Where the other forms of action are partial, it is complete.

A "validity claim" is a statement—usually implicit—about the relation of an utterance to one of the three worlds we have discussed: it claims that the conditions of the utterance are fulfilled by that world (TKH 1:65f/38f). There are, then, three and only three different validity claims raised and examined in communicative action: those to truth, appropriateness, and sincerity. These three claims are independent but systematically related. They are mutually independent because we cannot, or at least cannot always, decide, for example, that a statement is sincere or appropriate by deciding on its truth; differing forms of argumentation and warrant go with every validity claim (*TKH* 1:37-71/17–42; 2:98f). But any utterance in communicative action must claim all three, and they go together as a system (*TKH* 2:101–117).

Most validity claims are not explicit, and not all are "direct." An "indirect" validity claim is not raised by a given utterance but is presupposed by it. If I make a promise, which in J. L. Austin's terms is to perform a nonconstative speech act,[10] I have not made any truth claim about the world. My promise can be criticized for being insincere or inappropriate, but not for being untrue. Habermas argues that such nonconstative speech acts presuppose the truth of other statements. If, for example, I promise you that I will mail your letter tomorrow, I am presupposing that you will have a letter written by then, that I will be in the vicinity of a mailbox, and so forth. Also presupposed are more general beliefs, such as that I exist and am able to make promises (which implies, for example, that I am not a child), that the language in which I speak exists, and so on. Any of these presuppositions may be arguably wrong, and nonconstative speech acts can therefore be challenged with regard to truth (*TKH* 1:417f/311). Something similar holds for the appropriateness claim. A constative utterance, such as "the guinea pig is on the mat," does not claim appropriateness; but it can be inappropriate if, for example, one person is trying to hide the guinea pig from another who would kill it out of wanton hatred, thereby frightening the children and violating various social norms (cf. *TKH* I 418f./311f.). Hence, it presupposes the existence of social norms. Finally, we may say, any speech act presupposes a speaker's intentions in speaking and either reveals these for what they are or does not. In either case it makes a sincerity claim.

Discourse is the rational evaluation of validity claims and has three basic types corresponding to each of the three validity claims (*TKH* 1:38-45, 447ff./18–23, 333f.). The examination of the truth claim is carried out in "theoretical discourse." Such discourse is necessary to decide truth claims in the absence of a foundationalist account of knowledge. If we did have epistemic foundations, such as (for example) sense data or some other type of "primary" sensation, then an individual could in principle examine the truth of assertions for himself by reducing them to propositions about that foundation (though in practice, for any but a few relatively trivial propositions, he would presumably require the help of others). In the absence of any such foundation, truth can only be decided by examining the claim together with other people, attempting to reach the most rational decision possible (cf. *TKH* 1:424/316f.). Appropriateness claims are evaluated in "practical discourse." Here again, philosophical ethics may suggest that no final foundation can be found. But we ordinarily do discuss moral issues and occasionally reach consensus on them. Sincerity claims, finally, are examined in such forms as aesthetic and psychotherapeutic critique.

Discourse can, again, be regarded under three standpoints (*TKH* 1:47-49/24ff.). As a *process*, it is an approximation of a set of ideal conditions, which Habermas discussed in earlier writings as the "ideal speech situation." In such a situation, no possible interlocutor can be excluded from speaking; all participants must have an equal chance to speak; and no validity claim raised can be exempt from challenge.[11] As a *procedure*, discourse requires the interlocutors to

(1) be relieved from the pressures of action and experience;
(2) identify, or thematize, a problematic validity claim; and
(3) examine the claim with reasons, and only with reasons.

As the *production* of good arguments, discourse can have a variety of argumentative forms, depending on the specific nature of the validity claim discussed.

The goal of such activity, and of communicative action in general, is understanding. In Habermas's sense, this designates the achievement of unity among a group of interlocutors on the question of the validity of an utterance (*TKH* 2:184). As such, it has a normative component: it is not a mere factual agreement, but one reached through reason and argument.[12] It has a dynamic component as well: the achievement of understanding is, in fact, the overcoming of dissension through the adducing and examining of reasons, and is thus "mediated" by its negation (*TKH* 2:113f). As the goal of the most complete form of linguistic action, says Habermas, understanding "is the inherent *telos* of human speech" (*TKH* 1:387/287).

If an "emancipated" society is one in which decisions are reached by processes of communicative action (*TKH* 1:113/73f.), then Habermas can use his account of communicative action to formulate an interactive concept of freedom. In communicative action, the need for achieving understanding is met not by unchallengeable tradition (as in mythical world views) but by situation definitions worked out by the participants themselves (cf. *TKH* 1:456f./340f.; 2:118f., 232). Communicative action is then inherently "free" in the sense that it is directed by those who engage in it on a given occasion. The basic level of this type of freedom—that which opens up the "area of play" within which communicative freedom can come about—is the freedom of the interlocutor to accept or reject any utterance in communicative action. This decision is "free," not in the sense that it is made by the interlocutor's free will (about which Habermas is silent), but in that the party who makes the utterance cannot predict whether others will accept or reject it (*TKH* 2:95f, 113, 145).

Habermas connects this account of interactive freedom with two traditional concepts, one derived from Kant and the other, ultimately, from Hegel. Participants in communicative action act, not arbitrarily, but by reasons—"laws" which they enact for themselves (*TKH* 2:310). Understanding so reached cannot be forced; each participant who agrees on the validity of an utterance is able to give his reasons for agreeing (*TKH* 2:185). Further, since the participants are given over solely to rational examination of the validity of utterances, none of them can be operating from personal interests or pursuing personal aims (*TKH* 1:385/285). As thus rational, unforced, and disinterested, understanding approximates some aspects of what we saw was the Kantian idea of freedom in the first foundation. Thus, whoever is able to participate in communicative action is "responsible" for his acts. With the different forms of responsibility can be coordinated, Habermas tells us, different forms of autonomy (*TKH* 1:34/14).

This holds, as we might expect, particularly for practical discourse, whose similarity with the Kantian "discourse of legislation" is evident:

> What the categorical imperative was supposed to achieve can be accomplished with the help of the projection of a will-formation under the idealistic conditions of a universal discourse. The subject capable of moral judgment cannot examine by himself whether an existing or recommended norm is in the general interest and perhaps should take effect in society, but can do so only in community with all others affected (*TKH* 2:145).

But understanding is not merely static, communal legislation, as in Kant's Kingdom of Ends. It comes about through the dynamics of communicative action, and this means that it involves its opposite—dissension. In this respect, understanding approaches the Hegelian concept of reconciliation. This concept was in fact taken up by the classical Frankfurt writers who, following Lukács, tried to free the concept from the contemplative, metaphysical, and generally "philosophical" character it (supposedly) had in Hegel. But without Hegel's metaphysics, writes Habermas, the Frankfurt writers were unable to justify their use of the concept. In fact, the concept of reconciliation can be adequately formulated only interactively, a point Adorno was on the verge of making when he "dynamized" Kant's conception of freedom into a self-identity built up through "intact intersubjectivity."[13] Thus, what could not be rendered plausible in terms of the philosophy of consciousness, and what drove Hegel back to metaphysics in his attempt to articulate it (*TKH* 1:518f./386f.), can be given a clear and rational formulation in the theory of communicative action. Communicative action, as reconciliatory self-legislation, is then in my terms intrinsically emancipatory, and this is why societies to which it is basic deserve to be called "emancipated" for Habermas.

The concept of understanding thus captures certain traditional notions of freedom and can be validated as a fundamental presupposition of social action. Habermas uses it, with reservations, as an abstract basis on which to evaluate aspects of contemporary society. As an approximation to an ideal—to unlimited and undistorted discourse—interactive freedom is not to be used for guidance in the philosophy of history. It is not something that is realizing itself in the world, as Hegel thought, or even that can be realized. But it can give certain formal conditions of the good life, and it can aid in highlighting and clarifying social processes which, apart from its illumination, would remain unclear (*TKH* 2:163). It is, for example, in light of his concept of interactive freedom that Habermas can pose, as a basic problem for the theory of modernity, the question of why modernization has excluded

> the erection of institutions of freedom, which protect the communicatively structured action domains in the private and public spheres from the reifying peculiar dynamic of the economic and the administrative systems (*TKH* 2:484).

And it is the basis for some of the few prescriptions Habermas makes:

> In place of the law, used as a medium [for handling family conflicts], procedures of conflict-settling must enter which are appropriate to the structures of understanding-oriented action (*TKH* 2:544; cf. also the remarks on education at *TKH* 2:546).

True to the Kantian first foundation, in sum, Habermas has constructed an idea and then measured reality against it. But Kant's practical ideals, though counterfactual, were justified as constructions of reason. Our capacity to construct them was given transcendental foundation in critique. Habermas has abandoned transcendental foundations, and it would seem that he has abandoned the first foundation as well, going wholly over to the second as did Hegel and Heidegger in my narrative. Such, I will argue, is not the case: Habermas has not abandoned but reconceived the notion of an ahistorical, ideal justification of positive standards for social critique. To see this, we must examine the sorts of warrant he gives for his views on communicative action.

Two claims of that theory are particularly important in this regard. One is that there are three and only three such validity claims (cf. *TKH* 1:114/75). Had Habermas *defined* "understanding" as reaching agreement on three and only three validity claims, this would be a mere stipulation. But he has not. The passages cited above concerning understanding make no reference to the existence of three and only three validity claims; that existence must be argued for.

The other claim concerns the fundamental status of communicative action with respect to teleological action. If, as we saw, all action is fundamentally teleological, then communicative action seems to be merely a modification of it. This would undermine Habermas's whole project, for his basic critique of the modern world will be that rationality is a complex whole embodying not merely the criterion of truth, but also those of sincerity and appropriateness. The modern era, separating these off from one another, has allowed truth to dominate the public discourse of the age, and its correlate, teleological action, to dominate social action (cf. *TKH* 2:267–293). If it were to be shown that communicative action is merely a modification of the teleological variety, Habermas would be faced with a plethora of questions concerning whether it was a necessary modification or not. Indeed, much contemporary social science, fixed on the concept of teleological action, implicitly takes the view that communicative action can be dispensed with, both in giving an account of society and in actual practice. To avoid these problems, Habermas must not only show that communicative action always involves all three validity claims, but also that it is somehow basic to teleological action.

One could argue against the former claim by maintaining (a) that some of Habermas's validity claims are not really inherent in communicative action, i.e., are not made in all cases of action oriented toward reaching understanding, or (b) that there are other claims in addition to those three.[14] The first line of argument denies the fundamental status of communicative action as making all three validity claims. It would not reduce the field simply to teleological action, perhaps; but Habermas would have to show why it is important that communicative action make all three validity claims. If, on the other hand, it were to be shown that more than three validity claims are involved in understanding, the consequences would be less severe. Habermas's argument could go through, with an expansion to include further validity claims.

That all cases of communicative action make three and only three validity claims can, Habermas tells us, be tested against numerous examples

(*TKH* 1:412/307). It could be fully established only by a complete theory of speech acts (*TKH* 1:415/310). But Habermas undertakes to render it plausible prima facie by refuting some obvious objections to it, which I will simply note. One argument concerns indirect validity claims. To the view that, for example, making a promise raises no truth claim, Habermas responds with the view that if not directly raised, the truth claim is at least presupposed, and this means that the promise can be criticized with respect to truth. In this way, all three validity claims are, if only indirectly, made by every utterance in communicative action. Habermas also argues that sincerity cannot be reduced to truth. To criticize the claim that "it is raining now" on the grounds that the speaker does not believe it is different from arguing that it is, in fact, not raining now (*TKH* 1:412f./367f.). And he responds to Ernst Tugendhat's view[15] that only one validity claim is necessary (*TKH* 1:420-423/313–315).

In addition to truth, sincerity, and appropriateness, there are of course other claims that people in fact make for their utterances. One, which Habermas gets from H. P. Grice, is the claim that an utterance must be relevant.[16] Habermas argues that relevance is not a universal claim: there are situations (cocktail parties come to mind) in which relevance to a conversational whole is in fact out of place (*TKH* 1:418/312).

Habermas's second claim concerns the status of communicative action with respect to teleological action. It also cannot be definitively established in the current state of research. But it can be argued for by a "reliable procedure for testing reconstructive hypotheses" (*TKH* 1:65/38). The main set of such hypotheses is furnished by speech-act theory, which aims to reconstruct the basic intuitions that speakers have by virtue of their competences with language use. Habermas thus seeks to use speech-act theory as both a clue to the classification of communicative actions by validity claims and as a test for his theory as well: the concepts of understanding and those of speech-act theory "reciprocally interpret one another."[17]

This talk of "clues" and "tests" rather than of "foundations" (see *TKH* 1:415/310) points to the fact that speech-act theory is still incomplete and in some ways defective. Habermas does not simply lean on it in his arguments, but evaluates and changes it in so doing. Arguing with Strawson[18] against Austin, to begin with, Habermas claims that the distinction between "illocutionary" and "perlocutionary" speech acts cannot be drawn as Austin draws it. It is not a contrast between those effects of a speech act that are achieved conventionally—by conventions governing the speech act itself, and thus "internally" to the act—and those that are achieved nonconventionally, i.e., in virtue of circumstances that happen to obtain or of the ways the audience will happen to interpret the speech act. The distinction is rather between what Strawson calls the "essential avowability" of the illocutionary act, as opposed to the fact that perlocutionary acts cannot be avowed. Hence, for Habermas it is an illocutionary act to inform someone of something, as is shown by such avowing locutions as "I'm telling you that . . ." or "I want you to know that . . ." But to *mis*inform someone is a perlocutionary act, for if I avow that I am performing it, it fails (*TKH* 1:393-397/292-295). Perlocutionary acts are thus, Habermas concludes, manipulative: they are to be considered as "concealed strategic" acts. But as such, they presuppose illocutionary acts by means of which they are carried out. I could not misinform you if I could not seem to be informing you, i.e., if there were not a stratum of language in which I do make truth and sincerity claims. Hence, the illocutionary, or communicative, acts are the basic ones.

The theory which results from all this is what Habermas calls "formal pragmatics." It seeks to articulate, or reconstruct, the concept of communicative action in terms of the basic competences which language users possess, and hence to be true to certain of their basic intuitions about language. Such an approach is required both for orientation in the manifold empirical instances of language use and to explain certain things we do with language (*TKH* 1:444-448/331–334). But as a formal theory it begins from idealized examples rather than from actual cases of language use, and this opens the question of whether and how it can in fact relate to our actual speech. Habermas responds to this by listing (at *TKH* 1:441f/330) eight "idealizations" contained in the formal-pragmatic starting point. The most important of these is the absence of consideration of the role of background knowledge. Following Searle,[19] Habermas claims that even the literal, explicit, and direct meaning of an utterance cannot be grasped by its hearers without the application of background beliefs. Though literal meaning is not, for Habermas or for Searle, a mere fiction, it is at best only an abstract dimension of any speech act (*TKH* 1:448–452):

> Literal meanings are, then, relative to a deep-seated, implicit knowledge, *about* which we normally know nothing, because it is simply unproblematic and does not pass the threshold of communicative utterances that can be valid or invalid (*TKH* 1:451/337).

The reservoir of this background knowledge, as we will see, is the life-world. Since every utterance is thus relative to a life-world, it follows that those discourses in which participants in communicative action question and examine validity claims are themselves relative to their life-world. That life-world provides basic background beliefs with regard to the state of the various worlds presupposed in communicative action, as well as the nature of language and speakers. It also contains criteria for what makes a reason "good." All of these help determine the evaluations people actually make of validity claims.

The claim of discourse to evaluate claims "with reasons, and only with reasons" (*TKH* 1:48/25) is not, then, a valid one. In addition to explicitly advanced reasons, discursive evaluations, like all communicative action, also make use of the background beliefs of the life-world. But the claim is one which, in Habermas's view, we actually make. Even though there may, for example, be philosophical reason to doubt that we can reach "objective" decisions on ethical matters, we do—as we have seen Habermas note—attempt to reach such decisions, and we sometimes are satisfied with the results of our attempts. As he puts it elsewhere, the fact that we continually claim to engage in what really is an impossible form of interaction testifies to the "factual power of the counterfactual."[20]

Thus, like the ideal speech situation, discourse is counterfactual—and with it, discursive understanding. We never do in fact reach understanding with others in a wholly explicit and rational way, but always against an unchallenged background of life-world beliefs. Insofar as Habermas uses the concept of understanding to evaluate current social phenomena, he is proceeding along the lines of the Kantian first foundation, measuring social givens against a counterfactual ideal. But this ideal is not reached via a transcendental critique, or a metaphysical projection, or even by the thought experiment of maximally extending empirically given conditions for actual speech. It is reached by an abstraction: the bracketing of the life-world from the communicative context.

Narrative

The Theory of Communicative Action, as presented so far, can be narratively tied to Kant's first foundation and to Aristotle's concepts of purposive action and substance. As we might then expect, it leaves no room for poetic interaction.

The strategies of the first foundation were followed much more closely by Habermas in earlier writings, such as "Wahrheitstheorien" and "Towards a Theory of Communicative Competence," than in *The Theory of Communicative Action*.[21] That they have not simply been abandoned here is evident from Habermas's discussion of the idealizations on which the formal-pragmatic presentation of the concept of communicative action is founded. Because it is idealized, that presentation of communicative action is, I have said, counterfactual: it ignores the fact that all communication actually occurs in the context of a life-world. But the formal-pragmatic concept of communicative action is not counterfactual the way a Kantian idea of reason is. It is hardly Habermas's intention to claim that communicative action must be presumed to inhabit a noumenal realm, independent of the sensory domain for which it serves as an ideal standard. Communicative action is counterfactual, not in the sense that it never occurs, but in that it never occurs *as here described*: it is always empirically given as just one aspect of a larger, concrete whole. It is, I suggest, counterfactual in somewhat the sense that a description of a human hand playing a piano would be: we do empirically encounter hands playing pianos, but always functioning as parts of a whole human body. As such, the concept of communicative action is not the kind of thing Kant thought the categorical imperative was—a possible inhabitant of the noumenal realm. It is, however, like what *Hegel* thought Kant's categorical imperative was: what remains after the particular contents of concrete situations have been abstracted from them.

But the analogy of the disembodied hand fails to capture one aspect of the idealization of formal pragmatics which more clearly approaches Kant. The formal-pragmatic account of communicative action, by abstracting from the life-world, assimilates communicative action as a whole to that aspect of it Habermas calls discourse. In discourse, we actually undertake to examine validity claims "with reasons, and only with reasons:" to determine validity without appeal to the shared background of beliefs that constitutes our life-world. It is, to retain our analogy, like a pianist undertaking to play as if he were nothing more than a set of disembodied hands, or like a Kantian moral agent undertaking to act as if against all inclinations.

For present purposes, Habermas makes two important advances on Kant. The first is due to his empirical orientation. For him, the idealization which produces a counterfactual concept of communicative action is not the construction of a supersensible ideal but a methodological artifact, to be redeemed by the discussions of the life-world occupying much of volume 2 of *The Theory of Communicative Action*. And discourse itself, though motivated by counterfactual ideals, is an actual phenomenon. That individuals undertake to act as if such ideals could be realized is thus an empirical given and serves as an empirical image for those counterfactual ideals. Habermas's basic moral fact is thus no "fact of reason."

The second advance follows on this one. Not being conceived as part of a nonempirical, noumenal realm, discourse and communicative action are always presented as being within time. This means that the kind of thing Kant, in his formulation of the Kingdom of Ends, dismissed as mere "hindrances" to its realization can become intrinsic parts of the Habermasian reformulation. In particular, as we saw, all achieving of agreement essentially begins from disagreement and discord. In this respect, it approximates to what we saw treated in Hegel's *Phenomenology* as forgiveness, and in his *Aesthetics* as the interactive component of reconciliation. As such, the discursive overcoming of disagreement is not part of everyday activities: discourse presupposes that its participants are "freed from the pressures of action and experience," i.e., that they are not constrained to accept validity claims that have been problematized but not yet redeemed because of shortage of time or personal interest and purpose.

Habermas's remark that teleological action has been central to all action theory since Aristotle, and that it will not be central in his own theory, has extremely broad implications. First, it suggests that two millenia of viewing action as purpose-oriented are now coming to an end. But there is, as we saw, more to the Aristotelian concept of teleological action than this. For its concept of purpose or *telos* coincided, in the case of deliberate action, with the nature or self of the agent: purposive action was action which manifested, or actualized, the preformed self of the actor. That view was undermined by Kant, and rejected by Hegel and Heidegger; Habermas, in also rejecting it, places himself in their intellectual constellation.

The human self, then, is not "preformed" but takes shape only via its interactions with others; Habermas, like Hegel and Heidegger (but much more explicitly), returns to the "dialogical" orientation of the Platonic texts. My account of that orientation primarily concerned the *Phaedrus*, but it is surely no coincidence that in the earliest of Plato's writings, the *Apology*, Socrates begins his speech with reference to the four validity claims of Habermas's earlier work: truth, sincerity, appropriateness, and intelligibility.[22] Nor is it, presumably, accidental that the *Apology* and the *Phaedrus* discussions are both independent of the theory of Forms—the former because Socrates, whose views the *Apology* records, had no such theory; the latter because, though the theory of forms is present in the dialogue, the account of interaction in the Palinode is incompatible with it.

The view that action expresses the preformed self of the actor was prescribed by the Aristotelian substance metaphysics; and this, too, Habermas wants to reject. But, as Kant's example showed, the concept of substance is not so easy to get rid of. When Habermas speaks of understanding (*Verständigung*) as the "inherent telos" of communicative action itself, he is using Aristotelian substance language and is to a degree, I will argue, reinstating what we may call a substance approach. True, the sense in which Habermas understands *telos* as applied to understanding and communicative action is not that of purpose: he is not reinstating the

Aristotelian concept of teleological action itself. Rather, it is *telos* in the sense that the adult tree is the *telos* of the sapling: as the indwelling nature which, in the normal course of things, will be realized. And this is for Aristotle tied, if not to the concept of purpose, to the larger concept of substance.

We saw that the concept of substance, as the source of all activity within an entity, went together, in the Aristotelian texts, with a like conception of philosophy (or "science"): this conception was that one science, and indeed one concept within it, prescribed to other investigations. Every entity, to be understood, had to be interpreted as a substance; but not all entities really were substances. Those which were not were considered either as producing, adumbrating, or as manifesting substance and its activities. Thus, the children, women, and slaves in a houshold "led to" the "lord and master." He alone was capable of rational action, i.e., of self-actualization as a substance; they lived for his sake and were partial realizations of the rationality he possessed in full. The polis was a quasi-substance in that it was the field of manifestation of the deliberative acts of the substantial individual, and like that individual, it had a single source of all its action.

Similarly for the status of communicative action, on Habermas's theory: the other forms of interaction (teleological, dramaturgical, etc.) lead up to it, as the fullest expression of what they are. Historically, premodern life-worlds are "premodern" because they are not yet structured by communicative action (*TKH* 1:73-113/43−74), and this phrase "not yet" shows the concept of communicative action structuring phenomena which adumbrate it. And, finally, the modern life-world, which we have yet to discuss in detail, is defined as structured by communicative action: it constitutes the field of manifestation for such action, the space where it achieves effectiveness—as the Aristotelian polis did for teleological action.

Demarcation

My basic criticism of Habermas will not be that he has gone wrong in what he says so much as that his account of interaction and emancipation is incomplete and allows supplementation in certain respects. My demarcative aim will be to mark out the conceptual space his account leaves open for further development. Two limits to his presentation of communicative action so far can be taken to open up such space. Both can be seen from the claim that all utterances in communicative action make three and only three validity claims. If this were intended as merely a statement about the nature of communicative action, it could be regarded as a stipulation and hence would be trivially true. But it is not advanced as simply a claim about communicative action: the claim is rather about all cases of interaction which aim at achieving understanding or agreement on the validity claims of an utterance; this is why Habermas has to argue for the thesis.[23]

Do all utterances with which we seek to reach understanding make all three validity claims, even indirectly? Habermas's arguments are more developed for the truth claim and the sincerity claim than for the appropriateness claim (for which see *TKH* 1:418/311f). With regard to the truth claim, he introduces the idea of an indirect validity claim. We do, doubtless, make indirect truth claims. Any statement, in fact, presumably entails such claims as "I [the speaker] am now speaking," "there is such a thing as language," and "I am speaking this particular language." But is there not a distinction to be drawn between claims which, like the above, are raised by all utterances simply because they are utterances, and truth claims which—like some of the sentences we saw to be entailed by my promise to mail the letter—are raised by some utterances and not by others? If I utter something, is the claim that there is a language according to whose rules my utterance is formulated anything but trivial?

Let us distinguish between such trivial truth claims and the kinds raised by some utterances but not by others, which we will call "proper" truth claims. Are there utterances which raise no proper truth claims? An ambiguous utterance, I suggest, does not seem to do so in any definite way: we cannot, in fact, examine its truth because we do not know what it has said. And, since it is ambiguous, we do not know what other sentences are entailed by it—except for the trivial ones. When we reject it, we do so not because we think its truth claim is false, but because it has not yet made a proper truth claim. Only after the meaning of an utterance has been agreed upon—after understanding has been reached on that question—can a truth claim be accepted or rejected.

We might say that the fact that we reject the utterance because of its ambiguity means that it is at least *supposed* to raise a truth claim. We can thus underwrite the idea that all utterances in interaction oriented to understanding should raise truth claims, preserving the universality of the truth claim as something honored, here, in the breach. But this response will not work, I think, for two reasons. In the first place, it remains true that disambiguation is not verification: the cooperative undertaking to decide what truth claims have been raised by an utterance will use forms of argument which differ from those used to decide whether a truth claim is valid. These may include, for example, listing the possible meanings of the utterance; attempting to unravel what we suspect are metaphors it contains; imputing states of mind to the utterer; and using cultural background knowledge to disambiguate—all procedures which, we saw, were advocated by Aristotle in his account of how to understand, not language which claims truth in any normal sense, but the anomalies of tragic speech. In the process, we may decide the truth of various sentences—e.g., we may eliminate from our repertoire of possible construals interpretations of the utterance which make it obviously untrue—but our procedure will not be limited to these. And in all this, we aim at reaching understanding, not on the validity of the utterance's truth claim, but on what that claim is.

To say that the determination of the meaning of an ambiguous sentence is interaction oriented to reaching understanding does not mean, however, that it is communicative action or discourse in Habermas's sense. For in such determination, we do not examine the relation of the utterance to the "objective world" of states of affairs: instead, we may look to the meanings of the terms in it, i.e., conduct an investigation which is language-immanent; or we may look to background knowledge, in which case our investigation may be culture-immanent. Only when that is accomplished does the utterance raise a truth claim and become part of the context of communicative action.

Is it not possible, moreover, that there are ambiguous utterances which are intentionally so, and which are accepted by their hearer in all their ambiguity? Such acceptance would not entail the acceptance of any proper truth claim raised by that utterance. If the hearer went on to decide upon a meaning for such an utterance, he might make use of some of the same techniques that disambiguation uses. But would not his action be very different? Would he not aim, instead of uncovering a meaning which had been inadequately expressed, actually to create a meaning for the utterance? Or to assign it one on his own initiative? Such an undertaking would be, in my sense, poetic.

We can examine the question of whether the sincerity claim is as universal as Habermas maintains by looking at his argument that communicative action is really basic to teleological action. Using Strawson's critique of Austin, Habermas argues that illocutionary acts are essentially avowable: they accurately express the intention of the speaker. Perlocutionary acts are not, and for Habermas they represent a covert manipulation of the hearer: they are "concealed strategic actions." But this contrast seems to be overstated: a perlocutionary act, though not essentially avowable by the speaker, need not be concealed or even concealable by him. Consider the act of convincing a person of something. Persuasion, in such a case, is achieved through the speaker's utterances, and is,

Strawson notes, a perlocutionary effect of those utterances.[24] But it is not achieved simply in and through the utterance: the reactions of the hearer are also necessary. I, as a speaker, cannot avow that I am convincing you as hearer—I can at most avow that I am attempting to convince you, which is what Strawson calls an "illocutionary act of a kind not essentially conventional." But my inability to avow the perlocutionary effects of my utterance does not mean that I am concealing them; I cannot do so, because convincing another is not *my* act to hide or avow: being convinced is the audience's doing.

Habermas's basic point here is that strategic actions, in which the true intentions of the speaker are concealed, can be assimilated to perlocutionary acts. They then presuppose illocutionary acts, which as essentially avowable do claim to be sincere representations of the speaker's intentions, and this yields the conclusion that even strategic actions presuppose sincerity claims. The view that *all* perlocutionary acts must be concealed, however, is not necessary to establishing this point. It would suffice to say only that manipulative effects, as necessarily concealed, belong to the class of acts which are not essentially avowable. Even if they do not exhaust that class, they would still presuppose illocutionary acts, which do make sincerity claims.

What Habermas has done, however, has other implications. For by saying that all perlocutionary effects are concealed by the speaker, he excludes from consideration perlocutionary effects achieved cooperatively between speaker and hearer—as in the case of convincing. Among such acts, I will argue in chapter 22, may be acts which express intentions. It is perhaps quite possible for me not to know what my intentions in a given case are: indeed, it may be possible for me not to have any specific intentions at all. When I perform the kind of speech act that in English is called "blurting," do I not make an utterance which has no intention known to me? May my hearer not then help me clarify what my intentions in fact are, or should be?

Such an utterance, then, would neither express an intention nor conceal it: it would make no determinate sincerity claim. The case is analogous to that of an ambiguous utterance: before the utterance can be criticized as to whether or not it expresses the intentions of the speaker, it must first be determined just what those intentions are. Such determination, when carried on cooperatively between speaker and hearer, is interaction oriented to reaching understanding; but it does not examine the validity of a sincerity claim raised by the utterance. It seeks, as a prerequisite for such examination, to decide what that sincerity claim might be. As such, it, too, is speech-immanent: I do not look to the "subjective world" of the speaker's mental states to find out how the utterance relates to that world, since I have no access to it. I must turn instead to the words, tone of voice, etc., of the utterance itself, or perhaps to cultural background knowledge, to decide what mental states it might be expressing.

As with the case of ambiguous utterances, we could say that the fact that speaker and hearer undertake to decide just what intentions (or other mental states) are expressed in the utterance indicates that an utterance in interaction oriented to reaching understanding is *supposed* to express mental states accurately. And we might want to argue that, whereas an ambiguous sentence is clearly not true or false until its meaning has been determined, such is not the case here: whatever intentions the utterance expresses, it still claims to express some intention or other. In chapter 22, I will argue—parallelling what I will say about the truth claim—that there are some utterances which are made and accepted precisely as not expressing (or concealing) the intentions of the speaker: those where he or she has no intention to express, but simply "blurts."

Blurts and ambiguities thus constitute two cases that Habermas's analysis does not cover: two limits to that analysis. My narrative, however, suggests that something of value may be occluded by those limits. For Hegel, works of art are "ambiguous" in that a detail can be perceived either for itself alone or in terms of its relations to other details, through which gleams—but only gleams—the work's guiding conception. The detail, like the work itself, thus raises no proper truth claim: its aesthetic "truth" consists in the free play of occlusion which brings it into relation, not to an objective world, but to the immanent universal guiding the work of art itself. Nor does the work of art, because of Hegel's insistence that the artist is a mere "corridor," raise any proper sincerity claim. It claims to be, like any work of art, an expression of spirit; it expresses spirit, however, not through its content but through what we would call its form: through the free play of occlusion it presents.

Heidegger, too, insists, in "The Origin of the Work of Art," that the artist is a mere "self-destroying passageway" for the happening of artistic truth; in "From a Dialogue on Language," the "meaning" of what is said—the self-showing of the essence of language—comes about independently of the intentions, and even the knowledge, of the speakers. The various key words of that dialogue, not being propositional at all, do not claim to correspond to any objective world, but to further the dislocated series of meditations constituting the self-saying of language which comes about in and as the dialogue itself.

What if, as this suggests, blurts and ambiguities were not simply trivial mistakes in speech, but were connected with the broader realm of aesthetic discourse? Would we not find ourselves in a space of interaction where utterances are too vague to make definite validity claims? And might not interaction within that space partake of the emancipatory potential of aesthetic experience?

Twenty

The Second Foundation in *The Theory of Communicative Action*

Analysis

After Hegel, in Habermas's view, philosophy surrendered not only its totality claim—its pretension to yield substantive theories of nature and/ or of transcendental subjectivity—but also its claim to foundationality. It can no longer hope to present even the conceptual basis for such substantive theories. What remains of the unity of philosophy, if anything, is its concern for "reason's experience with itself" (*TKH* 1:15-24/1-7). But it appears from my previous account that reason can in fact have no experience which is exclusively "with itself." As interactive and linguistic, it is always situated in a life-world, and its various activities always include experiences of that life-world. Moreover it is, Habermas writes, only through the concept of the life-world that action theory—including, presumably, the theory of communicative action itself—can be connected to social theory (*TKH* 1:376f./279). The unsituated thought characteristic of the first foundation must thus pass over into something similar to the situated and situating character of the second. It does this, I will argue, in such a way as to put into question the "foundational" status of the first foundation. For if all speech and thought are indeed relative to life-worlds, the theory of communicative action itself must be as well. If so, how can it provide a "foundation" for judging society? This question has a complex answer in volume 2 of *The Theory of Communicative Action*. In order to understand it, I will first clarify Habermas's conception of the life-world.

Habermas arrives at this by reformulating the standard Husserlian conception.[1] Construed in dialogical terms, the life-world is no longer an indeterminate "horizon" of perception, as it was for Husserl, but a reservoir of unchallenged truisms, or background cognition, which individuals use for cooperative "processes of interpretation." This knowledge constitutes a cultural heritage and is linguistically organized.

Language, encoding the basic structuring principles (or beliefs) of the life-world, has in a sense a "transcendental" function with respect to possible components of situations. The existing "semantic capacities" of language are thus conditions for the possibility of speech, for we can speak about only that which we have the words to speak about (*TKH* 2:90f., 224). As linguistic, the life-world contains ordinary speech acts as well as more extended forms of speech. The latter include texts and theories, cultural "utterances" like artworks and technologies, and even institutions and structures of personality (*TKH* 1:159/107f). The life-world is thus produced by humans through their speech and is governed by the "operations" of language. It is therefore essentially different from the three worlds we have seen discussed before. The assertions of speakers in communicative action, for example, are linguistic events *in* the life-world which make claims *about* the other three worlds. Those worlds, by contrast, form a "categorial structure" in terms of which such claims are evaluated (*TKH* 2:186).

Communicative action, as a set of linguistic operations, itself exists within the life-world. It is, in fact, the life-world which grounds the discursive procedures of the first foundation. Those procedures are certainly not justified for Habermas because they somehow mirror reality. For one thing, they operate, in accordance with the general structure of communicative action, on the presupposition that three, and only three, worlds exist. This is not, as I noted in chapter 20, a presupposition that we can know to be true. For another thing, epistemic foundations do not for Habermas play an important role in how we decide truth claims. It is up to us—not "objective" structures of reality—to decide in specific cases whether or not a validity claim is justified. In the absence of epistemic foundations, discourse becomes, not logically definitive proof, but discussion and decision on the basis of the best available theory, according to criteria often quite specific to the particular object-domain involved. Habermas's position thus allows a considerable degree of skepticism as to whether or not individual validity claims can actually be decided.

Moreover, background knowledge, and hence the life-world itself, are holistically structured. All beliefs—including those about which criteria are appropriate for evaluating theories—entail indefinite numbers of other beliefs. We are not, however, directly aware of this holistic structure or of the entailment relations among our beliefs. Indeed, as background knowledge, the life-world is not something we are usually aware of at all. Only when a piece of background information becomes important for a given situation is it normally even a candidate for explicit awareness, and such thematizations are always partial. Hence, an individual can never become explicitly aware of the entire set of beliefs entailed by any one constituent of his life-world, let alone of the whole of that world.[2] And it follows that whether an utterance in communicative action is accepted or rejected depends, not merely on the facts of the case, but upon criteria for evaluating arguments whose own validity and scope remain only partially known. Since their validity is not known for sure, these criteria function, not because they adequately represent reality (though in fact they may), but because they form part of the life-world. Hence, both in its very general structures and in regard to individual decisions on concrete validity claims, communicative action is guided by the partially unknowable life-world of those who engage in it.

We must then explain why communicative action is undertaken at all, as well as the ways it unrolls in specific cases, by appealing to the life-world of its participants. In that sense, the life-world "grounds" communicative action and its specific procedures. True, in his discussion of Jacques Derrida, Habermas introduces what appears to be a second way of arguing that the practice of making validity claims should not be given up. His claim there is not only that such claims are *in fact* made continually by members of our society who engage in communicative action, but also that they *should be* made: for making them permits communicative action to occur, and this has pragmatic justification. Communicative action succeeds over time in building up independent fields of discourse which solve problems in organized ways.[3]

This pragmatic argument for communicative action, however, reduces to the kinds appeal to the nature of our life-world we have just discussed. This can be seen if one responds to Habermas with the argument that organized problem-solving is, perhaps, not something that would be appreciated by, e.g., a Zande tribesman, who prefers recourse to the ad hoc techniques of witches for his difficulties. Habermas's answer to this would have to be, I suggest, that preference for organized problem-solving is, if not a universally human given, not merely his own private whim. It is, rather, a deeply embedded increment of the modern life-world, one which no inhabitant of that world would want to give up. This suggestion is supported by Habermas's basic account of rationalization (*TKH* 1:72-114/43-74). The nature of the life-world changes historically. In premodern societies, the cultural heritage is articulated mythically and carried forward by tradition. In such societies, we may say, understanding in Habermas's sense cannot be reached because the preliminary dissent would not be allowed, or even understood. If social norms are viewed as generically identical to natural laws, then dissent from them is not merely untoward, but impossible: a Zande tribesman could, on this view, no more dissent from the social practice of consulting witches than he could from the law of gravity. Only in the modern life-world is myth replaced by communicative action as a means of reaching understanding. The differentiation of the three worlds from one another and from the life-world of the speakers is thus a precondition for the kind of rationality involved in communicative action, and it is the "liberation" of the rationality inherent in it.[4]

The structures of communicative action, including its highly idealized and counterfactual presuppositions, are thus distinguishing characteristics of the modern life-world. They, and the first foundation which rests upon them, are grounded, not transcendentally as Kant thought, but in the nature of the modern life-world. And this is sufficient, because we cannot transcend or even question the basic structures of our life-world:

> The life-world constitutes, in the situation of an action, a horizon we cannot get beyond. . . . For those belonging to a sociocultural life-world it is, strictly speaking, *senseless* to ask if the culture in whose light they come to understand themselves with respect to external nature, society, and internal nature empirically depends on something else.[5]

The life-world is thus the "necessary" foundation of communicative rationality in the Greek sense of *anankê*: not as what is logically deducible from self-evident premises or true in all possible worlds, but as what we must put up with. If we cannot challenge the totality of our life-world, we cannot globally challenge the structures which, like those of communicative action in the modern life-world, govern and define that totality. Those structures, in short, are indeed relative to a particular life-world; but it is *our* life-world, and there is in general nothing we can do about that:

> When [interlocutors] transgress the horizon of a specific situation, they cannot step into emptiness; they find themselves immediately in another, now actualized, but *pre-interpreted* realm of the culturally self-evident. In everyday communicative practice there are no completely unfamiliar situations. Even new situations rise up from a life-world, which is built up from a cultural supply of knowledge with which one is already acquainted (*TKH* 2:191; cf. 205f.).

A truly new situation, one which established knowledge does not cover, indicates a crisis in "cultural reproduction." It may call for the services of translators, interpreters, and therapists: but these can only proceed by relying on features of the life-world more general than those which have broken down. The interpreters must, for example, thematize the aspects of the life-world that are failing; this means identifying them as components of one or more of the three worlds (*TKH* 2:201–204, 212f.). In its basic and holistic structures, then, the life-world is "immune from total revision . . . situations change, but the limits of the life-world itself cannot be transcended" (*TKH* 2:201). Being thus necessary for us, the modern life-world suffices as ground—to some degree unknown—for the theory of communicative action. On this reading, it is as an articulation of the modern life-world that Habermas's entire theory—including the account of validity claims—is ultimately justified, and this, as we will see in the ensuing narrative, places it into the general category of the second foundation.

As with the notion of understanding, but independently, Habermas uses the concept of the life-world as a standard by which to judge contemporary society. In rough outline, the critique is as follows. The life-world, structured by processes of communicative action, is as necessary to us as are food and water. But not all processes for coordinating action are communicative, and they do not all belong to the life-world. In particular, money and power are mechanisms which coordinate action on nonrational grounds: if I have the power to order you about, for example, I do not need to give reasons for what I tell you to do. Insofar as the "steering mechanisms" of money and power take over more and more of the burden of coordinating human action, less and less space is left for the life-world, with its processes of communicative action and discourse. Since the life-world cannot, as necessary, be simply abandoned, various social pathologies result, which Habermas is able to diagnose.[6]

If my account is correct, the theory of communicative action must ultimately be understood as an articulation of basic structures of the modern life-world. How, we may ask, is this articulation accomplished? What are the standards by which it is to be judged? On the one hand, the theory is advanced as a set of propositions which claim validity (in the form, most importantly, of truth). This is shown by Habermas's refusal to limit his account of rationality merely to modern Western societies. Though different societies may manipulate Habermas's threefold scheme differently—in particular, by not sustaining it with communicative action—it is, he writes, the same scheme they are manipulating (*TKH* 1:86-102/53–66). And to Weber's question of whether or not rationalization (with its concomitant modernization) is a phenomenon restricted to the West, Habermas's clearest answer is as follows:

> [The three validity claims of communicative action] form a system—however fraught with internal tensions—that did indeed first appear in the form of Occidental rationalism but

that, beyond the peculiarity of this specific culture, lays a claim to a universal validity binding on all 'civilized men'" (*TKH* 1:259/184).

The reason for this is that, because it advances claims to be examined and decided upon rationally, the *theory* of communicative action is itself a *case* of communicative action:

> . . . the theory of communicative action aims at that moment of unconditionedness which is built into the conditions of consensus-formation by criticizable validity claims—*as* claims these transcend all spatial and temporal, all provincial limitations of the context of the moment (*TKH* 2:586f).

Because the theory of communicative action is itself advanced as a case of communicative action, it carries with it the kind of unconditional validity claim that communicative action in general contains. Habermas makes this point when he says that any social theory which rests upon the theory of communicative action,

> insofar as it relates to structures of the life-world, must explicate a background knowledge which no one can control at will. The life-world is "given," to the theorist and to the layman, in the first instance as his own life-world. . . . No more than for any social scientist does the totality of background knowledge constitutive for the construction of the life-world stand at his disposition. . . . The context in which it arises does not remain external to the theory (*TKH* 2:589–591).

But there are two problems here. First, formal pragmatics, in Habermas's view, aims to reconstruct basic linguistic competencies. It begins, not a priori, but from certain idealized examples. As Habermas notes in his "Rekonstruktive vs. verstehende Sozialwissenschaften," these examples may be, not merely idealized, but wrongly chosen. In such a case, the theory itself need not be false, for it may accurately reconstruct the competencies behind those particular examples. But if they are examples of some trivial and peripheral type of linguistic performance, rather than truly basic ones, the theory will universalize too strongly from its individual cases and obscure more important intuitions—not only, we may add, about language use, but also about the social implications of such use.[7] In that case, Habermas's formal pragmatics—and with it the theory of communicative action itself—would lose its grounding in the life-world. Rather than one of its central, and hence unchallengeable, structures, it might present a peripheral, changeable one.

The second problem is how, in the absence of a foundationalist epistemology, the truth of the theory of communicative action can be decided. If theories as wholes were like the propositions on which they are built, they would be true or false. But Habermas does not think highly of that analogy, in particular as applied to the theory of communicative action itself. He refers to the "strongly universalistic claim" of the theory, together with the merely "hypothetical" status of those universalistic claims; a status which is only "indirectly examinable" *TKH* 2:586f.).[8] Like other theories of high generality, the theory of communicative action cannot simply be tested against reality as simple propositions can, and Habermas is left only with the rule of thumb that if two theories contradict one another, one or both must be suspect. The proper procedure in such a case is usually not to test each against reality, but to attempt to remove their contradiction via rational argumentation. The revisions required by this, however, must be mutual: no theory or paradigm is entitled to primary status as an "unmoved mover" to which all others must conform. Habermas's picture is thus of a plurality of discourses, each adjusting itself to accommodate the rational insights of the others.[9]

There is more. One respect in which theories for Habermas differ from propositions is that theories, like living organisms, develop over time. Habermas generally refers to such developing conceptual "organisms" as *Forschungsrichtungen*, directions of research, or as "learning processes." Each is a "coherent argumentation developed around constant thematic cores."[10] The theory of communicative action has a nonfoundational claim to truth, not because it simply coheres with other discourses, but because, in their own immanent development, they *converge* on it. This convergence also means that the theory is not a merely peripheral part of the life-world, but it is central to it—and so, then, are the competencies it seeks to reconstruct.

I shall call the claim to be at the center of convergence of a number of distinct learning processes the "centrality claim." It is not a truth claim. For the achievement of centrality does not establish a relation to the objective world, which is the correlate of true propositions, but to other theories: to other linguistic "inhabitants" of the life-world. It appeals, not to the objective world, but to given circumstances of the contemporary life-world in which those theories have their place.

Habermas argues throughout *The Theory of Communicative Action* for what I have called the "centrality" of the theory of communicative action. That centrality, it appears, has three main aspects. While not a criterion of truth, the capacity to appropriate and work up the best traditions is certainly a sign of a social theory's capacity to be used by others [Anschlußfähigkeit] and strength of comprehension.[11]

This capacity is a sign that a theory is avoiding certain sorts of errors—specifically, that of "ideology" in the Marxist sense:

> the more freely it can take up, explain, criticize, and carry on the intentions of earlier theory traditions, the more impervious it is to the danger that particular interests are being brought to bear unnoticed on its own theoretical perspectives.[12]

"Taking up," "criticizing, " and "carrying on" are clearly references to the three moments of Hegel's concept of *Aufhebung* as the preservation, destruction, and raising to a higher level of entities and circumstances found in the world.[13] Let us examine each in turn.

Sometimes other paradigms converge, so to speak, of themselves: all Habermas has to do is reveal the convergence. Examples of this are: his claim that post-Hegelian philosophies, from logic to aesthetics, are becoming increasingly relevant to the theory of the formal conditions of rationality, and his claim that the mutual differentiation of validity spheres in modernity has now "meta-differentiated" itself into various centripetal moments of culture, all reconverging upon the theory of communicative action.[14] In such cases, learning processes which have developed independently from each other discover that they have something in common, and the researchers involved in each come into increasing dialogue.

But at other times, apparently, it is up to Habermas himself to bring into a common universe of discourse theories which are not converging of themselves. This is the case with system theory and action theory, which are not coming into mutual dialogue of their own accord, but are (in Habermas's telling phrase) the *disjecta membra* of a full theory of modernity.[15] In such cases, the convergence is not an "objective" fact which can be proven or disproven, but a task to be accomplished. And accomplishing it is not the job of a set of arguments distinct from the theory of communicative action, but is—as our above quote suggests—part of the work of the theory itself. We saw this in our discussion of Habermas's appropriation of speech-act theory: he does not remodel Austin and Searle in order to compare their theories with his own and then refute them where they diverge from it. Rather, the statement of Habermas's theory *is*, in fact, the remodelling of the other two thinkers. The interweaving of historical comment and theoretical analysis, which Habermas occasionally seems to apologize for (cf. *TKH* 1 : 114/75), is in fact central to his conception of theories as dynamically changing entities.

To participate in a common rational discourse means to be open to criticism from the other participants; for such discourse, as a case of communicative action, allows one's own validity claims to be challenged, examined, and abandoned if found wanting. Communicative action, in virtue of the criticizable validity claims it raises, thus contains an intrinsic critical potential which enables the participants in a common discourse to "penetrate a given context, to burst it open from within, and to transcend it." By providing a common universe of discourse for divergent paradigms in social theory, for example, the theory of communicative action unlocks their capacities for mutual and self-criticism; this, we may take it, is for Habermas another indication of its merit.[16]

The above reference to *Anschlußfähigkeit* suggests the third way, in addition to convergence and the unlocking of critical potential, in which a social theory can be evaluated for its centrality: through its effects. The usefulness of a theory for further research "can only be verified in its ramifications for research in the social sciences and philosophy" and is not for its proponent to judge. But Habermas is aware that it matters to a theory whether other research directions can make use of it, and he devotes much of the closing section of *The Theory of Communicative Action* to a discussion of such possible ramifications. Therefore, what makes Habermas's theory "central" is that other theories converge on it; have their "offensive" critical potential unlocked by it; and ramify from it into subsequent research.

The various paradigms and learning processes which converge on the theory of communicative action are, like all linguistic entities, parts of the life-world: they are

> internally connected with the social contexts in which they emerge and become influential. In them is reflected the world- and self-understanding of various collectives (*TKH* 1:201/140).

The theory of communicative action in general appropriates, criticizes, and helps other theories which themselves are dynamically developing components of the modern life-world. This justifies its claim to treat structures which are definitive for our life-world. This is shown—not argued for—by the theory itself, to the extent that Habermas can place his thought at the confluence—and, after critique, the effluence—of a large number of learning processes. The other discussions which converge upon the theory of communicative action are, as life-world realities with which it *must* deal, limits upon it, and it is situated among them. But the theory's ability to transform those discourses (as well as their capacity to transform each other) shows that they can be other than they are, i.e., they are in my sense parameters. It is the formulation of the theory of communicative action which, reworking other discourses, shows them to be parametric in nature. That formulation itself, then, is an exercise in situating reason.

But one problem with this suggests that Habermas has not fully articulated the relation of the theory of communicative action to the life-world. There are certain fields of discourse present in the contemporary world which Habermas excludes from his centrality claim: types of discourse that he does not want to claim are converging on the theory of communicative action. Two cases of this are instructive for present purposes. First, in Habermas's general account of rationalization complexes (*TKH* 1:326/238), along with spaces for the types of rationality we have seen him discuss—cognitive-instrumental, moral-practical, and aesthetic-practical—there is space for a "social-aesthetic" rationality. This would include interaction directed on the fundamental principle of art, which for Habermas is the expression of needs. Such rationality would presumably be the articulation of needs which are not merely individual, but social. But Habermas does not recognize this as a "rational" process: the space is filled, not with examples of such rationality, but with an "x." His reason for excluding aesthetic-social from his "rationalization complexes" is not that aesthetic articulations of social needs do not exist, but that they

> do not form structures that are rationalizable in and of themselves, but are parasitic in that they remain dependent upon innovations in the other spheres of value (*TKH* 1:326f./238f.).

As nonrationalizable, these phenomena of the life-world do not embody "learning processes" of the type Habermas views as converging upon his own thought.

Another instance of such exclusion is Habermas's account of action theory as developed in analytical philosophy. Though he does make piecemeal use of some of its findings (cf. *TKH* 1:143ff/95ff), Habermas does not attempt to deal with this domain of discourse as a whole. In addition to its restriction to the case of instrumental rationality—a restriction which, as we have seen, does not keep Habermas from dealing with speech-act theory—Habermas says that the investigations carried out under the heading of analytical action theory do not represent a unified approach, having in common only their method and the narrow formulation of their problems. They are not breaking new ground, but repeating battles long since fought. And finally, analytical action theory is carried out without regard to possible fruitfulness for other fields, in particular the social sciences (*TKH* 1:369f./273f.). We may conclude that in order to be a candidate for more than piecemeal treatment—in order to be the kind of theory that Habermas is ready to claim converges on his own—a "learning process" or field of discourse must satisfy the following conditions:

(1) It must be rational, i.e., built up through the making and discursive redemption of validity claims.

(2) It must be a unified approach, i.e., must, by virtue of Habermas's dynamic view of theories, be a development organized over time.

(3) It must not be parasitic on other approaches, importing all its insights from elsewhere, nor ignorant of the achievements of the past: it must build on these in its own ways.

(4) It must solve problems—not merely problems it formulates itself, but problems which arise in other fields, making it fruitful for those fields.

Two pragmatic motives for this set of restrictions are readily apparent. By insisting on the rationality of the learning processes with which he will deal, Habermas is able, first, to exclude what we might call entrenched ravings. We would not consider it a strong point for a social theory if it were able to accommodate the madness of, say, a Charles Manson, a Louis Farrakhan, or a Hitler—even though all three found disciples who were ready to take up and expand on their views. Two other restrictions serve, in addition, to filter out unnecessary labor. By insisting on the nonparasitic nature of learning processes, Habermas is able to avoid useless replication. By insisting that their fruitfulness be previously demonstrated, he is able to ignore much that is trivial.

Using these criteria poses difficulties as well. Thus, Habermas criticizes Horkheimer and Adorno for their "completely affirmative attitude toward the art of the bourgeois epoch," which delivered their critical theory over to the "measure of the age" (*TKH* 2:559f.). But his own reliance is on discourses which have developed in academic and other institutionalized realms of modern society, and this seems to reflect a rather affirmative attitude toward those institutions. It is more than possible that the learning processes carried on in the academy are not simply communicative articulations of the structures of the modern life-world, but that they are also conditioned by such factors as power and money. Habermas, in fact, recognizes that the specialized nature of many contemporary expert discourses cuts them off from the life-world (*TKH* 2:488, 521f.). But in restricting the centrality claim of the theory of communicative action to centrality among learning processes that have developed in the academy, Habermas seems to be delivering critical theory once again over to the measure of the age, i.e., of the modern world which has produced academies. This is, as Habermas maintains, in itself no objection to the "systematic status" of his account of rationalization complexes. But it does suggest, as Thomas McCarthy has noted, that certain possibilities are being screened out.[17]

Habermas has thus not solved the problem of showing fully how the theory of communicative action is related to the life-world in which it comes to be, and to that extent his turn to the second foundation is incomplete. We have seen enough, however, to understand how Habermas has reconceived the relation of the first foundation to the second. Neither is to be given up. But the former is to be viewed as a necessary and fruitful abstraction performed upon speech acts occurring in the life-world. Hence, when we operate in terms of the first foundation, we attempt to bracket as much as possible our own particular life-world from our examinations and redemption of validity claims. Such bracketing is in a sense a falsification, for we cannot ever really achieve it fully. But it is a pragmatically justified one: making validity claims which transcend one's own situation and life-world is a valuable mode of procedure, central to the modern life-world. The existence of the life-world does challenge the status of the first foundation to true foundationality. It deprives us of any claim to know the truth in the way that Kant thought he knew it, as certain for all possible rational beings. But it justifies "transcendent" truth claims as part of a counterfactual mode of procedure. Just as the Kantian moral agent was supposed to behave as if freedom were actual, so the rational person for Habermas behaves as if discourse were possible.

Though Habermas has not, if I have understood him correctly, fully clarified the status of his own thought as an articulation of the life-world, *The Theory of Communicative Action* provides a basis for doing so. At the end of the book, Habermas writes that the theory of communicative action does not merely make truth claims about the life-world or describe it theoretically, but it arises out of a set of specific disruptions in the life-world—disruptions caused by the threatening encroachments into it of the "steering mechanisms" of money and power. These call the theory forth through the pathologies they cause:

> Perhaps this provocative menace, a challenge that puts into question the symbolic structures of the life-world *as a whole*, can make plausible why those structures have become accessible for us (*TKH* 2: 592f.).

It is possible to view the theory of communicative action, arising out of dysfunctions as it does, as itself the articulation of a social need—the need for healing the life-world. This approximates it to the "social-aesthetic" realm—a realm to which Habermas would deny the theory is to be approximated (since he does not admit the existence of social-aesthetic rationality). In spite of the denial, *The Theory of Communicative Action*, I will argue, provides a basis for such approximation—a basis which recognizes the role of a sort of aesthetic judgment in the formulation of the theory, but which does not confuse that original formulation with the rational making and examining of validity claims which follow it.

Narrative

If formal pragmatics connects with Kant and Aristotle, the Hegelian and Heideggeran concerns of Habermas's account of the life-world are obvious. The whole topic of the life-world, in fact, has been reached in a familiar way: the need to have an empirical image for a non-empirically constructed concept of freedom.

Freedom as discourse, the kind of freedom present in the Habermasian first foundation, achieves its empirical instantiation when a group of individuals undertakes to examine validity claims "with reasons and only with reasons." This idealized undertaking parallels, on a communal level, the undertaking of a Kantian moral agent to act independently of all inclinations, or Socrates's individual undertaking to remain in jail in Athens rather than to escape. It also, we may say, parallels the main problems with those accounts. If Socrates was able to achieve self-mastery while still in the body, he was unique, and his way of life was nothing for others to aspire to. A Kantian moral agent could not even know whether he was able to act independently of all inclinations.

But the parallel is not complete. The community of discursive examiners may well be aware that they will not be able wholly to transcend the nondiscursive elements of their life-world. Their undertaking is not, strictly speaking, to examine "with reasons and only with reasons," but to do so as much as possible—exactly the kind of accommodation to reality that the categorical nature of the Kantian imperative forbids. Hence the problem of empirical imagery does not arise with the force it had for Kant, where no example of freedom was even possible. What does arise is the question of why, if discourse is unattainable, we should try to approximate it.[18]

Plato also gives us a question for Habermas. One central aim of formal pragmatics is to show that the community of examiners is enabled to undertake discursive examination by basic linguistic competencies, which excludes the view that they do so, in Socratic fashion, in virtue of a unique and divine fate. But something akin to the *Phaedo*-problem results when we consider Habermas's talk about the "selectivity" of his examples. For if the theory of formal pragmatics rests upon examples that have been badly chosen, then the community of examiners may be an idiosyncratic or socially irrelevant group of people: people whose way of life, like Socrates's in that dialogue but for different reasons, is nothing for others to aspire to.

Habermas's answers represent a major revision of Platonic and Kantian strategies. For he turns, not to metaphysics or critique, but to an empirically based account of the life-world and the learning processes it contains. In this he follows Hegel and Heidegger, who in my narrative also developed the second foundation. But unlike them, Habermas does not wholly give up transcendent universality claims: making such claims is recognized as necessary because of their status as basic structuring principles of the modern life-world. But there is no reason, other than ordinary experience, to think that any such claims can actually be redeemed.

We saw that Habermas's procedure in establishing the centrality of the theory of communicative action is an exercise of situating reason akin to Hegelian *Aufhebung*: its interpretation preserves (some aspects of) other discourses, destroys (some aspects), and raises others up. What we find in Habermas, but not in Hegel, is the claim that bringing diverse discourses together has an inherently critical function. Such was in fact the case for Hegel: putting the state together with aesthetic experience, for example, produced a major (but covert) critique of the state; when art came together with religion, a major (and overt) critique of art resulted. The difference is not merely one of whether critique dares speak its own name—a matter of external rhetoric and the tolerance of the surrounding society—but it lies in the hierarchical nature of the Hegelian narrative. One form of consciousness in the *Phenomenology* is able to criticize another only by virtue of its being located on a dialectically higher level: politics is not allowed to criticize art, nor art religion; and religion, certainly, is not allowed to criticize philosophy. The Habermasian perspective is, at first blush, much more "democratic:" no particular learning process is entitled to be the basic one to which others must conform. Any such process can make its critique of others, and if the critique is sustained discursively, the other process must adjust. This contrasts, not only with Hegel's hierarchical view, but also with Heidegger's nonview in which differing discourses simply go their own ways and ignore each other.

Such situating critique, in which one discourse clarifies the parametric status of another, is at the bottom of Habermas's account of the life-world as under attack from the state and the economy. In content, this is strongly reminiscent of Hegel's account of modern subjectivity as under attack from the state and civil society. The differences are two: First, the life-world is for Habermas structured interactively; for Hegel, modern subjectivity is an inner realm, considered to be of infinite value and therefore in infinite pain when attacked. Second, for Hegel there is the escape from such subjectivity, and its pain, to art: to a realm which is not subjective but absolute, and which is therefore more real than the harsh realities of modern life. There is no escape for Habermas from the threatened life-world: any such escape would be "stepping into nothing."

This lack of escape also, and more revealingly, distinguishes Habermas from Heidegger, whose views of the life-world he otherwise comes close to approximating. For Heidegger, the structures of the "world" are not susceptible to further articulation and hence cannot be further justified; for Habermas, to show that something is a basic feature of our life-world is to "justify" it quo ad nos. In both cases, this is because the life-world is a holistically structured network which is only partially disclosed at any one time. But for Heidegger, unlike Habermas, we can transcend our particular life-world by confronting a new one which is radically incommensurable with the old. This, I suggest, is because while for both Heidegger and Habermas the life-world is most basically structured by language, language functions differently for each. We saw that for Heidegger a word was the gathering point of a realm of presignificance he called "earth." This domain was essentially unknowable: anything might surge up from it, thereby changing the words of the language (such as "Being") and the language itself. For Habermas, by contrast, knowledge always has "propositional structure" (*TKH* 1 : 25/8); the basic function of language, the one realized most fully in the concept of communicative action, is to conform to states of affairs in the objective, subjective, and social worlds. It is not thinkable, then, that language could remain while those worlds vanished, or that people should cease to worry about worlds at all. And since those worlds are presupposed by central practices of the modern life-world itself, it, too, cannot change in its fundamental nature.

Habermas's view of the inescapability of one's life-world can be assigned ancient origins. He relates his concept of the life-world to Marx's formulation of the "realm of freedom" as opposed to the "realm of necessity"; and that distinction itself, as Hannah Arendt has argued,[19] is taken over from Aristotle, for whom the realm of necessity was the necessary condition of the polis, met via familial and economic arrangements. Marx's realm of freedom, then, is a modern rethinking of the Aristotelian polis itself. This, for Aristotle, was a quasi-substance, so constituted that one and only one entity within it—its "substantial form" or constitution—was responsible for all its acts. We may, then, expect the Habermasian life-world to exhibit some of the features of an Aristotelian substance.

That such may be the case is also suggested by my narrative of Kant. Substance, though no longer a metaphysical necessity, was retained by Kant, in his accounts of individual autonomy and the Kingdom of Ends, as a condition of moral activity. Habermas's accounts of ideal speech and discourse capture, we saw, the Kantian concept of transcendental freedom; they may, then, capture as well some traits of the conception of substance. Relocating them in the life-world then results in seeing that world as itself structured on a single conception: that of communicative action as the *telos* of language. Communicative action plays the prescriptive role for the life-world in general that Aristotelian substance played with regard to the polis.

True, Habermas is at pains to distinguish the life-world from the state. The life-world is not a political structure with a single constitution, but more like a series of small groups entering into and leaving situations of communicative action. But so was the Aristotelian polis, as a "network of friendships." What distinguished the polis from other types of social structure, such as the household, was that interaction within the polis primarily manifested one kind of action, rational choice, and was keyed to a single pursuit: that of nobility. Similarly, the Habermasian life-world, as fundamentally structured by processes of communicative action, is directed upon a single end—the "*telos* of language": understanding.

Hence Habermas's conception of the life-world, though clearly derived from phenomenology and motivated by problems concerning situating reason, bears on deeper levels traits of an Aristotelian quasi-substance: it consists of a variety of individuals, interacting in different ways, all of which are keyed to a single *telos*. That *telos*, and the basic social procedures for achieving it, structure that life-world in fundamental ways.

But the Aristotelian polis is conceived as natural; the Habermasian life-world is historical. The basic fixed distinctions of the polis—in particular, the distinctions between slave and free, male and female, adult and child—are all valid "by nature" and cannot be changed, no matter how much the constitution may vary in other respects. The Habermasian life-world, having arisen historically, has in general no such guarantees; its structures (though not its basic ones) can, in principle, be undone.

Demarcation

Habermas does not claim, of course, that his account of communicative action exhausts the structures of the life-world; if it did, he could hardly know it, since the parameters of the life-world remain to some degree unknown. But the traits of the Aristotelian substance metaphysics, surviving in the concept of the life-world the way they survive in the Kantian concepts of philosophy and discourse, occlude that fact: communicative action is the single structure in terms of which the life-world is to be comprehended in all ways important for social theory. Can we exploit this occlusion?

I have already suggested that there is space within the scope of action oriented to reaching understanding for a kind of disagreement and understanding that Habermas does not discuss, i.e., that in which we undertake to determine what sorts of validity claim a given utterance is making. And I suggested that such discourse may be related to aesthetic experience, as articulated by Hegel and Heidegger, so as to be emancipatory in the senses they assign to art: it would articulate both the basic structures of human reality and new structures which present themselves. In both cases it would operate critically. In Hegelian terms, it would have access to aspects of human reality which are occluded in modern life; in Heideggerean terms, it would refute current structures simply by presenting alternatives to them. As a clarification of language and as related to aesthetic experience, the kind of interaction for which we are here making room would be similar, as we will later see in more detail, to the interactive use of Kantian reflective judgment.

Habermas's concept of the life-world solves an important problem about such interaction: it gives it a locus. For Kant, as we saw, interactive reflective judgment had to be institutionalized, and Kant was unable to give a clear account of how that could come about: of why the state would tolerate the university let alone its philosophical faculty. Hegel also had problems with this, as we have seen, and finished by truncating the critical dimensions of his own project. And Heidegger largely restricted himself to writing on long-dead philosophers, to private discussions after dinner with foreign visitors, or to dialogues on country paths.

Habermas's concept of the life-world is as a holistically structured domain of shared background knowledge which, structured by communicative action, is (like the natural site of the *Phaedrus*) outside the realm of teleological and manipulative action that constitutes the political order. As Habermas has shown, and as Kant and Hegel felt, that order is essentially directed against the life-world. But it cannot control or eliminate it, as Kant and Hegel feared it might: for background knowledge can be eliminated or controlled only by being turned into foreground knowledge. And such complete articulation of the life-world is, as we have seen Habermas argue, impossible.

If the alternatives are the life-world and the state, then the type of discourse we are seeking to understand must be located in the life-world. But we cannot simply write the interactive use of reflective judgment into the Habermasian life-world until we have asked certain questions. How is Habermas's articulation of the life-world applied to aesthetics? To language-immanent investigations? What are the consequences of dethroning understanding, conceived in terms of communicative action, from its status as the "*telos* of language?" Must not poetic interaction, if it is to be true to the tradition I have narrated, be located in a portion of the life-world which is open to nature in a way that Habermas's account is not? Must not poetic interaction be open to nature, not in the sense of a "world" to which are assigned various propositional contents, but in Heidegger's sense of a domain of pre-significance; in Kant's sense of that which gives the rule to art; in Plato's sense of that which arouses erotic desire for another; in sum: to nature as a source of parameters for speech and action?

Twenty-one

Habermasian Accounts of Art: *The Theory of Communicative Action* and Albrecht Wellmer's "Wahrheit, Schein, Versöhnung"

Analysis

In Kant, Hegel, and Heidegger, concern for situating reason directs itself first to aesthetic experience. The aesthetic aspects of his own second foundation have not been systematically discussed by Habermas, who is suspicious of programmatic attempts to construe art as politically emancipatory.[1] His suspicions are raised by history. Marx's youthful effort at articulating an aesthetically oriented conception of labor as creative self-expression foundered on the fact that industrial labor simply was not in his day creative or self-expressive, and could not become so—a state of affairs that has only grown more obvious since (*TKH* 2:501f.).[2] Adorno's subsequent attempt to carry over the concept of reconciliation from Hegel's "metaphysical" aesthetics to critical theory was also unsuccessful. The "rational core" of Adorno's concept of aesthetic mimesis can for Habermas only be recuperated via an interactionistic reconstrual of it in the (notably un-aesthetic) terms of "understanding" (*TKH* 1:523/390). Finally, cultural tendencies to bring art and politics together lead, in general, either to authoritarianism (as in fascism), or to antiauthoritarian forms (such as anarchism). In all cases, the error lies at the roots of the undertaking, in the aesthetic concept of harmony itself: for both attempts "totalize" society as something that can and should be a harmonious whole. In view of the splits in the modern world, this is "visionary" as well as dangerous (*TKH* 2:520). In keeping with these suspicions, what Habermas has to say about aesthetic experience in *The Theory of Communicative Action,* as in his earlier writings, will be episodic rather than central.[3] But the episodes, I suggest, convey a unified view.

363

In keeping with his generally interactionistic approach, Habermas considers the aesthetic sphere, not in terms of works of art, but first and foremost as a mode of interaction, drawing his usual distinction between utterances themselves and the reflexive examination of them. Here, this takes the form of a distinction between art and art critique. Common to both is a particular form of judgment that Habermas calls "evaluative." Evaluative utterances raise a validity claim somewhere between that of expressive utterances, which claim to verbalize the subjective experiences of an individual, and normative ones, which claim to conform to expectations obligatory in a society. If (in an example Habermas takes from Richard Norman) I say, "I want a saucer of mud," I have made an "expressive" utterance: I have verbalized something entirely subjective and in fact idiosyncratic. If I were able to say, "I have a right to a saucer of mud," I would claim that my expression conforms to a social norm in force in my society: my utterance would claim a socially recognized right. And if I say, "I want a saucer of mud so that I can enjoy its rich river-smell," I have entered the middle ground of evaluative judgments. I have appealed to a criterion—the enjoyability of rich river-smells— which others can be expected to share, but which does not have the force of a binding social norm (*TKH* 1 : 35f./16f.).[4]

In a slightly less counterfactual vein, let us suppose that someone says, "I need a vacation." The person in question can express this need to others by articulating—describing and evincing with his behavior—the nervous fatigue in which he finds himself at work, the depression he feels at home when he sees all the household chores which have been left undone, and so forth. Such articulation can make use of vague but powerful predicates in locutions such as, "this nervousness is dreadful," or, "the chores at home are forbidding" (for these cf. *TKH* 1 : 139/92). Though vague, the predicates are what C. L. Stevenson calls "dynamic":[5] the attitudes they express are, unlike the attitudes in an expressive speech act, recommended to be shared by the hearers as well. When such sharing takes place, it is because those hearers have been able to recognize their own attitudes and needs in the speaker's articulation of his (*TKH* 1 : 139f./ 92). If the hearers cannot do this, the utterance fails: it is not truly "evaluative" but merely idiosyncratic (*TKH* 1 : 36f./16f.).

An "evaluative" judgment thus asks that the values and needs articulated in its predicate be shared by other members of the speaker's community. It cannot, however, expect this in the sense that a normative judgment can. Such a judgment claims that whatever rights it expresses are necessarily, i.e., obligatorily, recognized by its hearers, for they are sanctioned by universally binding social norms. That others share the values and needs of the utterer of an evaluative judgment is not necessary or obligatory but contingent—contingent upon their shared participation in a common form of life.[6]

I have referred to the basic states of mind articulated in evaluative judgments as "attitudes" and "needs." It is with the latter that evaluative speech acts for Habermas are primarily concerned. In contrast to non-affective states, such as beliefs and intentions, which are given to us as "subjective" only when (possibly) mistaken or not carried out, "needs" are feelings or desires, subjective from the outset. It is thus by and through our needs that a situation is given to us in a particular or unique way—one that differentiates us from others who may perceive it as well. In articulating needs, evaluative judgments serve to "make predilection understandable." When such a predilection is articulated in a way that is both honest and persuasive as well as innovative, the articulation deserves to be called a "work of art." Artworks, therefore, are to be interactively considered as evaluative utterances which, more than simply articulating someone's need of the moment, make a claim to "authenticity." They claim to be instructive presentations of an exemplary experience, i.e., an experience which others in the community will recognize themselves as sharing, perhaps to a lesser degree.[7]

An artwork which is innovative without being persuasive or exemplary is merely idiosyncratic. To avoid this, the artist's articulation must be created from the "material" of existing meaning conventions, and his speech acts (in linguistic art) must be "operationally" valid, i.e., must be recognizable by its audience as well-formed (*TKH* 2:30). Art is thus rooted in the life-world of its creator and its audience. But artistic communication does not belong to everyday interaction, particularly in the modern era. In art, subjectivity—in Habermas's term, the "inner world" of artist and audience—frees itself from the everyday conventions of perception and purposeful action in order to relate only to itself. It articulates its needs out of an "unrestricted commerce of the ego with itself," independently of the spatiotemporal conditions of the everyday, i.e., of actual situations (*TKH* 2:140, 584).

We may express this divorce from the everyday by saying that all art has an imaginative dimension, and verbal art a fictive dimension. This results, for Habermas, from a specific "mechanism of deception" which intentionally confuses basic modalities of language—in this case, the distinction between appearance and reality. The artist, through his imaginative craft, generates in the audience a suspension of disbelief in which they take the appearances he presents as being, for the moment, real (*TKH* 1:445/332). This is what Habermas, prior to *The Theory of Communicative Action*, had called a "category mistake" which founds an illusion—the illusion being the audience's suspension of disbelief.[8] It is also what he has referred to, subsequently to the book, as the "neutralization" or the "rendering ineffective" of the illocutionary binding forces of an utterance and the idealizations of communicative action.[9] By this suspension of the truth claim, an artistic utterance—a poem, novel, or play—is freed from its direct relation to the "objective world" and takes up what Habermas there calls a "world-disclosing" role, to which we shall return in connection with Albrecht Wellmer.[10]

In addition to suspended or neutralized truth claims, the work of art can make normative claims as well. This, indeed, is suggested by what was earlier said about the need for the artist to bear in mind the expectations of his public. For these are not merely linguistic in nature: if a work of art deviates too much from social norms for art, for example, it will not be recognizable by the audience as "art" at all. More importantly, the values articulated in a work of art can be candidates for adoption as social norms. When this happens in a particular subculture, so that a group of people tries to live in accordance with values presented aesthetically, we have the "avant-garde."[11] The avant-garde has specific problems in modern society because of the modern differentiation of the validity claims into three wholly separate spheres. It follows from this that the aesthetic sphere, that of subjectivity's "unrestricted commerce with itself," is wholly detached from both cognitive and moral, or practical, reasoning. One of the norms by which the modern world in general decides what is "artistic" and what is not is thus that the work of art is not supposed to make claims to social normativity at all.[12] Habermas's suspicion of attempts to construe political emancipation in aesthetic terms are thus faithful to an important parameter (or, perhaps, condition) of the modern life-world.

Habermas's discussion of the nature of works of art is admittedly incomplete and peripheral to his main concerns; but it does not lack all unity. We can pull together what we have found by saying that politically relevant art is for him a modified type of communicative action. As an expression of needs, any work of art is—like all evaluative utterances—rooted in the expressive speech act: it is an articulation of a subjective experience which claims authenticity as well as sincerity. In addition, any work of art raises the truth claim in what appears to be a suspended form and also, of course, raises indirect truth claims. Even *Finnegans Wake*, for example, presupposes the existence of the English language. Finally, some works of art also make claims to social normativity. This class would include all those which can claim political significance. In the view of *The Theory of Communicative Action,* however, the sincerity claim remains basic to art. Art's ability to raise (or provoke) other types of validity claims will be brought out, not by Habermas, but by Wellmer.

For Habermas, the significance of aesthetic experience is not limited to works of art. Also important is the reflexive medium to which they give rise, that of aesthetic critique. If the utterance constituting a work of art is primarily related to the expressive speech act, the type of interaction which examines and evaluates that utterance approximates to moral-practical discourse. Such discourse can examine whether or not an action conforms to norms currently in force in society, and it can also turn to question whether those norms themselves are justified. Similarly, aesthetic critique seeks to evaluate (a) the way a work of art expresses needs, and (b) those needs themselves. In the former case, this type of critique examines an individual case to see what needs it articulates or what values it exemplifies. The argumentation involved then has the effect of showing us the work in a new way. It guides our perceptions of the work so that its authenticity claim can be clearly seen (*TKH* 1:41/20). In its other form, aesthetic critique takes the work—once its authenticity has been validated—and evaluates the need it articulates. In this, we may say, aesthetic critique takes the work of art not merely as *presenting* values and needs, but as *advocating* them. It claims, in effect, that they should be recognized or adopted by others in the community, that they are "suitable" (*angemessen*) to the values and needs of the life-form of that community (*TKH* 1:42/20).[13]

But for Habermas aesthetic critique is not "discourse," in spite of the fact that it includes the reflective evaluation of utterances. This is because claims raised by works of art are not in Habermas's strict sense validity claims. They do not claim that a given utterance is valid with respect to the three worlds of communicative action, but only that it relates to the particular life-world of the utterer. The needs which a work of art expresses, even if "exemplary," are thus explicitly conditioned by the form of life of those whose needs and values they are. Evaluation of them is not, even counterfactually, considered to be motivated solely by the force of the better argument, but is admitted to be conditioned by the life-world. The community of such inquirers is far from the postulated community of ideal speech, which includes all possible interlocutors (even those belonging to other life-worlds) and requires them, as much as possible, to abstract from their situation within any specific life-world. Because it is not bound to the counterfactual presuppositions of ideal speech, aesthetic critique is not discursive in Habermas's sense (*TKH* 1:70f./41f.).

Such critique is then to be sharply distinguished from the "hermeneutical" explication of meaning, which for Habermas is oriented to questions of validity and hence is discursive (*TKH* 1:188-196/130–136). In this connection, he takes issue with theories which would reduce the "meaning" of an utterance either to the speaker's intention[14] or to its truth claim alone.[15] Rather, to understand an utterance is to understand what would make it acceptable to its hearers. And this requires attention, not merely to what the speaker hoped to achieve with his utterance, or to its truth, but to all three validity claims.[16] For in one sense, an utterance is "acceptable" if its validity claims are acceptable. To understand an utterance is then to understand the ensemble of validity claims it makes; and to understand a validity claim is to know the reasons for it. We can understand the truth claim of an utterance, for example, only by knowing what sorts of reasons could be advanced to sustain it. And to understand those reasons is, furthermore, to understand *why* they are reasons; to see what makes them good reasons for the claim raised. We must, in other words, understand why those reasons would require a hearer to assent to the original claim (*TKH* 1:167/115; 2:28). To understand this, in turn, we must enter into a process of discourse with its utterer. Such dialogue may be merely "virtual": if I am deciphering the meaning of an ancient text, its author is not present to tell me what his reasons are for the assertions he makes, and I must interpret them myself. But the interpretation must proceed from concepts of what a good reason must be; if the utterer's reasons are no longer good ones, my understanding of the utterance will be an explanation of why they are no longer good. In no case, then, can I understand an utterance without taking a position on its validity claims.[17]

So conceived, an understanding of the meaning of an utterance is related to Habermas's own technical sense of "understanding." In it I do not actually reach accord with the utterer on the utterance's validity, but I specify what such an accord would, in my view, have to consist in. The claim that an utterance is intelligible is then nothing more than the claim that it makes defensible validity claims, and the "meaning" of an utterance thus can be evaluated only by examining the validity claims it raises.

Such examination is obviously different from aesthetic critique. But Habermas has as well another sense of "meaning," which relates it not to grounds, but to rules. In contrast to the "full" meaning of "understanding" I have just described, there is also for Habermas a minimal sense, in which two hearers "understand" a linguistic expression if they both understand it the same way (*TKH* 1:157f., 412/106, 309). The circularity in this formulation can be removed by saying that such understanding concerns linguistic rules, rather than validity claims. Rules for Habermas formulate in general terms how something is produced, and they are general in two senses. First, to be a rule, something must apply to more than one case of production. Second, it must be valid for more than one person. Otherwise, as Wittgenstein argued, there would be no difference between following a rule and believing oneself to have followed a rule. That one may wrongly believe oneself to have followed a rule means, in other words, that to "follow a rule" is to perform an activity that by definition can be evaluated by others, and which is thus open, like an utterance in communicative action, to acceptance or rejection from them (*TKH* 2:31–39). Linguistic rules are thus not for Habermas merely private or subjective, but they are themselves parts of the life-world. The clarification of the operative rules by which a given utterance was produced—the clarification, in this second sense, of its "meaning"—is a clarification of structures of the life-world. As such, it approximates aesthetic critique.

Habermas leaves his account of linguistic rules undeveloped in two important respects. In the first place, he does not make clear what he considers the scope of linguistic rules to be. Do all the manifold regularities that can be perceived in our use of language come under the heading of "rules?" If not, which?

Surface syntax would clearly constitute a set of linguistic rules, and Habermas seems to have it in mind. Hence, if I usually form singular verbs by adding "s" to the root form, I am following a "rule" of English: I am producing utterances by procedures that cover a number of utterances and are valid for others as well as myself. Depth-grammar, in Noam Chomsky's sense,[18] would also, presumably, be included. And, Habermas says, someone who says, "I promise you that I was in Hamburg yesterday," unless he means "promise" in the unusual sense of "assure," has violated the grammar of English (*TKH* 1:401 n.43/441 n.43).

This final example pushes the concept of "grammatical rule" toward the lexical: the "grammar" of a word includes its operational meaning, the set of conjunctions the language allows it to have with other words. And here, matters become obscure. Is it a rule of the English *language* that certain animals in the field are "sheep," and that the same animals on the table are "mutton?" This regularity in English dates from the Norman conquest, after which the original Anglo-Saxon inhabitants of England found themselves in the fields tending sheep, while the French conquerers were at table eating them. One who violates it has perhaps said something ill-bred. But has he said something ill-formed?

Together with this vagueness on the scope of linguistic rules goes vagueness on the status of such rules and of the type of interaction which explicates them. Others can take up a "yes or no" attitude toward the grammaticality of an utterance and can examine that grammaticality rationally, in what Habermas calls "explicative discourse." Like other varieties of discourse, this comes under the counterfactual presupposition of ideal speech. This suggests, in turn, that Habermas views grammatical rules as akin to objective facts or social norms: a suggestion supported when he says, for example, that in order for an utterance to be rule-governed, the utterer must know, not merely how others *will* respond to it, but how they *must* respond.[19]

But this view would contradict some of Habermas's other statements. For one thing, Habermas is fully aware (in his discussion of rules at *TKH* 2:31–39) that linguistic rules are conventional, holding only for a specific language. As we have seen, language is the basic organizing principle of a life-world; indeed, to learn a language is for Habermas to participate in a life-world (*TKH* 1:165,181f./112, 125). It would seem from this that linguistic rules should rather be assimilated to the values and forms of life which hold within a life-world: the kinds of things that get expressed in works of art. But *The Theory of Communicative Action* does not pursue the topic.

One crucial step in the pursuit is taken in Albrecht Wellmer's account of the emancipatory potential of aesthetic experience from a communicative point of view, which, as I have noted, Habermas has endorsed. Wellmer accepts two of Habermas's points against the earlier Frankfurt writers:

(1) The present historical situation is not wholly negative, but contains some demonstrably positive aspects. This means that art is not restricted to the mere promise of future happiness, but points to a reality which is in latent operation in history (*WSV* 158);

(2) This in turn can be understood only if we take, as Habermas does, a communications-theoretical perspective on both the contemporary situation and the nature of art (*WSV* 152, 157f.).

Wellmer's suggestion is the following: Habermas is wrong to allocate art primarily to the category of expressive speech as an artist's articulation of needs. In fact, in a work of art the artist himself does not literally "say" anything. We should look rather to the discussion a work of art provokes in its audience, and if we do we find that it draws on the entire life-experience of those spectators. This means that assertions arise in such discussion that make all three validity claims (*WSV* 155, 159, 164f., 172). Art thus puts its spectators into unconstrained communication with one another and—true to Habermas's basic concept of freedom in terms of understanding—this is itself emancipatory. Adorno, Wellmer notes, had analyzed the "bourgeois subject" as inherently unfree because its unity was bought at the price of suppression and exclusion of some of its elements (the Kantian banishment of "inclinations" to the status of mere chains of natural causality here comes to mind). This exclusionary self can only be sustained by inner violence to the multiplicity of human desires and needs. It is itself imaged in the idealizing and organizing aspects of the traditional work of art, which excludes the imperfect and, via its composition, forcefully organizes the rest (*WSV* 148f., 156f.).

The open, or noncentered, and nonidealizing character of modern art—its new form of "synthesis"—therefore points to a new type of ego, one which can accommodate much more diffuse and heterogenous contents because it is itself organized, not by the dominance of one of its own internal constituents, but interactively, in a "communicatively fluent self-identity" (*WSV* 156f). The work of art relates functionally to these phenomena. Emancipation is not, as Adorno thought, something the work presents—a message that it conveys or part of its "meaning"—but the interaction it provokes among its spectators (*WSV* 145, 157f., 160). It provokes this because of its claim to "lay bare" the truth; for the claim of a work of art to exemplarity is its claim to express in an articulated and concentrated way diffuse and inarticulate strands of everyday experience. This claim can be intelligently evaluated only on the basis of the spectators' previous acquaintance with that experience (*WSV* 162f., 172). Such evaluation requires them to raise together all three validity claims: they must compare the work of art with the objective states of affairs with which they must deal, with their own mental contents, and with the norms of their own society. When the work of art does enable them to clarify those structures to one another, it possesses "aesthetic truth." Discussing it calls upon all facets of the egos of the spectators and puts them into "unrestricted interaction."

Such interaction is not to be confused with Habermas's own account of unrestricted interaction—ideal speech; for in aesthetic interaction as Wellmer conceives it, much more is achieved than simply the rational evaluation of validity claims. The experiences to which the interlocutors refer, and which they interpret in terms of the work, include their experiences of their life-world, of the values and needs which are shared among them as participants in a common form of life, and of that form of life itself. Hence, aesthetic interaction, unlike discourse, does not bracket the life-world, but articulates it.

In sum, a work of art is, in Wellmer's view, something which claims to reveal the truth of the contemporary life-world, including truths about the three-world categorical schema in terms of which members of the modern life-world pursue understanding. As such, it is dissociated from the dispersed, factual conditions under which inhabitants of the life-world pursue their activities—including the communicative activities of telling the truth, conforming to social norms, and revealing their subjective experiences. But it is not wholly closed off from those activities. Rather, it claims to reveal them in concentrated, "truer" form. In this, it provokes unrestricted communication among those who perceive it. Such communication itself, apart from any relevance to narrowly "political" matters, is emancipatory.

Narrative

The account of evaluative judgment in *The Theory of Communicative Action* clearly approximates closely the main features of the Kantian judgment of taste:

(1) It makes use of unclear predicates; the judgment of taste uses a predicate ("beautiful") which, as we have seen, is wholly vague.

(2) The contents it articulates are clearly subjective; in Habermas's case, needs, not pleasure.

(3) It imputes the agreement of others; it claims that others will come to share the needs it expresses, i.e., will recognize them as needs they themselves feel.

(4) As presupposing needs and the situations in which those needs are felt, it presumes that others experience those things in the same way as the speaker of the evaluative judgment, i.e., presupposes a sort of common sense.

(5) As proposing possible social norms, it approximates to the political use of Kantian reflective judgment—not as institutionalized by the state, however, but as resident within the life-world, which the state opposes but cannot wholly eradicate.

And as an extraordinary form of interaction, evaluative judgment may—though it is Wellmer who says so—stand outside such conditions as the need for particular actions. In Kantian terms, it is "disinterested"; in Hegelian terms, it reposes upon an extraneous externalization which simply leaves behind the confusion and contingency of reality; in Heidegger's terms it is, like his discussion with Tezuka, outside the normal context of world.

But Kant, in the third *Critique*, viewed aesthetic experience as in close connection with empirical concept-formation in general: beginning without concepts and sometimes providing them, reflective judgment was the vehicle for both. Hegel, we saw, followed Kant in this: the original building up of a language, the furnishing of its words, was accomplished by its poets. For Heidegger, too, the granting of new words was "poetic," in the sense of a sublime transport out of one's present world. For *The Theory of Communicative Action*, however, aesthetic experience and vocabulary formation are dispersed among divergent types of interaction.

This is first due to the book's restriction of evaluative judgments to the expression of "needs," which means that such judgment is too narrow to provide the broad foundation for language that we saw it to have in the earlier thinkers. This restriction is, I suggest, an attempt to root evaluative judgments in one of the three validity claims that the concept of communicative action prescribes to all interaction oriented to reaching understanding.

The second factor inhibiting *The Theory of Communicative Action* from developing a unified account of reflective judgment is its primary account of "meaning" as the ensemble of validity claims a particular utterance makes, and hence as decided in discourse. Though not the only account in the book, this is the one Habermas pursues most vigorously, and it too is obviously prescribed by the need to see all language use as exhibiting the structures of communicative action. Habermas's pursuit of this account has the effect of leaving his other characterization of meaning—linguistic rules—undeveloped and apparently unrelated to the lifeworld. This in turn leads him to miss the "world-disclosing" function of such rules and of evaluative judgment, and to occlude the similarities between aesthetic critique and the articulation of word meanings in terms of the life-world. And it leads him to miss as well the role of reflective judgment, and the second foundation in general, in the formulation of the theory of communicative action itself.

Decision on the validity claims raised by an utterance is reached for Habermas, as we saw, against an inexplicit horizon of background information: the first foundation reposes on the second; and the second includes information about the meanings of the terms contained in the utterance. Such "lexical background knowledge," as I will call it, is not provided by the grammar of a language (if "grammatical" rules for a given language are supposed to apply alike to all utterances in that language), for it is specific to the individual term in question. It can be assimilated to the account of grammatical well-formedness in *The Theory of Communicative Action* only if we take that phrase to refer to the specific grammar of individual terms. It is in providing lexical background knowledge—indeed, in providing the lexicon itself—that aesthetic experience and vocabulary formation meet.

The concept of lexical knowledge as knowledge of a life-world was articulated first in my narrative by Plato, who held that words convey, among other things, a cultural consensus: what the Athenians had agreed to call "free," *Republic* 8 argued, had little to do with what "freedom" really was. Aristotle denied this general claim, viewing words not as components of a life-world but as mirroring natural realities. But it was revived with Hegel's thesis that language is a product of social labor (and of the deformations of externalization). It was restated again in Heidegger's account of words as "accruing" to the significances articulated in a particular world.

If we take an Hegelian view, lexical background knowledge is the content of Spirit, i.e., the historical sediments of a quest for self-consolidation, articulateness, and cooperation. From the Heideggerean standpoint I analyzed, it reveals the gathering points of natural phenomena: the places at which the hidden parameters of earth emerge into the linguistic specificity of a name. Both interpretations can be covered by viewing lexical background knowledge as conveying parameters of a life-world which itself is dependent upon nature: the "inner nature" of the human mind as historically developed, and the "outer nature" of spatiotemporal states of affairs. These domains are then to be viewed, not as objective correlates of assertions, but as sets of parameters of human action and dwelling. The lexical structures of the life-world are themselves to be understood and evaluated as conditioned by these, and to share their parametric status.

The work of art, in Wellmer's view, exhibits such parameters, holding for a given time and place, in an exemplary way. The work of art is thus not true in virtue of any correspondence between the assertions it contains and the states of affairs in the world; it is, as with Aristotle, true in that it represents certain basic structures of life (or action), and thus brings about "learning" in its audience. With his functional account of aesthetic freedom, Wellmer expands the account of evaluative judgment in *The Theory of Communicative Action* into an account of emancipatory aesthetic interaction and takes a decisive move away from the aesthetic fixation on the art object and toward a truly interactionist picture of aesthetic experience: a picture which Hegel, in the *Aesthetics*, and Heidegger, in "The Origin of the Work of Art," began to articulate.

In sum, the work of Habermas and Wellmer shows us reason, once again, becoming situated. Habermas's formal pragmatic account of communicative action and discourse, abstracting from the concrete situations and parameters introduced by the life-world (whose role it intentionally ignores), is an account of reason in an unsituated form—a form corresponding to Heidegger's account of inauthentic discourse, to Hegel's externalized speech, to Kant's Kingdom of Ends, and to Plato's myths about the soul among the Forms. As with all of those thinkers, reason for Habermas becomes situated through the necessity for action. For even a simple utterance is an action and occurs amid circumstances which do not hold always and everywhere, some of which will be changed by the utterance itself. Hence, the importance of introducing the role of background information into formal pragmatics.

This opens a space for construing such background information *as* parametric, and hence for seeing reason as, not merely situated, but situating as well. But because of the limitations in its account of evaluative judgment, *The Theory of Communicative Action* adds little to the theoretical recuperation of situating reason begun, in my narrative, by Kant and carried forward by Hegel and Heidegger. From the present perspective, its accomplishment is rather that it finds a locus for situating reason, in particular for poetic interaction, which is outside the realm of the state and which therefore cannot be impeached by claims of the state, as a quasi-substance, to provide the field of all human interaction. This locus, which corresponds to Kant's philosophical faculty and to the banks of Plato's Ilyssos, is the life-world itself. Unlike Plato's nature and Kant's university, the life-world is neither a domain of mysterious, semidivine forces, nor a fantasied institution reposing on "dark ground." It is a domain of interaction which can be studied and whose structures can, at least in part, be exposed.

This means that the relation of aesthetic experience to the political sphere is open to investigation, as it was not for Hegel and Heidegger. This openness is not without consequences for our understanding of aesthetic experience itself. Witness for this is Wellmer's reformulation of Habermas's views on the liberating powers of art, which—looking at aesthetic experience in the full range of its emancipatory capacities—is able to amend Habermas's restriction of it to the articulation and evaluation of needs.

Demarcation

The conceptual basis for the full recuperation of poetic interaction (and ultimately, perhaps, of situating reason itself) is now largely at hand; we have only to demarcate space for that recuperation from the texts of Habermas and Wellmer. We can begin by asking this: Although Wellmer's account of aesthetic truth has freed art from *The Theory of Communicative Action*'s narrow view of aesthetic interaction as only being concerned with the expression of needs, does it suffice for a complete account of aesthetic emancipation? My assimilation of it to Aristotle's conception of "learning" suggests that it does not. For learning is not, for Aristotle, the only way a work of art can have effects on its audience: there is also catharsis, the emancipation of the audience from fear and pity. And this comes when the audience realizes that the play does *not*, in fact, apply directly to their own life-situations: indeed, the less the play has to do with those situations, the more the audience feels relieved. On this level, the play thus does not teach them about themselves but about general and rational structures of action and consequence, which may or may not apply, to varying degrees, to their own lives. It teaches them, as Aristotle says, about possibilities.

Is it not, indeed, through its *difference* from the concrete life-situations of its audience that the work of art can become, as it was for Hegel and Heidegger, an articulation of language itself—of lexical background knowledge? This point was made, in my narrative, by the *Phaedrus*'s reflection on the second of its speeches: for it was there made plain that, in order to examine word meanings, we must first be freed from the need to *use* the words whose meanings we are examining as well as from the concrete situations in which the words are used to state and argue for propositions. Is it then an accident that Hegel and Heidegger, in the course of elaborating their views of aesthetic experience in connection with the articulation of language itself, view it as operating, like Aristotelian catharsis, out of a discrepancy between art and the life-situations of the audience? For Heidegger, aesthetic experience is the confrontation with radically new significance that "transports" us from our world; for Hegel, it reveals that the true nature of Spirit has nothing to do with the current life-situations of individuals in the modern state, and hence yields a radical critique of those life-situations. Is it not then by virtue of its detachment from the structures of everyday life that aesthetic experience can move to the level of language itself?

We can clarify this further with reference to Aristotle. We saw that for him it is characteristic of tragic speech to contain words used in strange ways; correct critical procedure is to map out the possibilities, even the unusual ones, and then to decide charitably in favor of the playwright's usage. This procedure, we may say, is similar to the learning the audience undertakes in recognizing the general structures of action presented in the plot. But learning about words teaches little about the rational structures of action: a single word, or utterance, is abstract, where a work of art is a concrete whole. The mere word, then, cannot clarify to its hearers what their current situation is; it clarifies, at best, certain basic "ingredients" which can be components of many different situations. As long as we are experiencing a work of art with a view to clarifying something as complex as our own life-situation, then, we will be indifferent to what it has to teach us about language itself.

It is, we may say, due to its concreteness that, for Wellmer, the work of art can articulate the many diverse aspects that constitute a current life-world situation: without such concreteness, there will be no "aesthetic truth." It follows that an account keyed exclusively to the concept of aesthetic truth cannot articulate the connections between the concrete illumination of life-situations and the relatively abstract clarification of word meanings. Thus, Wellmer's concept of aesthetic truth, though one crucial step beyond *The Theory of Communicative Action,* prevents him from taking the next step: the one that we found in "From a Dialogue on Language," of viewing "poetic" quality as attributable, not solely or even primarily to works of art, but to ways of using language and forms of interaction themselves. Hence, Wellmer's account of aesthetic interaction, while valid as far as it goes, does not provide the only way to go beyond *The Theory of Communicative Action.* Also possible is interaction which reflects critically on a work of art, or more abstractly on an individual utterance, in ways which clarify, not the current situation of the audience, but general characteristics of their life-world and the "semantic capacities" of words in their language.

The gaps I have noted between Habermas and Wellmer, and between both and my previous narrative, are not simply mistakes or omissions; nor are they, as such, the effects of a Derridean play of "differance."[20] They cohere with each other in the following way:

(1) Blurts and ambiguities seem to be different in character from utterances which, directly or indirectly, raise proper validity claims. Do they not then require a form of interaction in which the aim is to agree, not on whether the validity claims of an utterance are valid, but on what those claims are in the first place?

(2) The view that the life-world is to be wholly comprehended, for purposes of social theory, in terms of the structures of communicative action alone seems to be a residue of Aristotelian substance metaphysics. Might not the life-world, as the linguistically structured repository of background knowledge, contain diverse forms of interaction, among which would be the type referred to in (1) above?

(3) The examination of the meanings of words, considered as the explication of the lexical background knowledge reposing in the life-world, is an abstract and simple form of what the philosophical tradition has referred to as "aesthetic experience." Might it not share the emancipatory effects of such experience?

Works of art, especially poems, and the interactive experiences with them and incited by them would on this view remain an unusually reflective, complex, and instructive paradigm for a larger class of interactions that we can call "poetic." But they are no longer definitive of, or even necessary for, such interaction.

Let us consider an example of what it could mean to extend aesthetic interaction beyond works of art in this way. In one well-known family of senses of the word "meaning," deriving in my narrative from Aristotle, it is possible to assimilate the meaning of a word to the traditional concept of truth. Let us take it, for example, that the word "water" refers to all and everything compounded of two atoms of hydrogen and one of oxygen: H_2O. On this sort of view, we can understand the meaning of "water" by examining the conditions for the term to be used in uttering true sentences. Among these will be a condition stating that something can be called "water" if and only if it has the chemical formula H_2O: "water" then means something with that chemical formula. [21]

But let us consider how "water" might form a structural part of a life-world. It would do so in virtue of how it organizes various components of the background knowledge shared by members of that life-world. Let us assume that, in some life-world, it is commonly agreed that water, among other things, is cold, that one can swim in it, drink it, bathe oneself with it, and baptize babies with it. These various properties and activities are linked with each other in that the term "water" is associated with each. Establishing these connections is, following Heidegger, (part of) the meaning of "water" in structuring the life-world in question.

These further predicates are not true of water the way "H_2O" is. Water is not always cold, and it is not always true that human beings can drink it, swim in it, or bathe with it—there are or have been cultures where they do none of these things. And the fact that some humans baptize others with water is a matter of cultural symbolism which in fact tells us very little about water (people have been baptized with sand). These assertions in general inform us, then, not about water itself, but about the *relation* of water to a certain group of human beings. And so understood, they can tell us a great deal about those human beings: about how they respond to certain natural phenomena, and about the parameters those phenomena offer to them.

The exploration of such life-world relationships, then, does not deal with a simple case of word-to-world correspondence; it explores cultural and natural totalities. To *ask* after the meaning of "water" in this background-informational sense is to ask about which other components of the given life-world that word is connected with. To *answer* such a question is to show the term to illuminate larger sections of the life-world, rather than to show how members of that life-world use it to organize their interactions with the objective world. It is to treat the word the same way the audience of a work of art, in Aristotle's sense, treats that work: to clarify rational possibilities of speech, though not necessarily possibilities relevant to one's current situation.

This sort of asking and answering has been treated often in the tradition I have narrated. Platonic dialogue employed it to uncover what was supposed to be (but cannot have been) the eternal realm of Forms. For Kant, it was the interactive use of reflective judgment as the vehicle of empirical concept-formation, especially—but impossibly—in the philosophical faculty. Hegel treated it as the reconciling articulation of the nature of Spirit presented in works of art. And Heidegger viewed it as the aesthetic interaction between worlds, which illuminated one's own world by contrast. Insofar as it articulates the lexical structures of a particular life-world which, as located in a *particular* life-world, could be other than they are, such interaction would be an articulation of what I have called "parameters." It would be the situating of reason in that life-world.

Habermas's dialogical account of the life-world provides, for the first time, a way to anchor such discussion: to clarify its role with respect to the state in ways unavailable to Plato, Kant, Hegel, and Heidegger. But the affinities of such situating reason for Habermas's account of evaluative judgment are obscured by the central position within the Habermasian life-world of processes of communicative action. While not denying that such processes take place, or that they have the emancipatory and critical significance Habermas attaches to them, we find that a place has been opened for another form of interaction. This form—on its elementary level, poetic interaction—is then to be seen as located within the Habermasian life-world. It takes as its material ambiguous, vague, and otherwise "strange" utterances, and seeks to understand them by looking to the life-world structuring properties of the words they contain. Such interaction, as I will argue in the following chapters, has emancipatory and critical potential of its own.

Twenty-two

Structures of Poetic Interaction

Analysis

The preceding historical analyses have shown, I hope, that the topic of intrinsically emancipatory interaction is no stranger to philosophy, and that keeping it in mind can be of service in illuminating texts which are otherwise recalcitrant to interpretation. In particular, we have seen that Plato, Kant, Hegel, and Heidegger all discussed interaction that is not only intrinsically emancipatory but which begins (in my sense) poetically, i.e., from utterances or other phenomena that cannot be univocally understood. Such interaction aimed in each case at supplying a meaning by clarifying parameters as parameters, and hence was (also in my sense) situating as well as emancipatory. My narrative has told how such interaction was occluded successively by metaphysics; then by its heir, transcendental critique; and finally by the modern way of distinguishing aesthetics and politics. And the demarcation suggests that, with the work of Habermas and Wellmer, these occlusions can be brought to an end.

The concluding two chapters of this book will trace intrinsically emancipatory interaction to its elementary form in ordinary language: poetic interaction. This is necessary for at least three reasons: to sum up the results of the previous investigations in the simplest possible way; to show that those accounts of intrinsically emancipatory interaction, for all their contentious complexity, are rooted if not grounded in the everyday; and to lay the basis for a fuller account of situating reason. In this chapter I will lay out the basic structures of poetic interaction; the following narrative will argue that those structures capture the kinds of interaction we have seen discussed by earlier philosophers. In the demarcation I will show how the theory of communicative action does not capture those accounts, arguing that the life-world as Habermas conceives it must be reconceptualized to allow space for poetic interaction. In the final chapter I will investigate claims that, in virtue of those structures, poetic interaction is both emancipatory and a source of norms for social critique.

The first requirement for articulating the structures of poetic interaction is a vocabulary in which to do so. I will begin, then, by stipulating definitions for some terms that can be used for the task. These stipulations, like many of Habermas's, are offered as makeshifts which can illuminate a limited set of phenomena for a particular purpose, not as a set of definite and final—still less proven—theses about language. The first of them is "expression."

An "expression" will be a sensible entity comprising both "conventional" and "nonconventional" components, and sometimes "unconventional" ones as well. By a "conventional" component of an expression, I mean any of its sensed features which is dependent for its existence on the expectations of others.[1] A "nonconventional" component is one for which the expectations of the hearers are not a necessary condition of its existence. The grammar of a language, then, is conventional: there would, for example, be no subjects and predicates if there were not people who expected them in speech. The mere sound of a word is nonconventional, for the human vocal apparatus could produce it even if that speaker were, like Adam naming all things, the only human being extant. But the presence of that sound in a particular utterance may, again, be conventional.

This distinction is fairly rough-and-ready, and illustration may be more helpful than precise formulation. Suppose, first, that I am all alone, am hammering, and hit my thumb. I may hop around, alternately sucking my thumb and waving it aloft, and my face may grow red. Since no others are present, we can presume that my behavior does not depend upon their expectations.[2] Though certainly in the ordinary sense expressive (of pain), such behavior does not constitute an "expression" in the sense I wish to take that term here. If I hit my thumb when others are present, some of my subsequent behavior is modified, but some is not. My face may grow red, but instead of sucking my thumb (which might be regarded as childish) I may say "ouch" or "damn it." My behavior here does contain components dependent for their existence on the expectations of others, and thus constitutes an expression. But it also contains components which do not so depend. These nonconventional components are any aspects of the second of these two examples which would also have been present in the first. An "unconventional component" of an expression, finally, is one which is present in it because the hearers do not expect it: the final word in André Breton's "the world is blue, like an orange," is an example of this. Unconventional components presuppose the conventions they contravene, and I will treat them as modifications of conventional speech.

An expression is then a sensory entity some of whose qualities are conventional, i.e., can be explained only by referring to the expectations

of a group of people. Conventions may be consciously induced and restricted in their validity to a specific text or investigation (my current
stipulations are intended to set up expectations of this type). They may
be culture-wide, such as the conventions by which Liverpudlians watch
soccer games. They may even, presumably, be species-wide.

An expression whose conventions are linguistic, i.e., a set of culture-
wide expectations concerning speaking and writing, will be an "utterance," and several types of linguistic conventions will be important to
us. The first distinction I want to make is between the grammar of a
language and that of a word. In order to understand an utterance, the
hearer must be in possession of the conventions by which all sentences in
that language are to be constructed, and this constitutes the "grammar"
of that language. But the hearer must also have knowledge of the meanings of the individual terms it contains. I will distinguish between the
rules which hold alike for all sentences of a language and those which
hold only for sentences containing a particular word of that language by
calling our knowledge of the latter "lexical."

Lexical knowledge of a term, as I want to understand it, extends beyond the set of truth conditions for sentences containing that term. We
cannot understand the phrase "the sun is rising" without knowing, as
Tarski's convention T has it, that it is true if and only if the sun is rising.[3]
But there is also a sense in which we cannot understand the sentence as it
would be uttered by a Greek (*ho helios anatellei*) without understanding,
for example, that *hêlios* for him designated a god whose status as such
was a matter of ambivalence and debate, partly for political reasons: by
the Hellenistic period, a Greek who uttered the sentence with a sufficient
degree of reverence could be construed to identify himself as a Roman
sympathizer.[4] But it is not the case that "the sun is rising" is true if
and only if I am (or am not) a Roman sympathizer. In this extended
sense, lexical knowledge can be viewed as the information accessed by a
particular term for competent speakers of the language. It amounts
to knowledge, not of the objective world, but of the specific culture
in which the term is used—to knowledge, as Habermas says, of its
"life-world."

In addition to utterances, I will talk of "responses." By this, I mean
an utterance for whose existence a determinate set of previous utterances is a necessary condition. All utterances, of course, have as a necessary condition for their existence an indeterminate set of previous
utterances—those by means of which the speaker learned the language
of the utterance. It may be that all utterances also have as necessary conditions for their existence determinate, but normally disregarded, sets of
utterances: that, for example, as Heidegger claims, all human utterances

are to some degree "responses" to the call of Being. If such is the case, the distinction between "utterance" and "response" will ultimately have to be retracted. But I will disregard this possibility here, using "response" to denote an utterance whose production is clearly occasioned by a determinate set of previous utterances.

We can simplify matters in what follows by speaking, not of "interaction," but of "interchange," which I take to be its minimal unit: an utterance plus a response. That we rarely engage in such minimal interaction—and that, almost by definition, it is uninteresting—is doubtless true. But, I will argue, interchanges do exhibit key features shared by the more complex types of interaction we actually experience and value. Instances of those types I will refer to as "encounters." In an interchange, as I have defined it, there are two types of utterances: one which elicits a response, and the response itself. Not all utterances provoke responses. Those which do—which form parts of interchanges—I will call "elicitors." The process by which an utterance provokes a response I will call "elicitation."

What distinguishes poetic interaction from other types is the way the response is elicited. My analysis thus focuses on the response and its elicitation, not on the eliciting utterance itself. But some responses themselves may elicit further responses and extend a basic interchange into an encounter. I will call these "eliciting responses." Those which do not, I will call "terminating responses." With respect to poetic interaction, it will be necessary to distinguish "terminating" an encounter from "breaking it off." We will say that to "terminate" a poetic encounter is to convert it into some other sort of encounter, such as communicative action; to break it off is to end the encounter altogether, e.g., by walking away.

With this as background, we can now discuss distinctive features of poetic interaction. The most important of these concerns the type of elicitation it contains, and this can be approached by contrasting it with the account of speech acts in J. L. Austin's *How to Do Things with Words*. Austin makes it a necessary condition of a successful speech act that there exist a "certain conventional procedure having a certain conventional effect, the procedure to include the uttering of certain words by a certain person in certain circumstances."[5] When a form of words prescribed by such a conventional procedure is uttered in appropriate circumstances, and the audience accepts that procedure, then the utterance produces its desired effect: "uptake" is achieved on the part of the audience.[6]

The Austinian account is clearly accurate as far as it goes. But not all interchanges, I suggest, come under it. For there are two obvious possible alternatives to the sort of situation it covers: there may be more than one conventional procedure which prescribes those words in this sort of situation, or there may be fewer, i.e., none. In the former case, we have an equivocation. It impedes the achievement of what Austin calls the "rhetic" act, which is the uttering of certain syllables with a definite meaning in mind, and Austin tends to dismiss such utterances as "primitive" or vague.[7] The latter case might be analogous to Austin's example of the man who first picked up a rugby ball and ran with it: but it is hard to tell because Austin does not discuss that example (except to indicate that it is "essential").[8] These two cases give us the two main sorts of poetic interaction, which is interaction that takes place in the absence of a single set of conventions and for which such a set must (usually) be supplied. I will begin my discussion of its main structures with some examples of the former sort.

(1a) Consider a modification of Sartre's famous treatment, in *Being and Nothing,* of the couple in the café.[9] Suppose Jack and Julie are having a business lunch, and Julie has just outlined her plan for a daring and resourceful *coup d'affaires.* Turning to her, gazing deep into her eyes, Jack says, "I think you're the most fantastic person in this firm."

This (admittedly sleazy) utterance instills, we may presume, sudden confusion about what set of conventions govern the interchange: those of friendly collaboration, of entrepreneurial inquiry, of flirtation, or perhaps of some other sort altogether. The question of whether the utterance secures its "uptake" or not cannot be resolved until the situation is further defined.

(1b) Let us now add the further hypothesis that Jack *does not know what he meant* by this utterance: that he just blurted it out, does not know what his feelings are, and therefore does not know what he is doing with his statement.

The situation, in his mind as well as in his hearer's, now has no "definition." In fact, it is up to the hearer to define it. Julie's task now is not to come to an agreement with Jack about what is in fact happening, but to make something happen—to decide what sort of context the utterance belongs in, what sorts of conventional procedure it should be viewed as instancing.

(2) At the end of *Ulysses,* Molly Bloom utters the words, "yes I will yes."

This can be construed in a variety of ways, depending, for example, on whether the reader takes Molly's final soliloquy to represent the musings of a faithless housewife or the primordial night-language of mother earth. In fact, *Ulysses* itself prescribes neither view. Such construal is up to the reader.[10]

(3) Another actual example, from politics: confronting France's inef-

fectual and vicious war to maintain control of Algeria, Charles de Gaulle went to Algeria and spoke to members of the French establishment there. They argued for continuation of the war, citing such factors as the glory and mission of France and, more to the point, their own personal interest in French domination. His response was, "Je vous ai compris," which the Franco-Algerians took to mean (a) "I have understood your position and am in sympathy with it." When de Gaulle returned to Paris, it became evident that what he actually had meant must have been (b) that he had "understood" their position to be that of members of an unjust and doomed elite. Once safely away from Algeria, he arranged for French withdrawal, resulting in Algerian independence and the loss of privileges for the French establishment.

(4) A scholar foraging through hitherto-undiscovered papers of Benjamin Franklin discovers a scrap of paper with the sole words, "The United States is a nation of shopkeepers."

This statement is metaphorical (a synecdoche) and can be understood in a variety of ways. It can, for example, be taken to mean that the United States is a nation of hard-headed, down-to-earth working people, in which case it is a compliment. It can also be understood to mean that the country is a land of limited, uncultured folk concerned only with their own survival and economic prosperity, in which case it is an insult.[11] Ben Franklin was a complex enough character that we cannot know which he meant. For unscholarly but understandable reasons of his own, the finder of the remark decides to take Old Ben as complimenting Americans.

These examples, for all their diversity (and still more diverse ones could easily be supplied) share a common characteristic: for one reason or another, the utterances in them leave it up to the hearer to decide how they are to be understood. So, of course, do many other vague, ambiguous, and idiosyncratic utterances. My thesis is that in such cases we must distinguish "infelicitous" utterances, which ought to convey a univocal meaning but fail to do so, from utterances which do not even make the attempt. An utterance may be infelicitous because it is ambiguous or otherwise ill-put, because the situation is unusual, because the speaker does not understand the circumstances, because the hearer mishears or perhaps willfully twists it, or for manifold other reasons. But in all such cases, a single meaning for the utterance—whether the one the author originally intended or not—eventually imposes itself and can be argued for.[12] Much—perhaps all—of language is of this type, in which the appropriate response is elicited by some sort of interpretive disambiguation. But there are also, I suggest, cases in which no single meaning or interpretation imposes itself, either because more than one does or (as we will see later) none can. In the present cases, the response must be elicited, not by disambiguation, but eventually by decision. We do not work through the utterance and its circumstances in order to find out what it means (or even what it probably means). We work through the various possibilities and then, since none imposes itself, select one as the meaning for the utterance.

The above examples can, I suggest, all be construed as cases of this type. This is clearest for (2), for we may take it that James Joyce, as one of the English language's great writers, intended precisely whatever ambiguity his words contain: he intended, in other words, to hand that sentence over to his readers, for them to understand as they would. In (3), it *could* be argued that de Gaulle really meant his utterance in sense (b) and was simply giving a false impression with his ambiguity. But it could equally well be the case that, at the time of his meeting with the Franco-Algerians, he did not know what his final opinion of their arguments would be and merely sought to buy time with some innocuous words. The same holds for (4): we do not know for sure how highly Ben Franklin valued shopkeepers in general, and neither, perhaps, did he.

Most interesting, I think, is (1). Austin has two main ways of handling it. It could be, first, that Jack's utterance is a mere misfire: that it simply fails to convey his meaning, does not secure the uptake he desires, and is therefore defective. This account presupposes that the language of the utterance—English—has the resources to make clear what Jack is doing, and that the man failed to make use of them.[13] But this applies much more perspicuously to (1a) than to (1b), for it is not so easy to label the utterance a "misfire" if Jack had no intentions in making it which he could fail to fulfill. To apply Austin's account, in fact, we must often invent purposes for speakers: if we do not know what de Gaulle meant by his utterance, we suppose that he "must have meant" it in sense (b). And indeed, *if he had to mean something definite by it*, later events proved that it must have been (b). Similarly, then, for the man in (1): we must suppose some vague yearning and attribute it to the speaker as what he was trying to convey—much as physicists trying not to accept the quantum theory "invented" causes for proton decay and attributed them to atoms. But protons do decay without cause: and, I suggest, people do speak without intending anything by their utterances. English has a perfectly good word to express such unintended speech: "blurting."

It is also possible that the speaker had some very definite intention, but circumstances are such that it is not able to impose itself. Franklin, in (3) above, may have meant something very definite by his utterance, but his intention is now unknowable and useless for interpretation. The point is that no single other interpretation can impose itself either. In general, whether or not the ambiguity of the elicitor is intended by the speaker or arises from other causes will not matter to my account here, which will remain focused on the production of the response, not of the elicitor.

Austin's second way of handling unclear speech acts is a value judgment (and a historicist one at that). It is possible to speak a language which has the resources to make clear what one is doing, and yet not to make it clear. In such cases, Austin writes, one's utterance

> preserves the "ambiguity" or "equivocation" or "vagueness" of primitive language. . . . This may have its uses; but sophistication and development of social forms and procedures will necessitate clarification.[14]

It is not just likely, Austin thinks, that language is evolving toward ever greater explication of speech acts, but it is "sophisticated," "developed," and therefore presumably good. This claim preserves Austin's model of a one-to-one correspondence between speech acts and conventional procedures by maintaining that the model has normative significance. Cases in which speakers do not make use of the resources their languages have developed to state explicitly what they are doing then do exist, but such cases are unsophisticated, undeveloped, and probably destined to disappear.

This is all extremely doubtful. Such highly sophisticated languages as Chinese, French, and Japanese, all older than English, are famed for being highly allusive and inexplicit. Perhaps, in a few hundred years, English will be as well. There is a good chance, in other words, that the real historical development is not toward a language in which all speech acts are made explicit but toward one in which, though the resources exist to make them explicit, those resources are only occasionally invoked. In that case, Austin's explicit speech acts do not stand at the *telos* of any historical development at all, but remain what I suggest them to be: models which cover some, but not all, cases of interaction.

But I need not appeal to the putative allusiveness of elderly languages to make my point here. I can also point out a mode of behavior, in English itself, which is far from primitive but which relies on this sort of ambiguity. This, on the analysis of John Sabini and Maury Silver, is flirtation. When we flirt with someone, we make utterances which can be taken either as "innocent" conversation or as sexually intended, and we leave it up to the other to decide how to take them.[15] Such linguistic behavior is neither unsophisticated nor primitive, and we may safely say that no developments in language, society, or the nature of the species (short of the elimination of sexuality itself) will put an end to it.

What is at issue in all this is the status of the fully explicit speech act as the paradigm from which to discuss all language use. I am not arguing here that all speech is or should be of the type in my examples. Such ambiguous language is not suitable, presumably, for Oxford dons, and we may well hope that Austin's prediction will continue, in that realm of discourse, to come true. But however important explicit speech may be for professors, there are those—in our examples including writers, politicians, and the flirtatious—who do not make exclusive use of it. It is not our *only* mode of speech.

I am also not claiming that this mode of speech is somehow independent of more literal forms. John Searle, for example, has argued that both metaphor and fiction are "parasitic" uses of language, presupposing univocal and literal uses of terms; Wolfgang Iser and Jacques Derrida have argued the reverse.[16] I claim only that the examples I have given so far are instances of a single underlying structure, in which the response is elicited through the hearer's deciding which set of a number of possible conventional procedures the utterance is to be understood to instantiate. Whether such speech is in ordinary language independent of, prior to, or parasitic upon literal or univocal speech is not at issue here.

In addition to such cases, in which more than one set of conventions is available for understanding an utterance, there are cases in which no such conventions are currently available to the utterance's hearers. Such cases violate expectations and correspond to what Richard Rorty has called "abnormal discourse."[17] The only way to formulate a response to such an utterance is to extrapolate a new procedure for interpreting it. An obvious example, already mentioned, is:

(5) "The world is blue—like an orange."

A less obvious example is Heidegger's famous:

(6) "Das Nichts nichtet."

In "Was ist Metaphysik?" this sentence is presented as, so to speak, entailed by the metaphysical attempt to render an account of everything. On a "metaphysical" approach, as Heidegger understands this, everything—including "nothing" itself—must be understood as an entity. The minimal way one can speak about the entity "nothing" is simply to repeat the subject of the sentence as a verb: *das Nichts nichtet*. But this cannot be understood in metaphysical terms, and a new way of understanding it—one which does not view the "nothing" as an entity—is called for.[18]

We can thus conclude that, in addition to speech acts which elicit responses on the Austinian model, there are other types of elicitation in which it is left up to the hearer to decide what the utterance means. Such a decision can take the form either of selecting one from a number of possible interpretations or of extrapolating new types of interpretation.

Because in each case the hearer plays a productive role with respect to the utterance's meaning, I call such interaction "poetic," retaining the breadth, if not the precise meaning, of the Greek *poiêsis*. When the response is selected, I will call the interchange "normally" poetic; when it must be extrapolated, I will call it "abnormal." My discussion here will be largely restricted to normal poetic interaction, for the simple reason that there is relatively little to say, on a general level, about the latter type.

If normal poetic elicitation can take a number of alternate paths, then the normal elicitor is by definition an utterance (or an expression) which can be understood in a number of different ways. One obvious mode of this is syntactic or lexical ambiguity: "flying planes can be dangerous" could, if uttered in the right circumstances, leave a hearer undecided about how to take "flying." One could conceivably tell someone "I went to the bank and got the money" and mean to allow the person to decide whether I drew it from an account or a cache in the water.

The hearer in poetic interaction cannot seek to understand the elicitor by reasoning back to it from the situation it describes, for it describes no single situation. He cannot attempt to clarify it by attributing mental states and intentions to the speaker, who in fact may have no clear ones. And he cannot appeal to the social norms governing interaction with the speaker, for he does not know what these are. He is thus, in the first instance, thrown back on the words themselves: nothing is left to "understand" except the meanings and forces (illocutionary and perlocutionary) which the utterance *might* have in some actual situation.[19] In particular, since the meaning of the utterance is indeterminate, the hearer is forced back on the *sounds* of the words it contains: he must articulate all, or as many as possible, of the meanings that could be attributed to those sounds in order to make his selection.

Though in the first instance we cannot appeal to circumstances to decide the meaning of the utterance for us, it does not follow that they are wholly irrelevant. We need to distinguish between linguistically ambiguous elicitors, which might remain ambiguous even if the situation were quite well-defined, and circumstantial ambiguity, in which an elicitor can be interpreted variously depending upon which of a number of nonlinguistic circumstances are considered by the hearer (a) to obtain, and (b) to be relevant. The adducing of such circumstances is a further phase of poetic elicitation. Example (1) offered a case of it. Jack's utterance could be understood in more than one way, not merely because it was vague, but because the circumstances were. If the hearer decides, for example, that the encounter is a flirtatious one, the meaning of the utterance will become quite clear; similarly, if she decides the encounter is a business one.

I will call the set of known possible interpretations of an utterance the "repertoire" of the hearer, and I will refer to that portion of the circumstances of the utterance which may affect the selection of one of those interpretations as "sets of influencing factors." Some of these influencing factors will, like the repertoire itself, be cognitive. Acquaintance with the language, and in particular with the various meanings of lexically ambiguous words, will be one element; others will be acquaintance with socially accepted conventions, personal knowledge of the speaker, and general beliefs about the state of the universe. Other factors will be noncognitive, or less cognitive, in character: the desires, feelings, plans, and goals of the hearer. In general, we can view influencing factors as falling under three main headings. One is psychophysical states of affairs—knowledge, intention, desire, etc.—which are present in the hearer, or which can be imputed to the utterer by the hearer. A second type is social conventions known to the hearer; and a third is the physical state of the world at relevant times and places.

In example (1), part of the reason the elicitor is poetic is that a variety of states of mind can be imputed to the speaker by the hearer in light of her background information about him. If she knows, e.g., that he is madly in love with someone else, she may be likely to take the elicitor as a business compliment. If he seems to be so nervous that he is unable to follow the plan as she outlined it, she may take it as flirtatious. But if the elicitor is poetic, the relevance of such facts must be up to the hearer to decide; a fact whose relevance the hearer cannot deny makes impositions on understanding. Freedom to deny the relevance of a fact does not, however, entitle one to deny the fact: indeed, for such an elicitor to be poetic, multiple imputation of states of mind to the speaker must be not merely possible, but correct. Otherwise, the speaker intends some single response, but fails to elicit it, and the utterance is merely ambiguous or vague. It follows from this that, although it is (within limits) up to the hearer to decide what a poetic utterance means, it is not up to him to decide whether or not it is poetic in the first place: there must actually be a variety of ways of construing the utterance, none of which is notably more warranted than the others.[20]

Similarly, the elicitation of the response may also depend on a variety of social conventions being available in terms of which to decide upon its meaning. These cannot be conventions which *might* be in force in society: they must be conventions actually accepted by speaker and hearer, all of which *do* apply to the situation and prescribe the utterance. In (1), these would be the conventions of business lunches, of flirting, and so on. Julie thus gets to decide which of these will govern her response, i.e., which will be permitted to be relevant. The same goes for social circumstances other than the present one: that she is engaged to someone else is something the woman can ignore or not, as she wishes.

Finally, various physical facts may or may not be permitted to enter into the production of the response. That Julie and Jack are of similar age and rather drunk, for example, may encourage the "flirtatious" reading of the utterance. But, again, encouragement does not command. If Julie has a headache, that is a fact about the physical world, and one which would mitigate against responding to the utterance as flirtatious. But she is free to disregard it.

Influencing factors are givens which rule out some responses, permit others, and encourage still others. They are what I have called situational limits for the hearer of the utterance. Insofar as it is up to the hearer to decide whether they will be allowed to play a role in eliciting the response, the limits to the situation could be other than they are, and hence influencing factors function as parameters. The elicitation of the response in poetic interaction thus undertakes, not merely the adduction, but the explication and selection of parameters which may not be objects of explicit awareness, or even (in abnormal poetic interaction) the articulation of new parameters. It is, when criticizable, an exercise in situating reason.

Thus, in normal poetic interaction, a hearer responds to an ambiguous utterance or a blurt by (a) formulating various possible meanings for it, (b) explicating to himself situational parameters which may influence a response to it, and (c) allowing some of those parameters actually to play a role in eliciting the response. In the first two steps, attention is directed not to features specific to the actual situation of the utterance but to factors which hold more generally, such as word meanings and social conventions. They can thus be viewed as a sort of step out of the concrete situation. In (c), the hearer steps back into the new situation created by the response.

In all this, the hearer constructs a narrative which moves from utterance to response by rationally organizing a mass of givens. Such a narrative, beginning with the utterance, sees that the response is constrained by, or fits into, previously existing states of affairs—the linguistic resources of the language, social conventions, the character of the speaker, and so on. Hence, in (1) above, Jack's utterance will eventually be fitted into the larger story of a business lunch, or of a flirtation, or of something else. Julie will construct that narrative with her response. But to the extent that only some of the relevant preexisting states of affairs are actually allowed to play a role in the elicitation of that response, the narrative cannot claim truth. It cannot claim, for example, that only one particular set of influencing factors in the speaker actually played a role in the production of the response, because it remains possible that others did as well. What it does claim is that the utterance will henceforth function *as if* it had been produced by that particular set of influencing factors and no others, and that in virtue of this functioning it will be fitted into an ongoing development. Like all narratives, those we construct in normal poetic interaction are only selections from a wider array of possibilities and do not mirror the actual complexity or vagueness of the circumstances.

Hence, (like poetry) narrative is not a type of discourse confined to a few easily recognizable genres such as history and fiction.[21] It extends from the way we produce responses to the most ordinary of single utterances up to the grandiose kind of philosophy introduced by Hegel. It ranges so far because humans are situated: they are governed by limits that do not hold always or everywhere. In narrative, participants interpret utterances in terms which they themselves have leeway to organize and to allow into the interpretive context. Such narrative is not only situated, it is situating.

In abnormal poetic interaction, the elicitor is recognized as apparently unintelligible, as not falling under any existent procedures for understanding. In such recognition, it is "demarcated" from the repertoire: a gap is opened up in the repertoire by its inability to cover the utterance in question. Such an elicitor, then, is not ambiguous, but bizarre: instead of too many possible meanings (more than one), it has too few (none). There are, of course, many bizarre utterances which do not reveal gaps in the repertoires of those who hear them; the ramblings of someone very drunk are an example. It follows that an abnormal elicitor must, though bizarre, be the kind of utterance that *ought* to have a meaning.

Such an elicitor will often have what we may call intelligent conventional features, i.e., features which are highly structured and clearly present because of the expectations of others, but without any indication as to what those expectations in fact are. The dedication to this book can, for most English-speakers, serve as an example. It seems to be an intelligent whole of parts which are related in obviously patterned ways and is thus, apparently, well-formed according to linguistic rules—but the rules of which language? It is only when the reader has demarcated the expression from, e.g., French, Spanish, and Italian, by noting anomalies to the conventions of those languages, that the path to understanding—a path of invention and hint, guesswork and dislocation—lies open.[23] Such demarcation, then, like narrative, begins with a stepping-out of the concrete situation of the utterance in order to see what the possible ways of understanding it are, and are not. In this case, the problem is not that there are a variety of equally plausible interpretations, but that no interpretation is plausible. A meaning must be guessed out. This extrapolation, when successful, creates a new situation in which new parameters are disclosed; when criticizable, it is an exercise in situating reason. So we can say that Heideggerean demarcation, like Hegelian narrative, has very basic analogues in (abnormal) poetic interaction.

If the response is itself determined by a variety of psychophysical states of affairs present in the hearer, it, too, may be poetic. Then the conversational ball is, so to speak, handed back to the original speaker. This often happens, we may note, in cases of flirtation: much of the pleasure in it comes from seeing how long the *double entendres* can be carried on without the undertones being put explicitly into words. A response which itself explicitly selects just one of the possible interpretations of the elicitor, and thereby defines the situation, terminates the encounter as poetic. But it may not be a break-off, which ends the interaction altogether; I call it a "terminating response." A response which continues the encounter as poetic will be a "nonterminating response." As an incomprehensible response to incomprehensibility, nonterminating abnormal poetic response might be thought to manifest mere stupidity or randomness, as Carnap thought Heidegger's "das Nichts nichtet" did.[22] But this has been excluded by my sense of "nonterminating." For if the response is taken as purely stupid or uninterestingly non-sensical, it will evoke, not a response or a termination on the part of the other, but what I have called a break-off of the encounter.

The discussion has now arrived at a typology of poetic interchange, or in a more extended form, of poetic interaction. First, with regard to the type of elicitation it contains, a poetic interchange can be either "normal," in which case the elicitation is a selection of one interpretation from a variety of possible ones, or "abnormal," in which case it is the extrapolation of a new response. And, depending on the nature of the response itself, a poetic interchange can be either "terminating" or "nonterminating," in which latter case it develops into a poetic encounter.

There are a number of ways in which the elicitor in such an interchange can be susceptible of a variety of interpretations, and this offers another way of classifying types of poetic interaction. If the elicitor is linguistically ambiguous, I will call the interchange "linguistically poetic." If it comes under a variety of social conventions, the interchange will be "socially poetic." If it is produced by a variety of psychophysical states of affairs attributable to the speaker, the interchange will be "aesthetically poetic." Among the psychophysical states of affairs which can function in this way, a particularly important group is those concerned with sexual desire, and I will refer to an interchange in which such factors help produce the elicitor as "erotically poetic." A given interchange may, of course, exhibit several or all of these features at once, and an encounter may oscillate between normal and abnormal.

Narrative

Poetic interaction can take on an enormous diversity of concrete forms (16 so far); poetic interchange can come about in ways equally diverse. But, by definition, these always contain just two broad types of elicitation: extrapolation and selection. *These, in turn, are elementary forms of narrative and demarcation—strategies which, writ large enough to be subject to criticism, we saw to be constitutive of the philosophies of Hegel and Heidegger, respectively.* Both thinkers, then, view philosophy as an activity of situating emancipation rather than truth telling, and both together would provide the basis for elaborating the present account of poetic interaction into a full account of situating reason as a form of intrinsically emancipatory interaction. I will renounce any such account here and confine myself to the characteristics of poetic interaction.

These have now been analyzed via a set of merely stipulated definitions. Those stipulations, however, are designed to capture my earlier analyses of intrinsically emancipatory interaction in the texts discussed. It is the task of this narrative to show that the major ones in fact do so. Four of those terms applied to language that extends beyond poetic interaction: "expression," "utterance," "convention," and "lexical" knowledge. I will look at the forerunners of these terms, especially in those thinkers who most closely adumbrated my own account: Plato, Hegel, and Heidegger. Then I will turn to my terms for the components for poetic interaction, and finally to the four categories I have suggested for it.

The concept of an "expression" as a sensory object, some of whose features are present because others expect them, has early roots in the *Phaedrus*'s account of a sensible being manifesting resemblance to a Platonic Form. On that account, we may say, the memory of the Form set up in the future lover a set of expectations concerning the vision of the Form itself, of which he was ignorant but which was triggered when he saw a beautiful person. The body of the other would not have been beautiful were it not that it induced in the lover expectations of seeing the Form of beauty, and in that sense the body was itself an expression—just as is the word "beauty." But beauty itself—the supersensible meaning of both body and word—was not merely an expectation or convention for Plato; it was an independent metaphysical entity. Hence, we may say that for Plato the conventions examined in dialectic were, or were supposed to be, metaphysically underwritten. If a body were not really beautiful but seemed to be, or if a word were used with the wrong meaning, its warrant would not be thus underwritten and would indeed be *merely* conventional (as in the second speech). Because words could have wrong meanings, knowledge of the meaning of a word was not the same thing as knowledge of a Form but could be knowledge of a mere linguistic agreement: "lexical" knowledge.

For Aristotle, too, a word had conventional features by which it became the sign of an affection of the soul, and those conventions might also be viewed as expectations that the word as used by one's interlocutor conformed to general usage: that it was, in Aristotle's term, "authoritative." But again, the meaning of the word could not be reduced to a set of expectations. A word meaning was a general feature of sensory experience, and hence existed, like a Platonic Form, independently of the users of the language. This view of all meanings as existing independently of the mind did not survive the Kantian critique, in which at least the basic concepts—the categories—existed only in the operation of rational minds, though as necessary conditions of that operation.[24] The Hegelian move was to abandon even those conditions and render meaning itself parametric.

In the "Battle of the Opposed Self-Consciousnesses," the primary operation of viewing an entity as meaningful was presented, Kant-fashion, as relating that entity solely to the ego of the viewer—but the "ego" there was completely empty, not outfitted with any of the Kantian categories. Thus, the battler approached the other in terms of an expectation: he expected to destroy the other and thereby to use the other to establish the value of his own ego. The other could not be approached in that way, however, without being viewed as the vehicle of a non-sensible meaning: as having an ego of its own. As with the *Phaedrus*, the body of the other was presented as what I call an expression. But the battler's expectation—that the other would affirm his ego—did not concern the vision of a metaphysical realm, but the institution of a social one. It was not, we saw, generalized into an enduring social agreement until the battle was over and both parties agreed that one would be master, the other bondsman. The master and bondsman were themselves, then, expressions in my sense: neither would exist were it not for the expectations of the other. But their "meanings"—the concepts of mastership and bondage—did not, like Platonic Forms, exist in some metaphysical realm, but were attained in the development the *Phenomenology* narrates. Unlike Aristotelian word-meanings, they were not natural but social. Unlike Kantian categories, they were, as narrated, capable of being transcended in later developments: hence, they were parametric in nature. This remained true when, as in poetry, the vehicle of meaning was no longer the body of a lover or an enemy but a word, and we arrived at "utterances" in my sense: at expressions whose conventions are linguistic. As one species of appreciating works of art in general, understanding poetry meant relating an individual word to the overall guiding conception of the poem, and hence was an exploration of the word's meaning in a paradigmatically rational context. Like Platonic dialectic, it provided "lexical" knowledge.

For *Being and Time,* the meaning of an entity was how it fit into the general structures of world. These structures, as basic horizons for the activities and projects of individual Dasein, also set up expectations—contexts of significance—in terms of which individual entities ready-to-hand were encountered; such entities were then encountered as expressive. These generalized expectations were, as for Hegel, social rather than metaphysical, natural, or transcendental. For they inhabited inauthentic consciousness and were inauthentic precisely because they were derived from others, rather than from the experienced entity itself. Authentic experience was then experience which was ready to have its expectations violated. Hence, Heidegger's thought, early and late, was concerned with unconventional, rather than conventional, utterances; with abnormal, rather than normal, poetic interaction; and with demarcation rather than narrative. Such abnormal utterances, with their disruption of convention, were warranted by other worlds than the current one of the interlocutor: the unique world set up by the work of art, or the world of a distant culture such as Japan. The experience of a word setting up such a world is then an exploration, indeed an instituting, of "lexical" knowledge.

An "utterance" for Plato, Hegel, and Heidegger is then, as I have analyzed it, not fundamentally something which raises a truth claim, but one type of "expressive" embodiment. What gets embodied are a set of "conventions," features present because of others' expectations. Such conventions differ for different words, and knowledge of them is, in my sense, "lexical." Hence, my use of these terms captures features of their accounts. Where those accounts primarily differed from each other concerned how the conventions themselves could be warranted. Such warrant could be, as for Plato and Aristotle, metaphysical, i.e., an appeal to a set of necessities; or in Kantian terms transcendental, with appeal to conditions of the operation of the mind. They could also be parametric in nature, in which case they were warranted for Hegel narratively, in terms of how they came to be; or demarcatively for Heidegger, by their function in other worlds. In the latter two cases, then, articulating those warrants was an exercise in situating reason.

We can now move from terms for general features of language to those I am using for poetic interaction itself. Ambiguous elicitation, to begin with, was first presented in the *Phaedrus,* where the body of the other was such that it could be responded to either animalistically or rationally; which of these occurred depended partly on the strength of the background expectations set up by the memory of the Forms, and hence was up to the viewer. Such elicitation was paradigmatically presented by an utterance when it contained members of the class of words with which we "wander," which have no clearly fixed meanings and could send us off on a variety of paths. These paths were explored in the dialectical examination of all the possible meanings of a word. The utterances in which such words occurred were then poetic elicitors. The "wandering" they provoked was the elicitation of a poetic response via the clarification of alternative interpretations and the choice of one of these for present purposes.

Thus, the *Phaedrus* presented, generally, what I call normal terminating poetic interaction. A simple and elegant example (though without any wander-inducing words) occurred, I suggest, at 244e. Socrates had decided to make his second speech, the one which would not dishonor love, and said: "Where is that boy I was talking to? He must listen to me once more, and not rush off to yield to his nonlover before he hears what I have to say."

Phaedrus then responded: "Here he is, quite close beside you, whenever you want him."

Socrates's utterance was ambiguous: "that boy" could have been the youth referred to in the first two speeches, who was present in words. Or it could have been Phaedrus himself, the lover of Lysias, present in body. Phaedrus's response, a nonterminating one, retained the ambiguity. If he were speaking as "the boy" of the first two speeches, the utterance expressed his willingness to hear more from Socrates. But he might also have been speaking as Phaedrus, who had been seduced by Socrates's earlier speech and was now ready for something quite different. Both types of psychophysical states were clearly in play, and it was up to Socrates to choose which he wanted to act upon. Socrates was clearly aware of both possibilities—though without the aid of dialectic. For (with admirable delicacy) he then identified himself as Stesichorus—a poet who, since he was blind, could not participate in the flow of particles that was eros—and began the Palinode. He had taken Phaedrus's words in the philosophical sense as soliciting speech, not body, thereby terminating the encounter.

For Aristotle all words had determinate meanings in the language as used by competent speakers, and all interaction had its "master," who in principle knew what he wanted to convey. Even the tragedian was presumed to know exactly what he meant with his words, and the analysis of "nonauthoritative" uses in tragedy had disambiguation as its purpose:

the aim was not to explore all possible meanings of a word, but to come up with that single meaning which would preserve the authority of the tragedian himself.

Though it is difficult to formulate Kantian viewpoints on the general issues of convention and utterance,[25] his discussions of the beautiful and the sublime could be given interactionist readings. For Kant, critical discourse on the beautiful selected from a beautiful object one single aspect and proceeded to formulate that as a concept. When the object in question was itself linguistic (such as a poem), it thus elicited an infinite number of interpretations and was, we may say, infinitely ambiguous. The selection and formulation of just one interpretation was, then, a case of normal poetic interaction. In contrast to Plato, the various concepts the beautiful object evoked could not for Kant, since they were infinite in number, be exhaustively examined; further interpretation was always possible. But in any particular case, the understanding was able to formulate a concept to capture the imaginative experience, and each such case was one of terminating normal poetic interaction.

We saw that Kant did not discuss the nature of discourse on the sublime in any detail, except to approximate it to the culture of reason. Yet I was able to hazard a few comments about what such discourse would be like. A sublime utterance would be one which could also be merely terrifying, and hence would be ambiguous: whether it were responded to with the respect for reason the sublime instills or with mere terror would be up to the hearer. Such an utterance, moreover, would not be one for which an interpretation was available in any current repertoire. For, as we saw, the experience of the sublime undid all empirical concepts, i. e., escaped all interpretation and drew us toward the infinite absence of the "abyss of reason." Such discourse would then be a case of nonterminating abnormal poetic interaction.

For Hegel, our dialogue with the work of art was one in which we could look at its details either for themselves or as conveying the overall guiding conception of the work, and in this sense the details were, once again, ambiguous. The analogy with the lover in the *Phaedrus* is a close one. There, the beautiful body could be viewed as just a beautiful body or in connection with a rational message. In Hegel's case, the rational message was not some supersensible Form, but was ultimately the organizing power of the work of art itself as a whole. We thus had, as with Plato, a definite repertoire of possible interpretations for any detail in the work of art: we could look to it alone, to its relations with other details, or to the entirety of the work. In each case, we would select one member of that repertoire and respond to the work on its basis. Hegelian aesthetic

experience thus corresponded to what I have called normal poetic interaction. It could be either terminating or nonterminating. An interpretation of a detail could be simply put on paper as something finished and
complete, which was what Hegel himself did in his *Aesthetics*; or it could
lead the reader on to further interpretations of further details. But the
entire process would eventually come to a halt, since the number of
details in any work of art is finite and their interrelationships must
be as well. This, then, distinguished the Hegelian conception from the
Kantian: for the work of art for Kant could provoke an infinity of
interpretations, and hence was inexhaustible. The finitude of aesthetic
meaning approximated Hegel, however, to Plato and Aristotle, for whom
meaning (of a word, a tragedy, or another person) existed as determinate. Hegel's account, then, is basically of normal terminating poetic
interaction.

For Heidegger, the work of art was essentially something new and
undreamed of, a violation of all expectations, and something which could
not be handled with the current repertoires of its audience: a meaning had
to be invented for it in line with its own prescriptions for its preservation.
Heideggerean aesthetic interaction was thus abnormal poetic interaction
and carried on the Kantian account of the sublime. Like Hegelian poetic
interaction, it could be either terminating—as when in "The Origin of
the Work of Art" the preservers of the work took their stand within the
new possibilities opened up by that work—or nonterminating, as when,
in "From a Dialogue on Language," each hint, when thought in terms of
the Twofold, yielded further possibilities and avenues for thinking. But
if, for Hegel, nonterminating interaction was merely provisional and
pointed to a final termination, for Heidegger the reverse was true: the
way of thinking had no intrinsic termination, and all stopping points
were merely provisional.

In general, then, the main components of poetic interaction—
ambiguous or bizarre utterance, narrative selection or inventive extrapolation of a response, and continuation or termination of the encounter—
are all present in aesthetic experience as treated by Hegel and Heidegger.
The characteristics in question are derived from the Kantian accounts of
the beautiful and the sublime in the third *Critique,* with the difference
that in Hegel and Heidegger their interactive dimension lies closer to the
surface—though not as close as in Plato's original treatment of normal
terminating poetic interaction. Because, as we have seen and will see
again in more detail in the next chapter, aesthetic experience is for all
these thinkers intrinsically emancipatory, it seems that my account of the
components of poetic interaction captures those earlier accounts of the

elementary components of intrinsically emancipatory interaction. There was, of course, much more in those accounts that mine does not capture, but consideration of that does not belong here.

We can now turn from the components of poetic interaction to its types. I have divided it into four categories, depending on the type of influencing factor that may play a role in the elicitation of the response: linguistic, social, aesthetic, and erotic. This division may or may not be exhaustive, but it suffices to capture the story of poetic interaction's long occlusion. For though all four types have previously been narrated, not all were present together at any one stage of that narrative. Thus, for Plato the aesthetic aspect was denied, since art was condemned as mimesis: the general emotionalism of art in the *Republic* was as bad as the specifically erotic mania of the *Phaedrus* was good, and the reason was that the work of art imitated sensible reality while the beautiful body imitates a Form. Because it was manic, the erotic response of the Palinode was, we may say, socially abnormal: it could not be handled in terms of the social conventions which, for example, distinguished slave from free man, and required the mutual improvisation of new types of relationship out in the countryside. When the relationship passed from the pursuit of the body to the examination of words, the affair passed to the examination of linguistic ambiguities, and became linguistically normal.

The metaphysical prescriptions of Aristotelian thought occluded poetic interaction altogether. Philosophy and other sciences, whose form was prescribed by that of Aristotelian metaphysics, could make no use of poetic utterances; the central doctrine of that metaphysics, its view of substance, meant that poetic interaction could not even be recognized as an independent form. All interaction was, in Habermas's sense, teleological and had to have a "master," one who knew what he was trying to do with his words and who could be (relatively) certain of the effects his words would have on others. Aesthetically, this master was the tragedian, whose authority should be preserved by critics. Socially, the repertoire of the Greek polis stood unchallenged: its ordinary language was "authoritative," the final court of appeal. And the erotic dimension, banished by Aristotle from the rational life of the polis, has yet to reappear in philosophy. It is as missing from Habermas as from Kant, Hegel, and Heidegger.

In the modern era, the common structures of poetic interaction have also been dispersed among a variety of practices which are usually held to be entirely distinct from one another. With the erotic definitively suppressed, these are aesthetic interaction, social critique, and linguistic analysis. The main agent of the dispersal in our writers was the modern conception of substance, playing its ancient prescriptive role in various new and not so new ways. This role weakened, however, as we moved from Kant through Hegel to Heidegger.

Aristotle's concept of teleological action, which followed from his substance metaphysics, had obvious residues in the views of Austin presented above. But the distinctively modern pattern of occlusions began, in my narrative, with Kant. For him, "substance" was no longer metaphysical reality. It was merely one of the categories in terms of which we organize the sensory manifold. Hence, it did not prescribe *theoretically* to all empirical reality: everything that exists is not necessarily a substance or like a substance, and does not have to be construed in such terms in order to be understood at all (in particular, the human mind did not). But in Kantian *practical* philosophy, substance reappeared: the autonomous self, as one which "gives the law" to itself, has within it its own source of action and, in this respect, especially when construed as the Kingdom of Ends, conforms to the nature of Aristotelian substance.

This conception of self, in turn, seemed to be undermined by the third *Critique* and the *Conflict of the Faculties,* in which a more interactive view of selfhood was adumbrated. In its paradigm—the interactive use of reflective judgment—new rules were given to art and new empirical concepts were formulated: aesthetic poetic interaction thus broadened to cover language in general. The aesthetic and the linguistic dimension here began to coalesce. Aesthetic experience was on the verge of being construed interactively, with the formation of vocabulary viewed as another experience of the same general type.

But these implications of the third *Critique* never quite become explicit. For one thing, Kant's emphasis on the beautiful object obscured the interactive dimension of aesthetic experience, and it kept him from viewing such experience as an experience not merely of sensory objects, as usually understood, but of linguistic ones as well. For another thing, though Kant rejected the truth claim of metaphysics and therewith the claim of metaphysics to prescribe theoretically to concrete investigations, he never rejected the general role of prescriber which metaphysics had formerly played; he merely reassigned it to critique. It followed that all concrete philosophical investigations had to be brought into conformity with the results of critique. In particular, the account of reflective judgment had to be harnessed to the substance conception of the autonomous self developed in the first two *Critiques.* The "harnessing" took two forms. One was that the original unification of the faculties experienced in the apprehension of something as beautiful was brought about entirely within the individual, rather than interactively. The other was that reflective judgment was to be carried out in institutionalized form by the philosophical faculty, which operated under the aegis of the state—the conception of which, as drawn from Kantian moral philosophy, was one of a quasi-substantial community. This attempt to harness reflective judgment to the state failed. As an instrument of social critique, reflective judgment was to be, as it is for Plato, abnormal: it was to uncover and articulate new social problems for which no adequate response had yet been devised. But Kant could not give an account of why the state would ever set up something as abnormal as a philosophical faculty. His concept of "disinterest," the formula for the subjectivization of aesthetics resulting from the first harnessing, could not carry over persuasively into the articulation of a socially effective use of reflective judgment.

The dispersions begun in modern form by Kant progressively lost force in Hegel and Heidegger. We have seen that Hegel's account of aesthetic experience strained to construe it interactively, and that the interaction in question was poetic. In his view, poetic interaction was basically what I call aesthetic, in that for him we responded to works of art, as we did for Kant, across the range of our entire being (except, apparently, for the erotic). But it was also linguistic, in that the highest art, poetry, was linguistic and indeed once helped create language. And, as we saw, it was social: aesthetic experience not only placed us outside the modern state, but taught us horrible things about it and its basic conventions. Hegel's own response to this subversive side of his aesthetic theory was to sublate it by an appropriation of Christianity which reconciled the individual to a truncated existence in the modern state. But, prior to sublating it, he allowed the critique to be stated. Hence, aesthetic experience was relevant both to linguistic experience and to the political realm.

The exemplary status of the state remained problematic in Heidegger. He, too, eschewed discussion of the political effects of his aesthetics—not by attempting some grand sublation to make art safe for the state, but by simply ignoring the issue altogether. Yet his account of aesthetic experience interpreted the work of art as something that could not be understood in terms of current social conventions, and which was thus socially abnormal; as a new use of language, it was linguistically abnormal as well. And as something mortals can dwell within, the work of art addressed all aspects of their Being, though Heidegger had no account of "faculties" or even of "psychophysical states of affairs." Hence, in Heidegger as in Hegel, all three general kinds of poetic interaction were articulated, with only the political one being strongly problematical. It remained for Habermas to conceptualize a locus for it that would differentiate it from the kind of interaction that takes place in the state without breaking all bonds to the political sphere.

In general, Kant's philosophy established, in my narrative, a distinctively modern pattern for the occlusion of poetic interaction. In contrast to Plato, in this modern constellation it is the erotic form of such inter-action that remains unnamed and unspoken (it will remain so until Freud—if we are entitled to construe psychoanalysis as in any respect poetic in nature). Further, because of the importance of beautiful objects to aesthetic experience, the aesthetic and linguistic types of poetic inter-action are dissociated from each other. And the social type is very care-fully put *hors de service*.

In contrast to Aristotle, the concept of substance plays no theoretically prescriptive role in modern philosophy: it tells us nothing about how the universe must be. But it continues, almost surreptitiously, to play other sorts of roles, and these dispersals can be traced to them. In erotic mania, another person suddenly intrudes into the core of my self and rearranges its basic elements. This has always been a threat to the self-containment of the substantial man, whether presented in his original guise as the Aristotelian citizen, reconceptualized as Kantian legislative reason or Hegelian consolidated self, or attenuated as an abstract Heideggerean thinker.[26] The occluding effect of the beautiful object is likewise a result of structuring aesthetics along Aristotelian lines: for then we are to study any domain by finding an exemplary type of object proper to it and studying that object. For Aristotle, this was the tragedy, itself quasi-substance with form (plot) and matter (incident and character); for Kant, it was the beautiful object offering material for the formative activity of the recapitulating imagination; for Hegel, it was the beautiful object as reconciliatory. The exemplary status of the work of art was only over-come in Heidegger's return to the "origin" of the work of art: by seeing that origin as a difference in worlds, Heidegger was able to break the constraints of the substantialist approach to aesthetics and to move (in "From a Dialogue on Language") to a level where language itself is aesthetic.

The same occlusive role for the concept of substance, in general, holds for the relation of poetic interaction to politics. There, the exemplary object is the state, and the social abnormality of poetic interaction oc-cludes it as long as the state can claim to be a quasi-substance. It appears from the previous narrative, moreover, that the status of the state is problematic for recent philosophers because the modern state, the would-be heir to the polis, is not merely to be studied *as if* it were the exem-plary field of all human interaction, but it actually tries to make itself into such a field and exemplar. This makes an account of interaction which is intrinsically emancipatory, rather than perpetuating the master-ship and dominance proper to the state, difficult and apparently even dangerous—if we may judge from Kant's and Hegel's problems with the Kaisers, (some of) Heidegger's with the Führer, and from the general circumspection of all three on the relevance of their respective views of poetic interaction to political matters.

If we are to believe what Kant, Hegel, and Heidegger thus indirectly tell us, the political sphere, historically conceived in metaphysical terms (the state as quasi-substance), makes the same sort of totality claim that metaphysics has always made: just as metaphysics claimed to be prescriptive or even foundational for human thought, so the state claims to have the prescriptions, or even (in Kant) the conditions, for human interaction. The problems we saw Plato, Aristotle, Kant, Hegel, Heidegger, and Habermas all having with the state are not prudential or sociological problems about the political acceptability of philosophy, but philosophical problems: once the dialogical turn is taken and we see that thinking *is* interacting, the state and metaphysics are one and the same.

Demarcation

The attempt to trace intrinsically emancipatory interaction to its roots in ordinary language means a departure from the tradition I have narrated, for in that tradition intrinsically emancipatory interaction was always somehow special. For Plato, it was an erotic encounter outside the polis and its norms. For Kant and Hegel, it had to do with the way we react to beautiful objects and talk about our reactions. For Heidegger, it was a rare, and rarified, encounter with a different world. For Habermas, it was the specialized and problematically structured practice of communicative action. Common to all was the view that intrinsically emancipatory interaction is not a necessary part of our experience with language. For it is easy to see that it is possible for a human being to pass a whole life without engaging in any of those practices—even in communicative action, if his life-world is premodern. To claim that intrinsically emancipatory interaction has roots in ordinary language is not to deny those other accounts of such interaction (though I have maintained that some of those I have presented are more complex forms of what I have been discussing); still less is it to level down intrinsically emancipatory interaction into what Heidegger calls the "everyday," or to deny its differences from other forms of interaction. Rather, I have argued that intrinsically emancipatory interaction is "ordinary" in that it is rooted in an experience that all human beings have with language, an experience so universal that it strains credulity to think of someone who has never had it speaking a language at all. This experience is, at bottom, that of persistent failure to understand someone's utterance, with a resulting turn to selection or invention.

My attempt to put intrinsically emancipatory interaction into ordinary language was inspired by Habermas's efforts, prior to *The Theory of Communicative Action,* to ground his account of validity claims in an account of the kinds of speaker's engagements made in ordinary language. I have not discussed those efforts, which were unconvincing and have been heavily remodeled in the account of formal pragmatics in *The Theory of Communicative Action.*[27] It is possible, perhaps, that Habermas simply made things too difficult. That all human beings have the experience I am discussing at some time is, I take it, in need neither of evidence nor of argument. It is an inescapable part of learning language, and the universality of poetic interaction is grounded on one of the few attributes we may without hesitation ascribe to all mankind: imperfection. That people view certain forms of this experience as "emancipatory," or indeed that they name it or think about it at all, is of course a cultural and historical matter.

The above account of poetic interaction enables me to demarcate it more clearly than I have done from Habermas's account of communicative action. Before moving on to more general matters, I will do so with two examples: one concerning a relatively abstract utterance, and one of the relatively concrete kind made by works of art.

My abstract example will revert to Julie's situation in example (1) in the preceding analysis. She cannot respond to the utterance in terms of communicative action, i.e., by accepting or rejecting the validity of the three claims it raises. Consideration of whether the utterance is true or not—whether she actually is the "most fantastic" employee of the firm—will not help her in understanding it, for it is too vague to have any truth value and, even if it were not, its truth or falsity would help little in responding to it. It is also irrelevant whether Jack is "sincere" in claiming that the woman is his "most fantastic" coworker, and just what his intentions are is also unclear, perhaps to him as well. Because of all this, Julie does not know which social norms are governing the encounter—those of flirtation, of business compliments, or of some other kind altogether—and the result is that *no* such norms are governing it: the question of whether the utterance is "appropriate" or not cannot even arise. Julie is thus in the uncomfortable position of not knowing what Jack's utterance actually means in the given situation—not because she does not know what the situation is, but because in a sense there will *be* no situation until she makes her response. The situation has thus been left up to her to "construct," by (for example) deciding that the utterance is to be taken as a business compliment. Only on the basis of that construction will she be able to reach Habermasian "understanding" with Jack on the acceptability (or, more likely, the unacceptability) of his utterance.

My more concrete example will be the *Iliad*. As a poem, the *Iliad* certainly does not raise a Habermasian truth claim: those in the modern world who take it seriously as "poetry" signal by this very seriousness that they are not prepared to discuss such matters as whether or not the Trojan War really took place as the poem describes. Nor does it necessarily raise a Wellmerian truth claim, either: its topic, the wrath of Achilles which sends him into a sulk for years, is barely comprehensible to us; as we saw Hegel argue, the life-situation of the epic hero does not, in general, present the aesthetic "truth" of our own. The poem also does not claim to express the intentional states of Homer the poet: indeed, we cannot tell from it whether there even was a Homer. Much scholarly opinion holds that "he" was a group of people who never even knew one another; one author suggests that "he" was a woman.[28] And finally, the social norms portrayed in the *Iliad*—such as they are—include slavery, concubinage, guest-friendship, and virtual ownership of wives. It is hard to see how they could be "appropriate" to readers in, say, Renaissance Italy, Victorian England, or romantic Germany. But readers from those cultures have been highly appreciative of the poem itself.

The *Iliad* thus cannot be readily accommodated either to Habermas's account of communicative action or to Wellmer's account of aesthetic truth. But it can, I suggest, be readily viewed as a case of abnormal poetic interaction. Coming to us from a culture so archaic as to be by now almost wholly alien, it nevertheless constitutes a clear and articulate whole of words: a "phenomenon," in the Heideggerean sense, which "rests in itself." In trying to put those words together, we must revise many of our own word meanings, extrapolating what for us are new meanings (to such terms as "wrath," for example). On a more concrete level, we do not measure Homer's words against the presupposed "three worlds" of outer nature, inner nature, and social norms, to see if they relate acceptably to those worlds: we construct a possible, or imaginary, world around them.[29]

Hegel's account of ideal art then amounts to an examination of the question of whether the modern reader can, in Heideggerean terms, "take a stand within" the *Iliad*. The conclusion is that although the "new" meanings one formulates are in reality very old, and come closer to articulating the nature of the human spirit than do the meanings and conventions of the modern state, it is not possible to return to the epic world. But the confrontation with that world highlights our own—it discloses the nature of modernity by contrast and "sets us more firmly" back into our own life-world—a demarcative move which Hegel recuperates for his narrative by arguing that modernity is superior to ancient elitism, using Christianity for (or reducing it to) his narrative link.

In Habermas's model, the hearer of an utterance has a simple choice: either to accept or reject the validity claims it raises. Habermas would presumably claim that it is possible to reject a validity claim, not merely for being false, but for being vague. It is important to see that such rejection is not what happens here: the utterance is not "sent back," as it were, because it is vague; rather, its vagueness or abnormality is *accepted* as the basis for the interpretive activity of the hearer. When the new formulation is achieved via selection from among a number of possible interpretations, it amounts to the disclosure of the life-world that Habermas adumbrates in his accounts of evaluative judgment in *The Theory of Communicative Action* and after. When elicitation is a matter of extrapolating new meanings, especially of taking a stand within them, it is a matter of transcending the life-world, either partially or altogether—possibilities which Habermas, because of the residues of substance-metaphysics in his thought, does not articulate. Both disclosure and transcendence of the life-world, I will argue in the next chapter, can be emancipatory.

Space for that argument can be opened up as follows. As a result of Habermas's diagnoses of the social pathologies caused by the state's intrusions into the life-world, the state can no longer be viewed as the overarching human community. It is one form of such community, and it is in opposition to others. My analysis of Habermas provided us with a space—the life-world—for poetic interaction. In order to locate poetic interaction within that space, we need (1) to subtract from Plato's account his appeal to a purported metaphysical reality, (2) to avoid the Aristotelian substance metaphysics altogether, and (3) subtract from Kant's thought the transcendental claims about the structures of a purported "consciousness as such." A space opens up which is, in virtue of (3), linguistic; in virtue of (2), interactive; and in virtue of (1), empirical. This post-Kantian space is occupied, in my narrative, by Hegel, Heidegger, and Habermas. But it is also occupied by forms of interaction which are "political," in which people pursue purposes in terms of fixed social distinctions (the primary distinction being that between those governing and those governed).

The state, I have suggested, is in my narrative the practical application of metaphysics, the science of substance. The "end of metaphysics," or of the exemplary status of the state, then means that, unlike Aristotle, we must recognize that poetic interaction cannot be made to inhabit the political part of the interactive space; unlike Kant and Hegel, we must not concede legitimacy to the efforts of the political sphere to prescribe and found all interaction; and unlike Heidegger, we must not ignore the political questions altogether. All these directions are taken by Habermas in his articulation of the concept of the dialogical life-world and its colonization by the state. With this, the space of human interaction is divided into the political-economic sphere, structured on its "steering mechanisms" of power and money, and the life-world, structured by communicative action. I suggest that a further distinction is to be made within the life-world: between encounters which raise and evaluate validity claims, and encounters which merely articulate them. The former relate to inner nature, outer nature, and the social world as domains to which contents are allocated by utterances; the latter relate to them as offering limits and parameters for understanding and articulation.

Finally, this also, perhaps, opens up a way to locate unsituated reason within the life-world—as a developed phase of poetic interaction. The elicitation of the response in both normal and abnormal poetic interaction begins, we saw, with a step outside the concrete circumstances in which the hearer seeks to measure the utterance against influencing factors. Some of these, like the desires of the moment, are specific to the current situation. But others are more general, such as linguistic or social conventions. Is not the move to consider such general factors a "desituating" of reason? And is it not, like narrative and demarcation themselves, writ rather large in philosophy? Does it not bear traces of the Platonic ascent to the Forms, the Kantian disregard of inclinations, Hegelian externalization, and the Heideggerean transport out of one's accustomed world? Is it possible that the evaluation of a poetic elicitor is at the root of unsituated reason? Then, it seems, the problem with philosophers until the *Critique of Judgment* would be that they tended to view all such nonspecific factors as, in the last instance, necessities (such as the Forms) or conditions (in the way that the categorical imperative was for Kant a condition of moral action). Once they are seen as parameters, does not a way open up for unsituated reason to be reconceptualized as the clarification of influencing factors of an utterance which are not themselves situation specific? Can unsituated reason be seen to have a role in poetic interaction? Would not the situating and desituating of reason, in fact, be the systole and diastole of poetic interaction?

Twenty-three

Freedom, Politics, and Poetic Interaction

Analysis

In the previous section I argued that poetic interaction is distinct from other types because of the kind of elicitation it contains. If now it turns out to be "free," then the question arises of whether it, and the kinds of freedom it exhibits, are wholly *sui generis* or whether they have implications for other forms of interaction. I will explore both questions here by first discussing various senses in which freedom can be ascribed to poetic interaction, as well as the kinds of standing it may have as a source of norms for social critique. Those senses will be admittedly simplistic and seemingly arbitrary. In the narrative, I will turn to strands of the philosophical tradition narrated earlier in the book to flesh them out and show that they are not willful, but coincide with formulations worked out in the only resource to which we can turn for a philosophical understanding of freedom: the tradition which has so largely created it. The two most problematic thinkers with regard to the status of poetic interaction for social critique are the two with which we began, Hegel and Heidegger. The problems they have with it point us to the relation of poetic interaction to philosophy, a relation which itself opens up, I suggest, a pathway to the future. I will adumbrate it in my final demarcation.

As its name suggests, and as all our writers would agree, human interaction is not a steady state. At the very least, it is an exchange of information. It can also amount to a redefinition of the interactors themselves, as in the Hegelian "Battle of the Opposed Self-Consciousnesses" or the Heideggerean preservation of the work of art. Any concepts of freedom that apply to it will then view freedom, not as the static quality of an object, but as a process. This processual dimension can be grasped by adapting a distinction we saw in Aristotle: I will look, on the one hand, to aspects of poetic interaction which *produce* freedom, and which I will refer to as "liberating" phenomena. I will also look at aspects which are *produced by* freedom and can be said to manifest it; I will call these "liberated." One departure from Aristotle in this should be noted: as we saw, he separated the production and manifestation of freedom from freedom itself, which was the internal state of a good moral agent. This view, I have argued, makes metaphysical commitments regarding the "substantial" nature of such a moral agent, which I will avoid. The processes by which freedom is produced and manifested are thus aspects of freedom itself.

It will be convenient to key my account to the response in poetic interaction, and to the process of elicitation itself. We saw there to be four types of such response. The first was terminating normal response. Such a response is elicited by the selection, from an available repertoire of interpretations, of one interpretation which is applied to the utterance. Since I cannot produce the response without making such a selection, my response manifests interactively one very well-known type of freedom, that of choice: the response is unconstrained by those conventions which govern the encounter, since there is no single set of such conventions.[1] But interactive freedom of choice is not wholly unconstrained, for the whole set of alternative conventions—the repertoire of intepretations available in the society and language for interpreting the utterance—will allow some responses but not others. In example (1) from the previous chapter, Julie may interpret Jack's utterance as either flirtatious or businesslike, but she cannot decide that he is calling out a base runner. Indeed, terminating normal response in effect reaffirms the repertoire which contains the alternatives it considers, just by validating one of those alternatives. That validation, then, both clarifies the parametric status of the alternative in question and is intrinsically emancipatory.

Though in this sense liberated, the selection of an interpretation has no intrinsic liberating function. The response may serve to cut off options for the other, as when I understand someone's chance remark as an insult and storm off. It may also impede other senses of "freedom" we have yet to discuss.

The second type of response was non–terminating normal response. This sort of response is elicited through a selection from among an available repertoire, and hence exhibits interactive freedom of choice. But it is itself ambiguous, and therefore a poetic elicitor. A case of this, in terms of example (1) of the previous chapter, would arise if Julie formulated a response which took Jack's utterance as both flirtatious and as a business compliment. She would then allow a number of heterogenous psychophysical factors into the conditioning of her response: her capacities for "business thinking," for example, and for erotic arousal. Her response, produced by the cooperation of divergent factors within her, would then manifest freedom as unification of the self. It would also, as non-terminating, be liberating: for it would require Jack to respond by selecting from among the repertoire of alternative interpretations it left open, and would thus occasion the use of his interactive freedom of choice—or, should he also respond in a non-terminating way, a further act of self-unification. This kind of response is also constrained by the repertoire of the hearer, and hence is also situated by that repertoire. It affirms, not just one, but several of its members.

The third type of response was terminating abnormal response, in which a univocal interpretation is extrapolated or conjectured and then applied to a previously incomprehensible utterance. Such a response is then produced by, and when recognizable as such manifests, what we might call freedom of improvisation. It is emancipatory in that, when successful, it adds a new rule to the repertoire of possible interpretations for utterances: it expands that repertoire and reduces dependence on its previously present components. An example of this would be, perhaps, the way James Joyce's *Ulysses* was received by other writers: as each gradually came to an understanding of the work, it opened up whole new worlds of possible writing. Such liberation is not constrained by any set of conventions or any repertoire. Indeed, by showing that the repertoire has gaps in it, does not cover all that it should cover, it is inherently critical of the existing repertoire. But it is constrained by the language itself, in which a meaning for the utterance must finally be formulated. In terms of my previous example, the dedication of this book is not in English, and the rules of English do not cover it. But if monolingual Americans are going to understand it, that meaning will have to be in English. In other words, the new repertoires which are added to the language by terminating abnormal poetic interaction are previously latent in the language itself. What is refuted is their latency, when they get articulated in new combinations of old words.

Finally, we have nonterminating abnormal response, in which the response is such that it cannot be understood by any currently available components of the repertoire. Like its terminating analogue, such a response manifests what I have called freedom of improvisation, in that it is not produced by the application of any currently existing rules. It is liberating, in that by responding to incomprehensibility with incomprehensibility it subverts, not merely the preexisting repertoires of the interlocutors, but the need for repertoires as such. Like a Zen riddle, it frees the interlocutors from overriding concern with finding interpretations for all utterances or from filling in all gaps. It is also liberating in that, as nonterminating, it requires the other to formulate a new type of response, evoking his freedom of improvisation.

Poetic interaction is thus "liberated" in that responses in it are produced by socially unconstrained choice, unification of the self, and improvisation. It is "liberating" in that nonterminating forms of it require the other to produce responses in these ways, and in that its abnormal forms reduce dependence on previously existing repertoires for interpretation. If, as will be shown in the ensuing narrative, the tradition qualifies these as senses of "freedom," then poetic interaction is intrinsically free.

The question of whether poetic freedom has implications for other types of discourse can be more specifically construed as that of whether it can provide standards by which to judge and criticize other modes. For this, two things are required. First, we must clarify what those standards are: we must articulate the concepts of freedom implicit in poetic interaction as standards which may apply more broadly. Second, we must determine the "standing" of poetic interaction with respect to other forms. By what right are its standards to be applied to other forms of interaction?

I will discuss three distinct types of standing. On the one hand, we might be able to argue that poetic interaction provides a positive model to which other forms of interaction ought to conform, and hence has "positive standing." Positive standing can be either "global," in which case its standards apply to all cases of interaction as such (as the Kantian categorical imperative applies to all actions), or "regional" in that they apply only to some. We can also, perhaps, claim that poetic interaction is not only different from other types, but should be and remain so. If such is the case, we could conclude that other types of interaction should not be allowed to encroach upon, or eradicate, the types of freedom it presents. Poetic interaction then would serve as a "negative" standard by which to judge other forms of communication, or would have "negative standing."

Whether poetic interaction has any or all of these standings depends upon the standards themselves that can be formulated for poetic freedom. Based upon what we have established so far, we can call a form of interaction "poetically free" to the extent that it makes one or more of the following allowances.

(1) The hearer of any utterance which occurs as part of its distinctive patterns is allowed to select a meaning for that utterance from his own repertoire of possible interpretations.

(2) No set of psychophysical factors in the hearer is excluded from cooperating in the production of the response.

(3) The hearer is also allowed, if necessary, to extrapolate an interpretation for the utterance: i.e., there are no predeter-

mined criteria by which an *utterance* is to be excluded as senseless.

(4) The form of interaction also has no predetermined criteria by which a *response* is to be dismissed as senseless; this, too, is in each case up to the hearers to decide.

The claim that poetic interaction has global positive standing—that it can serve as a positive model to which all other types of interaction ought to correspond—does not survive this list. An obvious counterexample is empirical science. If there is to be any such thing as "scientific" discourse, it is crucial that allowance (1) not be made: in order to be verifiable, in order to be determinable as either true or false, an utterance must have a single meaning. If it does not, it must be disambiguated before "scientific" discussion can begin. Further, the institutionalized patterns of scientific discourse require the rigorous excision of certain psychophysical factors from the production of utterances: a scientific utterance is not supposed to manifest a desire for spritual comfort, for material gain, or indeed anything except the passion for truth. Such factors are, of course, often if not always present: but they must be suppressed by the speaker when he presents his findings, and they are supposed to be ignored by others in formulating their response: the sole criterion by which scientific utterances are ideally evaluated is their truth.[2] Nor, finally, can science allow the hearers of an utterance to extrapolate meanings for it: any new term, for example, must be defined by the speaker when it is introduced. This again, is because science is in principle directed solely toward truth (or some other criterion of decidability). An utterance with no clear meaning cannot be true or false until it is assigned one, and discussion of an utterance which as yet has no single meaning cannot be scientific. Science thus does not make any of the allowances we have formulated from our examination of poetic interaction. It would not be science if it did: its non-poetic characteristics are conditions of its existence qua science.

Poetic interaction cannot serve as a model to which scientific discourse ought to conform, and hence it does not have global positive standing. On the other hand, there are forms of interaction for which it does seem to have regional positive standing. It has been recognized since Aristotle's discussion of "equity," for instance, that laws cannot prescribe everything fully. A law must be written vaguely enough to be adaptable to concrete circumstances:

> for the measure of the indefinite is indefinite, as is the leaden measure of Lesbian house construction: for it shifts towards the shape of the stone, and does not remain still; and the decree shifts towards the case (*NE* 5.10 1137b 29–32).

The "shifting" is of course carried out by the judge, who decides in a given case what the law means, and who thus has latitude to select an interpretation from the parameters given in the law. But if we can judge a law in terms of its flexibility, by how it approximates to allowance (1) of poetic interaction, there are even here limits to the positive standing of poetic interaction. Unlike the scientist, the judge is concerned with justice as well as with truth; but he, too, is required to exclude from the production of his response (or judgment) certain psychophysical factors: anger, envy, and pity, the *Rhetoric* tells us, do not "shift" the measure of justice: they warp it (*Rhetoric* 1.1 1354a23 seqq.). The applicability of poetic interaction as a positive model for legislation and legal judgment is then a matter of contextualized cases: how many interpretations a law should leave open is a matter which, presumably, varies with the law. Similarly, the psychophysical factors which a judge must exclude from the production of his judgment are a function of his particular status as judge and may vary with the circumstances of the judge and the case. When a crime is particularly heinous, for example, a judge can express the outrage of society with a stiff sentence.

This example indicates that the regional positive standing of poetic interaction is, as we should expect, a regional matter: how much latitude is to be allowed in the selection of the meaning of utterances, whether conjecture as well as selection is to be allowed, and precisely which psychophysical factors are to be excluded or admitted into the production of utterances are all up for contextualized debate. And this suggests that only empirical research can determine the regional positive standing of poetic interaction. Such "research" is not the kind that seeks impartially to uncover and explain statistical regularities, but is itself a form of situating dialogue.

I can sketch the course of such situating critique, briefly, as follows. It would begin, we may suppose, when we adopt the allowances above as standards of evaluation and then examine other forms of interaction to see whether or not they conform to them. Those other forms of interaction, as givens with which our critique must deal, are limits to our critical situation. Some of them cannot change to meet the standards of poetic freedom without ceasing to exist. But (as we saw in the case of science) to say this is not to render a final verdict upon them, because there may be other values (for science, truth) which they serve and which have their own warrants. Thus, to say that some form of interaction does not and cannot meet the critical standards provided by poetic interaction is not to condemn that form, but to admit that final judgment on it can be made only by some third discourse which is in possession of criteria for the values, if any, it does serve.

The other possibility is that the characters which keep the other form of interaction from meeting the standards for poetic freedom can be changed without destroying that form of interaction itself. Suppose, for example, that there is a type of interaction—say, Aristotelian friendship—which rigidly excludes erotic attraction from its established patterns. An argument could be made that this particular feature fails to meet allowance (2) above and should be changed. But this means that the absence of erotic features in Aristotelian friendship is a parametric feature of it, one that could be other than it is. Part of the task of our critique is to articulate this. We can do so by narrating the history of such friendship, perhaps on the model of my own narrative here, showing how it develops from a "substantialized" version of the erotic *paideia* of the *Phaedrus*. We might also open up space within the concept of such friendship itself, e.g., by showing that the exclusion of sexuality from relationships where it is appropriate is in some sense "unfriendly." In either case, our critique has clarified the parametric status of its object: it has been a form of situating reason.

Finally, if what I am suggesting here is valid, we cannot know in advance whether our critique of a given form of interaction will have validity or not. Hence, our critique is itself dependent upon feedback from its "objects" and, in that sense, is a form of dialogue with those objects. Indeed, by rejecting the claim of poetic freedom to serve as a standard for criticizing them, other forms of interaction will be taking my critique as *their* object, and will be indicating to me the parametric status of my own claim to criticize them. The regional positive standing of poetic interaction, then, can only be determined in specific cases by dialogue on a Habermasian model, in which representatives of distinct forms of interaction enter into mutual critique and adjustment. It is not for philosophers to set out in advance.

I have classified poetic interaction in terms of the types of circumstances that can enter into the elicitation of the response: linguistic and social conventions, psychosomatic states of affairs, and in particular erotic desire. My account of its negative standing will be keyed to these four classes; I will ask whether any of them can be wholly eliminated.

The elimination of erotic poetic interaction would be the elimination of flirtation, which would become, like Austinian speech acts, wholly prescribed by conventions—as if, in Strawson's words, "there could be no love-affairs which did not proceed on lines laid down in the *Roman de le Rose*."[3] It is safe to say that this is absurd: humans will always flirt, i.e., will always engage in erotic poetic interaction, and attempts to eliminate it are not so much dangerous as useless. This is true both for normal and abnormal flirtation. By the latter, I mean interaction in which the participants invent new erotic relationships, such as in the invention of courtly love by the troubadours of Provence, of romantic love in Victorian times—or of erotic *paideia* in the *Phaedrus*. We need not engage in moral argumentation to realize that this has always gone on and is going to continue. A similar argument can be made with respect to the wider field of aesthetic interaction: people's utterances are not going to cease to be expressive of several things at once, and they will presumably continue to express both psychophysical states which can be interpreted by an available repertoire and ones which cannot. In the course of doing this, they will trigger the articulation of social parameters.

In linguistic poetic interaction, the response is elicited, in the normal type of such interaction, by clarifying the various possible interpretations of the sounds contained in an utterance and by selecting one of them. The first part of this amounts to an examination and analysis of the utter-ance—language analysis, or the use of situating reason we saw in the *Phaedrus*. And, as was argued there, it cannot be dispensed with by so-ciety except at the price of remaining in ignorance of the most basic of conventions by which members of that society are bound together: the meanings of their words. Normal linguistic poetic interaction, as the ar-ticulation of the "hidden agreements" binding members of a society, can-not be dispensed with by that society unless it wants to become, like the community of master and bondsman, inarticulate. In its abnormal form, such interaction extrapolates new interpretations for utterances, i.e., forms new concepts and extends the lexical repertoire of the lan-guage. This activity can only cease if nothing new is being said, or if nothing happens for which new words must be found. And this, we may safely say, is not possible—even if entire cultures routinely follow on Hegel and convince themselves otherwise. The same holds, then, for abnormal social poetic interaction, in which groups of people articulate new modes of interpersonal relation. In both its types, then, linguistic poetic interaction is the establishment of a common public vocabulary and is a general presupposition of human community. It is thus not pos-sible to eradicate it, and it has negative standing with respect to other types of discourse. But this global formulation is relatively empty: other types of discourse, such as metaphysics and political interaction, may be inimical to poetic interaction to different degrees, and regional investi-gation is again called for.

In sum, then, we may conclude that poetic interaction has negative global standing with regard to other forms of discourse, and positive regional standing with respect to some of them.

Chapter Twenty-three

Narrative

Poetic interaction, I have argued, is in various senses and in various of its forms both "liberated" and "liberating." It is now to be shown that the meanings stipulated for these terms in the preceding analysis—pre-eminently, unification of the self and improvisation—actually capture, in an elementary way, the kinds of liberation claimed for intrinsically emancipatory interaction by the tradition I have narrated. I will conclude by discussing that aspect of the critical standing of poetic interaction which has proven most troublesome to that tradition: its relation to the state.

The first sense in which poetic interaction is free—that of interactive freedom of choice—is familiar territory to English-language thought on freedom, thoroughly explored by Mill and manifold other writers. It has ancient roots in the democratic conception of freedom as the ability to live as one wished, which was reformulated in *Republic* 8 as the opportunity to pursue whatever sensory objects offered themselves. We have seen the close connection between sensory objects and words as forms of expression for Plato, and if we substitute "interpretation" for "sensory objects" in the preceding characterization of democratic freedom, we see that we have the interactive freedom of choice we are now discussing: if democratic freedom was the opportunity to gratify surplus ("unnecessary") desires, freedom in the present sense is the opportunity to produce a surplus of interpretations. True, there is no reason to think, here, that whoever has the opportunity to pursue such interpretations will actually do so, and or that interactive freedom of choice would lead to the same kind of social ill effects as does democratic freedom in Plato's argument. But interactive freedom of choice (like all freedom) can be morally ambiguous, because it can leave me free to interpret what I hear in destructive ways.

The second sense of freedom in poetic interaction, that of unification of the self, could be found in my narrative of the *Phaedrus*. Such unification there formed the response to "beautiful words" which, on the one hand, entranced the hearer as a lover of beautiful words and bodies, and which, at the same time, led him upward towards the Forms. The responses of a participant in erotic *paideia*, then, were produced by body and soul in cooperation. The concept of such cooperation, though with "psychophysical states" doing duty for the elaborate Platonic views on the nature of soul and body, is then captured in an elementary way by the experience of nonterminating normal poetic response.

The *Phaedrus*'s presentation of freedom as unification of the self was, as my narrative of *De Anima* 1.3 showed, incompatible with Platonic metaphysics. But the Aristotelian writings did not simply take such unification on its own terms, as an interactive phenomenon: they sought to ground it in an alternative metaphysics, that of substance. Hence, they reconceptualized freedom as the unification of the self accomplished by the self under the domination of reason, the individual's "substantial form." It was no longer interactive, but immanent to the individual.

The third *Critique* suggested that the empirical image of noumenal freedom was the individual human being with his or her faculties put into "free play" by the experience of a beautiful object. This gave us, once again, freedom as the unification of the self; but it was now free from metaphysical conceptions in the sense of supposedly true accounts of a supersensible realm, as well as from the Aristotelian domination of reason. But the "self" thus unified was the self of critique: a self composed of the transcendental faculties of sensibility, imagination, understanding, and reason. As a feature of the structure of the human mind itself, free play had to be achievable a priori—immanently to the mind and independently of interactions with actually existing objects, including human individuals. It was only in Hegel's concept of reconciliation that freedom as self-unification in and through the encounter with an other received its full and concrete articulation.

That articulation, as I analyzed it, was not metaphysical. Hegel took aesthetic interaction as an empirical given and distinguished it from the kinds of interaction that take place in the political sphere of the will. There was no assertion, here, that such interaction led us to any nonempirical realm, or that it could be produced a priori. There was also—in contrast to the *Phenomenology*—no assertion that reconciliation was the necessary result of an ongoing narrative, itself unavoidable, of self-consolidation. It was thus the Hegelian philosophy of art which, free from metaphysical, critical, and narrative prescriptions, began to fulfill the promise of the *Phaedrus* for an account of freedom as unification of the self. My treatment above of freedom as conveyed by normal poetic response was directed to capturing the elementary aspects of that account, without the developed hierarchy of conceptual structures in which Hegel's account of art was embedded.

The "freedom of improvisation" manifested in abnormal response is not to be found articulated among the Greeks I have narrated, and this can be traced to their metaphysical presuppositions: if reality has a basic order, then all things conform to that order. Ingenuity and creativity, in the modern sense, will be either trivial or false. Hence, the only praise of originality in Plato or Aristotle was Phaedrus' early remark that the speech of Lysias was "clever" and of "extraordinary wording" (*Phdr.* 228c, 234c). Even this was dropped once Socrates began to attack the speech; from then on, Phaedrus defended it rather for its completeness

(*Phdr.* 234e, 235b). The whole second part of the *Phaedrus* was devoted to showing definite procedures for constructing discourses, taking such construction out of the domain of originality and creativity and reducing it to determinate procedures and knowledge (cf. especially *Phdr.* 277b seq). The downgrading of improvisation was also evident in the Palinode's presentation of the soul's first vision of the loved one: if the youth's body could be called an "expression" of beauty, it would seem to have been a new and unconventional expression, one which the perceiver did not expect and which he had to handle by improvising new patterns of behavior, "learning the way from any source that may offer or finding it out for [himself]." But the whole point of this was to realize that what was happening was not in truth anything new or different, and was really the awakening of a memory (*Phdr.* 251a seqq. 252e seq.).

In the Aristotelian texts all meaning existed prior to interaction: the deliberator reasoned from the preset end of happiness, which he either understood or did not; the teacher already had the knowledge he passed to the pupil; and even the tragedian merely gave rational form to an inherited myth. In my narrative, the modern rejection, shown by Kant, of a preestablished rational and normative order to the empirical world allowed for improvisation in the form of "genius," through which nature "gives a new rule to art." We may say that the creation, by a genius, of a distinctively new type of artwork called forth a new kind of response from the critic, and thus articulated a rule that was truly new: where "primary articulation" in the *Phaedrus* was the rediscovery of the Forms, in the third *Critique* it was the creation of a new concept. Such creation, as exercised by a critic or pupil, was truly interactive: it viewed the artwork as a new utterance (by assigning it to "genius"), and responded by conjecturing a new "rule" for the interpretation of such utterances.

But there were two problems with this in the Kantian context. The first was that the account of genius made "nature" ambiguous. In the first two *Critiques* and in the Third's "Critique of Teleological Judgment," nature was defined as the set of law-governed appearances, wholly dominated so far as we could know by Newtonian causality. In what sense could such a mechanical set of phenomena "give a rule to art"? What would the apprehension of such a rule be? How could nature in the third *Critique* be construed as a "site" for moral purpose? To answer such questions, for Kant, would require us to investigate the noumenal realm, and such investigation is impossible (*KU* 410). In short, the denial of moral significance to nature had gone so far that nature, far from being a source of moral norms, was not even a site for moral action. Second, the aesthetic idea, which provided an inexhaustible source of new formulations for the critic, could be distinguished from the sublime only by the role of the imagination in achieving the full presence of a unified form. This, as we saw, was an expression of the postulate of unified source: here, the single source for the apprehension of an object as beautiful is the imagination itself. But the postulate of unified source fell with the Heideggerean critique of metaphysics, and with this came new concepts of nature and liberation.

First, Heidegger reconceptualized nature as earth, as what I called the "domain of presignificance." It then became, not merely a network of mechanical causes and effects, but something which could provide guidelines and parameters for human dwelling. These parameters were not "merely empirical," as if opposed to some more fundamental realm, but could be the *basic* parameters for such dwelling. Second, Heidegger's account of the coming-to-be of new worlds saw them, not in terms of full presence, but as arising out of the earth in such a way as to remain in "strife" with it. The inarticulable dimension of Being itself was thus what I called a "sublime" ground for new significance.

The response called forth by the work of art—its "preservation"—was then an improvisation of new practices; insofar as the work of art was primordially poetic, an improvisation of new ways of interpreting words. Improvisation became subversion in two ways: first, the new addition to the repertoire—the patterns called forth by the work of art—"refuted all that exists" in its exclusivity. Dependence on previous ways of doing things—on the previous repertoire—was reduced. This could happen, in the Kantian framework, only within limits: critique itself provided a condition of the human mind, a framework which could not be refuted or transcended, to which no alternative was possible and from which human beings could not be emancipated; the political expression of this framework, we saw, was civil society. On Heidegger's account, the limits to change resided within the unknown depths of earth, or within the latent possibilities of one's own language, and all known limits could be other than they were. My discussion of the freedom of terminating abnormal responses was designed to capture this view of subversive improvisation with unknown limits.

The experience of the sublime was for Kant "emancipatory" in that it freed the individual from all determinate content and threw him back on reason itself. Again, we may say, the Heideggerean texts developed this notion more fully by freeing it from the transcendental conditions established for Kant in the first two *Critiques*. When the dialogue between Heidegger and Tezuka was brought back to the primordial, indeterminate happening of Appropriation, they were confronted by an "abyss" similar to that of reason in the Kantian experience of the sublime.

Each was freed from his world, in the sense that he recognized that world as conditional upon something else. But neither could go on and develop an account of what that "something else" might be: its true articulation would be a "keeping silent about silence." The result was that both were freed from the need to develop ultimate accounts and interpretations of things in general. Each was "set more firmly" into his own world through the recognition that all accounts had to be phrased, for him, in terms of that world. But that world, as the final legitimating factor for social and other parameters quo ad nos, was not susceptible itself of any further legitimation: seen as coming forth from an inarticulable abyss, all worlds—not just the present one—were subverted. This is what my discussion of the emancipatory possibilities of nonterminating abnormal discourse was intended to capture.

Improvisation and unification of the self are not, then, arbitrary stipulations of freedom. They are grounded the only way such meanings can be grounded: historically, by reference to the tradition which has produced the concept of freedom itself. In the development of that tradition, the concepts have gradually shed metaphysical and transcendental grounds, and with that process accomplished, both can finally be seen to have, if not grounds, then everyday roots in the give-and-take of poetic interaction. Those roots are humble. None of the philosophers I have dealt with here claims that poetic interaction is something to which all other forms of interaction ought to conform, and so none has advocated global positive standing for it—as I do not. Hegel, we saw, explored its regional positive standing as a model to which political interaction ought to conform—and rejected it. And Heidegger articulated it as being so rarified and unique as to have no positive standing at all.

My argument that poetic interaction has negative standing—that it forms a distinct type of human interaction, one which is not to be eradicated—is an analogue to Habermas's account of communicative action as under threat from the "steering mechanisms" of power and money. It would not be such an issue if there were not a whole tradition in which thinkers have occluded poetic interaction, if not eradicated it; banished it from theory, if not from practice. Those attempts began in the Aristotelian political writings, and they continued to influence the Kantian question of the institutionalization of reflective judgment and Habermas's exclusive concentration upon communicative action. Traditionally, they went together with prescriptive status for metaphysics. As long as metaphysical discourse—the production of true assertions about the universe as a whole—is the single recognized paradigm of reason, there is no way to articulate poetic interaction, which aims not at truth but at emancipatory articulation, and which is an exploratory groping rather than a deductive procedure. The same held when Kant, in his first foundation, replaced "metaphysics" with "critique": if the paradigm of nonempirical knowledge is the production of true determining judgments about the nature of the human mind as a whole, then there is no place for reflective judgment, or for its interactive exercise in poetic interaction. And the occlusion continues when Habermas instates communicative action, with its truth claims, as the most complete paradigm of interaction, with other forms adumbrating it.

But *The Theory of Communicative Action* is on a different level from Aristotle and Kant, because in spite of its residues of the conception of substance, it stands—with the Kantian second foundation, with Heidegger, and with Hegel—beyond the theoretical prescriptions of metaphysics to other forms of discourse. This is evident in that Habermas claims, not merely truth, but centrality. For the centrality claim of *The Theory of Communicative Action* cannot be understood as applying to the assertion and justification of true propositions, but to the primary articulation of basic features of the life-world—in particular, the pain of the threats to it in contemporary society. Hence, like Hegel and Heidegger, Habermas is able to recognize poetic interaction as distinct from other forms (though, unlike them, he does not actually do so).

Together with the theoretical occlusion of poetic interaction went, according to our writers, a set of practical occlusions. The political sphere was treated by Plato, Aristotle, Kant, and Hegel as the region in which people pursue purposes in terms of fixed social distinctions. In the Aristotelian texts, we had the view that the political sphere is structured like a substance, with a single source for all its activity. Plato, we may say, located the *Phaedrus* outside the walls of Athens with good reason, for as long as the state is conceived this way, manifold forms of poetic interaction seem to be inimical to it. We may admit, for example, that erotic poetic interaction may indeed be influenced by class distinctions: it is likely that, in most societies if not all, the rich tend to be viewed as good-looking. But though influenced by such distinctions, erotic attraction in general hardly reduces to them. From Achilles and Briseis to the recent South Africa of Alan Paton's *Too Late the Phalarope*, such interaction between members of different classes has been a major literary theme, and so has the fact that to some extent—as Aristotle feared—it undermines the structure of the state. The same is true, on a more relaxed level, of linguistic poetic interaction, which also does not proceed in terms of fixed social distinctions: the only requirement for it is naive command of the language, which almost everyone possesses. Hegel's aesthetic critique of the state, articulated from the point of view of normal aesthetic poetic interaction, was clearly inimical to modern political and economic structures. Abnormal social poetic interaction, articulating new forms of interpersonal relation, is also, as my narrative of Heidegger showed, a threat to established orders. Thus, if the realm of fixed social distinctions also undertakes to be the sole source of all action within its boundaries and the single field for all interaction, then it is bound to be inimical to poetic interaction.

But the relation of poetic interaction to politics is more complex than this. The other side of the political sphere, in addition to its fixed distinctions, is its purposiveness, and one cannot pursue a purpose until it has been formulated. This requires two things: (1) a language in which to formulate it: and (2) stability for that language, so that I will not find my purpose reinterpreted as I pursue it. The political order requires, for the first of these, situating reason and hence its elementary form, poetic interaction—but for the second it requires that such interaction be a thing of the past, completed and finished. If the political order is to be the total field of human interaction, as it is for Aristotle, then the establishment of a common vocabulary must be prior to all interaction; this means that it must—as we saw in the Aristotelian texts—occur in the individual before he steps into political pursuits.

The Kantian challenge to this was to recognize, in the second foundation, that empirical concepts cannot be formed "monologically" in this way: there is a variety of ways to articulate any given set of experiences, if they exhibit the kind of form which suggests that they can be articulated at all. In the absence of determinate concepts, the isolated individual is unable even to see whether the form he finds in the sensory data is really there or not. Hence, for Kant the paradox of the state and poetic interaction, suppressed by Aristotle, comes into the open: on the one hand, the state requires a developed vocabulary and must permit the kind of interaction that provides it; but on the other, such interaction would risk subverting the state's interests, and so it cannot be permitted. Such was the "dark ground" of the founding of the university in the *Conflict of the Faculties*.

The Hegelian attempt to clear up that dark ground, and do away with the paradox, was to harness aesthetic experience for political life through the final philosophical sublation of aesthetic experience into religious truth. The Heideggerean response was to allow them to go their separate ways, leaving their connection wholly unexplored. Both thinkers, then, are attempting—like Kant—to save poetic interaction, as they understand it, from what they see as the danger to it posed by the state. Because *The Theory of Communicative Action* stands beyond the view of the state as sole field of human interaction, Habermas opens up the lifeworld as a terrain within which the installation of a common public vocabulary can proceed, and he finally—though indirectly—establishes the negative standing of poetic interaction.

Demarcation

It was in my narrative the Hegelian and Heideggerean approaches which sought to articulate freedom, not in terms of a hegemonic or prescriptive metaphysics, nor in terms of a relation to a transcendental or noumenal realm, but in mind as empirically evident: in the manifold and changing experiences of human interaction. Their views are thus the outcome of long-term processes in our culture, and my account of freedom and poetic interaction was designed primarily to capture them. But it also distinguishes itself from them as well. We can clarify the distinction by noting that the aspects of their thought of which I have made use are not fully developed by Hegel and Heidegger themselves. Why not?

There are, of course, excellent prudential reasons why a German thinker, in 1827 or 1935, would want to leave embryonic his views on how aesthetic experience is intrinsically critical of the political sphere. But in Hegel's case, it is ultimately the narrative structure of his thought which cuts off the aesthetic critique by subordinating it to religion. And this move can ultimately be sustained only by an absolute commitment to the basic structuring principle of that narrative, its concept of self-consolidation. Such commitment, I suggested, was for Hegel warranted by history up to his time; and, as we saw, history since Hegel—particularly the thought of Heidegger—has refuted it. If self-consolidation thus turns out to be the structuring principle, not of the only possible narrative of freedom, but merely of one among many such narratives, then we are free to "buy out" of the Hegelian narrative: in the case of my own narrative, at the point where religion disarmed the aesthetic critique. We are then left with two realms of interaction—art and the state—the latter of which, from its own point of view, has some remarkably critical things to say about the former. But other narratives are possible. We could even, on the Habermasian model of mutually adjusting learning processes, construct, as Marx did, a counter narrative in which the economy is superior to, because more basic than, art—and, as Marx did not, put this into situating discussion with reflection on poetic interaction.[4]

Heidegger's views also reveal philosophical, in addition to political, problems. The concept of freedom I have derived from him has to do with abnormal response, terminating and nonterminating. Such freedom is subversive: Heidegger's thought concerns the refutation of a society's claim of absolute validity for the basic parameters it installs over human behavior. But in order for subversion to take place, there must be something specific to subvert. The Heideggerean perspective cannot distinguish between subvertible structure which can be affirmed for some reason and subvertible structure which is mere chains be cast off, and it cannot distinguish true reconciliation with what exists around us from the self-delusional stopping-point of a "wandering among worlds." Complementing Heidegger with the Hegelian account of freedom as residing also in normal poetic interaction enables us to see what it would be like to validate a political (or other) structure poetically: it would be to see it as founded upon or facilitating the unification of the self in poetic interaction. And the idea of situating critique, as developing from poetic interaction, opens up the possibility that other forms of discourse can validate structures that, from a poetic point of view, are repressive.

The topography of freedom opened up by poetic interaction thus lies beyond Hegel and Heidegger, who turn out to present complementary parts of a larger whole. That topography can be summed up as follows. Freedom, in its most generic sense—one intended to capture even Habermas's sense—is the capacity to engage in certain forms of interaction. The forms of interaction recognized as liberated or emancipatory vary with the status of interpretive norms. In Habermasian cases, where norms "govern," emancipatory interaction is communicative action, in which people define their situation together on the basis of accepted norms. Where norms do not govern from the outset but must be selected or extrapolated, two further, and traditional, senses of freedom come into play: freedom as unification of the self and as improvisation. These two must come into play together, located originally in complementary modes of handling utterances. I cannot allow for more than one set of conventions to be at play in an utterance unless, at the same time, I allow for fewer than one: I cannot have Hegel without Heidegger.

The *topos*, the situation of poetic interaction, is thus beyond metaphysics, in the sense that it is beyond all attempts to reduce language use to a single set of norms and parameters. Once human thought is freed from that, it is able to articulate radically heterogenous uses of language—uses which aim, for example, not at truth but at freedom, or presumably at other values than those two, such as justice or equality. As merely one among a number of ways of interacting, poetic interaction has no global standing for critique: it does not constitute a norm for all forms of interaction. The extent to which it is of value for understanding or evaluating other types of interaction is a matter to be decided on a case-by-case basis.

But poetic interaction need not furnish the absolute standards which have been so long sought by those who want to criticize existing realities.

Such standards are required only to the extent that the entire network of social relations can be condemned in a single breath: as Kant condemned all inclinations, or as the *Phaedo* condemned the entire sensory world. Such condemnation, when it is of a society, relies on the Aristotelian conception of substance, for it postulates a unity to the social givens and hence a single "form" for them. The recognition of truly heterogenous forms of human interaction leads to something else. It means accepting that each form of interaction is "relative" with respect to the others— none is the paradigm for all—without going on and asserting that the whole panoply of them is "relative" to anything. Each of those different forms can be used, in a negative or regionally positive way, to criticize and perhaps to correct the others. But, as Heidegger showed, it makes no sense to characterize the totality of them as either "relative" or "absolute," any more than we can say, from the fact that all things in the universe move, either that the universe itself moves or that it does not.

Situated outside metaphysics, poetic interaction is also situated outside the state—in the life-world, the only home of freedom. And it is, as interactive, situated outside the individual, for I can hardly undertake interaction by myself. It is the presence of other people, in fact, which provides me with my current "situation": with bodies I find beautiful, with psychosomatic factors to and with which I must respond, and with linguistic parameters that I do not invent or stipulate but that come from those I live among—and from those who taught them their language, and from the teachers of those teachers, and so on back in time. "Situating" reason exercised in solitude permits nothing, is subjective and whimsical; when exercised with a group, it becomes capable of revealing the basic parameters that bind its members together, and of formulating new ones. The group may consist, as in most cases of flirtation, of an other who is actually present; it may include the "virtual presence" of preceding generations who are collectively responsible for the language and society in which one lives; and it may include people who, like the authors I have discussed in this book, are present through their writings. As thus humanly situated, poetic interaction brings about what I have called a "reconciling relationship": it clarifies, or newly articulates, the common ground which one individual shares with another, or with a group. It is thus at bottom a form of friendship—a word at the root of the Germanic "free"—or of love—allied to the Romance root of "liberty."

I have analyzed basic structures of poetic interaction, shown them as the outcome of long standing developments in philosophical traditions, and demarcated them from those traditions. Many topics have been left undiscussed, and one large set of these concerns issues of the norms by which to discriminate better and worse forms and cases of poetic interaction. Are there criteria by which we can rank forms of poetic interaction? Are the activities of explication, selection, articulation, and extrapolation procedures for which standards can be formulated? When is a narrative well constructed, or a demarcation well made? Articulating such standards is beyond the scope of this book; it is work for the future. But that Hegel and Heidegger appropriated narrative and demarcation for their thought suggests that such articulation is possible. Only if it is carried out can poetic interaction become an articulation of current parameters and an improvisation of new ones, which is criticizably rational. Such interaction, we may say, would be a sort of wisdom. The Greek word for friendship is *philia*, and the Greek word for wisdom is *sophia*. Is there not a very ancient word which could be applied to such rationalized poetic interaction, situated in friendship and aiming at wisdom? Is not that word "philosophy"?

Notes

General Introduction

1. Berlin, Isaiah, "Two Concepts of Liberty," in Berlin, *Four Essays on Liberty*, Oxford: Oxford University Press, 1969, 121.

2. Skinner, B. F., *Beyond Freedom and Dignity*, New York: Knopf, 1971.

3. Barry, Brian, "A Grammar of Equality," *The New Republic*, May 12, 1982, 36–39.

4. Quine, Willard V. O., and J. S. Ullian, *The Web of Belief*, New York: Random House, 1978.

5. Dreyfus, Hubert, and Paul Rabinow, *Michel Foucault: Beyond Structuralism and Hermeneutics*, 2d ed., Chicago: University of Chicago Press, 1983, 263.

6. Foucault, Michel, *Histoire de la sexualité*, vol. 2: *L'Usage des plaisirs*, Paris: Gallimard, 1984, 91–107.

7. Cf. Barker, Ernest, *Greek Political Theory*, 5th ed., London: Methuen, 1960, 114f.

8. Klosko, George, *The Development of Plato's Political Theory*, New York: Methuen, 1986, xi.

9. Mill, John Stuart, "On Liberty," in Burtt, Edwin A. (ed.), *The British Philosophers from Bacon to Mill*, New York: Modern Library, 1939, 987.

10. Hobbes, Thomas, *Leviathan,* Oxford: Clarendon, 1909, 161ff.; Hume, David, *Enquiry Concerning the Principles of Human Understanding*, in Hume, *Enquiries* (L. A. Selby-Bigge, ed.), 2nd ed., Oxford: Clarendon, 1902, 95.

11. Locke, John, *An Essay Concerning Human Understanding* (Alexander Campbell Fraser, ed.), 2 vols., New York: Dover, 1959, 1:329.

12. Toulmin, Stephen, *The Uses of Argument*, Cambridge: Cambridge University Press, 1958, 94–107.

13. Cf. *KRV* B.371 for the distinction; also cf. Foucault, Michel, "What Is an Author?" (Josué V. Harari, trans.), in Rabinow, Paul (ed.), *The Foucault Reader*, New York: Pantheon, 1984, 110ff.

14. Cf. Nozick, Robert, *Anarchy, State and Utopia*, Oxford: Blackwell, 1974, 26–28.

15. Saner, Hans, *Kant's Political Thought* (E. B. Ashton, trans.), Chicago: University of Chicago Press, 1973, 19–26.

16. An excellent recent example of this approach is Taylor, Charles, *Hegel*, Cambridge: Cambridge University Press, 1975.

17. For an acute and sympathetic, but not uncritical, example of this approach cf. Caputo, John, *The Mystical Element in Heidegger's Thought*, Athens, Ohio: Ohio University Press, 1978.

18. Cf. Rorty, Richard, *Philosophy and the Mirror of Nature*, Princeton: Princeton University Press, 1979, 167ff.

19. Cf. Danto, Arthur C., "Narration and Knowledge," in Danto, *Narration and Knowledge*, New York: Columbia University Press, 1985, 342–363.

20. Cf. Peperzak, Adrien, *Le jeune Hegel et la vision morale du monde*, The Hague: Nijhoff, 1960.

21. Derrida, Jacques, "Differance," in Derrida, *Speech and Phenomena* (David B. Allison, trans.), 129–160, Evanston: Northwestern University Press, 1973.

22. Cf. Spinoza, Benedict de, "Ethics," part 5, preface, in R. H. M. Elwes (trans.), *The Chief Works of Benedict de Spinoza*, 2 vols, New York: Dover, 1955, 2:244ff.; for Descartes's method see Descartes, René, "Meditations on the First Philosophy," preface to the reader, in Descartes, *The Meditations and Selections from the Principles* (John L. Veitch, trans.), La Salle, Ill.: Open Court, 1964, 11f.

23. In addition to his writings on the history of metaphysics, we may note Derrida's "attempt to recapture the revolutionary potential of a *series* of the key texts of literary modernism—Mallarmé, Artaud, Joyce, a project which found its rationale in the situation of France in the 1960's." McCabe, Colin, "Forward," in Spivak, Gayatri Chakravorty (ed.), *In Other Worlds*, New York: Methuen, 1987, xi; emphasis added. The same case could be made for Heidegger's discussions of poetry.

24. Hegel, G. W. F., *Vorlesungen über die Geschichte der Philosophie*, in Hegel, G. F. W., *Werke* (Eva Modenhauer & Karl Markus Michel, eds.), 20 vols., Frankfurt: Suhrkamp, 1970–71 (hereinafter *Werke*), 18:501; also cf. Danto, *Narration and Knowledge*, 352f.

25. Plato, *Crito*, 47e seq.; cf. Aristotle, *Magna Moralia* 1.1 1182a15–22.

26. Heidegger, Martin, *Erläuterungen zu Hölderlins Dichtung*, Frankfurt: Klostermann, 1951.

27. Cf. *NE* 8.2; 9.5.

Part One

Introduction
1. Lauer, Quentin, S. J., *A Reading of Hegel's Phenomenology of Spirit*, New York: Fordham University Press, 1976, 2.

Chapter 1
1. I should perhaps note, in anticipation of future work, that there is a form of dialectical advance which comes about, not through contradiction, but through its utter opposite: boredom.

2. Since it is directed against the basic principle of Hegel's own narrative in the *Phenomenology,* that critique is external to the book itself. It has no place in the present analysis.

3. Hegel, to be sure, does not ultimately separate these two sides of language: as we shall see, making sense of the world is essentially a communal affair. But in "Sense-Certainty" the situation is so abstract that no discussion of language as functioning in an interpersonal relation is possible. Thus, the only distinction between "I" and "other" is as abstract and empty as the "I's" themselves: it is spatial location. When consciousness realizes that "truth" for it is a tree, while for another it is a house, it does not enter into dialogue with that other to try to sort things out: it moves to the level of the Hegelian "universal": *PhG* 81f./61. For an account of the linguistic implication of this passage, cf. Taylor, Charles, "The Opening Arguments of the *Phenomenology,*" in Macintyre, Alasdair (ed.), *Hegel: A Collection of Critical Essays,* Garden City, N.Y.: Anchor, 1972, 151–187.

4. For Hegel's view of the nature of signs and symbols cf. *Enz.* nos. 454–462.

5. The example is from *Enz.* no. 457 Zus. ("Zus." indicates a supplement, or *Zusatz,* added by Hegel's executors.)

6. Cf. Hegel, G. W. F., *System der Sittlichkeit* (Georg Lasson, ed.), Hamburg: Meiner, 1967, 23f.; English translation, *System of Ethical Life* (H. S. Harris, trans; T. M. Knox, ed.) Albany: State University of New York Press, 1979, 115f.; Hegel, *Jenaer Realphilosophie* (Johannes Hoffmeister, ed.), Hamburg: Meiner, 1931, 207ff. The concept of recognition was made central to understanding the *Phenomenology* by Alexandre Kojève, *Introduction to the Reading of Hegel* (James Nichols, trans.), New York: Basic Books, 1969.

7. This is mistranslated by Miller as "embraces many and varied meanings."

8. Hobbes, Thomas, *Leviathan,* Oxford: Clarendon, 1909, 94–98, 128–132.

9. In *RPh.,* this element of coercion is retained by modern society in the raising of children, the first concern of which is to raise the child out of his "natural immediacy"; such coercion cannot proceed via rational discussion, since the child is not yet rational: it must operate by force, and children "must be obedient": *RPh.* 158f./117f., 265.

10. For the "determinate reality" that thoughts acquire on being expressed, cf. *Enz.* no. 462 Zus.

11. Hegel, G. W. F., *System der Sittlichkeit,* 19ff./113f.; also cf. Blanchette, Oliva, "Language, the Primordial Labor of History," *Cultural Hermeneutics* 1 (1974): 325–382.

12. RPh. 173f/129.

13. Kojève, Alexandre, *Introduction to the Reading of Hegel.*

14. Marx, Karl, *Economic and Political Manuscripts of 1844,* in Robert C. Tucker (ed.), *The Marx-Engels Reader,* New York: Norton, 1972, 88.

15. For a critique of Kojève's interpretation, cf. Kelley, George Armstrong, "Notes on Hegel's 'Lordship and Bondage,' " in MacIntyre (ed.), *Hegel: A Collection of Critical Essays,* 189–217.

16. Hyppolite, Jean, *Genesis and Structure of Hegel's Phenomenology of Spirit*

(Samuel Cherniak and John Heckman, trans.), Evanston: Northwestern University Press, 1974, 196–215.

17. Only if that is so, in fact, can we hope to understand the series of *redefinitions* of the Unchangeable that forms much of the dialectical progression of the "Unhappy Consciousness," resulting in the human community as the "Mediator" between God and man. As Quentin Lauer puts it, "It is not this kind of God which makes for unhappiness; it is unhappiness which makes for this kind of God": Lauer, *A Reading of Hegel's Phenomenology*, 119.

18. Kierkegaard, Søren, *Fear and Trembling and the Sickness unto Death* (Walter Lowrie, trans.), Garden City, N.Y.: Anchor Books, 1941, 21–132.

Chapter 2

1. The Roman Republic is the standard example: *PhG* 330-346/279–294.

2. Aristotle, *Politics* 1.2.1253a; cf. part two, chapters 12–13 below.

3. It is also present, though I did not stop to show it, in the "Unhappy Consciousness," where the Unchangeable is a pure unity over against the multiplicity of consciousness itself.

4. Cf. *Metaphysics* 7.17.

5. The connection of externalization and alienation is why, for Lukács's Marxist interpretation of Hegel, the concept of externalization is as essential to the *Phenomenology* as that of recognition is for Kojève. And like Kojève, Lukács measures the concept directly against reality rather than viewing its uses internally to the *Phenomenology*; like Kojève, Marx, and Kierkegaard, he concludes that Hegel's *Aufhebung* of it is wrong. Lukács, Georg, *The Young Hegel* (Rodney Livingstone, trans.), London: Merlin Press, 1975, 537–567.

6. Also cf. Hegel, G. W. F., *Wissenschaft der Logik* (Georg Lasson, ed.), 2 vols., Hamburg: Meiner, 1932; English translation by A. V. Miller, *Hegel's Science of Logic*, New York: Humanities Press, 1976, 9f./31f.

7. Hence, even irony is for Hegel not an individual taking distance from his utterances, but the "general dissolution" of the content itself as the individual shrugs it off: cf. *PhG* 518/450f.

8. *RPh.* 74f./54–56.

9. Also cf. Findlay, J. N., "Analysis," in Miller's translation, p. 568.

Chapter 3

1. Hume, David, *A Treatise of Human Nature* (L.A. Selby-Bigge, ed.), Oxford: Clarendon, 1888, 402.

2. Aesthetic "reconciliation," in senses derived from but not identical to Hegel's, became an important normative concept for the classical Frankfurt writers, in particular Adorno. Cf. Benhabib, Seyla, *Critique, Norm and Utopia*, New York: Columbia University Press, 1986, 205–212, and Habermas's remarks discussed below in part three, chapter 19.

3. Hegel, *Wissenschaft der Logik* 2:260/619f.

4. Kaufmann, Walter, *Hegel: A Reinterpretation*, Garden City, N.Y.: Anchor Books, 1966, 136; also cf. Pöggeler, Otto, "Zur Deutung der *Phanomenologie des Geistes*," *Hegel-Studien* 1(1961): 255–294.

5. *PhG* 489-507/424–451; *Aesth.* 30f., 149/10f., 102.

6. For textual problems with the *Aesthetics,* cf. Knox's introduction to the English translation, *Aesthetics* (T. M. Knox, trans.), Oxford: Oxford University Press, 1975, vi–vii, and Moldenhauer and Michel's comments at *Werke* 15: 575–578.

7. Cf. *Aesth.* 82f., 109, 14.21/ 50, 71, 806.

8. Cf. *Aesth.* 14.210–215, 220-226/951–955, 959–962.

9. *Aesth.* 225, 14.73f., 168–171/163, 847f., 929–932.

10. *Aesth.* 230, 14.8, 233f., 237f./166f., 968, 972.

11. Not all details in a work of art get there as purifications of givens in the external world; some are simply products of the artist's imagination. But imagination itself is for Hegel a "purifying" power. We do not imagine things and events in all the concrete detail they would have if actually experienced. Our mind is itself selective and calls up for us only those features of what it imagines that are important for us. Imagination, too, always operates with a guiding conception and selects for the images it produces only those features which are significant for that conception; its products are ipso facto "stamped" with universality (*Aesth.* 227/164).

12. This does not mean that Richard cannot be presented without physical deformity, as Sir Laurence Olivier has done; it is precisely what makes such a presentation so striking.

13. Cf. *PhG* 517f./449–451 for a similar critique of Greek art—without, of course, the present contrast with the modern perspective.

14. *Aesth* 14.227, 233, 236f., 242f./964, 968, 972, 976.

15. *Aesth.* 43, 59f., 122-132/19f., 32, 82–89.

16. *Aesth.* 176f., 182, 202f./124, 128, 145.

17. *Aesth.* 34f., 164, 218/12f., 114, 157.

18. Cf. the translator's footnote on p. 184 of Hegel, *On Christianity: Early Theological Writings* (T. M. Knox, trans.), New York: Harper Torchbooks, 1961.

19. *Aesth.* 150f., 13.120-122/102f., 517–519.

20. *Aesth.* 304f., 13.141–144, 449/224f., 533–535, 778.

21. Where it may "exist" under some such description as "rat no. 1329674 completed maze 9D in 29.2 seconds."

22. Cf. *Aesth.* 81f., 142–150, 164f., 207–212, 264-266/49, 97–102, 114f., 148–152, 193f.

Chapter 4

1. *Aesth.* 48–50; cf. 153–160, 213-216/24f.; 106–115, 153–155.

2. *RPh.* 165–207, 253f./122–155, 189f.

3. Hegel, G. F. W., *Philosophie des Rechts: Die Vorlesungen von 1819/20* (Dieter Henrich, ed.), Frankfurt: Suhrkamp, 1983, 159, 193, 195f.

4. It is presented even in the admirable account of Shlomo Avineri, *Hegel's Theory of the Modern State*, Cambridge: Cambridge University Press, 1972, 176–184. Though Avineri tries "to draw on all Hegel's writings on social and political problems" in formulating his account (p viii), it is noteworthy that he never mentions the *Aesthetics*.

5. *Aesth.* 250–252, 264-266/182–185, 193f.

6. *Aesth.* 249f.; cf. 252, 254/182, 184, 189.

7. Hegel, *Wissenschaft der Logik* (Georg Lasson, ed.) 2 vols, Hamburg: Meiner, 1932, 2.478-483/818–822.

8. There are in fact three sorts of will operative in the political realm. The third type, which does not directly concern us here, is the "objective will." This is the will which wills the universal good but does so in an unconscious way—as when, for example, the actions of a number of individual entrepreneurs in a society have the effect, unintended by any of them, of increasing the general wealth.

9. Cf. *RPh.* 143f., 210; *Werke* 7:67f/105f., 107, 230.

10. Cf. *RPh.* at *Werke* 7:67f./230.

11. Lukács, *The Young Hegel*, 368f.

12. Hegel thus remains, in his *Aesthetics*, true to the claims of his youthful "System-Program": "So we must go beyond even the state!—for every state must treat free men as cogs in a machine; and this it ought not to do; so it must *stop*": Hegel, G. W. F., "Das älteste Systemprogramm des deutschen Idealismus," in *Werke* 1.234–236; English translation in Henry S. Harris, *Hegel's Development: Toward the Sunlight*, Oxford: Clarendon, 1972, 510–512.

13. *RPh.* 207–210, 222; *Werke* 7:434/155–158, 166, 285.

14. As Malcolm Knox has put it, "Even though religion necessarily takes on an external form, it knows itself to be too elevated ever to be satisfied in real life." Cf. Knox's translation, at 553n., and *Aesth.* 151f.; 13.165f./103f., 553.

15. Hegel, G. W. F., *Vorlesungen über die Philosophie der Religion*, in *Werke* 16:236–246; 17:330–333; English translation in *Lectures on the Philosophy of Religion* (E. B. Speiers and J. Burdon Sanderson, trans.), 3 vols., New York: Humanities Press, 1962, 1:246–257, 3:135–139; *RPh.* 220-233/165–174; also cf. Fackenheim, Emil, *The Religious Dimension in Hegel's Thought*, Boston: Beacon Press, 1967, 220–222.

16. Hegel, *Vorlesungen über die Philosophie der Geschichte* in *Werke*, 12:31, 311, 403f.; *Lectures on the Philosophy of History* (J. Sibree, trans.), New York: Dover, 1956, 18, 254f., 333f.

17. *Philosophie der Geschichte*, 31, 283/18, 229f.

18. *Philosophie der Geschichte*, 31, 283/18, 229f.; *Philosophie der Religion, Werke* 14:242/1:252f.; *RPh.* 111–113, 215–217, *Werke* 7:406-410/83f., 160f., 280f.

Chapter 5

1. Schürmann, Reiner, "Political Thinking in Heidegger," *Social Research* 45 (1978): 216f.

2. For the publication problems with *Being and Time,* cf. Heidegger, Martin, "Mein Weg in die Phänomenologie," in Heidegger, *Zur Sache des Denkens*, Tübingen: Niemeyer, 1969, 87f.; for those of the *Phenomenology*, cf. Kaufmann, Walter, *Hegel: A Reinterpretation,* Garden City, N.Y.: Anchor Books, 1966, 90–95.

3. Heidegger also maintains that such entities are not what we really experience anyway, but are theoretical constructs: *SZ* 59–62, 71, 74.

4. Frege, Gottlob, "On Sense and Meaning," in Peter Geach and Max Black

(eds.), *Translations from the Philosophical Writings of Gottlob Frege*, Oxford: Oxford University Press, 1952, 56–78. For the distinction as drawn in *Being and Time,* see *SZ* 145, 151, 161.

5. What follows is indebted to Sallis, John, "Language and Reversal," *Southern Journal of Philosophy* 4 (1973):109–124.

6. Wittgenstein, Ludwig, *Tractatus Logico-Philosophicus* (D. F. Pears and B. F. McGuinness, trans.), London: Routledge and Kegan Paul, 1961, no. 5.62, p. 114; Wittgenstein, *Philosophical Investigations* (G. E. M. Anscombe, trans.), 3rd ed., New York: Macmillan, 1958, nos. 199–207, pp. 80–82.

7. For this hypothesis, see Anthony Burgess, "The Syntax of Food Adds Spice to Language," *The New York Times*, June 2, 1982.

8. Heidegger, Martin, "Hölderlin und das Wesen der Dichtung," in Heidegger, *Erläuterungen zu Hölderlins Dichtung*, Frankfurt: Klostermann, 1951, 35; English translation "Hölderlin and the Essence of Poetry," in *Existence and Being* (Douglas Scott, trans.), Chicago: Regnery, 1949, 276.

9. Even Heidegger's own "fundamental ontology," pursued in *Being and Time*'s phenomenological analyses, thus turns out to be a wrestling with and modification of inauthentic interpretations of human life.

Chapter 6

1. *SZ* 250; also cf. 238–240, 263; Harries, Karsten, "Heidegger as a Political Thinker," in Michael Murray (ed.), *Heidegger and Modern Philosophy*, New Haven: Yale University Press, 1978, 310.

2. Kierkegaard, *Fear and Trembling*, 81f.

3. Heidegger, "Hölderlin und das Wesen der Dichtung," in Heidegger, *Erläuterungen zu Hölderlins Dichtung*, 4th ed, expanded, Frankfurt: Klostermann, 1971, 38ff.; English translation *Existence and Being* (Scott, trans.), Chicago: Regnery, 1949, 291ff.

4. The best discussion of the elusive facts of Heidegger's Nazi period is Palmier, Jean-Michel, *Les écrits politiques de Heidegger*, Paris: L'Herne, 1968.

5. To be subjugated or "enslaved" is a possible translation of *Verfallen*, which MacQuarrie and Robinson render more circumspectly as "falling" (cf. *SZ* no. 38). In terms of "The Origin of the Work of Art," world is the "ever non-objective to which we are subject," *dem wir unterstehen: UKW* 33/44.

6. Biemel, Walter, *Heidegger*, Reinbeck: Rowohlt, 1973, 97; The Nazi period was 1933–34, for which see Harries, "Heidegger as a Political Thinker," 304f. The chronological bibliography in Richardson, William J., S. J., *Heidegger: Through Phenomenology to Thought*, The Hague: Nijhoff, 1963, dates the writing of "The Origin of the Work of Art" from 1935 (p. 679); cf. also Kockelmans, Joseph, *Heidegger on Art and Art Works*, The Hague: Nijhoff, 1985, 76f.

7. See Hofstadter's translation at Heidegger, Martin, *Poetry Language Thought* (Albert Hofstadter, trans.), New York: Harper and Row, 1971, 86f.

8. The third view of the "thing," as the unity of a manifold of sensible givens, does not have any perspicuous application to the nature of language; it is treated at notably less length: *UKW* 14f./25f.

9. This association continues through the view of language as basically a "set

of propositions," in Frege and the early Wittgenstein, though the "bearer" of properties for them is no longer an Aristotelian substance but a mere object as such: Frege, Gottlob, "Function and Concept," in Geach and Black (eds.), *Translations from the Philosophical Writings*, 21–41; Wittgenstein, *Tractatus Logico-Philosophicus*, no. 4.001, p. 35.

10. This is then in the spirit of the later Wittgenstein's dictum that "the meaning of a word is its use in the language," or of Austin's "words are our tools": Wittgenstein, *Philosophical Investigations*, no. 43, p. 20; Austin, J. L., "A Plea for Excuses," in Austin, *Philosophical Papers* (J. L. Urmson and G. J. Warnock, eds.), Oxford: Clarendon, 1961, 129.

11. In the English translation, *eigenwüchsig* is rendered as "independent" and *In-sich-Ruhen* as "self-contained," thus missing Heidegger's careful contrast.

12. Applied to language, this means that both the ideal, "propositional" approach of the early Wittgenstein and Frege, and the contextualized, behavioral approach of the later Wittgenstein and Austin, fail to capture language's own phenomenality.

13. The question of how this happens is one of the deepest in Heideggerean scholarship; I will avoid it here. See Schürmann, Reiner, *Le principe d'anarchie*, Paris: du Seuil, 1982, for an extended discussion.

14. For Heidegger's main developments of this view see his "Andenken" in Heidegger, *Erläuterungen zu Hölderlins Dichtung*, 79–151; English translation, "Remembrance of the Poet," in *Existence and Being* (Scott, trans.), 243–269; and "Dichterisch wohnet der Mensch," in Heidegger, *Vorträge und Aufsätze*, 3 vols., 2d ed., Pfullingen: Neske, 1967, 2:61–78.

15. Cf. Gadamer, Hans-Georg, "Being, Spirit, God," in *Heidegger Memorial Lectures* (Werner Marx, ed.; Steven W. Davis, trans.) Pittsburgh: Duquesne University Press, 1982, 67ff.

16. Thus, for John Stuart Mill (to give one of many examples), proper names are denotative but not connotative: they "denote the individuals who are called by them, but they do not indicate or imply any attributes as belonging to such individuals." Mill, J. S., *A System of Logic*, London: Longmans, New Impression, 1970, 20.

17. For an empirical account of this, cf. Macnamara, John, *Names for Things*, Cambridge, Mass.: MIT Press, 1982, 18f.

18. There are, in fact, highly complex and subtle regulations for bestowing proper names in many cases, as is witnessed by the agonies that parents often go through trying to name their children. Certain names are, as well, more appropriate than others for certain *types* of entity: "Fido" is not, in English, an acceptable name for my son; "Pikes's Peak" is not, somehow, a wholly "proper" name for a dog.

19. Marx, Werner, *Heidegger and the Tradition,* Evanston: Northwestern University Press, 1971, 214; cf. pp. 211–256 for an acute development of this criticism.

20. Cf. *UKW* 59/71, on the "nothing," and 62/75f.

21. Schwan, Alexander, *Politische Philosophie im Denken Heideggers*, Köln: Westdeutscher Verlag, 1965.

22. This is presumably why Hobbes assigned a divine origin to language and specifically exempted it from his account of man in the state of nature, in the "war of each against all": Hobbes, *Leviathan*, 24, 94.

23. Cf. Heidegger's own refusal, when pressed, to talk about concrete political structures in his interview with *Der Speigel* magazine, "Only a God Can Save Us Now," *Graduate Faculty Philosophy Journal* 6 (1977):5–27.

Chapter 7

1. For antimethodological (and pro-"way") considerations, cf. Heidegger, *Nietzsche*, 2 vols., Pfullingen: Neske, 1961, 2:133f.; *Der Satz vom Grund*, 4th ed., Pfullingen: Neske, 1971, 185.

2. Cf. McCumber, John, "Language and Appropriation: The Nature of Heideggerean Dialogue," *The Personalist* 60 (1979):384–396.

3. He is elsewhere said to be "Prof. Tezuka, from the Imperial University of Tokyo": cf. "Hinweise," *UzS* 269.

4. The most important recent defender of the "single-grammar" view is Noam Chomsky; see his *Language and Mind*, New York: Harcourt, Brace & World, 1968; for the original formulation of the "Syntax as Conditioning World-View" thesis, see Whorf, B.L., *Language, Thought and Reality*, Cambridge, MA: MIT Press, 1956.

5. Few competent English speakers, for example, would know that a paper entitled "Long-Term Potentiation in Dentate Gyrus: Induction by Asynchronous Volleys in Separate Afferents" was about the nervous systems of rats. This paper is referred to in Browne, W. Malcolm "Wanted: Interpreters for the Frontiers of Science," *The New York Times*, January 6, 1987.

6. For further examples, cf. Edie, James M., *Speaking and Meaning*, Bloomington: Indiana University Press, 1976, 156f.

7. *FDL* 98f., 102f., 110f., 120, 123–125, 126f./12f., 15f., 21f., 28, 30–32, 33f.

8. *FDL* 114–117; also cf. 131/24–26, 37, where the German *Spur,* meaning trace or spoor, is rendered as "trail."

9. Heidegger, "Der Spruch des Anaximander," *HW* 302.

10. This incomprehension is illustrated most radically, perhaps, in the fact that the name of the Japanese is given, not in the dialogue itself, but in the references at the end of the book. This seems to put him on the same level as the other participant, who is explicitly identified only as an "Inquirer." In fact, the contrast is enormous: the "Inquirer," we learn in the course of the dialogue, is a Swabian former student of Edmund Husserl, who is interested in hermeneutics and wrote *Being and Time.* Obviously, then, he is the famous Martin Heidegger himself, about whom we readers have reams of background information. About the "Japanese," we have no such background information to go on, and the dialogue gives us little indeed. The asymmetry could not be stronger: where for the "Inquirer" no name is needed, for the "Japanese" none is possible.

11. Heidegger, *Nietzsche*, 2:138.

12. Biemel, Walter, "Poetry and Language in Heidegger," in Joseph J. Kockelmans (ed.), *On Heidegger and Language*, Evanston: Northwestern University Press, 1972, 77.

13. The German *vordergründig* is here misleadingly translated as "surface matters."

14. Cf. Heidegger, Martin, *The Question of Being* (William Kluback and Jean T. Wilde, trans.; German text with English facing), New Haven: Yale University Press, 1958, 104.

15. Cf. Marx, Karl, and Friedrich Engels, *The German Ideology*, in Tucker (ed.), *The Marx-Engels Reader*, 123.

16. See Pascale, Richard, and Anthony Arthur, *The Art of Japanese Management*, New York: Simon & Schuster, 1981, *passim* for a treatment of these issues, through in a vein no more "Heideggerean" than Marx's.

17. It remains the key to Heidegger's important discussion of freedom in his essay "Vom Wesen des Grundes" (which I therefore did not discuss): Heidegger, "Vom Wesen des Grundes," in *Wegmarken*, Frankfurt: Klostermann, 1967, 21–71.

18. For a defense of the view that we are in such an epoch (and that Heidegger thought we were) see Schürmann, *Le principe d'anarchie.*

Part Two

Chapter 8

1. For a general account of recent literature on Greek views of freedom, cf. Muller, Robert, "Remarques sur la liberté gracque," *Dialogue* (Canada) 25 (1986): 421–447.

2. Cf. *Rep.* 3.387b; 4.433d, 7.536e; 8.566e; 9.577c, 591a; *Laws* 7.808a; *Timaeus* 85e.

3. Ernest Barker maintains that "democracy," as the term was employed in ancient Greece, did not have the kind of wholly individualistic sense it has here but included reference to a common social will; he cites Pericles, to whom we might add the Protagoras of *Protagoras* (325a seqq.). But it is impossible to generalize about "the" meaning of such terms in ancient Greece (and Barker extends his generalization even to modern uses of "democracy"): Aristotle's remark that the idea I call "democratic freedom" has "arisen" in democracies reports a situation which is a couple of generations later than either Pericles or Protagoras. The easiest conclusion is that the terms "freedom" and "democracy" were, as befits parameters, in a state of flux, moving from the moderate usages of older generations to the more radical sense the term apparently had for younger ones—a flux which is precisely what the *Republic* describes. Barker, *Greek Political Theory*, 296; for Callicles as representing "a 'philosophy of life' of whose prevalence in the latter years of the fifth century we have much convergent testimony," cf. Plato, *Gorgias* (E. R. Dodds, ed.), Oxford: Clarendon, 1959, 12–15.

4. And indeed Aristotle denied it: *Pol.* 5.12.1316a24f.

5. The main statement of this is at 4.439a seqq., but it is repeated metaphorically throughout the dialogue. Unnecessary desires are compared to intruders who burst into the "citadel" of a young man's soul, which they force him to turn over to each of them in turn (8.561b seq.). They are likened to a drunken beast,

which gambols about and sallies forth (9.571c), and to winged drones which buzz about in the soul (9.573a). They are a "motley mob" of appetites (4.431b seq.), and it is said that those who are much devoted to "feasting and such things" are swept around in their quest for false pleasures, never having looked upwards to experience the "pure and stable pleasure" afforded by the Forms (9.586a seqq.).

6. For the ontological and moral status of "disorderly motion" in the Timaeus, see Vlastos, Gregory "The Disorderly Motion in the 'Timaeus'," in R. E. Allen (ed.), *Studies in Plato's Metaphysics*, London: Routledge and Kegan Paul, 1965, 397ff.; Vlastos argues there that his account of the *Timaeus* is in harmony with the *Laws*. As we shall see, it is in harmony with the *Phaedrus* as well; the applicability of its general account of goodness and badness to the *Republic* should be clear from the passages cited above.

7. Also cf. *Rep.* 4.444b, 9.589c–591b; *Gorgias* 503d seqq. (where the beauty of the soul is compared to that achieved by the artist), *Phaedo* 79e–80a; *Laws* 726–728b. For general accounts, cf. Vlastos, Gregory, "Justice and Happiness in the *Republic*," in Vlastos (ed.), *Plato: A Collection of Critical Essays*, vol. 2, Notre Dame, Ind.: University of Notre Dame Press, 1978, 66–95; Barker, *Greek Political Theory*, 165–208.

8. Thucydides, *History of the Peloponnesian War* 2.36; also cf. Pohlenz, Max, *Freedom in Greek Life and Thought* (Carl Lofmark, trans.), Dordrecht: Reidel, 1966, 17–38.

9. Cf. Maurer, Reinhart, *Platons "Staat" und die Demokratie*, Berlin: de Gruyter, 1970, 182.

10. Thucydides, *History* 2.59, 65.

11. Cf. Dorter, Kenneth, *Plato's Phaedo*, Toronto: University of Toronto Press, 1982, 82.

12. Cf. *Phaedo* 66b–67a; *Rep.* 10.611e seq.; *Phdr.* 246a.

13. Of the eschatological myths in Platonic writings—in the *Gorgias*, *Republic*, *Phaedo* and *Phaedrus*—only the latter two use the word *eleutheria*; chapter 9 will deal with the *Phaedrus*. For Phaedo's life, cf. Dorter, *Plato's Phaedo*, 9f.

14. Also cf. *Phaedo* 82e seq.

15. For liberation as *lysis,* or release, cf. *Phaedo* 67d, 82d, 83b, 84a.

16. The locution I have translated as "in accordance with itself" is *autê kath autên*, which is often applied to the Forms and means something like "in its true nature" or "as it really is." Cf. *Phaedo* 64d, 67a, 67d, 79d, 81c, 83b.

17. Cf. *Phaedo* 66b–d, 82a–c; also see *Rep.* 1.342e, 347a seqq.

18. For an attempt at extracting such unity as can be had, cf. Guthrie, W. K. C., "Plato's Views on the Nature of Soul," in Vlastos (ed.), *Plato: A Collection of Critical Essays*, vol. 2, 230–243; for a less unitary account see Robinson, T. M., *Plato's Psychology*, Toronto: University of Toronto Press, 1970, 39–46.

19. Cf. Allen, R. E., "Participation and Predication in Plato's Middle Dialogues," in R. E. Allen (ed.), *Studies in Plato's Metaphysics*, 43–60.

20. Cf. Mendelson, Alan, "Plato's *Phaedo* and the Frailty of Human Nature," *Dionysius* 5 (1981):29–39.

21. Gill, Christopher, "The Death of Socrates," *Classical Quarterly*, n.s., 22 (1973): 25–28.

22. Seeskin, Kenneth, "Socratic Philosophy and the Dialogue Form," *Philosophy and Literature* 8 (1984):181–194.

23. Cf. Plato, *Phédon* (Léon Robin, ed.), Paris: Budé, 1967, vii; Hackforth, R., *Plato's Phaedo*, Indianapolis: Bobbs-Merrill, 1958, 7.

24. The classic example of this is Popper, Karl, *The Open Society and its Enemies*, vol. 1: *The Spell of Plato*, 4th ed rev., Princeton: Princeton University Press, 1962; Reinhart Maurer has argued against this that Plato in the *Republic* is not an unequivocal enemy even of the "democratic" freedom he paints in such awful colors. "Er übernimmt jene anarchisch scheinende Freiheitsdefinition, fragt jedoch, wie man und die Besten wollen wollen, damit sie in der Polis leben können, wie sie wollen." Maurer, *Platons "Staat,"* 185.

Chapter 9

1. A class which itself is "democratic" in that it aims only at satisfying its desires: cf. *Rep.* 2.373b, 4.442a seq., 9.580d.

2. In Hackforth's phrase: Hackforth, R., *Plato's Phaedrus*, Cambridge: Cambridge University Press, 1972, 31.

3. For a recapitulation of some of the Platonic divisions, cf. McCumber, John, "Discourse and Soul in Plato's *Phaedrus*," *Apeiron* 16 (1982):31f.; Herman Sinaiko, on whose outline of the speech I base my account, makes no reference to the method of division: Sinaiko, Herman L., *Love, Knowledge and Discourse in Plato*, Chicago: University of Chicago Press, 1965, 29ff.; but cf. Helmbold, W. C., and W. B. Holther, "The Unity of the *Phaedrus*," *University of California Publications in Classical Philology* 14 (1950–52): 394; Rodis-Lewis, Geneviève, "L'Articulation des thèmes du Phèdre," *Revue Philosophique de France et de l'Étranger* 165 (1975): 10. For a general account of division cf. Lloyd, A. C., "Plato's Description of Division," in R. E. Allen (ed.), *Studies in Plato's Metaphysics*, 219–230.

4. Cf. *Philebus* 16e; also Hackforth, *Plato's Phaedrus*, 132n, 134–137.

5. Cf. *Phdr.* 236b, 252b, 257b

6. *Timaeus* 34a; *Laws* 893c seqq.

7. This has been summarized in Robinson, *Plato's Psychology*, 111–118.

8. Cf. *Timaeus* 34b seqq.

9. Demos, Raphael, "Plato's Doctrine of the Psyche as Self-Moving Motion," *Journal of the History of Philosophy* 6 (1968):33–45; as warrant for my general strategy here, cf. Charles Griswold: "The soul *is* the various motions or experiences which it originates and undergoes." If so, the only way to see in what sense the soul is self-moving in the *Phaedrus* would be to examine its experiences and motions in that dialogue, as I have done. Griswold, "Self-Knowledge and the 'Idea'" of Soul in Plato's *Phaedrus*," *Revue de Métaphysique et de Morale* 86 (1981): 483.

10. Cf. Griswold, Charles, *Self-Knowledge in Plato's Phaedrus*, New Haven: Yale University Press, 1986, 126 (which does not, however, go so far as to attribute self-motion to the couple as such). For Griswold's insightful discussion of self-motion in general, see op. cit., 78–87.

11. Robin, Léon, *Théorie platonicienne de l'amour*, Paris: Alcan, 1908, 141.

12. Cf. Sartre, Jean-Paul, *L'être et le néant*, Paris: Gallimard, 1943, 94ff. for an example of such a description—concerning a couple in a café—which will recur in part three of this book.

13. Schleiermacher, F. E. D., *Introduction to the Dialogues of Plato* (Wm. Dobson, trans.), London: Parker, 1836, 68; Chen, Chung-Hwan, "The 'Phaedrus' as the Transition from the Platonism in the Earlier Dialogues to the Dialectics and Theology in the Later Dialogues," *Studi Internazionali di Filosofia* 4 (1972):77–90; Nussbaum, Martha, "This Story Isn't True: Poetry, Goodness, and Understanding in Plato's *Phaedrus*," in Moravcsik, Julius and Philip Temko (eds.), *Plato on Beauty, Wisdom and the Arts*, New Jersey: Rowman and Littlefield, 1982, 79–124. Also cf. Santos, Gerasimo, "Passionate and Platonic Love in the *Phaedrus*," *Ancient Philosophy* 2 (1982): 105–114, for contrasts with the *Symposium*, and Bröcker, Werner, *Platons Gespräche*, 2nd ed., Frankfurt: Klostermann, 1967, 522, for the reference to Diogenes Laertius.

14. Not that this explains the matter fully: for a discussion cf. Robin, Léon (trans.), *Phèdre*, Paris: Budé, 1978, lx seqq.

15. Cf. *Rep.* 3.416d seqq., 4.420a seq., 5.458c–461a, 6.500b seq., 7.539e. The ambiguous account of definition at the beginning of the second speech, according to which definition is arrived at either by analysis of the appropriate form or by agreement among those party to the conversation (*Phdr.* 237c2–4), has the result of making the mode of discourse presented in the speech applicable both to the rulers of the *Republic*'s ideal state and to their helpers, the "auxiliaries": the former analyze Forms, and the latter simply agree with the analysis and carry out orders formulated on its basis. Cf. *Rep.* 2.375e seqq.; 3.412c seqq.; and Sinaiko, *Love, Knowledge and Discourse in Plato*, 32f.

16. For which see *Rep.* 3.413c seq., 5.473c seq., 6.484, 498e seq., 503a–c.

17. The *Phaedo*'s concept of self-mastery is by no means wholly abandoned after the *Phaedrus*. The *Laws* (627a) reassert it as the internal discipline of the soul. But there it is hardly what we would call a moral ideal. Far from being a moral achievement, it is something that can be legislated and enforced by the state—by enacting, for example, laws against sexual activity outside of marriage (*Laws* 838d–841e).

Chapter 10

1. For both, "acuteness" is required (*Phdr.* 250e2, 263c4).

2. Warrant for the presence of persuasive speech within the erotic relationship is further provided by two considerations. First, the distinction between persuasive arguments and dialectical ones is that the former are valid only for those possessing souls of a certain type; the latter, being ultimately truths about the Forms, are valid universally (*Phdr.* 249b seq., 271b). Any human being has a soul of a certain type and finds certain sorts of speech persuasive. A person who has not studied the soul dialectically (for which see 271d seqq.) will thus find some arguments persuasive but will not know why, and he will not know what sorts of argument would persuade people with soul-types differing from his own. Such

a person will be able to speak only with others who share his soul-type, which is precisely the case with the lovers who are "following the gods" up to the Forms in the Palinode (cf. 252c-253c). Second, rhetoric is said to cover, among other things, the kind of thing practiced in small groups by the "Palamedes of Elea," i.e., Zeno (261d). Since Zeno was known to have engaged in erotic *paideia* (for which see *Parmenides* 127b), "rhetoric," with its use of persuasive (but not necessarily true) speech would seem to cover the kind of interaction described in the Palinode, at least until the lovers adopt the philosophical way of life. Paul Friedländer has argued that the "Palamedes of Elea" was Parmenides; but in view of the *Parmenides* passage cited above, the point remains: Friedländer, Paul, *Platon*, 3 vols., Berlin: de Gruyter, 1960, 3:215f.

3. This is in contrast, for example, to the *Republic*, which is slightly removed from the city itself, taking place in its port of Piraeus (*Rep.* 1.328b). Even the *Phaedo*, for all its other-worldly character, takes place in the heart of Athens, near the court where Socrates had been tried (*Phaedo* 59d). The site of the *Phaedrus*, and its natural beauty, have been intensively investigated by Philip, A., "Récurrences thématiques et topologie dans le "Phèdre" de Platon," *Revue de Métaphysique et de Morale* 86 (1981): 452–476; also cf. Sallis, John, *The Way of Platonic Logos*, Pittsburgh: Duquesne University Press, 1975, 104.

4. Voegelin, Eric, *Plato*, Baton Rouge: Louisiana State University Press, 1966, 139. The sense in which I use "antipolitical" is related to, but broader than, that of Wayne Leys in his "Was Plato Non-Political?", in Vlastos, Gregory (ed.), *Plato: A Collection of Critical Essays*, vol. 2, 166–173. Leys takes the essential feature of politics to be the handling of conflicts that arise within the polis, and he argues that in the ideal state of the *Republic* such conflicts are not handled but eliminated; the *Republic* therefore presents a "non-political" ideal. The lovers of the *Phaedrus*, I am about to argue, reject even nonconflictual public action of the kind that takes place in a polis: they place themselves, with the poets, outside the "political" sphere altogether.

5. Gorgias's old claim, that rhetoric gives an individual "rule over all the others in his city" (*Gorgias* 452d), is thus partially sustained in the *Phaedrus*.

6. *Symposium* 210a-211b; also cf. Nussbaum, "This Story Isn't True," 104, and Santos, "Passionate and Platonic Love." Thomas Gould recognizes the persistence of attention to the beloved in the *Phaedrus* as versus the *Symposium*. But, as Gregory Vlastos has pointed out, he does not emphasize the continuing erotic nature of that ongoing attention: Gould, Thomas, *Platonic Love*, New York: Free Press of Glencoe, 1963, 120; Vlastos, Gregory, "Sex in Platonic Love," in Vlastos, *Platonic Studies*, Princeton: Princeton University Press, 1973, 38–42.

7. Cf. Maurer, *Platons "Staats,"* 185f.

8. As Jerry Stannard has put it, "an examination of eros is inadequate unless it reveals the hierarchical structure of eros, and . . . this hierarchical structure is, in the end, to be explained on metaphysical terms": Stannard, Jerry, "Socratic Eros and Platonic Dialectic," *Phronesis* 4 (1959): 121f.

9. Thus, "The *Phaedrus* is occupied in the main with matters far removed from the theory of Ideas": Ross, W. D., *Plato's Theory of Ideas*, Oxford: Clarendon Press, 1951, 80; also cf. Sallis, *The Way of Platonic Logos*, 145f.

10. Cf. *Phaedo* 74d seq.; *Rep.* 6.509d–510a, 7.514a–516c, 10.595e–597e; *Phdr.* 250b; *Timaeus* 37d; etc.

11. Thus, as W. J. Verdenius has written, the concept of mimesis has for Plato a "metaphysical foundation": Verdenius, W. J., "Plato's Doctrine of Artistic Imitation," in Vlastos, Gregory (ed.), *Plato: A Collection of Critical Essays*, Vol. 2, 267.

Chapter 11

1. The only mention by name is at *Rhetoric* 3.76.1408b20, which concerns irony. In addition to the present passages, *Topics* 6.3 and *Metaph.* 12.6.1071b37ff refer to the view that the soul is defined as a self-mover.

2. Cherniss, Harold, *Aristotle's Criticism of Plato and the Academy* 1, Baltimore: Johns Hopkins University Press, 1944, 391, n 311.

3. Cf. *Phys.* 8.7.260b1, 13; *De Generatione et Corruptione* 1.5.320a18; 1.6.322b9.

4. Aristotle, *De l'âme* (Jean Tricot, trans.), Paris: Jean Vrin, 1977, 28, nn1,4.

5. Cf. *Phys.* 6.8.215a1ff.; *De Generatione et Corruptione* 2.6.333b26ff.; *De Caelo* 2.1.300a20–27.

6. Cf. *De Generatione et Corruptione* 2.3.330b31; *Phys.* 8.4.255a2ff.

7. For problems with this sentence cf. Tricot (trans.), *De l'âme*, 30 n1.

8. Cf. *Phys.* 6.5.235b8–13; 8.7.261a20f.

9. Ross, W. D. (ed.), *Aristotle's Physics*, Oxford: Clarendon, 1936, 536.

10. *Metaph.* 9.1.1046a28ff.; cf. *Phys.* 3.3.202a32–35; 8.4.255b2ff.; 8.5.257b3f.; b9f., b25; for a general account of self-motion in Aristotle and the inconsistencies that arise in his views when they are applied to animals and to the cosmos as a whole, cf. Furley, David, "Self-Movers," in Rorty, Amélie O. (ed.), *Essays on Aristotle's Ethics*, Berkeley: University of California Press, 1980, 55–67.

11. *Phys.* 3.1.200b32–202a12.

12. My general account of actuality and motion follows Hagen, Charles, "The 'ENERGEIA-KINĒSIS' Distinction and Aristotle's Concept of Practice," *Journal of the History of Philosophy* 22 (1984): 263–280, which provides references to the growing literature on the subject, and Penner, Terry, "Verbs and the Identity of Actions," in Wood, Oscar P. and George Pitcher (eds.), *Ryle: A Collection of Critical Essays*, Garden City, N. Y.: Anchor, 1970, 405–411; also cf. Owens, Joseph, *The Doctrine of Being in the Aristotelian Metaphysics*, 2nd ed. rev., Toronto: Pontifical Institute of Medieval Studies, 1963, 403–409.

13. Cf. the articles cited in the preceding note, and Ross, W. D. (ed.), *Aristotle's Metaphysics,* 2 vols., Oxford: Oxford University Press, 1924, 2:251f.; Ross notes that Aristotle has no name for the wider "genus" of which motion and actuality are "species."

14. In the primary sense—not in the derivative senses I discussed in chapter 2.

15. Cf. Kamp, Andreas, *Die politische Philosophie des Aristoteles und ihre metaphysischen Grundlagen*, Munich: Karl Alber, 1985, 316. It would follow from this that *praxis* is not applicable to human actions alone, but it has a more general meaning as the proper motion of any entity which exists as a substance, i.e., any living thing, for which cf. Ritter, Joachim, "Die Lehre vom Ursprung und Sinn

der Theorie bei Aristoteles," in Ritter, *Metaphysik und Politik,* Frankfurt: Suhrkamp, 1969, 25f.

16. For general accounts of Aristotelian "science" cf. Owens, Joseph, *The Doctrine of Being in the Aristotelian Metaphysics,* 157–209; Owens, "The Aristotelian Conception of the Sciences," in Owens, *Aristotle* (John R. Catan, ed.) Albany: State University New York Press, 1981, 23–34; Ritter, "Die Lehre vom Ursprung," 9–32.

17. Cf. Larkin, Miriam Therese, *Language in the Philosophy of Aristotle,* The Hague: Mouton, 1971, 49–62.

18. The general relevance of Aristotle's metaphysics, especially the concept of substance, to his ethics has been traced by Irwin, T. H., "The Metaphysical and Psychological Bases of Aristotle's Ethics," in Rorty, Amélie, *Essays on Aristotle's Ethics,* 35–53; for politics, cf. Riedl, Manfred, "Politik und Metaphysik bei Aristoteles," in Riedl, *Metaphysik und Metapolitik,* Frankfurt: Suhrkamp, 1975, 63–84, and the much more detailed Kamp, *Die politische Philosophie des Aristoteles.*

19. *An. Post.* 1.2.71b10 seqq.; also cf. *Phys.* 1.1.184a9–b13; 2.5–6 passim.

20. *NE* 1.3.1094b13–28; 10.8.1179a18ff.; *Phys* 2.5.197a5–8.

21. Cf. Kamp, *Die politische Philosophie des Aristoteles,* 123f.

22. *NE* 3.12.1119b6–19; 9.4.1166a10–28; 9.8.1168b32–1169a2.

23. *Pol.* 1.2.1252b32ff.; *Metaph.* 12.10.1075a20ff.

24. *Pol.* 1.2.1252b30–1253a4, 3.3.1276b1–14; 3.4.1277a5ff.; 3.6.1278b10ff.

25. *Pol* 2.2.1261a18ff.; a24–30; *Metaph.* 7.17.1041b12ff.

26. Cf. *Metaph.* 1.9; 7.13f.; Ross, W. D., *Aristotle,* London: Methuen, 1964, 157–159.

27. Cf. Demos, "Plato's Doctrine of the Psyche."

28. Cf. Sartre, *L'être et le néant,* where the *néant* is, throughout, human Being.

29. E.g., in ethics, the *phronimos* or serious man; in metaphysics, the prime mover; in logic, the syllogism; etc.

Chapter 12
1. Cf. *Pol.* 7.8.1328a22–24; 7.9.1329a34–39; 8.1.1337a27–29.

2. *Pol.* 1.2.1253a2–30; *NE* 1.7.1097b7–11; 2.1.1103b20–26; 10.9.1179b32–34.

3. Cf. Kamp, *Die politische Philosophie des Aristoteles,* 106–117.

4. Cf. *De An.* 2.1.412a28ff. For the contrast between "matter," which is more or less homogenous throughout an individual thing, and "parts," which are nonuniform (and hence analogous to the different types of people there are in a polis), cf. Aristotle, *De Partibus Animalium* 640b16–29; for the application to the polis, which is not without its own subtleties, cf. Kamp, *Die politische Philosophie des Aristoteles,* 163–173, and Riedl, "Politik und Metaphysik bei Aristoteles," 67ff.

5. *Metaph* 5.16; also 5.17.1022a3–13.

6. Cf. Gauthier, René and Jolif, Jean-Yves, *Ethique à Nicomaque,* 2 vols., Louvain: Publications Universitaires, 1970, 2:217.

7. *Pol.* 5.9.1310a25–36; 6.2.1317b2–9.

8. *Pol.* 5.9.1310a25–36; 6.4.1318b39 seq.

9. For a brief and trenchant summary of Aristotle's views on women see Mulgan, R. G., *Aristotle's Political Theory*, Oxford: Clarendon, 1977, 44–47.

10. *Pol.* 1.2.1252a32ff.; 1.5.1254a20–55a3; 1.6.125564ff.; cf. Ross, *Aristotle*, 5th ed., London: Methuen & Colt, 1949, 240–242.

11. Cf. *Phys.* 4.8.215a1ff.; 7.4.254b12–17; *De Caelo* 1.2 269a7f.; 1.7.276a23; 3.2.300a23; *De Generatione et Corruptione* 2.6.333b29; *De An.* 1.3.406a22.

12. For an introduction to the various controversies see Broadie, Alexander, "Aristotle on Rational Action," *Phronesis* 19 (1974): 70–80; Cooper, John, *Reason and Human Good in Aristotle*, Cambridge, Mass.: Harvard University Press, 1975; and Wiggins, David, "Deliberation and Practical Reason," in Rorty (ed.), *Essays on Aristotle's Ethics*, 221–240.

13. Cf. also *NE* VII.3, *de An* III.2, and *de Motu Animalium* VII, 701a.

14. *NE* 7.3.1146b35ff.; cf. *De An.* 3.11.434a17–22; *De Motu Animalium* 7.701a13 seqq.

15. *NE* 1.13.1102b14–28; 6.2.1139a29–31; 7.1–10 passim; 9.4.1166a13f.; *Pol.* 7.13.1332a40ff.

16. *Pol.* 3.4.1277b9ff.; 3.5.1278b6–40; 4.7.1293b5f.; 7.4.1333a5ff.

17. *Pol.* 7.1.1323b30–36; 7.13.1331b26–37; 7.15.1334a12ff.

18. *Pol.* 4.14.1298a4–99a2; 7.9.1329a2–24; cf. *Rhetoric* 1.4–8 passim.

19. *De An.* 3.9.432b26f., 433a2–6; 3.10.433a22–25; also cf. *De Motu Animalium* 5.700b36f.; 10.703a4–7; *Metaph.* 12.7.1072a23–27, b3f.

20. *NE* 1.3.1095a10; 3.12.1119b9–18; indeed, of the two parts of the soul—that which has reason and that which merely apprehends it—the *telos*, or final cause, of the best life is in the superior of the two: *Pol.* 7.14.1333a17–24. Also cf. Homiak, Marcia, "Virtue and Self-Love in Aristotle's Ethics," *Canadian Journal of Philosophy* 11 (1981): 633–652.

21. *NE* 1.2.1094a18–22, 4.1095a14–20, 7.1097a34-b6.

22. *NE* 9.8.1168b3; also cf. *NE* 3.3.1113a6 seq.

23. As with "Being" in the *Metaphysics*, so with "human" here: it is said in many ways, one of which is—like the Prime Mover in the *Metaphysics*, and truth-telling for language—the paradigm for the others. Kamp has pointed out how many other Aristotelian political terms are, like Being, used in many ways: to them I add "human." See Kamp, *Die politischen Philosophie des Aristoteles*, 69–63 (*politikos*), 133f. (*politeia*), 187ff. (*politês*), 195ff. (*politikê, archê*), 166f. (*polis*), 318ff. (*praxis*), etc.

Chapter 13

1. For treatments of this sort of equivocity, cf. Owen, G. E. L., "Logic and Metaphysics in Some Earlier Works of Aristotle," in Düring, Ingemar and G. E. L. Owen (eds.), *Aristotle and Plato in the Mid-Fourth Century*, Goteburg: Studia Graeca et Latina Gothoburgensia 6 (1960):163–190; Owens, Joseph, *The Doctrine of Being in the Aristotelian Metaphysics*, 107–135.

2. *NE* 9.9.1179b14–33, 1180b3–14; *Pol.* 8.1.1337a7–32.

3. Cf. *Phys.* 3.3.202a32f., 202b6ff., 8.5.257a1–3, 257b3f.; also *Metaph.* 11.9.1065b19.

4. Hence, it is no accident that, where Plato wrote conversations, the works of Aristotle are derived from a very different oral practice: that of lecturing; cf. Owens, Joseph, *The Doctrine of Being in the Aristotelian Metaphysics*, 75ff.

5. *Poetics* 7.1450b21–25; 17.1455b1–3.

6. Cf. *Poetics* 6.1450b8–12; cf. *Pol.* 3.11.1281b10–15, and Barker's note at Barker, *Greek Political Theory*, 127f.

7. *Poetics* 13.1453a3–6, 3–16.

8. Cf. *Rhetoric* 2.8 passim.

9. Arendt, Hannah, *The Human Condition*, Chicago: University of Chicago Press, 1958, 35f., 187f.; *Politics* 8.7.1342a6–15; *Poetics* 14.1453b12ff.

10. Cf. *Rhetoric* 1.1.1354b30–33, 1355a4f.; 1.2.1356a4ff., 1356b27ff.; 1.3.1358b22–26.

11. The Greek *upenantiôma* is translated by Butcher and the Oxford translators as "contradiction"; but though this is adequate for other authors, the word never has that meaning in Aristotelian texts, where it refers to things *contrary* to good government or virtue (*Pol.* 7.6.1327a17; 7.9.1328b40); to the *anomalous* position of the uterus in some animals (*De Generatione Animalium* 1.11.719a27, 12.719b18f.); or to the *incongruity* of an incident to the plot (*Poetics* 17.1455a27ff.); cf. Butcher (ed.), *The Poetics of Aristotle*, London: Macmillan, 1911, 105, and McKeon, Richard (ed.), *The Basic Works of Aristotle*, New York: Random House, 1941, 1485.

12. Cf. Owens, Joseph, *The Doctrine of Being in the Aristotelian Metaphysics*, 108, 126ff. for discussions of this Aristotelian procedure and its presuppositions.

13. *NE* 1.7.1097b9–12; 8.6.1158a22–28; 9.4.1166a1f., a10–b2; 9.8.1168b3–6; 9.9.1170b1–12.

14. *NE* 8.1.1155a22–28; 8.9.1160a8–30; 9.11.1161a25–29, 1161a31–b10.

15. *NE* 8.3.1156b24–31; 8.6.1158a12f.; 9.5.1167a3–12; 9.10.1170b29–1171a21; 9.12.1171b29–1172a2.

16. *NE* 9.8.1169a11–1169b2.

17. Gould, Thomas, *Platonic Love*, New York: Free Press of Glencoe, 1963, 143.

18. *NE* 10.7; 10.8.1178a21f.; cf. *De An.* 3.5; also Erickson, Trond Berg, *Bios Theoretikos: Notes on Aristotle's Ethica Nicomachea X.6–8*, Oslo: Universitetsvorlaget, 1976, 114–118; Cooper, *Reason and Human Good in Aristotle*, 164f.

19. Cf. *NE* 10.7.1178b5ff. (though the reference there is only to the physical and economic prerequisites to theory, not to political ones); *Metaph.* 1.1.981b13 seqq.; Kamp, *Die politische Philosophie des Aristoteles*, 321.

20. Cf. Kamp, *Die politische Philosophie des Aristoteles*, 119ff., for a summary and discussion of previous views. Kamp wants to emphasize the critical nature of Aristotelian political philosophy, as against the traditional view that Aristotle is not critical of the polis, for which cf. Ritter, Joachim, " 'Politik' und 'Ethik' in der praktischen Philosophie des Aristoteles," in Ritter, *Metaphysik und Politik*, 126f.

21. Ritter, Joachim, "Das bürgerliche Leben," in Ritter, *Metaphysik und Politik*, 76f. (my translation).
22. *Pol* 2.1.1260b32–34; 4.1.1288b37 seq.; for an instance, cf. e.g., 7.8.1328a22-b22.
23. It must be kept in mind, however—as against some of Ritter's language in the passage quoted—that Aristotle's "hermeneutic" procedure develops political concepts not from raw facts, but from facts preinterpreted through the concept of substance.
24. Aristotle, *De Interpretatione* 1.16a3 seqq.; 4.17a1 seqq.; this is reaffirmed at *Rhetoric* 3.2.1405a11–13.
25. If a word has a number of interrelated meanings which run together at times, that is, as Joseph Owens has noted, only because it mirrors a reality in which those various designata are interrelated and run together: Owens, Joseph, *The Doctrine of Being in the Aristotelian Metaphysics*, 126ff.
26. *De Interpretatione*, 1.16a3 seqq.; 4.17a1 seqq.
27. Cf. *De Generatione Animalium* 5.2.781a26–30.
28. *An. Post.* 2.19; *Phys.* I.1.184a17-b14; *NE* 6.3–7.
29. *Rhetoric* 3.10.1410a10ff.; 3.11.1412a9ff.
30. Cf. Levin, Samuel R., "Aristotle's Theory of Metaphor," *Philosophy and Rhetoric* 15 (1982):24–46; in light of this, as Levin argues, Ricoeur's view that metaphors can break the established categorial structure of existing languages is, as attributed to Aristotle, anachronistic: Ricoeur, Paul *The Rule of Metaphor* (Robert Czerny et al., trans.), Toronto: University of Toronto Press, 1977, 197ff.
31. *Rhetoric* 3.2.1404b6f.; cf. Arnhart, Larry, "The Rationality of Political Speech," *Interpretation* 9 (1981):141–154.
32. Cf. Kamp, *Die politische Philosophie des Aristoteles*, 55, 74.
33. Cf. *Topics* 1.1; *Phys.* 3.3; *Metaph.* 1.9.992b24ff.; see also Evans, J.D.G., *Aristotle's Concept of Dialectic* Cambridge: Cambridge University Press, 1977, 7–48.
34. *Phys.* 8.5; *Metaph.* 7.8; 9.8; 12.3, 6; *Categories* 2; *De An.* 3.4; *An. Post.* 1.1
35. For the sorts of "quasi-friendship" that can subsist between master and slave, cf. *NE* 8.1.1161a32-b8; *Pol.* 1.6.1255b9–15.
36. This "separation" is not, to be sure, of the kind enjoyed by the Platonic Forms in their eternal separation from their fleeting, sensible instances. In a specific situation, the nobility to be actualized may be that of another, but nobility in general is something that can also be found within oneself and is, in fact, a characteristic of the unifying role of reason in an individual life. One's nobility is thus in the truest sense one's "self," and he who acts for the nobility of another is acting for his own highest self. But he is still acting for his own highest self as it is actualized in another.
37. The main complicating factor is that the divergencies and developments of the views *within* what are now viewed as distinct works is as great as the divergencies and developments *among* them. In general I would accept Ross's view that most of the extant works date from the period 335–323 B.C.: Ross, *Aristotle*, 17f.

38. Jaeger, Werner, *Aristotle*, Oxford: Oxford University Press, 1934, 243–246.

39. Thus, on Kamp's argument, the heavy emphasis of the early *Categories* on such substances, which would prescribe a radical democracy to political theory, is replaced in the *Metaphysics* with a more nuanced account: Kamp, *Die politische Philosophie des Aristoteles*, 16.

40. This in fact happens with respect to "Beauty" at *Symposium* 199cff. The "appeal to the Form" is presented as a sort of mystical insight, not only noninteractive but ineffable (*Symposium* 210e seqq.). But Forms can also be articulated in the mutual examination of word meanings presented in the Palinode, which takes the empirically given uses of terms to be mere conventions, and perhaps (as with Lysias) wholly wrong ones. The Aristotelian approach, e.g. in *Metaphysics* 5, takes the basic meanings to be already articulated and simply compares them with one another.

41. Epictetus, *Discourses* 1.17.22–26; 4.1.62–75; *Enchiridion* 1.1; 4; 7.8.

42. Epictetus, *Discourses* 2.22.18f.; 4.10.30.

43. Epictetus, *Discourses* 1.9.4f.; 1.12.7, 15,17–21; 2.10.3f.

44. Epictetus, *Discourses* 2.10.3f.; 2.7.20, 26; 2.24.36–38; 3.24.47, 117f.; *Enchiridion* 24.4f., 30.

45. *KU* 452f.

Chapter 14

1. Kant, Immanuel, *Briefe*, Academy Edition, 13:278; cf. also Lebrun, Gerard, *Kant et la fin de la métaphysique*, Paris: Armand Colin, 1970, 290f.

2. See Hume, David, *An Enquiry Concerning the Principles of Human Understanding* in *Enquiries*, 2nd ed., 25–55, 60–79.

3. Cf. *KRV* B.232–256, 263; 446n.; *KPV* 43; *KU* 410f.

4. With this compare the detailed treatment by Mary-Barbara Zeldin in her *Freedom and the Critical Undertaking*, Ann Arbor: University Microfilm International (for the American Society for Eighteenth-Century Studies), 1980, 22–38.

5. *KPV* 15, 48; *GMS* 437f.; *KRV* B.577f. Also cf. Kant, "Uber den Gemeinspruch: das mag in der Theorie richtig sein, taugt aber nicht für die Praxis" in Kant, Immanuel, *Werke* (Wilhelm Weischedel, ed.), 12 vols., Frankfurt: Suhrkamp, 1968 (hereinafter:*Werke*) 11:138f.

6. Kant, *Über Pädagogik*, in *Werke* 12:700f.

7. This characteristic is not clearly distinguished from the preceding one in *KRV*; cf. Beck, Lewis White, *A Commentary on Kant's Critique of Practical Reason*, Chicago: University of Chicago Press, 1960, 176ff.

8. *KRV* B.476, 585f.; *KPV* 21–29, 32; cf. Henrich, Dieter, "Der Begriff der sittlichen Einsicht und Kants Lehre vom Faktum der Vernunft," in Dieter Henrich & Walter Schulz (eds.), *Die Gegenwart der Griechen im Neueren Denken: Festschrift für Hans-Georg Gadamer*, Tübingen: Verlag J.C.B. Mohr, 1960, 77–115. The problem of associating rational spontaneity with moral law holds even if we accept Lewis White Beck's reading of the "fact of reason" as the "fact that reason is practical," i.e., as a fact not only known by, but about, reason itself. For from

the lawfulness of reason's immanent spontaneity we cannot, without additional premises, derive any obligatory laws about how an individual must act in a non-rational sensory world: L. W. Beck, "The Fact of Reason: An Essay in the Justification of Ethics" in L. W. Beck (ed.), *Studies in the Philosophy of Kant,* Indianapolis: Bobbs-Merrill, 1965, 200–214.

9. Cf., among many others, Walsh, W. H., "Kant and Metaphysics," *Kant-Studien* 67 (76):382; Habermas, Jürgen, "Labor and Interaction," in Habermas, *Theory and Practice* (John Viertel, trans.), Boston: Beacon Press, 1973, 151f. The difficulty of taking Kant in such a "monological" way has been argued by Nagl, Ludwig, *Gesellschaft und Autonomie,* Wien: Verlag der Österreichischen Akademie der Wissenschaften, 1983, esp. 40–51, 334–342. As we shall see, however, retrieving dialogical increments in the Kantian concept of autonomy does not settle all issues between Kant and Hegel, to say nothing of those between Kant and Heidegger.

10. Leibniz, G. W., *Monadology* 3, nos. 84–90, in Leibniz, Gottfried Wilhelm, *Philosophical Papers and Letters* (Leroy E. Loemker, ed.), 2d ed., Dordrecht: Reidel, 1969, 651f. This association with Leibniz does not contradict the derivation, mentioned by Robert Paul Wolff, of the Kingdom of Ends from Rousseau. But the Kingdom of Ends cannot be derived from Rousseau alone. As Wolff himself notes elsewhere; for example, Rousseau's republic does not have a king, while the Kingdom of Ends (like Leibniz's "Kingdom of Grace") does: Wolff, Robert Paul, *The Autonomy of Reason: A Commentary on Kant's Groundwork of the Metaphysics of Morals,* New York: Harper Torchbooks, 1973, 182; Wolff, "Introduction," Wolff (ed.), *Kant: A Collection of Critical Essays,* Notre Dame, Ind.: University of Notre Dame Press, 1967, xx–xxi. On the Kingdom of Ends, cf. also Heimsoeth, Hans, "Metaphysical Motives in the Development of Critical Idealism," in Moltke Gram (ed.), *Kant: Disputed Questions,* Chicago: Quadrangle, 1967, 170f.; and Hill, Thomas E., "The Kingdom of Ends," in Lewis White Beck (ed.), *Proceedings of the Third International Kant Congress,* Dordrecht: Reidel, 1972, 307–315.

11. A fact from which the second *Critique,* in its consideration of the moral law, abstracts: *KPV* 15, 21.

12. Cf. the "Preface" to the *Metaphysische Anfangsgründe der Naturwissenschaft, Werke* 9:11–24.

13. With this cf. Kemal Salim's account of culture in Salim, "Aesthetic Necessity, Culture, and Epistemology," *Kant-Studien* 74 (1983): 189–200. Details of this process of moral education are scattered throughout the Kantian writings (most notably, perhaps, in the *Über Pädagogik).*

14. Kant, "Über den Gemeinspruch . . . ," *Werke* 11:142.

15. As Eric Weill has argued: Weill, "Kant et le problème de la politique," in *Annales de Philosophie Politique IV,* Paris: Presses Universitaires de France, 1962, 1–32.

16. *KPV* 121f.; the Kingdom of Ends, if viewed as realized among temporal entities, would be the "ethical community" discussed in Kant, *Religion within the Limits of Reason Alone,* in *Werke* 8:753ff.; since such a community, it is asserted,

can be brought about by God alone, not by human effort, I will leave it aside from this discussion of political philosophy.

17. A second sort of concretion is seen to be required when the Kingdom of Ends is viewed, not merely as a goal toward which to work at any given moment, but as the goal of historical development itself. If the progress toward that goal is asserted to be the "real object of our willing," we are entitled to ask how "real" that object truly is. Progress toward the Kingdom of Ends cannot be an empirical object, because it is "progress" only when measured against a nonempirical ideal. That human history is to be viewed as the realization of a moral purpose is suggested by the concept of the culture of reason; but it needs more than mere "suggestion" to be persuasive: it, and indeed the idea of a cultivation of reason itself, requires some sort of validation via a philosophy of history. The main point of Kant's historical writings, which we will not consider here, is in fact to show how the idea of progress can be rationally validated in spite of its nonempirical status.

18. The "metaphysical motives" in Kant's account of the opposition of freedom and time are discussed at Heimsoeth, "Metaphysical Motives," 192–199. My claim is not that man, for Kant, takes over the metaphysical role of "primordial being," and that his philosophy thus remains, as Heimsoeth claims, metaphysical: W. H. Walsh is surely correct in his criticism of this in his "Kant and Metaphysics."

19. Heimsoeth, "Metaphysical Motives," 170f

Chapter 15

1. Hegel, G. W. F., *Wissenschaft der Logik*, 1:115/127.

2. The data are only relatively raw: as the "output" of my sensibility, they are structured according to space and time: cf. *KRV*'s "Transcendental Aesthetic."

3. Cf. *KRV* B.34, 118, 322f.; see also the "A" version of the "Transcendental Deduction" (*KRV* A.100–110) and the "B" version (B.151f., 162, 164f.).

4. *KU* 189ff., 197, 221, 229f, 240f., 244f. At *KU* 217, Kant refers to the faculties involved in free play as imagination and understanding; at *KU* 258 they are imagination and reason. *KU* 240f not merely omits the role of sensibility in the judgment of taste but denies it. This poses problems for Kant because he normally writes as if such judgment were exercised on public objects, and hence required sensibility. I restrict myself here to such cases, in which the free play involves a sensory object "supplying ready-made to the imagination just such a form . . . of the manifold as the imagination, if it were left to itself, would freely project" *KU* 241.

5. In introducing this second sense of "interest" here, I follow Paul Guyer. *KU* defines "interest" as the "delight we connect with the representation of the existence of an object" (*KU* 204f., 296). In *KPV* it is defined as a concept which founds a desire for an object, and which therefore is a basis for action (*KPV* 21, 79). Guyer has shown that the former concept cannot entirely convey what Kant has in mind when he calls aesthetic judgments "disinterested," and he argues for supplementing it with the second sense given above: Guyer, Paul, "Disinterest-

edness and Desire in Kant's Aesthetics," *Journal of Aesthetics and Art Criticism* 36 (1978):446–460.

6. Danielle Lories has traced this aesthetic conception of liberty in detail, with reference to later developments by Heidegger, in "Kant et la liberté ésthétique," *Revue Philosophique de Louvain* 79 (1981): 484–512.

7. *KU* 205–209, 212–216; 237.

8. Cassirer, Ernst, *Kant's Life and Work* (James Haden, trans.), New Haven: Yale University Press, 1981, 274f.; Stadler, Ingrid, "Perception and Perfection in Kant's Aesthetics," in Robert Paul Wolff (ed.), *Kant: A Collection of Critical Essays*, 378f.; also cf. Schaper, Eva, "Kant on Aesthetic Appraisals," *Kant-Studien* 64 (1973): 431.

9. Paul Guyer has brought together some startling remarks on this to be found in Kant's unpublished material: "the beautiful form seems only to be for society," "when we are alone we never attend to the beautiful," and "all solitary eccentrics have no taste" are examples. Guyer portrays Kant as vacillating in his development between two theories of aesthetic pleasure: that it is grounded on the unification of the faculties, and that it is grounded on sociability. These two theories are not necessarily incompatible, of course, and accepting both together would yield the position of the *Phaedrus*. Such joint acceptance lies very close to the surface of the Kantian texts: Lebrun, for example, has formulated it as follows: "la 'belle forme' n'était pas le plus exquis des produits de consommation, mais la symbole d'une communauté universelle possible,—l'absence de fin en elle n'était pas synonyme de gratuité, mais l'indice qu'elle ne servait plus à la satisfaction de *quelqu'un en particulier*": Guyer, Paul "Pleasure and Society in Kant's Theory of Taste," in Guyer and Ted Cohen (eds.), *Essays in Kant's Aesthetics*, Chicago: University of Chicago Press, 1982, 41ff.; Lebrun, *Kant et la fin de la métaphysique*, 386.

10. This development is very thoroughly and clearly presented in Deleuze, Gilles, *La philosophie critique de Kant*, Paris: Presses Universitaires de France, 1963, 33ff.

11. In thus looking to reflective judgment in the third *Critique* for Kant's account of empirical concept formation, I am following a suggestion of Stern, Carl, "Kant's Theory of Empirical Concept Formation," *Southwestern Journal of Philosophy* 8, no. 2 (Summer 1977):17–23.

12. Cf. the account of the *Critique of Judgment*'s treatment of nature and art in von Molnár, Géza, "Goethe's Reading of Kant's 'Critique of Judgment,'" *Eighteenth Century Studies* 15 (1982):402–420.

13. Jens Kulenkampff has argued this point but without the textual base adduced here: Kulenkampff, "Über Kants Bestimmung des Gehalts der Kunst," *Zeitschrift fur philosophische Forschung* 33 (1979): 68f.; also cf. the exposition in Luethe, Rudolf, "Kants Lehre von den aesthetischen Ideen," *Kant-Studien* 75 (1984): 65–74.

14. For detailed accounts of the structure of the sublime, neither of which deals with its interactive potential, cf. Makkreel, Rudolf, "Imagination and Temporality in Kant's Theory of the Sublime," *Journal of Aesthetics and Art Criticism*

42 (1984): 303–316; Guyer, Paul, "Kant's Distinction between the Beautiful and the Sublime," *Review of Metaphysics* 35 (1982): 753–783.

15. When the unification of the faculties under the guidance of the will does result in action for Kant, we have "prudence": its affinities with the Aristotelian tradition have been traced by Pierre Aubenque, who argues that Kant's exclusion of prudence from morality deprives him of any mediation between theory and practice. As we shall see, such is not quite the case: if the mediation is excluded from moral theory, its basis is still grounded aesthetically for Kant: Aubenque, Pierre, "La prudence chez Kant," *Revue de Métaphysique et de Morale* 80 (1975): 156–182.

16. Interaction is shown historically as the field of manifestation of aesthetic freedom, says the *Critique of Judgment,* by classical Athens, a society in which aesthetic communication was able actually to unite the cultured members of the society with their uncultured compatriots, thus making equality—and hence human freedom, in which all human beings share—a positive social force (*KU* 296ff., 306, 355f.). Also cf. Guyer, Paul, *Kant and the Claims of Taste*, Cambridge, Mass.: Harvard University Press, 1979, 52f.

17. *Timaeus* 49d seqq.

18. Cf. Gilson, Etienne, *Being and Some Philosophers*, Toronto: Pontifical Institute of Medieval Studies, 1949.

Chapter 16

1. These have been partially collected in English in Beck, Lewis White (ed.), *Kant on History*, Indianapolis: Bobbs-Merrill, 1963, and in Reiss, Hans (ed.), and Nisbet, H. B. (trans.), *Kant's Political Writings*, Cambridge: Cambridge University Press, 1971.

2. Arendt, Hannah, "Freedom and Politics" in Albert Hunold (ed.), *Freedom and Serfdom: An Anthology of Western Thought*, Dordrecht: Reidel, 1961, 207.

3. This foundational status is suggested by Beiner's observations on the "formal" nature of the various investigations in the third *Critique*: Beiner, "Interpretive Essay" in Arendt, Hannah, *Lectures on Kant's Political Philosophy*, (Ronald Beiner, ed.), Chicago: University of Chicago Press, 1982: 132ff.; also cf. Cassirer's remarks on what I have called the "subliminal" organization of the late Kantian writings with respect to the philosophy of religion: Cassirer, *Kant's Life and Thought*, 391.

4. The political philosophy of the first foundation is well summarized in the "Introduction" to Reiss, *Kant's Political Philosophy*, 1–48.

5. *EF* 372–377; cf. *KRV* B.372–374.

6. *GMS* 421, 429; *EF* 349f.; also cf. "Über den Gemeinspruch . . . ," in *Werke* 12:145–147, 150ff.

7. Cf. "Über den Gemeinspruch . . . ," in *Werke* 12:144f.

8. *EF* 365; cf. also the "Introduction" to the *Metaphysik der Sitten*, in *Werke* 8:339f.; *Religion innerhalb der Grenzen der bloßen Vernunft*, in *Werke* 8:754f.

9. *EF* 365f.; the coercion characteristic of the Kantian state has been exhaustively documented in Deggau, H. G., *Die Aporien der Rechtslehre Kants*, Stuttgart: Frohmann, 1983, 225–279.

10. *EF* 366f., 375n.; cf. "Über den Gemeinspruch . . . ," in *Werke* 11:148.

11. On this cf. Reiss, *Kant's Political Philosophy*, 20f.

12. Cf. *KPV* 29; *EF* 365f., 381–386; *Metaphysik der Sitten*, in *Werke* 8:323f.

13. *Metaphysik der Sitten*, in *Werke* 8:316f.

14. *EF* 350n.; cf. "Über den Gemeinspruch . . . ," in *Werke* 11:153f.

15. On the interplay of purpose and law within Kantian morality, cf. Reboul, Olivier, "Hegel, critique de la morale de Kant," *Revue de Métaphysique et de Morale* 80 (1975): 90ff.

16. Cf. *GMS* 389f., 410; *KPV* 20; *KU* 430, 436n.; *Metaphysik der Sitten*, in *Werke* 8:320; *SF* 359n.

17. The importance of reflective judgment to Kantian politics is argued by Dick Howard, "From Marx to Kant: The Return of the Political," *Thesis Eleven* 8 (1984): 77–91. Howard does not discuss, however, what we shall see to be the main problem with the use of specifically aesthetic judgment in politics: its "disinterested" character, which divorces it from most of life's ongoing concerns (including politics) and was of crucial importance to, for example, Goethe: cf. von Molnàr, "Goethe's Reading of Kant's 'Critique of Judgment.' "

18. See *SF* 19f.; also *Metaphysik der Sitten*, in *Werke* 8:336f., 429.

19. Cf. Kant, Immanuel, "Idee zu einer augemeinen Geschichte, in Weltbürgerlicher Absicht," in *Werke* 11:41. ("Idea for a Universal History from a Cosmopolitan Standpoint," Thesis 6).

20. Cf. *EF* 369. Dick Howard, regarding Kant in light of his connections with Sieyès, has argued that it is the executive which presents material to the legislator. This is supported, for example, by the reference to the "government," or executive power (cf. *EF* 351f) setting up the university without having any clear concept in mind, and thus presumably instituting legislation through a process of aesthetic judgment (*SF* 21f.). But the government, as we shall see the *Conflict of the Faculties* to argue, can never be disinterested: the use of aesthetic (as opposed, certainly, to other types of reflective) judgment in politics is then to be found in the philosophical faculty itself: Howard, "From Marx to Kant: The Return of the Political," 88.

21. *SF* 21f., 30, 34f.; cf. *Metaphysik der Sitten*, in *Werke* 8:437f.

22. Cf. "Über den Gemeinspruch . . . ," *Werke* 11:161.

23. *SF* 27–29; also cf. *EF* 369 for how this works with regard to the faculty of jurisprudence.

24. Cf. with this the account of interaction in the university given in Saner, Hans, *Kant's Political Thought* (E. B. Ashton, trans.), Chicago: University of Chicago Press, 1973, 96ff.

25. Cf. *EF* 374f.; also *KPV* 18f., 21, 33ff., 36, 67.

26. *EF* 369; *SF* 19f., 24f., 28f.; this function, we may note, is carefully disarmed by restricting the influence of the philosophical faculty to scholars in the other university faculties: *SF* 29, 34f., 89f. As thus denatured, the philosophical faculty becomes something like an institutionalized locus of the kind of "spectating" referred to by Arendt, (cf. Arendt, *Lectures on Kant's Political Philosophy*, 51, 54, 63, 65, etc.).

27. Unlike the social criticism of the philosophical faculty, art criticism ar-

ticulates both the successes and the failures of the artist. There is nothing, presumably, to prevent the philosophers fom articulating the successful components of their society as well as its injustices. But the "Secret Article" to *Perpetual Peace* suggests that such celebration has other institutional *loci* (*EF* 368f.).

28. Lebrun has pointed out the importance, in the third *Critique*, of not construing the beautiful as true (Lebrun, *Kant et la fin de la métaphysique*, 351). The sole concern of the philosophical faculty with truth would seem to imply, then, a strong disanalogy with aesthetic discourse. But truth decisions for Kant, as cognitive, must be based on a coherent employment of the cognitive faculties, which as Deleuze has argued is grounded in aesthetic free play (Deleuze, *La philosophie critique de Kant*, passim). It is thus impossible, on a Kantian view, to make truth decisions without some use of aesthetic judgment.

29. *EF* 349f.; cf. "Über den Gemeinspruch . . . ," in *Werke* 11:145.

30. When Patrick Riley defends the view that politics is for Kant instrumental to morality, he is claiming that the Kantian civil society is to be understood through its relation to the larger, "purposive" whole of culture, and not through its relation to the moral law. This clearly is in contradiction to my exposition of the first foundation, and to several of the texts cited in that exposition: but that it is an excellent reconstruction of Kantian ideas, and solves many problems with Kant's own explicit formulations, is evidenced, not only by the quality of Riley's argumentation, but by the similarity of his views with those of Schiller and Hegel: Riley, Patrick, *Kant's Political Philosophy*, Totowa, N. J.: Rowman and Littlefield, 1983. Against Riley's sort of interpretation as a restatement, rather than as a reconstruction, of Kant, cf. Marcuse, Herbert, "A Study on Authority," in Marcuse, *From Luther to Popper* (Joris de Brees, trans.), London: Verso, 1972, 79–94.

31. Cf. Arendt, Hannah, *Lectures on Kant's Political Philosophy*, 77, and Beiner's "Interpretive Essay," 126.

32. Cf. Guyer's discussion of the need to recognize "the complexity of [Kant's] aesthetic theory rather than reducing it to pure phenomenology or psychology or epistemology or linguistic analysis, each of which has a part to play in it but none of which exhausts it": Guyer, Paul, "Kant's Distinction between the Beautiful and the Sublime," 757.

33. In the aesthetic realm, such critical discourse is keyed either to the beautiful or to the sublime, which provides a further "pluralism"; but the latter is hardly adumbrated within Kantian aesthetics and is wholly absent from the political writings.

34. Cf. *KRV* B.537, 644, 672, 699.

35. Hofstadter, Albert, "Kant's Aesthetic Revolution," *Journal of Religious Ethics* 3 (1975): 172; also cf. Lyotard, Jean-François, and Thébaut, Jean-Loup, *Just Gaming* (Wlad Godzich, trans.), Minneapolis: University of Minnesota Press, 1985, 87f., 93.

Chapter 17

1. Kolb, David, *The Critique of Pure Modernity*, Chicago: University of Chicago Press, 1986, 42ff.

2. Hegel's reception of the third antinomy has been explored in detail at Gillespie, Michael Allen, *Hegel, Heidegger and the Ground of History*, Chicago: University of Chicago Press, 1984, 33–43; 47–55; my debt to Gillespie in what follows is heavy.

3. Gillespie, *Hegel, Heidegger and the Ground of History*, 53 n. 7.

4. Hegel, *Wissenschaft der Logik* 1:52/68; hence, the beginning of the *Logic* itself can be viewed as either the highly mediated outcome of the entire development of the *Phenomenology* (and thus, to some extent, of human history itself) or as the product of a "resolve, which can also be regarded as arbitrary" Hegel, (*Logic* 1:52-54/68–70).

5. *Enz.* no. 55.

6. *Enz.* no. 56.

7. *Enz.* no. 56.

8. Cf. *Enz.* no. 55.

9. Cf. Findlay's "analysis" in Miller (trans.), *Phenomenology*, 590.

10. Some of these are explored in my "Scientific Progress and Hegel's *Phenomenology of Spirit*," *Idealistic Studies* 13 (1983): 1–10.

11. It is so, then, in virtue of its *telos*: details of the narrative could be changed, as historical circumstances of consciousness changed, as long as the goal of the narrative stayed the same. This is compatible with Hegel's later downgrading of the *Phenomenology*, for which cf. *PhG* 578.

Chapter 18

1. The lovers in the Palinode, for example, work on each other as on statues—images, not of sensibles, but of a god: *Phdr.* 252d.

2. Carnap, Rudolf, "The Elimination of Metaphysics through Logical Analysis of Langue," in A. J. Ayer (ed.), *Logical Positivism*, New York: Free Press of Glencoe, 1959, 60–81.

3. Cf. Heidegger, Martin, *Kant und das Problem der Metaphysik*, Frankfurt: Klostermann, 1973; Heidegger, *Die Frage nach dem Ding*, Tübingen: Niemeyer, 1962.

4. Heidegger, Martin, *Der Satz vom Grund*, 4th ed., Pfullingen: Neske, 1971, 124–128, 131–134, 147f. Even Heidegger's discussion of Kant's relation to Schelling relies wholly on the first *Critique*, in spite of the obvious importance of the third for that thinker: *Schellings Abhandlung über das Wesen der menschlichen Freiheit (1809)*, Tübingen: Niemeyer, 1971, 42–53, 234–236; Schelling's debt to the third *Critique* is manifest in Schelling, Friedrich Wilhelm Joseph von, *System of Transcendental Idealism* (selections; Albert Hofstadter, trans.), in Hofstadter, Albert and Richard Kuhns (eds.), *Philosophies of Art and Beauty*, New York: Modern Library, 1964, 347–377.

5. Heidegger, Martin, "Vom Wesen und Begriff der *Physis*. Aristotles' *Physik* B.1," in Heidegger, *Wegmarken*, 309–371.

6. Heidegger, Martin, "Die Onto-theologische Verfassung der Metaphysik," in Heidegger, *Identität und Differenz*, Pfullingen: Neske, 1957, 51–67; cf. Schürmann, *Le principe d'anarchie*, 115–125.

7. Shapiro, Gary, "From the Sublime to the Political: Some Historical Notes," *New Literary Theory* 16 (1984–85): 213–235.

8. For a summary and discussion of the relevant texts, cf. Kockelmans, Joseph J., *On the Truth of Being*, Bloomington: Indiana University Press, 1984, 196–208.

9. In addition to the texts referred to above, cf. Heidegger, Martin, "Kants These über das Sein," in *Wegmarken*, 273–307.

10. Cf. my "Language and Appropriation: The Nature of Heideggerean Dialogue," *The Personalist* 60 (1979) pp. 384–396.

Part Three

Introduction

1. Heidegger, Martin, "Hegels Begriff der Erfahrung," in *HW* 105–192; also cf. McCumber, John, "Essence and Subversion in Hegel and Heidegger," in Hugh Silverman and Donn Welton (eds.), *The Future of Continental Philosophy and the Pragmatics of Difference*, Albany: State University of New York Press, forthcoming.

Chapter 19

1. Cf. Habermas, Jürgen, "Questions and Counterquestions," in Richard J. Bernstein (ed.), *Habermas and Modernity*, Cambridge, Mass.: MIT Press, 1985, 198.

2. *TKH* 1:109–113, 502ff./71–74, 375ff.; 2:550, 590f.

3. *TKH* 1:9/xli; 2:539f., 561–564, 586ff.

4. *TKH* 1:73, 86–103, 114, 370-373/44, 53–67, 75, 274–276.

5. *TKH* 1:82–85, 116f., 125f./50–53, 77, 124.

6. For this cf. *TKH* 1:126f.,129–132, 150f./84f., 87f., 101.

7. *TKH* 1:127 and n.139, 132—135/85, 88–90, 418 n.17.

8. *TKH* 1:128, 135-141/85f., 90–94; Goffman, Erving, *The Presentation of Self in Everyday Life*, Garden City, N. Y.: Anchor Books, 1959.

9. *TKH* 1:128f., 141-151/86, 94–101.

10. Austin, J. L., *How to Do Things with Words* (J. O. Urmson, ed.), Oxford: Oxford University Press, 1965, 156f

11. Habermas, Jürgen, "Towards a Theory of Communicative Competence," *Inquiry* 13 (1970): 371f.; Habermas, "Wahrheitstheorien," in *"Wirklichkeit und Reflexion" Walter Schulz zum 60e Geburtstag*, Pfullingen: Neske, 1973, 255f.

12. *TKH* 1:114, 142ff., 148, 412, 525/75, 95ff., 99, 307, 392.

13. *TKH* 1:484f., 500, 514, 523f./362f., 373, 384, 391; 2:9.

14. We could, of course, argue both at once; but this case is compounded out of the first two, and Habermas does not discuss it.

15. Tugendhat, Ernst, *Selbstbewußtsein und Selbstbestimmung*, Frankfurt: Suhrkamp, 1979.

16. Grice, H. P., "Logic and Conversation," in Donald Davidson and Gilbert Harmon (eds.), *The Logic of Grammar*, Encino, Calif.: Dickerson, 1975, 64–75.

17. *TKH* 1:387, 411, 427/287, 306, 319.
18. Strawson, P. F., "Intention and Convention in Speech Acts," *Philosophical Review* 73 (1964): 439–460.
19. Searle, John, "Literal Meaning," in Searle, *Expression and Meaning*, Cambridge: Cambridge University Press, 1979, 117–136.
20. Habermas, Jürgen, "Zur Einebnung der Gattungsunterschied zwischen Philosophie und Literatur," in Habermas, *Philosophische Diskurs der Moderne*, Frankfurt: Suhrkamp, 1985, 242.
21. Habermas, "Wahrheitstheorien," 252f.; Habermas, "Towards a Theory of Communicative Competence," 372f.
22. Plato, *Apology* 17b seqq.
23. On this and on Habermas' reading of Strawson (see below), cf. Wood, Allen, "Habermas' Defense of Rationalism," *New German Critique* 35 (1985): 145–164.
24. Strawson. P. F., "Intention and Convention in Speech Acts," 445.

    Chapter 20
1. Cf. Husserl, Edmund, *The Crisis of European Sciences and Transcendental Phenomenology*, Evanston: Northwestern University Press, 1970, 103–189.
2. *TKH* 1:149f., 188f., 451f./100, 130ff., 336; 2:189–205, 329, 589ff.
3. Habermas, Jürgen, "Zur Einebnung des Gattungsunterschieds zwischen Philosophie und Literatur," 232–234, 241, 242, 246n.
4. *TKH* 1:107f., 455/69f., 339; 2:163f., 218, 232.
5. *TKH* 2:225; also cf. 2:200f.; 1:451/336.
6. *TKH* 1:403-406/299–303; 2:489–583.
7. Habermas, Jürgen, "Rekonstruktive vs. verstehende Sozialwissenschaften," in Habermas, *Moralbewußtsein und kommunikatives Handeln*, Frankfurt: Suhrkamp, 1983, 41.
8. Cf. Habermas, Jürgen, "Moralbewußtsein und kommunikatives Handeln," in Habermas, *Moralbewußtsein und kommunikatives Handeln*, Frankfurt: Suhrkamp, 1983, 127f.
9. *TKH* 2:586, 588; also cf. Habermas, Jürgen, "A Reply to My Critics," in John B. Thompson and David Held (eds.), *Habermas: Critical Debates*, Cambridge, Mass.: MIT Press, 1982, 239f.; "Die Philosophie als Platzhalter und Interpret," in Habermas, *Moralbewußtsein und kommunikatives Handeln*, 25f.
10. *TKH* 1:16, 38f., 327/2, 18f., 239; 2:550, 562.
11. *TKH* 2:298.
12. *TKH* 1:201f./140.
13. Cf. Kaufmann, Walter, *Hegel: A Reinterpretation*, Garden City, N. Y.: Anchor Books, 1966, 144, 180ff., for brief discussions of these three meanings.
14. *TKH* 1:16, 504/2, 376f.; 2:12, 16, 86, 586.
15. *TKH* 1:460/343f.; 2:303, 550.
16. *TKH* 1:172-176/117–120; also cf. Habermas, Jürgen, "Wozu noch Philosophie?" in Habermas, *Philosophisch-politische Profile*, Frankfurt: Suhrkamp, 1981, 34ff.

17. *TKH* 1:327/239; McCarthy, Thomas, "Reflections on Rationalization in *The Theory of Communicative Action*," in Richard J. Bernstein (ed.), *Habermas and Modernity*, Cambridge, Mass.: MIT Press, 1985, 191.

18. The analogous question for Kant, which he never raises explicitly, is why, if a person can act freely, he should be required to do so: cf. Sherover, Charles, *Heidegger, Kant and Time*, Bloomington, Ind.: Indiana University Press, 1971, 161.

19. *TKH* 2:500; Arendt, Hannah, *The Human Condition*, Chicago: University of Chicago Press, 1958, 30f., 79–135; cf. 254 n.4.

Chapter 21

1. For the need for Habermas to incorporate aesthetic reason into his concept of rationality if the latter is not to be restricted to abstract moral argumentation, cf. Ingram, David, *Habermas and the Dialectic of Reason*, New Haven: Yale University Press, 1987, 58f., 73f., 99–103.

2. Also cf. Habermas, "Reply to My Critics," 222, 226.

3. Habermas, "Questions and Counterquestions," 202f.; Habermas, "Modernity: An Incomplete Project," in Hal Foster (ed.), *The Anti-Aesthetic*, Port Townsend, Wash.: Bay Press, 1983, 12; cf. Whitebrook, Joel, "Nature in Habermas," *Telos* 39 (1979):56.

4. Norman, Richard, *Reasons for Actions*, Oxford: Blackwell, 1971, 63f

5. Stevenson, C. L., "The Emotive Meaning of Ethical Terms," in Stevenson, *Facts and Values*, New Haven: Yale University Press, 1963, 18–21.

6. *TKH* 1:36, 41, 71, 139/16, 20, 42, 92.

7. *TKH* 1:36f., 68, 139/17, 40, 92; 2:448.

8. Habermas, Jürgen, "Some Distinctions in Universal Pragmatics," *Theory and Society* 3 (1976): 166f., to which Habermas refers at *TKH* 1:445n./445 n.86.

9. Habermas, Jürgen, "Zur Einebnung des Gattungsunterschieds zwischen Philosophie und Literatur," 238, 240.

10. Habermas, Jürgen, "Zur Einebnung des Gattungsunterschieds zwischen Philosophie und Literatur," 232f., 240.

11. *TKH* 2:286, 518, 520, 584, 586.

12. *TKH* 1:456, 467/340, 350; 2:520.

13. For a discussion of Habermas's concept of "suitability," cf. Nagl, Ludwig, "Ästhetik und Diskurs," *Wiener Jahrbuch für Philosophie*, 1985, 91–99.

14. *TKH* 1:371f., 450/274f., 335f.

15. *TKH* 1:424, 373-376/316f., 276–279.

16. *TKH* 1:167, 195, 374f., 400/115, 135f., 276f., 297f.

17. *TKH* 1:167–169, 191f., 426/113–116, 133, 318f.; 2:328.

18. Cf. Chomsky, Noam, *Syntactic Structures*, The Hague: Mouton, 1957.

19. *TKH* 1:43f., 71/20ff., 42; 2:28.

20. Cf. Derrida, Jacques, "Differance," in Derrida, *Speech and Phenomena* (David B. Allison, trans.), Evanston: Northwestern University Press, 1973, 129–160.

21. This is a much simplified version of the program presented in Davidson, Donald, "Truth and Meaning" *Synthese* 17 (1967): 304–323.

Chapter 22

1. Cf. Lewis, David, *Convention*, Cambridge, Mass.: Harvard University Press, 1969, 76. My account captures only the first two clauses of Lewis's definition; the last three make reference to "preferences," and I am not clear on how one can "prefer" the structures of one's own mother tongue to those of other languages.

2. This presumption is intended to beg the difficult issue of whether I am an audience for myself: of whether my behavior, even when alone, contains components that are present because I, as a sort of "generalized other" representing society at large, expect them to be. If such is always the case, there may be no cases of behavior which are not expressions. But this does not affect the point that there are components of behavior which do not depend on the expectations of *others*; it just makes it more difficult to give examples of it.

3. Cf. Tarski, Alfred, "The Concept of Truth in Formalized Languages," in Tarski, *Logic, Semantics, Metamathematics* (J. H. Woodger, trans; John Corcoran, ed.), 2nd ed. rev., Indianapolis: Hackett, 1983, 152–278.

4. Cf. Rose, Herbert Jenning, "Helios," in *Oxford Classical Dictionary*, Oxford: Clarendon, 1970, 494.

5. Austin J. L., *How to Do Things with Words*, 14f., 26–29.

6. Austin, *How to Do Things with Words*, 115f.

7. Austin, *How to Do Things with Words*, 72, 92–98.

8. Austin, *How to Do Things with Words*, 30.

9. Sartre, *L'être et le néant*, 94ff.

10. When applied to literary works, this analysis is in accordance with the *Rezeptionsästhetik* of Wolfgang Iser and Hans-Robert Jauss: cf. Iser, Wolfgang, *The Art of Reading*, Baltimore: Johns Hopkins University Press, 1978, 63f., 74; Jauss, Hans-Robert, "Negativität und Identifikation," *Poetik und Hermeneutik* 6 (1975): 263–339.

11. This account, though not this example, is drawn from Lakoff, George, and Mark Johnson, *Metaphors We Live By*, Chicago: University of Chicago Press, 1980, 12f., 52–55.

12. Such imposition of meaning independently (at least in part) of the speaker's intentions is treated under the rubrics of "situation boundness" and "fusion of horizons," at Gadamer, Hans-Georg, *Wahrheit und Methode*, 2nd ed., Tübingen: Mohr, 1965, esp. 375f.

13. Austin, *How to Do Things with Words*, 69f. Austin also discusses languages which do not have such resources. Suppose that Jack and Julie are not speaking English but some other language—pre-English—which has as yet no explicit formula by which to distinguish between attempting to flirt with someone and making a business compliment. Such speech acts, the nature of which cannot be made explicit in the language of their utterance, Austin calls "primitive" or "primary." This strategy will not apply to (1) because Jack is in fact speaking, not "pre-English," but English itself, which has the resources to make clear what he is doing—if he himself knows what he wants to do with his words: Austin, 71–73.

14. Austin, *How to Do Things with Words*, 72

15. Cf. Sabini, John, and Silver, Maury, *Moralities of Everyday Life*, Oxford: Oxford University Press, 1982, 107–123.

16. Derrida, Jacques, "Signature, événement, contexte," in Derrida, *Marges de la philosophie*, Paris: Minuit, 1972, 367–393; Iser, *Art of Reading*, 54–62; Searle, John, "The Logical Status of Fictional Discourse," "Metaphor," and "Literal Meaning," all in Searle, *Expression and Meaning*, 58–75, 76–116, and 116–136.

17. Rorty, Richard, *Philosophy and the Mirror of Nature*, Princeton: Princeton University Press, 1979, 320–322, 387.

18. Heidegger, Martin, "Was ist Metaphysik?" in Heidegger, *Wegmarken*, 1967, 1–19.

19. Cf. Austin, *How to Do Things with Words*, 99f. for these terms.

20. Nor, we may add, is such a decision always up to the speaker: it is possible to be unaware of some of the desires which nonetheless enter into the production of a response, and to be made aware of them in, say, one's sudden delight that what one thought was a business compliment is being happily taken to initiate flirtation.

21. Cf. Carr, David, *Time, Narrative, and History*, Bloomington: Indiana University Press, 1986.

22. See Carnap, "The Elimination of Metaphysics Through Logical Analysis of Language."

23. In fact the dedication is in Provençal.

24. The problem of how the categories can find linguistic expression is an interactionist formulation of one of the basic problems of Kantian critique, that of how the categories are known. I will avoid it here.

25. Cf. the preceding note.

26. For the last cf. Derrida, Jacques, "Geschlecht—différence sexuelle, différence ontologique," *Research in Phenomenology* 13 (1983): 68–84.

27. For Habermas's most extended attempt to carry out this grounding, cf. Habermas, Jürgen, "What Is Universal Pragmatics?" in Habermas, *Communication and the Evolution of Society* (Thomas McCarthy, trans.), Boston: Beacon Press, 1979, 1–68; for a trenchant statement of the general criticism it received, see Geuss, Raymond, *The Idea of a Critical Theory*, Cambridge: Cambridge University Press, 1981.

28. Butler, Samuel, *The Authoress of the Odyssey*, Chicago: University of Chicago Press, 1969; also cf. the article by C. M. Bowra on "Homer" in the *Oxford Classical Dictionary*, 2nd ed., Oxford: Clarendon, 1969, 524ff.

29. Cf. Iser, *The Act of Reading*, 63f.

Chapter 23
1. It may, of course, be constrained in other ways. In my first example in the previous chapter, Julie is "free" in that Jack's utterance does not uniquely specify how it is to be understood. But her eventual response may be determined by other factors: by the state of her hormones and brain cells, for example. The question of whether it is so determined or not is a metaphysical, not a political, matter: freedom of the will is, as John Stuart Mill noted, entirely independent of

the kind of lack of social constraints I am discussing here: Mill, "On Liberty," 949.

2. Cf. Broad, William, and Wade, Nicholas, *Betrayers of the Truth*, New York: Simon and Schuster, 1982, for examples of this being honored in the breach.

3. Strawson, P. F., "Intention and Convention in Speech Acts," 444.

4. Cf. Marx, Karl, *A Contribution to the Critique of Political Economy* (Maurice Dobb, ed.), New York: International Publishers, 1970, 20–22.

Bibliography

Aristotle

Central Texts:

Analytica Priora et Posteriora (W. D. Ross, ed.), Oxford: Clarendon, 1964.
De Anima (W. D. Ross, ed.) Oxford: Clarendon, 1956
Ethica Nicomachea (I. Bywater, ed.) Oxford: Clarendon, 1894
Metaphysica (W. Jaeger, ed.) Oxford: Clarendon, 1957
Physica (W. D. Ross, ed.) Oxford: Clarendon, 1950
The Poetics of Aristotle (S. H. Butcher, ed.) London: Macmillan, 1911
The Basic Works of Aristotle (Richard McKeon, ed.) New York: Random House, 1941 (contains marginal pagination to Greek edition)

Aristotle. *De l'âme* (Jean Tricot, trans.). Paris: Jean Vrin, 1977.
Aristotle. *The Rhetoric and Poetics of Aristotle.* New York: Modern Library, 1954.
Arnhart, Larry. "The Rationality of Political Speech." *Interpretation* 9 (1981): 141–154.
Broadie, Alexander. "Aristotle on Rational Action." *Phronesis* 19 (1974): 70–80.
Cherniss, Harold. *Aristotle's Criticism of Plato and the Academy.* Vol. 1. Baltimore: Johns Hopkins University Press, 1944.
Cooper, John. *Reason and Human Good in Aristotle.* Cambridge, Mass.: Harvard University Press, 1975.
Erickson, Trond Berg. *Bios Theoretikos: Notes on Aristotle's Ethica Nicomachea X.6–8.* Oslo: Universitetsvorlaget, 1976.
Evans, J.D.G. *Aristotle's Concept of Dialectic.* Cambridge: Cambridge University Press, 1977
Furley, David. "Self-Movers." In Rorty, Amélie (ed.). *Essays on Aristotle's Ethics,* 55–68.
Gauthier, Renée, and Jolif, Jean-Yves. *Ethique à Nicomaque.* 2 vols. Louvain: Publications Universitaires, 1970.
Gould, Thomas. *Platonic Love.* New York: Free Press of Glencoe, 1963.
Hagen, Charles. "The ΕΝΕΡΓΕΙΑ-ΚΙΝΗΣΙΣ" Distinction and Aristotle's Concept of Practice." *Journal of the History of Philosophy* 22 (1984):263–280.

Homiak, Marcia. "Virtue and Self-Love in Aristotle's Ethics." *Canadian Journal of Philosophy* 11 (1981): 633–652.

Irwin, T. H. "The Metaphysical and Psychological Bases of Aristotle's Ethics." In Rorty, Amélie (ed.), *Essays on Aristotle's Ethics*, 35–53.

Jaeger, Werner. *Aristotle*. Oxford: Oxford University Press, 1934.

Kamp, Andreas. *Die politische Philosophie des Aristoteles und ihre metaphysischen Grundlagen*. Munich: Karl Alber, 1985.

Larkin, Miriam Therese. *Language in the Philosophy of Aristotle*. The Hague: Mouton, 1971.

Levin, Samuel R. "Aristotle's Theory of Metaphor." *Philosophy and Rhetoric* 15 (1982): 24–46.

Mulgan, R. G. *Aristotle's Political Theory*. Oxford: Clarendon, 1977.

Owen, G. E. L. "Logic and Metaphysics in Some Earlier Works of Aristotle." In Ingemar Düring and G. E. L. Owen (eds.), *Aristotle and Plato in the Mid-Fourth Century*, 163–190. Goteburg: Studia Graeca et Latina Gothoburgensia, Vol. 6, 1960.

Owens, Joseph. *Aristotle* (John R. Catan, ed.). Albany: State University of New York Press, 1981.

———. *The Doctrine of Being in the Aristotelian Metaphysics*. 2d ed. rev. Toronto: Pontifical Institute of Medieval Studies, 1963.

Penner, Terry. "Verbs and the Identity of Actions." In Oscar P. Wood and George Pitcher (eds.), *Ryle: A Collection of Critical Essays*, 393–460. Garden City, N. Y.: Anchor Books, 1970.

Randall, John Herman. *Aristotle*. New York: Columbia University Press, 1960.

Ricoeur, Paul. *The Rule of Metaphor* (Robert Czerny et al., trans.). Toronto: University of Toronto Press, 1977.

Riedl, Manfred. "Politik und Metaphysik bei Aristoteles." In Riedl, *Metaphysik und Metapolitik*, 63–84. Frankfurt: Suhrkamp, 1975.

Ritter, Joachim. *Metaphysik und Politik*. Frankfurt: Suhrkamp, 1969.

Rorty, Amélie O. (ed.). *Essays on Aristotle's Ethics*. Berkeley: University of California Press, 1980.

Ross, W. D. *Aristotle*. 5th ed. London: Methuen, 1949.

——— (ed.). *Aristotle's Metaphysics*. 2 vols. Oxford: Oxford University Press, 1924.

——— (ed.). *Aristotle's Physics*. Oxford: Clarendon, 1936.

Wiggins, David. "Deliberation and Practical Reason." In Rorty, Amelie O. (ed.), *Essays in Aristotle's Ethics*, 221–240. Berkeley: University of California Press, 1980.

Habermas

Central Texts:

Habermas, Jürgen *Theories des kommunikativen Handelns*. 2 vols. Frankfurt: Suhrkamp, 1982

———. *The Theory of Communicative Action*. Vol. 1 (Thomas McCarthy, trans.). Boston: Beacon Press, 1984 (translations of volume 2 are the author's).

Wellmer, Albrecht. "Wahrheit, Schein, Versöhnung." In Ludwig von Freidebeurg and Jürgen Habermas (eds.), *Adorno-Konferenz 1983*, 138–176. Frankfurt: Suhrkamp, 1983.

Bernstein, Richard J. (ed.). *Habermas and Modernity*. Cambridge, Mass.: MIT Press, 1985.

Geuss, Raymond. *The Idea of a Critical Theory*. Cambridge: Cambridge University Press, 1981.

Habermas, Jürgen. "Labor and Interaction." In Habermas, *Theory and Practice* (John Viertel, trans.). Boston: Beacon Press, 1973.

———. "Modernity: An Incomplete Project." In Hal Foster (ed.), *The Anti-Aesthetic*, 3–15. Port Townsend, Wash.: Bay Press, 1983.

———. *Moralbewußtsein und kommunikatives Handeln*. Frankfurt: Suhrkamp, 1983.

———. "Moralbewußtsein und kommunikatives Handeln." In Habermas, *Moralbewußtsein und kommunikatives Handeln*, 127–206. Frankfurt: Suhrkamp, 1983.

———. "Questions and Counterquestions." In Richard J. Bernstein (ed.), *Habermas and Modernity*, 192–216. Cambridge, Mass.: MIT Press, 1985.

———. "Rekonstruktive vs. verstehende Sozialwissenschaften." In Habermas, *Moralbewußtsein und kommunikatives Handeln*, 29–52. Frankfurt: Suhrkamp, 1983.

———. "Reply to My Critics." in John P. Thompson and David Held (eds.). *Habermas: Critical Debates*, Cambridge, Mass.: MIT Press, 1982.

———. "Some Distinctions in Universal Pragmatics." *Theory and Society* 3 (1976): 155–167.

———. "Towards a Theory of Communicative Competence." *Inquiry* 13 (1970): 360–375.

———. "Wahrheitstheorien." In *Wirklichkeit und Reflexion. Walter Schulz zum 60e Geburtstag*, 211–265. Pfullingen: Neske, 1973.

———. "What Is Universal Pragmatics?" In Habermas, *Communication and the Evolution of Society* (Thomas McCarthy, trans.), 1–68. Boston: Beacon Press, 1979.

———. "Wozu noch Philosophie?" In Habermas, *Philosophisch-politische Profile*, 15–37. Frankfurt: Suhrkamp, 1981.

———. "Zur Einebnung des Gattungsunterschieds zwischen Philosophie und Literatur." In Habermas, *Philosophische Diskurs der Moderne*, 219–247. Frankfurt: Suhrkamp, 1985.

Ingram, David. *Habermas and the Dialectic of Reason*. New Haven: Yale University Press, 1987.

McCarthy, Thomas. "Reflections on Rationalization in *The Theory of Communicative Action*." In Richard J. Bernstein (ed.). *Habermas and Modernity*, Cambridge, Mass.: MIT Press, 1985, 177–191.

Nagl, Ludwig. "Ästhetik und Diskurs." *Wiener Jahrbuch für Philosophie*, 1985, 91–99.

———. *Gesellschaft und Autonomie*. Wien: Verlag der Österreichischen Akademie der Wissenschaften, 1983.

Norman, Richard. *Reasons for Actions*. Oxford: Blackwell, 1971.

Thompson, John P., and Held. David (eds.). *Habermas: Critical Debates*. Cambridge, Mass.: MIT Press, 1982.

Tugendhat, Ernst. *Selbstbewußtsein und Selbstbestimmung*. Frankfurt: Suhrkamp, 1979.

Whitebrook, Joel. "Nature in Habermas." *Telos* 39 (1979): 41–69.

Hegel

Central Texts:

Enzyklopädie der philosophischen Wissenschaften im Grundrisse, cited from *Werke* 8–10.

Grundlinien der Philosophie des Rechts (Johannes Hoffmeister, ed.). Hamburg: Meiner, 1955.

Philosophy of Right (T. M. Knox, trans.). Oxford: Oxford University Press, 1967.

Phänomenologie des Geistes (Johannes Hoffmeister, ed.). Frankfurt: Meiner, 1952.

Phenomenology of Spirit (A. V. Miller, trans.). Oxford: Oxford University Press, 1979.

Vorlesungen über die Ästhetik, Vols. XII–XIV, *Jubiläumsausgabe* (Hermann Glockner, ed.). Stuttgart: Frohmann, 1953.

Aesthetics (T. M. Knox, trans.). 2 vols. Oxford: Oxford University Press, 1975.

Werke (Eva Moldenhauer and Karl Markus Michel, eds.). 20 vols. Frankfurt: Suhrkamp, 1970–71.

Wissenschaft der Logik (Georg Lasson, ed.). 2 vols. Hamburg: Meiner, 1932.

Science of Logic (A. V. Miller, trans.). New York: Humanities Press, 1976.

Avineri, Shlomo. *Hegel's Theory of the Modern State*. Cambridge: Cambridge University Press, 1972.

Benhabib, Seyla. *Critique, Norm and Utopia*. New York: Columbia University Press, 1986.

Blanchette, Oliva. "Language, the Primordial Labor of History." *Cultural Hermeneutics* 1 (1974): 325–382.

Carr, David. *Time, Narrative, and History*. Bloomington: Indiana University Press, 1986.

Fackenheim, Emil. *The Religious Dimension in Hegel's Thought*. Boston: Beacon Press, 1967.

Gillespie, Michael Allen. *Hegel, Heidegger, and the Ground of History*. Chicago: University of Chicago Press, 1984.

Hegel, G. W. F. "Das älteste Systemprogramm des deutschen Idealismus." In Hegel's *Werke* 1:234–236. Frankfurt: Suhrkamp, 1970–71. (English translation in Henry S. Harris, *Hegel's Development: Toward the Sunlight*, 510–512. Oxford: Clarendon, 1972).

———. *Jenaer Realphilosophie* (Johannes Hoffmeister, ed.). Hamburg: Meiner, 1931.

———. *On Christianity: Early Theological Writings* (T.M. Knox, trans.). New York: Harper Torchbooks, 1961.

———. *Philosophie des Rechts: Die Vorlesungen von 1819/20* (Dieter Henrich, ed.). Frankfurt: Suhrkamp, 1983.

———. *System der Sittlichkeit* (Georg Lasson, ed.), Hamburg: Meiner, 1967, (English translation, *System of Ethical Life* (H. S. Harris, trans; T. M. Knox, ed.). Albany: State University of New York Press, 1979).

———. *Vorlesungen über die Philosophie der Geschichte.* In *Werke* 12. (English translation, *Lectures on the Philosophy of History* (J. Sibree, trans.). New York: Dover, 1956).

———. *Vorlesungen über die Philosophie der Religion.* In *Werke*, vols. 16 and 17. (English trans.: *Lectures on the Philosophy of Religion* (E. B. Speirs and J. Burdon Sanderson, trans.). 3 vols. New York: Humanities Press, 1962).

Hyppolite, Jean. *Genesis and Structure of Hegel's Phenomenology of Spirit* (Samuel Cherniak and John Heckman, trans.). Evanston: Northwestern University Press, 1974.

Kaufmann, Walter. *Hegel: A Reinterpretation.* Garden City, New York: Anchor Books, 1966.

Kelley, George Armstrong. "Notes on Hegel's 'Lordship and Bondage.'" In Alasdair MacIntyre (ed.), *Hegel: A Collection of Critical Essays*, 189–217. Garden City, N.Y.: Anchor Books, 1972.

Kojève, Alexandre. *Introduction to the Reading of Hegel* (James Nichols, trans.). New York: Basic Books, 1969.

Kolb, David. *The Critique of Pure Modernity.* Chicago: University of Chicago Press, 1986.

Lauer, Quentin, S. J. *A Reading of Hegel's Phenomenology of Spirit.* New York: Fordham University Press, 1976.

Lukács, Georg. *The Young Hegel* (Rodney Livingstone, trans.). London: Merlin Press, 1975

Macintyre, Alasdair (ed.). *Hegel: A Collection of Critical Essays.* Garden City, N.Y.: Anchor Books, 1972.

McCumber, John. "Scientific Progress and Hegel's *Phenomenology of Spirit*" *Idealistic Studies* 13 (1983): 1–10.

Peperzak, Adrien. *Le jeune Hegel et la vision morale du monde.* The Hague: Nijhoff, 1960.

Pöggeler, Otto. "Zur Deutung der *Phänomenologie des Geistes.*" *Hegel-Studien* 1 (1961): 255–294

Taylor, Charles. *Hegel.* Cambridge: Cambridge University Press, 1975.

———. "The Opening Arguments of the *Phenomenology.*" In Alasdair Macintyre (ed.), *Hegel: A Collection of Critical Essays*, 151–187. Garden City, N.Y.: Anchor Books, 1972.

Heidegger

Central Texts:

"Aus einem Gespräch von der Sprache" in Heidegger, *Unterwegs zur Sprache*, 4th ed., 85–156. Pfullingen: Neske, 1971.

"From a Dialogue on Language." In Heidegger, *On the Way to Language* (Albert Hofstadter, trans.), 1–56. New York: Harper & Row, 1971.

Sein und Zeit. 11th ed. Tübingen: Niemeyer, 1967.

Being and Time (John MacQuarrie and Edward Robinson, trans.). New York: Harper & Row, 1962 (contains marginal pagination to German edition).

"Der Ursprung des Kunstwerkes." In *Holzwege*, 4th ed., 7–68. Frankfurt: Klostermann, 1963.

"The Origin of the Work of Art." In Heidegger, *Poetry, Language, Thought* (Albert Hofstadter, trans.), 15–88. New York: Harper & Row, 1971.

Biemel, Walter. *Heidegger*. Reinbeck: Rowohlt, 1973.

———. "Poetry and Language in Heidegger." In Joseph J. Kockelmans (ed), *On Heidegger and Language*, 65–105.

Burgess, Anthony. "The Syntax of Food Adds Spice to Language." *The New York Times*, June 2, 1982.

Caputo, John. *The Mystical Element in Heidegger's Thought*. Athens, Ohio: Ohio University Press, 1978.

Edie, James M. *Speaking and Meaning*. Bloomington: Indiana University Press, 1976.

Gadamer, Hans-Georg. "Being, Spirit, God." In *Heidegger Memorial Lectures* (Werner Marx, ed.; Steven W. Davis, trans.). Pittsburgh: Duquesne University Press, 1982.

Harries, Karsten. "Heidegger as a Political Thinker." In Michael Murray (ed.), *Heidegger and Modern Philosophy*, 304–328. New Haven: Yale University Press, 1978.

Heidegger Martin. "Dichterisch wohnet der Mensch." In Heidegger, *Vorträge und Aufsätze*, 2:61–78. Pfullingen: Neske, 1967.

———. *Erlaüterungen zu Hölderlins Dichtung*, 1st ed. Frankfurt: Klostermann, 1951. Also 4th ed. expanded, 1971.

———. *Existence and Being* (Douglas Scott, trans.). Chicago: Regnery, 1949.

———. *Die Frage nach dem Ding*. Tübingen: Niemeyer, 1962.

———. "Hölderlin und das Wesen der Dichtung." In Heidegger, *Erlaüterungen zu Hölderlins Dichtung.*, 31–45. Frankfurt: Klostermann, 1951. (English translation, "Hölderlin and the Essence of Poetry." In Heidegger, *Existence and Being* (Douglas Scott, trans.), 291–315. Chicago: Regnery, 1949).

———. *Kant und das Problem der Metaphysik*. Frankfurt: Klostermann, 1973.

———. "Kants These über das Sein." In Heidegger, *Wegmarken*, 273–307. Frankfurt: Klostermann, 1967.

———. *Nietzsche*. 2 vols. Pfullingen: Neske, 1961.

———. "Nietzsches Wort: Gott is Tot." In Heidegger, *Holzwege*, 4th ed., 193–247. Frankfurt: Klostermann, 1963.

———. "Only a God Can Save Us Now." *Graduate Faculty Philosophy Journal* 6 (1977): 5–27.

———. "Die Onto-theologische Verfassung der Metaphysik." In Heidegger, *Identität und Differenz*, 51–67. Pfullingen: Neske, 1957.

———. *The Question of Being* (William Kluback and Jean T. Wilde, trans.; German text with English facing). New Haven: Yale University Press, 1958.

———. "Remembrance of the Poet" (Douglas Scott, trans.). In Heidegger, *Existence and Being*, 243–269. Chicago: Regnery, 1949.

———. *Der Satz vom Grund*. 4th ed. Pfullingen: Neske, 1971.

———. *Schellings Abhandlung über das Wesen der menschlichen Freiheit (1809)*. Tübingen: Niemeyer, 1971.

———. "Vom Wesen des Grundes." In Heidegger, *Wegmarken*, 21–71. Frankfurt: Klostermann, 1967.

———. "Vom Wesen und Begriff der *Physis*. Aristotles' Physik B.1." In Heidegger, *Wegmarken*, 309–371. Frankfurt: Klostermann, 1967.

———. *Vorträge und Aufsätze*. 3 vols. 2d ed. Pfullingen: Neske, 1967.

———. "Was ist Metaphysik?" In Heidegger, *Wegmarken*, 1–19. Frankfurt: Klostermann, 1967.

———. *Wegmarken*. Frankfurt: Klostermann, 1967.

———. *Zur Sache des Denkens*. Tübingen: Niemeyer, 1969.

Kockelmans, Joseph. J. *Heidegger on Art and Art Works*. The Hague: Nijhoff, 1985.

———. *On the Truth of Being*. Bloomington: Indiana University Press, 1984.

Marx, Werner. *Heidegger and the Tradition*. Evanston: Northwestern University Press, 1971.

McCumber, John. "Language and Appropriation: The Nature of Heideggerean Dialogue." *The Personalist* 60 (1979): 384–396.

Nicholson, Graeme. "Heidegger on Thinking." *Journal of the History of Philosophy* 13 (1975): 491–503.

Palmier, Jean-Michel. *Les écrits politiques de Heidegger*. Paris: L'Herne, 1968.

Richardson, William J., S. J. *Heidegger: Through Phenomenology to Thought*. The Hague: Nijhoff, 1963.

Sallis, John. "Language and Reversal." *Southern Journal of Philosophy* 4 (1973): 109–124.

Schelling, Friedrich Wilhelm Joseph von. *System of Transcendental Idealism* (selections; Albert Hofstadter, trans.). In Albert Hofstadter and Richard Kuhns (eds.), *Philosophies of Art and Beauty*, 347–377. New York: Modern Library, 1964.

Schürmann, Reiner. "Political Thinking in Heidegger," *Social Research* 45(1978): 191–221.

———. *Le principe d'anarchie*. Paris: du Seuil, 1982.

Schwan, Alexander. *Politische Philosophie im Denken Heideggers*. Köln: Westdeutscher Verlag, 1965.

Shapiro, Gary. "From the Sublime to the Political: Some Historical Notes." *New Literary Theory* 16 (1984–85): 213–235.

Sherover, Charles. *Heidegger, Kant and Time*. Bloomington: Indiana University Press, 1971.

Kant

Central Texts (all German is cited according to the following volumes of the Academy edition: *Kants gesammelte Schriften*, 29 vols. Berlin: 1902–, except for those to *Werke* and as noted):

Zum ewigen Frieden, vol. 8
Grundlegung der Metaphysik der Sitten, vol. 4
Kritik der praktischen Vernunft, vol. 5
Kritik der reinen Vernunft, vols. 3, 4
Kritik der Urteilskraft, vol. 5
Prolegomena zu einer jeden Künftigen Metaphysik, vol. 4
Der Streit der Fakultäten, vol. 7
"Perpetual Peace." In Kant, *On History* (Lewis White Beck, trans.), 85–136. Indianapolis: Bobbs-Merrill, 1963.
Fundamental Principles of the Metaphysics of Morals (Thomas K. Abbott, trans.). Indianapolis: Bobbs-Merrill, 1949.
Critique of Practical Reason (Lewis White Beck, trans.). Indianapolis: Bobbs-Merrill, 1956.
Critique of Pure Reason (Norman Kemp Smith, trans.). New York: St. Martin's Press, 1965.
Critique of Judgment (James Creed Meredith, trans.). Oxford: Clarendon, 1952.
Werke (Wilhelm Weischedel, ed.) 12 vols. Frankfurt: Suhrkamp, 1968.

Arendt, Hannah. "Freedom and Politics." In Albert Hunold (ed.), *Freedom and Serfdom: An Anthology of Western Thought*, 191–217. Dordrecht: Reidel, 1961.
Aubenque, Pierre. "La prudence chez Kant." *Revue de métaphysique et de morale* 80 (1975): 156–182.
Beck, Lewis White. "The Fact of Reason: An Essay in the Justification of Ethics." In Beck (ed.), *Studies in the Philosophy of Kant*, 200–214. Indianapolis: Bobbs-Merrill, 1965.
Cassirer, Ernst. *Kant's Life and Thought* (James Haden, trans.). New Haven: Yale University Press, 1981.
Deggau, H. G. *Die Aporien der Rechtslehre Kants*. Stuttgart: Frohmann, 1983.
Deleuze, Gilles. *La philosophie critique de Kant*. Paris: Presses Universitaires de France, 1963.
Guyer, Paul. "Disinterestedness and Desire in Kant's Aesthetics." *Journal of Aesthetics and Art Criticism* 36 (1978): 446–460.
———. *Kant and the Claims of Taste*. Cambridge, Mass.: Harvard University Press, 1979.
———. "Kant's Distinction Between the Beautiful and the Sublime." *Review of Metaphysics* 35 (1982): 753–783.
———. "Pleasure and Society in Kant's Theory of Taste." In Paul Guyer and Ted

Cohen (eds.), *Essays in Kant's Aesthetics*, 21–54. Chicago: University of Chicago Press, 1982.

Heimsoeth, Hans. "Metaphysical Motives in the Development of Critical Idealism." In Moltke Gram (ed.), *Kant: Disputed Questions*, 158–214. Chicago: Quadrangle, 1967.

Henrich, Dieter. "Der Begriff der sittlichen Einsicht und Kants Lehre vom Faktum der Vernunft." In Dieter Henrich and Walter Schulz (eds.), *Die Gegenwart der Griechen im Neueren Denken: Festschrift für Hans-Georg Gadamer*, 77–115. Tübingen: Verlag J. C. B. Mohr, 1960.

Hill, Thomas E. "The Kingdom of Ends." In Lewis White Beck (ed.), *Proceedings of the Third International Kant Congress*, 307–315. Dordrecht: Reidel, 1972.

Hofstadter, Albert. "Kant's Aesthetic Revolution." *Journal of Religious Ethics* 3 (1975): 171–191.

Howard, Dick. "From Marx to Kant: The Return of the Political." *Thesis Eleven* 8 (1984): 77–91.

Kulenkampff, Jens. "Uber Kants Bestimmung des Gehalts der Kunst." *Zeitschrift für Philosophische Forschung* 33 (1979): 62–73.

Lebrun, Gerard. *Kant et la fin de la métaphysique*. Paris: Armand Colin, 1970.

Lories, Danielle. "Kant et la liberté ésthétique." *Revue philosophique de Louvain* 79 (1981): 484–512.

Luethe, Rudolf. "Kants Lehre von den aesthetischen Ideen." *Kant-Studien* 75 (1984): 65–74.

Lyotard, Jean-François, and Jean-Loup Thébaut. *Just Gaming* (Wlad Godzich, trans.). Minneapolis: University of Minnesota Press, 1985.

Makkreel, Rudolf. "Imagination and Temporality in Kant's Theory of the Sublime." *Journal of Aesthetics and Art Criticism* 42 (1984): 303–316.

Marcuse, Herbert. "A Study on Authority." In Marcuse, *From Luther to Popper* (Joris de Brees trans.), 79–94. London: Verso, 1972.

von Molnár, Géza. "Goethe's Reading of Kant's 'Critique of Judgment.'" *Eighteenth Century Studies* 15 (1982): 402–420.

Nagl, Ludwig. *Gesellschaft und Autonomie*. Wien: Verlag der Österreichischen Akademie der Wissenschaften, 1983.

Reboul, Olivier. "Hegel, critique de la morale de Kant." *Revue de métaphysique et de morale* 80 (1975): 85–100.

Reiss, Hans (ed.), Nisbet, H. B. (trans.). *Kant's Political Writings*. Cambridge: Cambridge University Press, 1971.

Riley, Patrick. *Kant's Political Philosophy*. Totowa, N. J.: Rowman and Littlefield, 1983.

Salim, Kemal. "Aesthetic Necessity, Culture, and Epistemology." *Kant-Studien* 74 (1983): 189–200.

Saner, Hans. *Kant's Political Thought* (E. B. Ashton, trans.). Chicago: University of Chicago Press, 1973.

Schaper, Eva. "Kant on Aesthetic Appraisals." *Kant-Studien* 64 (1973): 431–449.

Stadler, Ingrid. "Perception and Perfection in Kant's Aesthetics." In Robert Paul Wolff (ed.), *Kant: A Collection of Critical Essays*. Notre Dame, Ind.: University of Notre Dame Press, 1967.

Stern, Carl. "Kant's Theory of Empirical Concept Formation." *Southwestern Journal of Philosophy* 8, no. 2 (Summer 1977): 17–23.

Walsh, W. H. "Kant and Metaphysics." *Kant-Studien* 67 (76): 372–384.

Weill, Eric. "Kant et le problème de la politique." *Annales de Philosophie Politique* Vol. 6, 1–32. Paris: Presses Universitaires de France, 1962.

Wolff, Robert Paul. *The Autonomy of Reason: A Commentary on Kant's Groundwork of the Metaphysics of Morals.* New York: Harper Torchbooks, 1973.

——— (ed). *Kant: A Collection of Critical Essays.* Notre Dame, Ind.: University of Notre Dame Press, 1967.

Zeldin, Mary-Barbara. *Freedom and the Critical Undertaking.* Ann Arbor: University Microfilm International (for the American Society for Eighteenth-Century Studies), 1980.

Plato

Central Texts:

Platonis Opera (John Burnet, ed.). 5 vols. Oxford: Clarendon, 1907.

Plato: The Collected Dialogues (Edith Hamilton and Hamilton Cairns, ed.). Princeton: Princeton University Press (Bollingen), 1961.

Allen, R. E. "Participation and Predication in Plato's Middle Dialogues." In R. E. Allen (ed.), *Studies in Plato's Metaphysics*, 43–60. London: Routledge and Kegan Paul, 1965.

——— (ed.). *Studies in Plato's Metaphysics.* London: Routledge and Kegan Paul, 1965.

Barker, Ernest. *Greek Political Theory.* 5th ed. London: Methuen, 1960.

Bröcker, Werner. *Platons Gespräche.* 2d ed. Frankfurt: Klostermann, 1967.

Chen, Chung-Hwan. "The 'Phaedrus' as the Transition from the Platonism in the Earlier Dialogues to the Dialectics and Theology in the Later Dialogues." *Studi Internazionali di Filosofia* 4 (1972): 77–90.

Demos, Raphael. "Plato's Doctrine of the Psyche as Self-Moving Motion." *Journal of the History of Philosophy* 6 (1968): 33–45.

Dorter, Kenneth. *Plato's Phaedo.* Toronto: University of Toronto Press, 1982.

Friedländer, Paul. *Platon.* 3 vols. Berlin: de Gruyter, 1960.

Gill, Christopher. "The Death of Socrates." *Classical Quarterly*, n.s., 22 (1973): 25–28.

Gould, Thomas. *Platonic Love.* New York: Free Press of Glencoe, 1963.

Griswold, Charles. "Self-Knowledge and the 'Idea' of Soul in Plato's *Phaedrus.*" *Revue de Métaphysique et de Morale* 86 (1981): 477–494.

———. *Self-Knowledge in Plato's Phaedrus.* New Haven: Yale University Press, 1986.

Guthrie, W. K. C. "Plato's Views on the Nature of Soul." In Gregory Vlastos (ed.). *Plato: A Collection of Critical Essays*, vol. 2, 230–243. Notre Dame, Ind.: University of Notre Dame Press, 1978.

Hackforth, R. *Plato's Phaedo.* Indianapolis: Bobbs-Merrill, 1958.

————. *Plato's Phaedrus*. Cambridge: Cambridge University Press, 1972.

Helmbold, W. C., and W. B. Holther. "The Unity of the *Phaedrus.*" *University of California Publications in Classical Philology* 14 (1950–52): 387–417.

Leys, Wayne. "Was Plato Non-political?" In Gregory Vlastos (ed.). *Plato: A Collection of Critical Essays*, vol. 2, 166–173. Notre Dame, Ind.: University of Notre Dame Press, 1978.

Lloyd, A. C. "Plato's Description of Division." In R. E. Allen (ed.), *Studies in Plato's Metaphysics*, 219–230. London: Routledge and Kegan Paul, 1965.

Maurer, Reinhart. *Platons "Staat" und die Demokratie*. Berlin: de Gruyter, 1970.

McCumber, John. "Discourse and Soul in Plato's *Phaedrus.*" *Apeiron* 16 (1982): 27–39.

Mendelson, Alan. "Plato's *Phaedo* and the Frailty of Human Nature." *Dionysius* 5 (1981): 29–39.

Nussbaum, Martha. "This Story Isn't True: Poetry, Goodness, and Understanding in Plato's *Phaedrus.*" In Julius Moravcsik and Philip Temko (eds.), *Plato on Beauty, Wisdom and the Arts*, 79–124. New Jersey: Rowman and Littlefield, 1982.

Philip, A. "Récurrences thématiques et topologie dans le *Phèdre* de Platon." *Revue de Métaphysique et de Morale* 86 (1981): 452–476.

Plato. *Gorgias* (E. R. Dodds, ed.). Oxford: Clarendon, 1959.

————. *Phédon* (Léon Robin, ed.). Paris: Budé, 1967.

————. *Phèdre* (Léon Robin, ed.). Paris: Budé, 1978.

Pohlenz, Max. *Freedom in Greek Life and Thought* (Carl Lofmark, trans.). Dordrecht: Reidel, 1966.

Robin, Léon. *Théorie platonicienne de l'amour*. Paris: Alcan, 1908.

Robinson, T. M. *Plato's Psychology*. Toronto: University of Toronto Press, 1970.

Rodis-Lewis, Geneviève. "L'Articulation des thèmes du Phèdre." *Revue Philosophique de France et de l'Étranger* 165 (1975): 3–34.

Ross, W. D. *Plato's Theory of Ideas*. Oxford: Clarendon Press, 1951.

Sallis, John. *The Way of Platonic Logos*. Pittsburgh: Duquesne University Press, 1975.

Santos, Gerasimo. "Passionate and Platonic Love in the *Phaedrus.*" *Ancient Philosophy* 2 (1982): 105–114.

Schleiermacher, F. E. D. *Introduction to the Dialogues of Plato* (Wm. Dobson trans.). London: Parker, 1836.

Seeskin, Kenneth. "Socratic Philosophy and the Dialogue Form." *Philosophy and Literature* 8 (1984): 181–194.

Sinaiko, Herman L. *Love, Knowledge and Discourse in Plato*. Chicago: University of Chicago Press, 1965.

Stannard, Jerry. "Socratic Eros and Platonic Dialectic." *Phronesis* 4 (1959): 120–134.

Thucydides, *History of the Peloponnesian War.*

Verdenius, W. J. "Plato's Doctrine of Artistic Imitation." In Gregory Vlastos (ed.), *Plato: A Collection of Critical Essays*, vol. 2, 259–273. Notre Dame, Ind.: University of Notre Dame Press, 1978.

Vlastos, Gregory. "The Disorderly Motion in the *Timaeus.*" In R. E. Allen.

(ed.), *Studies in Plato's Metaphysics*, 379–419. London: Routledge and Kegan Paul, 1965.

———. "Justice and Happiness in the Republic." In Gregory Vlastos (ed.), *Plato: A Collection of Critical Essays*, vol. 2, 66–95. Notre Dame, Ind.: Notre Dame University Press, 1978.

——— (ed.) *Plato: A Collection of Critical Essays*, vol. 2. Notre Dame, Ind.: Notre Dame University Press, 1978.

———. "Sex in Platonic Love." In Vlastos, *Platonic Studies*, 38–42. Princeton: Princeton University Press, 1973.

Voegelin, Eric. *Plato*. Baton Rouge: Louisiana State University Press, 1966.

Other

Arendt, Hannah. *The Human Condition*. Chicago: University of Chicago Press, 1958.

Austin, J. L. *How to do Things with Words*. (J. O. Urmson, ed.), Oxford: Oxford University Press, 1965.

———. "A Plea for Excuses." In Austin, *Philosophical Papers* (J. L. Urmson and G. J. Warnock, eds.). Oxford: Clarenden, 1961.

Ayer, A.J. (ed.). *Logical Positivism*. New York: Free Press, 1959.

Barry, Brian. "A Grammar of Equality." *The New Republic*, May 12, 1982, 36–39.

Berlin, Isaiah. "Two Concepts of Liberty." in Berlin, *Four Essays on Liberty*. Oxford: Oxford University Press, 1969, 118–172.

Bowra, C. M. "Homer." In *Oxford Classical Dictionary*. 2d ed., 524ff. Oxford: Clarendon, 1969.

Broad, William and Nicholas Wade. *Betrayers of the Truth*. New York: Simon and Schuster, 1982.

Butler, Samuel. *The Authoress of the Odyssey*. Chicago: University of Chicago Press, 1969.

Carnap, Rudolf. "The Elimination of Metaphysics through Logical Analysis of Language." In A. J. Ayer (ed.), *Logical Positivism*, 60–81. New York: Free Press, 1959.

Chomsky, Noam. *Language and Mind*. New York: Harcourt, Brace and World, 1968.

———. *Syntactic Structures*. The Hague: Mouton, 1957.

Danto, Arthur. *Narration and Knowledge*. New York: Columbia University Press, 1985.

Davidson, Donald. "Truth and Meaning." *Synthese* 17 (1967): 304–323.

Derrida, Jacques. "Differance." In Derrida, *Speech and Phenomena*, 129–160. (David B. Allison, trans.). Evanston: Northwestern University Press, 1973.

———. "Geschlect—difference sexuelle, difference ontologique." *Research in Phenomenology* 13 (1983): 68–84.

———. "Signature, événement, contexte." In Derrida, *Marges de la philosophie*, 367–393. Paris: Minuit, 1972.

———. "Signature Event Context." *Glyph* 1 (1977):172–197.

Descartes, René. "Meditations on the First Philosophy," Preface to the reader. In Descartes, *The Meditations and Selections from the Principles* (John L. Veitch, trans.). La Salle, Ill.: Open Court, 1964.

Dreyfus, Hubert and Paul Rabinow. *Michel Foucault: Beyond Structuralism and Hermeneutics.* 2d ed. Chicago: University of Chicago Press, 1983.

Fish, Stanley E. "With the Compliments of the Author: Reflections on Austin and Derrida." *Critical Inquiry* 8 (1982): 693–721.

Foucault, Michel. *Histoire de la sexualité,* vol. 2, *L'usage des plaisirs.* Paris: Gallimard, 1984.

―――. "What Is an Author?" (Josué V. Harari, trans.). In Paul Rabinow (ed.), *The Foucault Reader.* New York: Pantheon, 1984.

Frege, Gottlob. "Function and Concept." In Peter Geach and Max Black (eds.), *Translations from the Philosophical Writings of Gottlob Frege,* 21–41. Oxford: Oxford University Press, 1952.

―――. "On Sense and Meaning." In Peter Geach and Max Black (eds.), *Translations from the Philosophical Writings of Gottlob Frege,* 56–78. Oxford: Oxford University Press, 1952.

Gadamer, Hans-Georg. *Wahrheit und Methode.* 2d ed. Tübingen: Mohr, 1965.

Gilson, Etienne. *Being and Some Philosophers.* Toronto: Pontifical Institute of Medieval Studies, 1949.

Goffman, Erving. *The Presentation of Self in Everyday Life.* Garden City, N. Y.: Anchor Books, 1959.

Grice, H. P. "Logic and Conversation." In Donald Davidson and Gilbert Harmon (eds.), *The Logic of Grammar,* 64–75. Encino, Calif.: Dickerson, 1975.

Hobbes, Thomas. *Leviathan.* Oxford: Clarendon, 1909.

Hume, David. *An Enquiry Concerning the Principles of Human Understanding.* In Hume, *Enquiries* (L. A. Selby-Bigge, ed.). 2d ed. Oxford: Clarendon, 1902.

―――. *A Treatise of Human Nature* (L. A. Selby-Bigge, ed.). Oxford: Clarendon, 1888.

Husserl, Edmund. *The Crisis of European Sciences and Transcendental Phenomenology* (David Carr, trans.). Evanston: Northwestern University Press, 1970.

Iser, Wolfgang. *The Art of Reading.* Baltimore: Johns Hopkins University Press, 1978.

Jauss, Hans-Robert. "Negativität und Identifikation." *Poetik und Hermeneutik* 6 (1975): 263–339.

Kierkegaard, Søren. *Fear and Trembling and the Sickness unto Death* (Walter Lowrie, trans.). Garden City, N. Y.: Anchor Books, 1941.

Klosko, George. *The Development of Plato's Political Theory.* New York: Methuen, 1986.

Lakoff, George, and Mark Johnson. *Metaphors We Live By.* Chicago: University of Chicago Press, 1980.

Leibniz, Gottfried Wilhelm. *Monadology.* In Leibniz, *Philosophical Papers and Letters* (Leroy E. Loemker, ed.), 2d ed., 643–653. Dordrecht: Reidel, 1969.

Lewis, David. *Convention.* Cambridge: Harvard University Press, 1969.

Locke, John. *An Essay Concerning Human Understanding* (Alexander Campbell Fraser, ed.). 2 vols. New York: Dover, 1959.

Macnamara, John. *Names for Things*. Cambridge, Mass.: MIT Press, 1982.

Marx, Karl. *A Contribution to the Critique of Political Economy* (Maurice Dobb, ed.). New York: International Publishers, 1970.

———. *Economic and Political Manuscripts of 1844*. In Robert C. Tucker (ed.), *The Marx-Engels Reader*, 52–103. New York: Norton, 1972.

Marx, Karl, and Friedrich Engels. *The German Ideology*. In Robert C. Tucker (ed.), *The Marx-Engels Reader*, 110–166. New York: Norton, 1972.

Mill, John Stuart. "On Liberty." In Edwin A. Burtt (ed.), *The British Philosophers from Bacon to Mill*. New York: Modern Library, 1939.

———. *A System of Logic*. London: Longmans, New Impression, 1970.

Muller, Robert. "Remarques sur la liberté grecque." *Dialogue* (Canada) 25 (1986): 421–447.

Nozick, Robert. *Anarchy, State and Utopia*. Oxford: Blackwell, 1974.

Pascale, Richard, and Anthony Arthur. *The Art of Japanese Management*. New York: Simon and Schuster, 1981.

Popper, Karl. *The Open Society and Its Enemies*, vol. 1, *The Spell of Plato*. 4th ed rev. Princeton: Princeton University Press, 1962.

Quine, Willard V. O. *Word and Object*. Cambridge, Mass.: MIT Press, 1960.

Quine, Willard V. O., and J. S. Ullian. *The Web of Belief*. New York: Random House, 1978.

Rorty, Richard. *The Linguistic Turn*. Chicago: University of Chicago Press, 1967.

———. *Philosophy and the Mirror of Nature*. Princeton: Princeton University Press, 1979.

Rose, Herbert Jenning. "Helios." *Oxford Classical Dictionary*, 494. Oxford: Clarendon, 1970.

Russell. Bertrand. "On Denoting." *Mind* 14 (1905): 479–493.

Sabini, John, and Maury Silver. *Moralities of Everyday Life*. Oxford: Oxford University Press, 1982.

Sartre, Jean-Paul. *L'être et le néant*. Paris: Gallimard, 1943.

Searle, John. *Expression and Meaning*. Cambridge: Cambridge University Press, 1979.

———. "Literal Meaning." In Searle, *Expression and Meaning*, 116–136.

———. "The Logical Status of Fictional Discourse." In Searle, *Expression and Meaning*, 58–75.

———. "Metaphor." In Searle, *Expression and Meaning*, 76–116.

Skinner, B. F. *Beyond Freedom and Dignity*. New York: Knopf, 1971.

Spinoza, Benedict de. "Ethics," Part 5, preface. In R. H. M. Elwes (trans.), *The Chief Works of Benedict de Spinoza*. 2 vols. New York: Dover, 1955.

Spivak, Gayatri Chakravorty. *In Other Worlds*. New York: Methuen, 1987.

Stevenson, C. L. "The Emotive Meaning of Ethical Terms." In Stevenson, *Facts and Values*, 18–21. New Haven: Yale University Press, 1963.

Strawson, P. F. "Intention and Convention in Speech Acts." *Philosophical Review* 73 (1964): 439–460.

Tarski, Alfred. "The Concept of Truth in Formalized Languages." In Tarski, *Logic, Semantics, Metamathematics* (J. H. Woodger, trans; John Corcoran, ed.). 2nd ed rev., 152–278. Indianapolis: Hackett, 1983.

Toulmin, Stephen. *The Uses of Argument*. Cambridge: Cambridge University Press, 1958.

Wittgenstein, Ludwig. *Philosophical Investigations* (G. E. M. Anscombe, trans.). 3rd ed. New York: Macmillan, 1958.

———. *Tractatus Logico-Philosophicus* (D. F. Pears and B. F. McGuinness, trans.). London: Routledge and Kegan Paul, 1961.

Whorf, B. L. *Language, Thought and Reality*. Cambridge, Mass.: MIT Press, 1956.

Index

294–95, 298, 303–4, 418, 424; and Greeks, 66, 78, 79, 100, 101; and Habermas, 331, 358–59, 361; and Heidegger, 145, 321–23; and history, 303–4; and imagination, 433; and interaction, 46, 64, 87–105, 165, 289–93, 305; and intrinsically emancipatory interaction, 8, 9, 29–30, 64, 86, 105, 305–6; and irony, 432; and Kant, 10, 11, 46, 59, 60, 166–67, 289–306, 309, 321, 337, 454; and labor, 342–43, 46, 93; and language, 33, 36, 37, 43, 53, 75–77, 232, 290–92, 373–74, 375, 376, 431; and life force, 34–36; *Logic*, 7, 64, 89, 97, 98, 99, 260, 295; and narrative structure, 15, 16, 31–32, 43–44, 85, 151, 153–55, 165, 289, 297–99, 300, 301, 303, 304, 424, 427; and necessity, 72–74, 83–84, 294–95; and nonconsciousness, 32–33; and parameters, 20, 21, 165; and poetic interaction, 33, 66–67, 74, 205–6, 380, 394, 395, 396, 398–99, 409, 416, 421, 422–23, 425; and poetry, 74–77, 304; *Phenomenology of Spirit*, 14, 29–30, 31–45, 46–62, 63–86, 87, 89, 98, 99, 132, 151, 290–91, 298, 300, 301–4, 308, 338, 418; and philosophy, 299–304, 305; *Philosophy of Right*, 4, 7, 8, 9, 43, 92–93, 98, 99, 102–3; and Plato, 290, 291–92, 293, 297, 302, 305; and political theory, 66, 90–105, 166, 303–6, 317, 403–4, 407; and realm of belief, 50, 51; and reason, 48–49, 289–90, 296; and reflective judgment, 289, 297–99, 304–5, 309; and religion, 44, 47, 64–65, 66, 80–81, 103–4, 166, 423; and opposed self-consciousness, 33–45, 291, 409; and self-consolidation, 32–35, 165, 289, 301–4, 306, 307, 316, 322; and situated reason, 23, 45, 58, 83, 85, 87, 290, 296, 363, 374–75; and Spirit, 15, 31–32, 33, 46, 49–50, 60–61, 64–65, 75, 86, 107, 145, 289, 290; and state, 51, 55, 66, 90–105, 304–6, 307, 402, 422–23; and substance, 49–50; and the symbolic, 36, 43; and theoretical mode of existence, 89–90; and truth, 167; "Unhappy Consciousness," 432; and unsituated reason, 31, 40, 58; and wealth, 51–52, 55, 93–94; and will, 434; *see also* Externalization; Recognition; Reconciliation

Heidegger, Martin, 4, 106–23, 392; and aesthetics and art, 23, 128–42, 146, 166–67, 273, 308–9, 311, 316–18, 321–23, 343, 363, 374, 399, 409, 420–22; and Aristotle, 108–9, 128, 310; and authenticity, 30, 107, 109–16, 118–23, 124–26, 135–36, 143, 156, 308; and Being, 307, 316–18, 420; *Being and Time*, 4, 8–9, 106–23, 125–28, 134, 137–42, 143, 151, 152, 156, 307–10; and call of conscience, 125, 126; and communication, 119–23, 126–28, 137–42, 143, 156; and community, 106–23, 126–27; and contexts of involvement, 109–13, 309–10; and deconstruction of self, 322–23; and demarcation, 14, 15, 106, 124–26, 132, 141, 165–66, 315, 393, 394; *Der Satz vom Grund*, 309; difficulties of text, 8, 9, 106, 107; and discourse, 8–9, 116–23, 127–29, 153–54, 290; and earth, 132–33, 139–41, 151, 158, 294, 310, 315, 359, 420; and emancipation, 136–42, 157–61; and equipment, things as, 128; and freedom, 160, 424–25; "From a Dialogue on Language," 30, 107, 143–61, 166, 307, 308, 319–310, 315, 316–17, 343, 377, 403; and Greeks, 154; and Habermas, 358, 359, 361; and Hegel, 145, 321–23; and Heraclitus, 106; and hints, 153, 157; and Holderlin, 22, 106, 145; and inauthenticity, 30, 118–19, 120–21, 122, 435; and interaction, 307–11; and interpretation, 107, 113–16, 117; and intrinsically emancipatory interaction, 8–9, 106, 107, 123, 143–61, 165–66, 315–16, 404; and Kant, 166–67, 307–18, 455; *Kehre*, 128, 145; and language, 107, 116–19, 122, 127–42, 146–61, 232, 308, 323, 372–73, 376, 396, 403; and metaphysics, 158–59, 307–311, 388; naming, 133–34, 158; and Nietzsche, 106, 145, 155; "Origin of the Work of Art," 4, 30, 107, 128–42, 143, 147, 158, 294, 308, 309, 311, 343, 374; and parameters, 20, 21, 109, 155, 132, 135, 141–42, 157, 165–66, 315, 420, 424–25; paths (ways), 138, 145, 146, 149, 153, 309; and phenomenology, 107–8, 114–16; and Plato, 309; and poetic interaction, 106, 160, 380, 394, 395, 396, 399,